Russia's Economic Transitions

From Late Tsarism to the New Millennium

Russia's Economic Transitions examines the three major transformations that the country underwent from the early 1860s to the year 2000. The first transition, under Tsarism, involved the partial breakup of the feudal framework of land ownership and the move toward capitalist relations. The second, following the Communist revolution of 1917, brought to power a system of state ownership and administration – a *sui generis* type of war economy state capitalism – subjecting the economy's development fully to central commands. The third, started in the early 1990s and still unfolding, is aiming at reshaping the inherited economic fabric on the basis of private ownership, within a not yet fully determined market framework. The three transitions originated within different settings, but with a similar primary goal, namely to change the economy's ownership pattern in the hopes of providing a better basis for subsequent development. The treatment's originality, impartiality, and historical breadth have cogent economic, social, and political relevance.

Nicolas Spulber is Distinguished Professor of Economics, Emeritus, at Indiana University in Bloomington. He is the author of many books, including *Redefining the State: Privatization and Welfare Reform in Industrial and Transitional Economies* (Cambridge University Press, 1997), *The American Economy: The Struggle for Supremacy in the 21st Century* (Cambridge University Press, 1994), and *Restructuring the Soviet Economy: In Search of the Market* (1991). A leading specialist in comparative economic systems, Professor Spulber's teaching and research have focused on the complex role of the state – that is, governments and their administrations – in such varied cases as developing and transitional economies, centrally planned economies, and highly developed market economies.

Russia's Economic Transitions

From Late Tsarism to the New Millennium

NICOLAS SPULBER

Indiana University

CAMBRIDGE
UNIVERSITY PRESS

CAMBRIDGE UNIVERSITY PRESS
Cambridge, New York, Melbourne, Madrid, Cape Town, Singapore, São Paulo

Cambridge University Press
The Edinburgh Building, Cambridge CB2 2RU, UK

Published in the United States of America by Cambridge University Press, New York

www.cambridge.org
Information on this title: www.cambridge.org/9780521816991

First published 2003
This digitally printed first paperback version 2006

A catalogue record for this publication is available from the British Library

Library of Congress Cataloguing in Publication data
Spulber, Nicolas.
Russia's economic transitions; from late tsarism to the new millennium / Nicolas Spulber.
p. cm.
Includes bibliographical references and index.
ISBN 0-521-81699-8 (hardback)
1. Russia – Economic conditions – 1861–1917.   2. Soviet Union – Economic conditions.
3. Russia (Federation) – Economic conditions – 1991–   I. Title.
HC334.5 .S68   2002
330.947′08–dc21   2002024679

ISBN-13 978-0-521-81699-1 hardback
ISBN-10 0-521-81699-8 hardback

ISBN-13 978-0-521-02458-7 paperback
ISBN-10 0-521-02458-7 paperback

For Pauline, with love

Contents

Figures and Tables

Figures

Tables

Preface

The identification of the term *transition* with the passage to market-oriented reforms, of the post-Communist economies – now systematically designated as the "transition economies" – may convey the narrow, restricted view that no other major socioeconomic transition has occurred in the past, or could be unfolding anywhere else in the present. Actually, in its general sense, the term *transition* refers to *any* passage or progression through an intermediary situation between two different sets of conditions or circumstances. A socioeconomic transition refers hence to the period of transformations through which a country passes while experiencing the impact of newly emerging ownership and production relations.

Since the early 1860s, Russia underwent three major economic transitions that reshaped her socioeconomic structures and property relations. The main questions to be considered with regard to these and to any other conditions are: Which specific factors contribute to the rise of tendencies toward a country's socioeconomic transformation? Which ideas relating to the forms of government, the scope of the state's actions, and the socioeconomic relations confront each other and eventually gain popular interest and support at certain historical moments? How do these ideas, in conjunction with other major factors – such as war losses and the expansion of the popular mistrust in the prevailing socioeconomic framework – bring about vast structural displacements? These are the main problems related not only to the study of Russia's transformations but to the broader question of economic development in general. And, these are essentially the main problems with which this book is concerned.

Russia's first socioeconomic transition began in Imperial Tsarist Russia after the disastrous Crimean War (1853–6). It brought to the fore from 1856 onward the question of the emancipation of the peasantry from serfdom, the partial breakup of feudal frameworks, and the opening up of diverse pathways toward capitalist relations. The second major Russian transition began after another disastrous war leading to the collapse of Tsarist Russia in 1917; it put in power an all-encompassing state ownership and administration, imposed new patterns of socioeconomic relations, and placed the country's development under the aegis of central state command. Finally, the latest transition, the third, started in the early 1990s, after a series of internal crises tore apart the Soviet Union; since then, it has continued to reshape the country's economic fabric mainly on the basis of private ownership, with the aim of ensuring its development within an expanding market-directed framework.

The three transitions originated within different socioeconomic settings, evolved under the impact of different conceptions and measures, and resulted in different patterns of economic transformations. Yet the three of them have certain things in common. To start with, each of them changed the country's foundations, namely its ownership structure, on which its subsequent socioeconomic transformations were to evolve. The first cast away certain feudal barriers blocking the way toward broader capitalist relations. The second ruthlessly eliminated the private ownership forms and replaced them with all-embracing state controls over the means of production. Finally, the third, after inheriting the vast Soviet centralized ownership, dismantled it throughout various phases, reinstated private ownership, and let market relations grow in various directions. Extensive, conflicting, and highly passionate debates concerning the proper directions of the country's transformations and the measures needed to achieve these transformations took place on the political scene and among the intelligentsia, both before and during these socioeconomic transitions. These debates are of great interest from many points of view. I focus herein on the content and the interrelations between these debates, and on the wide divergences between what was aimed at and assumed to occur and what was actually achieved, at least in part, under pressure, through the policy makers' decisions and legislative acts.

In broad outline, during the Tsarist time, the main debates among the intelligentsia focused, on the one hand, on the country's eventual development with regard to the destiny of the masses of the peasantry and of its specific pattern of organization (the village commune) and, on the other hand, on to the country's basic ownership structure and of its pattern of growth and change in relation to those pursued in the advanced capitalist countries. Concerning the peasant communes, the great currents of change, such as the populist one, asserted that this pattern of organization was the foundation of the Russian life, and that it is on its soil "that a new social order will arise." As far as the general pattern of development was concerned, various famous populist leaders affirmed that Russia did not need to follow the Western path "step by step" but rather that it could, thanks to its exposure to Western ideas, take "a short cut instead." From the 1890s on, the increasingly influential Marxists rejected these approaches to both the commune and development in general. They asserted that the country could not advance without discarding the concept of the commune – an obsolete adjunct of the manorial organization – and some of them added that eventually a certain share of the peasantry would become rich and land-owning while the rest of the peasantry would become "proletarian." While the so-called right-wing Marxists claimed that the country was evolving toward capitalism, the left-wing Marxists, the Bolsheviks under the leadership of Lenin, eventually contended that the country was ready to transcend capitalism and was thus moving toward "the next phase, namely socialism."

After the collapse of Tsarism, the Bolsheviks nationalized all the means of production – creating in fact a *sui generis* state capitalism – instituting a centrally controlled system of employment on the basis of centrally fixed wages. After various conceptual and factual retreats and reassertions, the Bolsheviks attempted to direct all economic processes through centralized plans. All opposition views were rejected, and soon afterward opposition leaders were assassinated with or without judicial process. The peasantry was first deprived of land, then granted land, then again deprived of land, and finally enrolled in "collective farms," a Bolshevik reincarnation of the old village communes. The Bolsheviks, rebaptized as Communists, assumed the whole power, but willy-nilly had to create a vast strata of managers and administrators – the nomenklatura. Notwithstanding its theoretical complete dependence on the Communist Party's commands and directives, the nomenklatura felt increasingly capable of cheating the system, falsifying the results of its assignments, and finally asserting extensive controls over the activities of their enterprises, particularly in the 1980s. The Soviet press continued to claim higher and higher achievements while the system was in fact failing to meet most of its targets from its very inception. Eventually the Soviet Union started to break up in its outer empire – in Hungary in 1954–7, 1965, and then again in 1984–5; in Poland in 1956–7, in the early 1970s, and then in 1982; and in Czechoslovakia in 1967–8. Russia itself, plagued by a variety of poorly hidden planning and management distortions and crises, finally had to recognize openly, from 1986 on, that its system could not actually surmount its numerous and complex inefficiencies. It became thus increasingly evident, as the great economist Ludwig von Mises had pointed out already in 1922, that the "socialization" (nationalization) of the means of production precluded rational economic calculation; neither artificial markets nor artificial competition, nor manipulated prices, could indeed provide ways toward the rational allocation of resources.

After the collapse of the USSR in 1991–2, the state's lasting legacies explain the creation of the personalistic, presidential republic of the new Russian Federation. The new presidential administration combined from the outset unlimited central power in some respects with total lack of accountability, limited loyalty, and uncertain reliance on the new and old nomenklatura arising out of the remains of the old ownership system. The new regime was established within the framework of sharp socioeconomic and political debates over the most appropriate ways of a rapid transition to expanding market relations. The key issues in discussion concerned the resort to a "shock therapy" involving stabilization and price liberalization and the eventual recourse to vast privatizations. After an ineffective application of the "shock" solution, and following a massive inflation, two sequential privatization measures – one based on a voucher scheme, the other on a loans for shares scheme – finally achieved a broad but not fully complete transfer of production to private ownership. A certain number of new top owners of Russian enterprises – some of whom are the so-called tycoons or oligarchs who gained more or less legitimately high positions in production, and in trade – have thrived. The rest of the economy, however, has continued its process of increasing obsolescence and decay.

It is against this background that I present extensively both the widely ramified debates over Russia's economic transformations and eventual development, and the actual phases of the historical processes of transition toward a different economic system. The book is divided into three parts, identically structured, dealing with the same problems of change respectively under Tsarism (Part I), under the Soviets (Part II), and under the new presidential republic (Part III). Each part is in turn divided into three groups of studies of the varied and complex processes of transformations, involving respectively: i) the state, the economy, and society; ii) the economy's sectors; and iii) the handling of the social accounts. In turn, each of these three groups comprises three chapters. The first group defines the socioeconomic framework, the transition issues, and the economic policies. The second handles the sectoral transition in agriculture, industry, and trade. Finally, the third deals with money, credit, and state finance, and concludes with an overall view. The indicated identical structure of the three parts and of their subdivisions has two objects: first, the possibility of studying each transition in its respective interconnected processes of transformation; and second, the possibility of comparing the debates, decisions, and actions involved in each of the three transitions with regard to the key issues concerning the paths of transformation, the sectoral developments, the patterns of growth and change, and the final results.

The book as a whole aims to present the complex problems that arise in any large-scale transition from one systemic economic pattern to another designed to function under a different ownership structure. In the Russian case, the transitions involved first the passage from a system deeply rooted in a feudal framework into a mixed, half-free, half-controlled market system; second, the passage from the latter to an economy based on centralized state capitalism aiming to guide the economic processes via commands, as well as distorted prices and artificial markets; and third, the passage from that centralized and militarized Communist economy into a market-directed system – a transition resulting from a political choice rather than from historically spontaneous, long-term economic and social development. These transformations were not, as the reader will see throughout this book, the only ones that Russia or empire could have followed or was bound to follow. Indeed, the wide, complex debates that preceded the transition processes and continued through them show clearly the wide range of transformation options envisaged by different actors. As various observers noted about the sequence and speed of economic transformations in Eastern Europe as a whole, the processes of reform and change of the economy and of the state took place in a constant confrontation between "the new and the old," as many people continued to be uncertain whether the emerging new capitalist system has been the right goal, and whether the best possible variant of the capitalist system has indeed been the one selected. It is also clear that there are unavoidable vast discrepancies between the targets set by socioeconomic reformers and by political leaders, and the development patterns that ensued.

As for the future, the book sketches a broad outline of Russia's prospective developments. It underscores the existence of the numerous conflicts bound to arise between the complex, historical inheritances from the four hundred years of the Tsarist centralized autarchic state and from the seventy-five years of the equally centralized Communist system, and the drive toward an open society based on private property and on effective market relations capable of eventually surmounting the existing widespread corruption, barter, bribery, and tax evasion. The book notes in particular the continuing role of the "ownership" positions (explicit or implicit), of the old nomenklatura, struggling for the dominance of the economy against the new tycoons (or kleptocrats) emerging as a result of the privatization processes. It points to the peculiar division of powers and responsibilities between the center and the country's numerous regions, economically (and politically) autonomous in various respects, which the center wishes to limit and control. It draws attention to the efforts of the leader of the Russian presidential republic, Vladimir Putin, to strengthen his own powers and reduce those of the country's two chambers (the Duma and the Federation Council) to shrink the sphere of activity of the tycoons, to eliminate some of them, to expand the control of the center over the regions – and to do all of this while coping with the nagging problems of a widely decaying economy whose reconstruction and economic reorientation will require significant efforts over decades. The book finally suggests that the most probable pattern of the country's overall organization will be fashioned in many respects along the lines of East Asian and Latin American authoritarian and autocratic designs rather than on the Western European democratic models. Yet, as the great Russian poet Alexander Blok once put it truly and beautifully, historically Russia "could not sate her eyes" gazing and gazing with both "love and hate" upon the West (whose achievements obviously she wished to attain but failed). While the West, in its turn, has watched intrigued and confused, "like Oedipus before the Sphinx's enigmatic eyes," both the exaltations and the grieving of Russia.[1]

---

[1] Throughout the text and the notes I use only the Library of Congress' Romanization Table of the Russian alphabet. Various translators of Russian use at times different kinds of transliteration, hence the different spellings of various names and even of the same name (such as *Liashchenko* in the Library of Congress Romanization and *Lyashchenko* in a well-known English translation) in this book's notes.

This work is addressed to economists, sociologists, political scientists, historians, as well as the educated public at large. The three complex transition processes illustrate in many respects both the past and the current issues involved in the major processes of transformation of many developing countries. The research on which this book is based has been funded in part by generous grants in aid extended to me by the dean of research of Indiana University's Graduate School, Professor George Walker. I am also deeply indebted for his support to the former dean of the College of Arts and Science, Professor Mort Lowengrub. I am further indebted to my colleagues who have kindly read parts of or the entire manuscript and who have made numerous and valuable suggestions and recommendations, namely Professors Michael Alexeev, Robert Becker, Matei Calinescu, Robert Campbell, Roy Gardner, Michael Kaganovich, Elyce Rotella, and David Ransel (the Director of the Russian and East European Institute). I have also benefited greatly from free access to the valuable personal collections of Russian economics books and statistical materials of Alexeev and Campbell, for which I am deeply grateful.

I thank the librarians of the Reference Department and of the Government Publications Department of the Indiana University Library for the continuous and very useful help they extended to me during the preparation of this work. My debt is also great to Suzanne Hull, of the Graphic Services Department of Indiana University, who with understanding and ability produced the graphs included in the text; to John Hollingsworth of the Cartographic Services of Geography, who carefully designed the maps; and to Linda Baker, who intelligently and graciously typed the various versions of the manuscript.

Finally, I am greatly indebted to Andy Saff for his wise and precise editorial help, and I am also indebted to Robert Swanson, who constructed the index. I am responsible for all the remaining errors.

Nicolas Spulber

PART I

THE TSARIST ECONOMIC TRANSITION

CHAPTER I

The Socioeconomic Framework

1-1. Territory and Population

The humiliating defeat of the Russian Empire in the Crimean War (1853–6) by an Anglo-French expeditionary force of only seventy thousand men assisting Turkey, the "sick man of Europe," revealed clearly the Russian incompetence at the highest political and military levels, the inferiority of the quality of Russia's armaments, the absence of an adequate system of transportation for moving troops on her own territory, and Russia's overall backwardness. The military and diplomatic disaster shattered the stability of the Empire, threw Russia out of the Near East, destroyed its influence in Europe, and raised immediately the question of the future course of Russia's development.

Facing the necessary reorganization of its military establishment – increasing the combat effectiveness of its army and moving toward the modernization of its economy (and the underlying railroad network) – Russia needed, on the one hand, to ward off the widespread dissatisfaction and social instability of the peasantry concerning its postwar status, and, on the other hand, to overcome the deep-seated conflicts within the nobility concerning the increasingly evident necessity of handling as soon as possible the questions of land tenure and peasant serfdom. Finally, on February 19, 1861, Tsar Alexander II launched a historically decisive reform emancipating the peasantry from feudal dependence and also establishing a complex set of procedures intended to preserve as much of the gentry's control over most of the best land, as well as its privileged status in the society, as possible. On the other hand, the reform created along with the landowning gentry a landowning peasantry, and, in time, opened numerous ways and byways to transform Russian society. Notably, the reform increased differentiation among peasantry, shifted land ownership, increased agricultural output, expanded markets, and spread capitalist relations. However, the reform also maintained various legal differences among the country's social strata (the so-called social estates).

In these conditions, the question of Russia's path of development became of decisive importance not only for the Tsarist regime, its bureaucracy, and its policies, but for the country as a whole and for the public at large. In what direction should Russia's development be guided? Should Russia resolutely take the path pursued by various European states? Should it rather attempt to forge a new, unique path of growth and change that would "jump over" certain phases and stages of Europe's development? Should Russia actually reverse its course decisively and simply return to the old pre–Peter the Great path? Or, in fact, should Russia just try to adjust itself to the sporadic, spontaneous, largely unavoidable capitalist relations spreading willy-nilly throughout the economy? I will return in detail in the next two chapters to the passionate debates and to the action these issues brought forth. For now, I will first attempt to sketch in broad historical outline the evolving characteristics of the Russian Empire from the post-reform period up to the end of the Tsarist regime, the framework within which these debates and these actions took place. The questions to be considered in this respect are the following: Did the Russian Empire continue to expand territorially after the Crimean disaster? To what extent, and exactly in which directions? What was the pace of growth of the population, and what were its social characteristics? How did the rural society, on the one hand, and the urban society, on the other, evolve after the reform? How did the Tsarist command and control system actually function? In which particular ways did the expanding capitalist market relations combine with certain persistent feudal methods of production and with certain equally persistent feudal institutions?

Consider first the question of the Empire's territorial situation. After the Crimean defeat, Russia turned much of its attention toward the Asian continent. Consolidating the portions that it had acquired there from the beginning of the nineteenth century, Russia advanced successfully, first in the Eastern Caucasus, and then, after a series of campaigns and annexations in Central Asia, Russia took over the so-called Transcaucasian region, completing the Empire's full control over the Eurasian plain. Concomitantly, Russia started to change its boundaries in the Far East. The Empire obtained the southern half of the island of Sakhalin (in exchange for ceding to Japan the Kurils islands). By 1897 Russia acquired a twenty-five-year lease of Port Arthur and Talienwan (Dairen) – arrangements that were to be called into question after Russia's defeat in the 1904–5 war with Japan. Following that war, Russia was forced to recognize the "predominant interest" of Japan in Korea, ceded to Japan the lease on Port Arthur and Dairen along with the South Manchurian Railway (the so-called Eastern Chinese Railway), and returned to Japan the southern half of the Sakhalin island. On the other hand, Russia's conquests in the nineteenth century in the Caucasus, Central Asia, and the Far East made the Empire's southern boundary a lasting one; indeed, that boundary stretching from the Black Sea to the Sea of Japan assumed by the end of the nineteenth century the shape that it was to maintain until the collapse of the Soviet party-state in 1991 (see Figure 1-1).

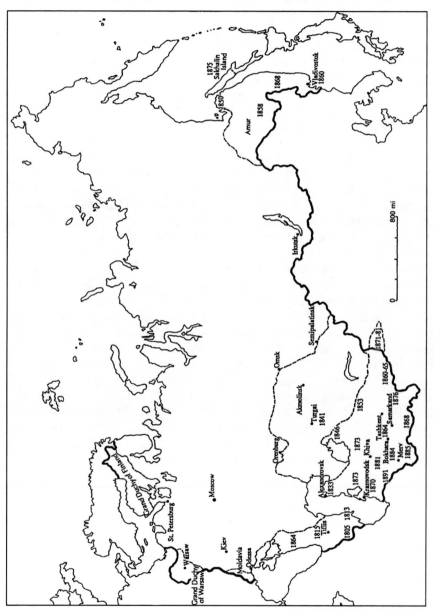

Figure 1-1. Russian Empire Expansion, 1800–1914

5

Russia's position in Eastern Europe started to improve unexpectedly fourteen years after the Crimean defeat, as a consequence of the Franco-Prussian War of 1870. In exchange for Russia's neutrality in that war, Germany supported Russia's demand for the abrogation of the dispositions of the post–Crimean War Treaty of Paris (of 1856) forbidding any Russian activity on and around the Black Sea. In 1876 Turkey had to accept a Russian ultimatum requesting the establishment of autonomous administrations for Bosnia, Herzegovina, and Bulgaria. Finally the Treaty of Berlin of 1878, ending the Balkan war, recognized the independence of the Romanian principalities, and of Serbia and Montenegro, sanctioned a special status for the three-way partitioned Bulgaria, and ceded Southern Bessarabia to Russia.[1]

By the end of the nineteenth century, the immense European-Asian Russian Empire extended over 22,430,440 square kilometers – over 8,660,390 square miles (in contrast to 7,770,882 square miles in 1862), a total including European Russia's 1,902,202 square miles, Caucasus' 180,843 square miles, Central Asia and the steppe region's 1,548,825 square miles, Siberia's 4,833,496 square miles, plus Poland's 49,159 square miles and Finland's 144,255 square miles. (In comparison, note that the giant United States extended in 1860 as well as in 1900 over 3,020,789 square miles)[2]

According to the estimates available, not always consistent from source to source, the population of European Russia increased from the morrow of 1861 to near the end of the nineteenth century (in 1897) from 69.9 million to some 94 million. From 1861 to 1914 – the entire period under review – the population of European Russia more than doubled, reaching 128.8 million. Imperial Russia, excluding Poland and Finland, increased from 1861 to 1897 from 69.9 million to 117.1 million, and also more than doubled for the entire period beginning in the early 1860s, rising by 1914 to 162.8 million (see Table 1-1). Including Poland and Finland, the Empire saw its population rise from 1897 to 1914 from 129.1 million to 178.3 million (with the population of Poland and Finland accounting respectively for 9.4 and 2.5 million in 1897 and for 12.2 and 3.2 million in 1914).[3] The growth of Russia's population was one of the critical factors that affected the processes of Russia's transformations from 1861 onward.

---

[1] See Pushkarev, Sergei, *The Emergence of Modern Russia 1801–1917*, Alberta, Pica Press, 1985, pp. 337–43, 353–8.

[2] *Appleton's Annual Encyclopedia 1899*, New York, Appleton, 1900, p. 756; *Statistical Abstract of the United States 1946*, Washington, DC, U.S. Department of Commerce, 1946, p. 4.

[3] Up to the general census of 1897, the population data for Russia consist of estimates not always consistent with one another notwithstanding the great efforts of Soviet demographers to surmount the difficulties involved and to produce reliable series for the nineteenth century. See, for instance, the numerous inconsistences present even in the important work of A. G. Rashin, *Naselenie Rossii za 100 let* (The population of Russia over one hundred years), *Moscow Gosstaizdat*, 1956. See notably pp. 26, 47, 48, and compare to *Rossiia 1913, Statistiko dokumental'nyi spravochnik* (Russia, 1913, Statistical Documentary Reference Book), used by the Russian Academy of Science, St. Petersburg, 1995, p. 16.

Table 1-1 *Russian Empire[a]: Population in Millions, 1863, 1897, in 1914*

Areas	1863	1897	1914	1914/1863
European Russia	61.1	94.2	128.8	210
Caucasus	4.1	9.4	12.9	314
Siberia	3.1	5.8	10.0	322
Central Asia	1.6	7.7	11.1	693
TOTAL	69.9	117.1	162.8	233

Note:
[a] Excluding Poland and Finland.
Sources: For 1863, Rashin, A. G., *Naselenie Rossii za 100 Let*. (The Population of Russia over one hundred years), Moscow, *Gosstatizdat*, 1956, p. 26; for 1897 and 1914, Rossiiskaia Akademia Nauk, *Rossiia 1913 god. Statistko – dokumental'nyi spravochnik* (Russian Academy of Science, Russia in 1913. Statistical – documentary reference work), St. Petersburg, Blitz, 1995, p. 16.

Table 1-2 *Russian Empire[a]: Rural, Urban, and Total Population,[b] 1811–1914, in Thousands and Percentages*

Years	European Russia			Imperial Russia			European Russia urban population Percent	Imperial Russia urban population Percent
	Rural	Urban	Total	Rural	Urban	Total		
1811	39,020	2,785	41,805	40,983	2,802	43,785	6.6	6.4
1867	56,007	6,543	62,550	66,193	7,395	73,588	10.5	10.0
1897	81,378	12,065	93,442	101,541	14,696	116,237	12.9	12.6
1914[b]	103,183	18,597	121,780	135,876	23,277	159,153	15.3	14.7

Notes:
[a] Excluding Poland and Finland.
[b] January 1, 1914, or the end of 1913.
Sources: Based on Rashin, A. G., *Naselenie Rosii za 100 let, op. cit.*, pp. 27, 45, 87, 88, 95, 98, 101; for the end of 1913 data, *Tsentral'noe statisticheskoe Upravlenie, Naselenie SSSR, 1973* (Population of the USSR, 1973), Moscow Statistika, 1957, p. 7.

A salient feature of Russia's pattern of population growth during the nineteenth century was the slow growth of the urban population. As can be seen in Table 1-2, over the 103 years from 1811 to 1914, the rural population increased massively both in European Russian and in the Empire as a whole. During the same period, the Empire's urban population increased only from 6.4 percent of the total population to 14.7 percent. If we take into account that Imperial Russia expanded its rule in the southeast and the east through unstable territories with imprecise boundaries and unreliable populations, and we focus only on European Russia's urbanization, we find that there, too, urban changes followed closely the same growth pattern: from 6.6 percent of the total population in 1811 to only 15.3 percent in 1914. In 1811, only two cities, Petersburg and Moscow, had populations of over one hundred thousand. By 1863, only one additional city reached the one hundred thousand level; by 1897, eleven additional cities did so as well, resembling "the pattern which had existed in Europe in the twelfth and thirteenth centuries." Besides Moscow, the large towns with a population of one hundred thousand and more that owed their progress to commercial relations with the foreign countries lay close to the frontier, stretching in an arc beginning with Petersburg in the northwest, continuing southward, and coming to an end with Nizhni-Novgorod in the east.[4] The contrast between Russia and West European countries such as France, Belgium, Germany, and England, where the towns included well over one-third of the population, was striking. The contrast is even more telling when one compares Imperial Russia to the United States, then clearly the opposite poles of modern civilization. In 1860, the total population of the United States amounted to 31.4 million, of whom 19.7 percent lived in urban areas; by 1890 the U.S. total population reached 62.9 million, of whom 35.1 percent lived in the cities; by 1910, out of a total population of 92 million, 45.6 percent lived in the rapidly growing industrializing cities.[5]

The inhabitants of Imperial Russia, amounting in 1897 to a total of 126.9 million including Poland and Finland, belonged to some 110 different nationalities, speaking 54 main languages, apart from various minor tongues. These nationalities can be grouped into four basic divisions: Indo-European, Uralo-Altaic, Semitic, and groups isolated by language. They accounted respectively for 80.6 percent, 13.7 percent, 4.1 percent, and 1.6 percent of the total population. The first group used nineteen and other languages, the second twenty-six and other idioms, the third mainly Yiddish and Hebrew (for religious services) and a very small percentage of other Semitic tongues, and the fourth, eight and other idioms.[6]

The indicated multinational divisions were reflected in different religious beliefs and devotions. Until the expansion of the Russian state in non-Slav areas, Russian religious homogeneity was secured under Russian Orthodox Christianity. From the end of the eighteenth century on, when large numbers of people were brought within the expanding state, the situation changed, at least away from the Empire's center. The growth of the Empire brought within its frontiers indeed a considerable number of Catholics (Poles and Lithuanians), Protestants (Finns, Estonians, and Latvians), Moslems (Turks and Iranians), Buddhists (Mongols and Kalmuks), and last but not least, a large number of Jews. The latter, treated as second-class citizens, were confined into seventeen

[4] Valentine, J. Bill, *The Forgotten Class: The Russian Bourgeoisie from the Earliest Beginnings to 1900*, New York, Praeger, 1959, p. 206.
[5] Peterson, John M., and Gray, Ralph, *Economic Development of the United States*, Homewood, IL, Richard D. Irwin, 1969, pp. 156, 308.
[6] See Miller, Margaret S., *The Economic Development of Russia 1905–1914, with Special Reference to Trade, Industry, and Finance*, London, P. S. King, 1926, pp. 10–13.

gubernias (regions, provinces, or governments) of European Russia and into the ten *gubernias* of Poland – jointly forming the "Pale (of Jewish) Settlement." "Western" in outlook and believers of an "alien" religion, most of the Jews did not fit easily into the traditionalist Russian world rendered particularly hostile to them by the paternalistic, intolerant, and deeply antisemitic Orthodox Church. Great Russian nationalism, which identified itself eagerly with the exaltation of the Orthodox Church, and whose policy of russification coincided with religious persecution, assumed its most brutal and outrageous antisemitic forms under Alexander III and his successor, Nicolas II. The pogroms of 1881–2 in southern Russia, the "quiet" pogroms organized all over by the police with the help of illiterate crowds, the bloody pogroms of Kishinev in 1903, the pogroms of 1905, along with all kinds of mischievous fabrications such as the Beilis Case (concerning an alleged Jewish ritual murder) and the *Protocols of the Elders of Zion* (a vicious, forged publication by the Russian secret police widely referenced by modern antisemites), became the indelible marks of the official Russian antisemitism. The results of this policy were momentous for the Jews and for the world. One of these results was the accelerated Jewish emigration from Russia and Poland, which greatly enlarged the Jewish communities of Britain and the United States. Another direct result of that official policy was that Russian Jews thronged into the revolutionary movements, a fact that many of them had to regret after the victory of Bolshevism, when again – as we shall see later on – antisemitism became woven into the fabric of political conflicts throughout the history of Communism.[7]

In Imperial Russia, individuals were not facing the state in a uniform way. The country's "administrative nomenclature" classified each human under a specific heading. As noted by Anatole Leroy-Beaulieu, the state did not have in front of it citizens or subjects, but only specific social categories – in Russian, *sosloviia* (a term roughly equivalent to *estates*, *categories*, or *orders*) – to which each individual belonged. The system distinguished, from 1649 on, four social categories or estates: *gentry*, *clergy*, *townspeople*, and *peasants*. These categories eventually acquired various subdivisions: The gentry was divided into hereditary and personal nobility; the clergy split at the margin into different, competing religious sects, and new religious beliefs besides the dominant one; the townspeople divided into several groups, including the growing number of professional people, the honorary citizens (hereditary or personal), the merchants (assigned to three and later to two "guilds"), the small traders along with craftsmen, artisans, and townspeople including industrial workers; and finally in the countryside, the peasants, comprised on the one hand of the peasants

---

[7] Rogger, Hans, *Jewish Policies and Right-Wing Politics in Imperial Russia*, Berkeley and Los Angeles, University of California Press, 1986, particularly pp. 25–39; see also various contributions in *The Jews in Soviet Russia since 1917*, Kochan, Lionel, ed., London, Oxford University Press for the Institute of Jewish Affairs, 1970; Setton-Watson, Hugh, *The Decline of Imperial Russia 1855–1914*, New York, Praeger, 1952, pp. 158–61.

of the nobles and, on the other hand, of the peasants of the crown. The state eventually added various accessory categories to take account of complex social changes. Thus the army started to be registered separately, particularly because of the use of a specially organized war caste, the Cossacks, with certain duties notably on the southern frontier of the Empire. None of these categories, nor their subdivisions, corresponded to Western social classes.[8]

The gentry (*dvorianstvo* – from *dvor* [courtyard]) did not form a closed caste. Peter the Great had established the rule that the highest grade of the civil service was to be granted the title of *hereditary* nobility, while the holders of lower positions in the civil service were to be accorded the title of *personal* nobility or of "honorary citizens." By competing for offices and court favors, the gentry remained divided and incapable of coalescing into a coherently organized status group, even though the summit of the hereditary gentry continued to retain the leading positions in the society even by the beginning of the twentieth century. The Orthodox Christian clergy (*duchovenstvo*) also continued to be viewed as forming part of the society's upper strata, even though the reforms of Alexander II deprived clergymen of the hereditary privilege on which their foundation rested until the 1880s. In the towns, the top social category was that of hereditary honorable citizen (*potomstvennyi pochtennyi grazhdanin*), usually awarded to influential or very wealthy merchants, financiers, and industrialists. Other merchants (the *kuptsy*) were divided for tax purposes into two "guilds." The first guild consisted of rich industrialists and professional people. Also among the townspeople, the last category – the broad group of small traders, craftsmen, and so on (the *meshchanstvo*) – was subject to military obligation and paid the head tax just like any peasant (although they were freed from the latter obligation in 1866, years before the peasants' tax burden was lightened).[9]

As shown in Table 1-3, at the close of the nineteenth century the hereditary gentry accounted for only 1 percent of the population of European Russia, and as I point out in the next section, vast differences existed within this upper stratum in terms of wealth, landholding, and number of peasant serfs. Both the gentry and the clergy, the traditional upper strata of the society, by 1897 registered sharp decreases from their relative leads of 1858 (on the eve of the great reforms of Alexander II). The 1897 decrease ranged from a joint total of 2.5 percent of the population to 1.5 percent. On the other hand the townspeople estate and the peasants estate registered massive increases. Within the townspeople, the actual growth was accounted for by the *meshchanstvo*, the

[8] Leroy-Beaulieu, Anatole, *L'Empire des Tsars et les Russes* (The Empire of the Tsars and the Russians), Vol. 2, *Le pays et les habitants* (The Country and the Inhabitants), Lausanne, L'âge d'Homme, 1888, reissued 1988, pp. 266–79.

[9] Pushkarev, Sergei, *The Emergence of Modern Russia 1801–1917, op. cit.*, pp. 324–7; Blackwell, William L., *The Beginnings of Russian Industrialization 1800–1860*, Princeton, NJ, Princeton University Press, 1968, pp. 101–4.

Table 1-3 *European Russia: The Population by Estates* (sosloviia) *in 1858 and 1897, in Thousands and Percentages*

Estates	1858			1897		
	Thousand	Thousand	Percent	Thousand	Thousand	Percent
Hereditary gentry	886.8		1.5	888.8		1.0
Clergy	601.9		1.0	501.5		.05
Townspeople estate including:	4,300.4		7.3	10,980.2		11.9
Honorary citizens[a]		347.5	0.6		794.6	.08
Merchants		399.6	0.7		239.6	.03
Small traders		3,553.3	6.0		9,946.0	10.8
Peasants estate	48,953		83.7	78,641.4		85.1
Military estate	3,767.4		6.5	1,439.7		1.5
TOTALS	58,510.0		100.0	92,448.6		100.0

Note:
[a] Including in 1897 also personal gentry and officials.
Source: Rashin, A. G., *Naselenie Rossii za 100 let, op.cit.*, pp. 259, 262.

vast and ill-defined mixed group including "declassés," members of the gentry, shopkeepers, craftsmen, and so on. The *meshchanstvo* grew from 6.1. percent to 10.7 percent of the much larger population of 1897. Finally, the peasants estate rose from 83.7 to 85.1 percent of the total population.

After this global view of the structure of the society of European Russia, I turn in the next section to the social structure and characteristics of the Russian countryside, and then to the demographic composition and characteristics of Russia's towns.

1-2. The Rural Society

The structure of Russia's rural society is only indirectly reflected in the respective size of the *sosloviia* of the hereditary gentry and the peasantry. On the one hand, the landholding, serf-owning core of the gentry was quite small, and, in addition, it was highly diversified in terms of wealth and power. On the other hand, the massive privately owned peasant serfs – those owned by the *pomeshchiki* (landlords) – represented only a part of the peasantry as a whole. According to the data furnished by I. D. Koval'chenko, in 1857 the total of 106,391 landlords of forty-seven *gubernias* (governments of provinces) of European Russia had in their private service a total of 10,694,000 "souls" (that is, male serfs only). The peasant male serfs were distributed as follows among the various categories of landlords: 3.3 percent of the "souls" in question were in the hands of the gentry with up to twenty serfs only; 15.9 percent were held by gentry with from twenty-one to one hundred souls; the balance of over 80 percent were held by the gentry with over one hundred "souls" each, a necessary condition for the owner to belong to the regional Assembly of the Noblemen. The petty gentry with up to twenty serfs lived little better than the serfs themselves. Those with twenty-one to one hundred serfs had a modest standard of living. But even within the privileged group with over one hundred serfs, further deep differences prevailed. The bulk of the serfs was accounted for on the eve of the 1861 reform by the gentry with one hundred to five hundred serfs; this group held 37.2 percent of the total. The gentry with five hundred to one thousand serfs held 14.9 percent of the serfs, and finally at the summit of the pyramid, those with over one thousand serfs, held at least 28.7 percent of the total "souls."[10]

All the land of the estates was divided into two parts: seignorial or *demesne* land, and *peasant* land. The serf's obligation to the landlord for the use of this land depended on the size and quality of the seignorial land, on the economic considerations of the landlord, and on his preferred method of organizing the farming of his demesne. Two basic systems of servitude were in use: the serfs' tilling the lords' demesne (the *barshchina* system), and the serfs' discharging their obligations to the landlords by paying a quitrent (the *obrok* system). The latter system was preferred by the landlord where the returns from land were low. As for the serfs, as farming alone was insufficient to feed them and allow them to pay the quitrent, many of them had to engage in various trades and/or to seek employment in the cities. The quitrent yielded thus a certain independence to the serfs, but this independence was insecure as it could be ended whenever the landlord chose to shift to a more onerous kind of servitude. The *barshchina* system bound the serf rigidly to the soil. Under that system, the peasants were supposed to till the lord's demesne with their livestock and implements for three days per week – but the latter limit was flexible and could be extended to seven days per week. In addition, the landlords aimed to reduce as much as possible the area of peasant landholding in order to expand the demesne land. At the extreme, certain serfs were entirely deprived of their holdings and converted into slave labor receiving a monthly ration from the landlord (hence their designation as *mesiachniki* – monthly paid serfs).

On the eve of the serfs' emancipation, the *barschina* system accounted for close to 72 percent of the serf population of European Russia, the *obrok* system for the balance of 28 percent. The first system was dominant in the black soil areas, the second in the less fertile areas. Within the indicated regions, and varying according to specific economic conditions, the *barschina* tended to predominate on the estates of medium size in as much as the method required not only the presence of the owner but also his active participation in farming

---

[10] Koval'chenko, I. D., *Russkoe krepostnoe krest'anstvo v pervoi polovine XIX v* (Russian Peasant Serfdom in the First Half of the Nineteenth Century), Moscow, Izd. Moskovskogo Universiteta, 1967, pp. 58–9.

the land. On the other hand, the *obrok* tended to predominate in both the very large and the very small holdings, in the former case because their landlords lived mostly in the cities, and in the latter instance because the amount of land was barely enough even for peasant farming.

As the 1858 data furnished by the economic historian Peter Liashchenko point out, the privately owned serfs of both sexes numbering 21.0 million accounted for 39.0 percent of the total peasant population of 51.5 million. (The landlords' serfs included not only the serfs under the *barschina* or the *obrok* systems, but also the serfs rendering service in the gentry's households, that is, the *manorial* serfs [*dvorovye*].) In addition, there were 2.0 million serfs of the Imperial family, and 518,000 private factory serfs. Workers in the mines and other peasants accounted for over 10 million people, while the remaining 18.7 million group – that is, over 36 percent of the total – was constituted by the state peasants (*gosudarstvennye krest'iane*) legally designated as "free rural inhabitants."[11] These peasants predominated in the northern and a few southern *gubernias*, as well as in Siberia. Their liberty has been often endangered by the manipulations of venal bureaucrats and by encroachments of landlords. Some of these peasants had been even reduced to direct bondage when a number of them had been transferred to the ownership of the Imperial family (notably under Nicholas I). Most of the state peasants were subjected to heavy fiscal burdens and experienced great poverty.

The rising pressures for expanding production and productivity, along with pressures for the growth and development of the defense industry, of trade, and of the towns following the Crimean War, called forth increasingly not only the need to import and assimilate the advanced industrial methods then spreading through Western Europe, but also and above all to modify the traditional concepts, methods, and technologies dominating Russia's economic foundation, namely farming. It became increasingly evident at various levels of the society that serfdom could not solve the problems of expanding agricultural production. The issues involved generated deep conflicts and brought forth various approaches and proposals about the path of development to follow and the measures needed to achieve real growth. Finally, the Tsarist regime launched the crucial reform of 1861, which cracked up the feudal legal framework, liberated the peasants from many harsh and demeaning feudal charges, and abolished various landowners' privileges, including the rights to

---

[11] Note the slight difference in the total peasant estate given by Rashin for 1858 (48.9 million, cf. Table 1.2) and by Liashchenko (51.5 million). Liashchenko indicates further that the privately owned male serfs amounted in that year to 9.8 million (compared to 10.6 million given for 1857 by Koval'chenko) and that the serfs of both sexes amounted to 20.1 million. The useful breakdown of the serfdom by both males and both sexes, and for each category given by Liashchenko, is used in the important study of Lazar Volin. See Liashchenko, P. I., *Istoriia narodnogo Khoziaistvo SSSR* (History of the National Economy of the USSR), Vol. I, p. 325, in Volin, Lazar, *A Century of Russian Agriculture from Alexander II to Khrushchev*, Cambridge, MA, Harvard University Press, 1970, p. 21.

resettle the peasants, to place them in workhouses, and to sell them. Almost half of the landowners' land – roughly the part that the peasants had been tilling for themselves – was set to become land allotable to the peasants at a "redeeming" price to be determined by intermediaries from the nobility. Put differently, the reform created among the landowning gentry a new land-owning peasantry that owned the allotted land. A number of years after the peasants' agreement with the landlord concerning the high price usually set for the allotted land and the difficulties of paying the great sums involved, the government stepped in and paid directly to the landlords, in interest-bearing notes, 80 percent of the balance due, the rest of 20 percent being left for the peasants to pay for in money or labor. The government's payment to the land-lords became a redemption debt for the peasants to pay to the government, divided into payment over a period of forty-nine years.

The new legal framework did not involve granting the peasants a status equal to that of the members of the other estates. The peasants indeed continued to be subjected to the payment of a head tax (until 1886) and to remain tied in virtual bondage to their specific peasant commune (*obschina*, administered by the assembly of the heads of households, the *mir*), then the dominant segment of peasant landholding and also an effective instrument of government control over the villages. The "redeemed" allotted lands (*nadely*) were handed out not to the individual peasants but to their commune, where these lands became the intangible and unalienable property of its entire membership. The freedoms granted to the landowners' serfs were extended to the state peasants (in 1863) and to the serfs of the Imperial family (in 1866). However, no land was made available for the household serfs. Notwithstanding the reduction (in 1881) of the high redemption payments for the *nadely*, the obligations involved turned out to be increasingly difficult to meet.[12] Finally, during the revolution of 1905, these payments were abolished and new agricultural reforms, introduced in 1906 and approved in 1910 (by the Third Duma [parliament]), finally broke up the rigid rules of the commune system and opened the doors to establishing a class of independent peasant farmers.

According to the data available for 1877, 1905, and 1914, the following basic displacements took place with regard to land ownership (see Table 1-4): The relative land share of the gentry that had started to decrease rapidly after 1861 accelerated its further contraction after 1887, notwithstanding the creation in 1883 of the Bank of Nobility, which mortgaged at favorable terms some of these lands. The share of the lands in question fell from 19.4 percent in 1877 to 12.8 percent in 1905 and then to 10.2 percent in 1914. A part of the nobility had

---

[12] Karycheff, N., "La Propriété Foncière" (Land Ownership), in Commission Imperiale de Russies a l'Exposition Universelle de Paris, *La Russie à la fin du 19ᵉ siècle* (Russia at the End of the Nineteenth Century), Kovalevskii, M. W., ed., Paris, Paul Dupont & Guillaumin, 1900, pp. 113–30.

Table 1-4 *European Russia^a: Landholdings, 1877, 1905, and 1914, Millions of Dessiatins^b and Percentages*

Holders	1877 Millions of dessiatins	Percent	1905 Millions of dessiatins	Percent	1914 Millions of dessiatins	Percent
State and Imperial family	157.8	41.9	145.2	37.5	143.7	37.1
Nobles	73.1	19.4	49.7	12.8	39.6	10.2
Peasants of allotment lands	118.2 (111.6)	31.3 (29.6)	160.9 (136.2)	41.5 (35.1)	170.5 (145.9)	44.0 (37.6)
All others	27.9	7.4	31.9	8.2	8.2	8.7
TOTAL	377.0	100.0	387.7	100.0	387.7	100.0

Notes:
^a Data for 1877 recorded in 49 *gubernias*; for 1905 and 1914 incomplete materials for 47 *gubernias*.
^b 1 dessiatin = 2.7 acres, or 1.09 hectares.
Source: Robinson, Geroid Tanquary, *Rural Russia under the Old Regime*, New York, Macmillan, 1932, pp. 268–72.

undoubtedly expected in 1861 that the redemption payments would allow it to keep much of its lands. But, many of these nobles had already been heavily mortgaged and they received only half of the redemption payments, the rest going for the repayment of these mortgages.[13]

In the meantime, the peasants started to buy land through employment outside the household and through emigration within the Empire or abroad. To assist the peasants' land purchases, a State Peasants' Land Bank was created in 1883, but its impact became effective only after 1895. As indicated in Table 1-4, the most massive transfers involved the allotment lands. Soon after the reforms of 1911, more than 2 million peasant households who had applied to leave the communes had left them and established their personal ownership of the land. The process of the destruction of the communes, which accelerated from then on, intensified the economic stratification of the villages. A well-to-do class of richer peasants emerged, while indigent peasants, on the other hand, often sold their allotments (which after 1906 they had been allowed to retain in their possession after leaving the communes).[14] As numerous sources have pointed out, in the half century that followed the emancipation, a stratum of richer families emerged from the almost uniform "gray" mass of the former serfs. But, fundamentally, the Russian countryside remained characterized "not so

[13] Gille, Bertrand, *Histoiré économique et sociale de la Russie du Moyen Age au XXe siècle* (Economic and Social History of Russia, from the Middle Ages to the Twentieth Century), Payot, Paris, 1949, pp. 177–9.
[14] Pushkarev, Sergei, *The Emergence of Modern Russia . . ., op. cit.*, pp. 265, 267–8.

much by the riches of a relatively few as by the great poverty of the mass. Otherwise the Revolution of 1917 would have taken quite another course."[15]

1-3. The Urban Society

Simultaneously with the basic postemancipation shifts in the economic and social structures of the countryside, broad changes were registered notably in the number of cities and in their socioeconomic development and overall growth – except in one respect: The cities' upper strata grew relatively little during the entire nineteenth century. Both before and after the emancipation reform, the joint share of the high nobility and the high civil servants accounted only for 5 percent of the urban population. Members of the hereditary gentry (old or new historically speaking) continued to provide the osseous framework of the state institutions, "a class of serving nobility" highly occupied with its state duties, but weak politically, legally, and economically, and incapable of playing an important independent role.[16] In addition, many members of both the hereditary and personal gentry began to participate also in various forms in the growing commercial, industrial, and financial enterprises.

Next in the upper hierarchy ranges, the upper clergy of the Russian Orthodox Church, like all the orthodox churches in Eastern Europe, identified itself with the state's policy and administration. Since Peter the Great, church and state were one, and no room was left for ambiguities regarding this relationship. When the clergy petitioned Peter to appoint a patriarch, he answered that that was his role and no one else's. As Tibor Szamuely put it, the Russian ruler could proclaim not only as Louis le Grand, "L'Etat c'est moi," but also, "L'Eglise c'est moi." Since that time, the Tsar administrated the church through the Holy Synod. The latter was the highest court for all ecclesiastical affairs, the guardian of the purity of faith, the guarantor that the clergymen (paid by the state) performed their duties, and the decisive opponent of heretics and religious dissent. The procurator general of the Synod had the authority of a minister in matters of church administration and served as the connecting authority between the Synod and all other state institutions. Since the officially recognized Orthodox Church failed to carve out for itself an autonomous sphere of activity, it drove significant parts of the population toward the dissident Old Believers (officially designated as "Splitters" [*Raskolniki*], and the "Sectarians" [notably the *Skoptsy*], an outgrowth of the Old Believers), as well as toward other sects.[17]

---

[15] Jasny, Naum, *The Socialized Agriculture of the USSR, Plans and Performance*, Stanford, CA, Stanford University Press, 1949, p. 149.

[16] Szamuely, Tibor, *The Russian Tradition*, Conquest, Robert, ed., New York, McGraw-Hill, 1974, pp. 41, 135–6.

[17] *Ibid.*, pp. 105; Pipes, Richard, *Russia under the Old Regime*, New York, Penguin Books, 1974, pp. 221–9.

According to the census of 1897, the "urban estate" – including the "honorary citizens," the merchants, and the small traders – represented 46.7 percent of Imperial Russia's city population. At that time, the "honorary citizens" accounted for 1.1 percent, the merchants 1.3 percent, and the small traders the balance of 44.3 percent. The merchants, industrialists and the financiers, jointly designated as the *kupechestvo*, did not constitute a closed category. Its members came from all the society's strata, including the gentry, and the members of sects or outcast minorities. The Old Believers and the Jews, for instance, excluded from the normal avenues of power and privilege in the army and the administration, turned much of their energies toward trading activities. The Sectarians built an underground trade network from Eastern Europe to Siberia. The Jews, who gained the right to participate openly in commerce and industry only in the 1860s, expanded in trade mainly as peddlers on the road, craftsmen, and shopkeepers, while a small number of rich and educated Jews began, in the 1860s and 1870s, to play important roles in railway construction, industry (especially textile and food), and banking. A few rich and enterprising Jewish industrial businessmen even received titles of "hereditary nobility" already during the nineteenth century or at the beginning of the twentieth – a situation typified by the career of Baron Joseph Ginsburg. Concomitantly, however, many very poor Jews were desperately seeking to escape through emigration from harsh persecution, mass discrimination, and the brutal and incessant attacks against them.[18]

The low category of the urban society, the small traders, the *meshchanstvo*, comprised besides the peddlers and the artisans also moderately wealthy traders and owners of small shops and small industrial establishments. It eventually included even certain nobles operating their own estates and small factories, who preferred to enter this lower guild of merchants because of the relatively inexpensive registration fees it required. After the emancipation, this guild received a vast inflow of various categories of serfs, including in particular the former domestic serfs, the *dvorovye ludi*, deprived of any landholdings and forced to look for work in the towns. The category massive increases also received from other peasant strata, in particular from those who were dissolving their personal and property relations that had kept them tied to the household land and to the commune – though not all peasants who looked for work in the towns broke off their accustomed connections with the villages.

The massive penetration of the peasants into the cities in search of work is easily illustrated by the following data. In 1858 the city population of European Russia amounted to 5,583,000 people, 1,128,000 of whom belonged to the peasant *soslovie*, while the balance of 4,455,000 accounted jointly for all the other social categories. In 1897 the population of the towns had increased to

[18] Bokhanov, A. N., *Delovaia elita Rossii 1914 g* (Russia's Business Elite in 1914), Moscow, Akademia Nauk, Institute Rossiskoi istorii, 1994, pp. 20–1, 36–7; Blackwell, William L., *The Beginnings of Russian Industrialization, op. cit.*, pp. 23, 237.

Table 1-5 *European Russia: Towns' Size and Number of Inhabitants in 1897*

Population in 1000	Number of towns	Inhabitants in 1,000	Percentages	
			Towns	Inhabitants
With more than 100	14	4,401.2	2.2	36.2
50–100	29	1,930.6	4.6	15.9
25–50	44	1,567.3	7.0	12.9
11–25	157	2,393.6	24.9	19.7
Less than 11	387	1,857.6	61.3	15.3
TOTAL	631	12,149.9	100.0	100.0

Source: Ryndziunskii, P. G., *Krest'ane i gorod v kapitalisticheskoi Rossii vtoroi poloviny XIX veka*. (Peasants and Towns in Capitalist Russia in the Second Half of the Nineteenth Century), Moscow, Nauka, 1983, p. 152.

12,065,000, of whom 5,255,000 belonged to the peasant *soslovie*. Thus, the share of the latter increased from 20.2 percent of the urban population of 1858 to as much as 43.5 percent of the towns' inhabitants of 1897.[19] The peasants born in locations other than the towns in which they had settled varied among the regions of European Russia from less than 20 percent to over 60 percent of the urban population. The massive inflow particularly of young male workers of the peasantry led to overcrowding and to severe living conditions, especially in the large towns. The peasants entered formally into the towns as temporary inhabitants but established themselves there definitively without changing their *soslovie*.[20]

Up to the 1860s, the majority of the Russian cities were administrative centers created by government fiat and affected only in a limited way by modern economic considerations. After the peasants' emancipation, the situation of certain towns changed appreciably due to developments in transportation, manufacturing, trade, and to the inflow of foreign capital (to which I will return in detail later on). The accelerated growth of certain towns widely increased the differences in size among them and the other cities. Between 1863 and 1897, the country's two centers, Petersburg and Moscow, increased their population from 539,000 to 1,264,000, and from 462,000 to 1,038,000 respectively. At the same time, twelve other towns passed the one hundred thousand limit by tripling, quadrupling, or quintupling their 1863 size. As can be seen from Table 1-5, the fourteen towns with over one hundred thousand inhabitants accounted for 36.2 percent of the total urban population, while

[19] Ryndziunskii, P. G., *Krest'iane i gorod v kapitalisticheskoi Rossii vtoroi poloviny XIX veka* (The Peasants and the Town in Capitalist Russia of the Second Half of the Nineteenth Century), Moscow, Nauka, 1983, p. 212.

[20] *Ibid.*, pp. 212–15; Rowland, Richard H., "Urban In-Migration in Late Nineteenth Century Russia," in *The City in Russian History*, Hamm, Michael M., ed., Lexington, KY, University Press of Kentucky, 1976, pp. 2, 119.

at the bottom of the scale, over 61 percent of the total towns were over-shadowed by the development of the great cities and were inhabited only by 15 percent of the total urban population. At the time, both in European Russia and in Imperial Russia as a whole, the urban population continued to remain quite small, fluctuating around some 15 percent of the country's total population.

At the end of the nineteenth century, the urban male labor force in European Russia amounted to a total of 6.0 million people, and in the country as a whole to a total of 24.5 million (of whom 13.3 million – over 54 percent – were in agriculture). Excluding the agricultural labor force, European Russia's male labor force amounted to a total of 11.2 million, of whom roughly half resided in the towns. Notwithstanding the significant development of industry, transportation, and trade, the country's male labor force – corresponding in fact to the total labor force outside agriculture – amounted in manufacturing to only some 2.3 million, less than 20 percent of the total nonagricultural labor force. On the other hand, modernization and industrialization stimulated the development of the professions and of the intelligentsia as a whole, which by 1897 numbered over 3.0 million in the European Russia. As indicated by P. G. Ryndziunskii, the big-industrial labor force in the country as a whole accounted for only 9.4 percent of the total labor force, while what the Soviet statisticians were to call "nonproductive" labor – the members of the administrative and military apparatus and the professions – accounted for 12.4 percent. (See Table 1-6.)

The massive immigration into the towns – mainly into certain centers, and mostly of young male workers from the peasantry – brought about not only evident demographic changes but also a whole set of shifts in the economic

Table 1-6 *European Russia: Professional Composition of the Urban and Non-Urban Population[a] in 1897, in Percentages*

Occupations	In towns	In non-urban locations	Total
Factory industry	15.0	7.6	9.4
Small-scale industry	14.2	4.4	6.8
Transport and communication	5.0	1.4	2.3
Trade	13.0	2.4	5.0
Agriculture	4.6	70.4	54.2
Domestic servants and laborers	19.6	6.7	9.9
Nonproductive population[b]	28.6	7.1	12.4
TOTAL	100.0	100.0	100.0

Notes:

[a] Excluding the members of the families.

[b] Including the administrative and military apparatus and members of professionals (doctors, lawyers, scientists, and men of independent means).

Source: Ryndziunskii, P. G., *Krest'ane i gorod . . ., op. cit.*, pp. 155, 174.

structure, notably with regard to the geographical distribution of the labor force and to an assembly of related issues concerning, in particular, housing, food, trade, and transport, which we will examine later on.

1-4. The Command and Control System

Until the great disaster brought about by the debacles of the war with Japan in 1904 and its ensuing socioeconomic and political perturbations, all the prerogatives of power – legislative, administrative, and judiciary – were fully concentrated in the hands of the Tsar autocrat. As the pertinent analyst of Russia of the second half of the nineteenth century, Anatole Leroy-Beaulieu, wrote in 1888, the Russian Empire was *"governed as a private domain* where nothing can be distributed, elevated or downgraded without a report to the master, and without the authorization of the proprietor." In this patrimonial system, everything in the Empire of any significance at the central or the local level had to be done on the Tsar's command.[21]

Peter the Great burned in 1722 the last of family ranks registers (*razriadnaia perepis*), which contained the claims of the noble families and put in their place, as the basis of the Empire's hierarchy, the *chin*, that is, the *Table of Ranks* designing the formal structure of the Imperial bureaucracy. It assimilated the civil service with the military service and defined simultaneously the framework of recruitment to the state administration and the qualification needed for promotion within it. To each grade of the *chin* corresponded a series of functions, and promotion in the system was set to take place, as in the army, hierarchically. Peter's Table underwent changes with the passage of time, but its basic concept endured. Table 1-7 lists the top ten of the fourteen ranks of the Table published in 1901.

All the key institutions of the country obeyed the will of the Tsar autocrat (see Figure 1-2). He had under his direct command the state council, the council of ministers, the governing senate, as well as the Holy Synod. In addition, he had at his disposal as a special means of government the secret instrument of state inquisition, of widespread spying, of political investigation, and of silent deportations to Siberia, the so-called Third Sector of the Imperial Chancellery, an independent, privileged authority placed outside and above the normal sphere of action of all the other authorities. Under Alexander II, a new,

---

[21] Leroy-Beaulieu, Anatole, *L'Empire des Tsars...*, *op. cit.*, pp. 63, 69, 100–1; Bennett, Helju Aulik, "Chiny, Ordena, and Officialdom," in *Russian Officialdom: The Bureaucratization of the Russian Society from the Seventeen to the Twentieth Century*, Pinter, Walter, and Don Karl, Rowney, eds., Chapel Hill, NC, University of North Carolina Press, 1980, pp. 162–4, 176–7. See also, on Tsarist patrimonial rule in general, Weber, Max, *Economy and Society: An Outline of Interpretative Sociology*, Vol. 2, Roth, Guenther, and Wittich, Claus, eds., Berkeley, CA, University of California Press, 1978, p. 1067; also Bendix, Reinhard, *Max Weber: An Intellectual Portrait*, New York, Doubleday & Co., Anchor Book edition, 1962, pp. 345–8.

Table 1-7 *The Ten Top Ranks of the* Chin

Class	Civil ranks	Corresponding ranks	
		Army	Navy
1.	Chancellor	Field marshall general	Admiral general
2.	Actual privy councillor	General of cavalry General of infantry General of artillery	Admiral
3.	Privy councillor	Lieutenant general	Vice-admiral
4.	Actual state councillor	Major general	Rear-admiral
5.	State councillor		
6.	Collegiate councillor	Colonel	Captain, 1st grade
7.	Court councillor	Lieutenant colonel	Captain, 2nd grade
8.	Collegiate assessor	Captain	
9.	Titular councillor	Staff captain	Lieutenant
10.	Collegiate secretary	Lieutenant	Warrant officer

Source: Vernadsky, George, senior editor, *A Source Book for Russian History from Early Times to 1917*, Vol. 3, *Alexander II to February Revolution*, New Haven, Yale University Press, 1972, pp. 760–1.

all-powerful organization, the *Okhrannoe otdelenia* (Secret Service), founded in 1878, directed all its forces against the revolutionaries. Abolished in 1889, the system of repression was based on the division of the country into six circumscriptions governed by general-governors, whose tribunals were used for various repressive measures, including capital executions and deportations.[22]

The State Council (*Gosudarstvennyi Sovet*) was empowered to exercise the basic legislative functions, but only under the Tsar's command. The initiative of new laws belonged exclusively to the Tsar. Even the submission of any project of law to the Council had to be authorized by the Tsar. After examination by the Council, the latter submitted to the Tsar both the suggested project of law and its proposed approval or rejection – but only the Tsar's decision became law. The Council deliberated also on the general measures to be taken for the application of laws, the measures needed in case of foreign conflict, and the projects of administrations and of the state.

The Council of Ministers (*Sovet Ministrov*) was the Tsar's principal consultative body on the questions of general administration. Functioning under a president appointed by the Tsar and including the presidents of the departments of the State Council, the ministers, and the members designated by the Tsar, the Council of Ministers, assisted by a host of permanent councils (such as the War Council, the Council of the Admiralty, and the Council of Finances), had the task of examining all the critical issues related to administration, as

[22] Leroy-Beaulieu, Anatole, *L'Empire des Tsars . . ., op. cit.*, pp. 144–5, 452; also, Slonim, Marc, *De Pierre Le Grand à Lenine* (From Peter the Great to Lenin), Paris, Gallimard, 1933, p. 159.

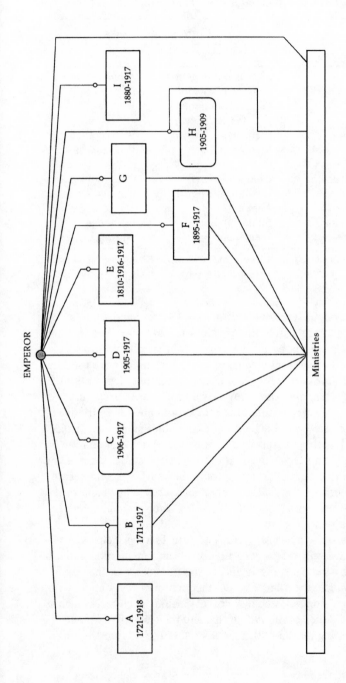

A   Holy Synod (Sviateishii Sinod)
B   Governing Senate (Pravitel'stvuiushchii Senat)
C   State Duma (Gosudarstvennaia Duma)
D   Council of Ministers (Sovet Ministrov)
E   State Council (Gosudarstvenyi Sovet)
F   Imperial Majesty's Chancellery (for complaints) (Kantselaria E.I.V.)
G   Imperial Majesty's Own Chancellery (Sobstvennaia E.I.V. Kantselaria)
H   State Defense Council (Sovet Gosudarstvennoi Oborona)
I   (Her) Imperial Majesty's Own Chancellery (Sobstvennaia E.I.V. Kantselaria)

Figure 1-2. The Imperial State Command Structure after 1905

Source: Rossiiskaia Akademiia Nauk. Institut Rossiiskaia Istorii (Russian Academy of Science, Institut of Russian History), *Rossiia 1913 god. Statistiko-dokumental'nyi spravochnik* (Russia, 1913. Statistical-documentary reference book), St. Petersburg, 1995, p. 229.

well as the charge of coordinating the measures taken separately by each of the ministers. In the early 1860s, Alexander II created the Council of Ministers, which was supposed to become the country's supreme administrative organ; but finally, this Council did not become permanent and did not fulfill any of the tasks for which it had been originally constituted.

The Governing Senate (*Pravitel'stvuiushchii Senat*), originally established by Peter the Great in 1711 as the highest state institution empowered to supervise all judicial, financial, and administrative affairs, became in time a partly deliberative and partly executive body that focused primarily on various problems of administration. It became notably the highest institution of administrative justice examining the complaints against administrative acts, and also assumed the role of principal supervisor and guarantor that the administration executed the orders of the Tsar. After important reforms of judicial matters carried out in the early 1860s, the Senate became the country's Supreme Court. That reform also established an independent court system for criminal and civil acts, a system that was to end direct government interventions in judicial matters. Actually, the state administration retained authority within the government setup and was often able to redefine the jurisdiction of the courts. The different legal orders represented by the courts and by the state administrations remained in conflict, with the frontiers between them continually in dispute.[23]

The country's bulky, cumbersome, and vastly dispersed local administrations were also mixing, at times in unpredictable ways, local and central powers' dispositions or commands. The Empire was divided into seventy-eight *gubernias* (regions, provinces, or "governments") – forty-nine in European Russia, seven in the Caucasus, and four in Siberia, to which were added ten in Poland and eight in Finland – and into twenty-three *oblasts* (territories), including one in European Russia, seven in the Caucasus, nine in Central Asia, and six in Siberia. The *gubernias* were in turn divided into districts, and the *oblasts* into *cercles*. In addition, four towns – Petersburg, Odessa, Sebastopol, and Kertch – formed what were called "prefectorial towns" that submitted directly to the central power. The chief of the *gubernia* or of the *oblast* was the *governor*, who represented both the central administration and the Ministry of the Interior, and who also controlled separately the police apparatus. As representative of the central government, the governor had the right to promulgate laws and to make any decisions on matters of public security, public health, and the economic interests of the region. At the level of the district, the closest power to that of the governor was that of the marshal of nobility, the chairman of the local Nobles' Assembly, responsible only to his peers. In 1866,

---

[23] On all of the indicated institutions, see notably Poutiloff, M. A., "Constitution Politique," (Political Constitution), in *La Russie à la fin du 19ᵉ siècle, op. cit.*, pp. 78–82; Wagner, William G., *Marriage, Property and Law in Late Imperial Russia*, Oxford, Clarendon Press, 1994, pp. 10, 379.

Alexander II created a new institution of local self-government, the *Zemstvo*, directly elected in each *gubernia*, territory, and district, and charged with the administration of various social and economic affairs (such as schools, roads, and health service) and empowered to tax the local agricultural lands and forests. Eventually, tensions arose between the most extensive form of self-government in Tsarist Russia, the *Zemstva* – elected by nobles and townsmen and indirectly by the peasants – and the government over revenue collection issues. Four years after the creation of the *Zemstva*, the government awarded to the cities the right of self-government, but this statute was revised in 1892, when the municipal governments were integrated into a unified system of state administration rather than being left as separate and parallel administrative units.[24]

Military defeats, along with various related causes, affected deeply the structure, depth, and development of Russian society. As James Mavor noted in 1914 in his *Economic History of Russia*, Sweden's defeat of Peter the Great at Narva occasioned the reorganization of the Russian military system and through it the reorganization of the entire Russian society. Napoleon's invasion increasingly drew Russia into the maelstrom of European diplomacy and politics, with external repercussions upon its own internal policy conflicts and priorities. The defeat of Russia in the Crimean War by England and France opened the door to the emancipation of the serfs and, on the other hand, to Russia's expansion into Southeast and Far East Asia. Japan's defeat of Russia compelled Russia *inter alia* to introduce reluctantly a quasiconstitutional system. In short, as Mavor astutely put it, "Russia has benefited rather by her defeats than by her victories" – a remark certainly valid at least until the cataclysm of 1917.[25]

After defeat by Japan, the epidemic of strikes and political assassinations and the outbreak of spreading revolutionary activities placed before the Tsar the following alternatives: to break all revolutionary actions through an absolute military dictatorship or, if this was not feasible, to grant the country limited, and subtly controllable, constitutional rights. Reluctantly, Tsar Nicholas II chose the latter solution. An Imperial manifesto of October 17, 1905, granted the Russian citizens civil liberties and a legislative assembly – the State Duma – based on a limited and unequal franchise favoring the nobles and the upper urban strata. The manifesto expressed the Tsar's will to establish a new governmental principle, namely that no law would take effect without the approval of the State Duma. Along with the manifesto, a companion decree created a new Council of Ministers suppressing and amalgamating the then-existing Committee of Ministers and Council of Ministers, to be presided by a chairman, the first "premier" in Russian history. Soon afterward, the revolution of 1905 and the armed uprising in Moscow of December 9 were suppressed, while a series of documents and decrees were finally consolidated in the Code

[24] Poutiloff, M. A., "Constitution Politique" in *La Russie à la fin du 19ᵉ siècle, op. cit.*, pp. 89–91.
[25] Mavor, James, *An Economic History of Russia*, New York, E. P. Dutton & Co., 1914, p. ix.

of Fundamental Laws (of April 26, 1906) defining the new legal framework and within it the functions of the Council of State, the State Duma, and the Council of Ministers.

The reorganized Council of State became the Upper Chamber, whose consent was made requisite for the passage of bills into laws. Half of the council could be elected by privileged groups, and half would be appointed by the Tsar. The elected members would represent the Church (six members), the high academic institutions (six), the provincial *Zemstva* assemblies (thirty-four), the provincial societies of the nobility (eighteen), commercial and industrial administrations (twelve), and assemblies of the landlords in provinces without *Zemstva* (twenty-two). The Upper Chamber thus acquired in fact functions identical to those of the Lower House with regard to initiative in legislation.

The Lower House – the Duma – was not set to evolve into a parliament in the Western sense of the term. It acquired in principle extensive rights, but many of these were in practice blocked by all kinds of limitations, particularly via the use of Imperial edicts and of orders in Council. The first Duma elected in March 1906 ran into direct conflicts with the government on various agrarian issues, and by July 8, 1906, an Imperial manifesto announced the Duma's dissolution. The second Duma, elected in January 1907, declined to discuss a series of proposals, including Premier Peter Stolypin's crucial reform of land ownership. Then, on June 3, 1907, the second Duma was dissolved while the government modified the electoral system in favor of the propertied strata. The third Duma, elected on November 1, 1907, on the basis of the new electoral law, finally passed the Stolypin reforms a few years later. Again, after dramatic strikes and dangerous economic conflicts that were evidently echoed in the Duma, the third Duma also was ended forcefully in 1912. A fourth Duma, elected in the fall of that year, functioned until the revolution in Petrograd in March 1917, when the real power started to shift toward the Soviet of Workers and Soldiers' Deputies.[26] All in all, the Dumas were in fact an open though reluctant admission of the new governmental principle, and the institutions did deliver in practice various legislative measures.

The Council of Ministers was set to exercise both executive and administrative responsibilities through twelve ministers appointed by the Tsar. The twelve were to be in charge of: 1) foreign affairs; 2) war; 3) navy; 4) finance; 5) justice; 6) ways and communications; 7) commerce and industry; 8) agriculture; 9) education; 10) internal affairs; 11) the Imperial Court; and 12) government control. All bills on all subjects scheduled to come before the Duma were to be brought first before the Council.

Finally, the Senate was designed to be the highest court of appeal in the Empire and was also granted the power to exercise control over the various

[26] Miller, Margaret S., *The Economic Development of Russia . . ., op. cit.*, pp. 23–7; Karpovich, Michael, *Imperial Russia 1801–1917*, New York, Holt, Rinehart and Winston, 1900, pp. 70–9; Pushkarev, Sergei, *The Emergence of Modern Russia . . ., op. cit.*, pp. 236–41, 250–63.

branches of the administration, including the right to examine the complaints brought against the actions of the ministers, governors, the *Zemstva*, and the town councils.

Within this new framework – derided by some as "sham constitutionalism," but recognized by others as a significant though reluctant step toward a constitutionalist regime – the Code of Fundamental Laws of 1906 still indicated in its Section 4 that, as in the past, "the Supreme Power is vested in the Tsar of All Russia," that is, the Tsar continued to hold the legislative, executive, and judiciary powers. But, in fact, this "supreme power" was more limited. Indeed, the Code specified that the legislative power had to be exercised by the Tsar in conjunction with the Council of State and the Duma; no new law could be promulgated without the assent of the Council of State and of the Duma, or enforced without the sanction of the Tsar. Moreover, the most important administrative acts of the Tsar henceforth had to be countersigned by one of the ministers "who are hereafter responsible to the Houses."[27] Finally, as Margaret Miller pointed out, as only a short period of twelve terms and unsettled years had passed between the Tsar's manifesto of 1905 and the outbreak of the revolution of 1917, it would be rather impossible to state with certitude what the future development of Russia might have been, namely toward a real representative government or back toward the full restoration of the Tsar's autocracy. Certainly, at least the Tsar's immediate circle would have preferred the restoration of autocracy. In 1913, Nicholas II did in fact consider returning to the former course of lawmaking "in accordance with the Russian tradition." Maybe the Empire's last head was indeed "without virtues or talents" commensurate with his responsibilities at such a critical historical juncture.[28]

1-5. Concluding Comments

The foundation of economic life of Russia until 1861 was the predominance of the landlords' farming estates, in the framework of a natural economy heavily dependent on serfdom. The 1861 reform – that is, the peasant emancipation aimed at suppressing the dependence of the serfs on the landlords and vice versa – ultimately increased the dependence of both on the state. As many of the landlords became increasingly incapable of coping with the burden of their debts, they found themselves compelled to sell much of their lands. The majority of the peasants – poorer than before, burdened by both taxes and redemption payments for their lands, and forcefully tied to their obsolete form

---

[27] *The Russian Yearbook for 1912*, compiled and edited by Kennard, Howard P., New York, Macmillan, 1912, p. 4.

[28] See Miller, Margaret S., *The Economic Development of Russia...*, *op. cit.*, pp. 27, 298; Rogger, Hans, *Russia in the Age of Modernisation and Revolution 1881–1917*, London, Longman, 1983, pp. 19–20.

of communal land ownership – were looking for work in the towns, and were incapable of giving a serious boost to the development of domestic markets. While the life of the country continued to depend mostly on agriculture, industrial development grew, particularly in the 1880s and 1890s – as we shall see in detail later on – due to the state's own initiatives and to the significant influx of foreign capital. Except for a small number of cities, the majority of the Russian towns continued to remain country towns rather than modern cities, and no marked division of labor arose among them.

Though the old *sosloviia* system was increasingly exhibiting various signs of decay, the set social structure did not change officially. One of the main apparent features of the underlying social change was the growth of the group of unclassifiable townspeople, the *raznochintsy*, literally people of a variety of ranks not clearly identified as a class. All in all, postemancipation Russia was developing in a variety of ways. The economy exhibited characteristics of a transitional economy – transitional not in the sense usually given to this term, implying a quasimethodic, fully previsible passage from one economic system to another but, rather in the sense given to this term by Werner Sombart, referring to a *mixed* stage amalgamating diversely the methods of production of the old system in some sectors along with the modern methods of production in other sectors.[29] In Russia, the feudal methods of farming production indeed remained predominant for a long time. The peasants' ties to the archaic system of the communes continued unaltered well after 1905, while markets, modernity, and capitalism were pushing at times only in a limited way toward expansion in farming and in the industrial and commercial fields. Until 1917, the upper strata of the *dvorianstvo* continued to be the key instrument of power, while the Tsar remained able to ceaselessly mix, in various doses, the rights that he had to concede to the Duma and the measures that he could or would actually take to hamper its effectiveness.

The feudal relations both before and after emancipation, as well as their amalgamation with the expanding market relations, eventually affected the scope but not the substance of patrimonialism as the basis of the conceptual system of command and control under the Tsar autocrat. Recall briefly the sources of patrimonialism. In the sixteenth century under Ivan the Terrible, and then in the early eighteenth century under Peter the Great, relations between the crown and the boyars (the old noble oligarchy) took a distinctive turn. In his fight against the boyars' power claims, Ivan the Terrible initially split the country in two. On the one hand, he created the *oprichnina* – from the word *oprich*, which means apart – in which he set up his own state and centralized administration, managed at his discretion by his new corps of servants, the cruel *oprichniki*. On the other hand, he left the other part of the country, the *zemshchina*, in the purview of the boyars' Duma. Peter the Great went further.

---

[29] Cf. notably Hoselitz, Bert F., "Theories of Stages of Economic Growth," in Hoselitz, et al., *Theories of Economic Growth*, New York, Free Press of Glencoe, 1960, pp. 225–7.

He decisively opposed the social independence of the feudal aristocracy. He burned the lists of nobility ranks and replaces them with his List of Ranks (the *chin*). He required that each member of the gentry join the state administration from the age of sixteen until the end of his days. Social rank became determined not by an ancestral patrimonial estate, but by the administrative rank. Nobility became a "court nobility," the *dvorianstvo*, the body of his administration. The compensation for service – the service-fief (*pomest'e*) with serfs, held by the *pomeshchik* – displaced the *votchinnik* – the landholder of the *alodial* estate (the *votchina*) inherited from the ancestor. While asserting, like the Byzantine king, the *basileus*, a patrimonial conception, both Ivan and Peter established under their rule fiefdoms for the *oprichniki* and eventually for the *pomeshchiki*, the members of their state bureaucracy. This same patrimonial conception with its despotic overtone had, however, disastrous consequences for the peasantry, pushed into serfdom for the benefit of the state and of its servant nobles until the great reform of 1861.

In his path-breaking studies on patrimonialism, Max Weber pointed out the adjacency of various kinds of socioeconomic relations with a patrimonialist administration, that is, with an administration in which the prince uses his political power as the exercise of his "patriarchal power." As Weber conclusively put it, "The majority of all great continental empires had a fairly strong patrimonial character until and even after the beginning of modern times." And further, "Patrimonialism is compatible with household and market economy, petty bourgeois and manorial agriculture, absence and presence of capitalist economy."[30] In short, while the underlying socioeconomic relations are determining the nature of the economic activities and the social structure of a society – feudal, transitional (in the Sombart sense or not), and even capitalistic – in a well-established patrimonialist system, the political administration is necessarily treated as the "purely personal affair of the ruler," and his political power is in practice "entirely discretionary." Put differently, patrimonialism shapes primarily a society's steering mechanism, that is, the nature, scope, and methods of its command and control system, and its ways of handling the legislative, judicial, administrative, and political issues of the underlying society.[31]

Later I will discuss in detail the concepts and the conflicts that developed in Russia concerning the prevailing institutions and the ownership relations. For

---

[30] Weber, Max, *Economy and Society . . ., op cit.*, p. 1013, 1029.

[31] Certainly the Tsar (and his bureaucracy) tended to "identify political power with the growth of territory, and the growth of territory with absolute domainal power." This does not mean, however, that under Russian patrimonialism the Tsar could without any kind of limitations "dispose of the country's entire human resources," as Pipes seems to suggest. Cf. Pipes, Richard, *Russia under the Old Regime, op. cit.*, pp. 23–4, 84, as well as Pipes, in his review of Hosking, G., *Russia, People and Empire 1552–1917*, in which Pipes states somewhat generally that under patrimonialism, "the state treats the realm as property and assigns its subjects no rights but only duties." Cf. *New York Times Book Review*, May 25, 1997, p. 13.

now, note that certain members of Russia's *intelligentsia* – a term of German origin, which in its Russian version designates intellectuals of all persuasions – played an increasingly decisive role in Rusia's socioeconomic and political turmoils, from the early 1800s on. Writers, philosophers, historians, men with a moral vision, a sense of political commitment, and a feeling of social responsibility, became, indeed, the judges and the critics of their country's institutions and patterns of administration, and of its political basis and economic perspectives. Was the Russian socioeconomic and political complex actually a unique and precious setup whose *originality* needed to be preserved by all means? Was it rather nothing more than a version of the feudalism that had reigned throughout Europe, but which Russia had lost the capacity to change? Or, was it the result of a marriage between Europe and Asia – a mixture of feudal European features and of some secondary Asiatic characteristics, pulling it in different directions?[32] And finally, after 1905, was Russia actually generating a new postfeudal and postcapitalist model that the rest of the world could eventually follow? It is around these basic issues and their ramifications that Russia's intelligentsia split in various ways during the nineteenth century and the early twentieth century, leading ultimately to the destruction of the Tsarist regime. I turn to these issues and to some of their implications in the next chapter.

[32] Leroy-Beaulieu, Anatole, *L'Empire des Tsars...*, *op. cit.*, pp. 199; Plekhanov, George, *Introduction a L'histoire Sociale de la Russie* (Introduction to the Social History of Russia), transl. from Russian by Mm. Plekhanov, Batault, Paris, Editions Bossard, 1926, pp. 152–8.

CHAPTER 2

The Transition Issues

2-1. Principles of Action

On the eve of the great reform commanding the peasant emancipation, the immense agricultural Russian Empire relied on feudal farming methods, on handicraft, small-scale industry, and a few larger-scale factories, on a barely be-gun railroad network, and on a slowly emerging banking system. If economic development is taken to mean expanding output, along with making continuous changes in the technical and institutional arrangements by which this output is produced and distributed, the Russian economy was then obviously far behind the changes that had been taking place in the Occident.

I will consider later on, in detail, the structural characteristics and the performance of each sector of the Russian economy. For now, recall in broad outline that on the eve of the emancipation, the country's landlord and peasant farming relied on archaic methods of sowing and plowing, yields were low, and very severe general crop failures were occurring often. The increase of population after the emancipation provided an expanding labor force, which remained poorly employed while the growth of capital and new technologies continued to be limited. The country's general economic and cultural backwardness made the native businessmen timorous, diffident, unadventurous, and dependent on the state, which in turn tended to rely heavily on imported foreign technicians, businessmen, and capital. The Empire's manufacturing output continued to be modest in the decade following the emancipation. In 1879, giant Russia accounted for only 3.7 percent of the world's manufacturing production, compared to 31.8 percent for the United Kingdom, 13.2 percent for Germany, 10.3 percent for France, and 23.3 percent for the rapidly expanding United States.[1] By that time, Russia's railroad network reached 10,700 kilometers, compared to the far larger networks of the far smaller European countries.

---

[1] League of Nations, Economic, Financial and Transit Department, *Industrialization and Foreign Trade*, Geneva, League of Nations, 1945, p. 13.

The network of the United Kingdom accounted then for 25,000 kilometers, of Germany for 18,700 kilometers, and of France for 17,900 kilometers. In the territorially comparable United States, the railroad network then extended already over 85,200 kilometers.[2] With regard to banking, the archaic methods were only slowly called into question. Prior to 1860, the main banking operations in the country as a whole were in the hands of small, decentralized government banks, namely state credit establishments, deposit banks, and boards of public charities. All of these were abolished in 1860 while the newly founded State Bank of Russia took over their operations. The growth of stockholder commercial banks became noticeable by 1870 while much of industry's growth of foreign trade remained attributable to foreign capital and to foreign concerns based in St. Petersburg.[3] As for the state finances, the first budgets of the Western type started to be drawn only after 1860.

Along with the abolition of serfdom, the setting of the direction of Russia's economic development became an imperious necessity. While the government did not formulate a coherent program in this regard, did not enact a consistent set of policies, and did not engage itself decisively in any early perceptive direction, it would be erroneous to assume that the regime did not try to cope with this problem, and did not consider and discuss it at its highest level. As we shall see later on (in Chapter 3), ministers and high-ranking officials debated the issue and suggested various crucial measures in this regard, some of which were accepted and some of which were neglected or carried out poorly, but which all in all helped a limited process of industrialization, expansion of trade and transport, increasing of banking activities, and a limited spread of market relations. The government actions, hesitations, and failures increased the pressures for broad changes, not necessarily as in the first half of the nineteenth century from the young nobles, but rather from the newly expanding plebian intelligentsia – the literati, journalists, and the growing professional strata.

The growth of general literacy and of the student population in the secondary schools (*gimnaziia*) and in the universities, along with the growth of the professional strata, became increasingly manifest after the big reform.[4] The data available on the number of students in the *gimnaziia* and the universities indicate a continuous progress throughout the postemancipation period. Thus, the number of students in the male *gimnaziia* rose from 31,000 in 1865 to close to 44,000 in 1875, 73,000 in 1885, and 75,000 in 1897–98. The number of students in the female *gimnaziia* rose in the 1880s to 30,000. In the process,

---

[2] Solov'eva, A. M., *Zheleznodorozhnyi Transport Rossii vo vtoroi polovine XIX v* (The Railroad Transport of Russia in the Second Half of the Nineteenth Century), Moscow, Nauka, 1975, pp. 20, 83.

[3] Miller, Margaret S., *The Economic Development of Russia . . ., op. cit.*, pp. 82–3.

[4] Rashin, A. G., *Naselenie Rossii . . ., op. cit.*, pp. 285, 291, 293; Thaden, Edward C., *Russia since 1801: The Making of a New Society*, New York, Wiley & Sons, 1971, p. 325.

the social structure of the student population changed in favor of the students coming from the taxpaying groups (that is, excluding sons of the gentry and of the clergy). Their share increased from some 25 percent in 1863 to close to 36 percent in 1874, and then close to 44 percent in 1885. The growth of the student population of the universities shows the same trends. In 1865, the country's nine leading universities (Moscow, Petersburg, Iur'ev, Kharkov, Kazan, Kiev, Odessa, Warsaw, and Tomsk) counted only 4,125 students. The number of students rose to 6,585 in 1870, 8,045 in 1880, 12,432 in 1890, and 16,295 by the end of the century. Data on the social structure of the students of seven of these universities (excluding Kiev and Tomsk) show that in 1880 the sons of the lower strata (that is, of small traders, craftsmen, peoples of unidentified estates, peasants, and Cossacks) accounted for 21 percent of the student population, and in 1900 for 25 percent. The growing universities, as Richard Pipes has pointed out, founded "the natural breeding ground of oppositional activities," particularly from the early 1860s on. As "unrest began then to engulf increasingly the universities, the Tsarist regime became involved in a state of 'permanent war' with the teachers, students, and scholars of every kind."[5]

As the nineteenth century unfolded, however, the growing intelligentsia of plebian origin became divided with regard to the crucial questions regarding the country's path of economic development. Which social estate and which social institutions would ensure the reaching of development comparable or even superior to that of Europe? Would Russia have to follow exactly the same road of development as Europe did, could it jump over some decisive intermediate steps along the way, or instead would it have to chart a totally *different path* than that which brought about Europe's advanced economic development? As Anatole Leroy-Beaulieu put it perceptively in 1888, the question of Russia's relations to Europe placed the following choices before the Empire: Should it consider itself the apprentice of Europe, and persist in trying to imitate the Occident, or rather should it see itself as being different from Europe, stop on the road to imitation, renounce to borrowings that do not fit its national genius, and assume the role of initiator of a new path? These issues, which historically had nourished many open or hidden conflicts, became from then on the source of lasting antagonisms between so-called Slavophiles and so-called Occidentalists or Westernizers (*Zapadniki*), as well as among the Occidentalists themselves, divided into various currents. The Slavophiles asserted that by Russia's origin and culture, its specific conceptions concerning land ownership, the family, the church, and the state authority, Russia was radically different from Europe, and hence its destiny was bound to be different. For the Westernizers – be they democratic liberal or left-wing revolutionaries – while Russia's past and traditions did evidently separate it from Europe, nothing

---

[5] Leikina-Svirskaia, *Intelligentsiia v Rossii vo vtoroi polovine XIX veka* (The Intelligentsia in Russia in the Second Half of the Nineteenth Century), Moscow, Mysl, 1971, pp. 51–2, 56–62; Pipes, Richard, *Russia under the Old Regime, op. cit.*, p. 263.

could prevent Russia now from assimilating whatever it considered appropriate from Europe's experiences, as in the past the Germanic peoples, for instance, beneficially assimilated parts of the dominant Roman culture.[6]

2-2. Russia and the West's Economic Patterns

The crucial question of the relations between Russia's and Europe's historical development was first raised publicly by Peter Ia. Chaadaev in 1836. His views, mixing at times paradoxically and not necessarily consistently a conservative orientation with a special Western bias, influenced in a variety of ways the ensuing divergence between the Slavophiles and the Westernizers, and even between the different Westernizing currents as well. The conflicts in question involved, on the one hand, asserting Russia's emancipation from European influences and even alleging Russia's superiority over Europe, and on the other hand, stressing Russia's dependence on Europe's experiences and Russia's need for further incorporating or imitating at least some of Europe's achievements. The debates centered on such specific issues of whether, since when, and in which ways Russia's *past* development diverged or not from that of Europe; on whether Russia's *existing* socioeconomic features constituted a decaying vestige of the past, or an indispensable component of a better future than that of Europe; on whether Russia's economic backwardness in relation to Europe could be bridged *in the future*, or whether Russia's specific personality already made Russia the bearer of a new, unique message for the entire world.

According to Chadaev, Russia should incorporate within its development certain past European processes and elements of progress, concerning in particular justice, freedom, and the pursuit of truth. Yet, while conceding that Russia could progress on the basis of Europe's past experiences, he also asserted that such progress was neither easy, inevitable, or even probable. Eventually he argued that Russia's backwardness was not a historical accident but rather a kind of historical privilege – that Russia should not become *assimilated* to Western Europe, though Russia should take over if possible some of the West's achievements and should then lead the way forward to attain a spiritual advance over Europe. As he put it: "One day we shall place ourselves intellectually in the heart of Europe.... That will be the logical outcome of our solitude. The greatest things emerge from the desert." Then, as Richard Hare noted, according to Chaadaev's contentions, Russia will be able to repay its moral debt to Europe, "by rescuing creative Europe of enlightenment and progressive religion from the suicidal Europe of socialist materialism and moral chaos."[7]

---

[6] Leroy-Beaulieu, Anatole, *L'Empire des Tsars...*, *op. cit.*, pp. 200–1.

[7] Hare, Richard, *Pioneers of Russian Social Thought*, New York, Vintage Books, 1964, pp. 8–16; Schapiro, Leonard B., *Rationalism and Nationalism in Russian Nineteenth Century Political Thought*, New Haven, Yale University Press, 1967, pp. 39–45.

Chaadaev's assertions that Russia stood alone, belonging neither to the
West nor to the East, that even its backwardness was an asset, that divine
providence intended Russia to surpass Europe and avoid its errors, influenced
deeply the Slavophile current asserting itself from the 1830s on. The term
slavophilism acquired a new meaning, associated with the contributions of
university teachers and scholars, increasingly interested from the 1830s on in
the historical problems of the Slavic peoples, their languages, literatures, and
overall social and cultural development. The Slavophiles – who were then led
by highly educated men, notable among them A. S. Khomiakov, Iurii Samarin,
and the brothers Konstantin and Ivan Aksakov – oriented their efforts against
the then prevalent tendency of giving preference to everything European and
stressed instead the alleged superiority of everything Russian. They became
the consistent advocates of the necessity of returning to the original, native
sources of the Russian past. Two basic issues gained predominance in the
conception of the Slavophiles: the historical role of the peasant commune, and
the impact of Peter the Great's reforms on Russia's state institutions and on
its overall development.[8]

With regard to the commune (*obshchina*), Konstantin Aksakov, along with
other Slavophiles, stressed what he believed to be its crucial functions as a
form of social organization and as the human embodiment of Christian living
throughout Russia's history. The commune appeared to those Slavophiles to
have been interconnected also with *custom* – rather than with *law* – as the
appropriate framework of social obligations, and with the stability of the *family*
and of family obligations. The opponents of the Slavophile conception of the
role of the commune, and particularly one of the earlier friends of Aksakov, the
historian S. M. Solov'ev, stressed as a keystone of Russia's social organization
the *clan (rod) order*, that is, the blood ties. While Aksakov accepted that the
clan order had existed among the early Slavs, he rejected the claim of its
persistence up to the sixteenth century. Actually, the commune had a long
and widespread existence, and, as Aksakov put it, up to Peter the Great,
the Russian peasant order was "completely communal among serfs as among
non-serfs." As mentioned in Chapter 1, the decomposition of the commune
accelerated only after the Stolypin agrarian reform in the early 1900s.[9] As to
the eventual end of *serfdom* – an issue that reflected first the interest of the
government, then of the gentry, and lastly of the peasants – the Slavophiles
had long since expressed their wholehearted support for much of the measure
in which they saw a decisive step toward strengthening the liberal tendencies

[8] On the "new meaning" of *slavophilism* from the late 1830s on, see Tsimbaev, N. I.,
Slavianophilistvo. Iz istorii ruskoi obshchestvenno-politicheskoi mysli XIX veka (Slav-
ianophilism from the History of Russian Social and Political Thought of the Nineteenth
Century), Moscow, Moscow University, 1986, pp. 17–19, 22, 28–9.

[9] Christoff, Peter K., *Aksakov, K. S.: A Study in Ideas*, Vol. III, *An Introduction to Nineteenth
Century Russian Slavophilism*, Princeton, NJ, Princeton University Press, 1981, pp. 272–92,
358.

in the country. Iurii Samarin, who had been working in the early 1850s on a well-known study on "The Status of Serfdom and the Passage from It to Civil Liberty" – one of a vast number of Slavophile projects and memoranda of the time – was to play an important part in the practical achievement of the emancipation.[10]

With regard to the Western-modeled reforms of Peter the Great and to his attempts to modernize the course of Russian development, the Slavophiles asserted that Peter had willfully interrupted Russia's organic growth, thwarted its uniquely national development, and imposed on Russia alien ideas and harmful practices. The Slavophiles idealized the Kievan and Moscovite periods as the epochs of harmony and of mutual confidence between the rulers and the intimately interrelated *narodnost'* (nationality), orthodoxy, and autocracy, unraveled by Peter. The Slavophiles' angry, nationalistic reactions against Peter's reforms were certainly not without precedent. Concern about and fervor against the impact of foreign influences had existed for centuries. As the famous writer Alexander Herzen was to put it facetiously, "Slavophilism as an indignant national feeling, as a dark memory and mass instinct, as a reaction against overwhelming foreign influence, already existed at the time when Peter the Great shaved off the first Boyar's beard."[11]

Slavophilism mixed in a very peculiar way its conception about the role of the Tsar with the Slavophiles' liberal tendencies concerning people's liberty of life, conscience, and thought. Their principles concerning the relations between the government and the people were summarized as follows: "for the government, unlimited power; for the people, complete liberty of life and conscience." These principles were presented as follows by Konstantin Aksakov in an 1855 memorandum addressed to Alexander II through Count Bulov:

1) The Russian people, containing no political elements within it, has divested itself of supreme power, and has no desire to govern. 2) Having no desire to rule, the Russian people assigns to the Government unlimited power. 3) In return for this, the Russian people reserves to itself moral liberty, liberty of life and of conscience.

The government must therefore "remove the yoke" it had placed on the moral life of the people; if it feels the need to ascertain the public opinion, it may, following past examples, call forth in "weighty occasions" a national assembly (*zemski sobor*). It may then obtain an expression of opinions, which it may then accept or reject.[12]

Slavophilism, as Franco Venturi remarked, represented a first "positive answer" to the spirit of inferiority nourished from the eighteenth century on in

---

[10] Schapiro, Leonard B., *Rationalism and Nationalism in Russian . . ., op. cit.*, p. 70; Tsimbaev, N. I., *Slavianophilistvo. Iz istorii ruskoi . . . mysli, op. cit.*, pp. 184–5.

[11] Quoted by Hare, Richard, *Pioneers of Russian Social Thought, op. cit.*, p. 75.

[12] Stepniak (Kravchinskii, S. M.), *King Stork and King Log: A Study of Modern Russia*, Vol. I, London, Downey & Co., 1896, pp. 29–35.

Russian contact with the West. The Slavophiles' positions did not derive from feudal ideas, but rather from their utopianism and from their adoration of the Russian customs and ways of life. They rejected the post-Petrine state and, with it, the whole process of imitation of Europe. Their hostility to rationalism and individualism, their efforts to assert Russian "superiority," undoubtedly influenced deeply, throughout the century, other tendencies, including above all the "popular terrorism" and its destructive views and processes, representing, as Leroy-Beaulieu defined it, "a kind of tragic emancipation of the Russian conscience."[13]

However, the ideology that influenced deeply the thought and actions of Russia's intelligentsia from the late 1840s to the mid-1880s, and then again in variously modified forms soon after the beginning of the 1900s, was not rooted in slavophilism but rather in the so-called populist conceptions and in their peculiar proposals for action against Tsarism. The diverse currents that were to constitute what came to be known as *narodnichestvo* (populism) asserted the necessity for Russia to assimilate Western training and experiences, but affirmed at the same time their opposition to large-scale industrialization (generating "pauperism and proletarianism").[14] Slavophiles contended that a backward country like Russia could bypass certain "intermediate" phases of Western capitalist changes and yet accelerate its own development. Finally, they maintained that Russia could even proceed "directly into socialism" through the application in the economy as a whole of the principles of communal ownership and management already present in Russian agriculture.

Let us consider now, in broad outline, the main proposals and the diverse contentions concerning the eventual characteristics of the process of transition of Russia to a new socioeconomic framework and its future development.

2-3. The Transition Path

The father of Russia's pre-mid-nineteenth-century radical thought concerning Russia's transformation, who exercised a great influence on all the intellectual currents of the second half of that century, was Visarion G. Belinskii, the passionate, enthusiastic upholder of the process of modernization initiated by

---

[13] Venturi, Franco, *Il Populismo Russo*, Vol. I, *Roma, Einaudi*, 1952, pp. LIV; Walicki, Andrzej, "Vladimir Solov'ev and the Legal Philosophies of Russian Liberalism," in *Russian Thought and Society 1800–1917: Essays in Honor of Eugene Lampert*, Bartoleti, Roger, ed., Kiel, University of Kiel, 1984, p. 154; Schapiro, Leonard B., *Rationalism and Nationalism . . ., op. cit.*, p. 71.

[14] On Hegel, see *The Philosophy of Hegel*, Friedrich, Karl J., ed., New York, Modern Library, 1953, pp. 112–13, 299; on the Slavophile-merchant partnership, see Owen, Thomas C., *Capitalism and Politics in Russia: A Social History of the Moscow Merchant*, 1855–1905, Cambridge, Cambridge University Press, 1981, pp. 32–3; on the Slavophile contributions, see Zilliacus, Konni, *The Russian Revolutionary Movement*, London, Alston Rivers, 1905, pp. 135–9.

Peter the Great, and the vigorous supporter of Russia's further assimilation of Western experiences and achievements. Belinskii became the censor of the "spiritual stagnation" of Russia, the resolute opponent of serfdom and of the Tsarist "timid and half measures concerning the landowners' 'white Negroes,' " and the harsh critic of the Orthodox Church committed, according to him, to "darkness, chain, and the knout." The most powerful cause of the dissension of the intellectual life of Russia of the 1840s was perhaps, as Leonard Schapiro suggested, the reaction against both Belinskii and the official doctrine, which he set out to oppose. His own career as a critic of letters and also of life under the Tsars reflected not only his development but that of many radical intellectuals of the time. It illustrated also the rise to notoriety in the intelligentsia of some of the *raznochintsy* – the members of classes other than the higher ups – who sought to pursue careers different from those that their background might have suggested.[15]

Some of the main ingredients of the soon dominant populist ideology were furnished in the 1850s and 1860s by the "forefathers of revolutionary populism" (as Lenin called them), namely the famous writer Alexander I. Herzen and the publicist Nikolai G. Chernyshevskii, whose notable articles in the *Sovremennik* (*Contemporary*) played a decisive role. Herzen contributed not only the basic elements of what became known as populist agrarian socialism, but also some personal views concerning economic development in general. According to him, the entire edifice of the Russian state was supposed to evolve on the following foundations: 1) the right of every man to land; 2) its communal possession; and 3) communal government. The village commune was supposed to be the bridge by which Russia would reach socialism. He assumed that the survival of the commune constituted an enormous advantage if one takes into account the socialist germ it contained and if one separated the commune from the serfdom to which it was historically connected. Concerning development in general, Herzen interpreted in his own way the critical question – by then in public debate since the Crimean War – of the relation between economic backwardness and advanced economic development. He asserted notably that Russia did not have to pass through all the phases of Europe's development; as he put it, "I absolutely deny the necessity of these repetitions." At most, he added, "we may have to pass through the difficult and painful trials of historical development of our predecessors, but in the same way as the embryo passes through all the lower degrees of

[15] Slonim, Marc, *De Pierre Le Grand à Lenine*, op. cit., pp. 66–9; Yarmolinsky, Avrahm, *Turgenev: The Man, His Art and His Age*, New York, Orion Press, 1959, pp. 74–9; Hare, Richard, *Pioneers of Russian Social Thought*, op. cit., pp. 39–81; Schapiro, Leonard B., *Rationalism and Nationalism . . .*, op. cit., pp. 62–4; Matlaw, R. E., "Introduction," and "Belinsky: Letter to N. V. Gogol," in *Belinsky, Chernishevsky & Dobrolyubov, Essential Writings by the Founders of Russian Literary & Social Criticism*, Matlaw, R. E., ed., Bloomington, IN, Indiana University Press, 1976, pp. vii–xii, 84–5.

zoological existence before birth." In fact, he noted, the results obtained by other countries "became the general possession of all who understand." In sum, backward countries may compress, or jump over, certain development phases, provided they understand how to use properly the experiences of the already developed countries.[16] These alleged "advantages" of backwardness or late development have been often repeated and elaborated ever since (and not only in Russia), even though "backwardness" or slow or retarded development takes obviously different forms at different historical junctures and may be due to a wide variety of combinations of causes.

Chernyshevskii agreed in some critical respects with Herzen, but he also diverged from him in some interesting ways. To start with, he agreed that the commune system had to be preserved since allegedly it could ease the passage toward a better society. Following the contentions of the Baron von Haxthausen, the famous German visitor and writer about Russia on the eve of the second half of the nineteenth century, Chernyshevskii also asserted that because of the communal land tenure – which preserved and developed "the spirit of association" – Russia could avoid the West European "illness" of "pauperism-proletarianism." "The best form of ownership of landed property for successful agriculture," he wrote, "is one that makes owner, manager, and worker one and the same person. Of all the forms of ownership, state ownership of property together with communal possession comes closest to this ideal." On the other hand, however, he also stated in other writings that the communal possession of land could be found in other societies and among other people, and he dismissed the idea that Russia could or should pride herself for having maintained the communes, which he qualified as "vestiges of an archaic antiquity" that bore witness only "to a slower, lazier historical evolution." The beginnings of Russia's industrial development did not escape him; he expressed the conviction that Russia had embarked upon the path of its modernization, and predicted the growth of factory production and utilization of modern machinery in agriculture, and the rapid expansion of the railroad network. But he then made a clear distinction between capitalism and the utilization of modern production methods, alleging that private property had become an obstacle to development, an anachronistic system incapable of ensuring further progress. According to him, the "analysis of production and capital" showed that all value was created by labor, that labor was responsible for all production, and that accordingly, "labor must be the sole owner of the value produced." Finally, with respect to backwardness, he also alleged, like

[16] Venturi, Franco, *Il Populismo Russo, op. cit.*, pp. 55–9; Vernadsky, George, ed., *A Source Book for Russian History, from Early Times to 1917*, Vol. 3, *Alexander II to February Revolution*, New Haven, CT, Yale University Press, 1972, pp. 634–6; Plekhanov, George, "Our Differences," in *Selected Philosphical Works*, Vol. I, London, Lawrence & Wishart, 1961, pp. 146–9; Barel, Yves, *Le development économique de la Russie tsariste* (Economic Development of Tsarist Russia), Paris, Mouton, 1968, p. 33.

Herzen, that a late-developing country could use the experience and knowledge of an advanced people, develop rapidly, and "rise from the lowest level directly to the highest bypassing the intermediate logical steps." Clearly, more than in the case of Herzen, Chernyshevskii's conflicting views concerning the simultaneous acceptance and downgrading of the commune arrangement, his rejection of the "anachronistic" character of private ownership and capitalism, and his views concerning the interrelations among value, labor, and the ensuing ownership title to production were to exercise a deep influence not only upon populist revolutionaries but also over the Marxists, as we shall see later on.[17]

How exactly would the transition from the commune to a "rational" socialist society take place? The "revolutionary populists" of the 1870s and 1880s elaborated various formulae and strategies. Herzen himself had asserted in a florid style that the transition was already in process as a "murmur, a groan," and was allegedly spreading through Russia, the first "roar of the ocean wave" that was beginning to "seethe rife with storm." Accordingly, he asked the revolutionaries to go "To the People! Toward the People," and become the people's dedicated warriors. Chernyshevskii tried less to elucidate the specific method of the transition; he only noted pessimistically that the people were ignorant and in nearly all countries were mostly illiterate, and that the liberals and the democrats were pursuing their own programs not necessarily for the good of the lower estates. He then added that only those institutions that the popular masses supported were "striving and powerful."[18]

Various strategies were formulated in the ensuing years for the fight against the Tsarist autocracy and the transition to another system. The simplest ideas were devised by the small groups of *nihilists* (a term forged by Ivan Turgenev in his famous novel *Fathers and Children*, in 1862). As their representative, the young D. I. Pisarev, put it at the time: "We refuse outright to work out a plan for future conditions of life. . . . We have but a single, unalterable plan – merciless destruction." The same kind of formulae was also used by the famed nihilist-terrorist S. G. Nechaev, the presumed author of the *Catechism of a Revolutionist* (1869), in which the father of anarchism, the aging M. A. Bakunin, was also supposed to have had a hand. According to the *Catechism*, the revolutionist "has no personal interests, no pursuits, sentiments, attachments, property,

[17] Plekhanov, George, *Selected Philosphical Works*, *op. cit.*, pp. 149–57; Vernadsky, George, ed., *A Source Book for Russian History*, *op. cit.*, pp. 636–8; Barel, Yves, *Le development économique . . .*, *op. cit.*, pp. 34–8; Acton, E., "The Russian Revolutionary Intelligentsia and Industrialization," in *Russian Thought and Society . . .*, *op. cit.*, pp. 100–3; Walicki, Andrzej, *The Controversy over Capitalism: Studies in the Social Philosophy of the Russian Populists*, Oxford, Clarendon Press, 1969, pp. 17–20, 83, 116–7; Hare, Richard, *Pioneers of Russian Social Thought . . .*, *op. cit.*, pp. 225–9, 246–8.

[18] Vernadsky, George, ed., *A Source Book for Russian History*, *op. cit.*, p. 646; Plekhanov, George, *Selected Philosophical Works*, *op. cit.*, Vol. 1, 1961, pp. 158–9.

not even a name." He knows "only one science, the science of destruction." The revolution he seeks "is one that completely eradicates any sort of state structure and annihilates all of Russia's tradition, institutions, and classes."[19] Neither the nihilists nor the anarchists formed a party. But their ideas influenced various currents in the Russian intelligentsia, including the so-called revolutionary populists of the 1870s and 1880s, who were also affected by opposing ideas about the organization of a popular party, the eventual role of the state, and the objectives of the revolution. In this respect, it is interesting to consider the influencing proposals notably of P. L. Lavrov, N. K. Mikhailovskii, and P. N. Tkachëv.[20]

Lavrov stressed (in 1873) that what Russia needed to "attain victory" in the drive for an equitable form of society was the organization of a party. The means of attaining "a completely equitable social order" was indeed, according to him, "the union of a majority of workers into a free association." Those who effectively desired the welfare of the people, he added, should aim at creating among the people a conscious conception of their goals, while making themselves not more than the executors of the social aspirations of the people toward these goals. In any case, according to him, the future socialist society needed to reduce – or even eliminate – the state (as the anarchists also believed).

Mikhailovskii asserted (in 1872 and 1875) that it was important first of all to distinguish between Europe's and Russia's social problems. In Europe, he stated, the labor problem had a revolutionary character since it raised the question of the transfer of the means of production. In Russia, allegedly, the labor problem had a conservative character, since it posed the necessity of the retention of the means of production by the peasant and the artisan "owners." In sum, what mattered in Russia was to develop further the relationship of labor and ownership already in existence, an aim that could be achieved through a large-scale state intervention, whose first action should be "the permanent stabilization" of communal property through legislation.

Tkachëv suggested (around 1875) quite different goals and means. The first objective, he said, was *political*, not *social*. It was to prepare a revolution whose direct and immediate aim should be for the revolutionists to seize governmental power. To achieve this, the revolutionaries must unite in a closely knit, disciplined, and hierarchical organization, which would serve as the necessary instrument for the "disorganization and destruction of the existing governmental power." After the seizure of the power, the revolutionary state should draw support from a National Assembly and through propaganda, while focusing

[19] Vernadsky, George, ed., *A Source Book for Russian History*, op. cit., p. 641–50; see notably the interesting comments of Leroy-Beaulieu, Anatole, *L'Empire des Tsars . . ., op. cit.*, pp. 164–73.

[20] Vernadsky, George, ed., *A Source Book for Russian History, op. cit.*, p. 650–7; Venturi, Franco, *Il Populismo Russo, op. cit.*, pp. 358–60, 364–73, 441–9.

on the social objectives and thus bringing about the expected social revolution through a series of reforms.

Under these and similar influences, many populists of the late 1870s finally organized themselves into a revolutionary party called *Zemlia i Volia* (Land and Freedom), which, as its program stated (in 1878), had as objectives the seizure of the land of the landlords and boyars, the expulsion and sometimes the general extermination of all superiors and representatives of the state, and the establishment of "free autonomous communes." These slogans had always allegedly constituted the "program" of all the leaders of the old peasant rebellions, redefined as "the revolutionary socialists from the people: Pugachëv, Razin, and their followers." The program further rejected expropriating the factories, because history, which had placed that problem in the forefront in Europe, has not posed it *at all* in Russia, which instead faced "the agrarian issue." The document then asserted that terrorism had "nothing to do against the foundations of the existing order," and that its own terrorists formed only "a protective detachment" against the blows of its enemies. Finally, the program concluded that the autocracy, attacked from all sides, will collapse, and then make way for the *privileged classes*, that is, "the bourgeoisie." To avoid this alternative, and to take full advantage of the confusion that always attends a change of system, the party must first dedicate its strength toward forging close bonds with the people.[21]

For a short while, *Zemlia i Volia* achieved a certain influence among the intelligentsia. But barely three years after its formation, the party collapsed ideologically and organizationally. It split into a minority group *Chërnyi Peredel* (Land Redistribution) and a majority group, *Narodnaia Volia* (People's Will) that broke openly with certain traditionalist populist views and oriented itself resolutely toward terrorism. On March 1, 1881, it thought it was "furthering its immediate task" by assassinating Alexander II, a criminal act that brought against it a vast and pitiless repression.

Let us first consider the case of *Chërnyi Peredel*. From the outset, its goal of "revolution in the countryside" soon proved ineffective. In addition, it rapidly lost quite a few of its members, first because of some damaging police raids directed against it in Moscow and Kiev, then because some of its early leaders, such as George Plekhanov, broke with the party, passing onto a path untrodden until then by the Russian revolutionaries, the path of Russian Marxism. Plekhanov, who emigrated to Switzerland, formed there with a handful of émigrés the group Liberation of Labor, and subsequently formulated there his antislavophile and antipopulist views in an influential book, *Nashe raznoglasiia*

---

[21] Karataev, I. K., "Narodnicheskaia literatura 60-90x godov XIX veka" (Populist Literature in the Sixties to the Nineties of the Nineteenth Century), in *Narodnicheskaia ekonomicheskaia literatura* (The Populist Economic Literature), Karataev, I. K., ed., Moscow, Social-Economic Literature, 1958, pp. 40–1; Vernadsky, George, ed., *A Source Book for Russian History*, *op. cit.*, pp. 662–3.

(*Our Differences*, first published abroad in 1884). The book methodically set out his arguments against the main competing currents in the intelligentsia, arguments that furnished the basic ideas of Russian Marxism until the end of the nineteenth century (as we will see later on).

In its program, the avowed terrorist group *Narodnaia Volia* asserted (in 1880) that as "socialists and populists," the group's goal was to seize power from the existing government and transfer it to the people via a freely elected Constituent Assembly (*uchreditel'noe sobranie*) that would adequately express and execute the people's will. The program added that in that future assembly, the party would defend a number of proposals, which were to influence Russia's democratic currents as well as the revolutionary groups of the time. The proposals notably included demands for permanent popular representation and for vast local and regional autonomy, as well as the attribution of all cultivable land to the peasants and of all the factories to the workers. The same document also indicated, however, that the purpose of the party's terrorist activities was to break the spell of governmental power and thus to strengthen the revolutionary spirit. The repression following the assassination of Alexander II, however, dealt crippling blows to *Narodnaia Volia*. The party continued to stay alive up to 1886, but it was persistently losing influence and supporters. A young terrorist group, which organized itself with the purpose of executing Alexander III, was caught the very day it had planned its attack. The group's leader, Alexander Ulianov, and four accomplices were executed in 1887. (Ulianov's younger brother, Vladimir, was subsequently to change his name to Lenin and become the chief of Communist Russia.) The disaggregation of *Narodnaia Volia* reached that year its final phase, as one of its main ideologues, Lev Tikhomirov, broke with his former friends, recanted his past, and was gratiated by the Emperor.[22]

Eventually, the great agricultural and industrial crisis of 1891–2, the disastrous grain harvest and the ensuing famine followed by the spreading of all kinds of epidemics, brought about a revival of the influence of populism during the last decade of the century. The works of certain populist writers – notably V. V. (V. Vorontsov), and Nikolai-on (pen name of N. Danielson) – gained increasing influence, as did certain populist magazines such as *Russkoe bogatsvo* (*Russian Wealth*).

V. V.'s book, *Fate of Capitalism in Russia* (1882), reasserted some of the old populist contentions – for example, that backwardness constituted a kind of "historical privilege" and that Russia could develop very rapidly by using the models created in the West. But then he added that Russian industries would have to compete frontally with the far more experienced industries of the

---

[22] Slonim, Marc, *De Pierre Le Grand à Lenine*, *op. cit.*, pp. 169–70, 199–203; Kuznetsov, I. V. , *Istoria SSSR* (History of the USSR), Moscow, Prosveschenie, 1971, pp. 182–5, 197–200; Offord, Derek, *The Russian Revolutionary Movement in the 1880s*, Cambridge, Cambridge University Press, 1986, pp. 28–35.

advanced countries, and that this competition would choke Russia's awakening capitalism. The latter, he added, lacked the foreign markets indispensable for development and could not produce massively for the domestic market without ruining the peasants and the artisans, thus reducing dramatically the population's overall purchasing power. At best, Russian industry could create only small islands of modern production for satisfying the requirements of the upper classes. The alternative for Russia's development, he added, consisted of an industrialization initiated and controlled by the state, built around the artisanal industries. The state could help the latter by providing supplies and the outlets needed for their production.

Nikolai-on subsequently expressed similar ideas in a number of articles and in his basic work, *Outline of Post-Reform Agriculture* (1893). Nikolai-on reasserted that Russia allegedly lacked foreign markets and reaffirmed that furthering large-scale industry – that is, capitalist development – was prejudicial to Russia's interests. He further condemned the policy of industrialization based on "outrageous protectionism" and suggested that it was still possible for Russia to go back to reliance on agrarian communes and artisanal production. In sum, he believed that Russia could avoid becoming "a tributary of more advanced counties" and that it could foster a non-capitalist, state-controlled industrialization that would increase both productivity and welfare.[23]

Toward the end of the century, notwithstanding the then-growing impact of Marxism (about which more in the next section), the populist ideology gained new prestige and increasing influence both in Russia and among the Russian émigrés in Paris, Zurich, and Geneva. Finally, toward the end of 1901, a new populist underground organization was formed under the name of the Socialist Revolutionary (SR) Party. The SR's doctrine and strategy became rapidly known. The new party proclaimed itself the successor of the *Narodnaia Volia* – that is, it adopted terrorism as a means of combat against the regime – and asserted further that it viewed socialism as the inevitable corollary of a society's evolution and as a guarantor of people's welfare. It then indicated that the passage to socialism could be modified in many ways to be compatible with a country's peculiarities with respect to race, climate, historical, and economic conditions. Since the peasants constituted the majority of the Russian labor force, the SRs affirmed that the success of a Russian revolution depended first on the peasants. Russia's revolution would not be a "bourgeois revolution," but rather a revolution carried out by the working masses and by the intelligentsia under the battle cry of "Land and Liberty!" Its task would be to abolish private landholding and to redistribute land to the peasants on the basis of collective landholding by the rural communes. The other immediate revolutionary goals

---

[23] Gatrell, Peter, *The Tsarist Economy 1850–1917*, New York, St. Martin's Press, 1986, pp. 14–16; Plekhanov, George, "Our Differences," in *Selected Philosophical Works, op. cit.*, pp. 216, 221, 270–1; Barel, Yves, *Le development économique . . ., op. cit.*, pp. 50–1; Walicki, A., *The Controversy over Capitalism . . ., op. cit.*, pp. 115–31.

were to abolish the autocratic regime, to elect a National Assembly, and establish a democratic federal state based upon the right of self-determination of all the national minorities. Eventually, during the tense years preceding the 1917 revolution, the Bolsheviks adopted various SR slogans. However, after the insurrection of November 7, 1917, and the Constituent Assembly elections held on November 25, the Assembly met formally on January 18, 1918. The SRs held an absolute majority of seats, but the next day the Bolsheviks dissolved the Assembly and for decades removed from the minds and from the habits of the Russian masses the notions of constitutionalism, parliamentary procedures, and effective civil rights.[24]

2-4. Alternatives

Unlike the Slavophiles and the populists, the Marxists did not believe in the existence of some special Russian socioeconomic destiny diverging from any and all European development patterns. Yet, while they had a single well-defined theoretical basis, as change began to unfold in postemancipation Russia, the Marxists began to split into various tendencies advancing different analyses of the country's conditions and its historical prospects.

Even before the existence of any Russian Marxist organization, Karl Marx and Friedrich Engels, like many other European intellectuals, focused their attention on Russia's evolution. In 1858, before the great reform of 1861, Marx rightly noted that the questions of serfdom were in Russia at the order of the day after the Crimean War, that the eventual liberation of the peasants was bound to "upset the entire state superstructure," and that Alexander II could not postpone this issue any longer.[25] Engels, in an 1875 polemical attack against P. N. Trachëv, derided the populist contentions that Russia's oriental despotism had no deep social roots, that the country lacked any capitalist and proletarian classes, and that the peasant commune was a lever of the socialist revolution. He then noted that the intelligentsia had an acute feeling of an imminent upheaval, but that it nourished the illusion that it could channel the disturbance into a peaceful direction.[26]

By the 1880s it was the turn of the Russian Marxists to focus their attention on the general characteristics of the postreform developments in their country, on the changing interrelations within agriculture and in the rest of the economy, and on the similarities and differences between these changes and those that

[24] Slonim, Marc, *De Pierre Le Grand à Lenine, op. cit.*, pp. 226–32; Charques, R. D., *A Short History of Russia*, New York, E. P. Dutton & Co., 1956, pp. 248–9.

[25] Marx, Karl, "The Question of the Abolition of Serfdom in Russia" (*New York Tribune*, October 19, 1858), in *La Russie par Marx et Engels* (Russia by Marx and Engels), transl. by Dangeville, Roger, Paris, Union Generale de l' Edition, 1974, pp. 210–3.

[26] Engels, Fredrich, "The Social Problems of Russia," April 16, 1875, in *La Russie par Marx et Engels, op. cit.*, pp. 236–54.

had taken and were taking place in Western Europe. In defining their positions, the Marxists necessarily delimited themselves vigorously, particularly from the populists, who continued to exercise a widespread influence at the time.

In 1884, Plekhanov, who wrote the first important Marxist study on the postemancipation changes in Russia, *Our Differences*, examined and rejected methodically each of the theses of Herzen, Chernyshevskii, Bakunin, and Tkachëv. In particular, Plekhanov repudiated their contentions concerning the alleged "communist instincts" of the Russian peasantry and the assumed importance of the commune as an instrument of progress. The commune, he pointed out, was not the vehicle of transition to a "communist form of communal life," but rather a declining, disintegrating system after the abolition of serfdom. In conclusion, he dismissed these writers' theses as an amalgam of the Slavophiles' scorn of the West and of their own simplistic and deficient investigations of peasant life and its evolution. He then pointed to the capitalist developments in the Russian home market, in agriculture, in handcrafts, in trade, and in industry, and asserted that the peasants' liberation from feudal dependence had constituted in Russia "the swan song of the old production process," even though the reform had been followed by certain legislative acts that aimed at hindering some of its consequences. He then stressed in particular the economic differentiation taking place among the peasantry as the communal life was disintegrating, the dismantling of the rural and domestic industry, the separation between agriculture and manufacturing, and the expansion of the latter while the economy continued to rely on various branches of the small handicraft industry. With regard to large-scale manufacturing, he stressed the role of capital in cotton spinning and weaving, then "the most advanced branches of modern capitalist industry," and in general, in the production of machinery and in the expanding use of modern technology. In conclusion, he raised the following crucial questions and provided certain perceptive answers that separated him and his partisans not only from the populists, but later on from Lenin and his followers. "Will Russia go through the school of capitalism? We shall answer without any hesitation: Why should she not finish the school she has *already* begun? ... *Capitalism is favored* by the whole dynamics of our social life, all the forces that develop with the movement of the social machine and in their turn determine the direction and speed of that movement."[27]

In his earliest writings, of 1893–4, Lenin expressed his agreement with the theses developed by Plekhanov in *Our Differences*. Thus, after asserting that "Russia had entered the capitalist path," Lenin also aimed at demolishing the populist positions – including those then in fashion, namely those of V. V. and of Nikolai-on (and their predecessors) – concerning: a) the alleged

---

[27] Plekhanov, George, "Our Differences," in *Selected Philosophical Works, op. cit.*, pp. 261, 263, 270, 274–5, 297, 309.

homogeneity and unity of the peasantry "as a single harmonious whole"; b) the identification of factory workers with *all* the workers engaged in capitalist production; c) the characterization of capitalism as "a false line of development"; and d) the intelligentsia's illusory attempts to "set out to seek 'different paths.' " With regard to agriculture, Lenin also stressed that the economic differentiation began among the peasants a process that he defined as a means of *depeasantization* leading from its earliest stages to the development of a commodity economy and to the growth of agricultural capitalism. Concerning what he called the "childish idea" of the populists that capitalism was confined to the employment of factory workers (then numbering 1.5 million), Lenin asserted that many other wage earners were engaged in capitalist production, as, for instance, the farm laborers, the handicraftsmen, the workers in the building industries, and so on. In opposition to the negativist populist views about capitalism in general, Lenin, like Plekhanov, also underlined at the time "the progressive character of capitalism" compared to the old feudal system, though he added that large-scale capitalism was opening the road to socialism through its creation of a new "working class." Finally, he rejected the "romanticist" contention that the increasing "bourgeois character" of the society was fortuitous and that some better path could be chosen – as if capital had not already made its choice, and reality had not yet shown most obviously that the "path" in question was that of the domination of capital.[28]

By 1895–7, in his first *Draft Program* of the Social Democratic Party, as well as in other papers of the time, Lenin put forth the ideas that capitalism was developing with "an ever growing rapidity" a new class of workers who could wage an effective struggle against capital, that this struggle was a political one aiming at the abolition of social estates, at equality of all before the law, and in addition, for the peasants, at the abolition of land redemption payments and at the return to them of all their lands.[29] Also in 1897, he further elaborated his views in a study entitled *The Development of Capitalism in Russia*, in which he stressed again the splitting up of the peasantry, this time in what he called "a rural bourgeoisie and a rural proletariat," the growth of commercial and industrial populations (in towns and in the colonized border regions), the increase in production and productivity along with the concentration of previously scattered agricultural and industrial production units, the expansion of overall employment and of wage labor in the economy, and thus the achievement by capitalism of its great "mission," namely that of replacing labor service with hired (wage) labor.[30]

However, from 1903 on, Lenin started to change these basic ideas and to separate himself increasingly from the underlying positions of Plekhanov and

---

[28] Lenin, V. I., *Collected Works*, Vol. 1, *1893–1894*, Moscow, Foreign Languages Publishing House, 1960, pp. 195, 219, 255, 285, 289, 311, 313, 316, 379.

[29] Lenin, V. I., *Collected Works*, Vol. 2, *1895–1897*, *op. cit.*, pp. 95–8, 336–7.

[30] Lenin V. I., *Collected Works*, Vol. 3, *1897*, *op. cit.*, pp. 316–34, 595–600.

his followers regarding the tasks of the industrial workers and, the role of the peasantry. Lenin asserted notably that the Social Democrats (SDs) should defend the demands of the wage workers *as a class* in all the branches of the national economy while sustaining only certain objectives of the peasantry since the latter no longer constituted an "integral class." For Lenin, the workers' objectives were henceforth directed against "the present-day (bourgeois) society," while the peasantry's demands were still directed essentially against the remnants of the old feudal system that subsisted in the succeeding social order. Yet, the evolution of agriculture involved also a capitalist evolution and hence was necessarily also engendering a "class struggle against the bourgeoisie" that should constitute the "fundamental concern" of the SDs.[31]

Subsequently, beginning in 1907, Lenin and his followers, the Bolsheviks, proceeded to revise the agrarian program of the SDs and deepened their differences with Plekhanov and his partisans, the Mensheviks, along the following lines. The SDs had agreed in 1903 that the agrarian question was the basis of the bourgeois revolution in Russia and that it determined the specific national character of this revolution; for the SDs the essence of the agrarian question was the abolition of landlordism and of the survival of serfdom in agriculture. But after the revolution of 1905, Lenin asserted notably that there were "two paths of objectively possible *bourgeois development*": one which liquidated medievalism, and one which did not. Medievalism could be disposed of either as a result "of the transformation of the landlord economy, or as a result of the abolition of the landlord latifundia – i.e. either by reform or by revolution." He then added that in the first case the feudal landlord economy could slowly evolve into a "bourgeois junker landlord economy" – like in the case of Prussia – while in the second case the bourgeois path could be opened when the landlord economy was broken up by a revolution "which confiscates and splits up the feudal estates" and transforms "the patriarchal peasant into a bourgeois farmer." This, according to Lenin, was supposedly "the American path." Lenin and his followers then added that in Russia, to establish really free farming, it would be necessary to break up not only the landlord system but also the peasant medieval system. This concomitant expropriation of both the landlord and the peasant landownership could be achieved only through nationalizing all the land, abolishing private ownership, and transferring all the land to the state. Furthermore, destroying all the forms of landownership would also require destroying the old political institutions of Russia: the monarchy, the standing army, and the bureaucracy.

While the Bolsheviks thus affirmed the needs of nationalization and of the destruction of the monarchical state system, Plekhanov and the Mensheviks asserted that the Russian revolution was a bourgeois revolution, that the SDs "must support the bourgeoisie in its struggle against the old order of things,"

---

[31] Lenin V. I., *Collected Works,* Vol. 6, *January 1902–August 1903, op. cit.*, pp. 113–16, 118, 124.

and that the solution of the agrarian problem that the SDs could support might involve dividing the landlord's estates among the peasants as private property, and/or the municipalizing the landlords' estates. Lenin retorted that the workers were certainly not indifferent to the development of capitalism either under a landlord monarchy with private ownership of land, or under a farm republic with the nationalization of land. They were evidently in favor of the latter, but even in this case the workers would have to fight simultaneously to abolish the old regime and its army and bureaucracy, because without their destruction, the agrarian revolution could not succeed. In sum, contrary to the Mensheviks, for Lenin and his followers the Russian bourgeoisie was not the driving force of the Russian revolution and, consequently, the days of bourgeois revolution had passed.[32]

2-5. Concluding Comments

In his work of the early 1880s, Plekhanov remarked that the question, "What path will the economic development of Russia follow?" was then discussed "lengthily and passionately" throughout the country's publications. This question, he added, could not be debated with "moderation" since it had become an immediate question concerning the future – a future that will indeed be shaped by the way that "the question of our economic development will be answered."[33]

To clarify the issues involved, Plekhanov, as we saw, examined carefully the positions of the Slavophiles and the populists, and sketched in the process the Marxists' views. As he rightly noted, Slavophiles and the populists propagated the idea of Russia's exceptionalism with regard to development – an exceptionalism implying Russia's capacity to devise and to follow a path unique from the one pursued in the West, particularly since the industrialization processes and the creation there "of pauperism and of the proletariat." The emphasis of both the Slavophiles and the populists rested on the assumption of the particular value in the present and in the future of the peasant commune. For the Slavophiles, the full benefit of the peasant communal socioeconomic setup could be realized if the country would eradicate the European influences and return to the pre-Petrine framework. For the populists, the reliance on certain European influences was welcome, but only those preceding Europe's industrial phases; the assimilation of the past influences was supposed to allow Russia to "jump over" the undesirable intermediate phases, avoid pauperism and proletarization, and, thanks to the commune, accede easily and directly

---

[32] See notably, Lenin, V. I., "The Agrarian Program of Social Democracy in the First Russian Revolution 1905–1907," *Collected Works*, Vol. 13, *June 1907–April 1908, op. cit.*, pp. 219, 239, 294–5, 347–55, and 421–8; and Lenin, V. I., "The Agrarian Revolution in Russia," *Collected Works*, Vol. 15, *March 1908–August 1909, op. cit.*, pp. 137–41, 147.

[33] Plekhanov, George, "Our Differences," in *Selected Philosophical Works, op. cit.*, pp. 700–1.

into socialism. As far as the existing autocratic system was concerned, the two currents diverged completely. The Slavophiles viewed this system as acceptable but only to the extent that it would rely on the following principles: for the government, unlimited power; for the people, liberty of life and conscience under a non-state-controlled Orthodox hierarchy. For the populists, the prevailing system was totally unacceptable; it had to be attacked and dismantled to open the door to the socialist society based on the communes.

From the 1880s on, the Marxists and the pro-Marxists perceived the crucial importance of the Tsarist reform of 1861, which to an extent freed the peasants from feudal dependence and constituted in Russia the "swan song of the old production process." They registered carefully the beginnings and the expansions of capitalism in agriculture and industry, in handicrafts, building, and trade. As these changes unfolded, Marxist unity broke down concerning the key question of the country's path of development. Was Russia evolving, as the Mensheviks thought, through a bourgeois revolution leading to the domination of the bourgeoisie, that is, to a Western type of capitalist system? Or rather, was Russia changing as the Bolsheviks thought, by the way of a peasant revolution – in which the peasantry was splitting up into bourgeois (*kulak*) peasants, and proletarian (wage-earning) peasants – ultimately generating a *sui generis* path of development based on the leadership of the working class associated with the "proletarian" peasantry?

Either of these two views – as well as those of the Slavophiles and the populists – resulted less from an exhaustive and objective weighing of the economic facts and more from the desire to trace a political direction based on political sets of tactics and strategies derived from various theories and conceptions of change considered as well fitting Russia's situation. Indeed, neither the Slavophiles nor the populists, neither the Mensheviks nor the Bolsheviks, paid close attention at the time to the preoccupations, the debates, and the specific choices of the Tsarist regime itself besides the great reform of 1861, impacting the country's patterns of development and within them the conditions and the forms of the growth of capitalism. I turn to these issues in Chapter 3.

CHAPTER 3

The Economic Policies

3-1. Agricultural Policy

The complex, tangled, ambivalent liberation of agriculture from its medieval shell in 1861 gave in time impetus to broader changes in agriculture, as well as in industry, transport, commerce, banking, and the government's receipts and expenditures. These changes were affected at times directly by clearly formulated governmental policies, at times indirectly and hesitantly by democratic policies evolved under circumstantial pressures domestic or foreign. I shall examine the character and scope of these policies in all the indicated sectors and conclude on their combined impact on the economy as a whole.

The liberation of agriculture from certain medieval bounds involved historically three key elements: first, the emancipation of the serfs along with the abolition of variously defined feudal rights; second, the liberation of the ownership of land from certain legal restrictions and greater mobility regarding land transfers; and third, the partial release of agriculture from the ancient culture and usages of cultivation methods and land management.[1] To what extent did the reform of 1861 and subsequent related measures actually help liberate agricultural labor through land ownership and offload ancient agricultural customs and methods?

The reform of 1861 certainly aimed at recasting the Russian agrarian society on new bases, by creating a landowning peasantry and by buttressing the management of the land allotted and purchased by the peasants through the authority of the communes. Recall that the reform abolished the bondage rights of the gentry over the peasants' serfs settled on their estates as well as over the manorial servants. Further, the peasants were set to receive from the gentry, in permanent use, beside their farmhouses, the fields allotted to them in exchange for a redemption procedure involving quitrents or labor services for

[1] Bogart, Ernest L., *Economic History of Europe, 1760–1939*, London, Longman, Green and Co., 1942, p. 1.

the gentry. The allotments were to be based on "voluntary agreements" forged under the gentry's heavy-handed influence, while the government retained in principle on the one hand the right to set a floor below which the gentry's land possession could not fall and, on the other hand, the right to protect the peasantry against insufficiency of the farm land they acquired. The party both to the separation procedure between the gentry landowners and the peasantry and to redemption procedure became the *mir*, the political counterpart of the commune (*obshchina*). Indeed, the charters setting forth both the land allotments and the peasant obligations were prepared for the collectivity of the peasants. This was true not only for the cases of field command organization but also for the areas where such an organization did not exist. The joint responsibility for the payment of taxes was indeed extended then to village communes where land was held by the individual household and not by the field commune. The latter did not exist in the Baltic area and amounted to less than 15 percent of peasant landholdings in the former Polish areas of the Ukraine. On the other hand, this percentage rose to between 33 and 40 percent in Belorussia and in other areas of the Ukraine, to 80 to 90 percent in the steppes of Novorussiia and in the easternmost part of the Ukraine, and to 96 to 97 percent in the regions populated by Great Russians, including the eastern steppes.[2]

The opportunity to combine the reform with inducements for the modernization of land was deliberately neglected. In the period from 1860 to 1890, only in certain black earth areas owned by the gentry did the agricultural commerce of grain develop through the use of machinery and wage labor. In other black earth areas, notably the central region, the methods of cultivation continued to be based on the old techniques. At the same time, the insufficiency of peasant land allotments and the high redemption obligations, along with the barriers to the individuals' breaking their ties with the commune, reinforced the traditional inefficiency of peasant agriculture. Agriculture did not supply massive labor for the nonagricultural branches. The abolition of serfdom and the upsurge of industrial growth were separated by close to twenty-five years, but these changes did eventually stimulate the growth of westernization and the spread of the monetary economy.[3]

By the 1870s and more so by the 1880s, Russian agrarian policy began to aim at correcting certain emancipation arrangements that were severely impacting the growing peasant population, notably regarding the small size of the lots and the burdensome financial obligations that they entailed. The possession of the land had become indeed not a privilege but an obligation enforced by

[2] Gerschenkron, Alexander, "Russian Agrarian Policies," in his *Continuity in History and Other Essays*, Cambridge, MA, Belknap Press of Harvard University Press, 1968, pp. 185–8.

[3] Gerschenkron, Alexander, "Russian Agrarian Policies," in *op. cit.*, pp. 193, 197, 208; Barel, Yves, *Le development économique de la Russie Tsariste*, Paris, La Hay, Mouton, et Cie, 1968, pp. 150–1.

the commune upon its members. Eventually the tax burdens were decreased, portions of the accumulated debts were canceled, the level of redemption payments was permanently reduced, and a limited attempt was made to remedy the scarcity of peasant land by helping the communes to finance land purchases. For numerous reasons, however, the last quarter of the nineteenth century brought very hard times for agriculture: The prices of agricultural produce were decreasing while those of industrial goods were rising, the agricultural population was increasing while the per capita index of agricultural output was falling. Aware of the peasant misery and discontent, the government began *inter alia* to consider with interest such ideas as peasant resettlements in Siberia. Of course, the construction of the Trans-Siberian Railroad (begun in 1891) facilitated the project, and in 1896 the Ministry of the Interior created a Resettlement Administration. While before 1895 fewer than one hundred thousand peasants moved to Siberia, beginning in 1895 the number of migrants rose to over one hundred thousand, in 1898 to over two hundred thousand. After a decline in 1905–6, their numbers increased in 1908 and 1909 to over seven hundred thousand in each of these years. Notwithstanding this kind of exodus, and notwithstanding the already indicated massive displacement of the peasants toward the towns (see Chapter 1), the proportion of landless peasants rose in the countryside from 7 percent of the peasantry in 1893–6 to as much as 19.4 percent in 1905.[4]

At the beginning of the twentieth century, for the first time since the emancipation, peasant revolts and disobedience increased sharply in numbers and intensity. After a short decline in 1902–4, peasant agitation and attacks against the gentry reached their summit in 1905. By 1906 the peasant disorders were finally contained while the government, especially under the influence of its newly appointed member P. A. Stolypin, turned its attention to the heart of the evil, namely the increasing poverty of the peasant population. Stolypin saw the solution of this problem as the creation of "a class of small proprietors – the basic cell of the state and in its very nature an adversary of all destructive theories." To achieve this objective, it appeared necessary to modify certain built-in regulations in the *obschina*, an institution whose early advantages as a source of cheap agricultural labor and high rents for the gentry were increasingly turning into an obvious disadvantage, as the communal villages were engaging in brutally destructive attacks against the properties of the gentry. Stolypin's aim of establishing a new economic order for the peasantry required the reorganization of the right of each head of household in the village communes to request at any time a formal transfer into his personal ownership of a portion of communal land, to consolidate his lands into a compact piece, and to sell his land if he so chose. These features adopted in 1906 were further elaborated in the law of June 14, 1910. By 1916 requests for acquisition of land

---

[4] Thaden, Edward C., *Russia since 1801: The Making of a New Society*, New York, Wiley-Interscience, 1971, pp. 320–1; Barel, Yves, *Le development économique...*, *op. cit.*, pp. 143.

in personal ownership were submitted by 2,755,000 households in European Russia.[5]

Evidently, the emancipation of the serfs and the subsequent related legislative measures were not concerned with liberating manpower for industrialization, but rather with keeping the peasants bound to land – a kind of new *adscripti glebae* – that was to ensure through the allotment's payments and their labor the basic support of the autocratic regime, the gentry's landownership. This system, however, had to be modified willy-nilly by relatively small adjustments until 1906–10. The partial breakup of Russia's feudal system began with the emancipation and ended with the 1910 reform, and was carried out from above with a modest input from the then publicly contending ideologies. The Russian changes have not been carried out like in France, for instance, under the increasingly decisive impact of the "bourgeoisie" – that is, of the expanding industrial and commercial strata in the society. The "transformation of the landlord economy and the abolition of the landlord latifundia" had not resulted in the West, as Lenin had contended, by way of a single, well-defined act: *reform* or *revolution*.

Consider, for instance, the changes in England and France, and then in Prussia and the United States (which Lenin chose to illustrate his allegations). The "transformation of the landlord economy" extended in England over centuries. The virtual abolition of serfdom took place by the middle of the fourteenth century, while the legal emancipation of persons was carried out fully by the end of the fourteenth century. The second step in the liquidation of feudalism, namely the liberation of the ownership of land from certain legal restrictions and the increased mobility in land transfers, occurred in the seventeenth century, though custom and law kept the great estates intact. The enclosure movement – allowing to each small tenant a plot of land roughly equivalent to his scattered strips – became important after 1750 and reached its high point in 1800–20. The third step, releasing agricultural techniques from ancient custom and usage, took several forms from the end of the eighteenth century through the following decades of the nineteenth century. This step concerned in particular the introduction of new crops, land drainage and manuring, skillful rotation of crops, the application of science to agriculture, and the thorough reorganization of agrarian life.[6]

In France, the feudalism of the eighteenth century bore little resemblance to its medieval origins. There was little actual serfdom by the time that the "bourgeois" revolution began in 1789. The vast majority of the peasants were

---

[5] Gerschenkron, Alexander, "Russian Agrarian Policies," in *op. cit.*, pp. 236–7, 246; Pushkarev, Sergei, *The Emergence of Modern Russia 1801–1917, op. cit.*, p. 256; see also "The Decree on Peasant Rights, October 5, 1906," "Decrees on Peasant Allotments, November 9, 1906," and "Stolypin's Speech to the Duma on the Agrarian Question, May 10, 1907," in Vernadsky, George, ed., *A Source Book for Russian History from Early Times to 1917, op. cit.*, pp. 802, 805.

[6] Bogart, Ernest L., *Economic History of Europe . . ., op. cit.*, pp. 3–16.

then free cultivators with certain seignorial and ecclesiastical dues. By August 11, 1789, the National Assembly abandoned officially the "feudal principle" and eliminated the feudal rights concerning serfdom, feudal dues, and other diverse obligations. What the Assembly did not do, however, was abolish the legal basis of the manorial system as well as various noble, ecclesiastical, corporate, and provincial privileges. The absolution of the old feudal rights was completed by 1793. As far as the ownership of land is concerned, various sources indicate that in 1789 about half of the lands held by some 4 million proprietors was in the hands of the peasants. The lands of the noble émigrés were confiscated in 1792 and were then offered for sale at low prices. As for the release of agriculture from the old cultural patterns and usage, progress was slow and remained modest even up to the middle of the nineteenth century.[7]

In Germany at the beginning of the nineteenth century, the conditions of the peasantry varied greatly. In eastern Germany, conquest and the holders of the Knights' fee had acquired the manors historically; the Junkers were the descendants of the conquerors. Their power over the peasants was strengthened by military and administrative functions. Unlike the English lord, who usually rented out his land or the French noble who seldom farmed his land, the Prussian Junkers, as Ernest L. Bogart has pointed out, "became capitalist cultivators at least after 1800, and farmed their land with the help of peasant labor." The mass of the peasantry was then unfree, yet there were many distinctions among the peasants in terms of the land owned by them and of the particular obligations they had toward the Junkers. The full emancipation of the peasants did not take place as it did in England, following a long historical evolution, or as it did in France, where all remaining seignorial and ecclesiastical burdens were removed between 1789 and 1793. In Prussia, the first measures in the interest of the peasants were taken at the end of the eighteenth century but it is only by 1850 that two crucial measures were taken there in their favor. The first abolished twenty-four different kinds of feudal rights, mostly remnants of early vassalage; the second provided for the establishment of rent-banks that were supposed to help the peasants redeem the rent-charges on their holdings. The transformation of the peasants into peasant proprietors was, however, handicapped in many ways. To start with, the peasants were not assigned any land, and moreover, the Junkers' estate managed to grow at the expense of the small peasant holdings. Only by freeing agriculture from antiquated techniques did Germany register remarkable results. In short, the "bourgeois Junker landlord economy" did not result from the 1850 reform – it predated it, because the Junkers, besides exercising their military and administrative functions were, unlike the English or French lords, true farmers.[8]

---

[7] *Ibid.*, pp. 16–27; Furet, François, and Richet, Denis, *La Revolution Française* (The French Revolution), Paris, Editions Marahout, 1973, pp. 87, 89.

[8] Bogart, Ernest L., *Economic History of Europe . . ., op. cit.*, pp. 27–41.

Throughout the American colonies, colonial administrators *attempted* to institute feudal forms of land tenure, but by the time of the Revolution, the feudal vestiges were eliminated. Land remained the most decisive element in the country's development until the end of the nineteenth century. It was plentiful and cheap, while labor and capital were scarce and dear. The government's law policy and the opportunity to acquire easily good land attracted many poor immigrants from across the oceans and encouraged the movement toward the West. A special plantation economy based on slavery developed in the South. Slavery, which became the characteristic feature of Southern society from the end of the seventeenth century, however, was not universal in the South: In the nineteenth century, over half of Southern families owned no slaves; only 2 percent owned more than fifty slaves, and only 4 percent owned enough to replace them without purchase. What was profitable for large slaveholders and for their large-scale agriculture based on cotton and to a lesser extent on sugar, rice, and tobacco was not necessarily profitable for the small slave owner, and not necessarily profitable for the South. The abolition of slavery became the *second* objective of the Civil War, whose first objective was the preservation of the Union. Lincoln's proclamation of the abolition of slavery in 1862 was viewed as "absolutely essential for the salvation of the Union." The emancipation had two effects: It destroyed part of the assets owned by whites by outlawing their rights over slaves, and added 4 million persons to the Southern free population. The old planter aristocracy suffered severely during the war and many of them gave up the struggle to maintain themselves on the land. On the other hand, small farmers and poor whites enlarged their farms in the prevailing disorder. Nothing was done, however, to help the Negro to become an independent landowner; the transition from slave to farmer was made "usually through the medium of tenancy, and for many it was never completely made."[9] Lenin's assertion concerning reform and/or revolution as the means of "transforming landlord economy" certainly does not fit either Prussia's or the United States' conditions and historical development (though the Soviet historians never ceased to repeat untiringly Lenin's simplistic formulae).

3-2. Industrial Policy

A government's main measures to promote industrialization and modernization in a backward country usually involve, in addition to direct support of

---

[9] Morison, Samuel, Commager, Eliot, Steele, Herbert, and Leuchtenburg, William E., *The Growth of the American Republic*, Vol. I, New York, Oxford University Press, 1969, pp. 700, 721–2, 733; Kroos, Herman E., *American Economic Development, The Progress of Business Civilization*, 3rd ed., Englewood Cliffs, NJ, Prentice Hall, 1974, pp. 71, 87, 91, 105, 115, 123; Unger, Irwin, *These United States, the Questions of Our Past*, Vol. I, 3rd ed., Englewood Cliffs, NJ, Prentice Hall, 1986, p. 369.

some state armament industries, the state's patronage of other ad hoc selected industries via loans, subsidies, or direct ownership. In addition, a government's strategy of development may involve various forms of transportation connecting at least some of the principal expanding urban industrial and commercial centers, the setting and adjustment of tariffs to protect certain industries and sectors, the mobilization of the domestic capital in chosen directions, and the encouragement of the influx of foreign capital. To what extent and in which ways did Russia's government resort to these measures in the period following the crucial reform of 1861?

As Alexander Gerschenkron has pointed out, the emancipation of the peasantry had certainly cleared the stage for industrialization to an extent, but the process of industrialization itself "had been initiated almost as an incidental and not quite desirable by-product of a political action *oriented to other goals*."[10] At the time, there were no immediate pressures on the government to orient its policies toward industrialization. The gentry was certainly not interested in large-scale urban and industrial growth. Further, the radical intelligentsia was divided regarding the "path of development"; some of its members, though not fully disinterested in industrialization, were mainly oriented toward the past (the Slavophiles), some others centered their attention and hopes on the peasant commune (the populists), while still others were divided on the kind of revolution they were witnessing or were preferring (the Mensheviks and the Bolsheviks). Eventually, the government's policies impacted directly the pace of industrialization – particularly the expansion of the railroads. With regard to their policies, a succession of ministers of finance, known since then as "the great reformers," played a crucial role. Indeed, since the 1820s and until 1905, the ministry of finance was in effect the agency increasingly responsible for Russian economic affairs. In addition to managing the government's credit and financial affairs, the ministry had also jurisdiction over the railroad policy, tariff policies, factory inspection, and virtually all the other key matters of economic policy (except those relating to agriculture).

The Russian government's goals and priorities in the period after the serfs' emancipation centered first on linking the various parts of Russia's Empire through an expanding railroad system and on developing certain industries connected with the needs of the railroad network. The government aimed also at the formulation of regulations compatible with rising industrial needs, with the extent of protective tariffs, and with the necessity of creating a climate favorable for both the mobilization of domestic capital and the influx of foreign investments and loans. The passage of the railroad construction from a minor role in the Tsarist policy to a critical and costly part of the Tsarist economics and politics began slowly at first but increased steadily from 1862

---

[10] Gerschenkron, Alexander, "Agrarian Policies and Industrialization of Russia 1861–1917," in *The Cambridge Economic History of Europe*, Vol. 6, Part 2, Postan, M. M., and Habakkuk, J. J., eds., Cambridge, Cambridge University Press, 1966, pp. 711–2, 792. Emphasis added.

to 1892, reaching finally its highest level by the turn of the century. During these thirty years, three ministers of finance played crucial roles: Mikhail Kh. Reutern (1862–78), Nikolai Kh. Bunge (1882–6), and Ivan A. Vyshnegradskii (1887–93). The most dynamic drive to industrialization based on railroad expansion finally took place under another minister, namely Sergei Iu. Witte (1893–1903).[11]

Both foreign and Russian entrepreneurs entered into the growing industry of railroad building, though until the 1900s they remained hesitant as to whether the system of state ownership or of private management should finally prevail. The state increased its participation even though the results seemed at times disproportionate to the enormous costs involved. Under Reutern's ministry, the length of open rail lines increased in sixteen years from 3,516 kilometers to the significant length of 22,371 kilometers. During Bunge's short ministry, the network increased further from 23,429 kilometers to 27,345 kilometers. Under Vyshnegradskii, in five years the network expanded from 28,429 kilometers to 32,870 kilometers. These expansions connected the Volga region with the Baltic Sea and the Western land frontier; it then reached the White Sea and finally under Witte established adequate communications also with Siberia and the Asiatic possessions. Under Vyshnegradskii in 1891, the state state undertook the costly and decisive effort to build the vast Trans-Siberian line, which was completed under Witte at the turn of the century. It was under Witte that the entire Russian railroad network increased impressively from 32,870 kilometers (1893) to 58,382 kilometers (1903), exceeding by then the networks of France (39,104 kilometers) and Germany (54,775 kilometers).[12]

The development of the railroads intensified the demand for certain key products of heavy industry. In the 1860s, the products needed for the expansion of the railroads besides bridges and railroad stations – rails, rail attachments, switches, wagons, and locomotives – were all imported from abroad. At the time, the state's intervention affected only certain limited objectives of the Russian industries concerning the railways. By the 1870s, the Tsarist regime started to support effectively the production of certain new industries that oriented some of their outputs toward the needs of the railways. The growth of the domestic production then allowed important limitations on the import of railroad materials. The tariff on the import of locomotives was sharply increased while premiums were granted for their domestic production. Soon, the Russian output of locomotives doubled while the domestic production of machinery covered more than 75 percent of the needs in rolling material.

---

[11] For detailed historical backgrounds, see the essays on Reutern, Bunge, and Witte in *Rossiiskie Reformatory, XIX-nachalo XX v* (Russian Reformers Nineteenth–Beginnings of Twentieth Century), Korelin, A. P., ed., Moscow, Mezhdunarodnye Otnosheniia, 1995.

[12] Mitchell, Brian R., *European Historical Statistics 1750–1970*, New York, Macmillan-Columbia University Press, 1975, pp. 316, 318.

By the mid-1880s, the state's intervention in favor of industrial expansion increased significantly, particularly with regard to heavy industry. Soon the tariffs on coal, coke, and iron ore were increased while the production of rails started to depend exclusively on domestic raw materials. At the same time, the state began a sustained effort to combine the private rail lines in a small number of private companies and thus to form a few consolidated networks. While during the 1860s the private rail companies had played the dominant role, the situation started to change from the 1870s on. From then on, the state also started to purchase the shares of various railway companies, and by 1901 the entire Russian railroad system belonged to the state. Interestingly, foreign investments in Russian railways also rose continually compared to the shares of this capital directed toward other state loans.[13]

The dichotomy between state and private enterprise was deeper in Russia than in any other industrial country, particularly with regard to the armament industry. As Peter Gatrell noted, the Tsarist officials bent on preserving the autocratic system were afraid to make the defensive industry dependent "upon the political mood of foreign suppliers or on the pecuniary appetites of native industrialists." The armament industry, the largest sector of Russia's industry, benefited from all kinds of special advantages. Most of the armament production occurred in the state's arsenals and dockyards, and only a small number of defense firms were privately owned. By 1900 the armament industry employed around seventy-five thousand workers – mostly "unfree labor"; indeed, these were military recruits directed to the state's arsenals and dockyards. An additional sixty thousand workers were employed in various military construction and engineering projects. Representatives of private industries complained bitterly about the state policies concerning the armament industry and urged unsuccessfully the government to renounce state ownership of industrial assets. In 1908 the shipyards were placed on a commercial footing, but they retained various privileges and traditional characteristics that distinguished them from "private enterprise."[14] In fact, not only the development of the key transportation network and the large armament industry depended on government's support: The *entire industry*, including private industry, depended heavily on a combination of state investments, state subsidies and laws (using either the Treasury or the Gosbank), low taxes, and the state's purchase of large shares of the industry's outputs.

The basic policies in the postemancipation era concerning the financial problems – the currency, the banks, the balance of trade, the budget, the

---

[13] Boykin, Valerij I., "Problems der industriellen Entwicklung Russlands" (Problems of the Industrial Development of Russia), in *Wirtschaft und Gesellschaft im vorrevolutionären Russland* (Economy and Society in Prerevolutionary Russia), Geyer, Dietrick, ed., Köln, Kiepenhauer and Witisch, 1975, pp. 191–4; Bertrand, Gille, *Histoire économique et sociale de la Russie du Moyen Age au XX e siècle*, Paris, Payot, 1949, pp. 168–73.

[14] Gatrell, Peter, *Government, Industry and Rearmament in Russia 1900–1914: The Last Argument of Tsarism*, New York, Cambridge University Press, 1994, pp. 27–38, 277, 281.

mobilization of the domestic capital, the influx of foreign capital – were also interconnected in numerous ways with the processes of industrialization, that is, with the patterns of expansion of industry, of its labor force, and of its factories' management and general regulations. I will turn in further detail to the financial policies in Section 3.4. For now, let us consider the evolving condition that existed in industry with respect to the characteristics of the labor force, the labor-management relations, and the factory legislation and regulations.

At the beginning of the postemancipation era and until late in the century and even afterward, patriarchal attitudes were dominant with regard to the conditions prevailing in industry. A significant part of the labor force maintained its traditional ties with the countryside. Unlike labor in the advanced European countries that lived entirely from wage labor, many of the Russian workers had to return regularly to till the land. There is strong evidence of the submissiveness of many of the industrial workers to the patriarchal tradition, long into the century.[15] On the other hand, the management of the industrial establishments, be they state- or privately owned, adjusted itself naturally to this situation, particularly since for a long time no legislation existed affecting labor hiring or employment practices. Under Reutern, no attention whatever was given to the eventual transformations that the processes of industrialization might eventually engender. The first minister of finance who focused decisively on these issues was Bunge. In his letters addressed to Alexander II in 1880 ("On the Financial Situation of Russia") and in 1885 ("Survey of the Activities of the Minister of Finance"), Bunge noted first the necessity of a system of laws instead of the prevailing royal administrative regulations concerning the financial system, its foundation, its connections to the development of industry – and in particular the modernization of the legal conditions of such a development – and its impact on the population's welfare. One of the central remarks of Bunge's messages was the need to decrease the tax burden on the peasantry (a measure that according to him would strengthen the peasant economy and would increase its capacity to absorb industrial goods). Bunge abolished all direct taxes on the peasantry except for the redemption dues, and given his concern with welfare, he paid close attention to the question of factory legislation and regulation. Notably, he introduced laws on industrial hiring and the protection of children and women, and further, he placed under the government's supervision the relationship between employer and employee in the factory.[16]

[15] Ibid., p. 39; Owen, Thomas C., Capitalism and Politics in Russia: A Social History of the Moscow Merchants, op. cit., pp. 120–1.

[16] Shepelev, Leonid E., Tsarism i burzhuaziia vo vtoroi polovine XIX veka. Problemy torgovo-promyshlennoi politiki (Tsarism and the Bourgeoisie in the Second Half of the Nineteenth Century. Problems of the Commercial-Industrial Policy), Leningrad, 1981, pp. 138–43; von Laue, Theodore H., Sergei Witte and the Industrialization of Russia, New York, Atheneum, 1969, pp. 20–1.

Bunge's successor, I. Vyshnegradskii, asserted different policy emphases. He stressed the need for a narrow nationalist-protectionist approach, proclaimed the necessity of Russia's independence from capitalist Europe, affirmed that the country's development must take place under the leadership of the state in its own interests, and further, contrary to Bunge, showed little concern for the welfare of the peasants and the workers. He limited the scope of the Peasant Bank and discontinued the further development of factory legislation. Clearly attached to the business interests, he focused his attention on the sharp expansion of exports, forced the peasants to surrender their crops for this purpose even though famine had broken out in the villages (in 1891–2), and inaugurated the highest tariffs in the world, which resulted in sharp increases in the prices of manufactured goods. At that time, the disastrous situation in the countryside forced him to resign.[17]

Vyshnegradskii's successor, Witte, rejected extremist conservatism, but was, however, also committed to a basically conservative approach. First, he asserted that the government's policy should aim at providing reasonable assistance to the development of the country's productive forces since this policy would increase both "the population's welfare and its paying powers" and thus the sources of government revenues. He centered his attention, as already noted, on modernizing and expanding the transportation network, as well as on strengthening its underlying industrial structures, spreading modern capitalist activities, and encouraging entrepreneurship. He showed unusual largesse in passing financial benefits to private entrepreneurs. Incidentally, with the Tsar Nicholas II's blessing, he left a centrally orchestrated, brutal antisemitic campaign of disturbances spread throughout the country. But he did manifest his opposition to the more severe measures of discrimination against the richer Jewish entrepreneurs (with important connections abroad).

The encouragement of private enterprise had an interesting impact on the scope of factory inspections. Under Bunge, the task of the factory inspectors had been to protect the workers against the employers. All this changed under Witte. The factory inspectors became agents of industrial promotion more than of the workers' welfare. Eventually, however, Witte introduced and carried out a bill limiting the hours of labor, and a law simplifying the issue of internal passports, indispensable identification of peasants working away from home. All in all, as Theodore H. von Laue has rightly pointed out, "no Tsarist minister of finance could boast of a more rapid pace of industrial advance during the tenure of office." Yet many of his critics have asserted that he forced the pace of industrialization, contributed to the lowering of the living standards of the mass of the population, and intensified the tensions between the modern and the traditional sectors of the Russian economy. Notwithstanding

---

[17] Shepelev, Leonid E. *Tsarism i burzhuaziia . . .*, *op. cit.*, pp. 143, 151; On the contrast between Bunge and Vyshnegradskii, see Stepanov, V. L., "Nikolai Khristianovich Bunge," in *Rossiiskie Reformatory . . .*, Korelin, A. P., ed., *op. cit.*, p. 209.

his industrial achievements, when Witte left power, he left behind menacing industrial disorders, a persistent agrarian crisis, and a disgruntled political establishment.[18]

Nevertheless, the great spurt of Russian industrialization in the prerevolutionary period took place in the 1890s under the leadership of Witte. The accelerated, large-scale construction of the railroad network provided the government with the crucial element needed for maintaining the demand for industrial products at high levels. In addition and in multiple ways, the government supplied or facilitated investments in industry in general and in the iron, steel, and machinery industries in particular. In these conditions, as Gerschenkron has pointed out, the average annual rate of Russian industrial growth during the 1890s was around 8 percent; none of the major countries in Western Europe experienced a comparable rate of change during the period.[19]

3-3. Commercial Policy

Domestic trade and foreign trade depend jointly on the patterns of demand (respectively, domestic and foreign), on the capacity of the country's productive forces to respond to demand, on the size and patterns of organization of trade, on the supporting means of transport credit and banking, on the objectives of the government's commercial policy – economic, political, or military – and on the effectiveness of the measures used to reach these objectives.

Consider first the characteristics of the Russian domestic trade. Due to the slow growth in disposable income, to the relatively small increases in the marketed produce of agriculture, to the small expansion in commercial properties, and to the low rates of urbanization, by the end of the nineteenth century, Russian retail trade at current prices was of the order of 4.4 billion rubles, and by 1913 of 5.4 billion – compared respectively to an annual average personal consumption of the order of 7.0 billion during 1885–9, and of 14.5 billion during 1909–13. Given the growth of the population, during the entire period 1899–1913 the per capita retail trade computed at comparable prices fluctuated around 85 to 90 percent of the 1899 level, reaching by 1913 the level of 88 percent of 1899. The overall level of the Russian domestic trade, including wholesale and retail trade, rose at constant prices, from 7.3 billion rubles in

---

[18] Bokhanov. A. N., "Sergei Iulevich Witte," in *Rossiiskie Reformatory . . .*, Korelin, A. P., ed., *op. cit.*, pp. 259–305; Moss, W. E., *An Economic History of Russia 1856–1914*, London, I. B. Tauris Publishers, 1996, pp. 130–2, 187, 203; Theodore H. von Laue, *Sergei Witte . . .*, *op. cit.*, pp. 34–5, 97–8.

[19] Gerschenkron, Alexander, "Russia: Patterns of Economic Development," in *Economic Backwardness in Historical Perspective*, Cambridge, MA, Belknap Press of Harvard University Press, 1962, pp. 124, 126, 129.

1899 to 8.8 billion in 1913.[20] In this general development, agriculture played a relatively limited role; the total production of agriculture is estimated to have reached 13.8 billion rubles in 1913, of which only 35.7 percent – that is, only 4.5 billion rubles – were accounted for by the consumption and production goods available on the domestic market. If one adds forest, fishing, and hunting products, the total products marketed reached 5 billion rubles. The most important agricultural products for sale were grain, flour, meat and fowl, vegetables and fruits, and flax and hops, while among the manufactured products the most important were textile products, metals, and oils.

As we shall see further on, the absence of a direct engagement of the government counteracted in various ways the development of this trade. Moreover, administrative measures hampered the commercial enterprises classified, licensed, and taxed according to differential rates. The government's discrimination policies excluded some private groups from either particular trades or particular locations. Yet, the government's sustained interest in the development of railroads as well as of certain industries certainly helped the expansion of the market and of vast interconnections. Indeed, at the beginning of the 1880s, Moscow was connected in the south, with Rostov and Vladikavkaz on the one hand, and with Sebastopol and Odessa on the other; in the south and southwest, it was henceforth connected to Kiev, and then further north with Minsk, Vilna, Riga, and Petersburg. In the north, Moscow finally reached by rail Yaroslovl and Vologda. The railroad, continued this expansion from the 1890s on into Sibera – turning Moscow and Petersburg into the true centers of a vast and increasing network.[21]

Indirect taxes weighed heavily on such standard products of Russian use as alcoholic beverages, tobacco, sugar, and petroleum products. In 1900, 1906 (the year after the 1905 revolution), and 1913, for instance, the direct taxes (on land and real estate, commerce and industry, and monetary assets) amounted to 131.9 million rubles, 163.2 million, and 272.5 million respectively. In the same years, the total of indirect taxes (on alcoholic beverages, tobacco, sugar, petroleum products, and matches) reached 301.8 million rubles, 252.9 million, and 355.2 million. Percentagewise, as can be seen in Table 3-1, the total direct taxes amounted to 7.7, 7.2, and 8.0 percent of the state revenues in the years considered, while indirect taxes amounted to 17.8, 11.2, and 10.4 percent in those years. Though declining, the revenues from excises continually exceeded the revenues from direct taxes. The causes of the declines are due to the sharp fall in the share of the excises from alcoholic beverages. But the figures in

---

[20] Dikhtiar, G. A., *Vnutrennaiaia torgovlia v dorevoliutsionoi Rossii* (Domestic Trade in Prerevolutionary Russia), Moscow, Izdat Akademii Nauk, 1960, pp. 79, 84; Rossiiskaia Akademiia Nauk, *Rossiia 1913 god. Statistiko-dokumental'nyi spravochnik* (Russian Academy of Science, Russia 1913. Statistical-Documentary Reference Book), St. Petersburg, 1995, p. 198.

[21] Ryndziunskii, P. G., *Utverzhdenie kapitalizma v Rossii 1850–1880* (The Assertion of Capitalism in Russia 1850–1880), Moscow, Nauka, 1978, p. 102.

Table 3-1 *Russia: Direct and Indirect Taxes as Percentages of Regular State Revenues in 1900, 1906, and 1913*

Direct Taxes on:	Percent of total revenues			Indirect taxes excises on:	Percent of total revenues		
	1900	1906	1913		1900	1906	1913
Land & real estate	2.7	2.7	2.6	Alcohol	9.7	1.8	1.6
Commerce & industry	4.1	3.6	4.4	Tobacco	2.4	2.6	2.4
Monetary assets	0.9	0.9	1.0	Sugar	3.8	4.8	4.4
TOTAL	7.7	7.2	8.0	Petroleum products	1.5	1.3	1.4
				MATCHES	0.4	0.7	0.6
				TOTAL	17.8	11.2	10.4

Source: A Source Book for Russian History from Early Times to 1917, Volume 3, *Alexander II to the February Revolution,* Vernadsky, George, senior ed., *op. cit.,* pp. 822–3.

this respect are in fact incomplete. In those same years, the state's revenues from its new monopoly on spirits (established in 1895) increased from 329.2 million rubles in 1900 (19.4 percent of the state's revenues) to 777.1 million rubles in 1906 (34.2 percent of the state revenues), and to 1,024.9 million in 1913 (30.0 percent of all revenues). Even if we deduct from these figures the state expenditures on the spirits monopoly, and then add to the net results the excise on alcohol, the state's actual revenues from alcohol in the years considered amounted to 321.9 million, 559.2 million, and 718.0 million, rubles respectively. That is, the revenues constituted its highest returns, exceeding by far all the direct taxes and even the total customs returns (amounting in the indicated years to 203.6 million, 241.3 million, and 352.9 million rubles).

Consider now the policy issues related to foreign trade. As in any other country, the measures concerning foreign trade affect not only the crucial aspects of the transactions involving merchandise trade, exchange of services, transfers of capital in both directions, the balance of payments results, and the state's customs revenues, but also all other financial, commercial, and industrial policies, as well as various political and military objectives.

Imperial Russia traditionally differentiated its tariffs in relation to Europe, on the one hand, and to Asia, on the other hand, as well as in regard to its trade with the Great Duchy of Finland. The frontier with Europe was evidently the most important one from the points of view of the quantity, diversity, and quality of the goods involved. Toward the end of the nineteenth century, Europe's share in the total trade amounted to 86 percent, that at the frontier of Asia for 10 percent, and that at the demarcation line with Finland for 4 percent. The consumer goods imported from Europe were taxed in 1895–7 on the average up to 75 percent *ad valorem,* the raw materials and the semimanufactured goods up to 27 percent, and the manufactured foods up to 21 percent, while at its frontiers with Turkey, Persia, and Afghanistan, all the imported commodities were taxed at only 5 percent *ad valorem*. On the frontier with China, no tariffs were applied except for tea, silver, and spirits. Within Russia, at the demarcation line with Finland, the tariffs applied to the imports from Europe were also applied on the imports of Finish goods.[22]

Choices between free trade and protectionism are shaped both by the complex dealings of a country with the other countries – commercial, political, and military – and by that country's own options and possibilities concerning its desired patterns of economic development. These choices are not necessarily coherent, consistent, or unchangeable over time. In Russia, after the great reform of 1861, these issues became of critical and immediate importance. The minister of finance, Reutern, pointed out cautiously, with reference to the prevailing tariff system, that even a change of "two or three articles" of the tariff legislation might eventually bring to a halt entire branches of industry, ruin the industrialists, and also change the life conditions in vast regions of the country. A few years later, he asserted in a report of 1860 and in other subsequent remarks that these issues were certainly of critical importance for him given their potential impact on finances, and then added that experience had shown that the prevailing tariff systems of 1850 and 1857 actually *did not* have "a favorable influence on the country's industry," and that in the future it might become necessary to "apply in their full strength" all the protectionist articles of the 1857 system. In the meantime, experience also showed that the 1857 system had indeed only a marginal impact on the customs revenues: The latter increased between 1857 and 1868 from only 35.8 million rubles to 37 million. Reutern contended that these poor results were undoubtedly due to the fact that a large share of foreign goods had actually been imported illegally – yet soon afterward he had to concede that given "the prevailing conditions of development of our industry," it might be necessary to increase certain protective tariffs. By June 1868 the State Council worked out a new tariff legislation. Yet, notwithstanding its protectionist bent, the new legislation still had to allow the free import of certain "essential materials for industry" (such as cotton, coal, and machinery) and to accept the application of small tariffs rates on other necessary imports (notably iron and other basic materials).[23]

Less than a decade later, a law of November 10, 1876, established that the custom duties must be paid in gold, a measure that implied a virtual addition of 33 percent to the tariff. By 1877, the very difficult situation created by the war with Turkey (which affected unfavorably the balance of payments), and by the needs for revenue, the state Treasury accented the orientation of the

[22] Chaposhnikoff, M. G., "Tariff Douanier" (Customs Tariff) in *La Russie à la fin du 19ᵉ siècle*, Kovalevskii, M. W., ed., *op. cit.*, pp. 546–53.
[23] Shepelev, Leonid E., *Tsarism i burzhuaziia ...*, *op. cit.*, pp. 113–17.

tariff policy toward protectionism. By 1880 and 1891 various tariff increases were added to certain types of imports. Bunge discarded Reutern's cautious approaches. The tariff rates were systematically increased in 1882, 1884, and 1895 on the average by 10 to 20 percent. Yet, the results did not turn out to be as advantageous as had been hoped; indeed the lack of easy access to certain basic imports hampered the activities of many industries. So in 1885 the government chose not to increase the tariff rates, notably on iron, during the next twelve years. Bunge thus cast himself in the role of the "defender" by all means of the national industry's interests, even though his basic orientation was actually in favor of complete protectionism.

Bunge's successor, Vyshnegradskii, continued the orientation toward the protection of the national industry and hence toward tariff increases. By 1890, tariff increases of up to 20 percent were applied to a whole range of industrial imports, including machinery and metals, as well as a series of consumer imports including cotton and woolen goods and sugar. The transition to an outright protectionist policy aiming at industrialization (without any regard for the interests of the peasantry), securing decreasing imports, and achieving good fiscal results along with a favorable balance of trade was accentuated in 1891 through various further increases of certain tariff rates up to 50 percent. The results of these increases were impressive in certain respects: The customs revenues had been of the order of 140 million rubles yearly between 1888–90; those of 1899 rose to 219 million. In addition, the influence of this increase appeared to be very favorable to the development of certain national industries. But, unexpectedly, a total calamity affected Vyshnegradskii's regime: the disastrous crop failure of 1891 and the ensuing widespread famine in the countryside. Vyshnegradskii tried to remedy this situation by stopping exports and negotiating for a foreign loan, but without success.[24]

Vyshnegradskii's successor, Witte, continued his predecessor's basic orientation concerning protectionism and industrialization but with the use of adjusted means. Though an even more resolute promoter of Russia's expanded industrialization, Witte imitated the examples of the methods then used in Western Europe for raising tariffs noting the differentiations of these methods' various applications. While affirming that the tariffs of 1891 continued to remain the "basic law" of the land, Witte asserted that as minister of finance he had the right to increase their rates for countries that did not grant to Russia the most-favored-nation status, notably for its exports of grains. Such increases were soon indeed ordered against Germany, then rapidly canceled after negotiations. Russia then signed favorable trade agreements with quite a number of countries, including France and the Austro-Hungarian Empire. From then on, the dispositions concerning the tariff, and the railroad transport rates were viewed as the basic item of the state's commercial and industrial policy. Witte viewed the tariffs as a key instrument for the development of the national

[24] *Ibid.*, pp. 166–9.

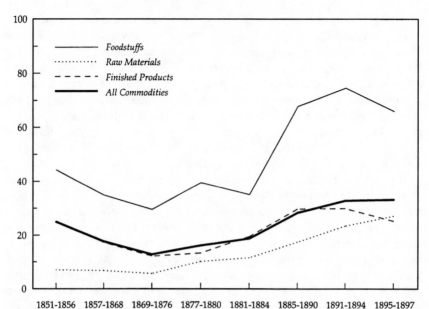

Figure 3-1. The Evolution of Tariffs by Commodity Groups, 1851–97, in Percentages and Averages per Indicated Periods

Source: Underlying data from *La Russie à la fin du 19ᵉ siècle* (Russia at the End of the Nineteenth Century), Kovalevskii, M. W., ed., Paris, Dupont & Guillaumin, 1900, p. 553.

industry; his aim was not only to limit certain industrial imports, but also to expand the national industrial exports even though he was conscious that in comparison with Western Europe and the United States, Russia remained in many respects backward and inadequately developed technologically.[25]

The fluctuations in the tariff rates during the second half of the nineteenth century are graphically illustrated in Figure 3-1. As can be seen from the graph and as indicated previously, the tariff rates on foodstuffs and manufactured goods, as well as on the total imports tended to decrease from 1852–6 to 1881–4, and then to increase sharply until the end of the century. Although the custom duties tended again to decrease in ways similar to the pre-1881 pattern, during the years preceding World War I (between 1905 and 1912 – for foodstuffs, from 90 percent to 67 percent, for raw materials and semimanufactured goods, from 28 to 22 percent, while remaining constant for manufactured goods around 26–7 percent), jointly for all the import classes of goods, the percentage fell only from 37 percent *ad valorem* to 30 percent – a rate of customs duty considerably above the rates that other countries impose on imports.[26]

---

[25] *Ibid.*, pp. 217–19; on the importance for both Germany and Russia of the Witte-Caprivi trade negotiations of 1894, see *Wirtschaft und Gesellschaft im vorrevolutionären Russland*, Dietrick, Geyer, ed., *op. cit.*, pp. 280, 285–7.

[26] Miller, Margaret, *The Economic Development of Russia . . ., op. cit.*, pp. 70–1.

The commercial policy, the combination of protectionism and free trade, and the governmental aim of achieving a desired *external* balance are all interconnected with the government's *internal* objectives concerning its preferred structure of the economy and its patterns of development. All these issues are reflected in the government's financial policy and in its ways of handling its expenditures, their financing, and their balances. I turn to the nexus of these issues in the next section.

3-4. Financial Policy

During the thirty-five years preceding World War I, Russia became the largest borrowing country in Europe. By 1914, the total foreign investments in Europe amounted to 27 percent of all long-term foreign investments in the world, followed by North America accounting for 24 percent, Latin America for 19 percent, Asia for 16 percent, Africa for 9 percent, and Oceania for 5 percent. Britain and France, the biggest world investors at the time, invested in Europe 218.6 million pounds and 27.5 billion gold francs respectively. Of the latter totals, Britain invested 50 percent in Russia, and France 45 percent. Jointly the British and the French investments amounted to over 50 percent of the total foreign investments in Russia.[27]

Before 1861 the Russian state debt was not very large. On the eve of the emancipation of the serfs, that debt was of the order of 1.2 billion rubles. From 1861 onward, the pace of increase of the debt quickened, notably because of 1) financial operations related to the emancipation of the serfs; 2) the military expenditures incurred in wars with neighbors; 3) the expansion of railroad construction; 4) the costs of stabilizing the currency and of strengthening the country's credit abroad; and 5) increasing difficulties with the budget deficit and the balance of payments.

Consider these issues in turn. Recall that financing the operations related to the emancipation involved government payments to the landlords with interest-bearing notes up to 80 percent of the balance due by the peasants for their land purchases, with the understanding that peasants would repay the government the money borrowed for the purpose – a repayment that became increasingly difficult to recover from the impoverished peasants, and which eventually had to be largely canceled.

Inflation and the borrowings of 1877 and 1878 – the "Oriental borrowing" that occured after the war with Turkey – further increased Russia's internal debt by over half a billion rubles. By 1876 the total state debt had already

[27] Feis, Herbert, *Europe the World's Banker 1870–1914*, New York, Norton, 1965, pp. 23, 51; Cameron, Rondo, *A Concise Economic History of Europe*, 2nd ed., New York, Oxford University Press, 1993, p. 290; see also Girault, René, *Emprunts Russes et investissements Français en Russie 1887–1914* (Russian Loans and French Investments in Russia 1887–1914), Paris, Armand Colin, 1973, p. 587.

amounted to 2.9 billion rubles. By 1886, a quarter of a century after the serfs' emancipation, the state debt reached 4.4 billion rubles, almost four times the 1861 level.

The expansion of railroads further increased the state debt, particularly under the leadership of Witte. In 1889, the state debt exceeded the 4.4 billion level by some 2.2 billion rubles – of which over 3 billion were accounted for by the state's own needs, and 1.3 billion were accounted for by expenditures for railroad construction. By 1902 the total debt amounted to 6.4 billion rubles, of which over 3 billion went for railroad expenses.[28]

The stabilization of the currency became an ineluctable necessity by 1897. Until then the Russian standard value had been the silver ruble, which served as basis for the monetary unit, the credit ruble. The demonetizations of the ruble over a large part of Europe and the declining price of silver introduced an element of deep uncertainty in Russia's commercial and financial connections with the West. The ensuing establishment of the gold standard in 1897 appeared hence indispensable not only for strengthening Russia's credit abroad but also for avoiding an economic collapse.[29]

Yet the country's financial situation continued to remain precarious, because of difficulties related to the balance of trade and payments, to the incapacity of meeting the foreign debt obligations from the proceeds of trade, and to the growing budget deficits. As we will see in detail later on (in Chapter 6), the balance of payments – that is, trade plus invisible accounts – was unfavorable in virtually all years and could not cover the payments needed on the foreign debt. Moreover, besides its exports, Russia did not have income from freight, while it had to pay large amounts of such charges for its imports; the Empire did not have any significant income from foreign investments abroad, but had to pay significant dividends and percentages for its indispensable foreign loans. The solution that Russia had at its disposal for equilibrating the balance of payment and for covering the deficits was often humiliating. Russia's credit was so weak that foreign investors demanded more and more security. Accordingly, the Russian government purchased land mortgage bonds on the Russian market, as well as existing railroad securities, and offered these to the foreign investors or sold them in foreign countries. On the other hand, the pressing need for foreign credit accented Russia's push for the country's industrialization, for the growth and diversification of its exports, and for the reduction of its imports at least up to the point beyond which further reductions would hamper the growth of its own industry. To say that Russia's industrialization was "a child of adversity" would be an overstatement, but as Leo Pasvolsky and Harold Moulton point out, "there is little doubt that the pressing need of

---

[28] Finn-Enotaevskii, A., *Kapitalizm v. Rossii (1890–1917)* (Capitalism in Russia [1890–1917]), Vol. I, Moscow, Finansovoe Isz., 1925, p. 206; Bertrand, Gille, *Histoire économique et sociale de la Russie . . ., op. cit.*, p. 165.

[29] Miller, Margaret, *The Economic Development of Russia . . ., op. cit.*, pp. 105–7.

improved credit with which to keep the state out of international bankruptcy played an important part in the beginning of Russia's industrial era."[30]

Other aspects of Russia's financial policies are reflected in the evolution of its state budget. For the moment, simply note that during the whole of the nineteenth century, Russian budgets ended with deficits. To mask this reality (as we shall see in detail in Chapter 8), the government divided the budget into an "ordinary" and an "extraordinary" budget, the latter including primarily military expenditures and repayment of domestic and foreign debts. After the Russo-Japanese War of 1904–7, budget revenues increased sharply due to the state's wine monopoly, a situation that inspired the popular saying that the state's budget was "drunk." With reference particularly to the period 1889–1905, Finn-Enotaevskii pointed out that the budget had been officially stated to be in balance, without regard to the fact that in 1891, 1892, 1897, 1898, 1899, 1901, and 1905, the country registered crop failures that had affected from one-eighth to a quarter and in some cases even half of European Russia, and also without taking into account the financial crises of 1899, jointly with the industrial crisis that extended until 1903 and ended with the war of 1904.[31]

The total state debt had rapidly increased from the mid-1890s to 1914 because of the fast growth of the state's foreign debt, which rose from 30 percent of the total debt in 1895 to 48 percent. Also, the ratio of the state's foreign debt to the country's NNP (Net National Product) also rose constantly from 1895 to 1909, notably from 14.5 percent in 1895 to 17.9 percent in 1899, 18.8 percent in 1904, and as much as 24.5 percent in 1909.[32]

But Russia's public debt – that is, the debt including, besides the state's debt, the state's guaranteed debt – reached even higher levels. According to the data presented in a study by Anton Crihan, the structure of the public debt was the following in 1914:

- *State debt*: general needs, 5,746 million rubles; railroads, 3,108 million; total 8,854 million
- *Guaranteed debt*: railroads, 1884 million rubles; two land banks, 2,069 million; total 3,953 million
- *Grand total*: (8,854 + 3,953) 12,807 million rubles[33]

[30] Pasvolsky, Leo, and Moulton, Harold, *Russian Debts and Russian Reconstruction: A Study of the Relations of Russia's Foreign Debts to Her Economic Recovery*, London, McGraw-Hill, 1924, pp. 35–6; Pokrowskii, Serafin A., *Vneshniaia torgovlia i vneshniaia torgovaia politika Rossii* (Russia's Foreign Trade and Foreign Trade Policy), Moscow, Mezhdunarodnaia Kniga, 1947, pp. 302–3.

[31] Finn-Enotaevskii, A., *Kapitalizm v. Rossii . . .*, *op. cit.*, pp. 170–4; Sofronoff, M. V., "Budget de l'Etat" (State's Budget), in *La Russie à la fin du 19ᵉ siècle*, Kovalevskii, M. W., ed., *op. cit.*, p. 778.

[32] Gregory, Paul R., *Russian National Income, 1885–1913*, Cambridge, Cambridge University Press, 1982, p. 132.

[33] Crihan, Anton, *Le capital étranger en Russie* (Foreign Capital in Russia), Paris, librairie générale de Droit et de Jurisprudence, 1934.

As indicated in Table 3-2, as of January 1, 1914, the state's foreign debt alone reached 4,229 million rubles; the guaranteed debt placed abroad amounted then to 870 million rubles; and also at that time, the Russian municipalities borrowed abroad 422 million rubles, on the basis of loans that were not guaranteed by the state. Together, all the loans placed abroad amounted to 5,521 million rubles – of which 4,416 million were placed in France, 773 million in Great Britain, and 331 million in Germany.

The foreign investments in Russia's commercial, industrial, and banking enterprises also increased sharply after 1895, reaching according to various estimates a total of 2,243 million rubles by 1917, of which 89 percent consisted of shares, the dividends of which varied from year to year, and 11 percent consisted of bonds bearing a fixed rate of interest. The Russian ministries of finance tried their best to oppose the French, British, German, and other foreign investors to make them compete as forcefully as possible in their lending of capital to the state and to the Russian enterprises – efforts not always devoid of success.

Russia's insatiable "hunger" for foreign capital increased as its economic development got under way. One of the dangers of this state of affairs was that it brought forth foreign tendencies toward the widespread colonization of Russia's economy, particularly from the French state and from French firms. Yet Russia certainly needed very much the broad participation of foreign capital for carrying forward the development of its economy and the needed structural modifications that had already taken place by then in the West. But by the end of the Tsarist regime, there appeared no way out of the dilemma arising from the danger of colonization by foreign capital, on one hand, and the Russian hunger for the same foreign capital, on the other hand. Russia's financial policy never confronted this dilemma systematically; it simply adjusted to it with the help of innumerable contradictory decisions.

3-5. Concluding Comments

What exactly is the balance sheet that can be drawn from the indicated governmental financial policies – namely, to what extent did the means taken actually help the government to attain its main goals, and to what extent did they lead to unwarranted or unexpected results? Consider in turn the main fields under discussion:

- The original agricultural policy aimed at maintaining, along with a more limited but secure land gentry, a stable landowning peasantry under the tutelage of the communes. But this policy eventually collapsed notwithstanding the state's great financial investments in its consolidation, because of often repeated agricultural failures, the financial difficulties of both the gentry and of the peasants, the latter's incapacity to fulfill their financial

Table 3-2 Russian Empire: State Debt, 1895–1914,[a] in Millions of Rubles

January 1 of specified year	Total debt		Domestic debt		Foreign debt			
	Amount of debt	Annual payments on account of debt	Amount of debt	Annual payments on account of debt	Amount of debt	Percent of total debt	Annual payments on account of debt	Percent of annual payments
1895	5,775	278.6	4,042	216.5	1,753	30	62.1	22
1899	6,122	266.6	3,857	168.6	2,265	37	98.0	37
1904	6,651	297.7	3,592	159.5	3,059	46	138.2	46
1909	8,850	396.4	4,779	215.5	4,071	46	180.5	46
1914	8,811	402.1	4,582	208.1	4,229	48	194.0	48

Note:
[a] At five-year intervals.
Source: Pasvolsky, Leo, and Moulton, Harold, in Russian Debts and Russian Reconstruction, op. cit, pp. 17, 117.

obligations, along with the desire of many of them to discard the communes' control and become fully independent.

- After the reform of 1861, the government did not engage itself resolutely in the domain of industrialization. But the political and military goals that preoccupied it and that centered on the strategic development of the railway network – a critical absorber of large investments – actually helped also the development of heavy industry and eventually affected the structure of industrial output and of trade. The government became aware of and partly interested in these developments only some thirty years after the emancipation.
- The government did not show any particular interest in the development of domestic trade. Certain actions that it took, notably taxing and licensing commercial enterprise, hampered trade, while its indirect taxation measures seriously restrained certain basic consumptions. However, the interconnections between the country's great centers, thanks to the railway networks, acted in the opposite direction, that is, they *helped* the development of domestic trade. With regard to foreign trade, the government was deeply concerned with the problem raised by the balance of payments. After 1881–4, the official policies moved increasingly toward protectionist tariffs in order to achieve a more favorable balance needed to cover the state's deficits, but the results were disappointing for many years.
- The nexus between the financial problems concerning agriculture, industry, trade, and the ensemble of financial policy had been continually shaped and reshaped by efforts to bring under control the growth of deficits – of the budget and of foreign trade – and the growth of borrowing. These attempts were far from successful on the eve of World War I, which further expanded both borrowing and the growth of deficits.

I will examine later on in detail the impact of these policies on the structural changes in each of the economy's sectors. What is apparent already is that the postreform transformations did eventually achieve certain significant shifts. As Paul R. Gregory has pointed out, over the entire period 1861–1913, the share of agriculture in the national income fell from 57 to 51 percent, while the share of industry – broadly defined to include construction, transportation, communications, as well as the factory and handicraft industry – rose from 23.5 percent to 32 percent, whereas the share of trade declined somewhat. Such tendencies are usually observed in any economy in the "take-off" process, whether this "take-off" occurs due to a coherent set of policies or through a mixture of often conflicting government measures and spontaneous developments, along with various foreign investments, as in the case of Russia.[34]

---

[34] Gregory, Paul R., *Russian National Income . . ., op. cit.*

CHAPTER 4

The Problems of Agriculture

4-1. Landholding

The abolition of serfdom created the preliminary conditions for changes in agriculture – eventually involving the diversification of outputs, the intensification of production, and the broadening of the market connections – along with deep permutations in the patterns of growth of population and its density in the various regions of the country. On the other hand, the agricultural reform's retention of the commune as the instrument of keeping the peasantry tied to the land, the acute scarcity of peasant land due to the expanding population, and the heavy burden of taxation and of the payments for the allotted lands generated increasing pressures of revolt and instability in the village and hampered rather than helped the desired modernization of agriculture.

As can be seen in Table 4-1, the total land surface of the Empire amounted to 1.952.2 million dessiatins, out of which European Russia accounted for 442.7 million. In the latter figure, agricultural utilization – in the broadest sense of the term (that is, including the forests) – accounted for 243.0 million dessiatins (close to 55 percent); in the Empire as a whole, the total agricultural utilization, as defined, amounted to only 25.7 percent.

With regard to the structure of landholding in European Russia, recall that the state and the Imperial family were stated to account in 1905 for 145.2 million dessiatins, and the peasants, on the allotted lands, for 136.2 million (refer to Table 1-4). The remaining private land ownership of the nobles, the peasants, and the other *sosloviia* could then be estimated to have amounted to 106.3 million dessiatins (49.7, 24.7, and 31.9 million for a total of 387.7 million dessiatins) for European Russia as a whole. Put differently, the structure of landholding was then accounted for 37.5 percent by the state and institutions (of which 35.8 percent rested in the hands of the state alone), while 27.4 percent belonged to the private owners (including peasants) and 35.1 percent were managed by the peasant communes (on the allotted lands).

Table 4-1 *Russian Empire^a: Total Land and Type of Use in 1914,
in Thousands of Dessiatins*

Area	Total land	Cultivated land	Meadows	Forests	Percent of $2 + 3 + 4 \div 1$
European Russia	442,782	78,808	22,198	142,060	54.8
Caucasus	42,950	9,075	1,495	4,887	35.4
Siberia	1,145,489	7,552	6,392	201,051	18.7
Central Asia	321,033	5,523	4,248	19,819	9.2
TOTAL	1,952,254	100,958	34,333	367,817	25.7

Notes:
^{a} Fifty-one *gubernias*.
^{b} Data excludes Poland and Finland.
*Source: Sbornik Statistiko-ekonomicheskikh svedenii po sel'skomu khoziaistvu Rossii i inos-
trannykh gosudarstv* (Collection of Statistical and Economic Data on the Agriculture of Russia
and Foreign Countries), Petrograd, Agricultural Ministry, 1916, p. 2.

Other detailed data of the evolution of private property from 1877 to 1905
and then until 1915 disclose very substantial land shifts among the various
subgroups of private owners during this period. As indicated in Table 4-2, the
share of the nobility fell from 79.9 percent of the total accounted for by these
lands in 1877 to 52.7 percent by 1905, and finally to 43.6 percent by 1915. On
the other hand, among the other subgroups, the shares of the townspeople of
higher standing (such as merchants and honorary citizens) and of the peasants,
Cossacks, and colonists increased significantly.

The data on the purchases and sales of land indicate, according to I. D.
Koval'chenko and L. V. Milov, vast land transactions from 1863 to 1910 involving a total of over 145 million dessiatins of land. The main purchasers and
sellers, namely the nobility, officials, and officers, purchased over 34 percent
of the land for sale and sold close to 65 percent of the land offered for sale.
Detailed data for 1906 to 1914, from the statistical reference work *Rossiia 1913
god*, indicate that during this crucial period, 37 million dessiatins were sold and
bought. The nobility, officials, and officers purchased 7.3 million dessiatins and
sold 17.5 million dessiatins; the private peasants purchased 7.2 million and sold
3.6 million dessiatins.[1]

Detailed data on the structure of ownership in 1905 show the striking diversity extant in the gentry's ownership of land and, in contrast, the quite tiny
holdings of the peasant households on the allotted lands. As can be seen in
Table 4-3, the lowest strata of the gentry, holding lands from ten dessiatins
to up to one hundred dessiatins, represented 57.6 percent of the gentry, but

---

[1] Koval'chenko, I. D., and Milov, L. V., *Vserossiiskii agrarnyi rynok XVIII nachalo XX veka*
(All Russian Agrarian Market: 1800 to Beginning of the Twentieth Century), Moscow, Nauka,
1974, pp. 255–6; *Rossiia 1913 god . . ., op. cit.*, p. 63.

Table 4-2 *European Russia^a: Private Land Ownership in 1877, 1905, and 1915 (in Millions of Dessiatins and in Percentages)*

Owners	1877		1905		1915	
	Dessiatins	Percent	Dessiatins	Percent	Dessiatins	Percent
Nobility, officials, officers	73.1	79.9	49.7	52.7	39.5	43.6
Clergy	0.2	0.2	0.3	0.3	0.3	0.3
Townspeople of higher standing	9.8	10.7	12.8	13.6	11.1	12.2
Townspeople of lower standing	1.9	2.1	0.4	0.5	0.4	0.4
Peasants, Cossacks, colonists, and individual ownership	5.8	6.3	13.2	14.0	16.8	18.5
Cooperative ownership	0.3	0.3	11.5	12.2	17.3	19.1
Various owners	0.4	0.5	6.4	6.7	5.3	5.8
TOTAL PRIVATE LAND	91.5	100.0	94.3	100.0	90.7	100.0

Note:
^a In forty-seven *gubernias* only.
Source: For 1877, Khromov, P. A., *Ekonomicheskoe razvitie Rossii v XIX–XX vekakh*, (Economic Development of Russia in the Nineteenth–Twentieth Centuries), Moscow, Gosizdat Polit. Lit., 1950, p. 395; for 1905 and 1915, *Rossiia 1913 god, op. cit*, p. 63.

possessed only 3.3 percent of the gentry-owned land. What may be called the middle gentry strata, holding from above one hundred dessiatins to about one thousand, represented 34.5 percent of the gentry, and owned 26.0 percent of the gentry land. Finally, the remaining 7.9 percent of the gentry (some 8,416 owners) owned 70.7 percent of the total of gentry land (some 35,192,000 dessiatins out of the total of 49,767,000). Clearly, the top gentry involved a small number of families, still highly differentiated in terms of wealth even above one thousand dessiatins per landlord. According to data available for 1915, the number of gentry owners had then decreased to 62,737, owning a total of 39,476.4 million dessiatins. The top gentry, then counting 7,141 owners, still possessed over 30,619 million dessiatins (more than 77.5 percent of the total gentry-owned land).[2] In contrast, in 1905, 12,277,355 peasant households

[2] *Rossiia 1913 god...., op. cit.*, p. 71.

Table 4-3 *European Russia: Land Ownership by the Gentry[a] and by Peasants on Allotted Lands, 1905*

Gentry			Peasants		
Size of land owned in dessiatins	Number of owners	Thousands of dessiatins	Size of land distributed in dessiatins	Households	Thousands of dessiatins
1–10	22,594	100.8	Up to 5	2,857,650	9,030.0
10–50	26,452	694.1	5–8	3,317,601	21,706.5
50–100	11,803	864.1	8–15	3,932,485	42,182.9
100–500	28,007	6,962.0	15–30	1,551,904	31,271.9
500–1,000	8,462	5,954.0	Over 30	617,715	32,695.5
1,000–2,000	4,671	6,456.5	TOTALS	12,277,355	136,887.1
2,000–5,000	2,591	7,851.3			
5,000+	1,154	20,884.3			
TOTALS	105,739	49,767.9			

Note:
[a] In forty-seven *gubernias* only.
Sources: On the gentry, *Rossiia 1913 god...*, *op. cit*, p. 71; on the peasants, Khromov, P. A., *Ekonomicheskoe razvitie Rossii...*, *op. cit*, p. 346.

owned tiny landownerships, below 8 to 15 dessiatins.[3] Between 1907 and 1917, the number of households requesting the acquisition of land in ownership amounted to 2,755,633. The number of families that actually succeeded to separate themselves from the communes amounted in that period to only 2,008,432, and the land involved covered 13.3 million dessiatins (on average, 6.6 dessiatins per household).

Clearly, by the end of the Tsarist regime, there existed in Russia principally two types of farming: farming of large domains, of at least over one hundred dessiatins, the gentry's landholdings; and farming of small strips of land, mainly peasant farming either under the communes' management or, to a far smaller extent, under peasant households' direct control. The major part of the peasant farms constituted a *subsistence sector*, and the limited rest, a *commercialized sector*.

4-2. Farming Methods

Except in the black earth areas, farming methods did not change significantly. No appreciable increases were registered concerning the capital stock, modernization, the utilization of fertilizers, or the diversification and specialization of outputs. In no mean measure, all this was due to the reformers' maintenance

[3] Semenoff, M. D.-P., "Agriculture," in *La Russie à la fin du 19ᵉ siècle*, Kovalevsky, M. W., ed., *op. cit.*, p. 145.

of certain prereform features, notably with regard to labor utilization and to the maintenance of the communes' stronghold over most of peasant households' activities.

The data available on agrarian machinery and equipment in use as late as the early 1900s indicate the country's continuing reliance on old-type implements. In 1910 there were in use in European Russia as a whole 6.4 million wooden plows, 6.3 million iron and steel plows, some 292,000 seeding machines, 412,000 threshing machines, and 17.1 million winnowing machines. Out of these totals, the peasant economy used over 95 percent of the wooden plows (6.1 million), 62 percent of the plows with more advanced features (3.9 million), 60 percent of the seeding machines (177,000), 90 percent of the threshing machines (371,000), and some 8 percent of the winnowing machines (1.4 million).[4] Commercial wheat production was centered in eight *gubernias* of the black earth (Bessarabia, Kerson, Taurida, Ekaterinoslav, Don, Saratov, Samara, and Orenburg) and on the utilization there of both more advanced machines and salaried labor.

Imperial Russia's 873 agricultural machinery and equipment factories (of which 770 were located in European Russia) produced in 1913 mostly old-type agricultural implements. In that year, this output consisted mainly of plows, seed-drills, mowers, sickles, rakes, and pitchforks, valued at some 35.6 million rubles (of which 25.7 million were accounted for by European Russia's factories).[5] Also in that year, the value of imports of agricultural machinery and equipment reached a total of 48.9 million rubles. These imports came mostly from Germany, followed by Great Britain and the United States.[6] The total amount of the equipment in use in agriculture was valued on average at 26.4 million rubles between 1896 and 1900, at 61.2 million between 1906 and 1910, and at 111.1 million in 1913.[7]

Both the gentry and the peasant landowners relied heavily on horses and cattle as beasts of burden. In 1864–9, European Russia disposed of 15.5 million horses, in 1910 of 19.7 million, and by 1913 of 22.9 million, of which 70 to 75 percent (namely horses of five years or older) were used for labor.[8] At the time, salaried laborers with one horse were paid between 145 to 159 rubles per day, laborers without a horse earned 63 to 80 rubles, while women were granted only 34 to 51 rubles per day.[9]

Changes over time in the composition of livestock are important indicators of the extent of the changes in agriculture as a whole. Actually, Russia

[4] *Rossiia 1913 god . . ., op. cit.*, pp. 86, 90.
[5] *Sbornik Statistiko-ekonomicheskikh svedenii po sel'skomu khoziaistvu Rossii i inostrannykh gosudarstv* (Collection of Statistical and Economic Data on the Agriculture of Russia and Foreign Countries), Petrograd, Agricultural Ministry, 1916, pp. 632–3.
[6] *Ibid.*, pp. 342–3.
[7] *Rossiia 1913 god . . ., op. cit.*, p. 85.
[8] Koval'chenko, I. D., and Milov, L. V., *Vserossiiskii agrarnyi rynok . . ., op. cit.*, p. 284.
[9] *Sbornik Statistiko-ekonomicheskikh svedenii . . ., op. cit.*, pp. 526–7.

registered only modest livestock changes and increases in the postemancipation years. The low levels of livestock (including horses) are dramatically
illustrated when compared to those registered, for instance, in the United
States. Thus, in 1911–14 there were in European Russia 16.5 horses per one
hundred people, compared to 51.8 in the United States; 23.6 horned cattle per
one hundred people compared to 237.8 in the United States; 30.2 sheep compared to 1,745.8 in the United States; 0.6 goats compared to 5.4 in the United
States; and 10.1 pigs compared to 16.4 in the United States.[10] The changes in
the Russian commercial exports of such products as butter, milk, meats, and
heads of livestock remained largely limited (for example, in 1911, these exports amounted to close to 100 million rubles out of the total exports valued
at 1591 million).

According to the calculation of Paul R. Gregory, the investments in the
country's agriculture in 1895 and 1910 amounted to 482 million rubles and
832 million respectively. Out of these totals, the share of investments in agricultural machinery and equipment was of the order of 2.5 percent and 7.9 percent,
the rest being divided between investments in livestock and farm structures,
with the latter absorbing 68.6 percent and 79.6 percent of the total. The credits
extended by the territorial governments for the amelioration of agriculture in
1914 amounted to only 15 million rubles.[11]

The system of cultivation continued to rely on the traditional, rather primitive method of crop rotation involving the alternation of the fallow land, winter
wheat, then summer wheat. The method – alleged by various Russian writers
to be "typical of the feudal system," and to have been at the root of the crisis
of Tsarist agriculture[12] – was strictly followed by the peasants, who relied on
cereals without any recourse to other types of plants such as potatoes or industrial plants. As Leroy-Beaulieu has pointed out, in the northern part of the
country, in the black earth area devoid of steppes, the natural fecundity of the
soil persisted for long periods even in the absence of fertilizers' use. Eventually, the decline of production brought about the need for massive utilizations
of manure or multiple alternations with fodder plants. All in all, the working
of the land, its seeding, mowing, treatment of the grains, and so on brought
forth a variety of procedures in the various parts of the country.[13] As for the
specific use of the cultivated land, some 73 percent of it was used in the early
1900s for the cultivation of cereals, among which the first places were held by

[10] *Rossiia 1913 god . . ., op. cit.*, p. 92.
[11] Gregory, Paul R., *Before Command: An Economic History of Russia from Emancipation
to the First Five Year Plan*, Princeton, NJ, Princeton University Press, 1994. Appendix A,
pp. 146, 148; *Sbornik Statistiko-ekonomicheskikh svedenii . . ., op. cit.*, p. 551.
[12] Confino, Michael, *Systemes Agraires et Progres Agricole. L'assolement Triennial en Russie
aux XVIII–XIXe Siècles* (Agrarian Systems and Agricultural Progess. The Triennial Crop
Rotation in Russia at the Eighteenth–Nineteenth Centuries), Paris, Mouton & Co., 1969.
[13] Leroy-Beaulieu, *L'Empire des Tsars . . ., op. cit.*, pp. 147–52.

Table 4-4 *European Russia: Output of Major Grains, 1886–1914, in Millions of Poods*[a]

Years	Rye	Wheat	Barley	Oats	Total	Index
			Major crops			
1886–90	970.5	251.8	183.0	519.4	2,024.7	82.2
1894–5	995.7	452.2	267.7	531.9	2,247.5	91.3
1896–1900	1,090.0	500.8	274.7	595.4	2,460.9	100.0
1901–5	1,183.8	734.0	350.2	666.2	2,934.2	119.2
1906–10	1,071.7	733.3	417.6	682.0	2,904.6	118.0
1914	1,221.3	770.4	412.3	613.3	3,017.3	122.5

Note:
[a] Pood = 36.11 lb.
Sources: 1886–90, Lyashchenko, P. I., *History of the National Economy of Russia*, transl. by Herman, L. M., New York, Macmillan, 1949, p. 453; for 1901–14, *Sbornik statistiko-ekononucheskikh swedenii po sel'skomu khoziastvu . . ., op. cit.*, pp. 32–3.

rye and wheat, followed by barley and various other cereals. I will examine further in Sections 4.3 and 4.4 the results of outputs and yields as well as the impact of these patterns of cultivation on the country's foreign trade. For the moment, note in conclusion with regard to all the aspects of farming methods the valid remark of Arcadius Kahan:

Facilities to foster agricultural research, improvement of breeding stocks of varieties of crops, were either in their infancy or grossly inadequate; the use of mineral fertilizers was minimal, so the modern agricultural revolution largely bypassed Russia at a time when other countries were already benefiting from it.[14]

4-3. Outputs and Yields

After the 1861 reform, agricultural output increased roughly at the rate of 2 percent per year. The principal increases were registered in crop production, particularly that of four major grains: rye, wheat, barley, and oats. On the basis 1896–1900 = 100, the index of the output of the major grains of European Russian rose from 82.2 in 1886–90 to 122.5 in 1914. Specifically, this output rose during that period from a total of 2,024.7 million poods to 3,017.3 million (see Table 4-4), constituting the major share of the total output of the Empire, which in 1914 reached 4,065.2 million poods. This figure represented 29 percent of the world's output of major grains. The most massive contributions to this total were due to the increase in rye and barley and less significantly to increases in oats and wheat.

[14] Kahan, Arcadius, *The Russian Economic History*, Chicago, University of Chicago Press, 1989, p. 10.

Crucial differences concerning yields[15] were exhibited in both the black and the non-black soil regions between the results obtained on the privately owned land and those reached on the peasant-owned lands. Through the 1900s until the war, each year the yields obtained in both areas and in European Russia as a whole were significantly and consistently higher in the privately owned lands for each of the crops. Incidentally, this was also the case for all the other cereals (that is, buckwheat, millet, and corn, as well as legumes, potatoes, and the many industrial crops, namely flax and hemp). The differences were due to the greater and more effective use of agricultural equipment on the privately owned lands.

Yet the higher yields of the privately owned lands were far below those obtained in Central and Western Europe. The highest rates for the main crops in the black soil regions – namely sixty-seven for winter rye, seventy for winter wheat, fifty for spring wheat, fifty-five for barley, and fifty-nine for oats – were closer to those of Serbia than of any developed country. The Russian Empire's yields compared to those of the then most advanced agricultural country, Germany, were lower than one-half of the latter's for rye, and roughly one-third for wheat, barley, and oats. The Russian Empire exceeded only neighboring Romania for rye and wheat, but even then it fell behind Romania for barley and oats.

At the time, Russian development of many industrial crops remained quite limited. For comparison, recall that in 1914 the major grain crops for the Empire covered 79 million dessiatins of cultivated land (67.2 + 11.8). In the same year, the major industrial crops besides potatoes, cultivated on 3.8 million dessiatins, covered relatively limited surfaces except for flax (1.4 million dessiatins), hemp (587,000 dessiatins), and sunflower (594,000 dessiatins); less land was used for rice (235,000 dessiatins), cotton (47,000), as well as for sugar beets and tobacco. The cultivation of potatoes, essential both for improving the human diet and for allowing the shifting of certain amounts of cereals toward raising livestock, covered between 1901–10 on the average 106,000 dessiatins, yielding an output of 64 million poods. The surface cultivated and the output decreased in the following years, falling by 1914 to a total output of 39 million poods.

It is evident that the poor performance of Russian agriculture can be attributed at least to an extent to the unfavorable climate and soil conditions reigning over much of its territory, to the predominance of the small-scale farming poorly managed by the communes as well as the larger privately owned farms often operated by absentee owners, and to the continuous reliance for increased output on the expansion of the area under cultivation rather than on the mechanization of agriculture and the modernization of the farming procedures. Yet just as before 1861, Russian agriculture throughout the period

---

[15] *Sbornik Statistiko-ekonomicheskikh svedenii . . ., op. cit.*, pp. 32–3, 58–9.

continued to be considered the most important sector of the economy, the main source of its employment, and the biggest contributor to its national income. The core of the Empire and its main producer, European Russia increased its output of major grains from 2,247.5 million poods to 3,017.3 million poods between 1894–5 and 1914 (that is, by 34 percent). This barely kept up with the increase of the population, which during the same period rose from 93.7 million to 128.6 million (that is, by 37 percent).

4-4. Exports and Imports

Russia's geographic conditions favored the development of its domestic trade rather than its foreign trade. The latter's growth was also hampered by various drawbacks along the country's long boundaries. A large part of Russia's continental frontiers is close to deserts, steppes, and the mountains of Asia, while only the small part of its maritime and continental boundary ties Russia to Europe and serves as the main channel of its contacts with the big world markets. By the end of the nineteenth century, more than 90 percent of Russia's foreign trade was carried out through the boundary with Europe (including that of Finland) and less than 10 percent was handled through the Asian frontier. Finally, the Tsarist tariff policy adopted since 1877 and dominant until the turn of the century also curtailed the growth of foreign trade.[16]

The agricultural sector played the decisive role in Russia's foreign trade. As we will see in detail in Chapter 6, the crucial agricultural items in the country's exports were foodstuffs and raw materials, while the largest items in Russia's imports were other raw materials and manufactured goods. From the turn of the century until World War I, the shares of these items varied little from year to year. Among the exported foodstuffs, cereals and flour products played the primary role. Jointly these two items accounted for over 70 percent of the value of foodstuffs and for over 40 percent of the total exports. Along with cereals and flour, the other main foodstuffs exported were milk products, fodder plants, oil-seed grains, oil cakes, and vegetable oils, as well as eggs, meats, legumes, and fruits. Among the exported raw materials, the main items were fibers of flax and hemp, timber products, followed by hides and furs. Live animals brought only a small share of the total value of exports. Among the imported raw materials, the crucial items were fibers – primarily cotton and wool – followed by fertilizers and wood products. Among the imports of manufactured goods, the imports of agricultural machinery played a surprisingly small role: Less than 11 percent of the import expenditures went for this equipment. Russia imported also cereals and grains – notably rice – as well as legumes, wines, meats, fish, fruits, and live animals.

---

[16] See Pokrovsky, M. B., "Commerce Exterieur," in *La Russie à la fin du 19ᵉ siècle*, Kovalevsky, M. W., ed., *op. cit.*, pp. 689, 722.

Russia's main customers in Europe were Germany and Great Britain. The Empire's main Asian partners were China and Persia. The largest shares of Russia's agricultural exports went to Germany. In 1913, Germany bought close to 30 percent of Russia's exports of foodstuffs, an equal amount of Russia's exports of raw materials, 77 percent of the exports of live animals, and only 7 percent of Russia's manufactured goods. In turn, Russia bought from Germany 23 percent of its imports of foodstuffs, over 44 percent of its imports of raw materials, and over 66 percent of its imports of manufactured goods. The Russian exports to Germany in that year amounted to 30 percent of the Empire's sales abroad, while Russia's imports from Germany reached over 47 percent of its total imports. Clearly, the role of Germany was decisive at the time with regard to Russia's needs to develop industry – as we will see in detail later on.

However, Russia's second important Western partner, Great Britain, bought far less from Russia, and exported to the Empire far less than Germany. Great Britain absorbed about 15 percent of Russia's exports of foodstuffs, 20 percent of its sales of raw materials, and about 7 percent of its manufactured goods. Russia bought from Great Britain less than 6 percent of its imports of foodstuffs, some 7 percent of its imports of raw materials, and 11 percent of its purchases of manufactured goods. All in all, the exports to Great Britain amounted to less than 18 percent of Russia's total exports and to less than 13 percent of its imports. (For comparison, note that France accounted for 4 percent of Russia's total imports and the United States for 5.5 percent.) Also, Russia's foreign trade with Asia remained very small. China and Persia (Iran) absorbed less than 6 percent of Russia's exports and furnished slightly over 9 percent of its imports. These countries bought mainly foodstuffs and manufactured goods, and supplied mainly foodstuffs and raw materials.[17]

During the twenty years preceding World War I, Russia's main exports, namely that of grains, did not keep up with its increasing production. According to Leo Pasvolsky and Harold Moulton, between 1891–5 and 1913, the share of Russia's exports of its growing grain crops had fallen for wheat, from 37.8 percent to 15.0 percent; for rye, from 5.7 percent to 2.9; for barley, from 34.7 percent to 34.2; and for oats, from 10.7 to 4.1 percent. As a result, by 1913 Russia was shipping only 15 percent of the total of these outputs instead of 40 percent as in 1891–5. Yet by 1910–12, Russia still accounted for 30.4 percent of the world exports of grains (including, besides the indicated crops, also corn) – that is, it still held the first place in such exports, followed in second place by Argentina (15.4 percent), then by Romania (9.8 percent), and by the United States (9.0 percent).[18]

[17] *Sbornik Statistiko-ekonomicheskikh svedenii . . ., op. cit.*, pp. 390–3.
[18] Pasvolsky, Leo, and Moulton, Harold, *Russian Debts and Russian Reconstruction . . ., op. cit.*, p. 71; Pokrowskii, Serafin A., *Vneshniaia torgovlia i vneshniaia torgovaia politika Rossii, op. cit.*, p. 349.

But Russia's share in total international trade remained very small. The expansion of its trade in total value was by far exceeded by the expansion of the other major countries' trade. Russia's share in world trade was in 1800 of the order of 3.7 percent; in 1850 still at 3.5 percent; in 1899 at 3.4 percent; in 1905 at 3.3 percent; in 1911–13 at 3.6 percent. (This share was equal to that of British India in the 1900s.) In contrast, in 1912, for instance, the shares of all the other great powers exceeded by far that of Russia: Great Britain's share was 4.7 times larger than Russia's, Germany's trade 3.7 times larger, and the shares of the United States and France were each 2.8 times larger.[19]

4-5. Concluding Comments

As Professor H. Gerschenkron has pointed out in *The Cambridge History of Europe*, the joint effect upon the growing agricultural population of both the inadequate land allotments and the burdensome financial obligations began to gain more serious attention from the government only after the assassination of Alexander II. Indeed, the tax levels began to be seriously adjusted only after 1881. The Empire abolished the poll tax, between 1881–5 for all the categories of the peasants of European Russia, and also at the time, reduced the level of redemption payments to about 9 percent of the debt. The state also made a rather modest attempt to remedy the scarcity of peasant land by creating the Peasant Land Bank, which, as already noted, was to help finance purchases of land by the communes, not by individuals. In fact, in the first decade of the Bank's existence, the extent of the peasant land financed by the Bank increased only by 1.2 percent. Legal prerequisites were subsequently created for deferment of tax arrears and for installment payments, notably in 1894, 1896, and 1899. Yet, it was only "the threatening disintegration of the Empire in the storm of peasant rebellions and in the mass strikes of factory and communication workers" that effected some deeper revisions of the agricultural policy, including notably the Stolypin reforms of 1906 and 1910.[20]

Notwithstanding the deep poverty of the mass of the peasantry, the total share of agriculture in the country's income and wealth far exceeded that of the rapidly growing secondary and tertiary sectors. This share in the national income was of the order of 57.4 percent between 1883–91, 51.2 percent between 1897–1902, and 50.7 percent between 1909–13. Over that entire period, the agricultural labor force grew at a rate slightly slower than that of the

[19] Khromov, P. A., *Ekonomicheskoe razvitie Rossii v XIX–XX vekah, op. cit.*, p. 251; Pokrowskii, Serafin A., *Vneshniaia torgovlia i vneshniaia torgovaia politika Rossii, op. cit.*, p. 383; *Statistisches Juhrbuch für das Deutsche Reich* (Statistical Yearbook for the German Empire), Berlin, Kaiserliches Statistiches Amt, 1913–14, p. 61.

[20] Gerschenkron, Alexander, "Agrarian Policies and Industrialization of Russia 1861–1917," in *The Cambridge Economic History of Europe*, Vol. 6, Part 2, *op. cit.*, pp. 768–80.

total labor force (that is, its share declined, but only modestly in the total labor force).[21] Agriculture failed to remain as productive as industry and the economy as a whole. Finally, at the beginning of 1914, agriculture, forestry, fishery, and hunting's share of the national wealth amounted to 34.8 percent, to which should be added the agricultural household wealth estimated at 9.5 percent. With certain adjustments, the total agricultural share fluctuated around 50 percent.

[21] Gregory, Paul R., *Before Command: An Economic History of Russia* . . ., *op. cit.*, pp. 29, 135; *Rossiia 1913 god* . . ., *op. cit.*, pp. 32–3.

CHAPTER 5

The Industrial Changes

5-1. Patterns of Growth

Most Soviet writers have contended that "commercial capitalism," or more modestly put, "capitalist manufacture," began to develop in Russia during the last years of the reign of Peter the Great (1682–1725). Certainly, Peter, with the specific goal of achieving a vast and powerful army for war and expansion, developed a number of large factories and used for the purpose an enormous amount of various resources. Yet most of this development was hardly "capitalistic." The factory workers were bonded to the state – they were so-called serfs of the Treasury – or were possessed by private owners. Thus, when the state established what was for the time a modern factory in the framework of a feudal society, its labor had to be drawn from the state's peasant-serfs; and when the state handed over this factory to a private entrepreneur, the bonded workmen were also handed over to him. The Russian factory workforce was thus, at its inception, based upon the same system as that of agriculture, namely upon bondage, and its wage rates were established by imperial edict.

Among the main results of Peter's industrial efforts were common foundries and armament works, tanneries, and woolen-cloth factories, the establishment of mining and metallurgy centers in the Urals, and the expansion of certain manufacturing industries in St. Petersburg and Moscow. After Peter's death, some of these establishments were leased to private persons or closed, and under Catherine the Great (1762–96), the state gave a certain industrial impetus primarily to the development of consumer goods manufacturing.[1] By the end of the eighteenth century, as M. E. Falkus has pointed out, Russian industry finally consisted of a complex mixture of state enterprises based on the bondage of state peasants, *votchinal* (manorial) enterprises using serf labor,

---

[1] Strumilin, Stanislav G., *Ocherki ekonomicheskoi istorii Rossii i SSSR* (Essays on the Economic History of Russia and the USSR), Moscow, Nauka, 1966, pp. 302–3; Falkus, M. E., *The Industrialization of Russia*, London, Macmillan, 1972, pp. 21–5.

Table 5-1 *European Russia: The Industrial Enterprises and Their Workforce in 1811 and 1860*

Industries	1811			1860		
	Enterprises	Workforce	Percent	Enterprises	Workforce	Percent
Textile materials	862	97,127	70.4	2416	303,832	60.1
Metallic products	77	13,4079	9.7	854	63,336	12.5
Chemicals	161	1,666	1.2	499	8,438	1.7
Ceramics/ crystal	143	6,696	4.9	250	14,093	2.8
Paper	68	6,701	4.9	207	12,804	2.5
Leather	1226	8,262	6.0	2515	14,151	2.8
Sugar	10	123	–	467	64,763	12.8
All other	374	4,060	2.9	2354	23,978	4.8
TOTAL	2921	138,042	100.0	9562	505,395	100.0

Source: Based on Rashin, A. G., *Formirovamie promyshlennogo proletariata v Rossii, Statistiko-ekonomicheskie ocherki* (Formation of the Industrial Proletariat in Russia, Statistical-Economic Essays), Moscow, Sotsialno-ekonomicheskoe Gosizdat, 1940, pp. 26–7, 30–1.

merchant enterprises using both hired labor and possessional peasants, and a variety of small-scale handicraft rural and urban workshops and plants.[2]

During the half century from 1811 to the emancipation of the serfs in 1861, factories and plants grew appreciably in numbers, and some of them began some mechanization and a larger utilization of "free" labor. First the consumer goods industries developed more vigorously while heavy industry stagnated. The traditional iron industries of the Urals, which accounted for over 80 percent of the country's production of iron, continued to rely on serf labor and languished because of various economic barriers that they proved unable to overcome. Table 5-1 presents an approximate image of the industrial changes that took place during the period. The term "approximate" refers to the very nature of Tsarist statistics, particularly until the 1880s. The statisticians used the terms "factories" and "plants" without clarifying the distinction between these terms with regard to size, level of mechanization, and utilization of wage labor. Nevertheless, the available data, indicate that the number of industrial enterprises increased about three times while their labor force expanded three and a half times. By far the largest employment was concentrated in the textile industries, followed by metal working and sugar production.

During the next half century, roughly from 1861 to 1913, two distinct periods are clearly noticeable. The first, extending over some twenty-five years from

[2] Falkus, M. E., *The Industrialization of Russia, op. cit.*, p. 30.

1861 to 1887, witnessed an increase in the number of industrial plants and their workforce by about two and a half times. And again, during the second period of roughly twenty-five years from 1887 to 1913, the industrial labor force increased two and a half times, within a roughly stable number of 30,000–39,000 enterprises. During the first quarter of the century considered, Euro-Russia accounted for 92 percent of the Empire's industrial labor force; during the next quarter of a century, this share fell to 76 percent, but Euro-Russia still controlled the vast majority of the Empire's industrial enterprises.

What were the short-term phases of the indicated periods and which factors accounted for the changes involved? Immediately after the reform of 1861 and roughly until 1866, the Empire's industrial development was severely handicapped by the problems posed by the consequences of the Crimean War, by the Polish insurrection of 1863, by bad harvests, by rising prices, and by the instabilities generated by the reform. The general malaise was further accented by the lack of large capital resources, skilled labor, a network of railroads, commercial banks and credit, and experience in the building of new industries. Eventually the beginning of the expansion of railways (with foreign capital help) gave a certain impetus to Russian industry providing various inputs for the railways, such as rails, switches, wagons, locomotives, and materials for bridges. The construction of railroads had been put high on the government's military-strategic agenda already by 1855, but methodic work in this regard had to wait until the late 1860s. The broad long-term targets that the government had in view were to draw the agricultural districts into commercial circulation, to connect the Volga region with the Baltic Sea, to connect Central Russia with the western border, and, on the other hand, to reach the White Sea and methodically expand the rail communications through the immense length of Siberia and through Central Asia. Strategic considerations always underlined the railway expansion decisions. The concomitant economic results were viewed as useful but of secondary import. In the absence of adequate funds, railroad construction was not pursued systematically and its impact was more decisive at some times than at others. The period of 1867–79 was in this regard a boom era, followed by a slowdown until 1891, then succeeded by another powerful construction boom until 1897. Between 1868 and 1877, railroads were built at an average pace of 1,900 kilometers per year; during the next fifteen years, this average declined to 710 kilometers per year; finally, during the five-year period from 1893 to 1897, the average pace increased to 2,600 kilometers per year. From 1866 to 1900, the Empire's rail network increased from 5,000 kilometers to 53,200 kilometers (including Poland but not the Duchy of Finland).[3]

From the 1800s to the mid-1870s and beyond, as the economic historian P. I. Lyashchenko has pointed out, the Russian economy intermingled its

[3] Westwood, J. N., *A History of Russian Railways*, London, George Allen & Unwin, 1964, p. 59.

Table 5-2 *Russia: The Industrial and Mining Enterprises and Their Workforce in 1887 and 1897[a]*

	1887			1897		
Industries	Industries	Workforce	Percent	Industries	Workforce	Percent
Textile materials	2,848	399,178	30.3	4,449	642,520	30.6
Mining/ smelting	2,656	390,915	29.7	3,412	544,333	25.9
Metalware	1,377	103,300	7.8	2,412	214,311	10.2
Chemicals	588	21,134	1.6	769	35,320	1.7
Ceramics	2,380	67,346	5.1	3,413	143,291	6.8
Paper	242	19,491	1.5	532	46,190	2.2
Animal products	4,425	38,876	2.9	4,238	64,418	3.1
Foodstuffs	14,508	205,223	15.6	16,512	255,357	12.2
Woodworking	1,093	30,703	2.3	2,357	86,273	4.1
All other	771	41,882	3.2	935	66,249	3.2
TOTALS	30,888	1,318,048	100.0	39,029	2,098,262	100.0

Note:
[a] Excluding Finland.
Source: Tugan Baranovsky, M. I., *The Russian Factory in the 19th Century* (1898), transl. by Levin, A., and Levin, C. S., Homewood, IL, Richard D. Irwin, 1970, p. 273.

slowly advancing industrial development with "the old elements of Russia's backward agrarian economy, and primitive forms of small-scale commodity production," and extributed a great lag in the production of machines and of the raw materials required for modern industrial development such as coal and petroleum. After an industrial crisis in 1873–5 primarily caused by the decline in railroad construction and to its direct impact on iron, steel, and fuel production, as well as to its repercussions on the other industries, new investment slackened and the industry did not begin to recover before passing through a new crisis in 1881–2.[4] As can be seen in Table 5-2, it is from 1887 to 1897 that industrial and mining development started at an increasing pace – thanks to massive foreign investments. The number of enterprises increased in Imperial Russia by 26 percent and their labor force grow close to 60 percent. Yet the underlying characteristics did not markedly change. The dominant industries remained the textile factories along with the mining and smelting enterprises and those engaged in metalware production. However, important locational shifts did occur in the period considered. Prior to 1887 there were only two metallurgical factories in the south; by the end of the 1890s there were seventeen full-cycle iron and steel plants in that area, with twenty-nine

[4] Liashchenko, P. I., *Istoriia narodnogo khoziaistvo SSSR, op. cit.*, pp. 493–4, 525.

blast furnaces in operation and twelve more under construction. The resulting regional shifts and growth were indeed impressive. Whereas in 1860 there was no production of iron and steel in the south, by the turn of the century the south was accounting for close to 58 percent of the output of pig iron and for 48 percent of the iron and steel of Russia (excluding Poland).[5]

Furthermore, two additional changes matured in the period beginning in the 1880s. The first concerned the increased concentration of the labor force in larger enterprises that emerged thanks to foreign investments with increased access to modernization and mechanization. The second concerned the growth of heavy industry in relation to the traditional dominance of the light industries. As can be seen from Table 5-3, the factories with over one hundred workers more than doubled between 1890 and 1914, while their workforce more than tripled. Within this group, the top large-scale industries with over one thousand workers continually increased their share in total employment. This share rose indeed from 37 percent in 1890 to 41 percent in 1901, 47 percent in 1910, and then 50 percent in 1914. Concomitantly, according to data furnished by S. G. Strumilin, total employment in the Russian factories and mines also expanded close to three times between 1887 and 1913, while the employment share of heavy industry finally surpassed that of the light industry by the end of the period considered. The increased concentration in large-scale industry along with the increase of the heavy industry in total industrial employment point clearly to expanding market-oriented relations in industry, particularly since the 1890s. But the Russian factory and mining labor force continued to remain only a small fraction of Russia's population. In this regard, it is interesting to recall the different outlooks of certain Russian analysts and that of Lenin and his followers. While various Russian publicists and sociologists saw in the medieval and semifeudal relics of Russia, and in the small ratio of industrial works to the total population, the proof that Russia was following "a path of development distinct of that which Western Europe followed," Lenin contended that Russia was developing along capitalist lines and that is was "absurd to equate capitalism with the number of factory workers." What mattered, according to him, was the total number of workers engaged in "capitalist production," which included all the society's wage workers, that is, besides the factory workers, the handscraftsmen who worked for merchants for ordinary wages, the farm laborers and the day-laborers who worked for wages in agriculture, the workers in construction, and so on. I will turn to some of these issues in the following section.[6]

[5] Fedor, Thomas Stanley, *Patterns of Urban Growth in the Russian Empire during the Nineteenth Century*, Chicago, University of Chicago, Dept. of Geography, Research Paper No. 163, 1975, p. 87.

[6] Lenin, V. I., "What the 'Friends of the People' Are and How They Fight the Social Democrats," *Collected Works,* Vol. 1, *op. cit.*, pp. 310-3.

Table 5-3 *European Russia: The Growth of Large-Scale Industry, 1890–1914,*
Number of Workers in Thousands

Number of workers	1890		1901		1910		1914	
	Factories	Workers	Factories	Workers	Factories	Workers	Factories	Workers
100–499	1,131	252.1	2,288	492.0	2,213	507.8	2,253	504.4
500–999	182	120.9	403	269.1	433	302.8	432	296.3
1,000+	108	226.2	243	525.6	324	713.6	344	811.1
TOTAL	1,421	599.2	2,934	1,286.7	2,970	1,524.2	3,029	1,611.8

Source: For 1890, Pogozhev, A. V., *Uchet chislennosti i sostava rabochikh v Rossii, materialy po statistike truda* (Calculation of the Number and Composition of the Workers in Russia, Materials for Statistical Work), St. Petersburg, 1906, p. 42; for the other years, Khromov, P. A., *Ekonomicheskoe razvitie Rossii v XIX–XX vekah 1800–1917* (Economic Development of Russia in the Nineteenth to Twentieth Century, 1800–1917), Moscow, Gosizdat Politlit, 1950, p. 301.

5-2. Workforce

The Russian historical-economic literature of the later 1890s and the beginning of the 1900s started to carefully accumulate data about, on the one hand, the large-scale manufacturing and mining industry and, on the other hand, the small-scale industry, including the urban arts and crafts and the rural *kustar* industry exercised by certain peasants and their families to create a supplementary income to the principal one generated from the agricultural work.

The factors that shaped the distribution of large-scale industry, besides the usual ones – the proximity of raw materials (for example, in the Donets, Ural, and Baku regions), the availability of foreign capital and foreign managerial abilities (mainly in the country's capitals), the presence of abundant and suitable labor (mostly outside the urban centers) – included also the impact of some specific conditions inherited from the sixteenth to the nineteenth centuries. Examples of these conditions include the key role of the Petrograd and of the Ural regions, as well as the consequences of various state policies on the development of Russian versus non-Russian regions. On the whole, according to data of the late 1890s until the beginning of 1902, the main concentration centers of the Russian industry were by then besides the two capitals, Moscow and Petrograd, the following four regions: 1) the Central Industrial; 2) the Right Bank Dnepr; 3) the Southern Steppe; and 4) the Northeast. According to the data available for 1902, for instance, besides the 37.9 percent of the total employment registered in the factory industry in the two capitals, the other four regions accounted for 16.3 percent of employment, thus amounting jointly to over 54 percent of the total. Excluding the capitals, most of the factory employment was located outside the urban areas. Of the fifty-four largest cities of the Russian Empire with a population of more than fifty thousand in 1897, only eleven cities had 30 percent of their gainfully employed in manufacturing.[7]

Why did the Russian factories locate preferably in the countryside and rely on the labor available there? A number of causes were at work. First, the factories spread outside the cities guaranteed the availability of the labor it needed: Various barriers prevented the peasants from going to the cities, so the factories had to go to them. The countryside offered also cheaper labor than in the cities (because of the differences in living standards) and, when needed, better trained workers from the *kustar* trades. The process of organizing a fully developed industrial labor force from the peasants was, however, a difficult, involved process, given the peasant mentality, traditions, and habits, particularly when the newly employed industrial workers retained their plots of land and kept close ties with their old village commune. Almost everywhere, these industrial workers returned periodically to the land when needed for agricultural work, or returned permanently to the countryside after accumulating

---

[7] Fedor, Thomas Stanley, *Patterns of Urban Growth . . ., op. cit.*, pp. 97, 175.

the money needed for buying a piece of land. In essence, while the Western European industrialization took place mainly in regions where industrial work had been practiced for a long time, Russian industrialization grew in a totally different framework, with a totally different labor basis. Moreover, since the Russian industrial expansion was due primarily to the necessity to provide new goods for new needs, this expansion could coexist on the one hand with the urban arts and crafts, and on the other hand with the small-scale rural *kustar* labor that was producing traditional wares for the country's traditional needs.[8]

The small-scale non-factory manufacturing was engaged notably in the processing of textiles – cotton, flax, wool, silk, and related materials – in the production of paper and polygraphic wares, in all kinds of woodworking, in metal and minerals processing, in the preparation of furs and of other animal products, in foodstuffs, and in chemical goods. According to data released by the Ministry of Trade and Industry, at the beginning of the twentieth century, the urban arts and crafts consisted of some 103,409 enterprises, 83.5 percent of which had only from two to four workers, 14.4 percent from five to fifteen workers, and 2.1 percent from sixteen to twenty-five workers or more. By 1910 their employment was estimated to have reached 900,000 or around 1.2 million.[9]

The rural *kustar* industry attached itself essentially to the production of the specific goods needed by the peasant families in agriculture and in their daily lives. Its main woodworking output, for instance, involved such goods as wheels, carts, sledges, barrels, buckets, rakes, and similar products. Concerning textiles, it delivered typical traditional articles of flax, hemp, wool, and cotton including shawls, scarfs, and knitted goods. In respect to animal products, it processed furs and leather, and besides tanneries it engaged in work on harnesses, boots, shoes, and gloves. With regard to metals, it focused on iron work, blacksmith's work, and the production of nails and spikes. In the case of minerals, large developments were usually registered in pottery work using the abundant clay available in the Russia soil.[10]

No fully reliable data are available on the size of the entire non-factory manufacturing sector. According to various calculations made in the early 1900s, total employment in small-scale industry reached at the time between 4.5 to 5 million workmen. The approximate relations in terms of employment

---

[8] Miller, Margaret,*The Economic Development of Russia . . ., op. cit.*, pp. 224–5; Barel, Yves, *Le development économique. . ., op. cit.*, pp. 186–91.

[9] *Rossiia 1913 god . . ., op. cit.*, pp. 55–7; Azhaeva, V. S., *Melkoe predprinimatel'stvo v Rossii, konets XIXV.-nachalo XXV* (The Small Enterprise in Russia, at the End of Nineteenth–Beginning of the Twentieth Century), Moscow, Rossiiskaia Akademiia Nauk, 1994, p. 8.

[10] Moratchevsky, M. V., "Petites industries, rurales dites de koustari" (Small Rural Industries, Called of Kustari), in *La Russie à la fin du 19ᵉ siècle*, Kovalevsky, M. W., ed., *op. cit.*, pp. 538–45; see also "Peasant Industries," in the *Russian Yearbook for 1912*, Kennard, Howard, ed., *op. cit.*, pp. 396–9.

Table 5-4 *Russia: Large-Scale and Small-Scale Industry at the Beginning of the Twentieth Century, Employment in Thousands and in Percentages*

Type of industry	Number of workers	Percent	Number of workers	Percent	Number of workers	Percent
Large-scale industry[a]	2,169	31.7	2,680	36.5	2,700	34.2
Small-scale rural industry[b]	3,755	54.9	3,755	51.1	4,000	50.6
Small-scale urban industy[c]	910	13.4	910	12.4	1,200	15.2
TOTAL	6,834	100.0	7,345	100.0	7,900	100.0

Note:

[a] Data for 1908. First two columns cover the processing industry only; the other columns cover the processing and the mining industry. Employment refers to workers.

[b] Data for 1904–13. Employment refers to workers (including artisans).

[c] Data for 1910. Employment refers to workers (including artisans).

Source: *Rossiia 1913 god . . ., op. cit.*, p. 56.

between large-scale and small-scale industry are indicated in Table 5-4. As can be seen in the table, the combined urban and rural small-scale industries provided around 65–7 percent of the total industrial employment. By far, the largest share was furnished by the rural *kustar* industry, which comprised the peasants who devoted part of their time to production for household use or for a local market.

Given the ties of the mass of industrial workers with agriculture, patriarchal attitudes prevailed among the factory workers just as much as among the handicraftsmen. The policy of the Russian authorities with regard to the mass of workers was adequately summed up by Margaret Miller as "an admixture of paternalism and absolutism." The workers' salaries were low. The factory employer provided and managed the barracks that the workers needed for their households, while the state regulated the various forms of insurance that applied to them. By the end of the 1890s, the industrial legislation restricted the working day for adults to no more than eleven and a half hours and night work to ten hours. Constant, detailed controls were exercised over the workers and any attempt to organize was looked upon as a criminal offence. Legal trade unions were finally accepted after the revolutionary movement of 1905. The industrial prosperity that gained momentum after 1909 created conditions favorable to the expansion of the labor movement.[11] Strikes took place increasingly from then on, accompanied by a tide of industrial disturbances. According to the historian P. I. Liashchenko, in 1910, 222 strikes involved 46,600 workers; in 1914, 3,500 strikes involved 1.3 million workers. The strikes

[11] Miller, Margaret, *The Economic Development of Russia . . ., op. cit.*, pp. 230–7.

spread from Petrograd to Moscow, Kharkov, Nizhni Novgorod, Baku, and other areas.[12]

Interestingly, Lenin and his followers rejected the populist idea that small-scale industry constituted a kind of "people's industry," and affirmed that such industries "were nothing but capitalism at various stages of development," and were mostly "purely capitalist organizations." On the other hand, Lenin affirmed that the craftsmen who worked for the merchants and on command for the large industries were just as much "proletarians" as the factory workers. That is why, while the non-Marxists asserted that Russia had only 2.7 million "proletarians" in 1913 – referring to the workers in the factory industry – the Marxists-Leninists retorted that the number of proletarians had reached in that year 18.2 million people, including 3 million working in the handicrafts workshops.

5-3. Output Levels

According to the calculations of Raymond W. Goldsmith, the rate of growth of the value added in manufacturing and mining, including both factory and small-scale industry, was within the range of 5 to less than 6 percent per year during the period 1860–1913. According to various other calculations of the Russian national income by sector of origin in 1913, the respective contributions of agriculture and of industry plus handicrafts had been of the order of 50.7 and 21.4 percent respectively – that is, by 1913 the net value of agricultural output amounted to 10,294 million rubles, that of industry plus handicrafts to 4,334 million (3,023 + 1,311), and that of the Net National Income as a whole to 20,292 million rubles.[13]

The increase of the output of Russian manufacture from its far lower levels of 1860 can be attributed to the growth of investments in ferrous metallurgy and in the fuel industry, to the increased utilization of more advanced mechanization and technology in such branches as textiles and metal working, to the boom in railroad construction, and more generally, to the growth of overall demand for overhead capital and for capital goods. The output of the basic products of black metallurgy grew at higher rates, particularly after 1880–1900. These were accompanied by increases in machine construction, especially after the 1900s, thanks to foreign investments and to the increased demand in various branches of industry, agriculture, transports, and shipbuilding.

---

[12] Liashchenko, P. I., *Istoriia narodnogo khoziaistvo SSSR, op. cit.*, pp. 692–4; Lenin, V. I., "What the 'Friends of the People' Are . . .," *Collected Works*, Vol. 1, *op. cit.*, pp. 218–9, 317–8; *Rossiia 1913 god . . ., op. cit.*, p. 223.

[13] Goldsmith, Raymond W., "The Economic Growth of Tsarist Russia," *Economic Development and Cultural Change*, Vol. IX, No. 3, April 1961, p. 469; Gregory, Paul R., *Before Command: An Economic History of Russia . . ., op. cit.*, p. 151.

Table 5-5 *Russia^a: Heavy versus Light Industry's Share in the Total Value of Output, 1887–1913*

	Heavy		Light		Total	
Years	Million rubles	Percent	Million rubles	Percent	Million rubles	Percent
1887	290	30.0	675	70.0	965	100
1897	769	41.3	1091	58.7	1860	100
1900	1047	46.5	1206	53.5	2853	100
1910	1359	38.5	2172	61.5	3531	100
1913	2237	47.0	2526	53.0	4763	100

Note:
a In the subsequent frontiers of the USSR.
Source: Based on Strumilin, S. G., *Ocherki ekonomicheskoi istorii Rossii, op. cit.*, pp. 511, 516.

In the expansion of both metallurgy and the fuel industry, a crucial role was also played by the development of new production fields. In this regard, the powerful growth of the "new South," led by foreign investments, involved the merging of the expanding mines of Krivoi Rog and of the coal basin of the Donets, sharply reducing the importance of the old iron industry of the Urals. Between 1887 and 1914, the percentage of the Urals in the production of pig iron, for instance, fell from 66 percent to less than 20 percent, while that of the South increased from 1.2 percent to over 70 percent. During the same period, the Urals' share in the total production of iron and steel fell from around 44 percent to 17 percent, while that of the South grew from about 9 percent to 60 percent. This growth proceeded apace with increases in the coal output due to a decisive shift involving the expanding output of the Donbass in relation to that of the Kuzbass and of the Urals.[14]

During the entire period considered, the textile industry continued to hold the first place in the total value of manufacturing and mining due in particular to great technological advances in the cotton industry. By 1913 the cotton production amounted to 1,817 million meters, compared to 138 million meters of woolen goods, 121 million of linen products, 81 million of hemp and jute, and 31 million of silk products.[15]

Notwithstanding the total increases in employment of heavy industry compared to light industry, the latter continued to account for the largest share of the manufacturing and mining output until World War I. Indeed, as can be seen in Table 5-5, heavy industry increased its relative share appreciably until 1910, when the detrimental impact of the crises of 1906–9 reduced to

[14] Khromov, P. A., *Ekonomicheskoe razvitie Rossii v XIX–XX vekah, op. cit.*, p. 456-8.
[15] Dewdney, John C., *A Geography of the Soviet Union*, 3rd ed., Oxford, Pergamon Press, 1979, p. 122.

rate of growth. Heavy industry recovered appreciably in 1913, but light industry remained the dominant sector notwithstanding its continuous decline until 1910.

From the point of view of industrial growth and change, the interval 1860–1914 clearly consisted of two basic periods of roughly twenty-five years each. As Alexander Gerschenkron once remarked, the first period of twenty-five years (from 1860 to the mid-1880s) might be viewed essentially as "an introduction" to the significant increases of certain industrial productions over the next quarter of a century until World War I.[16] However, notwithstanding the developments after the mid-1880s, Russian industry still remained far behind the technological advances and the industrial growth that were then taking place in Western Europe and in the United States. I will turn in some detail to the appropriate comparative data in this regard in the concluding section of this chapter. For now, let us first consider the role of industry in exports and imports.

5-4. Exports and Imports

What was the impact of Russia's industrial development on its foreign trade of manufactured goods (that is, of the products of industry less mining, building, and transport)? How did Russia's trade in manufactured goods compare with that of the Western industrialized countries?

Following the data worked out by the League of Nations and presented in Table 5-6, it is easy to see that Russia's exports as well as imports of manufactured goods were far smaller than those of the United States, the United Kingdom, Germany, or France.

Secondly, by 1913, for the United States, as for the United Kingdom, Germany, and France, the value of exports far exceeded that of its imports of manufactured goods. For Russia the situation was inverse: Its imports far exceeded its tiny exports. After years of industrial development, Russia's exports were exceeded sixteen times by those of the United States, forty-six times by those of the United Kingdom, thirty-seven times by those of Germany, and close to twenty times by those of France.

The structure of manufactured goods, raw materials, and semimanufactured goods varied greatly between Russia and the Western countries. Russia first needed to import various kinds of machinery – motors, various types of engines, machine tools, turbines, electrical apparatus, as well as some specific agricultural machines. In addition, Russia depended heavily on the imports of raw materials and of semimanufactured articles. In particular, its key textiles industries required imports of raw cotton, cotton yarn, wool, and silk; more

---

[16] Gerschenkron, Alexander, "The Rate of Growth in Russia since 1885," *Journal of Economic History*, Supplement VII, 1947, p. 144.

Table 5-6 *Russia: Trade in Manufactured Articles, Annual Averages in Millions of Dollars –*
1913 Prices

Period	Imports					Exports				
	U.S.	U.K.	Germany	France	Russia	U.S.	U.K.	Germany	France	Russia
1881–5	281	267	152	178	59	121	1113	521	425	8
1896–1900	250	386	183	168	104	248	1124	692	478	17
1906–10	416	488	286	282	146	473	1667	1191	725	32
1913	475	603	338	344	232	721	2029	1615	875	44

Source: Industrialization and Foreign Trade, New York, League of Nations, 1945, p. 160.

generally, other industries needed imported fuels, metallic ore (such as lead and zinc), chemicals, and rubber. As far as its exports were concerned, Russia had hardly any machinery to offer: Its manufactured exports consisted primarily of cotton fabrics, woolen goods, china, and pottery. Russia's exports of raw materials and of semimanufactured goods – which exceeded by far its exports of manufactures – involved notably flax and hemp, some iron and manganese, wood, and above all oil and oil products. Clearly, Russia's industrialization process exercised at the time still only a limited impact on its foreign trade of manufactured goods. In this regard, Russia's development fell far short of the great progress registered at the time by the major industrial countries of the world.

5-5. Concluding Comments

How far Russia lagged behind the major powers in manufacturing output can be readily perceived from the data presented in Table 5-7. From 1881 to 1913, certain industrial powers expanded massively both their production of manufacturing and their share in the total world production of such goods. The United States expanded its great share by an additional 7.2 percentage points, reaching over one-third of the total world output. Germany expanded its share by 1.8 points. The United Kingdom lost as much as 12.6 points and France 2.2 points – both of them still exceeding by far the share of the vast Russian Empire, whose total amounted by 1913 to only 5.5 percent of the world output (a total equal to the joint outputs of Sweden, Belgium, and Italy).

The deep differences between Russia and the major industrial world powers in certain basic manufacturing raw materials is in some respects even more striking. Except for copper and petroleum, Russia's shares of the world output were small or negligible compared to the shares of all the other great powers, such as the giant United States. The feeble state of Russia's industrial production is also evident in per capita comparisons. As noted by Liashchenko, in 1913 the smelting of pig iron, for instance, was 30.3 kilograms per capita in Russia compared to 326.5 kilograms in the United States, 206 kilograms

Table 5-7 *World's Manufacturing Production, 1881–1913,*
Percentage Distribution

Period	United States	United Kingdom	Germany	France	Russia
1881–5	28.6	26.6	13.9	8.6	3.4
1896–1900	30.1	19.5	16.6	7.1	5.0
1906-10	35.3	14.7	15.9	6.4	5.0
1913	35.3	14.0	15.7	6.4	5.5

Source: Industrialization and Foreign Trade, New York, League of Nations, *op. cit*, p. 13.

in England, and 250 kilograms in Germany. The extraction of coal reached a per capita figure of 209 kilograms in Russia, compared to 5,358 kilograms in the United States, and 2,822 kilograms in Germany. A further indication that Russia was continually falling behind the other major powers is that the per capita production in Tsarist Russia was one-eighth of the United States in 1900 and one-eleventh in 1913, and compared to Germany it was one-sixth in 1900 and one-eighth in 1913.[17]

Why Russia lagged behind the developed countries in the scope and pace of its industrialization is an issue of debate not only with regard to manufacturing, but also with regard to the entire heritage of Tsarism, be it with respect to its achievements or to its failures. For now, consider the complexities of the issues involved and recall the remarks of Gerschenkron, who noted that the factors that interacted in Russia were the inadequacy of its preindustrial and extraindustrial accumulation of capital, the widespread ignorance of the majority of its population, the corruption within the government, the feudal remains in agriculture, and, last but not least, the intensity of the popular discontent, all of which can be viewed as "obstacles placed in the path of industrialization."[18] I will return to these issues later on in Chapter 9.

---

[17] Liashchenko, P. I., *Istoriia narodnogo khoziaistvo SSSR, op. cit.*, p. 674.
[18] Gerschenkron, Alexander, "The Rate of Growth in Russia . . .," *op. cit.*, p. 151.

CHAPTER 6

Domestic and Foreign Trade

6-1. The Domestic Trade Network

Tsarist Russia's domestic trade was officially carried out through a number of ad hoc registered channels. According to an act of 1898, the registered stationary commercial enterprises were divided into four groups. Group I consisted of the wholesale firms handling agricultural products for over 300,000 rubles per year, the big drugstores, restaurants, and taverns. Group II comprised the establishments conducting transactions involving agricultural products for 50,000–300,000 rubles per year, as well as the wholesale stores selling alcoholic beverages either to small merchants or directly to private customers. Group III contained the small retail stores transacting agricultural products for 10,000–50,000 rubles per year, as well as the small tea and coffee shops and small drugstores. Group IV included the market stalls handling agricultural products for less than 10,000 rubles per year along with other types of commodities. A Group V was added for conveyance and delivery facilities.[1] In 1912, only 27.5 percent of the total commercial-industrial sales of the stationary commercial enterprises went to the villages, then inhabited by 86 percent of the total population; on the other hand, 72.5 percent of the total sales went to the towns, inhabited by 14 percent of the country's total population. If one considers only Euro-Russia, the amount bought by the town's population reached 212.75 rubles per capita, while it amounted to 13.04 rubles per capita in the countryside, that is, about sixteen times less. Further, according to the data of the Ministry of Trade, the yearly per capita commercial and industrial commodities in circulation, including also the imports and their sale by foreign trade firms, reached 90 rubles. Based on the same kind of calculation, it was asserted that the corresponding per capita figures were for England 420 rubles, for the United States 380, for Germany 290, and for France 220 rubles.[2]

[1] Dikhtiar, G. A., *Vnutrennaiaia torgovlia v dorevolutsionnoi Rossii, op. cit.*, pp. 66–70.
[2] *Ibid.*, pp. 79, 82–3.

100

One should not lose sight of the fact that the figures for the stationary enterprises did not cover all the domestic trade (and exchange transactions) that actually took place in the country. P. A. Khromov noted in this regard that if one takes into account all the sales of the industrial enterprises and of the handicrafts to the trade firms, then the total domestic trade figures would be far higher. Moreover, one should also take into account direct and second-hand sales, barter, and direct exchange of commodities in the villages, trade fairs, and later in the key railroad stations.

Finally, the official trade figures indicated that in 1885, 1,027,000 persons were engaged in the domestic trade, and in 1897, 1,600,000. These figures, however, did not take into account the millions actually involved in this trade.[3] Indeed, a great number of intermediaries participated in the domestic trade, including on the one hand the industrial, handicraft, and the credit firms, and on the other hand a vast number of intermediary brokers, jobbers, middlemen, small traders, and peddlers active in a variety of operations in foreign trade, in the small towns and in the villages.

The flow of industrial commodities was running through multiple channels. The most usual path was the following: A factory would deliver its products on credit to a great trading enterprise, which in turn would trade these goods throughout the interior of the country via the intermediary of less important provincial trade firms. In the villages and at the trade fairs, such goods would either be sold or exchanged for cereals, hemp, eggs, and so on. The goods handled in the domestic trade were largely the usual products of agriculture, cattle breeding, and forestry, along with such commodities as fruits, legumes, flax, and hemp. But after this group, along with the usual products character-istic of less developed countries – such as metals, naptha, kerosene, and salt – domestic trade included also a variety of industrial products specifically directed toward the expanding urban population (for example, haberdashery, cotton and woolen textiles, and various "modern" products). Also the sale of alcoholic beverages accounted for an important share of the trade.

In general, however, a wide variety of administrative measures hampered Russia's domestic trade. The classified firms were licensed and taxed according to different rates. Discriminatory features played a key role in their function-ing, including provisions against "nonindigenous" populations excluded from some trade branches or from some particular locations. The government estab-lished under close regulations short-term commercial trade fairs, particularly for the purchase of grain, fish, naphtha, alcohol, flour, sugar, as well as some statutory trade exchanges for other such products. The *Zemstva* established special warehouses with articles indispensable to the peasants, workshops for teaching various working methods to the small rural craftsmen, as well as trade outlets for their products. Domestic trade, in all its forms, suffered continually

---

[3] Khromov, P. A., *Ekonomicheskoe razvitie Rossii v XIX–XX vekah*, *op. cit.*, p. 229, 248–9.

from a shortage of capital and credit, which eventually led to the formation of intercommercial mutual credit societies.[4]

6-2. Trade Interconnections

As in all the developing countries, the increasing discrepancies between the small but expanding and modernizing capitalist-oriented industrial-banking sector and the vast lagging agricultural sector generated the need to rely on a wide variety of intermediaries between the two sectors and within them. "Nonindigenous" entrepreneurs, brokers, money-lenders, shop assistants, commercial travelers, and all kinds of peddlers were bound to play a decisive role in such a framework.

The dualistic pattern of development called forth the utilization of what the Russians called aliens (*inorodtsy*). These aliens included, on the one hand, a significant number of big importers-exporters, bankers, and industrialists from abroad as well as from some Russian minorities (including the Jews), and on the other hand, at lower levels, a widely discriminated-against mass of Jews, Armenians, Greeks, and other minority members, discharging the functions of small brokers, money-lenders, small firsthand buyers, shop assistants, commercial travelers, and the like. Many Jews discharged the intermediary functions in the Western frontiers of the Empire and also played a decisive role in such branches as the trade of bristles, feathers, hides, furs, and the like. In the Caucasus, the Armenians discharged some similar roles, and close to the Black Sea many such functions were in the hands of the Greeks. Rich and educated Jews as well as Jewish converts were allowed to leave the Pale of Settlement, and while some of them reached high positions in the 1860s and 1870s, the rest of the Jews lived under increasingly darkening clouds. From the mid-1860s on, violent attacks and bloody pogroms took place against them, and indeed for many of them life in Russia became unbearable. A large number of them eventually left Russia, while most of the remaining ones were confined increasingly to crafts and to work in the factories.[5]

The participation at great trade fairs of hundreds of thousands of businessmen and customers – many of them unfamiliar with the methods, the conditions, and the patterns of transactions there – opened wide fields of activity to all kinds of intermediaries. Often certain intermediaries concentrated in their hands a variety of commodity assortments to be presented to the incoming buyers not familiar with the market's suppliers, prices, and delivery conditions. As in the Middle Ages in Europe, a vast amount of

---

[4] Kahan, Arcadius, *The Russian Economic History*, op. cit., p. 35–8; "Commerce Intérieur" (Domestic Trade), in *La Russie à la fin du 19ᵉ siècle*, Kovalevsky, M. W., ed., op. cit., pp. 633–46.

[5] Ettinger, S., "The Jews in Russia at the Outbreak of the Revolution," in *The Jews in Soviet Russia since 1917*, Kochan, L., ed., London, Oxford University Press, 1978, pp. 15–28.

Russia's commodities continued to be sold through trade fairs. Besides the strictly regimented short-term fairs for specific agricultural products (grains, flours, wood, alcohol, and so on) whose transactions were under state supervision and were carried out on the basis of uniform weights and measures, and besides newly emerging weekly trade fairs in various parts of the country, Russia continued to rely to a large extent (particularly until the end of the nineteenth century) on its traditional trade fairs, which for centuries had served as the country's basic distribution centers. According to data of the official Statistical Committee, the operations of the transport and of the sale of commodities in the Empire's 16,604 trade fairs in 1894 reached 1,061 million rubles, that is, 64,000 rubles per fair. About 87 percent of these fairs were small, each handling and trading for less than 10,000 rubles; 12 percent were medium-sized fairs, trading between 10,000 and 100,000 rubles; only 1 percent of the fairs had the character of provisional commercial centers, with sales varying between 100,000 and millions of rubles. According to data released by the Ministry of Finance, 16,452 trade fairs were held in 1904 with a trade volume of 1,064 million rubles. The broad areas concentrating high numbers of fairs were the Central region (2,162 fairs), Eastern region (1,758), Ukrainian (2,597), Southern (1,071), Southwestern (1,078), Central agricultural (2,308), Baltic (1,484), Northern (378), Northwestern (1,661), Caucasian (196), Siberian (629), and Central Asian (130).[6]

The Empire's most important wholesale trade fair was that of Nizhni-Novgorod, still regarded in the early 1900s as "the world's greatest fair." During the six weeks when it was taking place, from July 26 to September 7, it was attended by about four hundred thousand persons from Europe and Asia. Located on the Volga, at the junction of the Volga and Oka, near the confluence of Kama, Nizhni-Novgorod constituted the center of an extensive system of navigation connected with all the parts of the Empire. Later, thanks to the railway linking it to Moscow, Nizhnii was thus joined by the Volga with the Caspian Sea and with the countries that surround it. The central core of the fair was the Gostinnyi Dvor, consisting of sixty blocks of buildings with 2,530 shops, surrounded by a canal beyond which an additional two thousand shops were added to the fair. Notwithstanding the continuous decrease in its transactions due to changes in the country's development patterns and to the impact of the railways expansion, the transactions carried out at Nizhni-Novgorod in 1899, for instance, still involved sales of the order of 162 million rubles. The main commodities traded there were cotton and woolen articles, hides, furs, copper, other metals, haberdashery items, perfumes, and drugstore products.

In the east, among the 2,758 trade fairs, by far the most important one was that of Ibrid, in existence since the seventeenth century. Held between

[6] "Commerce Intérieur" (Domestic Trade), in *La Russie à la fin du 19ᵉ siècle*, Kovalevsky, M. W., ed., *op. cit.*, pp. 646–51; Dikhtiar, G. A., *Vnutrennaiaia torgovlia v dorevolutsionnoi Rossii*, *op. cit.*, pp. 140–1, 143.

February 1 and March 1, the fair was a center of trade of commodities from Siberia, China, and Central Asia. Its importance started to decrease from 1885 on, at the time of the opening of the Ural rail line which established a continuous commercial road between Siberia and Euro-Russia going from Tumen to Perm. In 1910, it was estimated that 50 percent of the Siberia furs that found their way to the important German fur industry of Leipzig, and an additional 30 percent of furs that went to London, still came via Ibrid directly from the Siberian centers of supply.[7]

Under the impact of the expansion of railroads and in the conditions in progress in industrial, banking, and urban growth, the overall transactions of the trade fairs declined continually from the late 1890s on. Particularly significant was these fairs' loss of both wholesale and retail trade. According to the available data, between 1899 and 1908 the number of wholesale firms participating in the trade fairs decreased by 28.4 percent, while the number of retail firms decreased by 25 percent, particularly after 1908. Yet, the trade fairs still continued to play a significant role, but only for the short span of time then left to the Tsarist society as a whole.[8]

6-3. Concerns in Foreign Trade

As I underlined previously (in Chapter 3), prior to the outbreak of World War I, Russia had the largest foreign debt of any country in the world. Its foreign debt amounted in 1914 to 4.2 billion gold rubles. The main part of this debt had been contracted during the twenty-five years preceding the war. The debt had grown rapidly after 1892 because of the increasing need to borrow abroad as the gains from trade were ever more insufficient for paying for both the imports as well as for the services for which Russia was indebted to foreign creditors.

Yet the period of Russia's greatest expansion of its exports occurred after 1890. Indeed, after that year, Russia's opportunities in foreign markets increased significantly and its exports climbed from 692.2 million rubles in 1890 to 1,520.1 million in 1913, over eight times greater than Russia's exports of 1860. Imports also increased over eight times but at lower levels (see Table 6.1). A close look at the yearly exports and imports indicates how and why Russian debts were bound to accumulate. On the basis of the yearly data, one can note that imports exceeded exports in the interval 1860–81 during three periods totaling eleven years (1867–9, 1872–6, and 1880–1). After 1881 and up to 1913, exports exceeded imports – except in one year, in 1899 – but the surpluses achieved were too small to cover both imports and services for which Russia

---

[7] "Commerce Intérieur" (Domestic Trade), in *La Russie à la fin du 19ᵉ siècle*, Kovalevsky, M. W., ed., *op. cit.*, pp. 647–8; "Fairs," in the *Russian Yearbook for 1912*, Kennard, Howard, ed., *op. cit.*, pp. 401–4.

[8] Dikhtiar, G. A., *Vnutrennaiaia torgovlia v dorevolutsionnoi Rossii, op. cit.*, pp. 145–6.

Table 6-1 *Russia: Exports, Imports, and Trade Balances, 1860–1913, in Thousands of Rubles*

Years	Exports	Imports	Balance
1860	181,383	159,303	22,080
1870	359,958	335,927	24,031
1880	498,672	622,812	124,140
1890	692,240	406,650	285,590
1900	716,218	626,375	89,843
1910	1,449,084	1,084,442	364,642
1913	1,520,133	1,374,031	146,102

Source: Khromov, P. A., *Ekononucheskoe razvitie Rossii v XIX–XX vekakh, 1800–1917* (Russia's Economic Development in the Nineteenth–Twentieth Centuries, 1800–1917), Moscow, Gosizdt, Polit. Lit., 1950, pp. 468–70.

Table 6-2 *Russia: Schema of the Balance of Payments, 1898–1913, in Millions of Rubles*

Credits	1898–1913	Debits	1898–1913
Exports	17,435	Payments for imports	13,313
Foreign capital in:		Interest and dividends	5,000
Industries	1,500	Redemption of securities:	
Private railroads	—	By the banks	—
Banking	350	By the railroad companies	400
Construction	375	Spending by Russian	2,000
& municipalities		tourists abroad	
State borrowing	2,000	Other expenditures	415
Other sources	240	Increases of the gold fund	772
TOTAL	21,900	TOTAL	21,900

Source: Nötzold, Jürgen, *Wirtschaftspolitische Alternativen der Entwicklung Russlands in der Ära Witte und Stolypin* (Economic-Political Alternatives of the Development of Russia in the Era of Witte and Stolypin), Berlin, Duncker & Humbolt, 1966, p. 163; also, Khromov, P. A., *Ekonomischeskoe razvitie Rossii, op. cit.*, p. 490.

was indebted to foreign countries, namely interests on government and municipal obligations held abroad, interests and dividends on foreign investments in transport and industry and expenditures of Russian tourists abroad (see Table 6-2). As Leo Pasvolsky and Harold G. Moulton pointed out, there was not a single year between 1892 and 1909 when the trade balance was sufficient to meet the service charges and the interests on foreign debt. And, as I pointed out (in Section 3-4), Russia unlike the developed countries, had no international income from any other source except its exports. During 1892–1903, interest and amortization on the existing foreign debt averaged approximately

300 million rubles a year, and between 1904 and 1909 400 million rubles a year.[9] The surplus of exports over imports averaged during the period 1892–1903 only 157.4 million per year – excluding the year 1899, when the imports exceeded the exports – and during the period 1904–9, when the surplus reached only 276.9 million per year. During the remaining period to 1914, there were only three years during which new borrowing was not necessary. Thus, at its state of development, Russia had to borrow continually increasing amounts of capital and at increasingly higher rates. The only thing that Russia could do was to try to generate conflicts among its potential creditors – French, Belgian, German, British, and even North American – in order to secure the needed capital imports at the best rate.

As I indicated briefly in Chapter 4, Russia needed to export foodstuffs as well as raw materials and semimanufactured goods, and needed to import raw materials, semimanufactured products, and manufactured products. Table 6.3 reveals the great stability of the combined shares of the indicated groups.

Jointly, the indicated export groups accounted for around 93 percent of the total exports; jointly, the indicated import groups accounted for 72–82 percent of total imports. The main items of the exported foodstuffs were, as already stated, cereals and flours, to which were added in increasing quantities various new items (eggs, butter, meats, and caviar). In the semimanufactured goods, the increasing part was constituted by cotton and woolen fabrics, as well as by pottery.[10] In the import groups, steel, coal, and metallic ore, as well as fibrous materials needed for Russia's developing textile industry, began to account for large increases. In manufactured goods, the emphasis was placed increasingly on modern equipment for industry and on instruments of all kinds rather than on manufactured products.

Given Russia's level of development, its geographical position, and the regime of its tariffs, how broad was the distribution of Russia's international trade? Did Russia's predominant commercial connections coincide with its predominant financial relations? Put differently, in which ways did Russia's international economic relations rely on its commercial partnerships and its need for foreign capital? I turn to these issues in the following section.

6-4. The Foreign Trade Network

While the structure of Russia's trade did not undergo deep changes, the geographical direction of its trade underwent appreciable transformations. At the beginning of the nineteenth century, 88 percent of Russia's exports and 78 percent of Russia's imports used the maritime way. By the end of the nineteenth

---

[9] Pasvolsky, Leo, and Moulton, Harold, *Russian Debts and Russian Reconstruction . . ., op. cit.*, pp. 17, 31–2.

[10] Pokrovsky, M. B., "Commerce Exterieur," in *La Russie à la fin du 19e siècle*, Kovalevsky, M. W., ed., *op. cit.*, pp. 695–701.

Table 6-3 *Russia: Structure of Exports and Imports, 1896–1913, in Percentages*

Period	Foodstuffs		Raw materials & semimanufactured products		Live animals		Manufactured products		Totals	
	Export	Import	Export	Import	Export	Import	Export	Import	Export	Import
1896–8	58.2	17.3	35.5	52.7	2.3	0.6	4.0	39.4	100	100
1899–1903	58.7	18.7	34.4	51.3	2.2	0.7	4.7	29.3	100	100
1904–8	59.9	22.6	33.0	48.8	1.7	0.7	5.4	27.9	100	100
1909–13	60.5	18.1	33.2	48.7	1.8	1.0	4.5	32.2	100	100
1913	55.2	17.3	36.9	48.6	2.3	1.3	5.6	32.8	100	100

Sources: 1896–8, Pokrovsky, M. B., "Commerce Extérieur," in *La Russie à la fin du 19e siècle, op. cit.,* p. 695; 1899–1913, *Rossiia 1913 god . . ., op. cit.,* p. 212.

century, thanks to the expansion of railways, 27 percent of Russia's exports and 46 percent of its imports were made via land ways. At the beginning of the nineteenth century, the main trading outlet, accounting for 86–90 percent of Russia's exports and imports, was the Baltic Sea, followed far behind by the Black Sea, the White Sea, and the Caspian. By the end of the century, while the Baltic Sea maintained the first place for imports, the Black Sea acquired the first place for exports. Foreign trade escaped the impact of the changes brought about by the expansion of railways.[11]

Russia pushed decisively toward increasing its tariffs to protect the emergence of its industries from the 1890s on. In 1885–90, the tariffs on all imported articles amounted to 28.3 percent, compared to, 12.8 percent, in 1869–75, when the drive for higher tariffs originated. For the manufactured products, the 1885–90 level reached 29.7 percent and for the imported raw materials 17.4 percent, compared to 12.1 and 5.4 percent respectively in 1869–75. Germany, Russia's principal provider of industrial equipment and the main importer of Russia's cereals, answered to Vishnegradskii's and Witte's protectionist policies by increasing its tariffs on Russian cereals. The Russian-German tariff persisted through 1892–4, and ended in 1904 by reciprocal concessions.[12]

The general distribution of Russia's trade was very wide, but most of this trade war concentrated in Europe, primarily in Western Europe for Russia's exports and in Central Europe for Russia's imports. The pattern of exports and imports did not change significantly from the end of the last century until the war (presented in percentages in Table 6-4). However, the shares of Russia's main trading partners underwent critical changes. Russia's exports to Germany remained roughly within the same range (25.7 percent in 1896–8, 29.9 percent in 1913). But with regard to imports, Germany's role increased appreciably (rising from 32.4 percent of these imports in 1896–8 to 47.5 of Russia's imports in 1913). On the other hand, the second great trade partner of Russia, Great Britain, decreased its relative shares appreciably for both Russia's exports and imports. For exports, its share during this period fell from 21.1 to 17.6 percent and its share of Russian imports declined from 18.8 percent to 12.6 percent.

As Table 6-4 shows, Europe purchased about 91 percent of Russia's exports and provided over 78 percent of its imports. Russia's main export markets were in Western Europe, particularly in Great Britain and Holland, while the main providers of Russia's imports were in Central Europe, particularly in Germany, which alone accounted for 47.5 percent of the total, that is, a little more than all the imports provided by the indicated world groups (excluding the minor group, "All others"). Outside Europe, Russia's main trading partners were Persia and China, which jointly accounted for only 5.8 percent of Russia's exports, but provided over 9 percent of its imports.

[11] *Ibid.*, pp. 689–90.
[12] Chaposhnikoff, M. G., "Tariff Douanier" (Customs Tariff), in *La Russie à la fin du 19ᵉ siècle*, Kovalevskii, M. W., ed., *op. cit.*, p. 550; Girault, René, *Emprunts Russes et investissements Français*, Paris, A. Colin, 1973, p. 587.

Table 6-4 *Russia: The Network of Foreign Trade in 1913, in Percentages*

	Exports	Imports		Exports	Imports
Northern Europe	7.2	6.6	Near & Far East	6.5	10.1
Norway	0.5	0.7	Egypt	0.6	0.4
Sweden	0.7	1.2	Persia	3.8	3.2
Finland	3.6	3.7	China	2.0	6.1
Denmark	2.4	1.0	Japan	0.1	0.4
Western Europe	45.1	20.2	North & South	0.9	5.8
Great Britain	17.6	12.6	America		
France	6.6	4.2	United States	0.9	5.7
Belgium	4.4	0.6	Brazil	—	0.1
Holland	11.6	1.5			
Italy	4.9	1.3			
Central Europe	34.1	50.1	All Others	1.9	5.7
Germany	29.9	47.5			
Austria-Hungary	4.2	2.6			
Southeastern Europe	4.3	1.5			
Romania	1.4	0.1			
Greece	0.5	0.1			
Turkey	2.4	1.3			
TOTAL	90.7	78.4	TOTAL	9.3	21.6

Source: Based on Pasvolsky, L., and Moulton, H. G., *Russian Debts and Russian Reconstruction*, New York, McGraw-Hill, 1924, p. 74.

The analysis of the structure of trade further underlines the critical role played by the main industrial powers as Russia's export and import trading partners. Five countries – Great Britain, Germany, France, Austria-Hungary, and the United States – absorbed more than half of Russia's exports of food-stuffs and over 70 percent of the exported raw materials and semimanufactured goods, but only 16 percent of Russia's exports of manufactured goods (actually mostly textiles). They provided, however, 77 percent of Russia's purchase of raw materials and semimanufactured products and 87 percent of its purchases of manufactured goods (mostly machines and equipment). Germany alone accounted for 66.5 percent of Russia's purchases of manufactured goods, amounting to close to 300 million rubles (out of a total equipment purchase of 450 million). It would, however, be erroneous to limit one's view to these data only. Indeed, international relations cannot be fully grasped by focusing only on the commercial relations while overlooking the capital movements. Russia's relations with Germany, and with Central Europe as a whole, were primarily commercial. Russia's relations with the other European countries, primarily with France, were largely financial. While Russian exports to Central Europe were used primarily to purchase imports, 40 to 50 percent of Russia's direct exports to Western Europe were used as payments for various debts and services. At the time, Russia's credit was so weak that the foreign investors demanded adequate securities rather than just promises to pay. Because of this, Russia's government had to purchase on the Russian market land mortgage bonds and to offer them to foreign investors, and in addition it had to buy railroad securities, which it sold to foreign countries.[13] While conducting only minuscule commercial relations with Russia, France was making massive investments in the Empire; from this point of view, France had become, as René Girault noted, "a privileged economic partner of Russia." By 1913 France had indeed poured into Russia billions of gold francs into all kinds of investments – in commercial enterprises and in government securities – while Russia held in France, then the center of Russia's capital holding abroad, 431 million rubles (out of a total of 594 million held abroad) in order to pay for the increasing Russian debt obligations. France, the "privileged partner," was then plagued by the worry that Germany would profit from its vast commercial ties to Russia in order to expand German relations in the financial field. A multifaceted competition was then opposing France, the world's greatest banking power, with Germany, the great industrial power, but also with all the other foreign powers attracted by the increasing Russian industrial and financial interests. By the beginning of the twentieth century, Franco-Russian relations appeared to be faring very well. In fact, under this apparently calm front, each one entertained suspicions about the other, because each one wanted to use the other without being used.[14] (I will return to some of these issues in more detail later on in Chapter 7.)

6-5. Concluding Comments

The most decisive influence on the expansion and intensification of Russia's domestic and foreign trade in the postreform period was undoubtedly the development of railroads. As I pointed out in Section 3-2, in such a vast empire as Russia – with a widespread population, small number of urban agglomerations, great distances separating the producer and the consumer, poor roads, and navigable waters and lakes frozen and nonnavigable six and seven months during the year along with small stretches of seas bordering only limited parts of its territory – railroads were bound to play an increasingly crucial role in each section of the economy. The railroads were indeed drawing into commodity circulation the country's remote regions, and were bringing into trade ever greater amounts of grains and agricultural products, raw materials, and semimanufactured and manufactured products. Railroads were modifying in many ways both the scope and the content of production and of consumption. In 1860 Russia had 1,626 kilometers of railway lines open; by 1890 it had

[13] Pasvolsky, Leo, and Moulton, Harold, *Russian Debts and Russian Reconstruction . . ., op. cit.*, pp. 35, 83.
[14] Girault, René, *Emprunts Russes et investissements Français, op. cit.*, pp. 576, 578, 580, 582.

30,496 kilometers; by 1913 it had at its disposal 70,156 kilometers of which 53,240 kilometers were within its territory *excluding Poland and Finland*. The cost of constructing the railways was estimated in 1909 at 6.7 billion rubles.[15] The railroads' volume of freight increased from some 571 million tons per kilometer in 1865 to 14,925 million tons per kilometer in 1890. By 1913 they were carrying 69,731 tons per kilometer – an increase in freight faster than the expansion of the rail lines. Because industry was developing more rapidly than agriculture, soon industrial railroad freight exceeded agricultural railroad freight.[15]

The railroad also increased the routes used to supply the market, drew into commodity circulation an ever larger mass of diverse products, and moreover concentrated a high activity in a few railway centers collecting, transiting, and marketing a large part of country's trade. While the main trade fairs were declining in importance in the 1900s, the railway's marketing centers began to swarm with middlemen – the intermediaries, the brokers, the small traders, the exporters – constantly drawing the rural areas into the orbit of their cash turnover, increasing the role of the market in the economy, and augmenting the volume of goods available for both domestic and foreign consumption. The growth of the railroads, the changes in their techniques, and the growth of and the communications network involving the telegraph and the telephone further expanded the connections between production and the market, and significantly modified the patterns of growth of the domestic and foreign trade. Certainly, without the railroads, the commercialization of agriculture and the development of industry would have proceeded more slowly, the pattern of interregional and international trade would have been different, and the country's Gross National Product (GNP) would undoubtedly have grown much slower than it finally did.[16]

Yet, in spite of all this, Russia's railway network was still quite insufficient, compared to the developments in the Western countries. At the end of 1913, Russia had only one kilometer of railway to each 100 square kilometers of territory, compared to Great Britain, Ireland, and Germany each having 12 kilometers for the same amount of territory. Further, for each ten thousand inhabitants, the extent of the Russian railway net was 5 kilometers, compared to 8 kilometers in Great Britain and Ireland, 15 in Denmark, and 27 in Sweden. Russia had evidently a considerable task before it to satisfy the growing needs of the country for transport facilities.[17]

---

[15] Mitchell, Brian R., *European Historical Statistics 1750–1970*, London, Macmillan, 1995, pp. 316–7; Kahan, Arcadius, *The Russian Economy, op. cit.*, p. 30; *The Statesman's Yearbook 1914*, London, Macmillan, 1914, p. 1258.

[16] Kahan, Arcadius, *The Russian Economic History, op. cit.*, p. 31; Liashchenko, P. I., *Istoriia narodnogo Khoziaistvo SSSR, op. cit.*, p. 512.

[17] Miller, Margaret, *The Economic Development of Russia . . ., op. cit.*, pp. 200–1.

CHAPTER 7

Money and Banking

7-1. The Monetary System

For comprehension of the Russian monetary system prevailing after the Crimean War, a brief recap of its origins and evolution may prove helpful. The basic features of this system were established under Peter the Great. At the time, the state issued gold rubles, silver rubles (at the exchange rate of 13.8 silver rubles to 1 gold ruble), and small copper change. By 1755, under the Empress Elizabeth, the state issued a new set of gold pieces – so-called imperials and semi-imperials – at a high rate of exchange against the silver rubles. Finally, under Catherine II in 1759, paper money made its appearance under the name of assignat rubles. The price of the assignat was set almost equal to that of the silver currency. The number of assignats increased sharply afterward, particularly during the war with Napoleon, and their value declined appreciably. By 1810, under Alexander I, Russia finally decided to reduce the amount of paper rubles in circulation, increase their value, and ensure the country's monetary stability. To do so, the state adopted as a monetary basis silver monometallism, that is, it made the silver ruble the country's basic monetary unit. At the time, it had also been projected to give to the assignant a precise value in relation to silver, but the project was not carried out.

The metallic money and the assignants continued to circulate jointly but at a high premium of exchange for the silver ruble. By 1818 the emission of assignants was stopped and a certain number of them were withdrawn from circulation. It became then increasingly possible to return to the metallic monetary system, legally silver monometallism (but in reality bimetallism, as gold and silver were exchanged at the ratio 1:15.5). This return was carried out under Nicholas I, particularly between 1839 and 1843; the state repurchased the assignants, and a series of legislative measures ensured that credit ruble notes would circulate just like the silver money and would be easily exchanged against it.

The Crimean War brought once again trouble in the national finances, with the mass of credit rubles increasing sharply and their value decreasing appreciably. This havoc was to be brought under control through a series of measures taken between 1882 and 1903 under the ministries of finance of Bunge, Vyshnegradskii, and particularly Witte. To stabilize the value of the ruble, simplify government financial operations, facilitate foreign trade, protect foreign investors, and raise the confidence of foreign creditors, the Russian government decided to place the currency system on an "equal footing" with that of the European powers, that is, to place it on the gold standard. The monetary reform was prepared and then carried out by a number of steps, particularly between 1890 and 1897. The value of the ruble in terms of gold was fixed on the basis of the prevailing exchange rate of the credit ruble (which involved in fact a devaluation of the ruble to two-thirds of its previous nominal value); it was thus decided that the gold ruble was to be equal to 1.5 credit rubles. On the basis of an ukase of August 29, 1897, the state put into circulation gold monetary units, that is, coins of 10 rubles (the imperial) equal to 15 credit rubles, and of 5 rubles (the half imperial) equal to 7.5 credit rubles, along with silver monetary units, that is, coins of 25 kopecks, 50 kopecks, and 1 ruble (equal to 100 kopecks) as well as small copper change.[1]

The critics of the reform contended that Russia's backward economy had been unduly forced, through the adoption of the gold standard, to assume a position of "nominal equality" with Western Europe, a situation which forced it to accumulate gold reserves that it did not possess, and for which it had to depend heavily on the inflow of gold from abroad. This inflow, the critics asserted further, was obtainable only through disastrous means, namely by keeping imports at undue low levels notwithstanding the needs of the Russian industry (for example, raw materials), while pushing in opposition to the farmers for increases in cheap exports, notably of grain, that were decreasing home consumption to unacceptable levels. Those in favor of the gold monetary measure asserted that the establishment of the gold standard narrowed the fluctuations of the value of the ruble, decreased the costs in foreign trade, established Russia's credit, and significantly increased the needed confidence of the foreign investors.[2] Actually, various critical factors not foreseeable in 1897 – the war with Japan, the revolution of 1905, and the social instability that followed – shaped in unanticipated ways the role of the gold ruble and its interplay with the credit notes in the country's monetary circulation. As can be seen in Table 7-1, the credit ruble was the determinant instrument of the monetary systems before 1897. It then accounted for 94 percent of the

---

[1] See notably Chipoff, M. J., "Système monétaire – Circulation," in *La Russie à la fin du 19ᵉ siècle*, Kovalevskii, M. W., ed., *op. cit.*, p. 768–75; Miller, Margaret, *The Economic Development of Russia . . ., op. cit.*, pp. 105–9; Bertrand, Gille, *Historie économique et sociale de la Russie . . ., op. cit.*, pp. 163–4; *Rossiia 1913 god . . ., op. cit.*, p. 173.

[2] Miller, Margaret, *The Economic Development of Russia . . ., op. cit.*, pp. 110–14.

Table 7-1 *Russia: Monetary Circulation as of January 1, 1897,
to 1914, in Millions*

Rubles	1897	1900	1906	1914	1897	1900	1906	1914
Gold	36	641	838	494	3.2	50.2	38.5	21.6
Silver	30	145	133	123	2.6	11.4	6.1	5.4
Credit	1068	491	1208	1665	94.2	38.4	55.4	73.0
TOTAL	1134	1277	2179	2282	100.0	100.0	100.0	100.0

Source: Based on Khromov, P. A., *Ekonomiceskoie razvitie Rossii . . ., op. cit.*, p. 545.

monetary circulation. After the 1897 reform, the dominant element became, for a short while only, the gold ruble. By 1900, it accounted for over 50 percent of the circulation, with the credit ruble falling to the second place with 38 percent of the total but convertible to gold on demand. By 1906 the credit ruble became again the key element, as the State Bank was centering its efforts toward increasing the gold holdings in its vaults under the conditions of war and social instability. By the end of 1913, the credit ruble was holding by far the first place, namely 73 percent of the currency in circulation, with the gold ruble ranking second with only 21.6 percent. But by August 14, the credit rubles were no longer convertible to gold. Thus, the reign of the gold ruble lasted in the shadow of the credit ruble and of the silver ruble from 1897 to mid-1914. The return to the gold standard had been made possible and had been maintained *inter alia* thanks only to massive borrowing abroad – as we will see in detail later.

7-2. Development of Banking

Russia's backward economic conditions were evidenced before the 1860s by the absence of a broadly organized credit system – except for mortgage credit – and by the lack of powerful banks. This situation started changing from the 1860s on with the organization of state credit institutions, which were to play an increasingly important role in the country's growth of industry and trade. First, the state established at the center of the country's credit system the State Bank (1860), followed by the organization of Savings Banks (1862), the reorganization of the Banks for Lending on Securities (1862), and, subsequently, the creation of the Peasants' Land Bank (1883), the Nobles' Land Bank (1885), and the *Zemstvo* and Urban Credit Bank (1912). In addition, some of the duties of these credit institutions were discharged by the Ministry of Finance Special Chancellery for Credit and the Department of Direct Taxation, particularly duties related to the redemption of land.[3]

---

[3] *Ibid.*, p. 81.

Along with these state credit institutions, an increasing number of private banks and credit organizations were established. Among them were municipal banks, mutual credit societies, as well as banks and societies for agrarian credit, private loan offices, and above all, from 1872 on, big joint-stock commercial banks. Let us consider now in some detail the functions of the main state and private credit establishments.

The State Bank (*Gosudarstvennyi bank* – in short, *Gosbank*) was initially created with the chief function of a deposit bank, endowed with the right to make loans and discount operations, and also empowered to execute commissions for the Ministry of Finance, and to issue credit notes not independently, but only for the account of the Treasury. Following an important reform that took place in 1894, the bank's statute was revised. It then specified that the bank was a "state bank directly subordinated to the Ministry of Finance," and that its tasks were to safeguard the monetary system, facilitate the circulation of the currency, and assist the country's industry, agriculture, and trade with short-term loans. Subsequently, by the ukase of August 29, 1897, Gosbank was further authorized to issue credit notes for its own account against its reserve fund in gold. In sum, Gosbank was set up to act in a double capacity: as a central state bank and as a crucial commercial bank. As a state bank, it was dependent upon the government since the state was its most important creditor and in addition because it could rely on the Treasury's assistance when in need. The Treasury, in turn, could rely upon Gosbank if it had to cover a deficit. As a commercial bank, the state's bank could advance to the government the deposited money of private persons, and on the other hand, it could, within limits, lend the government's money to private persons and to all kinds of private institutions. Indeed, owing to the want of capital and ready money in the country, the bank would have had insufficient means to carry on vast operations without large state deposits. In 1899, for instance, the private deposits in the bank amounted to less than one-third of the state deposits. Clearly, by all these arrangements, the Ministry of Finance could exercise direct influence on various developments in the country. By the beginning of the twentieth century, the advances made by the bank, notably to various industrial companies, increased sharply. The risk involved in these operations also increased sharply, as many of these companies would have been unable to exist at all without such external support.[4]

Table 7-2 shows the distribution of the discount and advance operations of Gosbank in 1909 and 1913. The figures indicate that Gosbank was gradually assuming a predominant position in the money market and that, in particular, it was becoming the "bankers' bank."

Gosbank thus certainly became the central bank of the entire Russian credit system, while on the other hand it played only in a limited way the role of a

---

[4] Drage, Geoffrey, *Russian Affairs*, New York, E. P. Dutton & Co., 1904, pp. 263–4, 266–7.

Table 7-2 *Russia: Discount and Advance Operations of Gosbank, 1909
and 1913, in Millions of Rubles and Percentages*

	Amounts, million rubles		Percent	
Advances	1909	1913	1909	1913
To banks	1,004	4,530	52.3	73.4
Direct credits	873	1,448	45.4	23.5
To middlemen	39	188	2.3	3.1
TOTAL	1,916	6,166	100.0	100.0

Source: Miller, M., *The Economic Development of Russia, op. cit.*, p. 148.

true state bank of issue comparable to that of the central banks of the developed industrial countries. The critics of Gosbank's operations asserted that the predominant influence of the Ministry of Finance on the bank's activities provided the ministers with the power to carry out through the bank not only their schemes of economic development but also their own preferences concerning certain specific individual undertakings in which they were interested. Such cases were cited against Witte. The critics also condemned the attempts to place under the state's control the most important industries (such as those connected with coal, iron, sugar, and oil), while on the other hand they opposed the state's efforts to support industries that had demonstrated the inability to lead an independent existence. Finally, critics from the agrarian community complained about the Gosbank's "undue" attention to industry and its "neglect" of the agricultural interests. In reply to these and similar criticisms, a keen analyst of Russian affairs, Professor Gerhardt Von Schulze-Gävernitz, remarked that "when all commercial undertakings depend so largely upon the state's encouragement and regulations for their existence, it is inevitable that the state and the bank should be close." This is the "best that can be obtained, as it corresponds to the backward economic conditions of the country."[5]

The state assumed full responsibility of the sums and capital deposited in the State Savings Banks, and in addition, exempted them from certain stamp duties and the taxes levied upon interest paid on money capital. Further, by the statute of May 30, 1905, the state authorized these banks to transact with the government's guarantee various forms of life insurance, a type of business in which the banks became rapidly successful. The direction of the State Savings Banks was placed in the hands of a manager under the supervision of the manager of Gosbank. The banks grew rapidly in towns but quite slowly in the countryside. Their number increased to a total of 8,005 by the beginning of 1913, with 8.4 million depositors and deposits of 1.6 billion rubles. One of the main objections raised against the policy of these banks was that their

[5] Von Schulze-Gävernitz, Gerhardt, *Volkswirtschaftliche Studien aus Russland* (National Economic Studies from Russia), Leipzig, Duncker & Humblot, 1899, quoted by Drage, *op. cit.*, p. 264.

deposits, instead of being used to create small credits benefiting the people who accumulated them, were mainly directed into state securities.[6]

The State Land Banks founded in the early 1880s had the objective of assisting both the peasants and the landlords to cope with the increasing difficulties resulting from the land reform of 1861. The Peasants' Land Bank was set to advance money to the peasant households, the communes, and the peasants associations, and was also empowered to buy land on its own account in order to sell it eventually to the peasants. By 1914 the land bought by the bank amounted to a total of 4.2 million dessiatins; by the middle of 1913, the bank had sold to the individual peasants 2.4 million dessiatins, and to the village communes 666,000 dessiatins. Supporters of communal land ownership criticized the bank for its land sales to individual peasants, while the partisans of individual ownership criticized the bank for its "undue encouragement" of the acquisition of land by the communes.[7]

The aim of the Nobles' Land Bank was to assist the members of the nobility by advancing ready money on the mortgages of their estates for periods varying from eleven to sixty-seven years. The sum advanced was not to exceed 60 percent of the value of the mortgaged property, except in certain cases when this percentage could go up to 75 percent at the most. In 1860, the noble landlords were already indebted to the government for the sum of 425 million rubles, a situation that meant, as Margaret Miller has pointed out, that the landlords had mortgaged 69 percent of their serfs.[8] By 1880, the state had paid off over 300 million rubles of this debt, by crediting the landlords for the indemnities payable to them for their land allotted to the peasants by the reform. By 1890, following the revision of the statute of the bank, the bank's purpose was redefined as being to assist the nobility by advancing ready money on their estates for periods varying between eleven to sixty-seven years. This aid did not, however, decrease substantially the movement toward breaking up large estates and decreasing the lands held by the deeply indebted gentry; whereas in 1877 the gentry held 73 million dessiatins of land, by 1907 this amount had diminished to 48 million dessiatins. As can be seen in Table 7-3, by the end of 1911 the Nobles' Land Bank advanced to the gentry 709 million rubles, for 26,900 properties of 38.4 million acres of mortgaged land. At the same time, the Peasants' Land Bank lent to the peasants 147 million rubles, for the eventual purchase of 3.7 million acres (valued at 180 million rubles). Data comparisons from 1907–11 show the speed at which the gentry's properties were mortgaged, that the mortgaged land increased (twenty-three times), and that the amount of advances made by the Nobles' Land Bank expanded (twenty-seven times). The transactions of the Peasants'

[6] Miller, Margaret, *The Economic Development of Russia . . .*, *op. cit.*, pp. 88–93, 151; *The Statesman's Yearbook 1914*, *op. cit.*, p. 1259; Liashchenko, P. I., *Istoriia narodnogo Khoziaistvo SSSR*, *op. cit.*, p. 699.
[7] Miller, Margaret, *The Economic Development of Russia . . .*, *op. cit.*, pp. 98–101, 157–8.
[8] *Rossiia 1913 god . . .*, *op. cit.*, p. 159.

Table 7-3 *Russia: Activities of the Land Banks, Nobles, and Peasants, 1907 and 1911–12*

a. Nobles' Land Bank

Transactions	1907	Jan. 1, 1912
Number of properties mortgaged	280	26,988
Mortgaged land in 1,000 acres	1,660	38,462
Value in 1,000 rubles	43,527	1,232,885
Sums advanced in 100 rubles	26,164	709,007

b. Peasants' Land Bank

Transactions	1907	1911
Land bought with bank aid in 1,000 acres	2,518	3,773
Value in 1,000 rubles	120,598	180,234
Sums lent by the bank in 1,000 rubles	107,831	147,327

Source: *The Statesman's Yearbook 1914*, London, Macmillan, 1914, p. 1200.

Land Bank expanded during the same period at far lower speeds: The land bought by the peasants increased by 50 percent and the sums advanced by the Bank increased by 36 percent.

Consider now the development of the private credit institutions and the volume and range of their activities. These institutions – including notably the municipal banks, the mutual credit societies, and the joint-stock commercial banks – numbered jointly a total of 400 establishments in 1900 and of 1,467 in 1914. On the eve of World War I, the commercial banks could be divided in two groups: those with Russian capital only, and those with foreign participation. In the second group there were three major investors: France, Germany, and the United Kingdom. The principal banks with French participation were notably the Azov-Don Bank, the Russo-Asiatic Bank, and the Bank of Private Trade of St. Petersburg; banks with German participation included the Russian Bank of Foreign Trade and the International Bank of Commerce of St. Petersburg; banks with British participation included especially the Russian Bank of Commerce and Industry. All of these banks were among the main Russian commercial banks. According to the data available as of January 1, 1914, the total capital of the joint-stock commercial banks of Russia amounted to 581.2 million rubles, of which 434 million rubles, 74.7 percent, were accounted for by the banks with foreign participation. Of the banks sharing the 434 million rubles, the share of banks with French participation amounted to 53.2 percent, with German participation at 36.4 percent, and with British participation at 10.4 percent. The foreign capital in all the Russian banks reached 237.2 million rubles.[9]

---

[9] Crihan, Anton, *Le capital étranger en Russie, op. cit.*, pp. 220–32, 238; Gindin, E. F., *Ruskie kommercheskie banki. Iz istorii finansovogo kapitala v Rossii* (Russian Commercial Banks. From the History of the Financial Capital in Russia), Moscow, Gosfinizdat, 1948, pp. 401–2.

In a developing country like Tsarist Russia at the time, the banks had to fulfill much broader, less focused roles than those of the banks in the developed countries. The Russian banks had indeed to intervene actively and directly in virtually all the economic branches, including financing crops, helping industries tied to agriculture and their exports and imports, as well as facilitating activities of other old and new industries increasingly engaged in new processes of growth and change.

7-3. Foreign Capital

To gain an overall view of the crucial role played by the foreign capital in the developing Russian economy, one has to consider the origin, extent, and pattern of foreign investments in the Russian private enterprise of the late 1890s, early 1900s, and 1916–7, as well as the nature, volume, and importance of foreign capital in the public debt and in the municipal debt. Let me consider these issues in turn.

The available data on foreign investments cover only the joint-stock corporations. They do not cover the share of foreign capital in single-ownership enterprises. Moreover, the exact character of ownership was often obscured by the concern that Russian nationals might be controlled by stockholders and directors of another nationality, financed by institutions of yet another nationality. Nevertheless, according to these data – made available largely after the fall of Tsarism – before the reform of 1861, Russia was home to some 78 corporations with a total capital of 72 million rubles; by 1900 there were 1,595 such companies with a capital of 2.3 billion rubles. By 1914 this number had grown to 2,163 with capital of 3.9 billion, and by 1916–17 the capital had grown to 5.3 billion. The foreign investments increased very rapidly: from 97.7 million in 1880, to 911 million in 1900, 2125 million in 1914, and 2,242.0 in 1916–17. At the later date, about 12 percent of the indicated foreign investment was placed in firms incorporated under foreign laws – namely Russian branches of foreign corporations or firms organized solely for Russian businesses – while 88 percent (1.9 billion rubles) were placed in firms incorporated under Russian law.[10]

The heaviest foreign investments in the industrial joint-stock corporations were mainly in the mining and metallurgical industries and in machinery and metal working, and to a lesser extent in the textile industry. The mining and metallurgical corporations encompassed iron ore, coal mining, petroleum, copper, gold, silver, platinum, manganese and zinc mining, along with steelworks. The machinery and metal working included all types of machinery

---

[10] Eventov, L. I., *Inostrannye kapitaly v Russkoi promyshennost'* (Foreign Capital in Russian Industry), Moscow, State Sots-Ekon-Izd., 1931, p. 25; Lewery, L. J., *Foreign Capital Investments in Russian Industry and Commerce*, Washington, DC, Dept. of Commerce, GPO, 1923, p. 4.

works, electrotechnical and mechanical works, foundries, factories for metal specialities, locomotive works, and other industries. The foreign investments in the metallurgy and machinery branches accounted for over 63 percent of the total capital of these industries and for close to 55 percent of the total foreign investments. In all the industrial corporations, foreign investment reached 72.7 percent of the foreign investment in all the Russian enterprises, with the balance of 27.3 percent invested in finance, trade, transports, and municipal services.

The distribution of foreign investments by the country of origin presented in Table 7-4 shows the overwhelming importance of the French, British, German, and Belgian capital; these investments increased rapidly from the 1890s on. At that earlier time, French investments amounted to 31.4 million rubles; by 1916–17, to 731.7 million. British investments rose similarly, from 30.1 million in 1880 to 507.4 million by 1916–17. German investments rose from 29.8 million rubles in 1880 to 441.5 million in 1916–17. Finally, Belgian capital invested in the Russian enterprises rose even faster, from 1.7 million rubles in 1880 to 321.6 million in 1916–17.[11]

The French invested their capital in a total of 175 industrial corporations. Their investments in the metallurgical industries centered on blast furnaces and steel-works, distributed notably in southern Russia. French capital controlled the Donets iron and steel-works, the Taganrog steel-works, and the South Russian Dniepr works. In the machinery and metal working group, French capital controlled the locomotives and shipbuilding works, along with the joint mining and petroleum industries. The next great investor, Great Britain, was involved in a total of 144 corporations. British capital centered much of its attention on the petroleum industry: British investments were distributed notably among the principal oil fields – Baku, Embra-Ural, Groznyi, and Maikop. British capital also played important roles in the textile industries, and in the mining of copper, gold, silver, and lead. Next, German capital was involved in a total of 187 enterprises. Besides machinery and metal working, German capital was active notably in the chemical industry (where fourteen German companies were at work), the petroleum industry, textiles, and transports and municipal services. Like the French, the Germans made significant capital investments in banking. Belgian capital – the last of the four big groups of foreign investors – participated in 107 enterprises. It occupied the leading place in mining and metallurgy, namely in petroleum, gold mining, plate glass, municipal traction, and electric power.[12]

At the time of the expansion of foreign investments, relations between the Tsarist government and the Russian enterprises became closer and more

[11] Eventov, L. I., *Inostrannye kapitaly v Russkoi promyshennost'*, *op. cit.*, p. 25.
[12] For detailed data, see Ol', P. V., *Inostrannye kapitaly v Rossii*, Petrograd, Institut Ekon. Issledovanii, 1922, pp. 10, 42, 72, 100; Lewery, L. J., *Foreign Capital Investments in Russian Industry and Commerce*, *op. cit.*, pp. 8–27.

Table 7-4 Russia: Foreign Investments by Fields and by Countries of Origin, 1916–17, in Million of Rubles and in Percentages

Fields	France	G. Britain	Germany	Belgium	U.S.	All others[a]	Total	Percent
Industries								
Mining & metallurgical	317.1	307.7	73.5	116.9	—	19.1	834.3	37.2
Machinery & metal working	158.4	28.0	87.2	47.2	60.9	11.0	392.7	17.5
Textile	57.1	69.7	45.5	9.3	—	9.6	191.2	8.6
Chemicals	31.6	1.4	31.5	11.2	1.2	6.6	83.5	3.7
Paper	1.0	4.3	23.6	—	—	2.5	31.4	1.4
Woodworking	5.3	10.7	0.3	0.6	—	8.8	25.7	1.2
Mineral products	5.0	—	0.9	11.4	—	2.2	19.5	0.8
Foodstuffs	5.7	18.9	9.6	0.7	—	2.4	37.3	1.7
Animal products	0.4	10.0	2.1	1.9	—	—	14.4	0.6
Finance, trade, public service								
Banks	113.3	25.7	84.7	2.5	—	11.0	237.2	10.6
Insurance	1.0	0.9	3.0	—	1.0	2.8	8.7	0.3
Trade	3.5	8.2	2.8	—	54.6	11.6	80.7	3.6
Transport	1.5	0.6	6.0	10.5	—	8.0	26.6	1.2
Municipal public service co.	30.8	21.4	70.9	109.4	—	26.9	259.4	11.6
GRAND TOTAL	731.7	507.5	441.6	321.6	117.7	122.8	2,242.9	100.0
PERCENT	32.6	22.6	19.7	14.3	5.3	5.5	100.0	

Note:
[a] Swiss, Swedish, Danish, Austrian, Italian, Norwegian, and Finnish investments.

Sources: Based on Eventov, L. Ia., *Inostrannye kapitaly v. Russkoi promyshlennosti, op. cit.*, p. 95; Crihan, Anton, *Le Capital Étranger en Russie, op. cit.*, p. 249.

beneficial than before. The state was facilitating development in certain directions, notably due to its attention to railroad expansion and to its increasing need for numerous industrial goods. While the administrative controls of foreign business remained detailed and restrictive, the connections between a number of high officials and the foreign firms grew in many ways. (Effectively, certain of these officials, as well as some of those of lower ranks, saw important opportunities for personal gain in their own cooperation with foreign investors.)

7-4. Credit and Public Debt

From the middle of the nineteenth century on, first Great Britain and then Germany played a decisive role in Russia's borrowing abroad. After Russia's invasion of Afghanistan in 1885, the British financial market was closed to Russia, a situation that continued until 1907, when the formation of the Anglo-Russian entente opened up a period of better understanding between the two countries. After 1907, considerable impetus was given to British investment, particularly in guaranteed state loans for the Russian railways. The relations with Germany also deteriorated in 1887 because of Russia's increases in tariffs aimed at securing a favorable balance of trade. These relations did not improve much in the immediately following years. Given these changes, the Russian government turned its attention toward another potential foreign help, namely France. By 1888 the latter had indeed become Russia's principal source of foreign capital, a situation that continued unchanged until the revolution of 1917.

The Russian state debt, both domestic and foreign, rose constantly from 1.8 billion rubles in 1865 to 9.0 billion in 1910, after which it declined back to 8.8 billion in 1913 and 1914. This massive growth up to 1910 was due to war expenditures, various types of reforms (including the crucial monetary reform of 1897), and to a large measure to public constructions – principally the railroad network – and to the increasing pressures to resort to foreign markets in order to pay the interest and amortization of the growing foreign debts. According to the most often quoted sets of data, the state debt in 1889 amounted to 4.4 billion rubles, of which 1.3 billion were accounted for by the borrowing for the railways. By 1909 the state debt rose to 8.8 billion rubles, of which 3.1 billion were accounted for by the state constructing or acquiring the railroads and by the state's spending on other needs. By 1913, the different issues making up the public debt consisted of seventy-two loans – short-term, long-term, or nonredeemable at any fixed date – the majority of which had been received at relatively low interest rates ranging between 3.5 to 6 percent. As shown in Table 7-5, Russia's state debt increased continuously and appreciably between 1895 and 1914; a major component of this increase was the rising foreign debt, which increased from 1.7 billion rubles to 4.2 billion. Percentagewise, the share of the foreign debt in the total state debt rose from 30 percent to 48 percent, as did its share of the annual payments in the total

Table 7-5 *Russia: State Debt, 1895–1914, at Five-Year Intervals, in Million of Rubles*

Jan. 1 of year	Total debt		Domestic debt			Foreign debt			
	Amount of debt	Annual payments on debt	Amount of debt	Annual payments on debt	Amount of debt	Percent of total debt	Annual payments on debt	Percent of annual payments	
1895	5,775	278.6	4,042	216.5	1,753	30	62.1	22	
1899	6,122	266.6	3,857	168.6	2,265	37	98.0	37	
1904	6,651	297.7	3,592	159.5	3,059	46	138.2	46	
1909	8,850	396.4	4,779	215.9	4,071	46	180.5	46	
1914	8,811	402.1	4,582	208.1	4,229	48	194.0	48	

Source: Pasvolsky, Leo, and Moulton, Harold G., *Russian Debts and Russian Reconstruction, op. cit.*, pp. 17, 177.

payment in the account of the debt, which tripled during these years, rising from 62 million in 1895 to 194 million in 1914. However, as will become apparent during the discussion of the Net National Product (NNP), the latter rose faster than the total state debt, so that the ratio of this debt to the NNP, while remaining at high levels, fell from 1895 to 1913 from 75 to 44 percent.

Russia's public debt – the debt including the state's debt as well as the state's guaranteed debt, namely the loans issued by state institutions and guaranteed by the state – reached much higher levels. Part of the guaranteed debt was also placed abroad, particularly before the monetary reform of 1897; after the reform, most of this debt was placed on the domestic market. As of 1914, the public debt had the following components:

- State debt: General needs, 5,746 million rubles + railroads, 3,108 = 8,854 million
- Guaranteed debt: Railroads, 1,884 million rubles + Two Land Banks, 2,069 million = 3,953
- Grand total: 8,854 + 3,953 = 12,807 million rubles[13]

To these totals one may also add the debt of Russia's municipalities, placed abroad and reaching according to various estimates 422 million rubles by 1914. However, the state guaranteed only part of this debt.

Clearly, Russia's attempt to establish from 1895 to 1914 a broader foundation for its national industry along with the development of banking and the growth of the national money market involved heavy expenditures that could not be met out of home resources. Faced with these and other obligations resulting from wars and military necessities, transport expansion, and complex consequences of the fundamental reforms of 1861, the Russian state was forced both to increase its reliance on the home resources and to resort to massive foreign borrowing – an essential and unavoidable feature of the period under review.

7-5. Concluding Comments

To understand international economic relations, we must study jointly the commercial relations and movements of capital among countries. I considered Russia's commercial relations in Chapter 6 and the movements of capital in Chapter 7. As we saw in the preceding chapter, Western Europe absorbed over 45 percent of Russia's exports and provided over 20 percent of its imports. Central Europe absorbed 34 percent of Russia's exports and covered over 50 percent of its import needs. The crucial role of the main European powers was evident. In Chapter 7, in our survey of the capital movements – of both the foreign investments in Russia's private economy, and Russia's resort to

---

[13] Crihan, Anton, *Le capital étranger en Russie, op. cit.*, p. 72.

foreign borrowing – the crucial role of Europe's main industrial powers was again evident.

In 1861, following the important estimations of Professor P. V. Ol', the foreign capital invested in Russian private enterprise reached only a total of 9.7 million rubles. In 1895 the foreign investments in such enterprises increased to 280.1 million rubles, and finally by 1914 they reached the impressive level of 2,125 million rubles. Foreign capital accounted then for over 33 percent of the capital placed in Russia's private enterprises, specifically: 44 percent of the industrial capital and 38 percent of the capital in the financial and commercial enterprises and in the public services. Foreign capital brought to the country not only several basic industrial developments and new techniques. It also mobilized the Russian capital for its ventures, it used local personnel and local resources, and it established numerous patterns of cooperation with the local economies, and these patterns extended to complex customs and language divisions. Foreign capital was certainly of critical importance to Russia's expansion into new channels and played a great role notably in the development of basic industries in the mining, metallurgical, machinery, and metal working fields. It was also a decisive contributor to the development of banking and credit relations.

The amount of Russia's state debt and the guaranteed state debt increased massively from 1895 to 1914. The accumulation of debt was due in particular to balance of payments problems, to issues related to the railway's development, to the increasing pressure for foreign payments that the state could not meet without new borrowing, and finally to the limited amount of Russia's own resources. Concerning the balance of payments, there was not a single year between 1892 and 1914 in which the trade balance was sufficient to meet just the service charges and the interest on foreign indebtedness. The railroads' great share in the total state debt of 1889 had risen to 31 percent and in 1909 to 36 percent (of a state debt estimated by Professor A. Finn-Enotaevskii of 4.4 billion rubles in 1889 and 8.8 billion in 1909). With respect to the level of foreign payments, we saw in Table 7-6 the continuous increase in the annual payments on account of the debt. Finally, with respect to the amount of the domestic resources, Russian computations of the Net National Product of 1894–1913 asserted that less than 11 percent of that total was available for investment – a percentage that reflects the limited development of Russia's economy and the incapacity of its leadership to push more vigorously forward the drive for development. All in all, Russia's position remained precarious, both in the home economy and in the world market.

CHAPTER 8

State Finance

8-1. Size and Structure of the Budget

A law of 1862 defined the method of compiling the budget. Subsequently, from 1866 on, the budgetary accounts consisted of the following parts: 1) actual receipts and expenditures; 2) transferences of sums among different branches of administration; and 3) extraordinary revenues (loans, war indemnities) and extraordinary outlays (railways, military, public works). The second category was abolished in 1892. In accordance with a law of June 1894, the ordinary receipts included direct and indirect taxes, duties, and royalties and receipts from state property, funds, and other sources. The ordinary expenditures composed the following main branches: the higher state institutions; the clergy; the ministries and their related services; the ministers of war and of the navy; and the service of the state debt (see Table 8-1).

Faced with the need to increase its outlays, the state fell increasingly into debt. It had to rely not only on increases in direct and indirect taxes, but on expanding domestic and foreign borrowing. The growth of outlays was due notably to the obligations resulting from the land reform of 1861 and the measures involving the transfers of land, to the charges resulting from railroad construction, and to the costs of the wars with Turkey and subsequently with Japan. The purchases of land by the Treasury, which the peasants were supposed to reimburse, weighed heavily on the budget for over twenty years. The expansion of the railway network affected the budget expenditures strongly from 1867 on. Finally, the wars occasioned enormous outlays from 1877 on.[1] Hence the budget increased continually within the expanding yet underdeveloped frame of the growing Empire. Starting at the level of over 417 million rubles in 1861, budgetary outlays ordinary and extraordinary reached half a billion rubles by 1869, over one billion by 1877 and 1878 (during the war with Turkey), and then again over one billion from 1893 on (see Figure 8-1).

[1] Bertrand, Gille, *Historie économique et sociale de la Russie . . ., op. cit.*, p. 165.

126

Table 8-1 *Russia: Structure of the Ordinary Budget, 1900 and 1913, in Percentages*

Sources of revenue	1900	1913	Branches of expenditures	1900	1913
Direct taxes	7.7	8.0	Higher state institutions	1.5	1.3
Indirect taxes	29.8	20.7	Clergy	1.5	1.5
Duties & state royalties	24.6	36.8	Ministries	53.9	56.8
State property & funds	27.8	30.7	Ministries of war & navy	26.4	26.7
Miscellaneous	10.1	3.8	Service of state debt	16.7	13.7

Sources: Based on *A Source Book for Russian History from Early Times to 1917*, Vol. 3, *op. cit.*, pp. 822–4; Khromov, P. A., *Ekonomicheskoe razvitie Rossii v XIX–XX vekah, op. cit.*, pp. 524–7.

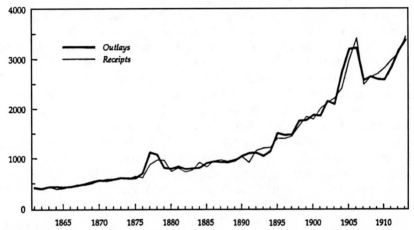

Figure 8-1. State Budget: Ordinary and Extraordinary Receipts and Outlays, 1861–1913, in Millions of Rubles

Source: Khromov, P. A., *Ekonomicheskoe razvitie Rossii v. XIX–XX vekah, op. cit.*, pp. 497, 501, 503, 517, 520, 521; Finn-Enotaevskii, A., *Kapitalizm v. Rossii, op. cit.*, pp. 206–7.

Officially, the magnitude of the budget outlays year in and year out equaled about 15–17 percent of the Net National Product, except in some exceptional years such as 1905, when the level of expenditures reached far higher levels. The per capita levels of the ordinary budget receipts rose from 10.4 rubles in 1895 to 20.8 rubles in 1913; the expenditures per capita rose from 12.5 rubles in 1895 to 19.8 rubles in 1913.

Consider now the basic components of the sources of revenues and of the branches of expenditure. As indicated in Table 8-1, the first class of ordinary receipts consisted of direct taxes. Recall that Chapter 3 (Table 3-1) pointed out that these taxes included taxes on land and other real estate, commerce and industries, and monetary assets. The indirect taxes, which yielded from

20–5 percent of the revenues, far more than the direct taxes, comprised excises on basic consumption items, namely on alcoholic beverages, tobacco, sugar, kerosene, naphtha, and matches, along with the important customs revenues. Next, the duties of various kinds, along with the state royalties – from mining, mint, the post, telegraph and telephone, and above all, from the spirits monopoly – yielded an increasing share of revenue, up to over 36 percent of the total. The revenue from property and funds included receipts from the state's extensive forests, other large estates, oil fields, gold mines, salt and mineral springs, collieries, fisheries, and, in addition to all this, the expanding state railway network. In the years considered, these also reached from 28 to over 30 percent of the total budgetary receipts. Finally, the most important receipts listed as miscellaneous were the redemption payments for the lands from the gentry, the crown, and the state. As we will see in detail in the next section, well over three quarters of the state receipts came from three principal sources: the indirect taxes, the spirits monopoly (the main item of the state royalties), and the state railways (the main item of the state property and funds).

On the side of ordinary outlays, the first branch of expenditure concerned the Ministry of the Imperial Court and the Higher State Organs, including the Senate, the State Council, and after 1906, the State Duma, as well as the state's Control Services. Next, the outlays for the clergy covered the expenditures of all the Orthodox Church's hierarchy and of all its churches and monasteries. The largest part of the expenditures – well over 50 percent in the data given in Table 8-1 for 1900 and 1913 – referred to all the ministries except those of War and the Navy – namely, the ministries of Internal Affairs, Finance, Justice, Foreign Affairs, Education, Communication, Trade and Industry (established at the end of 1905), and the Chief Administration of Land Organization and Agriculture (which before 1906 held the title of Ministry of Agriculture and State Property). The ministries of War and the Navy absorbed continually very large shares of the budgetary expenditures, including in 1900 and 1913 over a quarter of the total outlays. Finally the service of the state debt reached yearly around 14–15 percent of the state's outlays. As Section 8-3 will indicate, certain ministries redistributed large parts of their assigned outlays for various productive purposes, as well as for the operation of state undertakings, among which the railroads were by far the most important. The total expenditures on the railways were actually distributed under various headings and were part of the disbursements of a number of ministries (particularly the ministries of Finance and of Communications).

Table 8-1 focuses on the structure of the ordinary state receipts and expenditures – the most comprehensive part of the budget. The extraordinary receipts and outlays were not always consistently differentiated from the ordinary ones. Essentially, the extraordinary receipts grouped the revenues from the state loans, as well as the state's own deposits at the Gosbank. The extraordinary outlays concerned mainly certain disbursements for the railways and military purposes.

8-2. Analysis of the Receipts

The returns from direct taxes, as shown in Table 8-1, amounted in 1900 and in 1913 to 7.7 and 8.0 percent of the budgetary receipts. The Russians paid far less direct taxes than the French or the British. According to certain estimates, the direct taxes per capita in 1913 in Russia reached 3.11 rubles, compared to 12.35 in France and 26.75 in England; the development of direct taxes supposes, indeed, an already advanced economy.[2] The direct taxes on land and other real estate could not aim higher owing to the poverty of the mass of the peasantry, which bore many burdens. A general land tax was imposed in 1875, including from then on also the lands of the nobles, but the tax rates remained low. The poll tax, which had formerly been the chief tax, had been abolished by various laws passed between 1882 and 1885. The tax on trade and industry, comprising a basic tax (licenses) and an additional tax on capital and profits, became the most important direct tax yield in 1900 and 1913 – well over one-half of the total revenue from direct taxes.

The indirect taxes were far more beneficial for the Treasury. The excise taxes were levied on the basic goods of mass consumption except salt, on which the excise tax was abolished in 1881. The excise on sugar was raised many times (in 1863, 1873, 1878, and 1881), as was the critical excise tax on mineral illuminating oils (in 1813, 1878, and 1892). The excise on tobacco was also increased but without a general structural transformation. The total indirect taxes (as presented in Table 8-1) also include the customers' revenue, though many of these taxes were protective rather than fiscal. The only excise tax that decreased over time was that on spirits following the introduction of the state monopoly on the sale of spirits, first in part of the country in 1894, then in the Empire as a whole in 1902.

The next sources of receipts, the duties, reflected in a somewhat distorted fashion the country's personal and business transactions: Indeed, nothing in Russian life escaped the need for the stamp tax, either the simple official stamps ranging for any kind of document from 5 to 80 kopecks, or costly stamp sets proportional to the sums involved in any business act. The data for 1913 show the significant yield of all these stamps, namely 6.8 percent of the budgetary receipts, including notably stamps and registration fees (112 million), followed by transfer duties, port taxes, railway taxes, and fire insurance taxes – all totaling over 231 million rubles.[3]

The special entry on the state royalties concerning the receipts from mining, mint, communications, and so on were exceeded by far by the revenues from sales of the spirits monopoly. Government control of the liquor trade dated since the seventeenth century in Russia. Since 1767 four systems were tried

---

[2] *Ibid.*, p. 166.

[3] "Sources des Revenues de l'Etat" (Sources of State Revenue), in *La Russie à la fin du 19ᵉ siècle*, Kovalevskii, M. W., ed., *op. cit.*, p. 750–6.

to control the sale of spirits. From 1767 to 1819 the exclusive right of selling spirits was granted to certain private persons. Eventually the final results of this system were perceived as unfavorable, so a second system was tried from 1819 to 1827. This second system monopolized the distilleries, giving government stores rights to the wholesale trade, while confining the right of retail trade to a limited number of private persons. From 1827 until 1863, the state returned to the old system of leasing the retail sale of spirits to private persons who perceived that it was in their interest to push the sale of drinks by all means. Although the prices of licenses were high, it eventually became clear that this system diverted a rich source of revenue into private hands. This system was finally superseded by the fourth one, from 1863 to 1894. In this later system, the production of spirits was free; distilleries of a certain size were authorized once the set duty was paid. Distribution was also free once the tax imposed was paid, and the trade in alcohol was proclaimed "free" as any other trade. During the first year of this fourth system, called the "excise system," the consumption of spirits in Euro-Russia doubled, while three times as many public houses were opened. Finally, under the leadership of Count Witte, the state's spirits monopoly first tried on a part of the country in 1894 was expanded finally to the whole Empire in 1902. This system remained in force even after the collapse of Tsarism. It broadly excluded the private interest from the "drink trade" and transferred the public houses to salaried government agents but left distilleries to private enterprises (with the proviso that the amount produced would be fixed by the government and purchasable by the government) and that set the retail trade to be carried out by the government or by private persons specially licensed by the government.[4] The government's receipts from the spirits monopoly increased enormously, namely from 270.3 million rubles in 1900 to 899.3 million in 1913. However, one has to deduct from these totals the state's outlays on the spirits monopoly, which also reached considerable sums in some of the years considered. On the other hand, until 1902 the state continued to receive a large income from the excise on alcoholic beverages – of the order of 165 million rubles in 1900 – which because of the establishment of the spirits monopoly decreased appreciably from 1902 on. Indeed, the separate scope of the excise tax (on distilleries and on imports of liquor) decreased thereafter, yielding only 40 to 50 million rubles per year.

The revenues from the state's property and funds concerning notably the railroads and the state rent and leases of domains, forests, mills, and works, along with interests in banking operations and reimbursements of loan and advances, accounted jointly for around 25 percent of the total budgetary returns in 1900 and 1913. The main share of these returns came from the state railways. As I already indicated, the governments major interests in the development of the railways were military and strategic, and only incidentally

---

[4] See the "Spirits Monopoly," in Drage, Geoffrey, *Russian Affairs*, *op. cit.*, pp. 296–307.

economic. For a time, the state relied mainly on private construction of the railways while guaranteeing the stock of the railway companies. The outstanding period of railroad building occurred during the last thirty-five years of the nineteenth century. By 1889, the state owned only 24 percent of the railways, the remaining 76 percent being owned by numerous private companies. Though recognizing that foreign capital played an important role both in financing the system's construction and in providing it with specialized skills and technologically advanced equipment, the government decided by then to unify the railway tariffs (state and private) and to bring the entire system under the jurisdiction of the state. By 1900, after the state had taken over a few of the large private companies, over 75 percent of the system was in the hands of the state. (Refer to Section 3-2.) After 1905, the state allowed again new companies to build in underdeveloped areas, and by 1913 twenty-two private railroad companies still existed, with state-guaranteed debentures.[5] The state receipts from its railroads amounted to considerable sums – 21.2 percent of total receipts in 1900, and 23.8 percent in 1913. But, on the other hand, the ordinary outlays on the railways in fact exceeded the receipts in 1900 and left only a small surplus in 1913. Even this surplus disappears if one also takes into account the expanding expenditures – as we will see in Section 8-3.

The last significant receipts of the budget from miscellaneous sources (and only for early 1900) were the redemption payments for the land allotted to the peasants following the emancipation and paid off by the Treasury. The total land purchased by the peasants by 1900 accounted for 9.3 million allotments covering 33 million dessiatins priced at 895 million rubles. Given the enormous difficulties that the peasantry faced to pay both land taxes and the redemption charges, the government lowered the latter payments in 1881, and subsequent laws (of 1889, 1894, and 1896) extended the delays of payments of the arrears. Finally, by 1907, the government had to cancel the land redemption annuities, resulting in an annual loss for the Treasury of close to 100 million rubles.[6]

If one tries to assess the evolution of the Russian budgetary receipts from 1895 to 1913, for example, one may accept at least to an extent the remark of a careful analyst of Russian finance, Geoffrey Drage, who asserted that the state monopoly of the "drunk trade" and the "construction or acquisition by the state of the railways" were "the whole secret" of the rapid growth of the budget.[7] One could indeed note that in 1895, for example, the ordinary budget receipts amounted to 1,255 million rubles, and that they increased continually, reaching in 1900 1,704 million and in 1913 2,417 million. In 1895 the receipts from the excise on spirits amounted to 298 million rubles, while by 1900

[5] Westwood, J. N., *A History of Russian Railways*, *op. cit.*, 1964, pp. 59–61, 141, 143; other data from Table 8-1, *A Source Book for Russian History*, Vernadsky, George, ed., *op. cit.*, pp. 822–4; *The Statesman's Yearbook 1914*, *op. cit.*, p. 1240.
[6] Drage, Geoffrey, *Russian Affairs*, *op. cit.*, pp. 126–31, 277.
[7] *Ibid.*, p. 274.

they amounted to 164 million; on the other hand, the beginning of the spirits monopoly brought in an additional 270 million, bringing the total from spirits to 434 million. By 1913, the separate total from the excise alcoholic beverages brought 54 million rubles, while the spirits monopoly yielded 899 million, that is, a total of 953 million. Meanwhile, the railroad receipts, which amounted to 194 million rubles in 1895, also increased continually, reaching in 1900 361 million and in 1913 813 million.

However, these increases were not just the creation of the monopoly – which shifted some income from the private sector to the state – and the expansion of the railways and the state's, takeover of them. Another large factor was the continuous and decisive increase of the population in Euro-Russia as well as in the rest of the Empire (see Tables 1-1 and 1-2), along with changing interregional relations and various other transformations in the pattern of the country's development.

8-3. Analysis of Outlays

On its expenditure side, the Russian budget was constructed on the basis of the ministerial system – that is, all ordinary budget outlays were allocated according to the estimates submitted by each ministry. To ascertain exactly how large the ministerial disbursements were for state undertakings and in general the state's so-called productive expenditures (including railroad extensions and the improvements of ports), one encounters at times insuperable difficulties. Concerning certain state undertakings, we dispose of reasonable data. This is the case with respect to the disbursements on the railways made notably by the Ministry of Finance (whose main disbursements, however, were directed toward the needs of the state monopoly of spirits) and by the Ministry of Ways of Communications, along with disbursements made by the service of state control and by the service of the national debt. In addition, one must also take into account the capital outlays, that is, the special outlays for railroad construction extended through the extraordinary appropriations.

The expenditures on the railways alone amounted to around 28 percent of the ordinary budget expenditures for 1900 and over 23 percent of those for 1913, as well as of over 58 percent of the extraordinary expenditures for 1900 and of over 46 percent of those for 1913. These expenditures far exceeded the budgetary receipts for the railroads (361.7 million in 1900 and 813.6 million in 1913). Clearly, these were the most important state outlays on state undertakings. Other state expenditures were related mostly to the army's needs, and to the outlays for sea navigation and the ports and for the state's horse-breeding and agricultural properties. Important expenses were also incurred in relation to the war with Japan and to the military expenditures in China and Persia, along with certain specific outlays on the state's defense (fortresses and various other requirements of the army). The Ministry of Trade and Industry registered yearly expenditures of 40 to 50 million rubles between the date of its formation in 1902 and 1912, rising to 64 million rubles in 1913, but no breakdowns of these rather small expenditures are available.

The fiscal policies embodied in the ordinary and extraordinary budget outlays were often criticized in the Council of State and in the Duma. The critics asked that the government use its outlays as an instrument for a more effective economic development. They contended that a better policy would be to get out of debt eventually by going heavily into debt in the meantime rather than pursuing the official policy of balancing the budget and fulfilling the current foreign obligations in order to avoid the collapse of the entire credit structure. In short, the critics contended that if internal development were to be stimulated by new loans, the increase of the domestic production would eventually provide the means of both balancing the budget and of meeting the increased foreign payments. The critics were convinced that the state budget was in fact based on the precarious foundation of an overtaxed and restricted internal market for which the state was doing too little.[8]

8-4. Subnational Accounts

Along with the state's financial administration, Russia had regional administrations corresponding to the country's divisions into *gubernias* (territorial or provincial areas), districts, towns, and rural communities. The organs of the local administration, the *Zemstva*, had been established in thirty-six provinces of Euro-Russia by a statute of 1864. The rest of the country – the fourteen provinces of Euro-Russia, Transcaucasia, Siberia, Steppes, Livonia, and Estonia (excluding Poland) – were managed directly by the respective governors and others by agencies of the central government. A *Zemstvo* consisted of an assembly of deputies and of an executive bureau (*uprava*) elected by the assembly from among its members. By law, the proportion between the nobility and the peasantry within the assembly, first set at forty-two to thirty-eight, was subsequently changed to fifty-seven to thirty, with the difference assigned to the "third element," namely the salaried staff of the *Zemstvo*, doctors, nurses, teachers, and so on. To avoid any concerted action among the *Zemstva*, the government resolutely opposed the formation of a National *Zemstva* Assembly.

The principal role of the *Zemstva* was to look after the primary education and the sanitary needs of the population, watch the crop situation and take measures against approaching famine, take care of the "places of confinement," and keep roads and bridges under repair. Data for 1901 and 1913 show that their main expenditures were for public education, for which 19.2 percent and 31.0 percent respectively of the total outlays were disbursed, and public

---

[8] Pasvolsky, Leo, and Moulton, Harold, *Russian Debts and Russian Reconstruction . . ., op. cit.*, p. 58.

sanitation (including medical and veterinary care), for which 27.4 percent and 27.6 percent of the total *Zemstva* expenses were used. The principal sources of the *Zemstva* budgets were taxes on land and forests, and on houses, factories, and commercial establishments in the towns and the villages of their area. Just after the institution of *Zemstva*, their total receipts amounted to less than 6 million rubles; by 1900 their total receipts amounted to over 88 million rubles and by 1913 to over 253 million.

The towns also represented in the *Zemstva* or in provincial committees were in fact independent, with their own municipal governments. Like municipal governments everywhere else, they developed transport services by land and water, water supply, canalization, as well as banking and insurance services, and took care of all other types of collective needs. The towns' income came mainly from taxation of land values, taxes on trade and industry, duties, town undertakings and property leases.

The establishment of the *Zemstva* aroused hopes of special independent policies, forward-looking initiatives, and "liberalism" that were to be dashed. The improvements in educations, sanitation, agricultural methods, advances in transportation and communication, and overall development and modernization were limited by the general developmental framework of the country and by the limits of the resources disposable for each *Zemstvo*. While inevitable frictions were bound to arise between the central and the local governments, whose sphere of influence had never been clearly defined, the central government knew how and when to assert its powers. Finally, the local authorities were increasingly put under the control of the provincial governors. Various official reorganizations reduced the number of the delegates on the *Zemstva* assemblies and prevented their evolution into a politically effective national assembly.[9]

8-5. Concluding Comments

What do the budget data tell us about the role of the state in Russia's industrialization? Russian experts posit two main theses. One thesis, by Alexander Gerschenkron, asserts that the data reveal, from the beginning of the 1890s, "the basic substitution of the government's budgetary policies for the deficiencies of the internal market." Adds Gerschenkron, industrial policies became from then on "an accepted and in fact the central goal" of the government.[10]

---

[9] See notably Safonoff, M. V., "Budget de l'état et recettes et depenses des Zemstvos, des villes et des communes rurales" (The State Budget and the Receipts and Outlays of the *Zemstva*, the Towns, and the Rural Communes), in *La Russie à la fin du 19ᵉ siècle*, Kovalevsky, M. W., ed., *op. cit.*, pp. 787–802; Miller, Margaret, *The Economic Development of Russia . . .*, *op. cit.*, pp. 139–46; *The Statesman's Yearbook 1914*, *op. cit.*, pp. 1392–3.

[10] Gerschenkron, Alexander, *Economic Backwardness in Historical Perspective: A Book of Essays*, Cambridge, MA., Belknap Press, Harvard University Press, 1962, pp. 126, 128;

The second thesis, expounded by Arcadius Kahan, affirms that "during the period of industrial expansion of the 1890s the government exhibited little direct interference in the industrial sector (except railroads), and the amount of direct subsidies was modest indeed."[11]

Gerschenkron asserts that the thirty years preceding the 1890s represented a "period of preparation" for the changing governmental policies toward industry. From then on, the strategic factor in the spurt of Russia's industrialization was the following change in policy: The government ceased to view the growth of peasant demand for industrial goods as a prerequisite for industrialization and, on the contrary, considered the reduction of peasant consumption as the appropriate means for increasing investments and exports, and for ensuring the stability of the currency, and the availability of foreign exchange and of loans. Accordingly, the budget policies placed considerable fiscal pressure on the peasantry and impounded a large share of peasants' output. On the other hand, far from favoring indiscriminately all branches of industry, the government concentrated its attention on developing the output of iron and steel and machinery – in part because of the strategic interests of the railroads, and in part as a result of its new "substitutive budgetary process" for the deficiencies of the internal market. The budgetary data show clearly the efforts concerning the railroads and the underlying ferrous metallurgy, but are not as convincing concerning the "substitutive" budgetary process in other directions. Indeed, the budgetary railroad expenditures increased rapidly, from 98 million rubles in 1887 to 136 million in 1890, 242 million in 1895, and as I indicated in Table 8.2, to 448 million in 1900 and 742 million in 1913; if we add the extraordinary outlays, the total rose to 615 million in 1900 and 877 million in 1913. But the data for other "productive expenditures" are very uncertain. According to Margaret Miller, these "productive expenditures" amounted in 1913 to 17 percent of the budget. According to Theodore von Laue, however, under Witte, between 1894 and 1902, "more than two-thirds of the government's ordinary and extraordinary expenditures were poured into the economic development of the country." Von Laue arrives at this astounding figure by simply adding the expenses listed in the ordinary budgets "for the service on the government debt, for the Ministries of Finance, Communications, State Domains and Agriculture, State Control," and in the extraordinary budgets "for the expansion of railroads, ports and for the conversion of loans."[12] Clearly, such results are seriously questionable.

Gerschenkron, Alexander, "Problems and Patterns of Russian Economic Development," in *The Transformation of Russian Society: Aspects of Social Change Since 1861*, Black, Cyril E., ed., *op. cit.*, p. 217.

[11] Kahan, Arcadius, *The Russian Economic History, op. cit.*, p. 18.

[12] Miller, Margaret, *The Economic Development of Russia . . ., op. cit.*, p. 131; von Laue, Theodore H., "The State and the Economy," in *The Transformation of Russian Society: Aspects of Social Change since 1861*, Black, Cyril E., ed., *op. cit.*, p. 217.

Kahan asserts that the Russian government's policy with respect to industry and industrial development was neither uniform nor consistent throughout the postemancipation period. During the 1860s, and more so during the 1870s, the government increased tariff protection for both fiscal and general economic reasons. During the period of industrial expansion of the 1890s, "the government exhibited little direct interference in the industrial sector (except railroads) and the amount of direct subsidies was modest indeed." Under Witte, the official policies were closely related and coordinated to stimulate industrial development, but direct industrial subsidies remained modest. This does not mean, however, that if slump occurred, direct support of particular industries would not have been forthcoming. When the slump of 1900 took place, the government decided that Witte's expansionist policies outstripped the level of demand and that the government would have to avoid repeating such policies in the future. Indeed, in the industrial boom of 1909–13 the government limited its support of industrial development exclusively to tariff protection. Kahan notes further that certainly the railroads' contribution to the reconstruction of the ferrous metallurgy and to the location of this production in the southern region had been crucial. But, he adds, the stimulus for growth of the iron industry after the emancipation was exogenous to the previous development of this industry in Russia: The dynamism of the new South (merging the Donets coal basin with the iron mines of Krivoi-Rog) was nourished primarily "by the acceleration of investment of private capital in ferrous metallurgy." The protection tariffs provided favorable conditions for the growth of various industries and encouraged foreign firms to establish factories within Russia, but they also raised the costs of machinery to domestic users and hence discouraged the modernization of Russia's industrial plants.[13]

I believe that Kahan is right when he defines in broad terms the Tsarist government's policy toward industrial development as "neither uniform nor consistent" after 1861. I also agree that as far as the budget was concerned, besides the heavy outlays on the railways, "the amount of direct subsidies was modest indeed." Yet, the budgetary effort concerning specifically the expansion of the railways involved an increasing commitment on a far larger scale than one might have assumed in the early 1860 or 1870s. Subsequently, the actual spurts in railroad construction reflected only limited shifts in policy emphasis and more so the absence of adequate funds for a continuous and systematic expansion. While data on the railways' efficiency in the use of its assets and personnel are lacking, and while the revenues from the state's exploitation of the railways were rather limited, one could easily observe the wide-ranging impact of the railway on the expansion of commercial currents, the way that the railroad draw the agricultural districts and their grain products within these currents, and the general growth of supporting industries, including ferrous metallurgy. (This does not mean that Russia's industrial

[13] Kahan, Arcadius, *The Russian Economic History*, *op. cit.*, pp. 18, 20.

development from the 1890s on could have reached its higher level without the accelerated foreign and domestic investment of private capital in ferrous metallurgy and in other industries as well.) Furthermore, besides using the budget, the Ministry of Finance could and did use extensively, particularly from the 1880s on, Gosbank as an instrument of intervention in the economy to carry out its various schemes of development.

Though Russian capitalist growth and change remained very limited in relation to those of Western Europe, the emergence and expansion within the feudal backward Russian framework of the expanding, interlocking railway construction along with the increasing financial and commercial outspread did promote new patterns of development and did to an extent fit Russia into the broad patterns of European change characterizing the end of the nineteenth century and the beginning of the twentieth century – as we will see in detail in the next chapter.

CHAPTER 9

Overall View

9-1. Transition and the Agricultural Economy

Looking over the entire period after 1861 until the revolution of 1917, what conclusions can be drawn from the data presented throughout Part I about the extent of capitalist relations in the Russian economy in general and in the main branches of its primary, secondary, and tertiary sectors? In which specific ways were Russia's capitalist developments similar or different from those which took place simultaneously in the advanced West European economies? To what extent can the term "dual economy," which I used throughout this study, be considered as valid? Finally, which factors contributed to the collapse of Tsarism and to the emergence from the dual economy of a new economic order?

This concluding chapter on the Tsarist economy outlines the key aspects of the changes that occurred there from 1861 onward, presents some data on Russia's income and wealth, and methodically compares Russia's achievements with those in the West. I refer throughout this discussion continually to Lenin's work *The Development of Capitalism in Russia* in order to clearly indicate the ways in which these conclusions differ from those set forth by the founder of the Soviet regime.

Lenin's basic contentions concerning Russia's agrarian economy, which played a crucial role in the Bolsheviks' strategy and tactics against Tsarism, were from the end of the nineteenth century on the following: Russia's agriculture had become an "industry," that is, "a producer of commodities"; the peasantry lived henceforth in a "commodity economy" and was accordingly "completely subordinated to the market"; the surge of "property inequality" in the countryside dissolved socially the old peasantry and replaced it with "a rural bourgeoisie" and a "rural proletariat," that is, a class of commodity producers, and a class of wage workers. Lenin specified that "the development of commodity production and of capitalism had not emerged at once: first a transitional system had prevailed which mixed the corvée with the capitalist

138

system"; it was "the degree of the development of the home market which illustrated the degree of development of capitalism in the country"; and finally,
the division of the peasantry into classes was clearly perceivable when one considers "the distribution of the total number of horses belonging to peasants
in village communities." On this latter issue, Lenin presented a table based
on 1888 and 1891 data showing that in forty-nine *gubernias* of Euro-Russia,
22 percent of the 10.1 million peasant households who owned three horses or
more owned over 56 percent of the total horses available (17 million), while
55.9 percent of the peasant households had no horse at all or only one horse –
with the latter group owning only 17 percent of the horses available. On the
basis of these data, Lenin concluded that "if a fifth of the households possesses
half of the number of horses, one may unerringly conclude that no less (and
probably more) than half of the total peasant agricultural production is in their
hands."[1]

The data available on land ownership from some fifteen years after Lenin's
horses tabulation yield a different image of the situation in the countryside.
As shown in Table 4-3, in 1905, out of the 136.8 million dessiatins of land
then owned by the 12.2 million peasant households of Euro-Russia, at least
53 percent – that is, 73 million dessiatins – were owned by 10 million peasant
households with small patches of land of up to 15 dessiatins (a land size barely
sufficient for a household). This vast part of the land can be viewed as the
traditional subsistence sector, hardly able to provide any of its products for
the market. In addition, only a part of the 1.5 million households with landholdings varying between 15–30 dessiatins, covering 23 percent of the peasant
land, could have contributed a part of their output for the market. Most of
the peasant agricultural commodities must have come from the remaining
617,000 households with more than 30 dessiatins each, owning 23 percent of
the peasant land. Lenin's assertion that "more than half" of the total peasant
agricultural production was in the hands of the "peasant bourgeoisie" is clearly
contestable.

On the other hand, one should not overlook the changes that the gentry-
owned lands underwent. As of 1877, the gentry had in its hands 73 million
dessiatins. This amount decreased through sales to 49 million dessiatins in
1905 and then to around 43 million in 1915. According to the data provided
by the Nobles' Land Bank, in 1886–90, roughly 31–3 percent of the gentry
land was cultivated under the gentry's control, 30–2 percent of was leased,
and 35–9 percent was placed under mixed arrangements. By 1896–1900, only
20–2 percent of the available gentry land was cultivated under the gentry's
direct management. In the central and southern black earth regions, peasants rented the demesne lands in exchange for a share of the crops; many
landowners with little working capital found such arrangements convenient

---

[1] Lenin, V. I., *The Development of Capitalism in Russia," Collected Works,* Vol. 3,
pp. 67–69, 144–5, 172–9, 494.

Table 9-1 *Russia: Comparative Agricultural Yields for Grains and Potatoes in Poods per Dessiatin in 1914*

Countries	Wheat	Rye	Barley	Oats	Potatoes
Russia	45	51	47	46	459
United Kingdom	156	—	129	124	1047
Germany	132	110	132	137	900
Holland	170	98	158	147	—
France	86	70	90	85	631
Sweden	143	116	125	148	—
Switzerland	147	117	112	64	718

Source: Sbornik statistiko-ekonomicheskih svedenii ..., op. cit., pp. 115–16.

for avoiding costly inventory changes. Much of the other rented lands handled under mixed arrangements were not operated on the basis of sharecropping but on the basis of specific contracts with rural or urban entrepreneurs. The majority of the peasant households continued to be deprived either totally or largely of the land needed for a household. It is this situation that generated continuous opposition against the status prevailing in the countryside, an opposition accented by multiple harvest failure and by successive famines. The poor peasants had neither the financial resources to acquire land, nor the draft animals or the equipment needed to work on it. The majority of the peasants felt cheated of the land they believed belonged rightfully to them, and unjustly burdened by the price of allotments that were unable to support the increasing peasant population.[2]

Recall that the rural population of Russia (excluding Poland and Finland), while decreasing in relative terms from 90.5 percent of the total population in 1867 to 87.1 percent in 1897, and then to 84.7 percent at the beginning of 1914, in fact increased sharply in absolute terms, from 66.1 million in 1867 to 101.5 million in 1897 and to 135.8 million in 1914. This enormous rural population continued to rely on methods of cultivation long since discarded in Western Europe. Indeed, Russia's rural population still relied on the three-field system (fallow land, winter grain, summer grain) using primitive agricultural equipment, including the massive utilization of wooden plows and wooden harrows. Also, the peasants practiced these methods in communal lands on periodic reapportionments of peasants' land on strips allocated to different owners. The performance of agriculture fell far below that of the advanced Western European countries, as can be seen in Table 9-1.

[2] Gatrell, Peter, *The Tsarist Economy 1850–1917*, New York, St. Martin's Press, 1986, pp. 112, 115; Leon, Pierre, *La Domination du Capitalisme 1840–1914* (The Capitalist Domination 1840–1914); Garier, Gilbert, *Histoire economique et sociale du monde* (Economic and Social History of the World), Vol. 4, Paris, Armand Colin, 1978, p. 447.

While the agricultural output and the welfare of the Russian peasant continued to move "with the rhythm of droughts and of bumper crops," as Arcadius
Kahan noted, the government continued well until the revolution of 1905–6
to rely on "half-hearted measures" aimed at helping particular groups within
the agricultural population. None of these measures, however, was designed
to heal the fundamental problems of this principal sector of the country's
economy. After 1906 the government did introduce some dynamic elements,
including canceling the peasants' debts on the land redemption accounts and
intensifying local construction, irrigation, drainage, and land improvement
projects – but these policies remained insufficient and at variance with the
fiscal policies that continued to weigh heavily on agriculture. Stolypin's attempts in 1906 and 1910 to establish a new order in agriculture through the
creation of an increasing class of small proprietors came historically too late
and ultimately remained limited.

9-2. Transition and the Industrial Economy

As in the case of agriculture, I will now try to assess the complex impact of
capitalist relations in industry. The changes wrought by capitalism affected
handicrafts, small-scale industry manufacturing, the factory system, the structure of the labor force, the relations between the towns and the countryside,
the role of capital imports, and finally, Russia's share of manufacturing in the
international trade compared to that of the advanced capitalist countries.

With regard to the process of industrialization, Lenin drew attention in *The
Development of Capitalism in Russia* to the following broad outline emphasizing the "combinations of industry and agriculture." Patriarchal (national) agriculture, he stated, combined first with domestic industry for home consumption
and then with the corvée service for the landowner. Eventually the patriarchal
economy combined with artisan production and then with small-scale production of industrial products for the market. "Petty bourgeois" relations began
thus to emerge embracing not only industry but agriculture as well, combining wage labor in agriculture with wage labor in industry. As big workshops
with higher divisions of labor started to develop, we witnessed the genesis of
capitalist manufacturing. In time, this development linked the handicraft and
small-scale production, with its primitive forms of capital, with the large-scale
machine industry (the factory). Lenin then noted that "among our peasantry"
the combinations were "extremely varied," ranging from those that express the
most primitive economic system to those that embody "a high development
of capitalism." The most important factor concerning this development, Lenin
concluded, is the number of wage labor employed. In this regard, he asserted
that Russia had – at the end of the nineteenth century – about 10 million workers, namely 3.5 million agricultural workers (in Euro-Russia) and 1.5 million
factory, mining, and railway workers – that is, a total of 5 million "professional
workers." In addition, the country had about 1 million building workers,

2 million lumber workers and other "unskilled laborers," and 2 million workers in manufacturing not including in factory workers – again, a total of 5 million. Deducting from these 10 million the women and children, Lenin then pointed out that we get "7.5 million workers engaged in the production of material values in the country."[3]

Leaving aside for now the problems connected with Lenin's data (refer back to Chapter 5), let me recall in passing another outline of Russia's industrialization offered by another great revolutionary of the time, Leon Trotsky, in his work *The Russian Revolution of 1905*. According to Trotsky, Russian handicrafts had not detached themselves from agriculture and had not concentrated themselves in the towns but had remained attached to the agricultural population in the form of a domestic industry spread over the entire countryside. The big industry did not emerge in Russia via the "natural" or allegedly "immanent" path from manufacturing, because the handicrafts themselves had not had the time to tear themselves apart from domestic industry. It was foreign capital and foreign techniques that dominated the big industry from its birth onward. It was also Western capital and Western techniques that generated the conditions that allowed "the semi-Asiatic social conditions" to be endowed with the means of a great power able to mix in European affairs.[4]

Now recall briefly the path of development of Russian industry as it appears from different sources (see also Chapter 5). By the end of the 1850s, Russian industry consisted primarily of poorly developed handicrafts and small-scale commodity production, along with only a few manufacturing enterprises and large-scale factories and mines exploited primarily for the needs of the army. By 1860–70, the number of factories increased. However, with the exception of a few branches of industry, notably cotton spinning, calico printing, and some others such as paper, sugar, and tallow-melting, manual labor and technical backwardness still prevailed in industry, and mining. Eventually, by the 1890s, thanks to foreign capital, foreign techniques, and foreign entrepreneurship, large-scale mechanized capitalist industries began to appear in various branches, in the process growing and eliminating the backward craft establishments or transforming some of them into adjunct servicing facilities. In time, the transition to capitalist methods and techniques in certain industrial branches also promoted an increasing process of differentiation even among the factories themselves, favoring the expansion of those equipped with the highest technical standards. By the 1890s, the victory of the capitalist factory and the machine industry over the historical remnants of household production became evident in a number of industries. By the early 1900s, certain large firms combined and mergers took place in the advanced metallurgical

[3] Lenin, V. I., *The Development of Capitalism in Russia*, op. cit., 379–80, 385, 580–1.
[4] Trotsky, Leon, *Die Russische Revolution 1905* (The Russian Revolution of 1905), Berlin, Vereinigung Internationalen Verlagsanstalten, G.M.B.J., 1923, pp. 18, 21, 25, 28.

and mining industries of the south, in the petroleum industry, in the farm machinery factories, and in the railway car building plants. But, "despite their wide prevalence, great proportions and high degree of concentration," Russian monopolies, as Liashchenko pointed out, were still incapable of achieving any great international importance "comparable to the world monopolies of the advanced capitalist countries."[5] As H. J. Habakuk and M. M. Postan remarked in *The Cambridge Economic History of Europe*, "so long as the bulk of the Russian population was tied to a primitive agriculture the industrial enclave was bound to remain small and its progress impeded by a limited home market and inadequate supplies of domestic capital." The "salient feature of the industrial revolution" in Tsarist Russia continued to be its reliance on foreign capital and on foreign techniques.[6]

The total workforce, urban and non-urban, in the factory industry, mining, rail, and transport (as well as small-scale industry, to an extent) remained modest by the end of the 1880s but grew quite significantly from the 1890s until 1913, except for certain relatively short periods. According to various sources, the main changes in the workforce from 1865 to 1913 involved at the most an expansion from 706,000 to 3,929,000 in what Lenin called Russia's decisive "corner," embodying according to him "the quintessence of modern social relationships," that is, the "proletarian vanguard."[7]

Notwithstanding these changes, in fact modest for a country the size of Russia, the per capita outputs continued to remain far below those achieved in the West. The differences in the critical outputs of pig iron, steel, coal, electricity, and mechanical power, were enormous. In 1913 the per capita output for pig iron was one-eighth that of Germany and one-eleventh that of the United States; for steel again one-eighth that of Germany and one-eleventh that of the United States; for coal one-fifteenth that of Germany and one-twenty-sixth that of the United States; for electricity, the kilowatts per person was 16 in Russia, 320 in Germany, and 500 in the United States. (Utility generation did increase rapidly in Russia between 1905 and 1913, namely from 96 megakilowatts to 407 megakilowatts. Electricity spread widely during these years, but the vast majority of the country remained unelectrified.) In 1908 the mechanical power for every industrial worker (excluding mining) reached 91.9 horsepower in Russia compared to 152 horsepower in

---

[5] Liashchenko, P. I., *Istoriia narodnogo khoziaistvo SSSR, op. cit.*, p. 687.

[6] Habakuk, H. J., and Postan, M. M., eds., *The Cambridge Economic History of Europe*, Vol. 6, *op. cit.*, p. 23.

[7] These data are based on Liashchenko, P. I., *Istoriia narodnogo khoziaistvo SSSR, op. cit.*, p. 543; Ryndziunskii, P. G., *Utverzhdenie kapitalizma v Rossii 1850–1880, op. cit.*, p. 263; *Rossiia 1913 god . . ., op. cit.*, p. 223. (The figures differ somewhat from those of Tables 5-4 and 5-5 which offer other combinations by size of enterprises and by heavy versus light industry.) The quote from Lenin is from *The Development of Capitalism in Russia, op. cit.*, 584–5.

Table 9-2 *Russia: Comparative Exports of Manufactured Articles,[a] Annual Averages in Millions of Dollars at the Old Parity*

Period	Russia	Germany	U.S.	U.K. & Ireland	France	Austria-Hungary
1881–5	7	464	108	993	378	184
1886–90	10	509	111	996	385	179
1891–5	10	496	127	937	385	179
1896–1900	15	627	225	1018	433	198
1901–5	23	800	320	1172	520	238
1906–10	30	1110	441	1554	676	303
1911–13	39	1478	635	1902	817	350
1913	44	1615	721	2029	875	370

Note:
[a] According to the 1913 international classification.
Source: League of Nations, Economic, Financial and Transit Department, *Industrialization and Foreign Trade*, Geneva, League of Nations, 1945, p. 158.

the United Kingdom and 282 horsepower in the United States.[8] With regard to the creation and expansion of Russian industrial enterprises of the time, one must not overlook the decisive role of the foreign capital. For instance, out of the fourteen steel-works established in the south between 1888 and 1900, thirteen owed their foundation to foreign capital. Foreign capital also played a major role in the factories producing railway equipment, in the oil industry, in chemicals, and in related branches. In short, foreign control was overwhelming in the producer goods industries, whereas Russian capital was dominant in the consumer goods industries.[9]

In foreign trade, agriculture, not developing industry, held by far the dominant place. In particular, grains accounted for around 43–5 percent of the exports until 1900 and for 52 percent of Russia's exports of 1910. Russia's manufacturing exports remained extremely low compared to those of the West, as can be seen in Table 9-2.

In comparison with other countries, the level of Russian industry was certainly very low. According to Soviet computations, the value of industrial output of large-scale Russian industry amounted to as little as 6.9 percent of American production. In 1913, the net value of the output of Russian industry was equal to 47 percent of that of agriculture, while in the United States, the value of net output of industry was 170 percent of that of agriculture.[10] Clearly,

[8] Balzak, S. S., Vasyutin, V. F., and Feigin, Ya. G., eds., *Economic Geography of the USSR*, New York, Macmillan, 1949, p. 111; Coopersmith, Jonathon, *The Electrification of Russia 1880–1926*, Ithaca, NY, Cornell University Press, 1992, pp. 47, 68.
[9] Leon, Pierre, *La Domination du Capitalisme 1840–1914, op. cit.,* pp. 237–8.
[10] Gerschenkron, Alexander, "The Rate of Growth in Russia…," *op. cit.*, p. 155.

as Habakuk and Postan noted, in the prevailing conditions in Russia, the "industrial enclave" remained quite small within the surrounding mass of primitive agriculture. In his conclusion to *The Development of Capitalism in Russia*, Lenin himself finally noted, "the present rate of development of capitalism in Russia really must be considered as very slow." He then added that "it cannot be but slow for in no single capitalist country has there been such an abundant survival of ancient institutions that are incompatible with capitalism."[11]

9-3. Transition and the Tertiary Sector

To what extent and in which ways did the expansion of money relations, trade transport, and the population of the towns compared to that of the villages emphasize the development of capitalism in Russia at the end of the nineteenth and the beginning of the twentieth century?

Referring to these issues, Lenin as usual sketched first a kind of general Marxian theoretical framework of capitalist development and then tried to fit into it in a compulsory fashion the totally different conditions prevailing then in Russia. To start with he affirmed that the growth of commodity circulation and of capital accumulation had transformed merchant capital into industrial capital, while the growth of the industrial population at the expense of the agricultural one was "a requisite phenomenon" of every capitalist society, leading to the marked expansion of the towns. Yet, with regard to Russia, Lenin himself noted the existence within villages of "small local markets, primitive forms of artisan production, primitive forms of merchants and usury capital," the predominance there "of natural economy which accounts for the scarcity and dearness of money," and the assumption within these "pre-capitalist villages" of an importance "out of proportion to the size of their capital" by small traders, buyers, and rich peasants. Then, with regard to "commodity production," which he said depended on commodity circulation, he referred to the expansion of the railroads, the growth of the volume of foreign trade, and the growth of the turnover of the State Bank and of the state's Savings Banks. Finally, he added that the "most striking" expression of the growth of the country's industry and of its "separation from agriculture" was the growth of the towns, where population had increased from 1.6 million in 1863 to 6.4 million in 1897 – but he then also recalled that in Russia some parts of the industrial population tended to concentrate in "industrial villages" rather than in the towns.[12]

While Lenin paid close attention to the situation in Russia's countryside and put into relief its "pre-capitalist" characteristics, he referred only in passing to such related issues as the overall domestic trade, the growth and role of banking, the development of joint-stock companies, the importance of foreign

---

[11] Lenin, V. I., *The Development of Capitalism in Russia, op. cit.*, p. 599.
[12] *Ibid.*, pp. 383, 551–7, 565.

Table 9-3 *Russia: Comparative Length of Railways, 1860, 1880,
and 1900, in Percentages*

Regions	1860	1880	1900
World rail length (km)	106,311	357,395	749,793
Percentages	100.0	100.0	100.0
Europe minus Russia	46.7	37.9	28.4
Great Britain	13.7	7.0	4.0
France	8.9	6.6	4.9
Germany	10.9	9.1	6.9
Russia	1.0	5.0	5.9
North America	49.5	45.5	45.4
Rest of the world	4.1	15.7	26.4

Source: Léon, Pierre, *Histoire économique et sociale du monde*, Vol. 4, *op. cit.*, p. 148.

investments, and the relation of all these changes to those which were taking place in the developed capitalist countries. The absence of reference to domestic trade in general was certainly due to the Marxian contention that the workers in industry, agriculture, and, at times, also those in transport represented "the productive part of the population." The civil servants, the military, the rentiers, and the liberal professions constituted the nonproductive part, while those engaged in trade and communications and the servants constituted an intermediate semiproductive part. Indeed, according to Lenin's data – always referred to by the Soviet economists and historians – in 1897 the productive members of the population (without their families) numbered 23.4 million, the nonproductive 4.1 million, and the semiproductive 5.7 million, of whom only 1.6 million were in trade.[13]

While vast Russia had made significant progress on its railways after 1860, its system remained quite modest compared to the system of an advanced country of similar size, such as the United States (see Table 9-3).

Finally, with regard to the growth of towns – a growth representing, as Lenin put it, "the most striking expression" of a country's industrial growth – Russia again remained far behind the changes in the developed countries (see Table 9-4).

Lenin's own indicators – the "pre-capitalist" characteristics of the Russian villages, the predominance there of the "natural economy," the "scarcity and dearness of money," and within the country as a whole its relatively still "slow development of capitalism" – illustrate the overwhelming survival of pre-capitalist conditions in the countryside and the still limited development of capitalism in the towns within the Tsarist institutional framework at the beginning of the twentieth century.

---

[13] Khromov, P. A., *Ekonomicheskoe razvitie Rossii v XIX–XX vekah, op. cit.*, p. 229.

Table 9-4 *Russia: Comparative Town and Village Population,*
1908–14, in Percentages

Countries and regions	Town population	Village population
Russia	15.0	85.0
Euro-Russia	14.4	85.6
Caucasia	14.5	85.5
Siberia	11.9	88.1
Middle Asia	14.5	85.5
Great Britain	78.0	22.0
France	41.2	58.8
Germany	56.1	43.9
United States	41.5	58.5

Source: *Rossiia 1913 . . ., op. cit.*, p. 23.

9-4. Income and Wealth

According to the most detailed calculations available for Russia's Net National Product and National Income by sector of origin, for which we are in debt to Paul R. Gregory, Russia's Net National Product increased between 1887 and 1913, in billion rubles at 1913 prices, from 9.2 billion to 20.2 billion. During these years, the share of consumption fell from around 82.0 percent to 80.4 percent, while the share of government increased from 7.5 percent to 11.0 percent, and that of net investments (minus the net foreign interest and payments) rose from 9.5 percent to 11.4 percent. For a low-income country, government's share was extremely high due to wars and military expenditures and to its vast and costly administration.

The National Income by sector of origin changed in a number of interesting ways between 1883–7 and 1909–13. As can be seen in Table 9-5, the share of agriculture, by far the largest, fell from 57 percent to 50.7 percent, as did the share of trade, which shrunk from 9.8 percent to 8.1 percent. On the other hand, the share of factory industry increased appreciably from 9.6 percent to 14.9 percent, while an increase was also registered by transportation, which grew from 2.2 percent to 5.8 percent (see Table 9-5).

Aggregate production series at 1913 prices over the period 1885 to 1913 yield an annual rate of growth of approximately 3.25 percent on the basis of Gregory's end-use and sector of origin calculations. (These estimates are, however, higher than the two usual estimates cited in the literature, namely of S. N. Prokopovich and R. W. Goldsmith, respectively, of 2.6 percent and 2.7 percent, and closer to other estimates, such as these of M. E. Falkus and V. E. Vorzar, of around 3.1 percent.)

Gregory points out that in 1913 the total output of vast Russia almost equaled that of the United Kingdom. The high Russian result was evidently due to the volume of agricultural output. But the per capita output per worker

Table 9-5 *Russia: National Income by Sector of Origin, 1883–7, 1909–13, in Million of Rubles at 1913 Prices and Percentages*

	1883–7		1909–13	
Sources	Million rubles	Percent	Million rubles	Percent
Agriculture	5,044	57.0	10,294	50.7
Industrial factories	846	9.6	3,023	14.3
Industrial handicrafts	550	6.2	1,311	6.5
Transportation	199	2.2	1,173	5.8
Construction	445	5.0	1,035	5.1
Trade	869	9.8	1,640	8.1
Net government production	186	2.1	565	2.8
Net housing production	386	4.4	743	3.7
Other services	324	3.7	508	2.4
TOTAL	8,849	100.0	20,292	100.0

Source: Based on Gregory, P. R., *Russian National Income 1885–1913*, Cambridge, Cambridge University Press, 1982, p. 73.

Table 9-6 *Russia: Comparative per Capita Outputs in 1880 and 1913, Using the United Kingdom (= 100) as the Basis*

Countries	1880	Countries	1913
Switzerland	99.4	Switzerland	100.0
Belgium	86.6	Belgium	92.7
Netherlands	79.7	Denmark	89.3
Norway	68.2	Netherlands	78.1
France	68.2	Norway	77.6
Germany	65.1	Germany	76.9
Denmark	58.2	France	71.2
Sweden	44.5	Sweden	70.4
Russia	32.9	Russia	33.7
Continental Europe	48.6	Continental Europe	50.6

Source: Léon, Pierre, *Histoire économique et sociale du monde*, Vol. 4., *op. cit.*, p. 72.

in agriculture in Russia was much lower than that of the developed countries. The basic dichotomy between Russia's aggregate economic power and its low per capita achievements continued even during its more rapid growth between 1880 and 1913. According to the data presented in Table 9-6, comparing per capita outputs of 1880 and 1913, France, Germany, and the Scandinavian countries significantly increased their per capita output relative to that of Great Britain. Russia, however, continued to remain at a low level, on a par with such counties as Romania, Serbia, and Greece.

According to the estimates of the Russian economist A. L. Veinshtein, Russia's total wealth at the beginning of 1914 amounted to 69,193 million rubles. (The same year, the Net National Product reached 20,266 million rubles.) Agriculture, forestry, fishing, and hunting accounted in the total wealth for the largest share, 34.8 percent, to which should be added an additional 9.5 percent for wealth in the hands of the agricultural households. Further, according to Veinshtein, the share of large and small industry amounted to only 8.8 percent, and that of transport and communication to 10.5 percent, while that of the towns, including homes, construction, and trade, totaled 17.3 percent and the share of their population's wealth an additional 10.1 percent. Finally, the joint share of government and various institutions and their holdings reached 9.0 percent. The ratio of the share of agricultural installations and equipment to those of industry was then, according to Veinshtein, close to four to one (34.8/8.8) in 1914.[14]

9-5. Concluding Comments

The great events from February 1917 onward that marked the disintegration of the Tsarist government, the Imperial administration, the army, and the entire fabric of the society, leading to the revolution of October 1917, had as background the long, persistent, growing hostility of the peasantry and of part of the industrial workers toward the Tsarist state. The peasants' repeated revolts were part and parcel of Russia's socioeconomic reality long before the abolition of serfdom. The 1861 reform opened the door to many changes in agriculture as well as in the economy as a whole, but it intensified rather than assuaged the peasants' opposition to the situation prevailing in agriculture and its prospects. The peasants believed that the reform actually deprived them of what they viewed as their ancestral right, namely their ownership of the land. The increased land scarcity, in conjunction with the growth of the peasant population after 1861, the successive crop failures (of 1868, 1872, 1875, 1880, 1883, and 1895), the famines (of 1891, 1898, and 1901), and the heavy burden of the payments for the allotted lands increased peasant agitation and the danger of peasant uprisings. The insurrection of 1905 brought only limited concessions concerning the indemnity payments, but those concessions did not suffice to bring tranquility to the villages. The Stolypin reforms of 1906–10 aimed boldly at splitting the peasantry via the development of economically viable independent peasant landowners, but these reforms did not assuage the peasants' hostility to the post-1861 statute and to the nobles. As Lazar Volin put it, the historic contest between the peasant and the landlord shielded by the Tsarist state continued until the peasant won "a complete victory" in October 1917. But then, Volin rightly adds, this was a pyrrhic victory. Indeed, after the October Revolution, the

---

[14] Vainshtein, A. L., *Narodnoe bogatsvo i narodnokhoziaistvenoe nakoplenie predrevolutsion-noi Rossii* (National Wealth and National-Economic Accumulation of Prerevolutionary Russia), Moscow, Gosizdat, 1960, p. 419.

Bolsheviks eventually carried out their own objective, namely the collectivization of agriculture.[15]

An interesting parallel can be drawn between the ultimate causes and results of the French Revolution of 1789 and the October Revolution of 1917.
Marxian or non-Marxian historians long believed and often reaffirmed that
the bourgeoisie had carried out the French Revolution. Further, these historians believe that, the revolution was achieved through the substitution of the
"bourgeois capitalist order to the feudalist one." Since the 1960s, however, the
consensus concerning these beliefs has begun to change profoundly. The first
frontal attack against the old conception was pertinently carried out by Alfred
Coban in the early 1960s, followed since then by a number of various studies by
distinguished analysts. The thesis of Coban can be summarized as follows: The
revolutionary leaders of 1789 were mainly lawyers, petty office holders, and
government servants, and not businessmen or entrepreneurs of commerce or
industry. Not all the revolutionaries were hostile to seignorial rights and dues –
which the peasants, not they, destroyed; nor were they the "standard-bearers
of capitalism," even though their actions eventually favored capitalism's future
development. Moreover, the capitalists themselves were largely uninterested
in politics both before and during the revolution, and did not share the aspirations of the reformers. In fact, the bourgeoisie was far from being a united,
self-confident class with a clear self-conscious goal. In addition, the frontiers
between the feudal ownership and the bourgeois ownership were not always
easily traceable. In short, "it was the peasants rather than the bourgeois who
really opposed the systems and overthrew it." As another critic of the old
myths pointed out, the radical reforms of 1780 were the product of "a political
revolution with social consequences and not a social revolution with political
consequences."[16]

No comparable critical studies are as yet available concerning the revolution of 1905 and of February 1917, and of the Bolshevik Revolution of October
1917. The prevailing myth presents the latter as a "proletarian revolution." No
thoroughly documented studies have challenged the Marxian theories as formulated by Lenin, according to whom the revolution of 1905 already had the
unique character of being "bourgeois-democratic in its content but proletarian
in the methods of its struggle."[17] Having finally alleged that Russia had already
experienced the "bourgeois democratic revolution" in 1905, Lenin asserted

[15] Leon, Pierre, *La Domination du Capitalisme 1840–1914, op. cit.*, pp. 447–8; Volin, Lazar,
"The Russian Peasant: From Emancipation to Kolkhoz," in *The Transformation of Russian
Society*, Black, Cyril E., ed., *op. cit.*, p. 293.
[16] See the important study of Doyle, William, *Origins of the French Revolution*, Oxford, Oxford
University Press, 1980, pp. 2, 7–40; see also Furet, François, and Richet, Denis, *La Revolution
Française* (The French Revolution), Paris, Arthème Fayard, 1973, who note that their studies
make them "reject the concept of the bourgeois revolution as the key to the liberating
explosion of 1789" (p. 9).
[17] Liashchenko, P. I., *Istoriia narodnogo Khoziaistvo SSSR, op. cit.*, p. 662.

after the revolution of February 1917 that the latter had as rationale and purpose only, "as is always the case after the fall of absolutism," the "redistribution of the spoils among the bourgeois and petty bourgeois parties" (the Cadets, the Socialist Revolutionaries, and the Mensheviks). According to Lenin, a new revolution was hence needed to concentrate all its forces against state power, not to improve it but to "smash and destroy it." All this was to be done by the oppressed classes with "the proletariat at their head."[18]

Just like the French liberals of 1789 and 1792, Lenin and the Russian Bolsheviks of 1917 deliberately overlooked the critical role of the peasantry in bringing about the fall of the state machine. Lenin and his followers wished to fill in the Marxian framework the revolutionary events of 1905 and 1917 more or less appropriately by downgrading the significance and the implications of the peasant revolts against the gentry and their state protectors before and after 1861, and by upgrading the role of a "proletarian avant-garde" as a leading force of the insurrection. As the Bolshevik leader Grigori Zinoview put it in 1924, "The first new idea that Lenin introduced into Marxism was his outlook upon the peasantry . . . the union of a working class revolution with a peasant war."[19] The peasants, whether openly and brutally or not, incessantly aimed at acceding at full land ownership and at liberating themselves completely from the feudal shackles. It was the masses of the peasants who lost faith in the World War and brought about the disintegration of the Tsarist army and administration. The Bolshevik "professional revolutionaries" took over the disintegrating state machine after the collapse of the liberal gentry and intellectuals, who proved incapable of managing the post-Tsarist regime following the February 1917 revolution. The leaders of the October Revolution were not "proletarians" – any more than the leaders of the French Revolution had been "bourgeois" – and most of the actual proletarians did not associate with them. Lenin, Trotsky, and their associates – such as Nikolai Bukharin, Zinoview, Felix Dzerzhinsky, Karl Radek, Anatoli Lunacharski, Mikhail Frunze, and many others until Joseph Stalin's dictatorship – were middle-class intellectuals or semi-intellectuals of "petty bourgeois" origin. The Central Soviet Government, the Council of People's Commissars, and the Central Committee of the Communist Party were made up mostly of these middle-class intellectuals allegedly installing in the name of the proletariat its "revolutionary dictatorship." Actually, as we shall see in Part II, which examines the autocratic Soviet party-state that emerged through the Bolshevik coup d'etat, that state had nothing to do with the "dictatorship of the proletariat" either at its beginnings or during the long period of alleged "transition from capitalism to communism."

---

[18] Lenin, V. I., *The State and Revolution*, in *Collected Works*, Vol. 25, *June–September 1917*, Moscow, Progress Publishers, 1964, pp. 404–8.

[19] Quoted by Maynard, Sir John, *The Russian Peasant and Other Studies*, New York, Crowell Colliers, 1962, p. 357.

In sum, until the Bolshevik coup d'etat, Russia's semi-Asiatic socioeconomic structure and development had been shaped by the four hundred years' rule of the centralized, autarchic, absolutist, patriarchal traditions of the Tsarist state, built on feudal foundations. Notwithstanding the 1861 emancipation of the serfs, and the attempts at partial industrialization, by the beginning of the twentieth century, Russia was still a backward, agrarian, semifeudal country. The state's and foreign investments indeed achieved only the partial modernization of certain branches of industry. The drive for the desired economic shift toward modernity had been predicated on the expansion of the heavy industry needed for the growth of the railroads. But this primary, one-sided direction of investable resources remained in conflict with the need to expand the poor, small-scale, backward, peasant economy and to expand small and medium industry, the indispensable connecting links in the process of a sustained, balanced growth.[20] Thus, as noted throughout this study of Russia's transition under the Tsars, its system of autarchic centralized rule, patriarchal traditions and institutions, and targeted investment primarily in railroads and heavy industry proved incapable of bridging the expanding gap between its poor agricultural setting and the developed and rapidly advancing Western economies. As we will see in Part II, many of the characteristics of Imperial Russia were preserved in the succeeding system, which in theory was supposed to eradicate them completely.

---

[20] Haarland, Hans Peter, and Niessen, Hans Jachim, *Der Transformation prozess in Russland, Ergebnisse einer empirischen Untersuchung* (The Transformation Process in Russia, Results of an Empirical Research), Bonn, 1997, pp. 17–18.

THE SOVIET ECONOMIC TRANSITION

CHAPTER 10

The Socioeconomic Framework

10-1. Territory and Population

The Soviet Union succeeded the Tsarist reign after the revolution of October 1917. The Union lasted seventy-three years, after which it collapsed and was dismembered in 1990–1. During its existence, the Union's socioeconomic and juridical framework underwent a number of crucial transformations. Immediately after the revolution, during the Civil War, the Bolsheviks in power established what came to be known as the rule of War Communism (1917–21), which aimed on the economic plane at eliminating market relations and replacing them with an all-out system of centralized commands and controls. This system was in turn discarded in 1921 and replaced by a new coordinating mechanism called the New Economic Policy (NEP) (1921–8), which aimed at economic recovery and reconstruction and which for the purpose combined centralized command with the reestablishment of certain market relations. The NEP was followed in 1928 with an all-embracing policy of massive industrialization and of collectivization of the peasantry, inaugurating the era of Central Plans. After World War II, various attempts at reforming the planning system were undertaken, notably in the 1960s and then in the 1980s. The first became known as "The New System of Planning and Economic Incentives," the second, much vaster in scope, named perestroika (restructuring), aimed at eliminating many aspects of the inefficient and disintegrating central planning system and at returning in some respect to the organizational concepts of the NEP.

I will examine in detail each of these phases later on. For now, let me sketch briefly the principles of organization of the Soviet state and its officially established socioeconomic framework. These principles concerned notably the role of the Soviets and the Communist Party, and the targets of Soviet development. Principles and goals are well reflected in the four successive constitutions adopted between 1918 and 1977. All these documents affirmed that at the apex of the state's administration was the Supreme Soviet of People's

155

Deputies; that the state's leading force was, however, the Communist Party, the "nucleus" of all public organizations; and that the final goal was communism via a transitional socialist stage, under the worker's dictatorship. Besides affirming these principles, each constitution reflected the particular historical setting at its adoption and the leadership's evolving political concerns. The first constitution of July 1918 of Russia, then the only Soviet republic, asserted essentially (as did also many subsequent documents issued between 1918 and 1935) that the dictatorship of the proletariat was the basic instrument of Soviet development in the period of transition from capitalism to socialism. The constitution officially set up the Russian Socialist Federal Soviet Republic (RSFSR) and formally declared that the outcome of the revolution was settled. The second constitution, enacted in July 1923 and ratified in January 1924, followed the formation of the Soviet Union in December 1922; accordingly, it legally confirmed the establishment of the Union of Soviet Socialist Republics (USSR) as a multinational federation. The third Soviet constitution, called the Stalin Constitution, was adopted in December 1936 and ratified in January 1937, during the forward push of centralized planning. It affirmed that "socialism" had already triumphed in the USSR and that the Soviet working class could no longer be designated as a "proletariat." In the "intermediate" socialist period constituting "the first stage of communism," the Soviet dictatorial regime had allegedly become the dictatorship of the entire working class. These more or less confusing contentions prevailed officially until the collapse of the USSR – with some variations introduced by the fourth and last Soviet constitution adopted in October 1977. The latter added notably that the Soviet Union had become "a socialist state of the *whole people*," that its target was the building of a "classless communist society," that the political system of the socialist society "continued the state and social forms of the people's power," and that, as always, the people exercised this state power through the Soviet of People's Deputies while the Communist Party continued to act as "the guiding and directing force of Soviet society."[1]

Territorially, the Soviet Union's borders changed in the west in relation to those of Tsarist Russia, and changed again during and after World War II. In 1913, the USSR's area would have encompassed 22.3 million square kilometers. From 1917 until September 17, 1939, it extended over 21.7 million square kilometers. By 1940, after the occupation of parts of Poland, it increased to 22.7 million square kilometers and then, after various postwar adjustments and until its collapse in 1990–1, its territory covered 22.4 million

---

[1] On Soviet constitutional materials in English, see notably Feldbrugge, F. J. M., *The Constitutions of the USSR and the Union Republics Analyses, Texts Reports*, Leiden (Netherlands), Sijthoff, 1979; *Basic Laws on the Structure of the Soviet State*, transl. by Berman, J. Harold, and Quigley, John, D., Jr., Cambridge, MA, Harvard University Press, 1969; Scott, Derek J., *Russian Political Institutions*, New York, Praeger, 1961, pp. 81–9.

square kilometers. As far as its federal composition was concerned, at the time of the constitution of 1923, the USSR numbered only four Soviet Socialist Republics. By 1924 their number had increased to six, and by 1931 to seven. During the first phase of World War II, after various territorial changes, the number of federated republics increased to sixteen by 1940. Finally, after other readjustments, following a law of 1956, the number of the Union's federated republics was reduced to fifteen, a figure that remained unchanged until the collapse and dismemberment of the USSR in 1990–1. The changes in question involved not only the number of the republics but also their names and territorial ranges. Thus, for instance, the six republics of 1924 were, besides the RSFSR, the Ukrainian SSR, the Belorussian SSR, the Turkmen SSR, the Uzbek SSR, and the Transcaucasian SSR (which at the time included three autonomous republics: the Azerbaijan SSR, the Georgian SSR, and the Armenian SSR). The fifteen republics that finally composed the USSR are shown in Figure 10-1. Their populations in the year of their formation, in 1940 and in 1991 (January 1), as well as their territorial sizes at the time of the collapse of the USSR, are presented in Table 10-1.

As shown in the table, in the fifty years from 1940 to the end of 1990, the Soviet population increased from 194.1 million to 290.0 million – close to 95.9 million people. The RSFSR, the largest Soviet republic, encompassing 76 percent of territory of the USSR, accounted for 38.5 million of this increase (40 percent). The next two biggest republics, the Ukraine and Kazakhstan, covering jointly 15 percent of the territory of the USSR, contributed 21.3 million to the population increase (22 percent). Finally, the remaining twelve republics, embracing only 9 percent of the USSR territory, accounted for 36.2 million of the population increase (the balance of 38 percent). Put differently, in the fifty years considered (from 1940 until the end of 1990), the major population increase occurred not in the RSFSR but in the rest of the USSR.

A close look at the population changes in the USSR as a whole from 1913 to the end of 1990 reveals three periods of great decreases. The first occurred during the Civil War from 1917 to 1922, involving a fall from 163.0 million to 136.1 million – a decrease of 26.9 million. The second took place during the collectivization process. According to the data now available, in the four years between 1925 and 1929, the Soviet population increased normally by 10.4 million, from 143.0 million to 153.4 million; but in the next four years, between 1930 and 1934, the total population *decreased* by some 0.7 million, namely from 157.4 million to 156.7 million. The sharpest drop occurred between 1933 and 1934, when the Soviet population shrunk in one year by as much as 6.2 million, that is, from 162.9 million to 156.7 million.[2] The third drop in total population occurred during and after World War II. According to various Soviet sources, from 1940 to 1946, the Soviet population fell from 194.1 million

---

[2] *Naselenie Sovetskogo Soiuza 1922–1991* (Population of the Soviet Union, 1922–1991), Moscow, Nauka, 1993, p. 118.

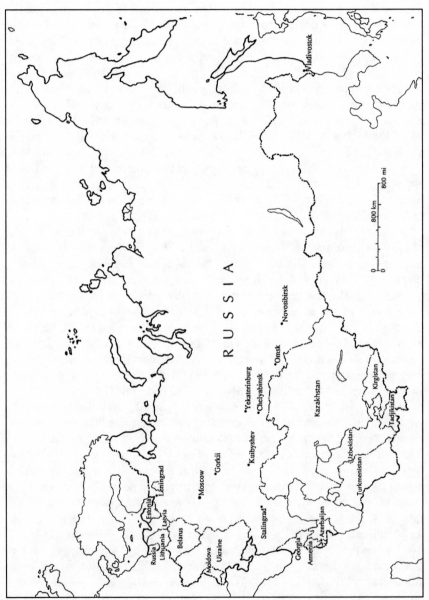

Figure 10-1. The Soviet Republics

158

Table 10-1 *USSR and Soviet Republics: Population in the Year of Formation[a], 1940 and 1991[b]*

Regions	Years of formation	Population in millions			Territory in thousands of sq. km. in 1991
		In years of formation	1940	1991	
USSR	1922	136.3	194.1	290.0	22403.2[c]
RSFSR	1917	91.0	110.0	148.6	17075.4
Ukraine	1917	27.5	41.3	51.9	603.7
Belorussia	1919	4.4	9.0	10.2	207.6
Uzbekistan	1924	4.2	6.6	20.7	447.4
Kazakhstan	1920	5.4	6.1	16.8	2717.3
Georgia	1921	2.4	3.6	5.5	69.7
Azerbaijan	1920	1.9	3.3	7.1	86.6
Lithuania	1940	3.0	3.0	3.7	65.2
Moldavia	1924	.2	2.5	4.3	33.7
Latvia	1940	1.9	1.9	2.7	64.5
Kirghistan	1924	.9	1.5	4.4	198.5
Tadjikistan	1924	1.0	1.5	5.4	143.1
Armenia	1920	.7	1.3	3.4	29.8
Turkmenistan	1924	1.0	1.3	3.7	488.1
Estonia	1940	1.1	1.1	1.6	45.1

Notes:
[a] Among the Soviet republics, the year of formation concerns their establishment as autonomous republics or regions.
[b] January 1, 1991.
[c] Including the surface of the White Sea and of Azov Sea, i.e., 127,300 square kilometers.
Sources: *Narodnoe khoziaistvo SSR 1922–1982* (National Economy of the USSR 1922–1982), Moscow, Finansy I statistika, 1982, pp. 11–12; *Narodnoe khoziaistvo SSSR v. 1990 g.* (National Economy of the USSR in 1990), Moscow, Finansy i statistika, 1991, pp. 68–73.

to 170.5 million – the staggering figure of 23.6 million. The 1940 level was reached again only between 1995 and 1996.[3]

The urban population's increases were continuous from the beginning of the Soviet industrialization drive in 1929. During the half century from 1940 to the end of 1990, percentagewise the sharpest urbanization increase took place between 1950 and 1960 – an increase of 10 percent; the lowest urbanization increase occurred between 1980 and the end of 1990, namely by 3 percent. Over the entire half century, the urban population doubled percentagewise but increased three more times in real terms, from 63.1 million to 191.6 million. Correspondingly the decreases in the rural population were massive from 1929 on. As a percentage of the total, the rural population was almost as large in

[3] *Ibid.*, pp. 118–19.

1929 as in 1913 or 1917 (81 percent compared to 82 percent). On the other hand, the change over the entire half century from 1940 until the end of 1990 brought about a sharp decrease of the rural population. In percentage, the decrease was from 67 to 34 percent and, in absolute figures, from 131.0 million to 98.4 million.

A close look at the urban and rural population changes by republic shows that the urban population increased significantly in all the federal republics. These increases were of course not identical. The most massive urban increases during the half century were registered in the RSFSR and the Ukraine, followed by Uzbekistan, Khazakstan, and Belorussia. (In the RSFSR, the increase amounted to 71.9 million out of a total of 128.5 million for the Union as a whole.) Percentagewise, the interrepublic urban population in 1940 ranged from a low of 13 percent to a high of 34 percent. By the end of the 1990s, the urban population ranged from a low of 31 percent to a high of 74 percent.[4]

With regard to the complex nationality structure of the Soviet Union, one must note that the Union, like Tsarist Russia, was home to over one hundred nationalities with as many different languages. But enormous differences in size existed among them. For instance, according to the 1979 official data, only twenty-two nationalities had a population of over 1 million. Among these twenty-two, the Russians and the Ukrainians were the most populous, with 43.4 and 16.2 percent of the Union's total population (137.3 million and 42.3 million respectively out of the total of 262.0 million). The other ten of this group accounted for 27.8 percent of the Union's total population, while all the other nationalities with fewer than 1 million each accounted jointly for the balance of the total, that is, for only 12.6 percent. This does not mean, of course, that in *each* of the other thirteen republics of the Union besides Russia and the Ukraine the dominant nationality – no matter its place in the Union scale – was not in full command even if it did not account for the majority of the population.

Under the impact of the policies of collectivization and industrialization developed from 1929 on, the Soviet leaders achieved massive changes in the structure of the labor force. The labor force in agriculture is estimated to have shrunk from 54.6 million in 1928 to 32.0 million in 1940 (including in the later year 29.0 million in the collective farms and 3.0 million in the state farms) and then fell to some 25 million in 1987 (over 12 million in the collective farms and 12.6 million in the state farms). All the other sectors registered crucial increases. To start with, the industrial manpower – excluding the managerial apparatus – more than tripled from 1928 to 1940, rising from 4.3 million to 13.1 million, and then again almost tripled between 1940 and 1987, increasing from 13.1 million to 38.1 million. Very significant increases

---

[4] See *Narodnoe khoziaistvo SSSR za 70 let* (National Economy of the USSR for Seventy Years), Moscow, Finansy i statistika, 1987, p. 378; *Narodnoe khoziaistvo SSSR v. 1990 g.* (National Economy of the USSR in 1990), pp. 68, 71–7.

Table 10-2 *USSR: Employment in the Economy's Sectors in 1928, 1940, and 1987*

National economy and its sectors	In millions			In percent		
	1928	1940	1987	1928	1940	1987
Total national economy	63.7	62.9	130.8	100.0	100.0	100.0
Industry	4.3	13.1	38.1	6.8	20.8	29.1
Agriculture & forestry	54.6	32.0	24.6	85.7	50.9	18.8
Transport & communication	1.4	4.0	12.0	2.2	6.4	9.2
Construction	.8	2.0	12.0	.9	5.6	9.2
Trade & related activities	.6	3.5	12.0	.9	5.6	9.2
Municipal economy	.1	1.5	5.0	.2	2.4	3.8
Health, education, culture	1.2	5.0	24.5	1.9	7.9	18.7
State apparatus	.7	1.8	2.6	1.1	2.8	2.0

Source: Computed from *Trud v SSSR, Statisticheskii Sbornik* (Labor in the USSR Statistical Collection), Moscow, Finansy i statistika, 1988, pp. 26–30.

were also registered notably in employment in construction, health education and culture, and the state apparatus. Percentagewise, by 1987, industry and agriculture accounted jointly for less than half of the total employment, while all the other sectors accounted for over one-half – namely for 52.1 percent compared to only 7.5 percent in 1928. It is interesting to note that by 1987 employment in the bloc of services – trade and related activities, the municipal economy, health education and culture – reached surprisingly close to one-third of the total employment (9.2 + 3.8 + 18.7 = 31.7 percent). (See Table 10–2.)

The changes in the interrelated patterns of employment in the state, cooperative, and private sectors can be dramatically visualized by considering these patterns at three crucial historical junctures: in the early NEP, on the eve of World War II, and in 1990 at the end of the Soviet system. In 1924, the state sector accounted for 14.8 percent of the employed population, the cooperative sector for 1.2 percent, the private sector for 75.4 percent, and other mixed ownership 8.5 percent. By 1939, the impact of administrative and structural policies of industrialization and agricultural collectivization changed dramatically the pattern of employment: The state accounted for 50.2 percent of the total, the cooperative sector (collective farms and cooperative *kustari*) for 47.2 percent, while the private sector had been reduced to 2.6 percent. Finally, by 1990, the massive shifts during the fifty years between 1940 and 1990 increased the state sector's employment to 81.6 percent of the total, the cooperative sector held 14.9 percent, and the "resurgent" private sector still held only 3.5 percent, with mixed ownerships accounting for the balance of 0.9 percent.[5]

[5] *Narodnoe khoziaistvo SSSR za 70 let, op. cit.*, p. 401; *Narodnoe khoziaistvo SSSR 1922–1982* (National Economy of the USSR 1922–1982), Moscow, Finansy i statistika, 1982, p. 11.

Table 10-3 *USSR: Monthly Income Levels per Family and per Capita in 1990,*
in Rubles

Social strata	Monthly income per family	Total population	
		Income levels	Percent
Workers and employees	179	Up to 100	18.3
Industrial workers	197	100–25	13.7
State farm workers	144	125–50	14.4
Collective farmers	147	150–75	13.1
Pensioners		175–200	10.8
Workers and employees	133	201–50	14.9
Collective farmers	150	Above 250	14.8

Source: Narodnoe khoziaistvo SSSR v. 1990 g., op. cit., pp. 112, 115.

Data on the monthly family income of the basic Soviet social categories –
workers and employees, industrial workers only, state farm workers, collective
farmers, and pensioners – as well as the per capita monthly income of all
the population's strata, are presented in Table 10-3. As can be seen in the
table, the highest family incomes were those of the industrial workers and
employees, the lowest those of certain categories of pensioners. Supplementary data (not included in the table) indicate that the monthly family incomes were increased from work on personal property by 3.1 percent for
the workers and employees, and by 25.6 percent for the collective farmers.
Thus, the workers' and employees' monthly family income was of the order of
202 rubles (197 + 5) and of the collective farmer's family income was 184 rubles
(147 + 37).

Nevertheless, a look at the per capita monthly incomes (column two of
Table 10-3) shows that the lowest part of the population's income receivers –
for example, those with up to 200 rubles per month – accounted for 70.3 percent
of the total, while those with monthly incomes above 200 rubles accounted for
29.7 percent. Among the latter, the highest stratum, namely those of income
receivers with over 250 rubles per month per capita, accounted for 14.8 percent
of the population. The latter figures actually misrepresent the real levels of the
incomes plus gifts and benefits received by the highest strata of the party-state
and economy's leaders, the nomenklatura. I will turn in detail to these issues
later on (in Sections 10-3 and 10-4). For now, I will first sketch the necessary
background for understanding these issues, by broadly examing the Soviet
rural and urban life and society.

10-2. Rural Society

The conflicts between the Soviet party-state bureaucracy and the peasantry
never came to an end during the existence of the Soviet regime. In principle, the Soviet state had been created on the basis of the "alliance"

between the industrial proletariat and the poor and middle peasants. Actually the Bolsheviks had always deeply mistrusted the entire peasantry. They believed that the peasants generated "incessantly" capitalist relations and that this situation would end only when collective agricultural production fully replaced the "transitional form" of individual production. As Lenin still asserted at the Eighth Congress of Soviets in December 1920, "The individual peasants are the stronghold of the capitalist roots in Russia."[6]

The Bolsheviks never fully acknowledged that the crucial political force that had overturned both Tsarism and its immediate successor, the provisional government, and that had torn asunder Russia's entire socioeconomic fabric, had been the poorly fed and disoriented 14 million or more of Russians under arms – in fact, the millions of peasants in uniform – who, jointly with the rest of the peasantry and the mobs of city dwellers, finally opened the doors to the Bolshevik system. The peasants accepted the Bolsheviks in the social Civil War of 1917–20 because the Bolsheviks kept stating that the land belonged to the peasants, while certain Whites asserted that they would return the land to the landowners. Already during the short-lived provisional government, the peasants had started to divide the estates. They continued to seize and divide the land during the Civil War while the Soviet government was proclaiming officially, in 1918, the "liquidation" of the large estates and the nationalization of the land, including the land belonging to individual peasants and peasant communities. While the peasants were carrying out this "nationalization" in their way – namely by directly seizing the landowners' land, cattle, and agricultural implements – the Bolsheviks had in view a different solution. They started to organize various "village communities" of poor peasants, along with "detachments of armed industrial workers," which they charged with the task of procuring by force at state-fixed prices agricultural produce, or of seizing the produce for delivery to state distribution institutions to feed the hungry towns. These compulsory methods increased for a time the amounts of food needed first of all for the industrial population, but built in exchange the peasants' resistance to the Soviet regime and prompted the hiding of food and the decline of the production of foodstuffs. The shortfalls in both production and in the marketable surplus of grain finally commanded deep changes in official policy concerning the peasants. The regime indeed had to inaugurate basic policy changes, recast its immediate economic objectives, set aside many of its old contentions – in short, to launch a New Economic Policy (the NEP). With regard to agriculture, the NEP first sought the recovery of production on the basis of individual peasant holdings. While in the other branches of the economy the state kept in its hands "the commanding heights," with private enterprise admitted only under strict control and within very restricted limits, in agriculture the Soviet regime granted independence to most of the landholders with regard to land leasing, investments, the hiring of labor, cattle,

---

[6] *Narodnoe khoziaistvo SSSR 1922–1982, op. cit.* p. 30; *Narodnoe khoziaistvo SSSR v 1990 g., op. cit.*, p. 97.

and agricultural machinery. The state also granted landholders the freedom to organize both the production and the marketing of goods. On the other hand, the government continued to support openly or underhandedly the poor peasants, and to encourage their cooperation with middle peasants against the rich peasants, the "kulaks." In 1926–7 there were in the USSR 22,773,000 individual farms, of which 2,560,000 (11.2 percent) belonged to industrial workers; 5,037,000 (22.1 percent) to poor peasants; 14,280,000 (61.7 percent) to middle peasants; and 896,000 (4.0 percent) to agricultural employers hiring labor and furnishing to them the necessary means of production. By 1928 the number of the industrial workers engaged in agricultural operations reached some 4,713,000.[7]

By the end of 1928, after years of critical debates, the Soviet government under the reign of Stalin discarded the NEP and established the central planning system aiming at rapid industrialization and the massive collectivization of agriculture. The terribly brutal and often murderous process of collectivization tore apart the villages and decreased their population, while substantially increasing the Siberian concentration camps with the deported peasants and sharply reducing agricultural production. In 1928, only 1.7 percent of the peasant households, controlling 2.8 percent of the country's sowing area, belonged to collectivized farms. By 1929, 2.9 percent of the peasant households were integrated in collectivization; by 1930, 23.6 percent; by 1931, 52.7 percent; and by 1932, 61.5 percent, then controlling 77.7 percent of the sown area. The collectivization process in the USSR's frontiers up to September 1, 1939, was virtually completed by 1937 when 93.0 percent of the peasant households were collectivized and were controlling 99.1 percent of the sown area.[8]

Besides various other agricultural policy changes (notably those undertaken under Nikita Khrushchev, which I will examine later on), the Soviet bureaucracy pursued indefatigably the transformation of the collective farms into state farms. The latter were continually reinforced by all kinds of measures and subsidies well into the 1980s, as the following figures will clearly show. In 1940, 236,900 collective farms (with 18.7 million households) existed; by 1950 their number was reduced to 123,700 (with 20.5 million households); by 1970 they counted only 33,600 (with 14.4 million households). Simultaneously, the state farms increased continually. In 1940 there were 4,200 state farms; by 1950, 5,000; by 1970, 15,000. By 1987 there were 26,600 collective farms facing 23,300 state farms. By that time, employment in the state farms involved 12.6 million people, in the collective farms 12.4 million.[9]

---

[7] Lenin, *V. I., Sobranie sochinenii* (Collected Works), Vol. XVII, Part II, p. 428, referred to by Baykov, Alexander, *The Development of the Soviet Economic System*, Cambridge, Cambridge University Press, 1946, p. 18.

[8] *Ibid.*, p. 135

[9] *Narodnoe khoziaistvo SSSR* (National Economy of the USSR), Moscow, Gosstatizdat, 1985, pp. 251, 259.

These processes led to continuous decreases in the village population – involving particularly the emigrations of young people, which reduced the agricultural population by 3 million in the 1960s and by 7 million in the 1970s – leaving behind the desolate wastage of many houses, the reversion of many fields to brush, and the abandonment of many ways and pathways. In the early 1980s (as we will see in detail in Chapter 12), a new Soviet leader, Mikhail Gorbachev, proclaimed the food problem as being Russia's "central economic and political problem." Again gigantic plans of change were drawn, notably for reorganizing agriculture, breaking up unprofitable collective and state farms, spreading land leasing, and increasing yields and the total output of grain and corn. However, many of these plans were not carried out and agriculture remained confined to its inefficient framework.[10]

Throughout all the afflictions, adversities, miseries, collectivization, deportations, and other ordeals, most villages barely benefited from the industrial expansion and from the towns' changes to which they contributed in many ways. As you approached the village, noted Hedrick Smith of the *New York Times* in the mid-1970s,

you see how modern conveniences come to an end. Follow the *narod* (the people) into the countryside and the modern world peels away with astonishing suddenness.... New apartment buildings give way to *izbas*, squat, low peasant log cabins...side roads are suddenly no longer paved but turn to dirt. Along the roadside every few hundred yards there is a hand pump and a well.... Much of Russian village life is shabby, drab, untidy and above all, muddy – with a mud that immobilizes life and movements....[11]

For good measure, add to these observations of an American journalist the following bitter remarks made by Gorbachev as leader of the Soviet Union, in March 1989:

The countryside is far behind the city in social and cultural development. The lack of good roads is a problem that affects all regions and it is a downright calamity for the Non-Black Earth Zone. The extent to which the countryside is provided with up-to-date, well appointed housing, municipal services, schools and medical and cultural institutions is extremely poor. A person often has to travel dozens, and sometimes hundreds of kilometers to deal with some very urgent matters – to obtain medical assistance, to avail himself of basic consumer services, to buy the simple goods.... In many regions the situation is such that people are simply abandoning the land and leaving the villages.[12]

---

[10] *Narodnoe khoziaistvo SSSR v 1985* (National Economy of the USSR, 1985), Moscow, Finansy I statistika, 1985, p. 179; *Sel'skoe khoziaistvo SSSR* (The Agriculture of the USSR), Moscow, Gosstatizdat, 1988, p. 6.

[11] See Smith, Hedrick, *The Russians*, New York, Quadrangle – The New York Times Book Co., 1976, p. 203.

[12] Gorbachev, Mikhail, speech to the Plenary Session of the CPSU Central Committee on March 15, 1989, on "The CPSU Agrarian Policy in Today's Conditions," *Izvestia*,

Gorbachev then added that the decay and decomposition of the village was well summarized by an official delegate at the Nineteenth Conference of the Soviet Communist Party in 1988: "The main and the most massive social injustice in our country affects the farmer.... For a long time we existed by robbing the farmer, by using the farmer's unpaid toil...."[13]

10-3. Urban Society

The urbanization of the Soviet Union proceeded very rapidly from the beginning of the industrialization drive. The republics' urbanization spread ranged between 1.9 and 28.0 percent in 1926, between 13.3 and 36.0 percent in 1939, and between 31.4 and 73.9 percent by the end of 1990. Clearly *all* urbanization levels increased from the late 1920s on, but at various speeds. Note that, for instance, the main Soviet republic, the RSFSR, when compared with all republics, ranked sixth in 1926, fifth in 1939, and finally first by the end of 1990, well above all the other levels. The natural growth of the dominant nationality of the republic, along with the massive migrations from the countryside into the cities and, in certain cases, the deliberate displacement of various minorities affected the relative importance of certain minorities in a number of republics. Examples include the Jewish urban population in the Ukraine and Belarus, the urban shares of the Tadjiks in Uzbekistan, the Armenians in Georgia, the Ukrainians in Moldova, and the Uzbeks in Kirghizstan.

The industrialization process brought about rapid increases in the *number* of cities and of urban-type settlements, as well as sharp increases in the population of the major cities. In 1926, the urban population of the Soviet Union amounted to 26.3 million people living in 709 cities and 1,216 urban-type settlements. By 1939, the urban population had more than doubled the 1926 level, reaching 56.1 million living in 923 cities and 1,450 urban-type settlements. Fifty years later, by 1989, the urban population had more than tripled compared to 1939, reaching the staggering figure of 188.8 million living in 2,190 cities and in 4,026 urban-type settlements, many of which were specialized company towns created with state investments.

In 1926 the Soviet Union had only two cities exceeding the level of 1 million inhabitants: Moscow, then with a population of 2 million, and Leningrad, with 1.6 million. By 1939 these were still the only two cities with a population of over 1 million, but they had greatly expanded in the intervening years: Moscow was then counting 4.5 million inhabitants, and Leningrad 3.1 million. By 1973, the number of cities with over 1 million had increased to ten: Moscow, in

March 16, 1989, transl. in *Current Digest of the Soviet Press*, Vol. XLI, No. 11, 1989, p. 4.
[13] Quoted by Medvedkov, Olga, *Soviet Urbanization*, London and New York, Routledge, 1990, p. 141.

the leading position, numbered 7.2 million, Leningrad 3.6 million, followed in descending order (from 1.8 to 1.1 million) by Kiev, Tashkent, Baku, Kharkhov, Gorkii, Novosibirsk, Kuibishev, and Sverdlovsk.[14]

The interrelated contributions to the growth of cities of the natural growth of the cities' population and of the rural migration into the cities are not easily quantifiable. According to a study carried out under the direction of the Science Academy of the USSR, the increases of the urban population of the Soviet Union between 1959 and 1969 amounted to 36.0 million, and between 1970 and 1978 to 27.6 million. In the first period, the natural growth of the population accounted for 40 percent of the increase (that is, for 14.6 million), the rural migration into the cities for 60 percent (21.4 million); in the second period, the respective percentages were similar, namely, natural growth 43 percent (12.0 million), rural migration into the cities 57 percent (15.6 million). Yet, population has increased under these influences at different rates in different periods and in the various republics. The migration into the cities mainly of young rural adults has generally contributed, on the one hand, to the general increase of the cities' population and, on the other hand, to the eventual growth of these cities' rates of natural growth.[15]

The development of the cities and the urban-type settlements was accompanied in time by significant increases of the country's infrastructure. In the case of the RSFSR alone, between roughly 1970 and 1990, the rail lines increased from 59,000 kilometers to 89,000, the waterway system from 91,000 kilometers to 108,000, the auto roads from 68,000 to 658,000. Yet, given the vast surface of the RSFSR and of the Soviet Union as a whole, the connections between producers and their customers continued to be far from adequate. The internal distances remained comparable to the distances of the international trade of the Western nations. Intercity flows remained heavy as each city had to bring from another distant city or place the necessary semiproducts and raw materials. Moreover, the interchanges between suppliers and customers had to be made by land transportation, with little help from shipping.[16]

The related chronic problems of urban food supplies had been generated not only by production, structure, transportation, pricing, and distribution, but also by a host of issues related to the policies governing investments,

[14] *Sovetskii gorod, sotsial'naia struktura* (The Soviet Town: The Social Structure), Aitov, N. A., Mordkovich, V. G., and Titma, M. Kh., eds., Moscow, Mysl', 1988, pp. 215–17. For 1926–39, Zlatopolsky, D., *State Systems of the USSR*, Moscow, Foreign Language Publishing House, 1960, p. 174; for 1989, *Nasselenie SSSR 1988* (Population of the USSR, 1988), Moscow, Finansy i statistika, 1989, p. 4.

[15] Khorev, B. S., *Problemy gorodov* (The Problems of Towns), Moscow, Mysl', 1975, p. 222.

[16] Zaionchkovskaia, Zh. A., and Velbanova, I. Iu, "Migratiia selskogo naseleniia SSSR v goroda" (The Migration of the Rural Population of the USSR into the Cities), in *Raselenie naseleniia i razmeshchenie proizvodstva* (The Settlement of the Population and the Placing of Production), released by the Academiia Nauk SSSR, Moscow, Nauka, 1982, p. 152; *Sovetskii gorod, sotsial' naia struktura, op. cit.*, pp. 152–62.

misallocations, and foregone opportunities – to which I will return in detail later on.

A critical urban problem that deepened with the growth of the cities was the inadequate quantity and quality of housing. In the 1920s, the Soviet leaders asserted that their system would provide everyone with the "sanitary norm of 9 sq. meters (96 sq. feet) of housing per person," exclusive of service areas. Actually, this quite modest goal proved unattainable by the end of the NEP. In 1928, housing space had declined in relation to 1917 from 7 square meters per capita, to 6 square meters. By 1940, as the industrialization drive was going ahead, the living space per capita reached 6.5 square meters – but soon after the terrible war destructions and subsequently the increased rural migration toward the towns officially brought the per capita level to 5 square meters by the early 1950s. By 1965 the per capita level was stated to have risen to 6.8 square meters of living space or to a total of 10.0 square meters including the service areas. Twenty years later, by 1985 the per capita living space is said to have finally reached 9.7 square meters and the total, including services areas, to 14.1 square meters. Clearly average distribution implies that many Soviets have had less than the average. (Moreover, significant deficiencies have persisted in the average level between republics.) In addition, one should remember that the middle and upper party-state ruling stratum has been systematically granted houses, apartments, and country *dachas*, while many poorer families often had to live two to three persons to a room, with only 2–3 square meters per person. As students of Soviet housing have pointed out, housing insufficiencies and inefficiencies have been the unavoidable result of planning choices concerning the needs of industrialization, and the simple neglect of the population's needs for housing, food, services, and medical care.[17]

No matter the size of the Soviet cities, their social structure evolved similarly under the Soviet regime. In all of the cities and towns, the percentage of workers has varied between 53 to 57 percent; that of the lower personnel between 3–5 percent; that of the medium specialized personnel between 16 and 24 percent; and finally that of the highly specialized personnel between 14 to 18 percent – except in the very big cities, where the latter percentage increased at times up to 23 percent. The best locations in the Soviet cities were reserved for the party's officials, the leaders of the administration, and the managers of the economy. The Soviet state indeed built its administrative and management foundations on the basis of the party's apparatus. A privileged "estate" or "class," the nomenklatura – that is, the appointees of the party – constituted the state's key instrument of policy. The appointees, like those previously selected by the Tsar, benefited in numerous ways in their choice of occupation, real income, type of housing (urban and recreational in the

[17] Seniavskii, A. S., *Rosiiskii gorod v 1960–1980 gody* (The Russian Town in the 1960s and 1980s), Moscow, Institut Rossiiskoi Istorii, 1995, p. 19; also, Medvedkov, Olga, *Soviet Urbanization, op. cit.*, p. 145.

countryside), food supplies, special stores, and all kinds of services, already in Lenin's time. Behind the Soviets supposed drive toward "socialist equality" thus arose sharp inequalities, deeply concealed but well known, reflecting in many respects the central power of the party's leader, the imprint of centuries of Tsarist history and tradition, and the old habits and submissive character of the Russian people.

10-4. Command and Control System

The official Soviet state documents always affirmed that the "working class" was the state's "ruling class" and that the essential organs of the Soviet power were the Supreme Soviet and its Presidium, the Council of Ministers of the USSR, along with the diverse directive organs of the federal and autonomous republics as well as the regional, counties, townships, and villages. Actually, the dominant institution of the Soviet state was from its inception the Communist Party. The real cabinet of the Soviet Union was the party's Politburo; the real parliament, the party's Central Committee; the country's absolute ruler, the secretary general, a *sui generis* reembodiment of the autocratic Tsar. The party's apparatus penetrated, overlapped, and controlled both the alleged legislative powers (the Soviets) and the executive powers (the Ministries) – that is, it clung to a unity of powers that ensured its complete dominance over the state's bureaucracy. However, the bureaucracy assumed formal responsibility for determining laws and selecting operational goals, allocating authority and resources, deploying personnel, and coordinating the processes of implementation. Unlike the situation in the fascist or the Nazi one-party system, the Communist Party's members did not confine themselves to roles of policy transmission belts to the state's bureaucracy or the economy's managers. They participated actively and directly in all the state's and economy's activities, as officials, administrators, managers, or workers.[18] (See Figure 10-2.)

The party had only a limited number of members in the early years of the Soviet regime. This began to change in 1922 when Lenin appointed Stalin as the party's secretary general. This apparently secondary, innocuous, "bureaucratic" leadership position focused on policy issues, but Stalin transformed it into the key instrument of his own accession to absolute power and of the reshaping of the party into his subservient apparatus. Stalin took under his direct control the supervision of the selection and appointment of the party's members to the crucial posts of command within the party itself and within the country's top bureaucracy. While maintaining the myth (or the illusion) that

---

[18] Cattell, David, T., "Soviet Cities and Consumer Welfare Planning," in *The City in Russian History*, Ham, Michael, ed., Lexington, KY, University Press of Kentucky, 1976, pp. 258, 259, 266; Alexeev, Michael V., "Soviet Residential Housing: Will the 'Acute Problem' Be Solved?" in *Gorbachev's Economic Plans*, study papers submitted to the Joint Economic Committee, Congress of the United States, Washington, DC, U.S. GPO 1987, pp. 283–4; *Sovetskii gorod, sotsial'naia struktura, op. cit.*, pp. 9, 141, 145.

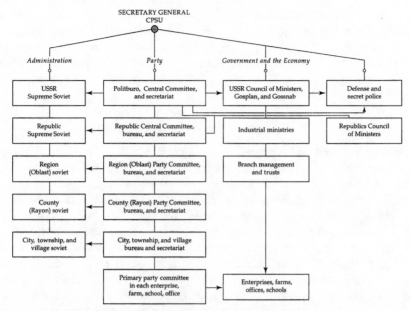

Figure 10-2. The Soviet Party – State Command System

"the ruling working class was managing the state and the economy" through its own technical and industrial intelligentsia, Stalin carefully staffed, under his control, a privileged stratum of command in the party itself, in the country's administration, and in the economy. The nomenklatura was, as under Ivan the Terrible, his *oprichniki*, his instruments of both terror and absolute control.

What was the de facto size of the command apparatus in that system? By 1941 the Communist Party had 2.5 million members and 1.5 million candidates (for admission into the party after various ad hoc tests). After the war, the party continued to grow, reaching by 1980 17 million members; compared to 1917, the party grew about forty times while the population grew by 62 percent. Not all the party members were in the state's key positions, though many of them did reach that level; one has to take into consideration the participation of engineers and other specialists also included in the nomenklatura. To suggest an answer to the latter's possible size, one has to consider in turn the extent of the party's upper echelons, of the Soviet's bureaucracy, of the ministerial administration, and of the economy's management.[19]

---

[19] Hough, Jerry, F., and Fainsod, Merle, *How the Soviet-Union Is Governed*, Cambridge, MA, Harvard University Press, 1979, pp. 262–3; see also Biscaretti di Ruffia, Paolo, *Lineamenti generali dell' ordinamento constituzionale Sovietico* (General Lines of the Soviet Constitutional Organization), Milano, Guiffré, 1956, pp. 107–21; Conygham, William, J., *The Modernization of Soviet Industrial Management*, Cambridge, Cambridge University Press, 1982, p. 1.

Table 10-4 *USSR: The Leading State Apparatus in 1985, in Thousands*

Apparatus	Number of personnel (in thousand)
Total Personnel of the Leading State Offices	2,376
Executive organs of ministries and departments	1,623
All union apparatus	107
Republics' apparatuses	140
Ministries of autonomous republics, territories, districts	280
Regions' and towns' departments	450
Organs of economy's management	646
Presidia of the Soviets	312
Judicial system	92
Executive organs of cooperatives of mass organizations	349

Source: Narodnoe khoziaistvo SSSR v 1989 g., op. cit., p. 50.

The highest party hierarchy – the central committees of the Soviet Union's party and of the Komsomol (the party's youth organization), the central council and the central committees of the trade union and of the social organizations including also the organizations at the level of the republics, territories, and regions – reached in the 1970s, according to a study of Michael Voslensky, a total of some twenty-five thousand persons; at the levels of districts and towns, the highest leadership reached about seventy-five thousand.[20] The highest state organ, namely the Supreme Soviet (comprising the two chambers, the Council of the Union and the Council of Nationalities), numbered fifteen hundred deputies. The persons "elected" under the party's control to these chambers included the top party members as well as deputies from various strata of the society. Those who served in these chambers discharged their duties in conjunction with their other occupations; they were not professional legislators. Their participation in law making was only pro forma. As indicated in Table 10-4, the executive organs of ministries and departments amounted to some 2.3 million. Finally, according to 1988 data, the apparatus of management of the economy's branches reached 14.9 million people, including notably 4.7 million in the industrial enterprises, 2.0 million in construction, 1.0 million in agriculture, and so on. Percentagewise, the managerial strata accounted to between 9 to 16 percent in the basic economic branches, and for about 13 percent in the economy as a whole.[21] Assuming that one-half of the management data

[20] Voslensky, Michael, *La Nomenklatura. Les privilegiés en URSS* (The Nomenklatura. The Privileged in the USSR), Paris, Belfond, 1980, pp. 146–7.

[21] *Narodnoe khoziaistvo SSSR v 1989 g., op. cit.*, pp. 50–1; *Narodnoe khoziaistvo SSSR v 1990 g., op. cit.*, pp. 100–1; note also that Gorbachev stated in 1987 that "in our country about 18 million people are employed in the sphere of management, including 2.5 million in the apparatus of various administrative agencies and something like 15 million people in the

incorporated lower personnel who should not be included in the nomenklatura, we may *grosso modo* infer that all the nomenklatura levels –
comprising highly different levels of income and power – accounted as
Gorbachev had stated for roughly 18 million of a total population of some
280 million.[22]

10-5. Concluding Comments

As Stalin stated at the twelfth Congress of the party, what mattered in the
selection of officials was that they should be able "to understand the party's
directives, consider these directives as their own, and transform these directives into realities." The appointment to the party's leadership, to high state
executive offices, and to high management responsibilities in the economy depended indeed less on competence and more on the political profile of the
candidate, a profile that had to suggest complete conformity in thought and
deed with the secretary general's directives, whatever these may be. Accession to a high position was a privilege granted only for as long as the supreme
leader or those closely connected to him wanted it to last. Under Stalin's
shadow, as under the Tsar's shadow – as the Marquis de Custine noted exactly
one hundred years earlier – all distinctions lost meaning; each distinction, like
everything else, was a product of the ruler's favor. "He could extend it; he
could withdraw it."[23]

The persisting illusions in the 1930s of socialist egalitarianism were swept
away by Stalin himself, who replaced them with another illusion, namely that
the "ruling working class" had to create and was indeed already creating *its own*
"technical intelligentsia" capable of upholding "the interests of the working
class . . . as the interests of the ruling class." Wage differentials in favor of this
"technical intelligentsia" of officials, administrators, managers, engineers, and
specialists were stressed as indispensable for increasing output and productivity. But these differentials were only one aspect (the one openly stressed but
quite secondary) of the increased differentials that were developing between
the upper strata and the alleged "working ruling class." The real differences
between them were concealed in the numerous hidden perks granted to these
upper strata concerning housing, country dachas, cars, food, health care, travel,
and state-paid excursion vacations. As Stalin explained it in 1930 in his Marxian
jargon:

Marx and Lenin said that the differences between the skilled and unskilled labor
would exist even under socialism, even after classes had been abolished; that only

management staffs of associations, enterprises and organizations." Cf. *Pravda* and *Investia*,
Oct. 2, 1987 (Gorbachev's speech in Murmansk).

[22] Voslensky, Michael, *La Nomenklatura . . ., op. cit.,* p. 90.

[23] Kennan, George, F., *The Marquis de Custine and His Russia in 1839*, Princeton, NJ, Princeton
University Press, 1971, p. 78.

under communism would this difference disappear and that, consequently, even under socialism "wages" must be paid according to work performed and not according to needs.[24]

The power of the secretary general became in time more extensive even than that of the Tsars. He became indeed absolute ruler with a system that *owned* the entire country and its economy. He became the virtual owner of the entire nationalized economy, and his nomenklatura embodied his "plenipotentiary representatives" – as Nikolai Podgorny, the Soviet president, once put it. These "plenipotentiary representatives" became in many respects much more powerful than the Tsar's ranked appointees of the *chin* – more powerful, but also more easily dismissed.

The upper strata lived in a world of its own, conscious of its status and full of scorn for all the other strata of the society, and particularly of the workers – of the alleged "ruling class" of this system. Once appointed, the executives at the highest levels in the ministries and administrations, in the factories, and in the giant plants and trusts, increasingly gained power. Indeed they continually strengthened their positions as that of the secretary general began to weaken after the death of Stalin, often because of a variety of personal rather than political conflicts at the highest level of the party. Concomitantly, the progress of the economy started to be hampered by widespread lying and corruption concerning the fulfillment and "overfulfillment" of the centralized economic plans. As these inner conflicts were developing, the nomenklatura engaged ever more decisively in all kinds of personal intrigues, and became united not by the official "ideology," but by personal concerns of power, privilege, and even illicit business deals. Even before the collapse of the regime in 1990, these executives indeed became entangled in all sorts of combinations in contradiction with the established laws, the moral and legal norms, and the public interest. After the collapse of the regime, they became finally the real owners of the properties they had managed in the name of the poor, disinherited, alleged "ruling working class."

---

[24] Stalin, J. V., "New Conditions – New Tasks in Economic Construction" (January 23, 1931), *Works*, Vol. 13, *July 1930–January 1934*, Moscow, Foreign Languages Publishing House, 1955, pp. 59, 69.

The Transition Issues

11-1. Principles of Action

What were the principles and rules of organization of the Soviet state from its inception? What were the concepts on the basis of which the economy was supposed to be reorganized and managed in order to transit toward "socialism"? How were production and distribution to be carried out, money and credit handled, wages and prices determined? To what extent would such changes reflect unalterable commitments to Marxian theories? Yet, why were some of the early principles eventually set aside, and then, later, reinstated as the guiding principles of the Soviet state?

The policies in question concerning notably the alleged transition from capitalism to communism, the dictatorship of the proletariat, and the specific pattern of organization of the socialist state and the economy that became central to Lenin's views and then to Soviet practice had been first enunciated by Karl Marx and Friedrich Engels, and then by certain German socialist theoreticians such as Karl Kautsky. Marx and Engels asserted in the *Communist Manifesto* of 1848 that the first steps in the communist revolution were "to raise the proletariat to the position of the ruling class." The proletariat would then use its political supremacy to "wrest" all capital from the bourgeoisie and to "centralize all instruments of production in the hands of the state," abolish private property on land, centralize credit and the means of transport and communications, and combine agriculture with manufacturing industry, gradually abolishing "the distinction between town and country."[1] In his *Critique of the Gotha Program* of 1875, Marx added that between the capitalist and the communist society lay "the period of transformation of the one into the other," a transition period during which "the state can be

---

[1] Marx, Karl, and Engels, Friedrich, "Manifesto of the Communist Party," in *Basic Writings of Politics and Philosophy*, Fener, Lewis, ed., Garden City, NY, Doubleday, 1959, p. 28.

nothing but the revolutionary dictatorship of the proletariat."[2] On this basis, Engels stated between 1877 and 1878, in a series of polemical articles directed against the German professor Eugene Dühring, that from the moment that society enters into the possession of the means of production it will be able to use them "in direct association for production." For this, society will not need to assign values to products. The useful effects of the various articles of consumption, compared with one another and with the quantities of labor required for their production, will determine the country's plan. In short, "people will be able to manage everything very simply, without the intervention of much vaunted 'value'."[3] All this was summarized by Kautsky in 1892 in the famous formula, "In the socialist society, which is after all a *single great industrial enterprise*, production and wages must be exactly, in a planned way organized, like they are organized in a modern large industrial enterprise."[4]

These Marxian theoretical views on the supposed patterns of political and economic transition from capitalism to socialism – namely, dictatorship of the proletariat, centralization of the means of production, planned valueless management of the economy reorganized as a single giant industrial enterprise – were considered by Lenin and by the Bolsheviks as their guiding principles of action. In *The State and Revolution*, written on the eve of the communist revolution, Lenin stated that such a revolution will necessarily lead to the dictatorship of the proletariat. The proletariat will use the state power to crush the exploiters and to lead the masses in the work of organizing a socialist economy. All the activities needed for the resulting unified economy to operate as a "country-wide state syndicate" were accounting and control, matters simplified by capitalism itself and allegedly reduced to "extraordinarily simple operations which any literate person can perform."[5]

Let me now sketch the specific measures taken by the Bolshevik Party (which became in 1917 the Communist Party) on the basis of these principles, during the period of War Communism, from November 1917 to the beginnings of 1921. The emerging communist state apparatus was set into place between December 1917 and January 1918. As Lenin put it, this allegedly "proletarian type of state" embodying the "dictatorship of the proletariat," proceeded first by eliminating all other parties except the communist one and by submitting all the political and social organisms (the Soviets and the trade unions) to the party. It then nationalized the banks, the means of production, the foreign trade, the domestic trade, and the land – of the landlords, of the Tsar's family,

---

[2] Marx, Karl, "Critique of the Gotha Program," *ibid.*, p. 127.

[3] Engels, Friedrich, *Herr Eugen Dühring's Revolution in Science*, Moscow, Foreign Languages Publishing House, 1959, pp. 389–90, 409, 426–7.

[4] Kautksy, Karl, "Erfurt Program," as quoted by Sutela, Pekka, in *Socialism, Planning and Optimality*, Helsinki, Finnish Society of Sciences and Letters, 1984, p. 28.

[5] Lenin, V. I., "The State and Revolution," *Collected Works*, Vol. 25, *June–September 1917*, Moscow, Progress Publishers, 1964, pp. 404, 470, 473.

of the churches and monasteries – and turned them into communes. Within this framework, the new state proceeded to extensive requisitions of peasants' production, and to administrative methods of organization of public works, sectoral and regional allocations, and compulsory distribution and utilization of labor, according to a centrally approved plan to address both military and civilian needs. The new system aimed to "naturalize" the economy, that is, to eliminate money from economic activities and to destroy the old capitalist "commodity system." In practice, a kind of dual economy arose: the first, the statewide economic setup, did away with direct money relations and replaced them with cashless clearings; the second, outside the state sector and still based on individual small-scale commodity production and exchange, continued to engage in market relations even though within a distorted, hidden, and illegal framework. Interestingly, the state itself resorted when needed to money emissions to handle its own purchases in the legally nonexistent free market.

The solutions improvised in the conditions of War Communism to operate the giant state economic sector were plagued by innumerable difficulties in production, planning, branch and sectors interconnections, and so on. The only "model" available in this respect was the German *Krigswirtschaft* – the wartime economic centralized organization of the Imperial German economy. Many Communist leaders were then impressed by its conception and by the ways of its operations. In this connection, Nikolai Bukharin, a Communist theoretician and a close collaborator of Lenin, asserted in a number of writings of 1919 and 1920 that under capitalism, the "finance capital" had organized the entire economy under its scepter through the banking capital, and the "monopolistic alliances of employers" combining enterprises, thus creating a new model of production that transformed the unorganized capitalist system into a new "*technical* division of labor within an 'organized' national economy." Bukharin, jointly with another Communist leader, Evguenii Preobrazhenskii, noted indeed that these were precisely the technical problems that the Soviet state had to solve, namely, how could production be best organized, that is, what was "the best way of *planning our economic life as a whole*, how should one branch of production be linked up with another, how should production be administered, what is the best way of allotting the reserve of raw materials, how can we best dispose of the available labor power." All these problems had to be solved "not in a single factory, or for a single factory, but for the whole of the huge country."[6] For these top Communist leaders, overall central planning was a necessary system of organization directly opposed to the market process and that will entirely supplant the market. *Commodities* – goods sold and bought by different owners – typical of capitalism, will be replaced in

---

[6] Bukharin, Nikolai, *The Politics and Economics of the Transition Period*, trsl. by Field, O., London, Routledge & Kegan Paul, 1979, p. 13; Bukharin, N., and Preobrazhenskii, E., *The ABC of Communism*, Ann Arbor, University of Michigan Press, 1966, pp. 263–4.

time by *products* stored in warehouses and delivered to those who needed them. Socialism, defined as incomplete communism, was a setup in which "by degrees, a moneyless system of account keeping" will finally come to prevail.[7]

By the end of 1919, on the military plane, the Red Army defeated the White Armies of Admiral A. V. Kolchak, and of Generals A. I. Denikin and N. N. Iudenich. But on the economic plane, the results of a centralized command and control method of planning and management based on requisitions and on nonmonetary relations, turned out to be disastrous. A New Economy Policy became imperative and had to be rapidly formulated and implemented. The underlying principles of War Communism had to be in part discarded, reinterpreted, and adjusted in a variety of ways to meet the new conditions. Yet the core *principles* of War Communism remained at the heart of the communist approaches to economic management, the hub of the Soviet system – modified, set aside, but not forgotten, as we will see in the next sections.

11-2. Russia and the West's Economic Patterns

The Soviet economy developed within the novel framework created by the NEP between the beginning of 1921 and 1927–8. Though the NEP was finally discarded and succeeded by the Central Planning era, eventually many of its concepts, orientations, and methods were again reaffirmed as valid and useful, and were resorted to by the Soviet leadership as we will see later on. When he launched the New Economic Policy, Lenin conveniently redefined the Communist assertions concerning socialism, communism, and the transition from one system to another. In launching the NEP, he affirmed notably that the Communists had made during War Communism the enormous error of believing "that there would be a *direct transition* from the old Russian economy to state production and distribution on communist lines." It was wrong, he added, "to attempt to go over straight to communism"; this meant to disregard the previous correct belief that "it would be impossible to bypass the period of socialist accounting and control in approaching the lower stage of communism." In this newly rediscovered period of socialist accounting and control, "capitalism need not necessarily be completely eliminated"; the NEP itself, added Lenin, actually meant "reverting to capitalism to a considerable extent."[8] This conceptual reversal implied the discarding of the War Communist ideas of the inevitable emergence of a new kind of economy without commodities (with "products" only), without markets, without money and credit, without prices and wages. It meant also the rejection of the total centralization

---

[7] See, Spulber, Nicolas, *Soviet Strategy for Economic Growth*, Bloomington, IN, Indiana University Press, 1964, pp. 29–32.

[8] Lenin, V. I., "The New Economic Policy and the Tasks of the Political Education Departments" (October 17, 1921), *Collected Works*, Vol. 33, *August 1921–March 1923*, Moscow, Progress Publishers, 1966, pp. 62, 64.

prevalent under War Communism – carried out in many respects on the model of the German war economy – in which, as Leon Trotsky put it, "the Supreme Council for National Economy allocated everything, organized everything, cared for everything: where should machines go to, where raw materials, where the finished products." From an economic perspective, Trotsky added, the mistake was to undertake something "beyond our low cultural level," and beyond the existing conditions in the country from "technical and production points of view."[9]

The new basic policy was oriented toward the end of compulsory requisitions of peasants' grain "surpluses" (and often of their own necessary food) and their replacement with a tax in kind – a tax containing half of the old appropriation system and half of the new system of commodity exchange – along with free market relations including, for local economic exchanges, the end of various trade restrictions, some development of private industries, and the granting to most state enterprises of the right to be managed on an economic basis taking account of the market. The NEP period evolved eventually through two distinct phases: during the first, from 1921 to 1925–6, the Soviet regime focused on the economy's recovery; during the second, from 1926–7 to 1927–8, it focused on the economy's restructuring. Toward the end of 1927 and the beginning of 1928, the party embarked decisively on a new drive to convert Russia from an agrarian to an industrial country. This new policy meant in fact totally discarding the NEP's concepts and management methods. The inauguration of the post-NEP policies took place at the Fifteenth Party Congress (in December 1927), which was baptized the Congress of Industrialization. The period that began on the morrow of that Congress became known as the Soviet Central Planning Era, that is, the Era of the Five Year Plans.[10]

During the NEP, the broad direction of industrial restructuring and development continued to be guided by the Supreme Council of National Economy (*Vesenkha*). But the state industrial enterprises were divided into two groups: the first, comprising the main means of production and the chief army and defense industries, remained under state management; the second, consisting of the other state enterprises that were grouped into trusts granted commercial autonomy. Put differently, the state kept under its control the "economy's commanding heights" – including most of the means of production industries – while it denationalized and thus relieved itself of the management of a number of enterprises of lesser importance. As the NEP aimed at reestablishing a mixed system including the "commanding heights" in the hands of the state

[9] Trotsky, Leon, *Protokoly XI s'ezda RKP(b)* (Protocols of the Eleventh Congress of the Russian Communist Party [Bolsheviks]), quoted by Szamuely, Lazlo, *First Models of the Socialist Economic Systems, Principles and Theories*, Budapest, Akademiai Kiado, 1974, p. 94.

[10] Jasny, Naum, *Soviet Industrialization 1928–1952*, Chicago, University of Chicago Press, 1961, p. 2.

and market relations all around it, the regime reestablished the State Bank (Gosbank) and proceeded to make a gradual transition to a stable monetary system, to create an expanding network of credit institutions, as well as to place public finances on a sound basis.[11]

During the recovery period in 1923–4, the country's production had the following components: Agricultural production accounted for 53.3 percent; factory and plant production for 26.8 percent; small commodity production for 10.9 percent; and construction and transport for the balance of 9.0 percent. Also in 1923–4, the state industry accounted for 63.5 percent of total industrial production, the cooperatives for 3.6 percent, the small handicrafts for 29.4 percent, and private industries for 3.5 percent.[12] During the years of recovery, it became increasingly evident that in the preceding years, the industrial dislocations that had plagued the economy during and after the war had hit hardest the more developed branches of industry, namely metallurgy and metal working, while the primitive branches of industry, agriculture, and handicrafts had held their own. The least disorganized had been the branches that served primary needs, namely food, fuel, and clothing, while the production of means of production had been stricken with paralysis. On the whole, during recovery, growth of the physical volume of industrial output was still based mainly on activating idle or underutilized equipment and on halting the erosion of fixed capital in various branches. But even where such services were available, activating them required great funds not always available. The basic productive funds of industry were not increased until 1925–6. Indeed, until that date, capital expenditures had been absorbed by capital repairs. The production funds of big industry estimated in 1920 at 8,090 million rubles (at 1926–7 prices) were valued at 8,105 million rubles in 1925. By 1926–7, when the USSR was officially crossing the line between *recovery* and *restructuring*, the process of restoring the inherited productive capacity and of fully utilizing the existing equipment was completed.[13]

At the time, state industry accounted for as much as 77.1 percent of the total industrial output, the cooperatives for 8.8 percent, the small handicrafts for 11.7 percent, and the private sector for only 2.4 percent. By then, total industrial production had not increased appreciably compared to 1913. In that year, industrial output amounted to 3,480.0 million rubles (at 1913 prices). After falling sharply during the early 1920s, industrial output reached the

[11] Akademiia Nauk SSSR (State Academy of Science), *Novaia Ekonomicheskaia Politika, Voprosy teorii i istorii* (New Economic Policy, Theoretical and Historical Questions), Moscow, Nauka, 1974, pp. 52–3, 116–20; Chakrabarti, S. C., Kundu, K. B., and Patra, M. M., *Economic Development of the Soviet Union*, Calcutta, Nabaharat Publishers, 1965, pp. 37–44; "Control Figures of the Economy, 1926/27," in *Foundations of Soviet Strategy for Economic Growth*, Spulber, Nicolas, ed., Bloomington, IN, Indiana University Press, 1964, pp. 401, 407.

[12] Popov, P. I., "Balance Sheet of the National Economy as a Whole," in *Foundations of Soviet Strategy . . ., op. cit.*, pp. 58–9; on the industrial production shares, Santalov, A. A., and Segal, Louis, *Soviet Year-Book 1929*, London, George Allen and Unwin, 1929, p. 109.

[13] Baykov, A., *The Development of the Soviet Economic System, op. cit.*, p. 120.

threshold of restructuring 5,000 million rubles in 1925–6, and, after the USSR had crossed the line between recovery and restructuring in 1926–7, output reached 6,033.0 million rubles (an increase of 72 percent over the low level of 1913).[14] Some of the Soviet leaders viewed these results as disastrous compared to the industrial developments then occurring in the West. As the new absolute leader of the USSR, Joseph Stalin, was to put it in 1928:

> We have assumed power in a country whose technical equipment is terribly backward. Along with a few big industrial units more or less based upon modern technology, we have hundreds and thousands of mills and factories in which the technical equipment is beneath all criticism from the point of view of modern achievements.... Look at the capitalist countries and you will see that their technology is not only advancing, but advancing by leaps and bounds, outstripping the old forms of industrial techniques .... our industry, which should be the basis of socialism and of Soviet power, is extremely backward technically. Do you think that we can achieve the final victory of socialism in our country so long as this contradiction exists?[15]

From the mid-1920s on, there was broad agreement among Soviet leaders about the need for rapid growth and industrialization, and about the need for faster growth of the socialist sector in relation to that of the capitalist one. But there were deep disagreements among them as to the path to follow in order to catch up with advancing capitalist Europe, and as to the specific measures to take to increase the volume of investment, change the composition of output and employment, and determine the interrelations of industry and agriculture. Two basic tendencies crystalized in these respects: The first advocated a strategy emphasizing the need for interacting agricultural-industrial development; the second, a strategy aiming at deliberately faster growth of the heavy industrial branches in preference to all other economic branches and sectors. The first strategy, of the so-called *right wing* of the party led by Nikolai Bukharin, and strongly supported by many of his followers such as L. Shanin and V. Bazarov, stressed the idea that the maximum and continuous rate of growth of the economy as a whole could be experienced only if industry would advance on the basis of a rapidly growing agriculture. As Shanin put it at the time,

> ...our economic strategy should involve, first, export of agricultural commodities, and second, investment of capital in the branches which serve that export. Relying on our agricultural basis, we must build grain elevators, refrigeration plants, and bacon factories, the investments required for these undertakings being infinitely small when compared with the expenditures which would be required for the immediate full-scale development of heavy industry.[16]

[14] Santalov, A. A., and Segal, L., *Soviet Year-Book 1929, op. cit.*, p. 109.
[15] Stalin, J., "Industrialization of the Country and the Right Deviation" (1928), *Foundations of Soviet Strategy . . ., op. cit.*, p. 267.
[16] Shanin, L., "The Economic Nature of Our Commodity Shortage" (1925), *Foundations of Soviet Strategy for Economic Growth . . ., op cit.*, p. 210.

The so-called *left wing* of the party, inspired by Leon Trotsky and defended by such theoreticians as Evguenii Preobrazhenskii, stressed, on the contrary, that what was needed for the economy's rapid growth was a massive agricultural tribute to industry so that the latter could shift to a higher technological plane. As Preoabrzhenskii put it at the time, "a country such as the USSR, with its ravaged and, in general, retarded economy, will have to pass through a period of primary accumulation, drawing very liberally upon presocialist forms of enterprise as sources . . . . to bank solely on accumulation within the socialist domain is to gamble with the socialist economy's very existence. . . ."[17] Stalin adroitly maneuvered between the two tendencies. After first rejecting the Trotsky-Preobrazhenskii position as "super-industrialist," Stalin took over its policies and emphasized even stronger than anybody else the Soviet need for heavy industry and, in addition, for a fully autarchic development ("Socialism in One Country"). The Stalin leadership, closing the debate on strategy, opened up by the end of 1928 the era of all-around planning and of maximum capital investment, in heavy industry in particular, and in industry as a whole in general.

11-3. The Transition Path

The early approaches of War Communism toward the structuring of the state, society, and economy were fully reinstated under Stalin's dictatorship, notably from 1929 to 1939. Four key characteristics defined the system consolidated under Stalin's reign: first, integration under the direction of the top leadership of the Communist Party (the secretary general and his Politburo) of state administration in all its aspects, in the entire Soviet Union as well as in each of its republics and regions; second, full "socialization" (nationalization) of industry, banking, transport, and trade, and the collectivization of agriculture; third, coordination under the formal responsibility of the Council of Ministers of economic policies, planning, and control, through the industrial ministries and the functional agencies for State Planning (Gosplan) and for Material-Technical Supply (Gossnab); fourth, assertion of the primacy of production over consumption, and of the state over the individual.

As an acute observer of the Soviet Union, Severyn Bialer, once put it, "the real Soviet Revolution took place [under Stalin] from 1929 to 1939." It is indeed then that the Soviet system finalized its shape and began to pursue inflexibly its targets on the basis of the Marxian theory alleging that it could essentially disregard the "law of value" cost-price calculations and impose on the economy the policy makers' own choices concerning scope and the rates of economic change. Already during the NEP, the Bolshevik commitment to both central planning and technological change was illustrated by Lenin's plan

---

[17] Preobrazhenskii, E. A., "On Primary Socialist Accumulation" (1926), *Foundations of Soviet Strategy for Economic Growth, op. cit.,* p. 235.

for the electrification of Russia (*Goelro* – a plan that incidentally contained Tsarist Russia's technological efforts after the 1905–6 revolution to use electric energy as a key factor in economy's development) and by the elaboration of the first Balance of the National Economy of the USSR for 1923–4 (a preliminary conception of the subsequent input-output modeling and analysis). From the mid-1920s on, the administration's State Planning Committee began to issue "tentative balance sheets for the economy a year and a half in advance" (so-called Control Figures) for 1925–6, 1926–7, 1927–8, and 1928–9, and then prospective five-year plans for 1925–6 to 1929–30 and for 1926–7 to 1930–1.

By 1929 the one functional agency, Gosplan, began to publish the first five-year plan to be implemented, namely the plan for 1928–9 to 1932–3, based "on the exhaustive politico-economic directives" of the Fifteenth Congress of the Communist Party. This plan, allegedly to be completed in four years, was to drive the country toward rapid industrialization, reconstruct the village on socialist bases, and strengthen the "socialist elements" in the economy as a whole.

Until the collapse of the Soviet Union, the state's central authority launched twelve so-called perspective plans (the twelfth to encompass the years 1986 to 1990). Four of these plans were carried out under Stalin's reign. If, for a moment, one could and would set aside Stalin's massive resort to terror and his generalized, massive murderous actions, and would consider only Stalin's policy objectives, one would have to recognize that these objectives did not differ from those of his colleagues and irreconcilable enemies, such as Leon Trotsky and Grigori Zinoview, whose execution Stalin managed. Nikolai Bukharin noted already in 1928 that "the ideologies of Trotskyism believe that a maximum annual transfer from peasant agriculture into industry secures the maximum rate of development of industry in general," and that "the growth of a planned economy means the possibility (on that dear old basis of withering away of the law of value) of acting any way one pleases."[18] Stalin's and Trotsky's ideas of socialism were in fact typical of those of most of the Marxists of the time.

The Soviet economic plans were a program of action based on the centralized coordination of information, forecasts, and directives for output and capital formation over the period. Key outputs, employment targets, and main consumption objectives were expressed in physical terms on the basis of a system of input-output and consumption balances. There were two types of plans: long-term expansion plans (for capital formation) and yearly working plans dealing with outputs, relation of production to consumption, and so on. Both types of plans had in principle to be coordinated and subdivided for operational periods (quarterly or monthly) and for sectoral and geographical operational levels (regional, district, or local).

---

[18] Bukharin, Nikolai, *Notes of an Economist at the Beginning of a New Economic Year* (1928), *Foundations of Soviet Strategy for Economic Growth . . ., op. cit.*, pp. 260–1.

The expansion plans for ten, fifteen, or twenty years, called *general* plans, laid out a tentative sequence of main projects to be constructed in some leading industries considered significant for both defense and economic growth, for example, electricity, electronics, nucleonics, and petrochemicals. The branch and sector plans were combined into a schematic structural model of the economy of the future. The Soviet plans integrating a set of specific targets for the economy as a whole were called *perspective plans* of five years, except one for seven years duration, providing, not necessarily consistently, the selected bases for the scheduling of yearly orders to the capital construction industries, that is, machine construction, building, and related activities. The five-year periods were selected as corresponding to the length of time needed for engineering, planning, constructing, and commissioning new industrial aggregates. The detailed yearly plans and their quarterly or monthly subdivisions were called *operational* plans.

The starting point for all plans was the formulation of political directives by the secretary general and the party's Politburo, based on political decisions and performance of the economy as indicated by the Central Statistical Administration. The scale of priority – the choice between the various basic tasks – expressed the preferences of the policy makers given the economy's estimated possibilities. Once the directives were formulated, it was the task of the State Planning Committee to translate them into concrete projects. These drafts included data in physical terms, specifying output targets by sector, branches, key commodities, rates of development, and sector proportions. The production phase was essentially viewed as a separate process that interacted with the equally distinct phases of distribution, exchange, and consumption. The drafts (called *control figures*) were submitted to the economic ministries and administrations for detailed working out of the scheduled tasks and for modification and adjustment. These bodies in turn transmitted detailed targets and indices to their enterprises. The enterprises worked out their specific plans and determined their claims within the established framework for equipment, raw materials, and fuels. The projects worked out at the bottom of the state pyramid were transmitted back through the hierarchy, adjusted, recast, and consolidated for all the supervisory agencies. On the bases of these projects, Gosplan prepared the final program to submit to the party for approval. After its approval, the plan became the law of the land.[19]

The excessively detailed plan targets and central commands are illustrated by the number of the material balances concerning production and consumption, elaborated by Gosplan and by Gossnab. In the mid-1980s, Gosplan coordinated production and consumption through the completion of four hundred balances for the five-year plan, and of two thousand balances for each of the one-year plans that approximated the current production. Gossnab

[19] Iun', O., "Developing Management's Planning Mechanism," *Problems of Economics*, Vol. XXIX, No. 7, November 1986, p. 10.

detailed up to fifteen thousand items that were produced and distributed. The ministries drafted up to fifty thousand balances. When Gossnab assigned the respective balances to the producers, the balance mix was enlarged another ten to fifteen times. Finance and credit were for the most part treated as independent categories, as the monetary form of the distribution and redistribution of the national income and product. The indicated balances were not well interconnected: The material (physical) balances were not united in a single system, and the balances in value terms (the national accounts) were not coordinated with the intersector relationships of production and distribution. The gaps in the plans and the divorce between the two aspects occurred because the planners could concentrate only on certain key branches of production and could not go beyond first-order inputs because of the enormous practical difficulties involved. Further, the centralized decisions on the size and nature of capital construction – that is, the intensity of industrialization, the choice of growth branches, the determination of their outputs, and the gradation of plans' efficiency – were all made solely on the basis of technological considerations, independently of prices. Soviet pricing deliberately adopted the regime of centralized physical controls and various restrictions of choices imposed on both producers and consumers. Thus pricing was seriously impaired as an instrument for allocating resources.

The Soviet planners remained incapable of formulating a planning theory that could unite all the physical plans into a single system, and that could in addition integrate them with the financial balances. In these conditions, the core of the Soviet plans continued to consist only of selected physical targets, predicated on the key balances of capital construction, equipment, raw materials, fuel and power, and manpower. Further, the ideas that production and distribution could be carried out primarily on the basis of material accounting and engineering without much regard to "values" (prices) remained dominant, even though increasing discrepancies and disequilibria kept piling up in planning with regard to the efficiency in use of capital resources and of labor and with regard to the quantities, qualities, and design of the products.

Yet, already in the early 1950s, disproportions between sectors, branches, incomes, and goods available continued to increase. Stalin himself asserted, shortly before his death, that the "law of value" – which supposedly was acting blindly under capitalism but not at all under socialism – could bring benefits under socialism if the planners would use it appropriately for rational resource utilization. According to him, the law of value could reign spontaneously only at the periphery of the state complex, but on the other hand it could "nudge" all the socialist sectors toward rational resource allocation, rigorous accounting discipline, and methodical production efforts.[20] The question of

---

[20] Stalin, J. V., *Economic Problems of Socialism in the USSR*, New York, International Publishers, 1952, pp. 19–20.

price, value, and economic calculation finally gained broader attention in the USSR itself in the 1960s *inter alia* under the influence of various deep crises that occurred throughout Eastern Europe (notably in Hungary in 1954–7, in Poland in 1956–7, and in Czechoslovakia in 1963–8), where the numerous dysfunctional consequences of the centralized, coercive Soviet-type planning and management system became literally unbearable. In the USSR, in the early 1960s, the Soviet academician V. S. Nemchinov proposed a critical change in planning methods – a change widely debated at the time, involving notably the possible passage in planning from commands to contractual obligations, based on cost accounting. According to Nemchinov, this cost accounting was to be built on prices acceptable to both the respective planning agency and the respective enterprise, prices, and contracts that the signing parties would view as definite, unchangeable obligations. In the prevailing system of planned assignments (*zadania*) to the enterprises, added Nemchinov, there were only unilateral obligations; the enterprises were indeed receiving the plan targets without the superior agency having any responsibility for discrepancies and miscalculations in the plans.[21] While the Nemchinov proposals were not carried out, the focus on value and price remained the order of the day. By the mid-1960s, the so-called Alexey Kosygin reform aimed at improving planning via the administrative rationalization of prices and the use of sales – instead of gross output, profits, and profitability – as indices for evaluating an enterprise's performance. All this, however, was supposed to coexist obligatorily with the fulfillment by the enterprises of "the planned contractual deliveries in *physical* form with respect to quantity, quality, and assortment." Ultimately, the Soviet reform, referred to as "the New System of Planning and Economic Incentives," brought about some administrative price overhauls, increased responsibility of suppliers for products, and restructured budgetary deductions – but it did not indicate how the authorities could achieve a system of correct prices. The planners remained as before unable to coordinate the various production processes, and moreover to create a consistent set of millions of prices continually adjusted to changes in priorities, technologies, and factor supply. The overall practical results proved disappointing, and many cardinal principles of the reform were soon circumvented.[22]

The last secretary general of the Communist Party before the collapse of the Soviet regime, Mikhail Gorbachev, tried in the mid-1980s to engage the Soviet Union in a vast process of decentralization and reorganization down to its foundations. With regard to economic calculation, he stated notably

[21] Nemchinov, V., "Socialist Economic Management and Production Planning" (*Kommunist*, No. 5, March 1964), trsl. in *Current Digest of the Soviet Press*, Vol. XVI, No. 18, 1964, pp. 3–8.
[22] Halm, George, N., "Mises, Lange, Liberman: Allocation and Motivation in the Socialist Economy," *Weltwirtschaftliches Archiv*, Band 100, Heft 1, 1968, p. 31; Spulber, Nicolas, *Restructuring the Soviet Economy in Search of the Market*, Ann Arbor, MI, University of Michigan Press, 1991, p. 186.

in 1987 that commodity-money relations were certainly an organic part of the socialist economic system and that their skillful use "through prices and financial credit levers, and through planned mastering and management of the market," would facilitate the creation of an appropriate mechanism for holding down costs. He did not, however, go far beyond these generalities.[23] In 1988, he took a step further and stated with regard to the "revolutionary restructuring" of the Soviet system that much of this kind of transformation depended on the reform of pricing. He then added that the "unsettled problems of the revision of wholesale, purchase and retail prices" were indeed greatly complicating the implementation of overall economic changes. As he put it, "without a price reform we will be unable to create normal economic relations in the national economy, ensure a valid assessment of outlays and production results and equivalency in the exchange of goods and services." Until the end of its existence, the Soviet system proved, however, consistently incapable of achieving these "normal economic relations," notwithstanding Gorbachev's laments and warnings that the pricing problem had to be solved "no matter how difficult it may be and no matter what doubts and apprehensions it may cause."[24]

The Soviet system's evident incapacity to solve efficaciously the problems of economic accounting, and its inability to combine in a satisfactory fashion central planning commands with some rational forms of pricing, largely justified an old contention of the Western economist Ludwig von Mises. Von Mises argued that the market and its functions in the formation of prices – which, as he put it, are "the essence of capitalism" – cannot be "artificially imitated under socialism," no matter the scale of efforts spent in this regard. Already in 1922 von Mises warned that socialization of the means of production precluded rational economic calculation: Neither artificial markets nor artificial competition could provide ways out of the problem of rational allocation of resources. Neither the various attempts of "rationalizing" the system of pricing under socialism proposed by such notable socialist economists as Oskar Lange and Evsey Liberman, and then by such top Soviet leaders as Kosygin and finally Gorbachev, could perform the task of consistent price determination across factors and goods and solve the problems of rational resource allocation and of adequate labor and management incentives. Decentralizing – but with limits on the centrally determined capital construction involving the bulk of economic resources, centrally normed profits and

---

[23] "On the Party's Tasks in the Fundamental Restructuring of Economic Management," Report by Gorbachev, Mikhail, Secretary General, at the Plenary Session of the CPSU Central Committee on June 25, 1987, *Current Digest of the Soviet Press*, Vol. XXXIX, No. 26, 1987, p. 12.

[24] "On Progress in the Implementation of the Decisions of the 27th CPSU Congress and the Tasks of Deepening Restructuring," report by Gorbachev, Mikhail, Secretary General, at the Nineteenth All-Union CPSU Conference on June 28, 1988, *Current Digest of the Soviet Press*, Vol. XL, No. 26, July 27, 1988, pp. 9–10.

wages, and centrally determined prices – could not yield efficient answers to the problem of economic calculation, and could not put an end to the misallocation and wastage of resources.[25]

11-4. Alternatives

In the Soviet system of planning and management built under Stalin, the state intervened directly and continually in setting the key quantitative and qualitative production targets and in carrying out the processes aimed at meeting these targets. But, as the economy expanded and diversified, wide disproportions arose among the various branches of the economy, and as the planning miscalculations inevitably multiplied, the possibility for the managers of the enterprises to deviate from certain plan commitments while apparently fulfilling all the plan's targets also increased significantly. The central pressures upon resources to make them yield a maximum product inevitably generated complex evasive practices throughout the entire socioeconomic setup.

The managers began to develop sets of methods for simulating the plan's fulfillment in order to avoid the risks incurred when the commanded tasks were not carried out. It became increasingly evident already before the war that the managers produced certain outputs in the quantities required but without regard to their quality, since the buyers were not in the position to be choosers, and since many of these buyers constituted the best outlet for the disposal of rejects. Further, the managers began increasingly to hoard various goods and to build up extensive reserves of labor and materials on which they would rely in case of urgent and unexpected needs. Moreover, the managers developed close contacts with ministries' officials in order to reduce their assigned production tasks, and with banks' officials so that they would overlook unplanned uses of the enterprise's funds. Finally, the entire managerial structure generated the development of a network of intermediary pushers and go-getters – called *tolkachi* – whose tasks were to obtain, through influence, mutual understandings, direct exchange and/or graft goods in short supply, of better quality and at lower prices, plus various other plan accommodations. This ramifying effect of the plans' rigid commands and vast miscalculation generated what the Russians called *blat* – a complex combination of protection, pull, graft, and outright thievery – throughout the economy as a whole.[26]

---

[25] Von Mises, Ludwig, *Socialism, An Economic and Sociological Analysis* (published in German in 1922), transl. by Kahane, J., from the second edition of 1932 and some additions of 1936), Indianapolis, Liberty Classics, 1981, pp. XIX–XXIV, 5–14, 473–8.

[26] See Berliner, Joseph S., *Factory and Manager in the USSR*, Cambridge, MA, Harvard University Press, 1957, pp. 182–205; Ledeneva, Alena V., *Russia's Economy of Favors, Blat, Networking and Informal Exchange*, Cambridge, Cambridge University Press, 1988, pp. 117–19.

These undermining processes of the Soviet planning mechanism, affecting also all relations both in the economy and in the society, continued to expand to the point that by the mid-1980s, Gorbachev had to recognize openly their widespread deleterious consequences, which he wanted to overcome. In his report to the Central Committee of the Communist Party, in January 1987, Gorbachev, then the party's general secretary, detailed openly a host of examples of what he called the "adverse process" corroding the party, the planning system, and the society at large. He noted that planning was "subverted by subjective approaches, imbalances, instability, the striving to embrace everything down to trifles," combined with a host of decisions taken "without regard for real possibilities." Further, there were misconceptions about the role of monetary-commodity relations and voluntaristic attitudes in the economy that had led to "loss of accountability, to wage leveling and to subjective approaches to price formation." Communist leaders had been proven guilty in numerous regions and towns of "embezzlement, bribe taking and report padding," but "inertia, a tendency to brush aside all that did not fit into conventional patterns," continued to prevail in "policy-making and practical work." Thus, notwithstanding the preceding assorted reshuffling undertaken since the 1980s concerning in particular the number and kind of functions of the formal planning organizations, the specific rights and obligations in the line of duty, and the sets of incentives and controls and their obvious lack of results, certain Soviet leaders, including Gorbachev, continued at the time to believe that out there, somewhere, was "the perfect organizational structure and the perfect set of instructions governing inter-hierarchical relationships"[27] that will allow a happy, lasting combination between a properly modified Soviet system and a carefully managed expanding scope of the market.

However, by the end of the 1980s, the decomposition of the Soviet system and society became so complete and evident that the question of transition from central planning to some kind of restoration of market relations became imperative. The leadership's differences coalesced around three basic strategies: The first focused in particular on the new legal framework that would be needed for this purpose; the second centered its attention on the questions of denationalizations and on the speed of price changes; the third, finally, concentrated on the financial and monetary improvements, the gradual transition to market prices, and the broadening of "the sphere of market relations." The first strategy, embodied in the so-called Ryzhkov Plan, was a product of archetypical technocrats; it concerned itself very much with the shaping of the legal foundations of a market economy – especially with reforming prices and reducing administrative restrictions – with the whole reform extending

[27] Gorbachev, Mikhail, *Reorganization and the Party's Personnel Policy*, Report and Concluding Speech by the General Secretary, January 27–8, 1987, Moscow, Novosti, 1987, pp. 10, 12–14.

over a period of five years (1990–5). The second strategy, devised by Stanislav S. Shatalin – which, after its approval by Boris N. Yeltsin, became known as the Yeltsin Plan – stressed the need of changing "in 500 days" the extent of existing nationalizations and the liberalization of prices while avoiding "price shocks," ensuring market stabilization, and finally privatizing no less than 70 percent of the industrial enterprises. The third and last strategy proposed by Gorbachev (who was then still at the head of the USSR) advocated the transition to a full-fledged "market" to be implemented over an unspecified period of time. This task, however, was to be achieved in four sequential stages: The first would improve financial and monetary aspects of the state budget, suppress the emission of money, and restructure the banking system; during the second, a gradual transition would be achieved with regard to the "liberalization of prices" for a broad range of production and technical outputs; in the third stage, market relations would be broadened in various directions; finally, the last stage, would effect an "accelerated" formation of self-regulatory mechanisms, notably with regard to demonopolization, denationalization, and privatization.[28]

All this collapsed by 1990–1, as the entire Soviet Union was literally disintegrating and as the population was losing at an incredible speed all interest in the maintenance or mending of the old Soviet setup.

11-5. Concluding Comments

To set in relief what he viewed as the changing phases of capitalism, and using for the purpose a Hegelian kind of imagery, Marx focused in *Capital* on the changing nature and status of private property. According to him, first, the capitalist private property based "on the exploitation of the so-called free labor" constituted a negation of the self-earned individual private property that it increasingly replaced. Second, the subsequent expanding centralization of capital involving the expropriation of many individual capitalist private properties constituted in its turn a "negation of the negation." Eventually, capitalist private property would be replaced by the socialist property after the expropriation of the "few usurpers" who were finally owning it.

Of course, many evolutionary phases could be viewed à la Marx, as subsequent "negations" – as *reversals* of previous situations. In the case of the Soviet Union's evolution, the NEP could be viewed as the "negation" of War Communism, the Stalinist system as a "negation of the negation," that is, as

---

[28] Schroeder, Gertrude, E., "The Soviet Economy on a Treadmill of Reforms," in *Soviet Economy in a Time of Change: A Compendium for the JEC, 96th Congress, 1st Session*, Vol. I, Washington, DC, GOP, 1979, pp. 312–13, and Schroeder, Gertrude, E., "Organizations and Hierarchies. The Perennial Search for Solutions," in *Reorganization and Reform in the Soviet Economy*, Linz, S. J., and Moskoff, W., eds., Armonk, NY, M. E. Sharpe, 1988, pp. 3–20.

a rejection of the NEP and as a return in many respects to the concepts and methods of War Communism. Finally, the Gorbachev perestroika (and to an extent various preceding attempts at reform) involved in their turn a "negation of the negation," that is, a rejection of the Stalinist system and implicitly also of War Communism, and a return to various concepts and orientations of the NEP.[29]

The parallels between War Communism and the Stalinist setup are indeed evident as are in key respects those between the NEP and the Gorbachev perestroika. Under War Communism and under the Stalinist setup, the top hierarchy of the fused party-state assumed the task of building a socialist socioeconomic system as defined by Marx and Engels in their 1848 *Communist Manifesto*, that is, a postcapitalist transitional command and control administration inevitably leading to the ideal Communist society.[30] In the ongoing process of building socialism in the regimes of War Communism and Stalinism, the elimination of all private property in production and distribution posited the need to manage centrally the economy and all of its branches as a whole. The determination of the tasks involved and the supervision of their execution were patterned on those of a war economy and were eventually based on a single overall command and control. The only differences between the two regimes centered on the uses of money and price; both excluded market relations between the state undertakings, but the Stalinist setup did not exclude such relations also *outside* the state complex, that is, in relation to wages and distribution. The parallels between the NEP and perestroika – both "negations" of the closely interrelated War Communism and the Stalinist setup – involved various conceptual retreats from markets and prices, and various limitations on management and the scope of the central commands and controls. The main break concerned the interrelations of the party-state and the nature and object of "socialist" socioeconomic relations. In War Communism and in the Stalinist regime, the party's and the state's tasks, means, and methods coincided fully; in the NEP and perestroika, party and state were recognized as different entities, whose objectives and means coincided only in certain respects. The reduction of the scope of the state's ownership in the economy, and the search for diversity in ownership forms, posited deep reconsideration of the nature and extent of the subsistence of centralized commands and controls, changes in the roles of money and price and in the scope of market relations, and finally some concrete decisions with regard to the speed and extent of the transition toward a market-directed economy.

---

[29] Spulber, Nicolas, *Redefining the State. Privatization and Welfare Reform in Industrial and Transitional Economies*, Cambridge, UK, Cambridge University Press, 1997, p. 108.

[30] Marx, Karl, *Capital*, Vol. I, pp. 761–4; cf. Marx, Karl, *Economy and Social Revolution*, Jordan, Z. A., ed., London, Michael Joseph, p. 239.

War Communism lasted for a short period. So did the NEP, as well as perestroika's attempted changes. The Stalinist setup alone endured from its coalescence in 1929 to its virtual collapse in 1985–90, apparently without any crucial modifications. In fact, as we will see in further detail, the Stalinist setup suffered complex and well-hidden continuous processes of internal deterioration and decay, some of whose consequences perestroika tried in vain to overcome, until the complete collapse of the entire Soviet system.

CHAPTER 12

The Economic Policies

12-1. Agricultural Policy

The Soviet policies on agriculture, industry, trade, and finance cannot be properly understood without keeping in view the changing frameworks within which the Soviet leadership tried to handle the question of the relations between market and what they viewed as its antimony, namely socialism. Recall that under War Communism, the Bolsheviks, notwithstanding World War and Civil War destruction, attempted to transform the economy completely and eliminate from it market relations, which they considered the generators of capitalism. Under the ensuing insuperable necessity of coping with the economy's total collapse, the Bolsheviks resorted to the NEP, that is, to the restoration of market relations at the borders of the economy's "commanding heights," which they kept firmly in their hands. They maintained the ensuing "mixed" system, defined by Lenin as state capitalism, until they perceived the achievement of full economic recovery. Afterward, Stalin engaged the country in a global planning and industrialization process aiming to transform Russia from an agricultural country into an industrial one on the basis of "socialist" dictatorship but with the use of variously controlled and distorted market relations. Finally, as multiple, complex, internal dislocations became increasingly hard to handle, the return to a kind of "mixed" economic framework of the NEP type appeared as indispensable to avoid if possible the expanding pressures for a direct transition to a market-directed economic system.

Let me sketch now the evolving agricultural policies within these frameworks. During War Communism (from the middle of 1918 to March 1921), the Bolsheviks in power under Lenin's leadership issued a number of decrees concerning the nationalization of land, its partitioning among collective farms, the requisition by the state of the peasants' "surplus" of grain, and the elimination of market-oriented activities. As Lenin stated it, "the bourgeoisie arises from market based production." Simply put, the peasant "who has 100 poods of surplus grain (1 pood = 36 pounds) that he doesn't need for his family

192

and doesn't turn over to the workers' state – what is that? Isn't that the bourgeoisie? Isn't that where it arises?" As for individual land use, Lenin's views, embodied in February 1919 in the "Statute on Socialist Land Use Policy and Measures to Accomplish the Transition to Socialist Agriculture," were also simple and direct: "all forms of individual land use should be viewed as transitional and obsolete." Accordingly, the Bolsheviks organized special ruthless detachments that the state sent throughout the countryside to procure grain at fixed low prices, and in case of refusal, to confiscate it. As a result of these and related antipeasant measures, great declines took place in sown areas, crop outputs and yields, and livestock numbers. By 1920 these declines resulted in widespread famine in certain regions. Yet, as far as land ownership was concerned, while the class war in the villages led ultimately to the elimination of landlords' estates as well as of many of the larger peasant holdings, the turmoil in the villages and the disaster in the towns led many landless peasants back to the countryside. Thus, the number of small family farms rose sharply over time; simply put, the poorer peasants gained land at the expense of their neighbors.[1]

The disastrous economic consequences of War Communism forced the Bolsheviks to change policies, remove many of the brutal restrictions placed on some of the middle and the upper strata of the peasantry, and focus their attention on the recovery of production, first in agriculture, and then in all the other branches of the economy ruined by their previous policies. The first, primary measure of the NEP was to replace the requisitioning of agricultural produce with a food tax. Further, during the NEP, a whole system of measures aimed at giving full support to the poor peasants, organizing various forms of cooperation with the middle peasants, and restricting the growth of the rich (*kulak*) peasant households. While upholding the nationalization of land – as state property left largely to peasant management – the state recognized the rights of the actual occupiers in their investments in the land, authorized the hiring of machinery, implements, cattle, and labor, and accepted even land leasing. By 1926, as the harvested grain crops finally reached the 1913 level, the government revised its policies, increased substantially its pressure (via taxation) on the *kulaks*, while at the same time fanning discord in the countryside and multiplying the development of agricultural cooperatives among the poor peasants. Toward the close of 1927, the drive toward the liquidation of the *kulak* farms and toward the collectivization of agriculture received an increasingly powerful impetus that was to transform itself into a vast and brutal mass reorganization of the village and the economy as a whole.[2]

---

[1] Selyunin, Vasily, "On Early Soviet Policies" (*Novyi Mir*, No. 5, May 1988), *Current Digest of the Soviet Press*, Vol. XL, No. 40, pp. 14–17; Nove, Alec, *An Economic History of the USSR*, New York, Penguin Books, 1972, p. 106; Baykov, Alexander, *The Development of the Soviet Economic System, op. cit.*, pp. 16–24.

[2] Baykov, Alexander, *The Development of the Soviet Economic System, op. cit.*, pp. 132–9.

By 1929, the Communist party-state under Stalin's leadership launched the country on the path of the all-out collectivization of agriculture. As Stalin put it on the eve of this drive, in November 1928, the Soviet system could not proceed indefinitely with two different foundations, namely a large-scale industry and "the most scattered and backward small economy and peasantry." Accordingly the Soviet party-state had to engage, as Stalin put it, in the "amalgamation of small peasant farms into large collective farms . . . and in the squeezing out of the capitalist elements from agriculture." As Alec Nove rightly pointed out, as this process unfolded, the lowest peasant strata that had not been destroyed in the turmoil could not have survived its consequences without the eventual official toleration in and after 1930 of some limited private food growing and family raising of some domestic animals. Great bitterness had been caused even in the lowest peasant strata, in the hungry villages, by the collectives' forced acquisition of livestock, especially of cows, and by the ensuing absence of milk for the peasants' children. Agriculture reached its lowest point in 1933. After that date, even though the collectivization drive continued, household private farming registered the beginnings of a slow and painful recovery. In the meantime, the peasants were deprived of all political influence and found themselves completely confined to the periphery of Soviet life.[3]

During the critical period 1929–40, much of industrial growth and urban construction were due to the use of agriculture as the basis of industry's development in terms of capital transfers and of the shift of labor and agriculture toward industry and urban construction sites. From the beginning of the planning era and throughout all its years, the basic element in the planning of agricultural production was the state procurement of agricultural produce at state-determined prices. These purchases, which reached very high shares of various marketable farm produce, were meant to be sufficient to supply the population with foodstuffs and the industries with cotton, flax, sugar beet, tobacco, wool, and hides fully (or almost fully) sold to the state. Within the collectives, members' pay was low, while the terms of trade imposed on the villages were extremely unfavorable, and the practice of compulsory deliveries of grains and all the other products at low prices was inflexibly imposed. The practice of paying the collective farm members in kind, with some cash in arrears only after the sales proceeds had been realized, put the collective's peasant members in an inferior position to that of farm or industrial workers.

After Stalin's death in 1953, it was recognized officially that investments per farm were insufficient, that the peasants were paid too little, and that productivity continued to be very low. During the leadership of Nikita Khrushchev, the increasing evidence of the impossibility of rapidly increasing agricultural yields led to the launching in 1954 of a new agricultural policy, namely that

---

[3] Stalin, J. V., "Speech Delivered at the Plenum of the Central Committee" (Nov. 19, 1928), *Works*, Vol. 11, in *Foundations of the Soviet Strategy . . ., op. cit.*, p. 271; Nove, Alec, *An Economic History of the USSR, op. cit.*, p. 84.

of immediately expanding the sown areas by bringing into cultivation some 13 million hectares of virgin lands, to be expanded eventually to 28 or 30 million hectares in Northern Kazakhstan, the southern parts of Siberia, and the southeast of European Russia. All this necessitated a vast amount of resources of which the traditional agricultural regions were to be deprived. Ultimately, the results of this policy turned out to be wasteful and ineffective. By 1964, the new leaders of the USSR, Leonid Brezhnev and Alexey Kosygin, adopted a new strategy concerning this unfortunate sector. Their new policy aimed at modernizing and rehabilitating certain villages and limiting emigration from the countryside. But of the existing 705,000 villages, only some 120,000 were declared as having a "viable" outlook (*perspektivnye*), while the rest of 585,000 were declared as devoid of development prospects (*bezperspektivnye*). The plan set a twenty-five-year target for the transformation of the "viable" villages into productive urban-type settlements. But after years of effort and of important investments, the plan was finally abolished as yielding only minor results and, moreover, as further disrupting appropriate food supplies for the cities.[4] All these policies were conducted while pursuing indefatigably the consolidation and the transformation of the collective farms into state farms, continually reinforcing the latter with all kind of subsidies and support well into the 1980s.

Under Mikhail Gorbachev's leadership – first from 1978 to 1983 as the party's senior agricultural official, and then as secretary general until the collapse of the USSR – gigantic plans were again drawn about the reorganization of agriculture and the growth in labor productivity, crop yields, livestock, and the variety and quality of foodstuffs. By the mid-1980s the Council of Ministers set up under its direction a State Agro-Industrial Committee (*Gosagroprom*) as the state's super-agency for the management of the country's entire agro-industrial complex, involving in its work all the ministries related to agricultural production (those of Procurement, Light Industry, Land Reclamation, Farm Machinery, and so on). *Gosagroprom* was supposed to improve the national distribution of agricultural products and to increase the specialization and the concentration of production, but its activities were often blocked by the divergent objectives of its component ministries, and its actual results remained in many respects far below the reformers expectations. Gorbachev also stressed the need to change radically the state's ways of exercising the rights of socialist land ownership, by recognizing the equality of the different farms of actual land distribution and management, namely state farms, collective farms, and peasant auxiliary farms. By 1988, he aggressively promoted the idea of massive long-term land leasing as a way to increase output by freeing

---

[4] Friedgut, Theodore, H., *The Persistence of the Peasant in Soviet Society*, Jerusalem, Mayrock Center for Soviet and East European Research, Hebrew University of Jerusalem, Research paper No. 64, May 1987, pp. 6–7.

agriculture from the state's paralyzing controls. At the time, about one-fifth of the state and collective farms were already leasing land and equipment to individuals, families, and small cooperatives. Long-term land leasing, the growth in the number of cooperative farms, and the expansion in the amount of goods that farmers could sell in the open market were supposed to combat waste, to maximize the output of agriculture rapidly, and notably to increase food supplies and to reduce imports. As Gorbachev put it in March 1989: "the reality is this: We do not produce enough agricultural output. The state is forced to make large purchases abroad of grain, meat, fruit, vegetables, sugar, vegetable oil and certain other products.... Up to now, we have been unable to resolve the food question in a fundamental way."[5] Much resistance developed, however, in the state's vast agricultural bureaucracy against Gorbachev's ideas and tutelage. The conflict broke into the open in the Politburo, which in 1989 finally appointed a Gorbachev adversary, Igor K. Ligachev, to run agricultural policy. Ligachev opposed notably Gorbachev's proposals of liquidating unprofitable collective and state farms in favor of new cooperative owners, ending the requisitions of the agricultural "surpluses," relaxing the prevailing price curbs, and, eventually, granting farmers the right to choose freely the ways of marketing their products.[6]

Many party bureaucrats viewed with displeasure Gorbachev's approval of the key NEP policies replacing grain requisitions with the tax in kind, encouraging the development of cooperatives, authorizing land leasing, and eventually establishing "equivalent exchanges" between the city and the countryside. These bureaucrats particularly considered unacceptable his assertions that Stalin and his entourage, after rejecting the NEP rationale, had simply "implemented to all intents and purposes Trotsky's and Preobrazhenskii's concept...of primitive socialist accumulation through the virtually uncompensated pumping of money out of agriculture and into industry." Yet, under the pressure of the entourage of the party's cadres, Gorbachev hesitated to be consistent, to put into practice his own views, or to accept the idea of the transition of Russian agriculture to full-scale private property. As he put it in an interview granted to a correspondent of the *New York Times* one year before the downfall of both his government and the Soviet Union, private property was not "a precept" of his program. Perhaps, he added, "as our economy is reformed, we will develop a new type of economy, perhaps there will appear

[5] "Report by Mikhail Gorbachev at the Plenary Session of CPSU Central Committee on March 15, 1989" (*Pravda*, March 16, 1989), transl. in *Current Digest of the Soviet Press*, Vol. XLI, No. 11 (April 1989), p. 3.

[6] See notably Gorbachev's speeches and reports: "Put Cooperatives' Potential in the Service of Restructuring," speech at the Fourth All-Union Congress of Collective Farmers on March 12, 1988 (*Pravda*, March 24, 1988), transl. in *Current Digest of the Soviet Press*, Vol. XL, No. 12 (April 20, 1988); "Develop Leasing, Restructure Economic Relations in the Countryside" (*Pravda*, October 14, 1988), transl. in *Current Digest of the Soviet Press*, Vol. XLI, No. 2 (February 21, 1989).

farms that will in some way resemble small scale private property," but, he concluded "to make it a program, I would not do this."[7] That's as far as the official policy of the Communist Party leadership could go before the regime's final breakdown.

12-2. Industrial Policy

From the moment of their arrival in power, the Bolsheviks set out to dismantle at great speed the remnants of Russia's feudal-capitalist system and to replace them with a so-called socialist organization based on Marx and Engels' concepts as embodied in their *Communist Manifesto* of 1848. In the few months that followed the country's military debacle, the disintegration of its socio-economic fabric, and the collapse of its administration, the Bolsheviks rapidly concentrated state power in their hands, resorted to the nationalization of the economy, and attempted to run its operations on the pattern of organization of war economies. In November 1917, they set up a Supreme Council of the National Economy (SCNE) with the tasks of shaping and handling the economy's organization and preparing appropriate plans for the economy's development. Also at the time, the government issued a decree introducing workers' control over all enterprises' "production, purchases, storage and finance," with the aim of engaging the industrial workers in the actual management of administration of the economic apparatus. These programs, however, instead of raising labor's productivity, weakened labor discipline and furthered the processes of production decline. After the party issued a number of decrees concerning obligatory work for all citizens, a law of January 29, 1918, finally introduced the conscription of all labor and the attachment of all workers to their place of work. With neither the SCNE nor another council set up to coordinate the activities of the economic commissariats (the future ministries), the Council of Labor and Defense worked out a plan of development for the economy as a whole. A state plan for the electrification of Russia (*Goelro*), including projects of engineering development and of construction of large-scale regional powerstations, was issued in 1920 and attributed to Lenin himself. Then, the following year, in February 1921, on the eve of the introduction of the NEP, the government set up under the leadership of the Council of Labor and Defense a State Planning Commission (*Gosplan*) with the task of working out a "General State Plan as well as the means and order for carrying it out." However, several years went by before Gosplan drew up in 1925 the "Control Figures of National Economy 1925–1926," and, years later, as we will see further on, Gosplan's control figures became an overall plan for the national economy.[8]

---

[7] Keller, Bill, "Gorbachev Says It's Not Time for Soviet Private Property," from Moscow, *New York Times*, November 17, 1989.

[8] Baykov, Alexander, *The Development of the Soviet Economic System, op. cit.*, pp. 424–6.

At the Tenth Party Congress, in March 1921, Lenin openly stated that "on the economic front, in our attempt to pass over to Communism, we have suffered by the spring of 1921, a more serious defeat than any previously inflicted by Kolchak, Denikin, or Pilsudski." The NEP was then set up with the immediate targets of increasing by all means the goods produced and reintroducing trade in lieu of the prevailing barter, while maintaining in the hands of the state only the economy's "commanding heights." In short, the state kept in its hands the large industrial enterprises, but denationalized most of the small enterprises and leased them to cooperatives or to private entrepreneurs. Of the 165,781 enterprises officially accounted for at the time, only 8.5 percent were to remain in the hands of the state, but these accounted for 84.1 percent of the total employed workers. Yet, at the Twelfth Party Congress of April 1923, the Soviet state openly recognized that the large-scale industry had its basic capital worn out and that its deficiencies in working capital resulted in low utilization of production capacity and in economic instability that showed that the state had placed under its administration "more enterprises than it was feasible in the present conditions." Accordingly, the state decided to concentrate production in the best-suited enterprises and to close temporarily or liquidate some of its smaller trusts. By 1923–4, while agricultural production had reached 75 percent of its 1913 level, industrial output reached only one-third of its prewar level. From 1924–5 on, the state financing of industry began to exceed the revenue that the budget derived from that sector. In the last years of the NEP, the renovation and the further expansion of industry proceeded on the basis of increased funding by the state budget. By 1926–7, the process restoring industrial capacity and fully utilizing existing equipment was completed. Side by side with the state industry's recovery, the economic regulation of private industry increased. Only twenty-three foreign concessions in the manufacturing industry were still operational in 1927. By 1928 the total employment in industry reached the figure of 4.3 million, compared to 1.9 million in 1922, and 3.1 million in 1913.

From the launch of five-year plans (FYPs), the Soviet system continually aimed, as Stalin once put it, "to create such an industry in our country as to be able to rearm and reorganize not only industry as a whole, but also transportation and agriculture, on the basis of socialism." Emphasis was placed from the beginning on the expansion of producers' goods ("industries A") and secondarily only of that of consumers' goods ("industries B"). Between 1928 and 1942, the Soviet Union launched three FYPs. During the first (1929–32) – an FYP allegedly completed in four years – capital investments reached twice the total of the preceding ten years. Three-quarters of the capital earmarked for industry went to heavy industry. Certain of the latter, such as motor-works, ferrous metallurgy, chemical, and aviation industries, were built from scratch. New major state enterprises were established during the period, including the Magnitogorsk and the Kuznetsk metallurgical combines, along with tractor-works, engineering stations, power centers, and mines. During the second FYP

(1933–7), the ambitious, skewed industrialization drive continued unabated. Capital investments reached twice the level of the first FYP. New industrial centers were created in Siberia and Central Asia. According to the official data, forty-five hundred major industrial enterprises were built and put into operation, including important metallurgical plants. In the meantime, in 1937, a vast bloody purge of the party, state administration, and industry's management was carried out without any officially registered declines in the supply of equipment, construction schedules, or contract obligations; by then, Stalin's dictatorship was in absolute control, capable of the bloody liquidation of any of its former political adversaries in the party and of striking terror throughout the country as a whole. Nevertheless, the third FYP (1938–1942) was launched with the usual fanfare, but had to be stopped after three and a half years, when Nazi Germany attacked the USSR. Before World War II, some three thousand major industrial enterprises were said to have been put into operation during the FYPs; by 1940 the industrial labor force had officially risen to 13.1 million, well over three times the 1928 level. The war brought about enormous destruction of the Soviet industrial machine. Yet by 1946, it was officially stated that some seventy-five hundred factories demolished during the war had been restored and that new enterprises had been developed, notably in heavy industry.

The fourth FYP (1946–50), the first after World War II, aimed to attain the prewar production levels and to launch new programs concerning notably trans-Caucasus metallurgical works, heavy machine-tool work, and prefabricated structures for construction. Finally, throughout the fifth FYP (1951–5) – during which Stalin died (in 1953) – most allocations for heavy industry focused on the power engineering branches, new mines, and oil fields. By 1955 the labor force engaged in industry reached 19 million, compared to 10.7 million at the end of the war (1945). As the prewar overall industrial levels had been significantly surpassed, the planners turned their attention to the "intensification" of various industrial outputs. The sixth FYP (1956–60) – replaced in 1959 by another long-term plan, discussed later – set as targets the building of five thousand industrial enterprises, including notably hydroelectric plants, metallurgical plants, and powerstations in Siberia, the Ukraine, and Kazakhstan. By 1960, the total employment in the Soviet industry was stated to have reached 22.6 million, a level achieved by United States manufacturing in 1929 (22.4 million). In 1959, under Nikita Khrushchev's leadership, the "extraordinary" Twenty-first Party Congress decided to launch a seven-year plan (1959–65) to speed up the development of the chemical industry, superphosphate enterprises, and high powerstations. During this period, 3,290 enterprises were said to have opened, including the Bratsk station, stated to be the world's largest powerstation. By 1965 employment in the Soviet industry reached 27.4 million, compared to 26.5 million in the United States in 1959, a date when profound technological developments and new interrelations between industry and services, and between the national and the global world market, were leading to *decreases* in U.S. industrial employment, while industrial employment continued to grow in the technologically lagging Soviet industry.

The eighth FYP (1966–70) did officially accentuate both production efficiency and certain highly advertised industrial shifts. Some nineteen hundred industrial enterprises were to have been put into operation during that period, including major steel, cement, and mineral fertilizer plants. Moreover, for the first time in many years, increased allocations were to have been made for expanding and reconstructing various light industry factories and food industry plans. The next FYP, the ninth (1971–5), aimed officially even more resolutely to boost living standards through agricultural building programs and through agricultural "industrialization," thanks to the building of livestock complexes, poultry-dressing plants, chemical fertilizer warehouses, and agromachinery repair stations. Yet, the real accent of the plan continued to be placed as usual on heavy industry, and concerned notably the building of a nuclear plant (in Leningrad), blast furnaces (at Krivoi Rog), automobile works (the Volga), and chemical combines. Under the tenth FYP (1976–80), the official accent was finally placed on modernizing and reequipping the existing plant facilities. From the beginning of the central planning era, the Soviet system aimed first to allocate the largest share of investments to new construction projects while relying in the already available industries on keeping their increasingly obsolete equipment in production. Besides accentuating reequipment, the tenth FYP also directed important investments to the development of mineral resources (of iron ore, bauxite, and chalk), notably of the so-called Kursk Magnetic Anomaly. The policy of renovating and reequipping existing facilities was set to continue also through the eleventh FYP (1980–5). In the meantime, a heated debate arose among the country's economists about the regime's industrial policy in general and about the appropriate size and pattern of investment allocations. In his first year in the country's top office, Gorbachev tried to establish a long-term recovery plan, with the stated goal of modernizing Soviet industry and reaching during a decade of overall technological expansion the level of the leading Western economies. The targets of the twelfth and last FYP (1986–90) began to be debated in 1984, when Gorbachev was still "second" secretary of the party; he was then pressing for more ambitious targets than the Gosplan was ready to accept, a conflict that finally resulted in the drawing of multiple drafts of the twelfth FYP. The final plan aimed at propelling the modernizing economy on a higher growth trajectory of more than 5 percent per annum from the late 1980s on through 1990, relying on the engineering branches and the domestic machinery building and metal working industry rather than on foreign supplies. It should be noted that since the 1960s, the technologically lagging Soviet Union had experienced the most rapid industrial employment growth among the major industrial economies. By 1989, while the Soviet industrial workforce – operating with much technologically backward machinery and equipment – had *increased* to 36.4 million, that of the most technologically developed economy, the United States, had *decreased* to 18.4 million.

The allocation of Soviet investable resources during the successive FYPs displayed indeed a basic consistency in its policy choices. From 72–80 percent of the total investable resources were allocated to material production, and a decreasing share of 28 to 20 percent was left for the "nonproductive" sphere (that is, for services excluding trade and transport, which Soviet statistics included under material production). Systematically, more than a third of the country's total investments went to manufacturing, and as much as 90 percent of them were provided for the industries of Group A, the producer of intermediate products and equipment. Inevitably, the country's capital stock acquired the skewed structure commanded by the skewed investments allocation pattern. From 1985 on, Gorbachev denounced the policy of incessantly emphasizing the building of new productive assets, and emphasized instead the need to renovate the existing ones; he recommended reductions in the fuels and raw materials bases, and pointed to the need for conservation and better use of the output available. Asserting that growth depended to a crucial degree on machine building, which embodies fundamental scientific and technological ideas, he pushed for a vaster concentration of resources in the engineering branches than ever before. Gorbachev, and along with him the Twenty-Seventh Party Congress (1986), asserted that engineering was the priority sector to which investment must be allocated. But by that time, Soviet industry had to cope with expanding imbalances, obvious technological retardation in comparison with the west, and uncontrollable waste and inefficiencies, which made the goal of modernization practically inaccessible. At the collapse of the Soviet Union, the country was left with the results of the long-standing, skewed pattern of allocation of resources, which had systematically emphasized the continuous expansion of the military and heavy industries without much regard to the other needs of the population as a whole.[9]

12-3. Commercial Policy

At the beginnings of Soviet power, private trade continued legally in all goods and products not monopolized by state organizations. But the vast economic dislocations caused by World War I and the Civil War, the fall in production,

[9] *The Development of the Soviet Economic System, op. cit.*, pp. 423–75. On the plans' sequence, see *Soviet Economy, Results and Prospects*, Sarkisyants, G. S., ed., Moscow, Progress Publisher 1977, pp. 192–210. On the conceptual basis of Soviet planning as defined under Stalin and continued since then, see Blackwell, William L., *The Industrialization of Russia: A Historical Perspective*, 3rd ed., Arlington Heights, IL, Harland Davidson, Inc., 1994, pp. 116–27. On the relations of the Soviet planning strategy with the Marxian schema of reproduction, see Spulber, Nicolas, *Restructuring the Soviet Economy in Search of the Market*, Ann Arbor, University of Michigan Press, 1991, pp. 53–8.

the rapid loss of the ruble's purchasing power, and the peasants' reluctance to bring their products to the market led to an acute scarcity of goods. Step by step, the Soviet government closed the private banks, abolished commercial secrecy, and resorted to the establishment of state monopolies for particular goods (foods, implements, and machinery), and to confiscations, requisitions, and repression of trade, thus creating a highly uncertain situation in which money, prices, and credit ceased to play their usual role. On April 22, 1918, the government adopted the nationalization of foreign trade, asserting its control over all export and import transactions. On November 21, 1918, it proceeded also to nationalize all internal trade, which made all non-state trade illegal and at the same time liquidated all the old networks of trade. Interestingly, all these were key features of War Communism – the wide state controls, the demonetization of a large part of the economy, the replacement of money with barter transactions between state's departments, and the rationed supply of some essential goods and services. All of these contributed to the further disorganization and disintegration of the failing economy, but were viewed by certain Communist leaders to constitute the "bones and flesh of the ideal Communist society." For them, the passage to the NEP was simply a retreat from socialism to state capitalism.

On the contrary, for other leaders, the transition to the NEP was necessary and inevitable. It was a transition, however, that they considered as involving only a *temporary* reliance on capitalist practices before a new expansion of the struggle to build socialism. As the NEP began, the Soviet administration hoped that it could limit the free market to local transactions while organizing barter on a national scale between the towns and the countryside. But the attempts to limit free sales to local markets failed. The restrictions on trade had to be lifted not only among the public but also among the state enterprises, and among the state enterprises and the public. At the time, the state engaged mainly in the wholesale of manufactured goods, while cooperatives, which had become independent of the state apparatus, were involved in retail trade. According to data for 1922–3, the state and the cooperative trade accounted then for 14.4 percent of the total trade. A uniform stable ruble currency was launched in that year. Further, the government tried to reduce the enormous gap (the "scissors crisis") that had been developing between the constantly rising industrial prices and the declining agricultural prices. On the other hand, the state decided to favor stricter regulation of the industrial prices and systematic expansion of cooperative trade. Gradually, the purveyance of grain, meat, and industrial crops was concentrated in special state and cooperative organizations. By 1926 cooperative trade was accounting for 49.1 percent of retail turnover, state trade for 27.7 percent, and private trade for 23.2 percent. By 1927–8 the share of cooperative trade rose to 61.6 percent of the total, while that of state trade fell to 15.9 percent and that of private trade maintained itself at around 22.5 percent. (Meanwhile the total retail trade turnover had increased between 1922–3 and 1927–8 over four times.) Finally, by 1929, as the Soviet Union discarded the NEP and engaged itself in the new phase of extensive industrialization, collectivization of agriculture, and rationing, it abolished the relations that had prevailed until then in the field of home trade and substituted a new system of organized trade.

During the planning era, the new ad hoc economic levers put to use for "guiding the private consumption" included, beside the central determination of the proportions between the projected growth rates of the producer goods industries (group A) and of the consumer goods industries including a great part of the agricultural output (group B), also the central determination of the proportion between the overall size and structure of consumption, and the level and structure of disposable income and savings. The leaders tried to match the pace of growth of the consumer goods outputs to the income growth of the population so as to stifle the inflationary pressures and avoid the dampening effect of unfulfilled consumer demand. Yet, wide discrepancies arose continually between the projected demand and supply of consumer goods, as reflected in variations in the volume of the population's savings deposits – equal to the unsatisfied demand plus the savings for coping with unexpected cash needs. The reduced availability of the scarce inputs needed for the production of consumer goods, the obsolete and deteriorating character of the equipment of many light industries, the ups and downs of agricultural outputs, the priority claims of exports, and, last but not least, the incapacity of distribution to choose among producers and select among their products – except in the case of the shops reserved for the nomenklatura – severely limited the access to goods and the range of choice among them left to ordinary households. Foreign as well as Soviet analyses of the supply of consumer goods stressed the narrowness of choice with respect to style, design, assortment, quality, durability, convenience, reliability, and attractiveness of the goods that were offered to the consumer. The imbalances of supply forced the Soviet consumer to spend inordinate amounts of time searching for products, trudging from store to store, and standing in endless and exhausting lines. Eventually all this helped the development of all kinds of black markets.

The black market, defined by certain Western economists as "a second economy" or as "a parallel market," and by certain Soviet writers as "the shadow economy," traded illegally in all kinds of goods from all kind of sources, including state stores and factories. Goods available only to the privileged bureaucrats either in the special state stores or from trips abroad commanded high black market prices that were significantly advantageous for the seller. Moreover, not only the supply of goods but also everyday services fell far short of the most elementary demands; this was the case for such things as repair and maintenance of appliances and furniture, tailoring and repair of clothing and shoes, and any kind of household repair needs. Also in short supply were services, such as laundries, cleaners, barber shops, recreational and cultural needs, and many other facilities including hotels and rooming houses. For most citizens, however, the worst problem was notably that of housing: Most urban families lived in crowded, state-owned, subsidized, but neglected apartments, or in communal facilities in which the shadow market was widely represented. The amount spent on services offered by *chastniki* (private providers of services) was at least twice as much as officially estimated; the reasons for this were shortages of both construction materials and of available qualified personnel.

The allocation of Soviet investable resources during the successive FYPs displayed a basic consistency among the main choices. For instance, from the sixth to the eleventh FYP (from 1956 to 1985), systematically more than a third of the total investment allocations went to manufacturing. From this total, Group A received around or over 95 percent, and Group B, from 3.5 to 5 percent. The country's capital stock acquired an increasingly skewed character. Between 1970 and 1986, for instance – a period in which the central planner was supposed to grant benevolent attention to agriculture and light industry – the share of the latter in the capital stock fell from 12.6 percent to 10.9 percent while that of the heavy industry increased from 87.4 percent to 89.1 percent. During the same period, the performance of agriculture underlying both light industries and food processing facilities went from bad to worse, registering poor harvests notably in 1972, 1975, 1979, 1980, and 1981. During this span of time, the share of light industry fell in the total industrial production from 18.8 percent to 13.8 percent, while that of food processing industries declined from 18.9 percent to 15.4 percent.

Yet, during the ninth FYP (1971–5), agriculture was supposed to be industrialized and its production stepped up in all its branches. During the tenth FYP (1976–80), it was officially claimed that "an immense land reclamation program would be implemented creating a major zone of guaranteed grain production." To all this was added in 1985 a "Comprehensive Program for the Development of Consumer Goods and the Service Sphere in 1986–2000," scheduling substantial increases in the production of fabrics, clothing, and footwear, along with all kinds of other consumer goods as well as services. It was also stated in 1985 that by 1990 the population's requirements for the services concerning all the household needs "will be completely satisfied." To carry out measures of a "fundamental restructuring" aimed at improving planning and management in light industry, it was decided that by January 1, 1987, planning in the Ministry of Light Industry would be based "on orders filled by trade, formulated with an eye to the result of wholesale fairs for the sale of goods." To accomplish this, the state decided to reduce the number of indices confirmed by centralized procedures, to enhance the role of incentives, and to eliminate the practice of petty tutelage over the production enterprises.

But, a 1986 resolution of the party's Central Committee recognized also, that "the economic levers" had little influence on increasing production, improving quality, expanding the assortment of consumer goods, and accelerating their sale. In addition, the economic relationship between industry and trade did not "adequately facilitate the accomplishment of these tasks." In 1988, in a report on "Practical Work to Implement the Decisions of the Nineteenth

Party Congress," Gorbachev himself had to recognize and to state officially that notwithstanding the adequate supply of such consumer goods as salt, flour, and sugar, these were "vanishing from the trade network in various places" as if someone had a stake in maintaining a shortage.[10] An experienced observer who had firsthand experience in Soviet planning, Fyodor I. Kushnirsky, pointed out (in 1982) that the real power of the Soviet planning bureaucracy lay in its authority to distribute resources, and that it was this distribution that led inevitably to intricate processes of bargaining, swapping, bribing, and padding, and to reports of falsification within ministries and between ministries and central agencies. Distortions, and even the eventual "vanishing from the trade networks" into the black market, had deep and complex sources within the planning system itself, including the planners' solutions, which allegedly were not subjective but rather "objective outcomes of plan calculations."[11]

Gorbachev's chief economic adviser, Abel Aganbegyan, asserted in the late 1980s that only a true reversal of planning priorities, leading to the subordination of production to consumer demand, could put an end to the waste of resources and the perennial production of shoddy goods, and finally bring about a rapid increase in the quantity and quality of the consumer goods produced. Certainly such a reversal of the Soviet planning strategy – which did not actually take place – would have changed the structure of Soviet planning priorities. But even such a momentous change would not have put an end to the planning and management setup, to the centralized power of the Soviet planning bureaucracy, and to its ability to distribute resources – that is, its generation in the plan fulfillment of what Kushnirsky called the processes of bargaining, swapping, bribing, padding, and falsifying reports – which involved a vast array of plan simulations until the final disintegration of the Soviet system in 1990–1.[12]

12-4. Financial Policy

When the Bolsheviks took over the state power, they attempted to carry out a kind of collaboration with the private banks, reserving for the state the right to exercise control over all their credit operations mainly to prevent them from using any of their resources against the regime or for transferring capital abroad. This attempt, however, was short-lived, as inevitable conflicts developed with the banks' leadership. By November 12, 1917, the private banks were closed and commercial secrecy abolished. Finally, a decree of December 27, 1917, declared banking a state monopoly, and the State Bank absorbed all

---

[10] Resolution "On Improving Planning and Economic Incentives and the Management of Consumer Goods Production in Light Industry" (*Pravda* and *Izvestia*, May 6, 1986), transl. in *Current Digest of the Soviet Press*, Vol. XXXVIII, No. 13 (1986), pp. 12, 22–3.

[11] Spulber, Nicolas, *Restructuring the Soviet Economy . . ., op. cit.*, p. 67.

[12] *Ibid.*, p. 27.

private joint-stock companies. Certain credit institutions (such as municipal banks and regional credit institutions), continued to function up to the middle of 1919, but by then the nationalization of all banks was completed and the State Bank was renamed the People's Bank. All this was carried out as the moneyless economy was unfolding and as a swift inflation was undermining the basis of all credit transactions. In this situation, the activities of the People's Bank became fused with those of the Commissariat of Finance. By January 19, 1920, the People's Bank was liquidated and most of its assets and liabilities were transferred to the Commissariat of Finance. At the time, the main source for covering the state's expenditures was the issue of money, as revenues from taxation were negligible and the disintegration of money relations proceeded rapidly. A decree of February 8, 1921, discontinued the collection of money.

The transition to the NEP started – as we already saw in the discussion on agricultural policy – with the food tax replacing requisitions of agricultural products. As Alexander Baykov remarked, the NEP thus started with a financial measure. A number of other financial measures soon followed. In August 1921, the state instituted payments for the goods and services it obtained from private persons. In October 1921, profitable state enterprises were authorized to buy and sell on the market, while some of the smaller enterprises were leased to private entrepreneurs. During 1921–2, the state financial apparatus was reorganized, and a financial controlling administration was set up as a department of the Commissariat of Finance. The restoration of the credit system began in November 1921 with the reestablishment of the State Bank, whose capital was supplied by a Treasury grant. Other key banks of the Soviet banking system – the central Agricultural Bank, the All Russian Cooperative Bank, the Bank of Foreign Trade – were organized subsequently. The fiscal apparatus began to be gradually restored, as were various sources of the budget. Parallel to the taxation in kind of the agricultural population, monetary taxation started to be reestablished through various measures in 1921–2, and the Eleventh Congress of the party (in March–April 1922) soon proclaimed the taxation policy as "the principal instrument" of the party's revolutionary policy. Yet, since taxation together with the revenues from the state enterprises continued to be insufficient for covering the state's budget expenditures, the state continued to rely on note issue, even though it had recognized officially the imperative need of a "gradual transition to a stable monetary unit." Finally, while the budget deficit continued to induce the state to issue the depreciating currency (the *sovznak*), it also influenced it to introduce alongside it a stable currency with a limited sphere of circulation (the *chervonetz*). The issue of the latter by the State Bank started in October 1922; the *chervonetz's* steady penetration in circulation aided the rapid depreciation of the *sovznak*. Finally, by January 1924, the Twentieth Party Conference decided to let the state undertake a vast monetary reform involving the issue of a new paper currency – "gold rubles" granted the right of legal tender – the cessation of the printing of the *sovznak*, and the minting and issue of small silver and paper coins. As far as revenue was concerned, the state carried out the transition from taxation in kind to monetary taxation by 1924, and gradually transformed the agricultural tax into a kind of progressive income tax between 1924 and 1927. Control over expenditure was strengthened and various campaigns were undertaken to increase expenditure economies in the state institutions and enterprises. Price regulation became more strict and covered increasingly more items from 1927 on.

After the NEP, from the beginnings of the centralized planning system, finance was viewed as the monetary form of the planned distribution and redistribution of the national income and of the social product. The production phase, based on the targets set and on the supporting planned material balances was regarded as a distinct process interacting with the equally distinct phases of distribution, exchange, and consumption. The system of financial plans was viewed as subservient to the economic plan; it served to facilitate and to control various aspects of the economic plan's fulfillment. It was comprised of: a) the financial plans (the balances of income and expenditure) of the state enterprises, construction sites, state farms, transport and economic organizations, ministries, and associations; b) the central state finance, including the state budget, state life and property insurance plans, and the social insurance budget; and c) the credit plans of the State Bank, the Foreign Trade Bank, the Construction Bank, and the savings banks. The summary financial plan – the national income and expenditure balance – was not an operational plan, and unlike the state budget, was not approved by the government. It constituted only an economic estimate based on the macroeconomic plan.

The main sources of finance available to the state were determined in the light of the macroeconomic planning indicators for production and sale of output. The difference between the income of the state enterprises, collective farms, and cooperatives and their costs represented their net income, or for the economy as a whole, the social net income. Part of the net income was scheduled to be paid into the state budget in the form of a turnover tax and deduction from profits of the state enterprises, and in the form of an income tax from the cooperative enterprises. Other financial resources were to come from state loans. The volume of profit by sector was calculated in the national income and expenditure balance in the light of the macroeconomic plan. The turnover tax was determined on the basis of projections in the various production plans. The social insurance funds were calculated on the basis of the total wage bill laid down in the macroeconomic plan. On the other hand, the scheduled investments and expenditures on major repairs were included in the financial balance also on the basis of the amount laid down in the macroeconomic plan.

The chief instrument of economy's financial management was the state budget; the latter constituted a consolidated account of the all-union, republican, and local budgets. It consisted of a central budget, some twenty-eight budgets of autonomous republics, and of about fifty thousand regional, urban, and rural budgets. The State Bank (with its three hundred thousand branches) was the government's fiscal agent, an administrative, not a policy making, agency responsible for collecting all the government's revenues, regulating the note circulation, and servicing the credit payments and the households' savings needs. In the socialized sector, money performed the function of a unit of accounting for recording costs and as an instrument of planning, rather than as a measure of value. All the prices involved – except those prevailing in the farm markets – were planned prices, made to include both the costs of production and the planned accumulation earmarked for expanding production.[13]

Throughout the centralized planning era, the Soviet system operated on the basis of the subservient role of the enterprise to the party-state–planned economic-management decisions. The *perestroika* envisaged to change this situation over a number of years, with 1990 as its target of completion. The principal decisive change that it undertook was to transform the enterprise from a subservient tool into the principal sector in the economy, a fact bound to change radically its relationships to Gosplan, Gossnab, and Gosbank. Indeed, this transformation of the role of the enterprise was not to discard the planning system, but only adjust it to this new situation. Thus, in June 1987 the Central Committee of the Communist Party adopted a resolution entitled "Basic Provisions for the Radical Restructuring of Economic Management," representing the product of more than two years of Gorbachev's and his allies' attempts to reform the Soviet economic system. This particular resolution, as in the past, allowed the central planners in Gosplan and in the all-union ministries to develop long-term, five-year, and yearly plans for the economy as a whole and for its sectors on the basis of "control figures" set by the Politburo. But both the "control figures" and the plans were to become henceforth indicative rather than directive – that is, central planning was to become normative rather than commanding in principle. Likewise, state enterprises would become financially autonomous and would operate on a self-accounting basis; the state would no longer subsidize enterprises that could not generate revenues to finance their own activities. (Yet it is not certain whether this would have applied to enterprises in the military-industrial complex, and also to various crucial but unprofitable enterprises that could not have continued to function without subsidies.) The enterprises would draw their own plans, but obviously could not ignore the state's "normative" control figures, nor the state's orders and allocations. The enterprise's plans would be carried out on the basis of contracts with the state, and the necessary inputs would be purchased from the wholesale stores run by Gossnab. The resolution did not precisely define the rights of the enterprises to dispose of their own products. Nevertheless, the

[13] On the financial policies during War Communism and the NEP, see notably Baykov, Alexander, *The Development of the Soviet Economic System, op. cit.*, pp. 29–39, 364–420; on the central planning era, see Garvy, George, *Money, Financial Flows, and Credit in the Soviet Union*, Cambridge, MA, Ballinger Publishing Co., for the National Bureau of Economic Research, 1977.

relationships between the enterprise and the financial institutions were also set to change. Gosbank rather than the state budget was to become an active participant in the country's economic activity: Gosbank's loans rather than the state budget funds were to become the main source of capital investments and the source of indemnification of losses. A subsequent resolution of 1988 stated that the enterprise's officials, elected and not dismissible by the party, would determine the format and system of workers' compensation. No consensus was reached among the party leaders concerning the reform of prices. While this leadership did set forth the basic principle of the autonomy of the enterprise, and while it did try to integrate the economic activities and the financial operations, it did not prove ready or capable of discarding the old frameworks and organizational structures. The only thing it could attempt was to modify either their scope or their impact on the economy.[14]

12-5. Concluding Comments

To what extent did these different sectoral orientations and policies reflect a well-integrated strategy of development? What were the origins and the sources of the concepts and means combined in this strategy? In which ways and why did the application of this strategy ultimately lead to counterproductive results?

To start, recall that the differences between the sectoral Soviet policies, as well as their strategic interrelations, constituted a reflection of the "marriage" between the Marxian conception of economic growth and the organizational methods of a war economy, as developed during World War I by the German high command. The Marxian conception was embodied in Marx's famous two-sector model set forth in the *Capital* (Vol. II). It divided the physical output of the economy into two categories: producers' goods and consumers' goods produced respectively by producers' goods industries, or industries of sector I, and consumer goods industries, or industries of sector II. Producers' goods embraced both raw materials and capital goods. Each output was in turn equated to capital depreciation and raw materials used (c), wage bill (v), and surplus value (m) (that is, property income). The model sought to portray the mutual relations between the components of each output and the demand and supply of producers' and consumers' goods in either "simple reproduction" (that is, in conditions of zero net investment) or in "expanded reproduction" (in conditions of positive investment). In Marx's examples of the model, the organic composition of the capital (the ratio of c to v) remained unchanged and the output of the two sectors' development, stayed at an unchanged rate.

---

[14] On the perestroika changes, see Litvin, Valentin, "On *Perestroika*: Reforming Management," and "On *Perestroika*: Analyzing the 'Basic Provisions,' " both in *Problems of Communism*, Vol. XXXVI, July–August 1987, pp. 87–92, 93–8.

The proportions in which new investments were to be distributed between the two sectors could be varied, and the growth rates of that output could be increased, kept constant, or decreased.

Lenin grasped this idea in his work *The Development of Capitalism in Russia* (1899) and stressed that the development of the consumer goods industries might even be completely arrested while heavy industry forged continually ahead. Concentration of investable resources in heavy industry – starting with the production of electrical power and then iron and steel, machinery, and armaments – became indeed the hallmark of the Soviet strategy for economic growth. In fact, from the beginning of the Soviets' activities in the early 1920s, Gosplan's theory and practice of planning, along with the works of many Soviet economists, as well as the political debates on the paths of industrialization, centered on the Marxian schema, on the interrelations between sectoral rates of growth, and on the limits the Soviets might set to the process of industrialization.[15]

The methodic and consistent application of this strategy required total control over the economy's activities, its outputs, and their allocation. Such total control could be exercised in an economy organized and managed like a war economy (*Kriegswirtschaft*) such as the one organized by the German high command during World War I. The war forced all the belligerents to reorient their human and material resources into new channels. The necessity of this shift generated a number of experiences and ideas about industrial organization and management aiming at the production of the greatest volume of goods and services essential for military use. Means had to be found for "commandeering" production investments, and agents for directing them according to the estimated war needs. A number of factors (including the blockade) pushed German policies forcefully in that direction. Under the direction of Walter Rathenau, the leader of the German power industry, and under the surveillance of the war ministry, the Germans developed a vast apparatus for the detailed surveillance and control of virtually all commodities circulating in the economy. By 1916, the German military leadership, in order to expand its outputs of munitions and of other defense materials forcefully, proceeded toward the total mobilization of the labor force. By November 1916, the totality of the war machine was integrated under the War Emergency Office headed by General Wilhelm Gröner. According to Gröner, that office was leading Germany "as a colossal firm which includes all production of every kind, and it is indifferent to the kind of coat, civil or military which its employees wear." It was this type of "colossal firm," the fully developed *Kriegswirtschaft*, that became the model of organization and management of the Soviet economy.

---

[15] See *Foundations of Soviet Strategy for Economic Growth*, Spulber, Nicolas, ed., particularly Part I ("Macro-Economic Models") and Part III ("Planning Theory and Methods"), *op. cit.*, pp. 3–203, 359–503.

Incidentally, that system of organization fitted perfectly Marxian conceptions, formulated in the nineteenth century, concerning the evolution of capitalism. According to Marx, the organization of the capitalist economy was forcefully directed toward the creation of a single, centrally run, multibranch, multiplant corporation. This process began, according to him, with the appearance of the factory and machine manufacture. The private owners of factories were inevitably involved in a process of eliminating "absolute" market competition and concentrating in fewer and fewer hands the control and operations of the economy. The capitalists could not, however, carry out this process to its logical conclusion – that of ultimate total concentration – since they could not reconcile such an organization with the system of individual appropriation. Only the Communists could expropriate *all* the owners of the means of production and run the "socialized" economy as a single, centrally commanded complex. This idea was alive not only during War Communism, but also under the NEP, and it became the undisputed basis of the centralized planning system from 1929 on. It was enshrined in the 1977 Soviet Constitution (Article 16) and continued to be accepted well into the 1980s. Numerous official works of the 1980s – such as the collective work of the time of the Soviet leading economists, entitled *The Socialist Economic System* – continued to assert that the Soviet economy had become "an integrated, single national economic complex," thanks to the capacity of "socialism" to surmount all the so-called particularism of industrial branches and regions.

In the long run, however, the system of centralized commands of an entire economy, setting fixed, incontrovertible targets of production for every branch and unit of the economy led to increasingly widespread distortions, falsifications, and simulations concerning the targets set. It is in the continuous central effort to emphasize the growth of heavy industry and armaments on the backs of the "secondary" sectors – agriculture, light industry, and consumer goods in general – that the discrepancy between the targets set and the actual achievements grew incessantly, resulting, as well-known Russian author Feordor Burlatsky put it in the *Literaturnaia Gazeta* in February 1988, in "an increasingly impoverished and essentially half destroyed country, technically backward industry, grave shortage of housing, the population's low standard of living, millions of persons in jail and camps, the country's isolation from the outside world."

CHAPTER 13

The Problems of Agriculture

13-1. Landholding

The basic factors that shaped the framework of Soviet agriculture and determined its landholding, farming methods, and performance were, the nationalization of land, the collectivization of the peasant farming, the growth of
state farms, and the state policies on investments and taxation in this sector.
In 1928, as much as 80 percent of the Soviet Union's population were still
in agriculture and forestry, while 8 percent were in industry and construction,
2 percent in transport, 3 percent in trade, and the balance of 7 percent in all the
other sectors. By 1940, the population in agriculture accounted for 54 percent,
that in industry and construction for 23 percent, and the balance of the other
23 percent in all the other sectors. As the deep processes of sectoral changes
continued, by 1987, only 19 percent of the population were stated to be in
agriculture, while 38 percent were accounted for in industry and construction,
and the balance of 43 percent in all the other sectors.[1]

The process of collectivization developed at rapid speed from 1930 on. In
the precollectivization period, toward the end of the NEP in 1927, barely
0.8 percent of the peasant households were in the agricultural collectives.
By 1928 this percentage had risen only to 1.7 percent and by 1929 to 3.9
percent. As the massive process began to unfold in the centralized planning
era, the percentage of peasant collectivization rose by 1930 to 23.6 percent,
by 1931 to 52.7 percent, and finally by 1940 to 96.9 percent. As I already
indicated in Chapter 1, the Soviet process of collectivization involved also
two concurrent processes: one of consolidation of the collective farms, and the
other of continuous development of state farms. A few data will illustrate these
processes and put in evidence the very rapid growth of the state farms, whose
privileged position in relation to that of the collective farms was continually

---

[1] Goskomstat SSSR (Soviet State Committee on Statistics), *Trud v SSSR*, *Statisticheskii sbornik*
(Labor in the USSR, Statistical Collection), Moscow, Finansy I statistika, 1988, p. 14.

Table 13-1 *USSR: Collective and State Farms, 1940 and 1960–87*

	1940	1960	1970	1980	1987
Collective farms[a] (thousands)	235.5	44.0	33.0	25.9	26.6
State farms (thousands)	4.2	7.4	15.0	21.1	23.3
Interbranch agricultural enterprises (thousands)	—	3.1	4.6	9.6	7.2
Collective farmers[b] (millions)	29.0	22.3	17.0	13.5	12.4
Employment in state farms (millions)	1.8	6.8	10.0	12.0	12.6
Employment in interfarm associations (millions)	—	—	0.0	0.5	0.4
Additional employment from other enterprises (millions)	0.1	0.5	0.6	1.3	1.4
Total employed in all the branches of agriculture (millions)	30.9	29.6	27.6	27.3	26.8

Notes:
[a] Excluding collective farm fisheries.
[b] Employed in collective work.
Source: *Narodnoe khoziaistvo SSSR*, 1985, p. 179; and 1987, pp. 251, 259.

reinforced. In 1940, the collective peasant farms were taking care of over 78 percent of the country sowing area, compared to 7.6 percent then handled by the state farms. By 1960, these percentages had changed as follows: The share of collective farms fell to 59 percent of the sown area, while that of the state farms increased to 33 percent of the total. From the 1980s on, these percentages shifted further so that by 1987 the collective farms' share amounted to less than 44 percent of the sown area while that of the state farms had risen to over 53 percent of the total. As can be seen in Table 13-1, the number of collective farms fell from 235,500 in 1940 to 44,000 by 1960 and then to 26,600 by 1987; during the same span of time, the number of collective farmers shrank from 29.0 million to 22.3 million by 1960, then to 12.4 million by 1987. On the other hand, during the entire period considered, from 1940 to 1987, the number of state farms rose from 4,200 to 23,300, while their workforce increased from 1.8 million to 12.6 million. The interbranch agricultural enterprises comprising intercollective farm associations – mainly for construction purposes, repairs of agricultural machinery, and some interfarm feed factories – increased from the 1960s on, particularly after the liquidation of the agricultural servicing units called machine and tractors stations. By 1987, these associations reached a total of some seven thousand units employing four hundred thousand people.[2] Notwithstanding the sharp reduction and consolidation of the collective farms, the expansion of the number of state farms (including that which occurred through the state farms' absorption of weak collective farms), and the fact that

2 *Naradnoe khoziaistvo SSSR v. 1985 g.* (National Economy of the USSR in 1985), Moscow, Finansy i statistika, 1986, pp. 278, 187.

both reached roughly the same number of units (around twenty-five thousand each by the mid-1980s), in various respects the differences between the two types of farms were not much narrowed over time.

In focusing on the changes in agriculture, one must not lose sight of a third factor besides the collective and the state farms, namely that of the private sector of farming and gardening. Since the early 1930s, a relatively small portion of the land was left for the personal use of the collective and state farmers. Depending on the political situation and on the food supply, the private plots were limited or slightly expanded (notably from the late 1960s into the 1970s). By 1986, the collective farms held in collective use 169.8 million hectares of the total agricultural land, the state farms 379.3 million, and the mixed organizations and enterprises 1.8 million, a total of 550.9 million out of the country's 559.0 million. The other 8.1 million hectares (3.7 + 0.4 + 4.0) were privately handled by the collective farmers' families and by the workers and employees of both the collective and the state farms. The collective farm household was entitled to a personal plot of land and to the ownership of a dwelling house, farm buildings, livestock, and equipment for working the personal plot. At least one member of the household had to contribute labor to the collective. The distinction between the plots and livestock holdings of the collective farmer and those of the workers and employees (some of whose plots were located in urban areas) eventually lost much of its early significance. All in all, the fundamental Soviet ideological position on private farming did not change over time, but the practical situation forced the Soviet leadership to shift its policies in this regard in order to cope with the increasingly difficult problems of the food supply. The leaders indeed had to rely on the private producers' plots and livestock holdings in order to cope with these nagging problems; the regime attempted to increase the outputs of the collective and state farms continually but without much and consistent success, so the reliance on the private sector remained markedly unavoidable (as we will see further on).[3]

On his private plot, the private landholder (including since World War II also urban plots granted to retired officers) could grow mainly potatoes, vegetables, as well as other crops. But his most important contribution to the country's food supply was livestock and animal products (meat, milk, eggs, as well as wool). The private sector disposed indeed in the mid-1980s of about 20 percent of the country's horned cattle, 18 percent of its hogs, 22 percent of its sheep, and a large share of its poultry, and produced by 1987 as much as

[3] On the role and development of the private sector, see notably Wädekin, Karl-Eugen, *The Private Sector in Soviet Agriculture*, Berkeley, University of California Press, 2nd ed., 1973, particularly ch. 1 and 3, pp. 1–9, 20–49; Kalinikina, A. F., *Lichnoe podsobnoe khoziaistvo* (The Private Subsidiary Economy), Moscow, Kolos, 1981, pp. 11, 13, 36–41; Shmelev, G. I., *Lichnoe podsobnoe khoziaistvo* (The Private Subsidiary Economy), Moscow, Izd. Polit-lit., 1983, 58–70; Litvin, Valentin, *The Soviet Agro-Industrial Complex, Structure and Performance*, Boulder, CO, Westview Press, 1987, pp. 1–13, 18–45.

26 percent of the country's meat, 21 percent of its milk, 26 percent of its eggs, and 22 percent of its wool. The Soviet bureaucracy compelled the private producers to market large shares of these products through the state procurement organs and through the semistate consumer cooperative network, as we will see further on.[4]

13-2. Farming Methods

The processes of collectivization and of industrialization have deeply changed the patterns of landholding, the methods of land cultivation and improvement, and the reliance in this sector on specialists, machinery, equipment, and electric power. By the end of the NEP, the work of individual peasants accounted for 98 percent of the agricultural output. The gross agricultural production, which in 1925–6 reached the prewar level, exceeded this level by 6 percent in 1926–7. The amount of the peasants' investments and the size of their output depended on the size of each family and on the number of workers in the household. In 1928 total investment in the rural economy amounted to 17.7 million rubles, the number of tractors in use to twenty-seven thousand, and the electric power used to 21.3 million horsepower. Agriculture had only some two thousand grain harvester combines, and lacked seed machines, cargo cars, and a variety of basic implements. The very small amounts of equipment owned by nearly all peasant households, and the insufficient draft power, led often to a great deal of coownership, pooling, and hiring of means of production. According to a 1926 survey, only about 50 percent of the peasant households worked their land with their own work stock and implements.[5]

By 1940 the processes of collectivization and industrialization had raised the amount of investment in agriculture to 21.3 million rubles (in comparable prices with the preceding 1927 data) and had provided agriculture with important agricultural machinery, including 531,000 tractors, 182,000 grain harvester combines, and 228,000 cargo cars, and with electric power reaching 47.5 million horsepower. In time, particularly from the 1960s on, the size of each collective and state farm tended increasingly to stabilize around a certain magnitude – reaching in the mid-1980s about 6 million hectares for a collective farm and around 16 million hectares for a state farm – while the amounts in each of production assets, agricultural machinery and implements, and electricity in use, and the number of specialists and machinery operators, reached increasingly high levels. According to the official figures, the productive assets in agriculture, including livestock, increased, on the basis 1940 = 1, to 3.1 by 1960, 6.6 by 1970, 15.8 by 1980, and 21.3 by 1985. In the 1980s, agricultural production assets amounted to around 13 percent of the country's production assets

[4] *Narodnoe khoziaistvo SSSR v 1985 g, op. cit.*, p. 241.
[5] Jasny, Naum, *Soviet Industrialization 1928–1952, op cit.*, pp. 161, 169, 202.

(a share closely comparable to that of all transport and communications assets). Capital investments in agriculture amounted to 18.5 percent of the country's total investments in 1981–5 and to 16.9 percent of the total of 1986–9. In the state and the collective farms, the structure of the productive assets was similar: Construction accounted for 62 to 63 percent of the total, machinery and equipment for 16 to 17 percent, the means of transport for 4 percent, the working and the productive cattle for 10 to 11 percent, and the balance for diverse needs.

With regard to the level of mechanization, one should note that the total tractor park increased substantially from 1960 to the 1980s. Significant increases were registered for each type of tractor – tractor-plows, tractor-seeding, tractor-cultivators, tractor-mowing – as well as for grain harvesting combines, potato harvesting combines, maize harvesting combines, and other machinery. Electricity used in agricultural production also increased appreciably. The labor force decreased in the collective farms between 1980 and 1989 (from 13.5 million to 11.9 million), while it stayed roughly at the same level in the state farms (namely 12.0 million in 1980 and 11.9 million in 1989). The total number of specialists and of machinery operators also increased significantly. While the number of specialists and mechanical operators increased in the total employment in the collective and state farms, the vast majority of the labor force of either of these kinds of farms remained devoid of any specialized training and continued to perform work under the direction of ad hoc organized brigade leaders. Various types of farm tasks were mechanized, while others continued to be done manually.

As in the past, the state and collective farms continued to produce, even during the perestroika, under a vast bureaucratic apparatus. They continued to receive planned targets concerning the volume of state purchases of agricultural produce, as well as various directives from the central economic authorities. In addition, they had to submit to a multilevel bureaucracy supervising the carrying out of the targets set. Further, to coordinate the agro-industrial interrelations insufficiently discharged by the existing agro-industrial organizations for agricultural supply of raw materials and produce, for food processing, and for mechanical repair, construction, and transport, Gorbachev launched a vast institutional reform that established in 1985 a state Agro-Industrial Committee, which assumed the functions of a number of dissolved ministries involved up to then in agro-industrial relations. The key elements in the final product of the Agro-Industrial Complex (*Agropromyshlenni Komplex*, in short, APK) concerned, as can be seen in Table 13-2, agriculture, the industries processing agricultural raw materials (light industry and food industries including flour mills and the meat and milk industries), and state procurement along with trade and service machinery repair and construction.

Historically, Soviet agricultural work suffered from low productivity, far below that of the advanced countries. Yet, as Karl-Eugen Wädekin has pointed

Table 13-2 *USSR: The Structure of the Agro-Industrial Complex, 1989,*
in Percentages

APK and participants	Production funds	Employment	Final product
APK	100	100	100
Agriculture	71.5	69.5	51.0
Forestry	0.5	1.0	0.2
State procurement	2.7	1.3	0.9
Industries processing agricultural raw materials	14.0	8.7	34.1
Trade and services	3.6	6.2	2.2
Machinery repair	2.3	2.3	1.8
Construction	5.4	11.0	9.8

Source: *Narodnoe khoziaistvo SSSR v 1989 g, op. cit.,* p. 413.

out, the Soviet Union disposed of as much arable land per head as the United States; but then, the United States has been self-sufficient on 70–80 percent of its arable land, a fact that suggests that the potential for self-sufficiency existed at least theoretically for the Soviet Union even though its land was of lower quality than that of United States. The Soviet Union did not reach this level and remained dependent on heavy imports of grain.[6] One may certainly attribute this to – besides the impact of the land's lower quality, harsh climate, and brief growing season – the lower levels of agricultural mechanization, the unequal and insufficient training of the largest strata of the labor force, and the complex bureaucracies that weighed heavily over the activities of the entire agricultural complex.

13-3. Outputs and Yields

It is not possible to establish a fully reliable account of the exact performance of any of the Soviet economy's sectors. The central planners were consistently setting high targets, while the managers, under compelling obligations to fulfill them, applied not only exhaustive efforts to reach them, but also a whole gamut of devices to obtain lower goals or simulate their completion. The data available do provide, however, a measure of the scope and limits of the Soviet performance, particularly when, in periods of crisis – notably in the 1980s – the Soviet leaders themselves help us to better evaluate what had been aimed at and what had actually been achieved.

[6] Wädekin, Karl-Eugen, "Soviet Agriculture: A Brighter Prospect?" in *The Soviet Economy on the Brink of Reform,* Wiles, Peter, ed., Boston, Unwin Hyman, 1988, p. 212.

After the turbulent prewar years of disorganization of the villages and collectivization, and after the immense upheavals of World War II, Soviet agriculture seemed by 1960 to have largely overcome its convulsions, and to have at least become able to face more effectively the country's food problem. Actually, the food problem became increasingly harder to solve given the poor yields of agriculture and the massive increases of the country's population. Let me consider now closely the following data for the decisive twenty-nine years from 1960 to 1989 concerning the growth of the value of agricultural output, its basic structure, the claimed crop yields, and the issues related to the expansion of livestock and animal products.

During these twenty-nine years, total agricultural production rose by 84 percent (from (122.1 billion 1983 rubles to 225.1 billion); the increase was due to a 64 percent growth of plant growing and to a 102 percent growth of livestock breeding. Interestingly by 1989 the shares of European Russia were only of the order of 47 percent in both these types of agricultural outputs. The corresponding quantitative data on the critically important part of plant growing, namely that of grains – besides the other components such as cotton, sugar beets, potatoes, and vegetables – were the following. The total amount of grains increased in million tons from 1960 to 1989 by 121 percent, but its wheat grew only by 35 percent, and the rye and corn, which remained small components of the total, grew only by 11 and 56 percent respectively. The most significant increases were those of barley, oats, and other grains. (The share of European Russia in the total grain output was also of the order of 50 percent.) The data on the grain yields, measured in centners (100 kilograms) per hectare, show increases not fully reconciliable with the total output figures or with the targets. Nevertheless, according to various Soviet sources, the yield of grain increased during this period by 72 percent from 10.9 centners to 18.8, while the target set by Gorbachev was 21 to 22 centners by 1990. The yield of wheat remained roughly stationary, while those of rye, corn, barley, and oats showed various increases. Besides grain, the other components of plant growing, in particular potatoes and vegetables, showed more significant growth rates, namely of the order of 25 and 60 percent respectively.

The changes in livestock breeding and their impact on the food problems, namely that of the crucial animal products, have been hindered by multiple causes, such as unsuitability of breeds, quantitative and qualitative deficiencies of the livestock feed rations, limited veterinary service, as well as shortages of skilled labor and appropriate machinery and equipment. Yet the program of increase of meat supplies had been at the heart of the official consumer policy since 1965. Over the twenty-nine-year period considered, no increases were registered in the number of cows and sheep; the only increases were in hogs and poultry. It should also be noted that by 1989 the private – or "subsidiary" – sector accounted for 31 percent of the total number of cows, 18 percent of the pigs, 23 percent of the sheep and goats, and a large part of the available poultry.[7] The official data on the basic animal products for food consumption indicate that the total outputs of meat, milk, and eggs increased significantly during this period.

Yet, one should not forget that during this period, the Soviet population increased by over 74 million people (from 212.3 million in 1960 to 286.7 million in 1989) and that the targets set by the Soviet leaders for overcoming the country's food shortages had not at all been reached. Indeed, note that in March 1965 these leaders had set as their key target "an upswing in agricultural production" required to overcome both the need in food production and the crisis in feed grain, and that after a number of years and party congresses (from the twenty-third to the twenty-sixth), the leadership had to recognize in the early 1980s that the food problem had become "both economically and politically the central problem of the current decade." Accordingly, the plenary session of the Communist Central Committee approved on May 24, 1982, the "USSR's Food Program for the period of up to 1990" – a program planning to increase the average annual production of grain from 238 million to 243 million tons during the eleventh five-year plan (FYP) (1980–5) and from 250 million to 255 million tons during the twelfth FYP (1986–90). Actually, by 1989, the officially registered level of grain output was 211.0 million tons, far below the targets set in 1982 even for the mid-1980s. The goals considered indispensable for meat, milk, and other food programs proved barely reachable.[8] In reviewing the agrarian policy, Mikhail Gorbachev had to point out distressingly, "the reality is this: We do not produce enough agricultural output." The USSR was indeed trailing behind the developed countries in labor productivity, crop yields, livestock productivity, and the quality of foodstuffs. As Gorbachev had to state it officially, "we have been unable to solve the food question in a fundamental way."[9]

Indeed, the countryside as a whole was increasingly falling behind economically, and in many regions people were simply abandoning the land and leaving the villages. The population outflow from rural areas had already been exceeding the natural growth of the population for many years. The party proved incapable of changing its system of agricultural management and giving the peasantry real opportunities for independence, enterprise, and initiative, while taking the appropriate measures for increasing the peasant income, housing, roads, and transportation means. Unlike the industrial workers, the peasants

---

[7] Severin, Barbara, "The USSR: The Livestock Feed Issue," in *Socialist Agriculture in Transition, Organizational Response to Failing Performance*, Brada, J. E., and Wädekin, K-E., eds., Boulder, CO, Westview Press, 1988, pp. 344–59; *Sel'skoe Khoziaistvo SSSR . . . 1988, op. cit.*, p. 244, and *Narodnoe khoziaistvo SSSR v. 1989 g., op. cit.*, p. 462.

[8] See "The USSR Food Program for the Period up to 1990" (*Pravda* and *Izvestia*, May 27, 1982), transl. in *Current Digest of the Soviet Press*, Vol. XXXIV, No. 21, 1982, pp. 10–11.

[9] "Report by Gorbachev, M. S., at the Plenary Session of the CPSU Central Committee" (*Pravda* and *Izvestia*, March 16, 1989), transl. in *Current Digest of the Soviet Press*, Vol. XLI, No. 11, 1989, p. 3.

had to rely to a great extent on their "subsidiary" economy rather than on the income from collective farms. According to the official sources, in 1960 the average monthly income of a worker or employee amounted to 80.6 rubles while the monthly farm's payment of a collective farmer amounted to 28.3 rubles. By 1987 this gap narrowed: The corresponding figures were 202.9 rubles and 170.2 rubles – but the gap continued in housing and accessories. An industrial worker's wage accounted in 1960, and then in 1987, for 75 and 79 percent respectively of the income of the worker's family. In the same years, the income of a collective farmer from the collective farm accounted for 35 and then for about 52 percent of the worker's family income. That family had to rely for no less than 43 percent of its income in 1960 and then for over 24 percent of its income in 1987 on the sales of its "subsidiary" economy, that is, on the output of its personal land plot, rightly called the *semisubsistence* economy.[10]

13-4. Exports and Imports

I will discuss in Chapter 6 the basic principles of Soviet trade policy that shaped and guided the country's foreign trade, then examine the specific impact of the central economic plan and of the monopoly of foreign trade. For now, let me focus exclusively on the relations between agriculture and foreign trade.

Between 1950 and 1986, the shares of foods and of the materials needed for their production decreased continually in the total Soviet exports. In 1950, that share amounted to 21.1 percent; in 1960, to 13.1 percent; in 1970, to 8.4 percent; in 1980, to 1.9 percent; and in 1986, to 1.5 percent. The Soviet imports of agricultural products, notwithstanding appreciable differences from year to year, remained continuously at significantly high levels. That share amounted in 1950 to 19.7 percent of the total imports; in 1960, to 13.1 percent; in 1970, to 15.8 percent; in 1980, to 24.2 percent; and in 1986, to 21.1 percent. With regard to the crucial problem of grains, Soviet exports decreased appreciably from the 1960s on, while Soviet imports increased substantially, notably in the 1980s. As can be seen in Table 13-3 the imports of grain reached, 27.8 million tons in 1980, and 26.8 million tons in 1986.

The data available on the hard currency trade show that the Soviet agricultural exports amounted to only $167 million in 1970, $458 million in 1980, and again to only $274 million in 1986. But the value of just the imports of grain, which amounted to only $101 million in 1970, rose to $4,503 million in 1980, and then to $5,253 million in 1985. The total of other agricultural goods imported from the nonsocialist countries rose from $512 million worth in 1970, to $4,301 million in 1980, and to $2,872 million in 1985. Grains had been the only product in the Soviet-American trade for which the USSR accounted for a substantial share in the American exports – namely 13 percent

[10] For family income data, see *Narodnoe khoziaistvo SSR v. 1985 g.*, *op. cit.*, pp. 418–19; *Narodnoe khoziaistvo SSR v. 1989 g.*, *op. cit.*, pp. 88–9.

Table 13-3 *USSR: The Grain Trade, 1960–86, in Millions of Tons*

	Exports				Imports			
Items	1960	1970	1980	1986	1960	1970	1980	1986
Grains:	6.8	5.7	1.7	1.4	0.2	2.2	27.8	26.8
Wheat	5.6	4.7	1.5	1.1	0.1	1.8	4.7	15.7
Barley	0.3	0.5	"	"	—	—	2.3	3.6
Oats	"	"	"	"	—	—	—	—
Corn	"	—	—	—	0.1	0.3	9.9	7.2

Note:
" = below 50,000 tons.
Source: *Narodnoe khoziaistvo SSSR za 70 let, op. cit.*, pp. 641–2.

in 1982–5 – and for which the United States had been a major, and at time the dominant, supplier. Incidentally, the U.S. grain output reached 269.7 million tons in 1980 (compared to 186.8 million in the USSR) and 281.1 million tons in 1987 (compared to 211.4 million in the USSR). Another major component of U.S.-Soviet trade has been fertilizer shipments in both directions. Besides the United States, the USSR's other main exporters of grain had been Argentina and Canada.

Given the basic Communist strategy of economic development and its impact on the structure of the economy and on its pattern of growth, foreign trade played only a limited role. In 1985, for instance, the ratios of both exports and imports to the official Soviet GNP estimates amounted each to only 4 percent. Major efforts began to unfold in the USSR in the organization and development of foreign trade, but, as we will see later, the results achieved remained limited by the time of the collapse of the entire Soviet system in 1990–1.

13-5. Concluding Comments

Gorbachev's concept of agricultural reorganization encompassed not only production, processing, sale of products, and technological services, but also substantial changes in the structure of state and collective farms. He posited notably the reorganization of the agricultural complex as a single, multilevel setup, beginning with the peasant family, the team, the brigade, the rental contracts running through the state farms, collective farms, and cooperatives, and culminating with agro-industrial associations at the level of provinces. It involved further assigning a leading role to agricultural policy in the entire course of Soviet policy, and shaping what he called "new notions about socialism as a whole and about its social and economic prospects."

But these targets were not achievable, and indeed were not reached. The dominant factor continued to be that a whole set of issues affected the food problem that the Soviet system could not solve. The Soviet Union could not produce enough agricultural output, and could not diminish its dependence on large purchases of grain, meat, fruit, vegetables, sugar, and other such products from abroad. As Gorbachev himself noted on the eve of the collapse of the Soviet system, "we continue to trail behind the developed countries – large and small – in labor productivity, in crop yields from fields, in livestock productivity, and in the variety and quality of foodstuffs." Farm labor productivity – estimated between 10 to 25 percent of U.S. farm labor – remained low not only because of the agricultural management systems, the wages and the bonus system, the lack of incentives, and the pattern of investments, but also, among other factors, because of the limited and poor mechanization and equipment in such branches as vegetables, sugar beet, cotton, and flax growing as well as in feed production and auxiliary farming operations. The machine builders, as the Soviet leaders themselves had pointed out, had taken advantage of their monopoly positions in order to unload on the countryside outmoded models of machinery with low levels of dependability and efficiency. Further, the Soviet's fields' fertility continued to decrease in most regions, as large areas of land abandoned to wind and water erosion were undergoing widespread deterioration. Collective farms, state farms, and various enterprises of the agro-industrial complex were deeply in debt, and were unable to get out of debt as the state itself became incapable of helping them.[11]

The reverse side of the state and cooperatives' inability to provide sufficient goods and services was the continuous development and diversification of the shadow economy. The latter concerned not only production by self-employed persons hidden in the shadow, outside the fields of the state's accounting and oversight, or the sales by smugglers of imported scarce foreign goods, but above all, all kind of activities by persons involved in semilegal or outright unlawful operations *within* the state's established production and service structures. Much of the private production had indeed become part of the "socialist" production, as for instance when a state enterprise fulfilling the plan was also producing *nalevo* (illegally), and not for the benefit of the state, all kind of commodities. As certain Soviet writers pointed out, as the shadow economy became an active part of the daily process of consumption, it struck vitally important centers of the official economy. In short, one could no longer draw a strict line between "the official and the unofficial economy."[12] The shadow

---

[11] "Report by Gorbachev, M. S., at the Plenary Session of the CPSU Central Committee," *Current Digest of the Soviet Press*, Vol. XLI, No. 11, 1989, *op. cit.*, pp. 3–6.

[12] See Ioffe, Olimpiad, S., and Maggs, Peter, B., *The Soviet Economic System, A Legal Analysis*, Boulder, CO, Westview Press, 1987, p. 14; Osipenko, O. V., and Kozlov, Iu. G., "What Is It Casts a Shadow?" and Koriagina, T. I., "Shadow Services and Legal Services," both from *Ekonomika I organizatsiia promyshlennogo proizvodstva*, No. 2, 1989, transl. in *Problems of Economics*, Vol. 32, No. 7, November 1989, pp. 29–48.

economy ultimately drew into itself not only the multiple issues related to food supplies and consumer goods and services, but also (as I have already noted in Chapter 12) complex managerial interfirm relations engaged in vast operations of bargaining, swapping, bribing, and simulating plan fulfillment – all in all, a highly vitiated heritage for the society that will succeed the collapsing Soviet regime.

CHAPTER 14

The Industrial Changes

14-1. Patterns of Growth

Throughout the central planning era, from 1928 on, the Soviet manufacturing industry operated within the framework set by detailed central directives enforced and supervised by the party and by a hierarchical, complex planning and managerial administration. The industry's pattern of growth was shaped by the central plans on the basis of a set of policies, of which the determinant ones were: the Soviet strategy of rapid industrialization with emphasis on heavy industry and military needs; a sustained drive toward wider and wider concentration of plants, workshops, and employment into larger and larger enterprises; and reliance over a long period of time on obsolete equipment within various industries, combined with modernization of other industries and vast investment in new construction. In the second half of the 1980s, a complex project of renewal aimed as usual at accelerating the technological progress, catching up with the technologically advanced industries of the West, and eventually changing the planning system by establishing the enterprise as the primary actor in the Soviet economy. Let me illustrate these policies with some appropriate data.

The Soviet strategy of industrialization commanded the rapid infusion of fixed capital, labor, and raw materials into industry. According to the Soviet data, the industry's capital assets grew after the post–World War II reconstruction and restructuring, in comparable prices by well over nine times in thirty years, namely from 99.6 billion rubles in 1960 to 926 billion by 1990.[1] During the same period, the industrial labor force grew from 22.6 million to 35.3 million, an appreciable though not necessarily healthy increase for a country whose pre–World War II industrial labor amounted to 13.1 million (1940 data). The available data on the distribution of capital assets and of labor by industrial

---

[1] *Promyshlennost' SSSR Statisticheskii sbornik* (Industry of the USSR Statistical Collection), Moscow, Finansy I statistika, and Infoizdat tsenter, 1988, 1991, pp. 49 and 9.

Table 14-1 *USSR: Distribution of Capital Assets and Labor by Groups of Industries, 1960–87, in Percentages*

Years	All industry	Capital assets[a]			Labor		
		Heavy ind.	Light ind.	Food ind.	Heavy ind.	Light ind.	Food ind.
1960	100	76.6	4.6	10.2	73.5	17.2	9.3
1970	100	79.9	4.5	8.4	75.0	15.8	9.2
1980	100	86.4	4.1	6.5	77.5	14.1	8.4
1987	100	89.5	3.7	6.4	78.5	13.4	8.1

Note:
[a] Totals do not amount to full 100 percent as certain industries were not included (e.g. the porcelain industry and others); the 1960 and 1970 data for capital assets stand for January 1, 1962, and 1972.
Source: Narodnoe khoziaistvo SSSR v 1961 g. and *Narodnoe khoziaistvo SSSR 1922–1972* (National Economy of the USSR in 1961 and 1922–72), Moscow, 1962 and 1972, pp. 186, 152–3; *Promyshlennost' SSSR 1988, 1991* (The Industry of the USSR), Moscow, 1988, 1991, pp. 70, 48.

groups, presented in Table 14–1, show clearly the decisive emphasis on the heavy industry group, that is, on massive increases notably in fuel and power, metallurgy and machine building, and chemicals.

The drive toward industrial concentration accelerated first in the late 1950s. According to a statistical compendium published in 1957, *Achievements of the Soviet Power in Forty Years*, Soviet industry was already the "most concentrated industry in the world." Actually, as indicated by the first Soviet statistical yearbook published after Stalin's death, *National Economy of the USSR in 1956*, also published in 1957, in addition to 206,000 "large and small industrial enterprises owned by the state," there were 107,000 small-scale industrial cooperatives and 28,000 industrial consumer cooperatives. Cooperative industries accounted for 7 percent of industrial output, to which was added a 1 percent contribution of 350,000 blacksmiths and other small workshops in the agricultural sector. This situation led to change by the end of the 1950s. Industrial cooperatives were disbanded, their property was handed over to the state, and the industry was reorganized. By the beginning of the 1960s, the industrial enterprises were merged into 46,500. After an increase of this total to 49,383 state enterprises by 1970, their numbers declined to 44,172 by 1980 and then settled around 45,000–46,000 by 1990. The available data on the size distribution of these enterprises from the 1960s on, by employment capacity, share in total industrial employment, and share in total output – which we will examine in detail in the next section – confirm the tendency toward concentration in plants with more than one hundred employees.

The reliance on obsolete equipment in many industries along with continuous emphasis on new construction was a characteristic of Soviet development

Table 14-2 *USSR: Structure and Effectiveness of Capital Investments, 1971–82, in Percentages*

| | In percent at end of the period | | Effectiveness of expenditures ruble/ruble | | | |
| | | | Projected | Actual | Projected | Actual |
Structure	1971–5	1976–82	1971–5	1976–82	1971–5	1976–82
New construction	42.1	41.8	0.319	0.246	0.319	0.246
Expansion & maintenance	37.3	33.5	0.299	0.250	0.299	0.250
Reconstruction	11.5	10.7	0.289	0.122	0.289	0.122
Technical reequipment	9.1	14.0	0.515	0.252	0.515	0.252

Source: Malygin, A. A., *Planirovanie vosproizvodstva osnovykh fondov* (Planning the Structuring of Capital Assets), Moscow, Ekonomika, 1985, p. 160.

until the 1980s. (See Table 14–2.) Until then it was officially considered that the average service of an industrial machine lasted 21.5 years and that the period up to its first restoration would take six years. For the following fifteen to sixteen years, the planners' estimates were supposed to rely only on this restoration of the machinery's power within its old technical parameters. This kind of approach did not favor technological progress. Moreover, the planning levers had little or no influence at the enterprise level on such problems as increasing production, improving quality, or expanding the assortment of goods. In April 1985, Mikhail Gorbachev asserted that the Soviet leadership was finally accentuating a widespread industrial modernization and technological change because, as he stated, "the urgency of this problem stems from the fact that in the past few years the country's productive apparatus has largely become obsolete and the rate of renewal of main production facilities has declined." Gorbachev then added that in the twelfth five-year plan, from 1986 to 1990, "top priority must be attached to a substantial increase in the rate of equipment replacement."[2] By then the productive apparatus had become increasingly obsolete for more than "the past few years," and, in addition, the Soviet leadership did not have a sufficient life span ahead of it to undertake such a vast operation.

The emphasis on modernization necessarily coincided with an officially affirmed orientation toward replacing the old planning concepts and methods with a new "flexible economic mechanism." In June 1987, a plenum of the

[2] Gorbachev, Mikhail, "Report at the Plenary Meeting of the Central Committee of the CPSU, 23 April 1985," in Gorbachev, M. S., *Speeches and Writings*, Oxford, Pergamon Press, 1986, p. 136.

party's Central Committee ratified a document entitled *Basic Provisions for the Radical Restructuring of Economic Management*. These provisions stated that the Politburo would continue to issue a plan and "control figures," but that the latter would be only indicative rather than directive, aiming to inform the direction of the Soviet economic development over the next fifteen years. On the other hand, the five-year plan would set "planning aims," but the enterprises and the industrial associations would be allowed to construct their own plans on the basis of "state orders," that is, of contracts with the state, with the guaranteed freedom to buy their needed production resources from appropriate departments of wholesale trade. This system, meant to establish the enterprise as the "primary economic actor" on which to predicate the restructuring of the Soviet economy, was to be implemented over the next "four to five years." In short, the central idea of the "Basic Provisions... of creating a more favorable environment for the enterprise" remained only a project before the collapse of the entire Soviet system.[3]

14-2. Workforce

The leadership's commitment to the numerical increase of the industrial labor force, as well as its conviction of the workers' efficiency, discipline, and devotion to public property, started to give way as the overall performance of the economy continued to deteriorate more and more visibly from the late 1960s on. Between 1940 and the mid-1980s when Gorbachev took full power, the total of the gainfully employed in the economy more than doubled, rising from 62.9 million to 130.3 million, compared to a population growth of 62 percent. Simultaneously the gainfully employed in industry rose from 13.1 million in 1940 to double that amount in the 1960s, and almost treble in 1985 (38.2 million). The Soviet Union crossed over from a primarily agricultural country, in which 51.4 percent of its manpower was engaged in agriculture, to a primarily non-agricultural one through the 1950s. From the 1960s to the 1970s, agricultural employment fell to 24 percent of the gainfully employed in the economy, while employment in manufacturing rose to 29.6 percent. With big output targets systematically built on the presumed "already achieved levels," with taut allocation of scarce resources, and with increasingly aging and obsolete equipment requiring above all greater inputs of labor, the Soviet leadership became challenged by both the *apparent* labor shortages and by the increasingly evident falling productivity levels. Eventually, the leadership became quite conscious of the fact that the real problem it faced was not the specter of labor shortage but rather the already bloated employment in manufacturing and in the economy at large, its retarding technology, its declining productivity, and the spreading of dissatisfaction among workers and employees with the decline of the economy.

---

[3] Litvin, Valentin, "On Perestroika: Reforming Economic Management," *op. cit.*, pp. 88–92.

Table 14-3 *USSR: Industrial Managerial Personnel, 1985 and 1988, in Thousands*

Industrial managerial personnel	1985	1988
Manufacturing workforce	38,103	37,736
Managerial personnel of enterprises	12,464	13,131
TOTAL	50,567	50,407
Managerial percentage	24.6	26.0
Apparatus of ministerial management	2,376	1,831
Total management	14,840	14,962
GRAND TOTAL	52,943	52,338
Managerial percentage	28.0	28.6

Sources: *Promyshlennost' 1991, op. cit.*, p. 9; State Statistics Committee "Where are the Managers, and How Many of Them are There?" (*Izvestia*, March 7, 1989) transl. in *Current Digest of the Soviet Press*, Vol. XLI, No. 10 (1989), p. 8.

Incidentally, the Soviet statistics on the manufacturing workforce have always included data only on workers, apprentices, messengers, typists, security personnel, and other lower personnel. They never specified the size and the numerical importance of the managerial and higher administrative personnel in direct relation with the industrial enterprises. Late in the history of the USSR, such data became available through a press release of the State Statistics Committee (see Table 14-3). Clearly, besides the vast managerial personnel of the enterprises, a large apparatus of ministries, committees, and administrations exercised an additional complex administrative control over all of the enterprises' operations. Put differently, the real manpower involved in the enterprises' work amounted in 1988, for instance, not to 37,736,000 but to 52,338,000. The Soviet policy makers and planners have always perceived as key elements of planning the size and structure of the wage fund, as well as its original distribution and subsequent "redistribution" for services. As might be expected, the ratio of the "social surplus" (profits) to the wage fund had tended to fall through the 1970s and mid-1980s as did the rate of return to total outlays on the use of machinery and raw materials. The share of wages in the industrial production expenditures decreased from 18.0 percent in 1965 to 16.1 percent (1970), 14.8 percent (1980), and 13.9 percent (1987), and then recovered to 14.2 percent in 1990. In 1990, the highest shares on wages in total industrial expenditures amounted to 21–2 percent, notably in machine building and in construction; in heavy industry, the total share of wages amounted to 16.9 percent, while it reached only 9.0 percent in light industry and just 6.8 percent in the food industry.[4] On the basis of the pay scale, Soviet society

---

[4] *Promyshlennost' SSSR, 1988 and 1991, op. cit.*, pp. 42 and 39 respectively.

Table 14-4 *USSR: Size Distribution of Manufacturing Plants, Employment, and Output in 1960, 1975, and 1987, in Percentages*

Size distribution by employment	Total number of enterprises			Share in total personnel			Share in total output		
	1960	1975	1987	1960	1975	1987	1960	1975	1987
Up to 100	43.6	27.7	27.2	5.6	2.2	1.7	7.0	2.7	1.8
101–500	40.7	41.3	43.3	25.3	15.3	13.2	25.3	16.9	12.9
501–1000	8.6	12.5	13.1	15.8	12.5	11.7	14.9	11.2	11.4
1,001–5000	5.5	12.1	13.8	24.2	35.6	36.2	24.0	35.3	38.0
5,001–10,000	1.4	1.6	1.7	18.9	15.4	15.6	19.4	16.1	15.7
10,000 +	0.2	0.8	0.9	10.2	19.0	21.6	9.4	17.8	20.2

Note: Excluding the powerstations and their personnel. For 1960, the range was 1,001–3,000 and 3,001–10,000.
Sources: *Narodnoe khoziaistvo SSSR* (National Economy of the USSR) for 1973 and 1984, pp. 244–5, 159 respectively; and *Promyshlenost' SSSR*, 1988, *op. cit.*, p. 14.

exhibited the following stratification. The top layers were represented in descending order by members of the executive organs of the state and the economy, the engineering-technical personnel, and the scientific and cultural personnel. These layers were followed, again in descending order, by workers, collective farmers, employees, and finally at the bottom, the pensioners, whose situation deteriorated continuously since the mid-1950s. As the *Ekonomicheskaia gazeta* of October 1989 (No. 42) pointed out, by that time 41 million Soviet citizens lived on an income below the official poverty line.

The various aspects of the organization and functioning of industry and of its concentration – to which I referred in the preceding section – are clearly observable in the grouping of industries by size, in their shares in industrial employment, and in total output. As can be seen in Table 14-4, by 1987 three groups of manufacturing enterprises were sharing the manufacturing workforce and the manufacturing output as follows. The largest number of enterprises, those with up to one thousand employees, employed 26.6 percent of the manufacturing workforce and produced 26.1 percent of the output; next, the enterprises with one thousand to five thousand workers employed as much as 36.2 percent of the manufacturing labor force and produced 38.0 percent of the output; finally, the largest enterprises, with over five thousand workers, employed as much as 37.2 percent of the workforce and accounted for 35.9 percent of the total output. Interestingly, the shares of the three groups of enterprises in the number of workers were similar to their shares in total output; the per capita output did not increase in the factories with presumably higher technology.

Legal foundations were established in the second half of the 1980s for creating individual family and cooperative enterprises, partnerships, and possibly also joint-stock companies. Both individual and cooperative enterprises were forbidden to engage in activities considered "ideologically, socially and morally dangerous" (such as marketing alcohol and narcotics, organizing lotteries and gambling, and buying and selling precious metals), but in addition they were also prohibited from providing private professional services, notably in medical assistance and engineering. While the enterprises of this "second economy" were supposed to operate on an equal footing with those of the first, their real situation was far from equal. Enterprises of the second economy indeed had to overcome numerous hurdles. They had to operate under the arbitrary supervision of the bureaucratic hierarchy, hostile to their activities. The enterprises had to depend on the bureaucracy in many ways; the bureaucracy could provide or deny the needed leases, grant or withhold work authorizations, impose licensing charges, vary their tax bill, and provide or deny the necessary tools and raw materials. The bureaucrats did not look upon the cooperatives as a necessary road to the market, and paradoxically, the members of the cooperatives viewed the bureaucrats essentially as a means of defending small producers against the newly expanding market. Notwithstanding the indicated handicaps and the conflicting perspectives in question, by 1989 some 734,000 individual enterprises and 77,548 cooperatives were operating with 1,396,000 workers, out of which 16,152 cooperatives were engaged in the production of industrial technical materials (the rest of the cooperatives were active in the production of goods of mass consumption and in trade). In short, the enterprises of the "second economy" did not grow at the rates expected when the leaders of the perestroika adopted the appropriate laws.

14-3. Output Levels

Between 1960 and 1987, the Soviet industrial labor force increased from 22.6 million to 38.1 million. The share of the heavy industry (the so-called Group A) increased in this employment from 73.5 percent in 1960 to 78.5 percent in 1987, while the share of the so-called Group B (the joint light and food industries) decreased from 26.5 percent to 21.5 percent. Relying mainly on its own resources and only marginally on foreign trade, the Soviets developed massively the country's iron, steel, and similar industries. Notwithstanding the Soviets' great efforts, according to the Central Intelligence Agency of the United States, the average annual rates of growth of industrial production, industrial materials, total machinery, and other goods decreased sharply from 1976 to 1987, as can be seen in Table 14-5.

While the average annual rate of industrial growth declined, the share of manufacturing value added in the Soviet GDP continued to increase from the 1970s through the 1980s. The Soviets strived incessantly to increase iron and steel production. The outputs of crude and rolled steel, destined particularly

Table 14-5 *USSR: Average Annual Rate of Growth of Industrial Production, 1961–87*

Industrial categories	1961–5	1966–70	1971–5	1976–80	1981–5	1987
Total industrial production	6.5	6.0	5.6	2.4	2.0	3.1
Industrial materials	6.7	5.8	5.3	2.1	2.0	2.6
Total machinery	7.1	6.1	7.1	3.1	2.0	3.8
Nondurable consumer goods	4.8	6.1	3.4	1.9	1.7	2.7

Source: Directorate of Intelligence, *Handbook of Economic Statistics 1990*, Washington, DC, 1990, p. 67.

for the Soviet defense industry, were not used exclusively for the production of military hardware, but also, as it became increasingly known in the 1980s, for the silent, semilegal supply of various "technical" consumer goods, from motorcycles to televisions and other household machines. In no mean measure, this production, as we will see later, conveniently supplied the Soviet "shadow economy."

Evidently, from many points of view in many crucial industrial fields, the USSR remained far behind the Western powers, as we can see from a closer comparison with the main industrial power, the United States. As shown in Table 14-6, in terms of total population and of the size of the nonagricultural labor force, the USSR was comparable to the United States. On the other hand, the Soviet industrial labor force increased much faster than that of the United States. Starting with similar totals in 1960, from 1980 to 1987 the Soviet industrial labor force increased by 15.5 million, that of the United States by less than half that amount, namely by 7.2 million. While the USSR employed many low-skilled manual workers, the United States relied on labor-saving technologies and on increasing productivity. While the Soviet Union held the lead in the output of various industrial commodities, qualitatively its goods were below the standards prevailing in the Western markets, a fact that prevented Soviet manufacturing products from gaining appreciable selling shares in these markets. The stock of productive capital was huge in both the United States and the USSR, but the USSR had to rely mostly on aged, obsolete, and backward plants and equipment. Among other things, the Soviet Union remained far behind the United States in the consumption of primary energy and electricity, crucial ingredients of development for both industry and the society at large. The Soviet hopes of rapidly retooling the economy on the basis of increased domestic production and of massive imports of machinery of all kinds and of machine tools proved ultimately unattainable. Yet, in only one respect did the Soviet Union reach its primary goal: Disregarding all costs, it built for its army

Table 14-6 *Comparisons of the United States and the USSR, 1960–87*

	1960	1970	1980	1987
Population[a]				
U.S.	180.7	205.0	227.7	242.8
USSR	212.4	241.7	264.5	283.1
Nonagricultural labor force[a]				
U.S.	65.9	81.3	105.0	118.2
USSR	64.7	88.6	112.6	120.9
Industrial employment[a]				
U.S.	22.0	26.6	29.1	29.2
USSR	22.6	31.6	36.9	38.1
Primary energy production[b]				
U.S.	21,143	30,819	32,567	32,541
USSR	9,250	17,070	25,740	32,560
Primary energy consumption[b]				
U.S.	20,628	21,810	37,125	36,369
USSR	8,499	14,790	22,470	26,187
Electricity production[c]				
U.S.	893.7	1,742.7	2,437.8	2,747.0
USSR	292.3	740.9	1,293.9	1,665.0

Notes:
[a] In millions.
[b] Thousands of barrels per day of oil equivalent; data for coal, crude oil, natural gas liquids, hydroelectric, and nuclear electric power expressed in terms of oil equivalent.
[c] Billion kilowatt hours.
Source: Handbook of Economic Statistics 1988, op. cit., pp. 67, 98, 99, 113.

a heavy industry and nuclear foundation comparable to that of the United States.[5]

14-4. Exports and Imports

Soviet foreign trade in industrial raw materials and products constituted a very small part of the world trade. A look at the structure of this trade (Table 14-7) shows that over the period 1960–87, the main items of Soviet exports, by order of magnitude, were first fuels and lubricants, followed by machinery and equipment, and finally by ferrous metals. The fuels and lubricants share increased massively after 1970 due particularly to the crucial increase of petroleum and petroleum products. In 1960, the share of petroleum and petroleum products in total exports amounted to 11.8 percent; in 1980

---

[5] Belousov, I. S. Chairman of the State Military-Industrial Commission, interview on the Defense Industry by Pokrovski, A. (*Pravda*, August 28, 1989), transl. in *Current Digest of the Soviet Press*, Vol XLI, No. 35, September 27, 1989, pp. 1–2.

Table 14-7 *USSR: Exports and Imports of Industrial Materials and Products, 1960–87, in Percentages*

Type of goods	Exports				Imports			
	1960	1970	1980	1987	1960	1970	1980	1987
Machinery and equipment	20.6	21.5	15.8	15.5	29.7	35.5	33.9	42.8
Fuels, lubricants	16.2	15.5	46.9	46.4	4.2	1.9	1.6	3.7
Ferrous metals	11.5	10.5	4.6	4.4	6.6	5.0	6.8	5.7
Chemicals	2.7	2.6	2.6	2.8	2.6	4.2	3.8	4.7
Wood and wood products	5.5	3.6	4.0	3.3	1.9	2.1	2.0	1.2
Textiles raw materials & manuf.	6.4	3.4	1.8	1.5	6.4	4.8	2.2	1.5
Industrial consumer goods	3.7	2.5	1.6	1.9	1.7	1.8	12.0	13.7
TOTAL	70.9	62.8	78.6	76.9	58.6	57.9	64.7	73.3

Source: Computed from *Handbook of Economic Statistics 1988, op. cit.*, pp. 165–6. Underlying data: Official Soviet statistics using dollar exchange rates for Soviet foreign exchange rates. Exports are free on board (f.o.b.).

that share rose to 36 percent and in 1987 to 33.5 percent of a total export volume, nineteen times larger than in 1960.[6] Soviet exports of machinery and equipment were directed, for over one-half to two-thirds of the totals, to the socialist and the less developed countries. Finally, the third important item of the industrial exports, ferrous metals, involved predominantly the export of rolled steel and other metals. The exports ranged from 63 percent of the total Soviet exports to 77–8 percent, the rest including mainly agricultural goods. As indicated in Table 14-7, the highest share of imports was accounted for by machinery and equipment, which increased from roughly 30 percent in 1960 to over 42 percent in 1987. The only other double-digit item was that of industrial consumer goods, which increased from 1.7 percent of the imports of 1960 to 13.7 percent of those of 1987. The increasingly decisive role of fuels and lubricants in Soviet exports and the relatively small share of the exports of machinery compared to over twice as large a share in the import volume suggest certain evident limits of the Soviet economic development. These limits may be more clearly perceived when considering the mechanical engineering exports and imports of both the USSR and the group of developed industrial countries, the G7. The Soviet exports of machinery were by far the lowest compared to those of any of the G7 countries. As far as imports were concerned, the Soviet evolution from 1970 to 1989 paralleled only that of Italy.

[6] U.N., *Handbook of Industrial Statistics 1990*, U.N. Industrial Development Organization, Vienna, 1990, p. 85.

Japan imported less than the USSR, but its export capacity was close to eleven times that of the USSR. Of course, the Soviet Union did not match in any significant way the great exports and imports of the dominant United States, or of Germany, France, or Great Britain.

14-5. Concluding Comments

Many of the fundamental problems of Soviet industry along with various critical issues facing the Soviet economy as a whole became continually more evident and open to debate by the time that the perestroika was launched in the 1980s. First, a key pressing question was how to move industry from the usually exclusive emphasis on heavy industry – Group A – toward a more balanced development, including the light and food industries – Group B – some of the latter tied directly to the increasingly compelling food problem. A second key question was how to overcome the problems generated by the vast obsolescence of plants and equipment, and how and with what means to achieve the imperative need for industrial reequipment and modernization. How, in fact, could such changes be effectively carried out given the widespread alienation of managers and workers alike with regard to state property? Moreover, how could the system as a whole cope with the pervasive inertia engendered by the prejudices against private property, overcome it, and push forward toward the development of competition among the state enterprises and between them and the hopefully expanding cooperatives?

Certainly, solutions to these issues depended in turn, as the economist L. Albakin pointed out at the time (in *Voprosy ekonomiki* of December 1987), on whether such new tasks could actually be achieved within a system functioning upon a formal identity between the party-state and its employees, whether bold departures from old conceptions, policies, and methods could actually be carried out within old organizational forms and with the old personnel, or whether that system could enlist the confidence of the masses in the often reported and clearly often failing centralized efforts to improve their lives. The imperative changes needed by industry concerning reequipment, modernization, and the overcoming of obsolescence on a gigantic scale had to be effectively carried out at an accelerated pace. Alas, characteristically, in the Soviet economy, completing any project took from two to three years, constructing an enterprise required an additional five to seven years, and setting enterprises on a new basis took some two to five additional years. A progress achieved after nine to fifteen years was evidently not one that increased rapidly the effectiveness of investments.[7]

---

[7] Collective authorship, *Ekonomicheskii stroi sotsializma. Ispol'zovanie ekonomicheskikh zakonov v planovom upravlenii khoziaistvom*, (The Economic Building of Socialism. Utilization of the Economic Laws in the Planned Management of the Economy), Moscow, Ekonomika, 1984, Vol. 3, p. 366.

Many of these and related elements could not change before the collapse of the system in 1991. The growth of the capital assets and the workforce of the heavy industry continued to hold priority; the percentage of technical industrial reequipment remained low compared to the capital investments directed toward new construction and toward plants' expansion and reconditioning. The drive toward industrial concentration continued unabated in conjunction with the arrogant, prejudiced, and discriminating attitudes toward the cooperatives and the individual enterprises. The industrial labor force continued to grow without any appreciable results in technological change and labor productivity. In terms of the overall level of industrial development, any further comparisons with the highly industrialized members of the G7 continued to reveal little change. Restricted within the confines of the old planning framework, the closed Soviet economy had to barter most of its foreign trade exchanges with the equally backward countries of the "socialist camp."

CHAPTER 15

Domestic and Foreign Trade

15-1. Domestic Trade Network

The Soviet Union provided its population with most consumer goods through the state-owned network of retail establishments, the state-dominated cooperatives, and farmers' markets. In addition, the state managed the public catering services through its food services (buffets, restaurants, coffee houses, snack bars, and such) and non-food services (clothing stores, printed matter stores, technical stores, and so on). Employment in the state and cooperative domestic trade increased between 1940 and 1987 from 2,246 to 7,977: yet during this period, the relative share of employment in trade remained roughly the same, namely around 6.7 percent of the total labor force. In addition, this trade workforce was managed by an enormous apparatus of ministerial directors and bureaucrats numbering by January 1, 1988, 5,995 persons (dominating the 7,977 employees directly involved in trade).[1]

The bulk of the retail trade was carried out through the state and the cooperative stores: From 1940 to 1987, the share of the state stores in the total retail sales consistently increased from 63 percent to 71 percent and that of the cooperatives from 23 to 26 percent. The relative share of the collective farms' market – numbering some six thousand outlets – dropped from 14.3 percent to 2.7 percent. (However, with regard to foodstuffs only, the farms' market share dropped from 19.7 percent to 5.3 percent.)

Both the state and the cooperative stores were small and poorly equipped. On the average, a retail establishment in 1940 had a sales area of 43 square meters and in 1987 of 98 square meters. Except for the very large stores in the capital cities, the retail stores had outmoded and poorly equipped facilities. In the officially registered retail sales, the share of foodstuffs (including bread, flour, flour products, meat, milk, fish, fats, eggs, sugar, potatoes, vegetables,

---

[1] Goskomstat SSSR (State Statistical Committee), *Torgovlia SSSR, Statisticheskii sbornik* (Trade of the USSR, Statistical Collection), Moscow, Finansy i statistika, 1989, p. 285.

and alcohol) decreased from 54 percent in 1940 to 47 percent in 1987, while correspondingly, the share of non-foodstuffs (including all kinds of textiles, clothing, as well as a variety of so-called cultural-technical goods) increased from 46 to 53 percent of the total. There were considerable differences in the volume of sales in the towns and the countryside. According to the official data, out of the total retail sales of 1940, 70 percent occurred in the towns, 30 percent in the countryside; by the mid-1980s, these percentages shifted to 80 percent in the towns and 20 percent in the rural areas. Most of the residents of the capital towns, Moscow and Leningrad, shopped mostly in the state stores (97 percent) and little in the other outlets. However, the biggest differences in shopping patterns occurred between the various social groups. Managers at the various state levels were in the most advantageous positions: They had privileged access to the state trade, to a privileged system of orders and bonuses, and to all the other markets. The intelligentsia had limited access to the system of orders, and for certain scarce supplies, particularly meat, they had to rely on black market salesmen. Most of the workers, particularly pensioners, had no access either to the special system of orders or enough money for special purchases on the black market.

Increasingly, from the 1960s on, a vast amount of buying, selling, and bartering began to be carried out under multiple semilegal and illegal forms in what the Soviets used to call "shadow markets." The hundreds of central directives, orders, and instructions, increasingly contradictory, opened a variety of loopholes and allowed all kinds of cheating, fraud, and misappropriation of resources. Illicit acquisition of goods could involve special administrative allocations and closed distributions of goods. Coupons were more valuable than bank notes, and invitations bearing stamps of given institutions entitled the bearer to obtain scarce goods diverted for the use of the personnel (and their friends) of large enterprises and influential organizations (such as trade union committees). Networks of distribution with their own rules emerged forcefully, particularly in the 1980s, along the established trade channels. Since the center's priorities deviated substantially from the population's wants, and since the basic planned flows of production and income mismatched, widespread doors opened to taking bribes, padding reports, setting unwarranted pay and bonus levels, and pushing people toward illicit deals. Branches of the defense industry provided all kinds of "technical" goods – such as non-food consumer goods ranging from motorcycles to televisions and to all kind of household machines – but avoided relinquishing their specially converted facilities to civilian use. These semilegal activities of defense industries, which by 1989 turned out one-fifth of all non-food commodities in the country, did not, however, either end the scarcity of a wide variety of goods or hamper in any way other branches further expanding the shadow markets. The increasing quandary of the leadership confronted with these and other developments made it incapable to solder the system's ill-assorted parts, namely the rigid old supply administrative system and the flexible illegal and semilegal shadow markets.

The retail prices in the state stores were set below prime cost for certain highly necessary products such as meat, milk, salt, sugar, and flour, while the prices of other products were set deliberately high; this encouraged increased demand for the "cheap" basic products, a demand that could not be met satisfactorily since many of these goods started to be diverted massively toward the "parallel" markets. It was this situation that led Gorbachev to assert quite innocently at a Communist Central Committee Plenum (*Pravda*, July 30, 1988) that as salt, sugar, flour, and many other goods are continuously vanishing from the trade network in various places, one automatically gets the idea that someone "has a stake in maintaining a shortage, or at least is devoid of any sense of responsibility to the people." But, of course, more than "someone" was involved in the process of diminished commodities on the trade network.

Except for such products as alcohol, fruit, and coffee, the other food prices were officially kept at their 1960 levels. There were three kind of prices for agricultural goods: state procurement prices, negotiated prices, and free market prices. The sales to the state, in fulfillment of mandated state orders, were made at low procurement prices; the negotiated prices were used for the official cooperatives – which operated their stores mainly in the rural areas – or for direct interenterprise trade. The free market prices concerned the products sold directly to the consumer in the free market or collective farm markets, the only fully legal parallel markets with flexible prices; these were, however, thin markets through which flowed only a small volume of foods, mainly vegetables and fruit.

In the 1960s, the Communist leaders launched a great program set to provide for the Soviet citizens "the highest living standard in the world by 1980." In fact, by 1980 real per capita consumption in the Soviet Union was estimated to be less than a third of that in the United States. According to a study prepared for the U.S. Congress in 1981, at the time, Soviet consumers came nearest to their American counterparts in the consumption of food, beverages, and tobacco (54 percent) with regard to consumer durables. On the other hand, with regard to alcohol and more especially to hard liquor, the Soviets exceeded the United States in per capita consumption.[2] According to 1988 Soviet data, Soviet per capita consumption amounted then for 66 kilograms (compared to 126 in the United States) for meat, 101 kilograms (compared to 126 in the United States) for vegetables, and 55 kilograms (compared to 99 in the United States) for fruit. On the other hand, the Soviets allegedly exceeded the U.S. per capita consumption of bread, milk, eggs, and potatoes. No comparative Soviet data are given for light industry products or for "cultural-technical" products such as televisions, refrigerators, washing machines, and so on.[3]

---

[2] *Consumption in the USSR: An International Comparison*, study prepared for the use of the Joint Economic Committee Congress of the United States, 97th Congress, 1st Session, August 17, 1981, Washington, DC, GPO, 1981, p. v.

[3] *Torgovlia SSSR, op. cit.*, p. 23.

15-2. Trade Interconnections

At its beginnings, the Soviet system set as one of its basic targets the complete elimination of market relations from the economy. The economic collapse that followed War Communism, however, led to the establishment of the NEP, that is, to an open door to wide market relations. After liquidating the NEP and launching the planning era, the Soviet leadership sought to bring all trade relations under the complete control of the state. Connections between all the state's enterprises were to be carried out (as I will point out in the next chapter) through bookkeeping without any direct currency transfers. The Soviet leadership would plan and control the volume and structure of the consumer goods, taking into account first all the primary interests of the state, and then the planned output levels of agriculture, of a great number of industries, and of their interconnections. The leadership would consider the main factors affecting demand – including the size of the population, its social make-up, the division of town and country, the patterns of employment, and the levels of disposable income and savings – and their impact on the general volume of expenditure and of the demand for each type of product and service available. The leaders and state planners viewed the planned bulk of supply and demand at prices set by the state as a replacement for free market relations under socialism. All this was also connected to such problems as the controlled volume and pattern of investment in trade and the controlled imports and exports.

One of the major considerations with regard to agricultural outputs was the availability of the foods needed for urban requirements, exports, and the state reserves, at the modicum purchasing prices determined by the state. The state's planned purchases (the targets for delivery of produce to the state) were by far the most important element in the planning of agricultural production. The targets indeed enabled the state to determine the patterns of agricultural production and to coordinate its purchases with the distribution of agricultural outputs by zones and districts, taking into account the available area and quantity of land. From 1940 to 1987, the state took over regularly at its fixed prices over one-third of the grain output and one-third of raw cotton output as well as almost the entire production of flax fiber and of sugar beets, along with increasing shares of vegetables, milk, eggs (rising to or near 70 percent), and potatoes.

As far as the producer goods were concerned, in the planned economy of the USSR, just as in a market economy, every industrial activity required material supplies and equipment. The architects of the Soviet reconstruction envisaged in the 1980s the eventual transition from the central allocation of the producer goods to a system of intersectors, interbranches, interenterprises, and competitive purchasing. But such a changeover first required the abolition of the tutelary central controls and obligations concerning inputs, outputs, and scheduled interconnections, measures that were not then on the policy makers' reconstruction agenda. The attempts to move away as much as possible from directly assigning inputs and outputs without systematically expanding whole-sale markets for producer goods proved not feasible. Innumerable difficulties stymied the changeover from the central system of allocations to a system of industrial purchasing even remotely similar to the one prevailing in market-directed economies. The raison d'etre of the State Planning Committee, of the State Supply Committee, and of the State Bank (Gosplan, Gossnab, and Gosbank) had precisely been to control the vast concentration of enterprises and to match the producers with the particular suppliers of their inputs and with the specially designated users of their products. The changeover to whole-sale trade in producer goods, along with open conversions of an increasing part of the military industries and of their advanced technological equipment for the production of technically complex consumer goods and of medical and other equipment, were hampered not only by the sheer weight of the plan-ning mechanism but also by the fear of both the policy makers and of the state bureaucracy of moving too fast in these directions, of losing control over the main input-output relations, and of bringing about unmanageable results throughout the economy.

Wholesale in producer goods was officially set to begin in 1987. Actually, as indicated by V. Romaniuk in *Izvestia* of January 3, 1989, by that time only 3 percent of the means of production were sold wholesale, while the central mechanisms for allocating resources remained unchanged. A basic hindrance to the development of such trade, as Romaniuk pointed out, was the existence of numerous monopolies in production; not only the ministries but also nu-merous large enterprises held 100 percent of certain markets in their hands, a situation that developed countries such as the United States would long be-fore have addressed through antitrust legislation. The problem of monopolies could not be solved only by expanding the wholesale market even in conjunc-tion with the free use of free market prices. The customers must also have had access to the use of alternative financial resources and of various kinds of services – a situation that did not exist at all in the USSR, and which the Soviet restructuring leaders were not ready or able to consider.

15-3. Concerns in Foreign Trade

From the inception of the Soviet system, Soviet policy makers, planners, and theoreticians rejected the underlying theories and practical approaches domi-nant in market economies in regard to international trade, commercial policies, exchange rates, balance of payments adjustments, and flows of productive resources across frontiers. The Soviet leaders assumed that a truly centrally managed economy needed to resort to international market relations only in the state's interests and only under the complete control of the state. Accord-ingly, the Soviet Union made foreign trade a state monopoly, accompanied by a state monopoly of foreign exchange, and created a foreign trade organi-zation meant to ward off capitalist penetration, provide maximum protection to domestic capital formation, and turn all foreign trade transactions into subservient elements of the overall economic plan. This organization and its underlying principles were not affected by any major restructuring until 1986, and even then, as we will later see in detail, the state monopoly was not fully dismantled. To understand the extent to which the measures taken from 1986 onward affected the old system and the extent to which they left some of its crucial parts standing, let me recall briefly the system's main historical characteristics.

In the traditional Soviet system of foreign trade, the objectives of the overall economic plan commanded the dynamics of imports, and in turn, the dynamics of exports. The government determined the overall volume, structure, and direction of the country's trade. Tariffs were reduced to a secondary role. The Ministry of Foreign Trade, the head of the foreign trade system, had authority to plan all the relevant elements of foreign transactions so that they fit the domestic output plan and various policy considerations and commitments. The planning department of the ministry prepared the draft plan of international trade in close contact with the State Planning Committee. The draft took into consideration the basic proportions planned for the economy as a whole, existing commercial commitments, and the foreign exchange available. It specified the volume, prices, transport cost, structure, and direction of foreign trade. The importing and exporting state corporations in turn drafted their specific plans on the basis of the physical balances (output and its allocation in physical terms) submitted to them by the producing organizations and their selling and purchasing departments. The corporations of foreign trade suggested, fitted in, or completely modified the basic blueprint, which they presented to the planning department of the ministry for a final evaluation.

After World War II, a group of Soviet-type economies led to a special foreign trade market distinct from the rest of the world market – namely, the interplanned economies market. Stalin proudly (and erroneously) asserted that this was "a second world market" destined, in time, to reach and surpass in importance the first, intercapitalist world market. To coordinate its activities at the level of trade and, eventually, at the level of output, the participating countries formed (in January 1949) a Council of Mutual Economic Assistance (CMEA) in which the Soviet Union was to play the dominant role. The stated political aim of the interstate commercial agreements concluded among the CMEA countries was to help them "construct socialist societies" while the commercial aim was to provide them with a well-defined basis for achieving their domestic economic plans. The capitalist countries concluded trade agreements bilaterally, with accounts in clearing and with the values involved expressed in the currency of the partner or in dollars (just as in the case of the trade with the socialist countries). The balance of these accounts involved gold or foreign exchange, or shipment of additional commodities. After June 1957, the State Bank of the Soviet Union started to act as a clearinghouse for intersocialist multilateral compensations. Given, however, that the bulk of trade continued to flow on the basis of bilateral agreements and through bilateral channels, the amount multilaterally compensable remained rather small for a long time. Since the socialist domestic prices were looked upon as an element that could be manipulated at will to meet various planned objectives, these prices reflected only in part the underlying factor endowments. Further, since the various rates of exchange were established at arbitrary levels, the planners of foreign trade were handicapped when trying to ascertain the efficiency of the foreign system as a whole, though the planners might have been able to compare in a crude manner the profitability of one transaction to that of another. Each socialist country used a different system in this field, though their users found all these methods extremely deficient.

Possibly under the "persuasive" influence of the Soviet Union, each socialist country eventually perceived that it need not develop all the branches of heavy industry and that cooperation was achievable without changing in any way the basic Marxian tenets of "enlarged reproduction" within each economy. This division of labor was to be achieved through centralized coordination of the production plans and administrative commands passed down to the producing enterprises. However, this kind of coordination could not be easily executed. A major obstacle was the impossibility of establishing some meaningful relation between the distorted interior prices and the accounting prices of the goods to be traded. Another handicap was the built-in tendency of each plant, industry, sector, region, or country in the area to forego trade and other goods needed to fulfill the domestic output plan. Of course, the Soviet Union itself was reluctant to agree to any scheme that would have implied weakening its central position in CMEA, reducing its control over its own output plan, or sharing with other socialist countries its planned investable resources.

The official downgrading of past policies and practices concerning foreign trade began in 1986 under the direction of the perestroika leadership. The latter questioned extensively the premises of the old Soviet theories on foreign trade and condemned CMEA for its inability to foster a meaningful division of labor among its members. In the words of a Soviet economist, the incorrect ideas that prevailed for many years concerning the place of foreign trade in the national economy stemmed from the perception of foreign ties only as a means of eliminating the imbalances that were constantly arising in the economy. While maintaining the principle of the monopoly of foreign trade – that is, that foreign economic activities are part of the overall national economic plan – the Gorbachev leadership proceeded, on the one hand, to restructure and redefine the components of its centralized system of foreign trade management and, on the other hand, warn the other members of CMEA that the system had to be fundamentally restructured and that it had to cease its existence as a *sui generis* market functioning only on the basis of rigid, bilateral barter exchange. On August 19, 1986, the Central Committee of the CPSU adopted two crucial joint decrees that changed profoundly the administrative system that had prevailed for close to seventy years in the management of Soviet foreign economic relations. The direction and coordination of foreign economic activities, were placed henceforth in the hands of a newly formed State Foreign Economic Commission attached to the USSR Council of Ministers. This commission was empowered to direct the work of the Ministry of Foreign Trade, the State Committee for Foreign Economic Relations (which had been managing the cooperation with the CMEA countries), the Foreign Trade Bank, the State Custom Administration, and all ministries and departments active in foreign trade. Further, the commission curtailed and dispersed the monopoly rights of the Soviet foreign trade organizations. A number of ministries, departments, enterprises, and associations received for the first time since the NEP the authorization to engage directly in import-export operations, starting January 1, 1987. Financial measures were adopted giving enterprises and associations direct involvement in foreign currency transactions. Further, for the first time since 1930, the formation of joint ventures with non-socialist firms was authorized. Then, a further reform introduced on January 15, 1988, merged the USSR Ministry of Foreign Trade and the State Committee for Foreign Economic Relations and charged it with drafting the foreign trade plan, taking into account the draft plans of all the entities authorized to engage in foreign trade relations. Finally, as of January 1, 1989, the USSR Council of Ministries authorized *all* enterprises, associations, and production cooperatives (including the agricultural cooperatives) to engage in import-export operations if their products or services were competitive on foreign markets. Moreover, the ministerial council also allowed the voluntary formation of various types of foreign trade organizations, consortiums, joint-stock companies, trading, and other interbranch associations.

The broad opening of these innumerable channels toward the world market, remained, however, at least in principle, still to be coordinated centrally so as to preserve the state's "monopoly of foreign trade," while creating new, and as time was soon to prove, insuperable difficulties. This modified monopoly indeed continued to be accompanied by the old monopoly of foreign exchange – that is, the enterprises were still not the genuine masters of the foreign currency that they earned. Instead of receiving actual foreign currency, the exporters received rubles and a right to only a part of the foreign currency they had earned. In practice, the enterprises were thus compelled to sell part of their revenues to the state at the official exchange rate. Moreover, the enterprises were still not allowed to take the foreign currency remaining at their disposal and deposit it in foreign currency accounts at interest rates comparable to those of Western banks. The indicated restructuring of the managerial system and procedure in foreign trade seriously affected inter-CMEA business deals, their structure, their prices, and the currency used to carry them out. From 1987 on, discussions on these issues in CMEA became increasingly contentious. The Soviet Union put forward various proposals in this council to improve its own terms of trade, including a new configuration of specialization and structure of the national economies, and an eventual changeover from muted convertibility of national currencies to the creation of a collective monetary unit convertible into freely convertible currencies. While this was not all put into practice, the Soviet prime minister, Nikolai Ryzhkov, asserted that CMEA should start trading at world market prices by 1991 and replace its existing system of accounting with one based on hard currency. Of course, by 1991, the Soviet Union ceased to exist.

Also at the time, the Soviet leaders as well as the leaders of the other CMEA countries became highly interested in multiplying their direct contacts with foreign companies, and if possible also with forming joint companies with them and encouraging foreign investments in their countries. After the promulgation of a Soviet Joint Venture Decree in January 1987, amended subsequently in October 1987 and in December 1988, by July 1989, 685 joint ventures engaged, with Soviet participation, in the coproduction of certain commodities rather than in "trade of commodities." (At the same time, a large number of joint companies were created, most notably in Hungary and in Poland.) But most of these companies were still made only between fairly small entities anticipating only modest initial revenues. Concurrently, the ruble was to be scheduled to have a single commercial rate replacing the thousand "currency coefficients" that set in effect a special exchange rate for almost every foreign currency. Soviet economists believed then that the Soviet ruble would be properly convertible by the end of the century, but as we know, a decade before that, the Soviet system ceased to exist.

15-4. Foreign Trade Network

Before the perestroika as well as during its existence, Soviet shares in world trade remained extremely small. In 1970 Soviet exports accounted for 4.0 percent of world trade, in 1980 for 3.8 percent, and in 1989 for 3.6 percent. In the same years, Soviet imports accounted for 3.6, 3.3, and 3.6 percent respectively. In the largest category of world trade, manufacturing exports, the Soviet shares in the 1980s amounted to 0.4 percent in 1980 and 1985, and to 0.6 percent in 1988. The Soviet exports, computed in dollars on the basis of Soviet statistics (using for the Soviet foreign exchange ruble the rate indicated by the Soviet State Bank), amounted to $12.7 billion in 1970 and to $107.6 billion in 1987 – levels far below those of any of the big industrial countries of G7 such as the United States. They compared poorly indeed to $43.2 billion exports in 1970 and to $252.5 billion in 1987 by the United States. Soviet imports amounted in these years to $11.7 billion and to $95.9 billion, compared to $39.9 billion and to $422.4 billion for the United States.

Consider now the pattern of the Soviet trade in 1950 to 1989. As can be seen in Table 15-1, the biggest shares in the Soviet exports and imports were accounted for by the intersocialist CMEA. This council counted six socialist countries in 1949: Bulgaria, Czechoslovakia, Hungary, Poland, Romania, and the USSR. In 1950 East Germany was included in the group, followed in 1962

Table 15-1 *USSR: Pattern of Foreign Trade, 1950–89, in Percentages*

	1950	1960	1970	1980	1989
Exports (by group of countries)	100	100	100	100	100
To: Socialist	83.6	75.7	65.4	54.2	61.6
Developed capitalist	14.6	18.2	18.7	32.0	24.4
Developing capitalist	1.8	6.1	15.9	13.8	14.0
Imports (by group of countries)	100	100	100	100	100
From: Socialist	78.1	70.7	65.1	53.2	62.0
Developed capitalist	15.6	19.8	24.1	35.4	29.1
Developing capitalist	6.3	9.5	10.8	11.4	8.9

Sources: Computed from *Narodnoe khoziaistvo SSSR za 70 let, op. cit.*, p. 640, and *Handbook of Economic Statistics 1990, op cit.*, p. 165.

by Mongolia, in 1972 by Cuba, and in 1978 by Vietnam. From the 1950s to the 1980s, the CMEA's shares in both the Soviet exports and imports decreased substantially – to roughly one-half of each – accompanied by the parallel increase in the shares of the developed and developing non-socialist countries. Paradoxically, in the 1980s, the relative intersocialist shares increased while those of the trade with the capitalist countries decreased: The Soviet Union could not expand massively its trade with the latter, as it would have preferred.

The main CMEA buyers from the USSR were Bulgaria, Czechoslovakia, East Germany, and Poland, which were also the main CMEA exporters to the USSR. The main Western buyers of the Soviet exports, and the main Western exporters to the USSR, were West Germany, followed by France and Japan. The latter countries absorbed jointly in 1989 7.6 percent of the Soviet exports and contributed 10.3 percent to Soviet imports. The United States absorbed only 0.8 percent of Soviet exports but accounted alone for 4.0 percent of Soviet imports. Great Britain, once a great exporter to and importer from Russia, absorbed in 1989 only 1.3 percent of the Soviet exports and contributed only 1.4 percent to Soviet imports.

The structure of the Soviet foreign trade compared to that of the big industrial countries of the G7, as well as to that of the United States alone, show strikingly the less developed character of the Soviet economy. As can be seen in Table 15-2, machinery and equipment accounted for a small share of Soviet exports. The USSR's main exports were those of fuels, accounting for close to half of its exports. On the side of imports, the share of machinery and equipment of the G7 and of the United States exceeded substantially the corresponding share of the Soviet Union; the latter's exports or imports of fuels, raw materials, and foodstuffs exceeded its trade in machinery and equipment.

A leading group of the Institute of Economics of the USSR Academy of Science drew at the end of 1987 the following balance sheet of the Soviet achievements and losses in foreign trade (in *Izvestia*, October 10, 1987). First, the group underlined the fact that the bulk of the Soviet exports toward the

Table 15-2 *G7, USSR: Commodity Structure of Foreign Trade, 1987,*
in Percentages

Commodities	Exports			Imports		
	G7 100	U.S. 100	USSR 100	G7 100	U.S. 100	USSR 100
Machinery & equipment	81.0	71.1	15.5	68.6	75.5	41.4
Fuels	3.4	3.1	46.5	11.8	11.1	3.9
Raw materials	4.4	6.6	15.2	7.2	4.4	27.5
Foodstuffs	7.5	11.4	2.6	10.4	6.5	16.2
Other unspecified	3.7	7.8	20.2	2.0	2.5	11.0

Sources: Computed from *Handbook of Economic Statistics 1990, op. cit.*, p. 152, and *Narodnoe khoziaistvo SSR v 1989, op. cit.*, pp. 664, 666.

industrial countries had continued, in the 1980s as before, to consist mainly of fuels and raw materials, a fact that led the group to assert that the Soviet Union had become "a raw materials appendage" of the developed (capitalist) countries. Second, the group noted that the Soviet Union imported massive amounts of machinery, but added that the prevailing Soviet economic mechanism failed to give to the USSR's enterprises any stake in using this equipment efficiently. Further, the Soviet Union was also importing yearly 30 to 40 million tons of grain, a fact that showed that agriculture was holding back Soviet foreign trade; indeed, whatever the Soviet Union was gaining from its exports, it had to spend on food from abroad. All this was attributable to the incorrect ideas that had prevailed in the Soviet Union, namely that foreign trade was only "a means for eliminating the imbalances arising constantly in the economy." Thus the Soviet Union "doomed itself to economic and technological backwardness," stagnant thinking, and lack of initiative.

15-5. Concluding Comments

The efforts of changeover in domestic trade from the central planning of supply and demand to the continuous expansion of free markets appeared insuperable in many respects during perestroika. But equally insurmountable were the problems posed by the evident need to rethink and reform the rationale of Soviet foreign trade, effectively break up the monopoly foreign trade, and grant to the enterprises both real autonomy and appropriate incentives for engaging in foreign interrelations. The prevailing concepts of foreign trade and the existing exchange arrangements were not broad and supple enough to permit the creation of a new, internally consistent foreign trade system, even though in various respects the measures beginning in 1986 did represent some notable breakups of the previously fully dominant monopolist system.

But these breakups brought along with them also new inconsistencies and new difficulties.

Consider the relation of two basic issues: the rights granted to certain enterprises to engage in import-export operations, and the rights granted to them with regard to the foreign currency earned. As of January 1989, the Soviet Council of Ministers granted specifically to the enterprises and cooperatives "whose products were competitive on the foreign markets" the right to engage directly in foreign trade provided that "the foreign trade expenditures were offset by revenue." But, on the other hand, the resolution granting this right also added, first, that this right could be suspended "in cases in which there is unscrupulous competition" or when the trade activities were damaging to the interests of the state. Secondly, it specified that the exporting enterprises had to credit part of the money in their foreign exchange funds to the enterprises and organizations that provided their supplies, taking account of the participants' "contribution to the exported goods."

As a Soviet writer noted at the time, until the end of 1988, "nobody paid attention to exchange rates, and all foreign ties were firmly enclosed in the state budget." Attention began to be paid then to the foreign activities of the enterprises, but symptomatically, no official mention was made as to the Soviet government's effective foreign currency monopoly and to the right of the enterprises to become genuine masters of the foreign exchange they earned. In addition, what was effectively needed at the time was a shift to a single, economically justified exchange rate, to a foreign currency policy in keeping the state's contradictory administrative involvement in foreign trade – objectives hardly achievable in a country accustomed to using physical units as the basis for its administrative command system, and to relying confidently on the absence of the free movement of resources toward the areas where they would yield the highest returns.

CHAPTER 16

Money and Banking

16-1. The Monetary System

To what extent and in what ways did central decisions about income, capacity expansion, and manpower shape the state's financial plan, its budget, and the control of money and banking? From the beginning of the planning era, the financial plan took into account the scheduled expansion of the gross value of output and of its components, as well as the "sources" that this expansion would generate. It surveyed the obligations that these resources had to cover – obligations embodied in a capital construction plan and in a manpower plan – and specified in this connection the funds to be allocated to the banking system for short- and long-term credits, for investments, for grants, as well as for the fiduciary means of circulation (bank notes). During the planning era, the centralized plans (and funds) managed by the Ministry of Finance were the state budget, the budget of the Social Security system, the state insurance budget, the currency and credit plans of the State Bank, and the balance of income and expenditure of the population. The decentralized funds – managed by the enterprises, collective farms, cooperatives, and their organs – concerned their respective activities and obligations. The government budget was the main instrument for implementing the financial plan, that is, the principal tool for centralizing and disbursing the country's financial resources. I will examine in detail the evolution and the structure of the budget – that is, of its receipts and expenditures – in the next chapter. For now, let us look in succession at the questions of the currency, banking, and then credits.

Financial planning concerned two interrelated but clearly distinct spheres of activity: the state's interfirm transactions, and the relations of the firms with the households (as well as the interhousehold transactions). Since the state firms' transactions and those of the households were segregated, the supply and holding of money were bifurcated. The firms' and the government agencies' transactions required clearing transfers through the State Bank, while the payment of wages required cash flows for the purchase of consumer goods

248

and services. In Lenin's interpretation, interfirm transactions did not reflect "commodity-monetary relations," but rather relations among entities belonging to a single owner, the Soviet state. Eventually, in the 1960s, this conception was partially discarded, but the dichotomy between noncash and cash flows remained. In the interfirm transactions, the scriptural bookkeeping (or clearing ruble) served as a unit of account, as a medium of exchange only in a prescribed way (namely for accounting for the movement of specified goods at predetermined prices) separated from the means of payment, but traditionally bundled together in the term *money*. The Soviet system relied not only on the separation of money management of the state firms and of the households, but also on the separation of foreign exchange management. The Soviet currency had also the special feature that it could not be either exported or reintroduced into the Soviet Union. Only in 1987 did the convertibility of the ruble (that is, its free exchange on the international market) begin to be seriously envisaged. Interrelations were finally established at the beginning of 1989 between certain Soviet enterprises created with foreign firms, as we will see later. Let me note in passing that in the 1980s the Western New Monetary Economics (NEM) asserted that, indeed, under laissez-faire, the unit of account and the means of payment, traditionally fused under the term *money*, could be easily handled separately. Referring to earlier economics writers who shared this view, as well as to recent contributors to the NEM, Tyler Cowen and Randall Kroszner stressed (in the *Journal of Political Economy* of June 1987) that many of the insights of such analyses (without any reference to the Soviet experience or to its particular rationale) were "relevant to modern monetary theory." (Certainly, in the present Western world, electronic transfers replacing check payments are increasingly picking up speed – though a completely checkless society is still a long way off.)

The Soviet monetary system underwent various phases during its existence. Under War Communism, the Soviet leaders aimed at the total abolition of money. They claimed at the time that money subsisted only on the fringes of the state economy, with a short-term life span, namely until the liquidation of the private farms and of the black market (which incidentally the government was then funding for its purchases with increasingly depreciating rubles). After the ensuing enormous inflation and the monetary disorganization brought about by the Civil War, the Soviets introduced in 1924 a uniform and stable currency. During the planning era, noncash transactions continued to involve the circulation of goods and services within the state-owned system of production and distribution, and the cash transactions continued to involve the relations of the state-owned system with the households. The cash plan aimed then to bring receipts of currency into balance – mainly from state retail trade and transport, taxes, salaries, transfers, and advances for state agricultural purchases. To keep the quantity of currency at a minimum and enforce controls over its circulation, the Soviets ordered each state enterprise to hold as little currency as possible, and required each retail shop to deposit its daily receipts with the respective

State Bank office. The credit plan was in principle closely related to the cash plan; in practice, it aimed systematically to siphon off resources from the efficient state companies and shift them to the inefficient ones to keep them afloat and able to fulfill their output plans. In theory, the Soviet currency consisted of "tokens" of gold. In fact, and increasingly so over time, the performance of the Soviet ruble had nothing to do with its purported connection with gold. For all practical purposes, the Soviet currency could not be converted into gold, was unaffected by changes in Soviet gold reserves, was impervious to international price fluctuations, and was entirely severed from other currencies. Its purchasing power at any moment depended on the attempts at equilibrium in the key planned balances. The Soviet leaders still asserted by the beginning of 1989 that the ruble's exchange rate was $1.60, but this rate had nothing to do with the reality. Indeed, not a single rate applied to the Soviet factories, which at the time dealt with about six thousand "currency coefficients" setting different exchange rates for virtually every product. As a step toward a single commercial rate applied to importers and exporters, the USSR announced toward the end of 1988 that it would devalue the ruble by 50 percent against convertible currencies from January 1, 1989 – but on the black market, the ruble was then worth from 10 to 20 cents. A new pricing system was supposed to be set in place in 1991 with the ruble freed from its shackles, but by then the Soviet Union ceased to exist.

During the entire planning era, the main structural flow of the Soviet economy was the impossibility of freely moving any kind of resource to address changing needs and into areas where they could yield a maximum return. Theoretically, the planners' decisions already accounted for all these concerns, but in fact the planners' priorities deviated continually from society's needs and, as far as certain outputs were concerned, the monopolized state enterprises met only a small portion of consumers' demand. As a well-known Soviet mathematical economist, A. D. Smirnov, pointed out at the time (in *Pravda* of October 21, 1989), this situation could evidently change only by the elimination of the centralized apportionment of input-output assignments in physical terms, a fact that required making the ruble a freely exchangeable currency. Today, added Smirnov, the ruble is a lottery ticket rather than a bank note: If one is lucky, he or she can buy something with it. This kind of currency, as it was on the threshold of the Soviet collapse, exacted indeed a heavy price both directly and indirectly in mismanagement, low efficiency, corruption, and speculation, accompanied by public discouragement, misgivings, and uncertainly.

16-2. Development of Banking

Until mid-1988, the State Bank serviced all the currency, credit, and payment needs of the economy. It acted as the fiscal agency of the government and constituted an all-encompassing center for the settlements and clearing transactions of all associations and organizations. After a number of reforms, the State Bank had become, as Lenin had willed it in 1917, the country's monobank. It was a single giant state bank with branches in every factory and rural district, achieving as Lenin had envisioned "countrywide bookkeeping and general state accounting of the production and distribution of goods."

Let us consider first the ways in which the concentration of powers occurred in the State Bank and then the process of its transformation started in mid-1988. The State Bank was constituted in July 1923, on the basis of the RSFSR State Bank founded two years earlier. Besides the State Bank, the banking system of the mid-1920s comprised a host of interbranch and territorial joint-stock banks, cooperatives, commercial and agricultural banks, savings banks, and credit unions. During the early 1930s, a thorough reform liquidated all these banks except the State Bank and adjoined four newly constituted all-union sectoral banks for financing long-term capital construction: in industry (*Prombank*), in agriculture (*Sel'khozbank*), in trade (*Torgbank*), and in building (*Tsekombank*). In addition, the reform consolidated a system of saving depositories (*Gostrudsberkassy*) and maintained a bank for foreign trade and foreign economic relations (*Vneshtorgbank*) under the control of the State Bank. Subsequently the latter became not only the bank of issue but also the center for crediting and accounting the production and distribution of all state-owned firms, and moreover, absorbed the Sel'khozbank and extended also its control over the saving depositories. Simultaneously a single bank for capital investment in the country as a whole, *Stroibank*, was constituted on the basis of Prombank and replaced all other investment banks.

By 1988, the giant State Bank operated 4,500 branches and was handling the business operations of over 825,000 enterprises and organizations, managing over 4 million accounts – besides some 178 million savings deposits. In time, the vast multiplication of mutually compensatory transactions led to the establishment of various interbranch, interindustry, or regional mutual-offset clearing schemes within the State Bank. Schematically, the State Bank's balance sheet consisted, on the side of assets, of gold holdings, Treasury notes, foreign exchange, and loans, and on the side of liabilities, of currency and deposits. Finally, its net worth included its charter capital and its reserves. The State Bank charged and paid interest, except on budgetary accounts; the difference between charges and payments represented its income. As the government's fiscal agent, the State Bank discharged numerous duties, including collection of taxes, disbursement of expenditures, and control of the execution of specified budgetary tasks for the all-union or republic ministries of finance. The second key element of Soviet banking was the bank for capital construction, Stroibank. Its assets were augmented periodically by budget appropriations, specific parts of depreciation allowances, and shares in the profit of enterprises. The bank extended both non-interest-bearing grants and long-term credits – the grants going to the state enterprises, and the credits to collective farms, cooperatives, and local industries, as well as to individuals for building houses. Finally, the Soviet Union maintained the Bank for Foreign Trade (*Vneshtorgbank*) as a subsidiary of the State Bank, as well as a number of banks abroad (notably in Paris, London, Zurich, Frankfurt, and Vienna).

Following the decisions of the party Central Committee of July 1987, the Council of Ministers launched a broad reform of the banking system. In the framework of this reform, the State Bank continued to be the country's central bank. In this role, the State Bank participated at the highest levels in formulating the planned direction of the country's development, framing the government budget, planning the balance of incomes and outlays of the population, and drawing the financial plan. It continued to be the country's bank of issue, coordinator of the monetary circulation, and primary decision maker concerning the conduct of credit operations. But it no longer had direct credit deposits and accounting relations with the state enterprises; these functions were transferred to five new, specialized all-union banks superseding also the former Construction Bank. The new banks (the Industrial Construction Bank, the Agro-Industrial Bank, the USSR Bank of Housing and Municipal Services, the Bank for Foreign Economic Activity, and finally, the Bank of Labor Savings and Public Credit), still under the leadership of the State Bank, were not the result of a competitive process, but still the outcome of an administrative decision.

The Law of the State Enterprises of 1987 gave the enterprises the right to transfer materials and monetary resources to other enterprises for their services. The discount papers created, moving from bank to bank, began to expand the scope, rapidity, and flexibility of credit, as well as the financial maneuverability of both the banks and the enterprises. Many different branches began to think about having their own banks. It was hoped that a network of co-operative commercial and other banks reaching in the several hundreds would soon use credit to maximum effect and would open the door for eliminating monopolism and developing competition in banking. By the end of 1988, work got under way on drawing up a draft law on banks. Certain partisans of commercial credit forcefully stressed that all these activities would actually allow the all-union banks to concentrate on major transactions, while increasing the self-control of associations over their own financial resources. The critics of the reforms asserted that the ensuing expansion of the scope of credit would in fact hamper the all-union bank activities, increase credit beyond control, and multiply bank bureaucracy and accounting procedures. The critics expressed notably the fear that the eventual curtailment of the State Bank's credit and its replacement by commercial credit would weaken bank oversight by the ruble and allow the enterprises to "veil" the real state of affairs.

In the meantime, forceful inflationary pressures continued unabated, fueled by the consumers' apprehension of accelerated price increases due to the evident discrepancies between supply and demand as well as to the announced price revisions in the 1990s. Other factors increasing inflationary pressures were the "overhang" of the unaccustomed large government budget deficits, the push of prices by self-financing enterprises that had to cover their rising costs, and the unusually large ruble holdings by the population (in the savings bank and in "strong boxes"). As it was pointed out openly at the time, the planned economy had no reliable antidote to inflation, and even the mention of eventual price increases exacerbated the fears of more inflation. The price reform, continually postponed to 1990 and beyond, increased the fears of higher inflation under the impact of the dangers of reduction in subsidies and of the increasingly obvious imbalances generated by the perestroika.

16-3. Foreign Capital

Soon after the 1917 October Revolution, the Bolshevik leaders repudiated all national and foreign loans contracted during the Tsarist regime, expropriated the foreign properties, and proclaimed the state's monopoly over foreign trade. But after the beginnings of the NEP, the same Soviet leaders aimed at redeveloping foreign trade, opening the doors to foreign investments, and establishing joint companies with foreign enterprises. All these attempts, however, were only partially successful. Western conferences held at Cannes and the Hague in 1922 had asserted that the Western powers were ready to restore relations with Russia provided the latter would "recognize all public debts and obligations" contracted or guaranteed by the Imperial government. The Soviet government refused, however, the demand of payment of all the past debts, and asserted only that it would provide "real guarantees" for the credit and loans extended to it for the reconstruction of new Russia. (The question of the old debts resurfaced only in the late 1980s.)

In the meantime, Soviet foreign trade started to develop (though at a very slow pace), the ruble became convertible (after the currency reform of 1924), a number of joint enterprises with foreign capital were formed (on the basis of a 1922 decree and of the civil codes of the various Soviet republics), and the Soviets also leased forests, mines, and oil fields directly to foreign enterprises. With regard to foreign trade, at comparable prices, exports, which had reached 1,192 million rubles in 1913, amounted only to 50 million rubles in 1921, 264 million in 1924, and 630 million by the end of the NEP in 1928. Imports also fell from 1,078 million rubles in 1913 to 212 million in 1921–2, 204 million in 1924, and 747 million in 1928. The ruble remained convertible until 1926; the exchange for gold or foreign currency was then ended, and the export of Soviet currency was prohibited. Exchange rates thereafter became theoretical rather than real, and payments abroad were made in other currencies.

The extent of the development of private, cooperative, and foreign enterprises in the USSR is well illustrated by the following data provided by the Soviet writer I. Gladkov. According to these data, in 1924–5, the state institutions and enterprises controlled 47.3 percent of the USSR's exports and

86.6 percent of its imports. The mixed companies with foreign capital controlled 5.5 percent of the exports and 1.3 percent of imports, while purely
foreign companies were involved in 1.1 and 1.3 percent of exports and imports
respectively. Cooperative and private companies handled the balance in both
directions.[1] By 1930, the mixed companies were dissolved; already in 1929,
most of the 128 concessions agreements to which the Soviet Union had entered were discarded. The USSR established a special form of Soviet mixed
companies in Eastern Europe at the close of World War II. The bases of these
companies were Soviet reparations claims involving the transfer to the USSR
of properties that the Germans had acquired either legally or illegally.

The past experience of Soviet association with foreign capital was put to
new, ample use in Eastern Europe, beginning in 1945. In Hungary, the Soviet
ownership involved seventeen financial institutions, eighty-two mining and
manufacturing firms of all types, ninety-four miscellaneous businesses, a railroad line, and two shipping companies. According to data released in 1948,
the forty Soviet undertakings and the eight Soviet-Hungarian joint companies, with a total of 3,876 plants, employed 3.1 percent of the total gainfully
employed in Hungarian manufacture. In Romania the Soviet Union acquired
397 commercial and industrial enterprises, 33 oil and mining firms, and 97 banks
and insurance corporations. The USSR instituted in Romania fifteen "joint
partnerships" in oil exploration, manufacturing, air transportation, insurance,
and other fields. A number of joint companies were also formed in Bulgaria
and Yugoslavia until 1949. The entire network in Hungary, Romania, and
Bulgaria of Soviet companies and joint partnerships was dismantled in the
autumn of 1954.[2] It was not until 1971 that CMEA envisaged the formation of
joint companies with the USSR. Romania allowed them in 1971, Hungary in
1972, and Bulgaria and Poland in 1977. According to Soviet data, the USSR
granted "economic and technical aid" to CMEA and to developing countries,
and established, on the basis of mutual understandings, various enterprises
in manufacturing, agriculture, transport, and communication, as well as other
fields. In the meantime, in 1978, the Soviet Union refocused its attention on
the eventual reestablishment in the USSR of joint partnerships with foreign
capitalist firms. The first step in this direction was the foundation of a Center
for Technology and Automation between the German firm Siemens and the
Soviet ministry for automation equipment. A further official expression of the
Soviet interest in joint partnerships was given by the Soviet deputy I. T. Grishin
during his visit to Japan in 1984. Yet it was only in 1986 that discussions on this
issue began in the press. Finally, by December 1986 the Politburo approved

---

[1] Cited by Muntung, Roger, *The Economic Development of the USSR*, New York, St. Martin's
Press, 1982, pp. 191, 202.
[2] For a detailed description of the companies and of the assets involved, see Spulber, Nicolas,
The Economics of Communist Eastern Europe, Cambridge, MA, Technology Press of MIT,
and John Wiley & Sons, New York, 1957, pp. 166–223.

a proposal allowing the establishment of such enterprises, and by January 13, 1987, the Supreme Soviet issued an edict on "The Creation and Operation on the Territory of the USSR of Joint Enterprises, International Associations and Organizations."

The Soviet Union's leaders noted that China (after Yugoslavia and Hungary) had already moved resolutely in this direction. Indeed, since 1979, China had opened the door not only to the formation of joint partnerships but also to companies entirely owned by foreigners. In addition, China had established four "special economic zones" and fourteen "open cities" for the implantation of such enterprises. In the ten years from 1979 to 1988, approximately ten thousand companies had been created in China, 2 percent of which were entirely owned by foreigners. Foreign investments in China were estimated to have reached 6 to 8 billion dollars.

The Soviets' hesitant moves yielded, however, very poor results. In the spring of 1988, only thirty-seven joint enterprises were registered in the USSR. By the summer of 1988, their number increased to fifty-two, seven of which were American. By December 1989, the Soviet Union counted 685 joint ventures – close to one hundred of which were American. The key problems in this slow development were the conflicting demands of the state-run enterprises and of the market-driven joint ventures, the absence of satisfactory dispositions for converting currency, and the lack of understanding that the growth of such enterprises imposed the need to dip into the scarce reserves of foreign currency and that the profits of foreign investors had to be "brought home."

By 1990, the deterioration of the Soviet economy reached increasingly worrisome proportions for the Soviet leadership. By June 1990 the Gorbachev government issued two new corporate laws (the second concerning regulations of joint-stock companies and limited liability companies) advancing broad market principles that no previous Soviet leader would have dared to put forward. Certainly by that time the economic (and political) situation was very uncertain and the leadership's opinions were deeply divided. A new Russian law of December 1990 contained only sketchy provisions concerning the functioning of joint companies, and generalities about the capitalist institutions that were to emerge in Russia. All this took place as an extreme anxiety was gripping the population and the leaders agonizing over the unavoidable collapse of the USSR and over the imperative transition to the market.

16-4. Credit and Public Debt

No credit market existed in the Soviet Union. The short-term and long-term credits were extended by the State Bank through the banks, to fulfill the economic plans. In contrast to the budget, which disbursed grants, credit offered to the enterprises loan funds that they had to repay to the bank within a set period of time and use only for the planned purposes for which they had been given. Until 1987, the state and the cooperative enterprises had to maintain all their liquid assets in a current account at the State Bank, and the building organizations at the Construction Bank. After 1987, the current accounts assets were transferred to the specialized all-union banks (indicated in Section 16-2). The maintenance of the liquid assets in the current accounts allowed the banks to dispose of the assets that were not currently being used, as a source of short-term credits for production, construction, and trade. Most of these short-term credits were directed toward industry.

The credit plan, on all territorial levels – local, regional, and central – was a combination of identifiable credit requirement projections with potentially unforeseen needs. It was a crucial means of the centralized regulation of the entire economic activity. The continuously high rates of credit allocations to industry were clearly predicated on the basic strategy of development, temporarily adjusted in the early 1980s under the pressure of the food problem. The large allocations to retail trade involved rapid turnover. No relation was established between the rates of return for any particular credit use. Enormous credits were indeed allocated to various industries whose rates of return were problematical. At the same time – and unlike the situations that prevailed during the late years of the Tsarist economy – only relatively low credits were allocated to transport and communications.

To avoid economic disruptions, a legal resolution of the 1970s specified that when a state purchaser was short of money, the State Bank would pay the purchaser's invoices so that the planned processes would continue without delay. Yet, given the increased abuses of credit obligations, the Fundamental Statutes of Bank Credit, issued in 1982, specified that the bank would limit or suppress altogether new loans to the enterprises that violated credit discipline. Such measures encouraged the expansion of interfirm commercial obligations. As *Pravda* correspondent Alexander Nikitin put it (on October 8, 1985), mutual nonpayment among enterprises was snowballing: There seemed to be "no end to the claims on one another, everyone owes and everyone is owed." Day by day, the effectiveness of centralized credit measures became questionable.

As far as foreign capital was concerned, the central planners had aimed from the beginning, to isolate the Soviet economy from outside influences. The combination of the monopoly of foreign trade with the monopoly of foreign exchange was the instrument of that policy. No foreign currency market was needed in the USSR since no foreign operation could be carried directly by a Soviet enterprise. Until the late 1980s, foreign currency problems were virtually nonexistent except within the State Bank. No one received foreign currency, nobody paid attention to exchange rates, and all foreign ties were firmly enclosed within the state budget. But even in the late 1980s, when the Soviet enterprises were allowed to engage in trade operations with foreign firms, the enterprises still did not receive the actual foreign currencies they had earned. The state maintained in its hand the foreign currency funds and gave to the exporters rubles along with "a right" to the foreign currency funds.

Table 16-1 *USSR: Hard Currency Debt to the West, 1971–89, in Billions of U.S. Dollars*

	1971	1975	1980	1985	1989
Commercial debt	0.4	8.2	11.0	19.5	39.0
Government backed debt	1.4	4.3	9.5	9.5	8.8
Gross debt	1.8	12.5	20.5	29.0	47.8
Assets with Western banks	1.2	3.8	10.0	13.3	14.5
Net debt	.6	.7	10.5	15.7	33.3

Source: *Handbook of Economic Statistics*, 1990, *op. cit.*, p. 76.

A foreign currency market emerged, but in a peculiar fashion: It provided officially for the free exchange of foreign exchange fund entitlements and for the sale and purchase of these entitlements for Soviet rubles, at negotiated prices at foreign currency auctions organized by the All Union Bank for Foreign Economic Activity. Thus sixty years after the last exchanges were done away with (in the late 1920s), the Soviet Union still did not arrive at the point of distributing the centralized foreign currency resources predominantly by the means of the real foreign currency market and credit.

The Soviet participation in the world trade remained quite modest from 1970 until the end of the 1980s, and in its crucial relations with the West, the USSR's hard currency gross debt rose from only 1.8 billion in 1970 to 47.8 billion in 1989 (see Table 16-1). Many people in the USSR considered this debt unfortunate. As the Soviet writers Nikolai Shmelëv and Vladimir Popov noted at the time, using foreign credit was "shameful, abnormal." They stated further that a country's successful development should be accompanied by a surplus or by equilibrium in its balance of payments. Shmelëv and Popov observed, however, that artificial restraints on economic cooperation with the West would only intensify the isolation of the USSR from the basic processes of international cooperation.[3]

In any case, with the aim of broadening the participation of the Soviet Union in the world market and of providing more realistic assessments of the effectiveness of its exports and imports, the Soviet leadership was planning for a changeover, by January 1991, in the use of a new exchange rate for settling accounts in foreign economic operations – a measure that arrived too late, increasing the turmoil that tormented the Soviet Union before its collapse.

16-5. Concluding Comments

Even in the late 1980s, Soviet foreign trade continued to remain heavily oriented toward CMEA, notwithstanding the tendencies to change the underlying

[3] Shmelëv, Nikolai, and Popov, Vladimir, *The Turning Point. Revitalizing the Soviet Economy*, trsl. by Berdy, Michele A., New York, Doubleday, 1989, pp. 242–3.

conceptions and the administrative structures of foreign trade management, and the need to orient the country toward broader contacts with the West. The indispensable measures for successfully expanding these contacts were *inter alia* to shift toward a single, economically justified exchange rate, to create a real foreign exchange market, and to expand the enterprises' economic activity to borrow funds from one another, from banks of their choice, and from the population as well, without a plan, and directly on the basis of agreements and negotiated interest rates. But while all this was under discussion in the late 1980s, little was done legally. Autarchy was abandoned in principle, but the growth of the volume of international trade, the expansion of the formation of important joint companies, the modification of the backward and archaic structures of credit, and the development of technological imports were still shackled in various ways by the old centralized controls.

In the meantime, the planners and the bank administrations' rules and regulations were increasingly challenged by the enterprises' use notably of the interenterprises' commercial loans, and by their various tendencies toward independence. On the other hand, the banks became hesitant to apply to the enterprises the stern rules concerning the deficient banks – namely the cancelation of credits or the total discontinuance of credit payments – because of the inevitable impact of such measures not only for the culprit, but also for the suppliers who were meeting their own obligations. Indeed, just one enterprise declaring itself "insolvent" sufficed to cause a chain reaction of insolvency affecting tens of thousands of economic organizations. The banks were hence compelled at times to menace with sanctions (but not to apply them), to make compromises, and to render the regulations increasingly meaningless. In short, the Soviet Union proved at the time incapable of restructuring the relations among the planners, the enterprises, and the banks.

All this opened the door, more than one might have suspected, to the willingness of the managers of the Soviet enterprises to carry out trade operations and other arrangements independently with the foreign firms. But it soon became evident that the Soviet producers had neither the appropriate personnel disposable nor the experience in making deals on the world market. In short, while the old mechanisms were receding here and there willingly or unwillingly, the new mechanisms were still not yet able to replace them effectively.

CHAPTER 17

State Finance

17-1. Size and Structure of Budget

The state budget constituted the center of the Soviet financial system and Soviet financial planning. It disposed of different resources than those of the government budgets in market-directed economies and spent these resources for different purposes. It was an instrument of the state as owner and manager of the economy, an instrument for coordinating the material and financial plans, correlating the centralized and decentralized funds, controlling the activities of enterprises and associations, and channeling a large part of the state's resources and of various kinds of subsidies toward the selected branches of the economy.

The budget system was hierarchically consolidated. The USSR state budget (*Gosudarstvennyi biudzhet SSSR*) included the Union budget (*Soiuznyi biudzhet*) as well as the budgets of each of the fifteen union republics (*Gosudarstvennyi biudzhet soiuznoi respubliki*). The latter, in turn, included the republic budget itself as well as the budgets of the autonomous republics and the local budgets (*mestnyie biudzhety*). In keeping with the principle of all-union centralization, only the budget of the USSR had the right to levy taxes, whether all-union, republic, or local; the budgets of the lower level had the right to their "own" revenues, but these were designated from above. In the system that prevailed until the late 1980s, there were no clear-cut indications as to which specific budget collected which revenue and which specific expenditures were made by each budget. Data on the structure of budget revenues and expenditures indicated only the total distribution by levels. Until the late 1980s, the budgets for the whole USSR – both plan and budget – were presented for approval to the Supreme Soviet. Year in and year out, all these budgets were proclaimed to yield a surplus, and there was never a state deficit. There was no public discussion of defense expenditures, and most other key issues of the budget were not even mentioned before the Supreme Soviet. The one-day "debate" of the Supreme Council, usually praising the economy's

259

Table 17-1 *USSR: Size of the Budget Receipts and Outlays Related to National Income, 1950–90, in Billions of Rubles and Percentages*

Items	1960	1970	1980	1990
National income	145.0	289.9	462.2	700.6
Budget receipts	77.1	156.7	302.7	471.8
Percent of national income	53.2	54.0	65.5	67.3
Budget outlays	73.1	154.6	294.6	513.2
Percent of national income	50.4	53.3	63.7	73.2

Sources: *Narodnoe khoziaistvo SSSR za 70 let, op. cit.*, pp. 122, 628–9; *Narodnoe khoziaistvo SSSR v 1990, op. cit.*, pp. 5, 15–16.

performance, was followed up by a summation by the minister of finance, and then the final budget version was published as a "law" in the daily press. The information released contained planned figures and only at times referred partially to actual results.

According to the official data – that is, the working data of the planners and managers of the economy – the budget absorbed an increasing part of the growing national income, and then directed the state's resources toward material production as well as toward the so-called nonproductive sphere encompassing a vast variety of services. As can be seen in Table 17-1, from a yearly GNP stated to have increased between 1960 and 1990 from 145 billion rubles to 700 billion, the budget receipts absorbed a total of 53 to 67 percent of the budget and redistributed it roughly in toto throughout the economy, according to its scheduled development needs. Crucial deficiencies, however, have obviously affected these data, first seriously questioned by Western analysts. Yet, by 1988, Soviet Minister of Finance Boris I. Gostev also recognized officially for the first time since 1944 (in *Pravda* and *Izvestia* of October 28, 1988) that contrary to the official data released until then, "the state expenditures have run ahead of its receipts *for many years*," and that these imbalances have been sharply exacerbated "in the last five years." Gostev added forthrightly that these problems were not something that arose all of a sudden, but that they were "the consequence of imbalance in the economy, large subsidies, enormous losses – all things that were caused by extensive methods of economic management, dependence, and a passive financial policy." A well-known pro-perestroika critic, Nikolai Shmelëv, also noted about that time (in *Novyi Mir*, No. 4, 1988) that the state revenues and expenditures were "often a fiction, merely thin air, the illusion of money with no kind of material support." The most obvious manifestation of this kind of fiction was the taxation of enterprises by the budget "*before* their products were sold or regardless of whether they will ever be sold." Shmelëv also recalled that a similar negative role was played by the massive granting of credits to industrial and agricultural enterprises, "a considerable part of which [became] nonreturnable finance," that is, they constituted deliberate inflationary financing, exceeding by far "what we can materially support."[1]

Clearly, the data on state financing, as well as the figures on national income, must be viewed as projections of the central planners' aims of economic development, rather than as consistent actual results. As a rule, the deviation of results from projections was never disclosed. Yet, these data do allow us to perceive the basic tendencies of Soviet economic policies and management and broadly of the financial means mobilized to execute them. What follows is an analysis of the structure and volume of revenues, and then of outlays, the question of the deficits, and the historical trends with respect to the interrelations between all-union, republic, and local budgets.

17-2. Analysis of Receipts

The receipts of the Soviet budget were usually aggregated as indicated in Table 17–2. The receipts were essentially grouped into two main categories: from the national economy, and from the population. From 1940 to 1990, the first category of receipts was set around 89 to 91 percent of the total receipts, the second at around 9 to 11 percent. The receipts from the economy consisted mainly of the turnover tax and of the payments from profits. Why this distinction between the two? Increasingly the two acquired well-defined, different roles and exercised different impacts. Planned or authorized profits were split between the enterprise, its higher-level agency, and the state budget. The division was meant not only to provide the budget with the investment funds and the higher-level agencies with centralized funds and reserves, but also to provide the managers of the enterprises with various funds to be used for incentives and development. The turnover tax (indirect commodity tax) had different functions: Besides providing investable resources to the state budget – at a different pace and with a different predictability than that of profit deductions – the turnover tax also functioned, in principle at least, as an anti-inflationary tool in the poorly supplied consumer goods market.

The legislation adopted during Stalin's tax reform of 1930 obliged the state enterprises to transfer to the state budget 85 percent of their planned profits. The accounting of the actual transfers was made at the end of the year. Eventually, the deductions from profits were adjusted to take account of the different needs of each enterprise, and the range of payments was differentiated to between 10 and 80 percent of the profits. Until the mid-1960s, the set deductions from planned profits and above-plan profits were transferred to the budget independently of the funds that the enterprises actually used

[1] Shmelëv, Nikolai, "Novye trevogi" (New Anxieties), *Novyi Mir*, No. 4, 1988, transl. in *Problems of Economics*, Vol. 31, No. 10 (February 1988).

Table 17-2 *USSR: Structure of Budgetary Receipts, 1960–90, in Percentages*

Items	1960	1970	1980	1990
Total receipts	100.0	100.0	100.0	100.0
From the economy	91.0	91.2	91.4	88.7
Turnover tax	40.7	31.5	31.1	25.7
Payments from profits	24.2	34.5	29.7	24.7
Taxes on cooperatives	2.4	0.8	0.6	1.4
For social insurance	4.9	5.3	4.7	9.2
Unspecified	18.8	19.3	25.3	27.7
From the population	9.0	8.8	8.6	11.3
Taxes	7.3	8.1	8.1	10.3
Loans	0.1	0.3	0.2	0.9
Unspecified	1.6	0.4	0.3	0.1

Sources: Computed from *Narodnoe khoziaistvo SSSR za 70 let, op. cit.*, pp. 122, 628–9; *Narodnoe khoziaistvo SSSR v 1990, op. cit.*, pp. 5, 15–16.

to discharge their obligations. The 1965 reforms set the deductions on the basis of new criteria and strengthened their managerial incentive functions. Other reforms determined that the transfer to the budget of the deductions from profits was to be made not on the basis of the enterprise but rather of its respective higher-level authority. After the adoption of the Law on the State Enterprise in 1987, the deductions from profit were set to comprise a charge for productive assets (paid on the basis of a similar norm for all enterprises); reimbursement for the training of the workforce and various other services; differentials rents (for special natural and locational advantages); and an additional charge levied on the residual profits left after the payment of the indicated charges plus the repayment of bank credits and interests. Various other changes were contemplated afterward, but were not made.

The turnover tax evolved since its creation in 1930 into a highly differentiated kind of tax – differentiated by type of product, type of enterprise producing it, and the jurisdiction to which that enterprise was subordinated. When it was created, the turnover tax was applied with different rates to the products of some forty industrial administrations, including certain branches of heavy industry. By 1948 the turnover tax started to be levied at the wholesale stage of almost all the products of the food and light industries. By the mid-1960s, the scope of the turnover tax was expanded; it was added at the level of the Union republics by type of goods, taking into account the specific technical-economic conditions of each enterprise. Turnover tax receipts were transferred to the state budget daily or at most within two weeks by the state banks, and were paid by the industrial administrations, associations, supply-wholesale organizations, as well as by cooperatives (excluding collective farms). While by then the tax was applied to producer goods (at very low rates) and to consumer goods (excluding staples and a few other products), its major yields were due, as in the 1930s, to the imposition first on alcoholic beverages, and then on sugar, tobacco, and textile products.

The magnitude of the tax on alcohol was staggering. Gorbachev's anti-alcohol campaign, launched in 1985, rapidly created a big hole in public finance, led to the rapid expansion of moonshine production, and eventually brought about the rationing of sugar (the principal input in this kind of production). In his speech to the Central Committee of the Communist Party, on February 18, 1988, Gorbachev stated (as reported the next day in *Pravda* and *Izvestia*) that the country's rate of economic growth had been achieved "in large measure on an unhealthy basis" – namely, thanks to the trading of petroleum on the world market at high prices... and to a "totally unjustified step-up in the sale of alcoholic beverages." Gorbachev added that if the influence of these factors was removed from the Soviet economic growth indices, then the Soviet Union had no increase in the absolute growth of the national income over four five-year plans. In his report on the 1989 budget of October 28, 1988, Minister of Finance Gostev indicated that the projected turnover tax losses due to the production and sales of wine and vodka would amount in 1989 to more than 36 billion rubles, that is, exactly to the total budget deficit projected for that year. Actually the budget deficit turned out to be much larger than this figure: It amounted to 80.7 billion rubles.

The individual enterprises (authorized since 1987), the cooperatives, the public organizations, and the collective farms payed various taxes, including taxes on personal incomes. The collective farms paid taxes in a variety of forms, including notably an imposition on the collectives' taxable net income and a tax on the wage fund, that is, on the collective funds used to pay for the labor of collective farmers.

Traditionally, direct personal income taxation played a limited role in Soviet budget receipts, even though the personal income tax was imposed on all factory and office workers, writers and artists, and professionals and artisans. Separate tax scales were established for each group with a slightly more favorable scale for the first two groups. The income tax on workers' income was never progressive. The tax was constructed to minimize disturbances to the resource allocation function of wage differentials. Moreover, a number of taxes were applied both on enterprises and organizations, as well as on individuals (notably taxes on buildings, land, ownership of vehicles, and so on). Personal income taxes were supposed to increase sharply in the 1990s. Up to then, progressive taxation had been regarded in the Soviet Union as interfering with the established incentives; moreover, contrary to modern capitalism's attempt to redistribute income through progressive taxation, the Soviet Union had systematically shied away from such measures.

17-3. Analysis of Outlays

Throughout the Soviet speeches and publications referring to the budget – be they reports at the Supreme Soviet, annual statistical handbooks, or five-year statistical compendia of the state budget – the budgetary data were always presented in highly aggregated forms, frequently amalgamating incompletely assorted information and resorting time and again to incomplete and ambiguous presentations. Yet these data do convey the main budgetary choices, and so illustrate the tasks assigned to the budget components of the underlying planning goals – goals not always fully carried out.

As can be seen in Table 17-3, the basic budgetary outlays concerned the financing of the national economy, the bloc of sociocultural measures, and the state administration and national defense. The financing of the national economy aimed to supplement the economic accountability monies, the allocations to economic branches and sectors, and the subsidies. Besides capital investments, these outlays included working capital advances and bank credit allowances, certain operational expenses for geological surveys and the introduction of new techniques, subsidies for the sale of agricultural and other products, as well as outlays for reserves (inventories) and foreign economic activities (including noncommercial operations). The capital investments alone, with priorities for defense, according to various estimates amounted to between 25–35 percent of outlays. The most deceptive data were those listed under the national defense itself: They were inconsistent with the observed expansion, size, theaters of operation, as well as the land, aerial, and naval strength of the army. Also, according to various sources, at least until the late 1980s these data accounted only for the feeding, clothing, housing, and pensions of the army. The most detailed budgetary data (in the Soviet statistical yearbooks) were those concerning the sociocultural measures (education, science, public health, social security, and so on).

Table 17-3 *USSR: Structure of Budgetary Outlays, 1960–90, in Percentages*

Items	1960	1970	1980	1990
Total outlays	100.0	100.0	100.0	100.0
Financing of the national economy	46.7	48.2	54.7	44.1
Sociocultural matters	34.1	36.2	33.5	33.1
Education & science	14.1	16.0	13.6	11.7
Social welfare	8.9	8.2	8.1	5.7
State administration & defense	14.2	12.6	6.7	14.5
National defense	12.7	11.5	5.8	13.5
State apparatus	1.5	1.1	0.9	1.0
Residual expenditures	5.0	3.0	5.1	8.3

Sources: Narodnoe khoziaistvo SSSR za 70 let, op. cit., pp. 122, 628–9; Narodnoe khoziaistvo SSSR v. 1990, op. cit., pp. 5, 15–16.

Some of the state budget receipts were based on planned projections, before products were actually sold and regardless of whether these goods would be sold. Further, the State Bank extended above-plan credits that were often nonreturnable. In practice, the budget accounts (minus bank advances) had never been in equilibrium since such balances required the conjunction of innumerable plan elements. To understand the complexity of the factors involved, it is useful to recall the October 1988 speech of Minister of Finance Gostev, who indicated that "still" one out of five enterprises in industry and constructions (and one out of four in machine building) had not fulfilled its yearly financial obligations toward the budget; specifically, twelve thousand enterprises or organizations and twenty-three ministries had not fulfilled the planned obligations. The same deficiencies were shown by branches and republics (concerning the turnover tax). The biggest failures were registered in foreign trade operations, where exports toward hard currency areas were only 43 percent fulfilled.

In his 1981 study on the *Secret Incomes of the Soviet Budget*, Igor Berman remarked before anyone else that the Soviet budget was a deficit budget, covertly but systematically covered by State Bank grants. Gostev, in 1988, was the first Soviet government official to state that the Soviet Union had been running large budget deficits for years. According to the official data available only for 1985 to 1990, the deficits rose to as much as 80 billion rubles in 1988 and 1989. When considered as percentages of the expenditures, the deficits reached yearly 3.6, 10.9, 12.1, 17.5, and finally 8.1 percent in 1990.

Historically, various significant changes occurred in the structuring of both receipts and outlays. The state revenues fluctuated around the relatively stable axis of the personal income taxes ranging from 7 to 10 percent of the budget receipts and from 9 to 11 percent if we add the loans from the population. Incidentally, the total internal state debt rose between 1985 to 1990 from 141.6 billion rubles to 566.1 billion, that is, from 18.2 percent of the official Soviet data on the national product to 56.6 percent. A key factor in this increase was the increase of the budget deficits. The crucial composites of the revenues were, as indicated in Table 17-1, the receipts from the enterprises (turnover taxes, receipts from profits, and social insurance). These have tended to fall from 1970 on (from 71.3 percent of the budget revenues in 1970, to 65.6 percent in 1980, and to 59.6 percent in 1990) due to the larger share of profits left in principle at the disposal of the associations and enterprises, a share that was scheduled to increase further in the 1990s as a consequence of the 1987 Law on the Soviet State Enterprises.

Over time, the operative state expenditures – those on state administration and defense and on sociocultural matters – have tended to decrease (mainly in 1980), while the expenditures on the national economy have tended to increase (except in 1990). A major component of the first defense expenditures has been the hardest to pinpoint with confidence. It is worthwhile to record that the minister of finance affirmed in October 1988 that the 1989 spending for defense was of the order of 20.2 billion rubles. Gorbachev asserted that the real defense expenditures amounted to 77.3 billion rubles, if one includes the defense industry's contracts with industry. Interestingly, the *Statistical Yearbook for 1990* (*Narodnoe khoziaistvo SSSR v 1990 g*) recorded (on page 16) the following budgetary figures for defense for 1985 to 1990: 19.1 billion rubles each for 1985 and 69.1 billion for 1990. The second bloc of outlays – that on the expenditure on economic branches, including capital grants for both defense and nondefense industries, increased at a rapid pace until 1990 (see Table 17-3), due to an accelerated growth of subsidies. A close look at the available data on the state outlays on industry, agriculture, and housing shows that these outlays have tended to exceed the receipts from these sectors. Conversely, the receipts from transport, communications, and trade have tended to exceed their authorized outlays.

17-4. Subnational Accounts

The budgetary relations among the Union, republics, and localities (including the autonomous regions) reveal some interesting indications concerning the interactions between the Soviet center of policy making and planning and the Soviet territorial subdivisions. As Donna Bahri has pointed out in a 1987 study on budgetary policy in the Soviet republics, a variety of dilemmas confronted the Soviet Union in its efforts to establish an appropriate mix of center-regional authority. Programs had been introduced to adjust and readjust the connections among central planning agencies, industrial associations, and variously determined "territorial production complexes." Programs had been shifted from central to republic jurisdiction and back; regionalization schemes had been devised, applied, and then discarded. The degree of centralization and the rule of each specific republic had varied depending on the level of subordination of a given program and a given industry and sector, the issues to be decided, and the ability and possibility to muster both central support and regional power conditions within the institutional setup.

As can be seen in Table 17-4, from 1966 to 1990 the share of the Union and of the republics in total budgetary outlays tended to increase, while conversely, the share of the localities (that is, of territories, oblasts, districts, cities, regions, and rural settlements) significantly decreased. Indeed, over the period considered, the Union budget absorbed from over 51 to over 53 percent, that of the republics from 28 to 31 percent, while that of the localities decreased from 20 to less than 6 percent. The major underlying factors accounting for these allocations shifts were the complex patterns of control of the economy's branches and sectors. Manufacturing was almost entirely under Union jurisdiction: Mining, utilities, light, and construction materials industries were under Union authority; agriculture, agricultural procurement, and smaller food-processing installations were under the republics' command. Notwithstanding repeated campaigns for initiative at the local level, budgetary

Table 17-4 *USSR: Budgetary Outlays of the Union and of Republics, 1966–90, in Percentages*

	1966–70	1971–5	1976–80	1981–5	1990
Budget of the USSR	100	100	100	100	100
Budget of the Union	51.5	51.7	52.3	53.2	53.1
Budget of republics and localities	48.5	48.3	47.7	46.8	46.9
Budgets of the republics	28.6	30.0	30.8	31.1	—
Budgets of the localities	19.9	18.3	16.9	15.7	—

Sources: *Gosudarstvennyi biudzhet SSSR* (State Budget of the USSR), 1966–70, 1971–5, 1981–5, Moscow, Finansy I statistika, 1972, p. 24, 1977, p. 21, 1987, pp. 12, 13; *Narodnoe khoziaistvo SSSR v 1990 g., op cit.*, p. 17.

expenditures and, hence, administrative power tended to decline at the local level. Gorbachev promised to reverse the trend, but many such promises had also been made in the past without results.

A detailed examination of the budgetary receipts at all the indicated levels reveals that profit deduction played the major role at the Union level, while the turnover tax played the major role at the republic and local levels. Personal income taxes played a much larger role in the republic and local budgets than in the Union budget. On the side of expenditures, allocations to economic branches played the highest role in the Union budget, the lowest in local budgets. In the local budgets the sociocultural expenditures played a major role.

Ranking the Soviet republics by levels of economic development and tabulating per capita budgetary outlays furnishes an interesting perception, as shown in Table 17-5.

The leftmost column arranges the republics in the standard way in which Soviet handbooks presented them – an arrangement that is neither correct historically, geographically, or by size of population. The rightmost column ranks the republics by per capita outlays. As the table shows, the Baltic republics (Estonia, Lithuania, and Latvia) were still at the top of the list, the Tadzhik, Azerbaijan, and Uzbek republics were at the bottom. The ranking of Russia (RSFSR) in sixth place should not imply that it did not play the central role in all interrepublic relations. In fact, the RSFSR concentrated approximately 60 percent of the Soviet Union's economic potential and commanded large human and material resources, including key branches of the Union's manufacturing. Like the rest of the USSR, however, the RSFSR remained poorly developed outside its main urban centers. Notwithstanding the interplay between interrepublic specialization (to take advantage of both natural conditions and large-scale production) regional diversification (to promote all-around development in each area), the dependency of the republics on the RSFSR continued to be decisive until the collapse of the USSR.

Table 17-5 *USSR: Budgetary Outlay per Capita and Ranking of the Republics in 1985*

Republics	Outlays (in rubles)	Rankings
Russian	703.9	6
Ukrainian	621.2	9
Belorussian	775.0	4
Uzbek	451.1	13
Kazakh	720.9	5
Georgian	620.7	10
Azerbaijan	449.8	14
Lithuanian	1,072.9	2
Moldavian	632.0	7
Latvian	994.6	3
Kirghiz	541.7	11
Tadzhik	380.6	15
Armenian	624.0	8
Turkmen	490.7	12
Estonian	1,124.5	1

Source: Computed from *Gosudarstvennyi biudzhet SSSR*, 1981–1985, *op. cit.*

17-5. Concluding Comments

Traditional Soviet budget theory viewed the operative budget outlays – on state administration (excluding defense) and on sociocultural matters – as allocations for the system's nonproductive sectors, appropriation to be minimized in favor of larger expenditures for the productive branches of the economy, above all, for the heavy industry branches. The military outlays were viewed as losses, incurred to the detriment of the national economy. In the 1980s, these views were somewhat altered. The term *nonproductive sectors* was increasingly shunned. Attention was drawn to the importance of education and science in technological development, but the old rationale continued to shape the content of the budget.

Over the years, the USSR's budget exhibited a strong tendency toward expansion, as illustrated by its increasing percentage of the official national income data (see Table 17-1). The expansion was due less to the growth of the economy, and more to the expanded deficits, inflated currency emission, and the upward drift of prices. When the budget expenditures exceeded receipts (and short-term credits exceeded the State Bank's receipts), new currency was injected into circulation. Gorbachev recognized publicly that "for many years the state budget's expenditures grew more rapidly than revenues," and that the deficit was undermining "the stability of the state and the monetary circulation in general" (*Pravda*, June 29, 1988), but nothing was done or could be done by then to change the situation. By 1990, the budget outlays exceeded the budget receipts by over 41 billion rubles, that is, by 8.8 percent.

The Soviet tax system had not been construed with the aim of doing justice to both incentives and equity. In fact, the greater the tax requirements, the more difficult it became to satisfy both incentives and equity. The failure of the Soviet system to exempt the lowest income strata from personal income taxation placed a terrible strain on the lowest paid workers, pensioners, and other disadvantaged taxpayers. The turnover tax weighed heavily on these strata and its impact was offset only marginally by the distribution of free social services and by various subsidies.

In principle, the center alone had the power to levy taxes, whether these were all-union, republic, or local. In practice, the allocation of funds always involved complex and hidden apportionments between consumption and accumulation, as well as among various sectors and branches, and among the center, the republics, and the lower levels. (According to the official data, in 1990 the actual consumption of the population absorbed 67.4 percent of the national income while accumulation plus state services accounted for the balance of 32.6 percent.) As Igor Berman pointed out in his 1981 study on *Secret Incomes of the Soviet Budget*, there were in fact no clear answers to the questions of which expenditures were made by each budget, and how and which budget exactly collected which revenues. There were many exceptions even to the cardinal rule that the appropriations of each budget followed the administrative subordination of organizations. What is clear is that budget allocations implemented the planned choices concerning basic targets for the economy and aimed to develop first the Russian heartland, the seat of heavy industry, rather than to equalize the living standard of the population as a whole. While asserting that the strength of the USSR must be grounded "in the strength of the republics," Gorbachev also added, in 1988, that the republics had "a vital stake in a strong center, capable of insuring the accomplishments of nation-wide tasks" (*Pravda*, November 30, 1988). Of course, less than a year and a half later, all this proved to be completely out of touch with reality.

The partisans of the perestroika directed some of their more virulent criticisms against the ways in which the financial authorities credited the budget with fictitious revenues and then circulated these fictitious revenues as outlays for various purposes. As the economist Leonid I. Abalkin pointed out at the time, crediting the budget with the turnover tax at the wholesale level and before the products were sold had no connection either with cost accounting or with the enterprises' performance. Another Soviet economist, Nikolai Shmelev, also asserted that it was imperative that the turnover tax cede its place as a basic budgetary revenue source to the taxing of the real incomes of the industrial and agricultural enterprises, and moreover, that investment financing needed to be shifted from the state budget to the industrial and agricultural enterprises, with financing achieved on the basis of their income. The much heralded price reform scheduled for 1990 "will not improve anything" noted a discouraged Gorbachev (in *Pravda*, June 29, 1988), unless, as he put it, "questions of financial balance and bringing order into the credit and financial system, the activity of the banks, the budget, etc. are solved at the same time." By then the Soviet system was assailed from all sides by the innumerable problems it had created not only in the financial sphere but in the underlying production, planning, and management structures, then in a process of unstoppable disintegration. (I will return in detail to some of these issues in the book's concluding chapter.)

CHAPTER 18

Overall View

18-1. Transition and the Agricultural Economy

The social transformation of the peasantry and the industrialization of agriculture were central to the Soviet conception of Russia's transition from a semifeudal capitalist system to a so-called socialist and thence to a communist system. In the Bolshevik conception, as Lenin affirmed many times on the eve of 1917, as long as Russia lived in a small peasant country, there was "a surer economic basis for capitalism in Russia than for communism." Capitalism, he asserted, depended on small-scale production; the only way to undermine capitalism was to place the economy, including agriculture, on the basis of "modern large-scale production." Emphasizing Lenin's thesis, Stalin affirmed on the eve of the planning era, in 1928, that Russia had to replace "the scattered and backward small-scale economy of the peasants" with an agricultural system based on the new technological foundation of "large-scale production." Either we place the economy on the foundations of the most large-scale industry and of an agriculture of a new technical basis, added Stalin, "or we turn away from it and do not accomplish it, in which case a return to capitalism may become inevitable." In essence, the transition to socialism was predicated on industry as the main foundation, but also on a reconstructed, industrialized, and collectivized agriculture, viewed as the necessary basis of industry's own development.[1]

In the Bolshevik conception, the transition to socialism required not only the destruction of small-commodity production but also the concomitant elimination of the market and its replacement with complete central control over production, interfirm connections, and intersector relations. When Lenin had to discard War Communism, establish the NEP, and restrict full state controls over only a part of the economy – viewed as a single factory with a

---

[1] Stalin, J., "Industrialization of the Country and the Right Deviation," in *Foundations of Soviet Strategy for Economic Growth, op. cit.*, pp. 270–1.

single owner, the state – he defined this new system as *state capitalism* using within its now confined limits the methods of War Communism. All this was, however, alleged to embody the "dictatorship of the proletariat" exercised through the hierarchy of Soviets, but only with the Communist Party in control of the whole. From 1924 on, when Stalin took over full power – a man embodying, as the Soviet writer Vasilii Grosman once put it, "the Asian despot and the European Marxist" – he dominated absolutely the party, the state, and the economy, determined the basic patterns of its development, and laid down the line to be followed by the population and by the country as a whole.

Small private ownership in the countryside was replaced with collectivized farming, the policy of "primitive socialist accumulation" – that is, pumping money from agriculture into industry – was executed. However, agriculture was industrialized only marginally, and not at all brought on a par with industry. Agricultural practices, as well as industrial activities and mining methods, brought about a continuous deterioration of the national resources base. According to official reports, the diminishing soil fertility became an additional factor in low returns to investments in agriculture. Also, as Gorbachev noted on March 15, 1989 ("Report," *Pravda* and *Izvestia*, March 16, 1989), "the situation with respect to the preservation and rational use of the land … is extremely unfavorable. In the past 25 years, 22 million hectares of developed plow land have been lost." Almost from their inception, the collective and state farms had not been specialized: Only 20 percent of the collective farms and 30 percent of the state farms could be considered specialized. Moreover, the system of mandatory procurements continuously hindered farm specialization. Indeed, the overwhelming majority of the farms were assigned quotas for cattle production, while many if not all of the farms that had unfavorable soil or climatic conditions were obliged to provide the state with grain. The central agricultural planning and management bureaucracies were heavily intrusive in the activities of the farm enterprises and smothered all local initiative. With its poor-quality equipment dating back to the 1950s and 1960s, Soviet agriculture as a whole experienced deep problems concerning notably the mechanization of its various branches, in particular livestock (where 80 percent of the labor was manual), sugar beet, cotton and flax farming, and vegetable growing. Losses were enormous during harvesting, transport, storage, and procurement, equal to the purchase abroad of agricultural products. As Shmelëv put it, "we have no need to increase gross output: we ruin, spoil, rote, or lose at least 20 percent of our annual production of grain, 60–70 percent of our fruit and vegetables, and 10–15 percent of our meat."[2] Investments were particularly low in the industries processing agricultural products, and the integration of production and processing was deficient in many respects. The enormous debt of the collective and state farms and of the other enterprises of the so-called

---

[2] Shmelëv, Nikolai, "Novye trevogi", *Novyi Mir … , op. cit.*

agro-industrial complex, debt that accumulated over many years, hampered in many ways useful initiatives. Low overall productivity due *inter alia* to the fact that much of the collective farmer's remuneration was mostly symbolic compelled much of the agricultural labor to rely heavily on its auxiliary farming operations. It should also be remembered that the countryside remained far behind the cities in transportation, housing, municipal services, schools, medical services, and so on, which encouraged the people to abandon the land and leave the villages.

The central output plan targets for agriculture were always out of correspondence with the actual situation and the actual results. The "USSR Food Program for up to 1990" (*Pravda* and *Izvestia*, May 24, 1982) set as a target for the eleventh five-year plan (1980–5) an increase of the average annual production of grain from 238 million to 243 million tons, and during the twelfth five-year plan (1986–90) from 250 million to 255 million tons. Actually, the average annual grain output during the eleventh five-year plan reached 168.7 million tons, and during the twelfth 196 million. The target for the average animal production during the eleventh five-year plan was 17.5 million tons, and during the twelfth 20 to 20.5 million tons. The actual results were for the eleventh FYP 16.2 million tons and for the twelfth 19.3 million. The other targets for fish products, vegetables, fruits, and so on, were also unrealistic. Notwithstanding these results, Gorbachev himself set in 1988 (*Pravda*, March 28, 1988) the obviously arbitrary target of 260–280 million tons of grain per year "during the next five-year plan."

Yet, Gorbachev knew very well the real situation. As he stated in another speech on March 15, 1989, "We do not produce enough agricultural output... we continue to trail behind developed countries, large and small, in *labor productivity*, in *crop yields from fields*, in *livestock productivity*, and in *the variety and quality of foodstuffs*. The gap is not getting smaller, it is growing." Then after condemning the concepts and policies of Stalin, Trotsky, and the other Soviet leaders for the "enormous damages done to agriculture," Gorbachev asserted that "it would be wrong to use all this as a basis for denying the need for socialist transformation in the countryside." What he recommended at the time was only a transitional period during which new "interconnecting systems" of purchase wholesale and retail prices would be geared toward intensifying production in that sector. By October 18, 1990, however, Gorbachev had to set aside willingly or unwillingly the "socialist transformation in the countryside" and the transitional period interconnecting its purchases – sales – and prices, and argue instead for the "stabilization of the national economy and the transition to a market economy."

18-2. Transition and the Industrial Economy

Stalin asserted in 1928 that a fast rate of production of means of production was "the underlying principle of and the key to the transformation of the country along the lines of socialist development." The maximum rate of growth of industry was not to be achieved via the combined advance of industry and of agriculture, but via the maximum annual transfer of capital from agriculture to industry. This was supposed to ensure that the Soviet Union would "overtake and outstrip" economically the advanced capitalist countries, always keeping in view the need of "the maximum capital investment in industry."[3]

The centrally administered Soviet industrial system grew rapidly throughout the planning era. Toward the end of the 1980s, it numbered some forty-six thousand enterprises employing over 30 million workers, administered directly in the enterprises and managed centrally by a vast bureaucracy of some 15 million people. But this centrally run system could not achieve what a competitive system does: It could not be run efficiently or economically, avoid waste, combat cheating and falsification of results, be alert to competitive technological changes, increase labor productivity, or avoid overemployment. Under the aegis of its single owner, the state, and under the combined directions of Gosplan (for output targets), Gossnab (for supplies), and Gosbank (for deposit and interindustry transactions), the Soviet industrial establishment tended toward extreme concentration in certain branches and toward uneconomical vertical integrations, without any consideration of cost and efficiency concerning the availability of the inputs needed to fulfill the plan and to avoid uncertainties and time lags. For the same purpose, many enterprises resorted to building all kinds of stocks (including labor), to hoarding materials, and to developing their own options of supply and unofficial interenterprise channels of goods interchanges. Inputs and tools were of poor quality – according to various estimates, 30 to 40 percent of the industrial equipment in operation had been in use for fifteen to twenty years or more – and thus were not worth much beyond salvage value. In some cases, even the new equipment was based on outmoded technologies. The directors of the enterprises had to accept increasingly absenteeism, idle time, drunkenness, and reciprocal concessions with an overblown labor force. In the late 1980s, it was estimated that at least 25 percent of the industrial labor force was superfluous even according to Soviet technical norms. The tendency toward wage leveling in the enterprises and the absence of economic incentives – along with the poor availability of consumer goods on sale, at distorted prices – further accented labor disinterest in production and overall inefficiency. The industrial linkages effectuated by Gosplan and supplied by Gossnab were not suited *inter alia* for assessing in each case and in each plant efficient choices among alternative technologies and methods of production. The emphasis on new construction and continuous expansion went hand in hand with the maintenance in operation of decrepit giants (such as Stalin's steel city Magnitogorsk) and

---

[3] Stalin, J., "Industrialization of the Country and the Right Deviation," pp. 266–7, 269–70; Bukharin, N., "Notes of an Economist at the Beginning of a New Economic Year," p. 260, both in *Foundations of Soviet Strategy for Economic Growth, op. cit.*

the neglect of reequipping and restructuring old enterprises. In addition, vast inefficient constructions (such as the Baikal-Amur-Main [BAM] line unnecessarily joining the Trans-Siberian Railroad), along with all kinds of protracted construction of new plants and facilities in selected areas, and the large scale of steel establishments, chemicals, pulp and paper, and various defense industries brought about hidden, uncontrolled, massive contamination of lakes, rivers, subsurface water supplies, and a significant number of cities.

The perestroika aimed to free the Soviet industry of many of its obvious ills. In June 1987, eleven decrees were adopted on the restructuring of industrial planning, financing, and material-technical supply. The main objective was to scrap at least in part the administrative methods of management based on yearly assignments of targets and to let the enterprises formulate their portfolio increasingly on the basis of customer orders. Actually, this transition did not take place as the reformers assumed it would. As the economist Tatiana Zaslavskaia pointed out at the time, the old system proved "terribly inert." Another economist, V. Efimov, recalled then in a cogent article in *Sovetskaia Rossia* (March 27, 1987) that what was wrong with the old economic mechanism was the perpetuation of such negative phenomena as shortages of production, slow scientific and technical progress, low output, low quality, excessive inventories, large accounts of unfinished construction, and low labor productivity. All this was attributed to the old system of plan indices and assignments, formal economic accountability, and multilevel management. That's what the reformers of 1987 wanted to change, but what resulted after a variety of compromises was in many respects an ineffective hybrid that could not eliminate the widespread shortage of goods, the undue accumulation of inventories, and the low productivity. Other economists suggested that all these phenomena could be remedied by limiting, or better, by discarding the system of state orders that introduced priority in supplies, handicapped the drive toward wholesale trade, and circumscribed the independence of the enterprises. Yet according to a State Statistical Report of 1989 (*Izvestia*, March 7, 1989), between 1985 and 1989 the apparatus of ministries, departments, and other agencies decreased by 23 percent, namely from 2.3 to 1.8 million persons, but the managerial personnel in the enterprises and in the industrial associations increased by 4.8 percent, namely from 12.5 to 13.1 million. In addition, the state orders continued to weigh heavily on the volume and structure of industrial output. In 1988, 90 percent of the manufacturing output was still subject to state orders. This rate was supposed to go down in 1989 to 35 percent, but this reduction did not take place. By 1990 the state's share varied between 40 and 100 percent of total production according to the state's interest in various product groups. The adoption on June 4, 1990, of the "Law on Enterprises in the USSR" expanded significantly the rights of operation of individual, family, cooperative, partnership, and joint-stock companies, but it did not affect the hierarchical system of organization, nor the modus operandi of the state enterprises. The drive toward private industrial cooperatives remained weak.

Most of the industrial cooperatives (80 percent of them) worked under the orders of the state enterprises according to their needs; they did not orient themselves toward the population's demand.

This system, as underlined by the valuable work *A Study of the Soviet Economy*, issued in 1991 by the IMF, the World Bank, the OECD, and the European Bank for Reconstruction and Development, had not reached in most of its industries a labor productivity equal to more than 40 percent of that of the United States. This was due to the unbreakable combination of poor work planning, poor-quality inputs and tools, inadequate incentives, and overemployment. The key Soviet machine building center used 1.7 percent more labor than the United States. Rejection rates of industrial products continued to be very high, and most of the Soviet industrial goods remained internationally noncompetitive. To "overtake and outstrip" economically the advanced capitalist countries, which was the incessantly repeated goal of the Soviet system, proved increasingly less attainable, notwithstanding the immense human sacrifices brutally imposed upon the population of the USSR by the Communist Party and its ideologies.

Finally, by October 18, 1990, Gorbachev recognized in his report to the Supreme Soviet entitled "Basic Guidelines for the Stabilization of the Economy and for the Passage to a Market Economy" (*Pravda* and *Izvestia*, October 18, 1990) that the economy was deteriorating, production was declining, the economic links were broken, separatism was intensifying, and the state solvency had reached critical levels. He also stated that the USSR had "no alternative to *switching to the market*." This transition, he noted, was necessary since the self-regulatory mechanisms characteristic of the market would ensure the rational use of labor, and of material and financial resources. It took over sixty years of war economy planning and management to arrive officially at this conclusion.

18-3. Transition and the Tertiary Sector

Soviet thought and practice attributed secondary importance to retailing, wholesaling, personal selling, and advertising. It paid little attention to such things as stores, trading space and equipment, transport facilities of the merchandise, storage, and warehousing. Trade was viewed as the nonproductive, passive outcome of production. It suffered from continuous disruptions in supplies, shortages and low quality of goods, as well as insufficient trading space, selling equipment, and sales personnel. This situation began to change somewhat in the 1970s, and then gained more effective attention only in the second half of the 1980s. At that time, the Communist Party adopted a so-called comprehensive program, the "Development of the Consumers' Production and the Service Sphere in 1986–2000" (*Pravda* and *Izvestia*, October 9, 1985). The program envisaged an all-out increase in the production of consumer goods, in the expansion of their assortment, and improvements in their quality, along with increases in the range of services provided to the consumers in public catering, housing, transport, and various other services such as repair and maintenance of homes, equipment, and appliances.

The Soviet distribution system involved, with regard to production, the handling of the material-technical supply of the industrial enterprises (carried out by Gossnab on the basis of the plans drawn by Gosplan), and, with regard to the consumer sector, the management, on the one hand, of the state procurement of agricultural produce (*zagatovki*) and, on the other hand, of the wholesale as well as the retail trade network. Both the "noncash" settlements and clearing of interfirm transactions, and the "cash" transactions concerning wages and salaries and the consumer goods purchasing, were handled by the Gosbank. In the second half of the 1980s, suggestions were made to move away from directly assigning inputs and injunctions on outputs, and to expand wholesale trade and freely negotiated contracts among producers and users, but these suggestions were not followed. While the leaders were stressing the idea that the trade in producer goods had to play "a decisive role in the formation of a socialist market" (*Izvestia*, January 3, 1989), in fact the changeover from the system of central allocation to a system of industrial purchasing even remotely similar to the one prevailing in market-directed economies proved stymied by innumerable difficulties.

The changeover to an expanded wholesale trade indeed could not be achieved without industrial deconcentrating, the surge of competitive suppliers, and the opening of the economy to world market influences. The changeover could also not be achieved because of the fear of the top bureaucrats handling the material-technical supplies that their loss of control over this crucial element of central planning would, according to them, bring about total economic collapse. The changeover was also hampered even by the managers of the state enterprises who were clinging to the old game they knew – central deliveries of the buildup of excessive inventories, of low outputs, and of valuable bonuses for "overfulfilling" the targets. The party leaders had first assumed that by the end of 1989, 30 percent of the produced capital goods would not be assigned centrally but would be carried out through wholesale trade, and that by 1990 the traded share would rise to 60 percent, and by 1992 to 80–90 percent. Actually, however, by the end of the 1980s, wholesale accounted for only 3–5 percent of the movement of capital goods. In short, as in the case of agriculture, the leaders and their bureaucracies, who had been reluctant to give away the state's procurement of agricultural products at administered prices (the *zagatovki* supplies), were not reluctant to rely in theory, with respect to the producers goods, on the spontaneity and unpredictability of wholesale market relations.

Special plans were also then drawn up for the eventual expansion of the retail network, supported by various calculations of the growth of outputs and the use of ad hoc norms for establishing the number of outlets, the sales floor surface, and the personnel needed to manage such facilities in the towns and in the countryside. But in practice, the expansion of the state retail network, notwithstanding the increased size of the population, remained slow, irregular, inadequate, and primitive. The nomenklatura continued to have access to special stores with low prices and wider assortments, but the mass of the consumers had to continue to rely on poorly located and poorly provided state shops, cooperative shops, and on the more expensive collective farm markets. The system of public catering remained also, as before, the most neglected part of the system of distribution, in dire need of better supplies, facilities, and equipment. Wholesale, retail, and public catering continued to function under hundreds of frequently contradictory directives and orders, and continued to be prey to all kind of subterfuges, cheating, fraud, and misappropriation of resources. The only real market operations involving a vast amount of buying and selling were carried out under multiple semilegal and illegal forms in the "shadow markets." Since the central priorities continued to deviate substantially from the population's wants, and since the main flows of the economy did not move fully according to the officially stated goals, the people became increasingly skeptical about the official pronouncements about an impending "movement toward the market." Historically, as the American experience shows, as the U.S. private industrial firms grew and expanded their production facilities, they shifted from a production-oriented philosophy to a distribution-oriented policy and strategy. No such normal change could have occurred in the USSR, where the state-run industry was managed on the basis of a production-oriented ideology, which could not be abandoned without bringing about the collapse of the entire system. Indeed, as Gorbachev himself put it in his October 1990 "Basic Guidelines" on the transition to the market, what was necessary for such a "breakthrough" was "that the state tutelage, freeloading and leveling, and apathy and mismanagement bred by the administrative-edict system be replaced by *freedom of economic activity*," that is, by a change involving the real discarding of the basic principles and methods of what had constituted the Soviet system.

18-4. Income and Wealth

At the beginning of 1988, *The Economist* remarked that in theory the USSR had been ripe for the sort of modern economic miracle performed since 1945 by West Germany, Japan, and South Korea. Yet notwithstanding that the USSR had vast riches in raw materials and a large strata of educated workforce, the archaic structure of industry that it acquired over sixty years of central planning, its bad habits, inertia, and enormous bureaucracy (of 18 million, equal to the entire working population of South Korea) brought about not an economic miracle but rather a continuous decline in its rate of development.[4] Indeed, the Soviet system's protracted economic slowdown and growing "malaise,"

---

[4] "The Soviet Economy: Russian Roulette," *The Economist*, April 9, 1988.

Table 18-1 *USSR: Rates of Economic Growth, 1961–90*

Period		Official data[a]	Seliunin & Khanin[b]	CIA estimates[c]
7th FYP	1961–5	6.5	4.4	4.8
8th FYP	1966–70	7.8	4.1	5.0
9th FYP	1971–5	5.6	3.2	3.1
10th FYP	1975–80	4.3	1.0	2.2
11th FYP	1981–5	3.2	0.6	1.8
12th FYP ⎱	1986–9	2.7	—	1.4
⎰	1990	–2.5	—	—

Notes:
[a] Net Material Product at comparable prices.
[b] Net Material Product.
[c] GNP rates adjusted to be comparable to the official estimates.
Sources: Nardnoe khoziastvo SSSR za 70 let, op. cit., p. 51, and Goskomstat data, cf.
A Study of the Soviet Economy, op. cit., Vol. 1, p. 84; Seliunin, V., and Khanin, G.,
Nardonaia khoziaistvo SSSR-Lukavaia Tsifra (The National Economy of the USSR –
Deceptive Figures), *Novyi Mir*, No. 2, 1987, pp. 192–5; Directorate of Intelligence,
Revisiting Soviet Economic Performance under Glasnost, Washington, DC, September
1988, p. 9.

treated at the beginning of Gorbachev's perestroika as correctable deficiencies, eventually became recognized as incurable diseases of the all-embracing
party-state order. As can be seen in Table 18-1, according to the official figures
as well as of various estimates, the rates of growth of the Soviet Net Material
Product declined continually beginning in the 1970s. According to Vasilii
Seliunin and G. Khanin, as well as Central Intelligence Agency (CIA) estimates, the decline had been much more severe than officially recognized. Yet,
neither the official figures nor the indicated estimates are fully illustrative of
the deep decreases in the Soviet rates of output growth. Thus, in a speech to
the plenary sessions of the Communist Party's Central Committee, in February
1988, Gorbachev pointed out that the official growth rates had been reached
"largely on an unhealthy basis," namely on the basis of the exports of petroleum
at the high prices then prevailing on the world market, and of the high sales
of wine and vodka on the domestic market. If we remove those influences
from the economic indices, added Gorbachev, "the result is that we had no
absolute growth of the national income over virtually four five-year plans, and
that it even began to decrease in the early 1980s." Gorbachev concluded that
the country was going to run into "an extremely serious financial situation"
given the change in the price of fuel, and given the reduction in the Soviet
production of wine and vodka that the state mandated to maintain "the social
health of the population."[5]

[5] Gorbachev, Mikhail, "Provide an Ideology of Renewal for Revolutionary Restructuring,"
Pravda and *Izvestia*, February 18, 1988, transl. in *Current Digest of the Soviet Press*, Vol. XL,
No. 7, 1988, p. 7.

A close look at the patterns of output growth in industry and agriculture shows sharp decreases in both, but, much more severe decreases in agriculture. These decreases also brought forth all kinds of explanations besides those of Gorbachev concerning the real impact of the sale of petroleum and alcohol. Thus, various Soviet writers viewed the Soviet production in general as being vitiated by innumerable afflictions, including pervasive "theft, bribery, extortion, fraud," and countless violations of the officially established rules and regulations. According to O. Osipenko, who focused on the sources of widespread "unearned" incomes, the latter resulted from the distortions of the reports concerning wages and bonuses, the production of defective and unsalable products, violations of construction rules, illicit uses of state equipment, the resort to low norms resulting in "overfulfillment" figures that had no relation to labor productivity, and so on.[6] Other writers asserted that the "critical nature of the economic dynamics in the 1970s and early 1980s" hampered the implementation of social programs (notably the food program), a fact that "negatively affected public sentiments and attitudes."[7] Still other authors asserted that the lagging of the Soviet national product in relation to those of the capitalist countries was due to a host of elements, including the absence of proper organization, loose discipline, and the inefficient use of resources. Certain other commentators, who tried to excuse the evident aberrations of the Soviet planning system, suggested that *all* the economic failures were actually essentially due to "the initial lagging of pre-revolutionary Russia in applied science and technology, the low cultural and technical development level of labor force, the underdeveloped infrastructure of Siberia, the Far East, the North and Central Asia," and finally, to "the disastrous consequences of the First and especially the Second World War, the ensuing arms race, and other factors out of control."[8] While it is certainly true that all these circumstances had a disastrous impact on the Soviet economy, it is equally true that the pretentious, brutal, authoritarian, and in many respects inefficient "state capitalism" – as Lenin rightly named it – and its centralized planning system proved in many respects incapable of surmounting its innumerable shortcomings.

Other Soviet writers, well aware of the numerous contradictory manipulations of the "out of control factors," pointed out, for instance, the ways in which the reigning bureaucracy manipulated the shares of consumption and investment in the national income. As Seliunin remarked, it was stated officially that three-fourths of the national income went to consumption and one-fourth to

[6] Osipenko, O., "Unearned Income and Forms of Its Manifestation," transl. from Russian in *Problems of Economics*, Vol. XXX, No. 4, August 1987, pp. 50–61.

[7] Kulikov, Vsevolod, "Accelerated Socio-Economic Growth as a Basis for Social Progress," in USSR's Academy of Sciences, Institute of Economics, *The USSR: Acceleration of Socio-Economic Development*, Moscow, Social Science Today, 1987, p. 17.

[8] Kravchenko, Sergei, "The Strategy of Acceleration and Its Bourgeois Falsifiers," in *The USSR: Acceleration of Socio-Economic Development, op. cit.*, p. 168.

accumulation. But, added Seliunin, the state's statistics use different rubles to measure consumption and accumulation – in one case the value of goods is calculated in the higher retail prices, in the other case in the lower whole-sale prices. When the differences between the two are eliminated, it appears that the share of consumption has steadily "declined for many decades," while the share of accumulation has increased sharply. The colossal investments in heavy industry have not benefited the standard of living.[9] In this regard, the economist R. R. Simonian, department head at the Soviet Academy of Sciences, noted in mid-1988 (*Izvestia*, July 8), "our per capita individual con-sumption is only about one-third of that of the United States. Note that the lag in the level of consumption is essentially equal to the lag in labor productivity. That is natural. The way we work determines the way we live."

In short, by the end of the 1980s, on the eve of the complete decomposition of the USSR, it became increasingly evident to a large part of the Soviet intelligentsia that the Soviets could certainly not achieve the postwar eco-nomic miracle realized by West Germany, Japan, and South Korea. The Soviets had irreconcilably failed in the competition with the advanced capitalist coun-tries with regard to the growth of output, productivity, standard of living, and general speed of economic development. Inevitably, an increasing part of Russia's population forever lost confidence in the pretentious Soviet idea of "reaching and surpassing" the achievements of the market-directed capital-ist countries through the state's planning methods. In one respect, Stalin was right: As he put it at the launching of the central planning era, Russia would either succeed in basing the Soviet regime on the "foundation of the most large-scale united industry," or a return to a market-directed economy would become inevitable.[10] Indeed, after over sixty years of ineffective, brutal, bu-reaucratic, overall centralized commands and controls, this transition became unavoidable.

18-5. Concluding Comments

As stated officially, Russia had transited in 1917 from the Tsarist semifeudal capitalist economy to a "Soviet, proletarian, socialist economy." But in fact, it had transited to a state capitalist economy anchored on the state's ownership of all industrial factories, tolerating for a time, at the margin of its complex, private economic relations in agriculture, small production, and trade. This economy was run throughout its existence with war economy methods, under the absolute power of the secretary general of the Communist Party. This state had eliminated since 1928 the private economic sectors, proceeded to the

[9] Seliunin, Vasilii, "A Profound Reform or the Revenge of the Bureaucracy?" *Problems of Economics*, Vol. XXXI, No. 11, March 1989, p. 9.

[10] Stalin, J., "Industrialization of the Country and the Right Deviation," *Foundations of Soviet Strategy for Economic Growth, op. cit.*, p. 271.

collectivization of agriculture with the goal of transforming it into "factories in the field," and launched successive central economic plans aimed to "catch up with and surpass" the most advanced capitalist countries.

Under Stalin and his successors, the USSR achieved important targets in heavy industry, but continued to remain technologically far behind the Western countries in all fields, except the military-nuclear one. From its beginnings, the callous planning system started to be corroded by all kinds of hidden unbalances and subterfuges aimed at fulfilling its inflexible targets. Deviousness, deceptions, evasions, and manipulations of all kinds of data, along with cheating and reciprocal favors, spread throughout the economy, concomitantly with an increasing indifference of labor to work. Ideas of reorganizing the Soviet system started from the 1950s on in the Soviet Union and its East European satellites. The satellites reached revolutionary stages before these ideas impacted the Soviet Union's conceptions about its own ways of handling its socioeconomic problems. Still, even in the early 1980s, Gorbachev treated the Soviet protracted economic slowdown as the consequence of correctable deficiencies; he did not aim at discarding the Soviet system, but rather at finding the appropriate changes that would keep it alive and functioning properly. He stated early in 1986 that he would not take "a single step away from Marxism-Leninism," but that he would, however, "resolutely reject" the "dogmatic, bureaucratic, legislative legacies" of the preceding regime (*Pravda*, February 19, 1986). Subsequently, he indicated that he wanted to reverse "the unfavorable tendencies" that had led since the 1970s to the decline of the output growth rates, and to increase these rates through an all-out intensification of production along with structural restructuring, effective forms of management, and stimulation of labor (*Pravda*, February 26, 1986). Over a year later, he specified that he aimed to achieve a new kind of centralism that would determine the basic priorities and objectives of the economy and the areas of structural investment policy but which would combine "the advantages of planning" with the skillful use of commodity-monetary relations (*Pravda*, June 26, 1987). Soon afterward, after condemning the party's policy concerning the peasantry and the villages, he took another important step away from Stalin's legacy. By 1989, he stressed the necessity of clearly demarcating the functions of the party and of the Soviets; he proposed that the party should continue to be the "vanguard of the proletariat," while the Soviet administration should become the real instrument of state power (*Pravda*, July 19, 1989). Under increasing pressures tearing apart the Soviet system and the Soviet empire, he finally asserted that the country had to "renounce the primitive views on *socialist ownership*" and "the neglect of *commodity-monetary relations*" in order to find the solution to the "organic *combination* between planning and market methods" (*Izvestia*, February 13, 1990). By October 1990, Gorbachev had to take the last step before his fall from power, namely the assertion of the need for the transition to the market (*Pravda*, October 18, 1990).

Gorbachev's evolution from "a new kind of centralism," to a "combination of the advantages of planning with commodity-monetary relations," then to the "renunciation to the primitive views on socialist ownership," and finally to the acceptance of the necessary "transition to the market," reflected in many ways not only the disastrous difficulties of the Soviet system but also the conflicts, debates, and inevitable changes in process throughout its empire. As the Polish economist Leszek Balcerowicz put it, one can subsume the concept of the development of the reformed system begun in Eastern Europe to "the imitation of capitalism under increasingly relaxed constraints." In Balcerowicz's frame, Pekka Sutela indicated as follows the stages of the evolution from Lenin's type of economy to the market economy: 1) Start with Lenin's conception of socialism as a "single [hierarchical] factory"; 2) proceed through simulated commodity markets in the "corporation" model; 3) shift to a mixture of real commodity markets and simulated capital markets in a "public sector" model; 4) accept the existence of real capital owners, that is, "capitalism in a technical sense."[11]

Neither Gorbachev nor his successor to the presidency of Russia were the liquidators of the decrepit Soviet system. That system started to decompose itself long before the perestroika. When the party's right wing tried to retake power violently and failed, the power fell into Boris Yeltsin's hands. As Vladimir Buckovski remarked with regard to Gorbachev – and this applies perfectly also to Yeltsin – "nothing in his previous career would indicate that he was in any way different from the so-called 'old guard' which had indeed brought him up, educated him, and promoted him."[12] What had changed at these critical moments was not Gorbachev or Yeltsin's training, prejudices, and methods, but the unstoppable decay of the Soviet economy, of its empire, and of its satellites.

In short, what the Communists had established was a semi-Asiatic, centralized, autarchic state, similar in many respects to the preceding Tsarist one. Within this framework, its crucial choices concerning development were embodied in the concepts and procedures of a war economy. Their five-year plans ordering the allocation of resources in determined directions, setting the key targets, specifying the methods of implementation, and commandeering their execution reflected indeed perfectly the concepts of a war economy operating under the tutelage of an inflexible bureaucracy. Paradoxically, as under the late Tsars, the country's investable resources were directed toward the expansion of certain heavy industries – but now not for increasing the railroad network but for modernizing and expanding of the armament industry and its underlying bases – steel, machinery, nuclear power, and so on.

---

[11] Sutela, Pekka, "Rationalizing the Centrally Managed Economy: The Market," in *Market Socialism or the Restoration of Capitalism?*, Aslund, Anders, ed., New York, Cambridge University Press, 1992, p. 67.

[12] Bukovsky, Vladimir, "Glasnost," *Commentary*, Vol. 86, No. 5, November 1988, p. 2.

The existence over seventy years of a war economy commandeering the country through unreachable goals generated all kind of devious methods and habits meant to circumvent the official targets, lie about achievements, and falsify the processes of execution. A whole illegal set of procedures grew within the projected "single factory," entertained by all kind of ties between the managers and the workers. The inflexible direction of investable resources toward one sector – in an impoverished country, with a production apparatus largely obsolete and ineffective – brings to mind an appropriate remark of Adam Smith in the *Wealth of Nations*:

It is thus that every system which endeavours, either, by extra-ordinary encouragements, to draw towards a particular species of industry a greater share of the capital of the society than what would naturally go to it; or, by extraordinary restraints, to force from a particular species of industry some share of the capital which would otherwise be employed in it; is in reality subversive of the great purpose which it means to promote. It retards, instead of accelerating, the progress of the society towards real wealth and greatness; and diminishes, instead of increasing, the real value of the annual produce of its land and labour."[13]

The resulting skewed character of the Soviet economy's capital stock, the poor productivity of most of its sectors, and the manifest underdevelopment outside of the main urban centers led to a multiplication of unlawful operations within the country, disregard of state commands, and alienation of managers and of workers with regard to "state property" and leaders' objectives. The longer the existence of the odious, retarding Soviet war economy, the deeper its decomposition and vaster its contrast with the developing West.

[13] Smith, Adam, *An Inquiry into the Nature and Causes of the Wealth of Nations* (1776), New York, Modern Library, 1937, pp. 650–1.

PART III

THE POST-SOVIET ECONOMIC TRANSITION

CHAPTER 19

The Socioeconomic Framework

19-1. Territory and Population

The disintegration of the Soviet Union in December 1991, and its replacement by a Russian Federation and by a "commonwealth of independent states," had been preceded by a dramatic series of conflicts and maneuvers between two Communist leaders, Mikhail Gorbachev and Boris Yeltsin. Already in 1989, Yeltsin had positioned himself as the main antagonist of Gorbachev and as an alternative leader. At the time, Gorbachev himself was trying to strengthen his capacity to circumvent the Soviet bureaucracy's opposition to reform, by creating an executive presidency of the USSR and by being appointed to this position. The measures were finally enacted in 1991, but Gorbachev's powers remained in fact limited. His presidential decrees were disregarded as the Union was increasingly torn apart by innumerable difficulties and conflicts. In the meantime, the powers of Yeltsin grew appreciably. He was elected as leader of the Supreme Soviet in May 1990, and then established through a Declaration of State Sovereignty ratified by the Congress of the Russian Republic the primacy of Russian law over Soviet law on its territory and, at the same time, the idea of economic sovereignty for all the other Union republics. By February 1991 he insistently called for Gorbachev to resign as president of the Soviet Union, and soon afterward, on June 12, 1991, Yeltsin succeeded in being elected president of Russia.

Between August 19 to 21, as Gorbachev was away on vacation in Crimea and while Yeltsin was officially housed in Russia's center of power of its parliament, the Russian White House, the anti-Yeltsin right wing of the Communist Party attempted a disastrous putsch on the White House. In the absence of Gorbachev, Yeltsin proclaimed himself supreme commander of the armed forces, denounced the plotters publicly from above a tank facing the White House, and finally triumphed against the putschists led notably by Valentin Pavlov, the Soviet prime minister, Dimitri Iazov, the defense minister, and Vladimir Kruickhov, the KGB's chair. Late on August 21, Gorbachev returned

287

meekly to a liberated Moscow. The plotters had been arrested and indicted, while Yeltsin saw his power strengthened with an extra dose of respect and legitimacy.

In this situation, after a number of contradictory measures, Gorbachev tried in December 1991 to regain power by strengthening the position of the Communist traditionalists, of the military, the police, and the KBG, and by cutting significantly into the legislative functions of the Supreme Soviet. But his prestige as a creditable political actor was in shambles. After a secret meeting of Yeltsin with the leaders of the Ukraine and Belarus, on December 8, 1991, it was decided that a "Commonwealth of Independent States" would replace the USSR. Shortly afterward, Yeltsin issued a number of decrees ordering the Russian government to seize the Kremlin and replace the functions of the Soviet central government. Gorbachev declared the decrees illegal but lacked the means to block them. Finally, on December 23, 1991, Gorbachev gave up his power, which passed, as far as the new Russian Federation was concerned, into the hands of Yeltsin. The collapse of the Soviet Union wiped out hundreds of years of imperial conquests and expansion – conquests maintained under a firm rule, also during the seventy-four years of the Soviet system. But the Russian Federation did inherit much of the political arrangements of the RSFSR, including a constitution adopted in 1978. Finally, the latter was replaced by a new constitution adopted by a referendum on December 12, 1993. While this constitution is the country's supreme act, many of its provisions are general and ineffective unless rendered implementable by legal acts of various kinds, including federal laws and codes, presidential decrees and orders, cabinet decrees, and administrative rules.

The present frontiers of the Russian Federation contained in 1959 117.8 million people. By 1989 its total population reached 147 million, and it maintained this figure over the next decade. Big changes in urbanization were registered between 1959 and 1989: The ratio of the urban to rural population shifted during that period from 52/48 to 74/26, and this ratio prevailed during the 1990s. (See Table 19-1.)

Table 19-1 *Russian Federation: Total Population, Urban and Rural, 1959–99, in Millions and Percentages*

Population	1959	1989	1991	1995	1999
Total	117.5	147.4	148.5	148.3	146.3
Urban	61.6	108.4	109.8	108.3	106.8
Rural	55.9	39.0	38.7	40.0	39.5
Percent					
Urban	52	74	74	73	73
Rural	48	26	26	27	27

Sources: Goskomstat, *Rosiiskii statisticheskii ezhegodnik 1998* (Russian Statistical Annual 1998), Moscow, 1998, p. 98; Goskomstat, *Rossiia v tsifrakh* (Russia in Figures), Moscow, 1999, p. 70.

Table 19-2 *Russian Federation: Territory and Population by Regions, 1998,*
Totals and Percentages

Federation and regions	Territory – 1,000 Km	Population in 1,000	Percent[a]	
			Territory	Population
Russian Federation	1,707.54	147,105	100	100
Northern	1,466.3	5,785	8.6	3.9
North Western	196.5	7,989	1.2	5.4
Central	483.0	29,651	2.8	20.3
Volga-Viatka	265.4	8,376	1.6	5.7
Central Black Earth	167.7	7,846	1.0	5.4
Lower Volga	536.4	16,886	3.1	11.5
North Caucasus	355.1	17,707	2.1	12.1
Ural	824.0	20,406	4.8	13.9
West Siberia	2,427.2	15,109	14.2	10.3
East Siberia	4,122.8	9,071	24.2	6.2
Far East	6,125.9	7,336	36.4	5.0

Notes:
[a] Rounded figures.
Source: Rossiskii statisticheskii ezhegodnik 1998, op. cit., pp. 33–5.

The Russian Federation's most populated regions – namely the Central, Lower Volga, North Caucasus, and the Ural – accounted jointly in 1998 for over 57 percent of the country's population, but for less than 13 percent of its territory. On the other hand, the country's most sparsely populated but largest regions – namely the Far East, East, and West Siberia regions – accounted jointly for almost 21 percent of the country's population, but for close to 75 percent of its total territory. (See Table 19-2.) The highest urban/rural ratios were registered by the North Western and the Central region (namely 86/14 and 83/17); the lowest by the North Caucasus and the Central Black Earth region (55/45 and 63/37). All the other regions had an urban population of 70 to 75 percent and a rural population of 25 to 30 percent.

The Russian Federation inherited its administrative and political frontiers from the Soviet Union. The Federation comprises eighty-nine units: twenty-one autonomous republics, forty-nine provincial areas (*oblasti*), an autonomous (Jewish) *oblast*, six territories (*okruga*), ten districts (*krai*), and two federal cities treated as *okruga*, Moscow and Petersburg. Yeltsin has emphasized this federal arrangement from 1990–1 as a new, democratic beginning in the relations between the center and the ethno-republics. At the time, he saw in the support of the autonomous republics – with relatively high ethnic populations – a way of both counteracting Gorbachev's power and strengthening his own base. The federal arrangement was indeed viewed as an appropriate means for preventing Russia's own breakdown. Subsequently, numerous autonomous republics as well as various *oblasti* pursued policies counteracting many of the central power's objectives, laws, and edicts. Finally, after the end of the Yeltsin regime, Moscow has increasingly aimed at curtailing the powers of republics and of the *oblasti*.

As can be seen in Figure 19-1, the twenty-one republics are located in the following regions:

- Two: *Karelia* and *Komi* are in the Northern region.
- Seven: *Adygea, Karachai-Cherkassia, Kabardino-Balkaria, North Ossetia (Alaniia), Ingushetsiia, Chechniia*, and *Dagestan* are in the North Caucasus region.
- Five: *Chuvashiia, Mari El, Mordovia, Tatarstan*, and *Kalmykiia* are in the Volga-Viatka and Lower Volga regions.
- Two: *Udmurtia* and *Bashkortostan* are in the Ural regions.
- Four: *Altai, Khakassia, Tyva*, and *Buriatiia* are in the East and West Siberian regions.
- One: *Sakha (Iakutiia)* is in the Far East.

According to the 1989 census data, the Russians accounted for 81.5 percent of the population of the RSFSR. Only six of the autonomous republics had non-Russian ethnic populations exceeding 50 percent; all the others had non-Russian ethnic populations that were below 50 percent, and among them six had less than 25 percent non-Russian populations. While certain autonomous republics – such as Chechniia – as well as certain *oblasts* had incessantly claimed powers that in fact they could not fully obtain or exercise, other regional, territorial, and even district administrations may have obtained various kinds of powers that far exceeded their legal status.

With regard to employment, massive displacements were registered in the 1990s in conjunction with the overall changes in the levels of economic performance, in the forms of ownership, and in the sectoral economic activities. Let me note for now only that the Gross National Product decreased through the 1990s by 43 percent. (I will return in detail to this key issue later on.) Total employment decreased sharply through the 1990s; in relation to the 72.0 million employed in 1992, the total reached in 1995 involved 66.4 million persons, and in 1998 63.6 million. Registered unemployment increased from 3.8 million in 1993 to 6.7 million in 1995, and then to 8.8 million in 1998. Employment by underlying forms of ownership, administrations, and enterprises also shifted appreciably; thus significant decreases were registered in the state and municipally owned enterprises, while notable increases were accounted for in the privately owned firms. The share of state and municipal workforce decreased from 68.9 percent of the total workforce in 1992 to 38.3 percent in 1998; on the other hand, the workforce in the private sector increased from 18.3 percent to 41.8 percent, with the mixed companies (particularly those with foreign participation) accounting for the balance.

The shifts in the sectoral workforce reflect also the underlying changes in the economy's activities. As can be seen in Table 19-3 in absolute figures, large decreases were registered in industry, agriculture, construction, transport and

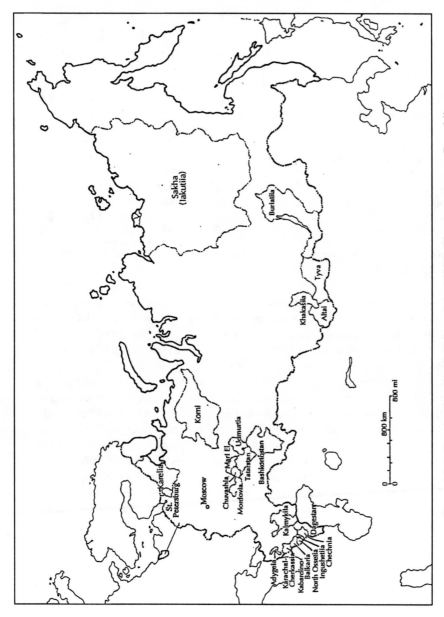

Figure 19-1. Russia after the Collapse of the USSR: The Autonomous Republics

Table 19-3 *Russian Federation: Total Workforce in the Economy's Sectors in 1990, 1995, and 1998, in Thousands and Percentages*

Workforce	In thousands			In percent		
	1990	1995	1998	1990	1995	1998
Total	75,325	66,441	63,642	100	100	100
Industry	22,809	17,182	14,150	30.3	25.9	22.2
Agriculture	9,965	10,003	8,282	13.2	15.1	13.0
Construction	9,020	6,208	5,410	12.0	9.3	8.5
Transport & communication	5,818	5,253	5,043	7.8	7.9	7.9
Trade & public catering	5,869	6,679	8,900	7.8	10.1	13.9
Housing & communal service	3,217	2,979	3,691	4.3	4.5	5.8
Health & physical culture	4,238	4,446	4,500	5.6	6.7	7.1
Education, culture, & art	7,231	7,316	7,200	9.6	11.0	11.3
Science	2,804	1,688	1,370	3.7	2.5	2.2
Financial services	402	820	760	0.5	1.2	1.2
State administration	1,602	1,893	2,570	2.1	2.8	4.0
Other employment	2,350	1,974	1,766	3.1	3.0	2.8

Sources: For 1990, *Rossiiskii statisticheskii ezhegodnik 1998, op. cit.*, p. 79; for 1995 and 1998, *Rossiia v tsifrakh, op. cit.*, p. 81.

communications, and science, while appreciable increases were accounted for in trade and public catering, state administration, and financial services. In the comparable positions in the yearly rankings, sharp increases were registered in trade, education, and state administrations, while the most notable decrease was in industry.

As far as the pattern of monthly wages was concerned, throughout the 1990s the lowest wages were those paid in agriculture – where they accounted for only a part of the total peasant income – followed by education and the arts. The highest wages were obtainable in finance, geology and geodesy, information, transport and communication, and finally in industry. In 1998, the monthly wage in agricultural enterprises amounted to 452,000 rubles, compared to 1,309,000 in industry, 1,554,000 in transport, and 2,191,000 in finance. The wage differentials – reflecting *inter alia* the structural changes and the shifts in the pattern of output and employment – were part and parcel of the marked increases in economic inequality. According to the official data, the distribution of money incomes by 20 percent of population groups evolved as shown in Table 19-4. The first group of 20 percent of the population obtained a share of the monetary income amounting to around 6 percent of the total; at the opposite end, the fifth and last group of 20 percent of the population acquired a share increasing from 37 percent to 47 percent of the total. The Gini coefficient, the index of the concentration of income, rose from 0.289 in 1992 to 0.379 in 1998 after reaching 0.409 in 1994. According to other official data, incomes below the subsistence level amounted to 33.5 percent (49.7 million) of the population

Table 19-4 *Russian Federation: Distribution of Money Income by 20 Percent of Population Groups, 1992–8*

Money income by 20 percent of population	1992	1993	1994	1995	1996	1997	1998
Total	100	100	100	100	100	100	100
First group	6.0	5.8	5.3	5.5	6.2	6.0	6.2
Second	11.6	11.1	10.2	10.2	10.7	10.2	10.5
Third	17.6	16.7	15.2	15.0	15.2	14.8	14.9
Fourth	26.5	24.8	23.0	22.4	21.5	21.6	21.0
Fifth	38.3	41.6	46.3	46.9	46.4	47.4	47.4
Gini coefficient	0.289	0.398	0.409	0.381	0.375	0.381	0.379

Source: *Rossiia v tsifrakh, op. cit.*, p. 110.

of 1992 and to 20.8 percent (30.7 million) of the population of 1997. At least as far as 1997 is concerned, we may conclude that the below subsistence level group, amounting slightly to over 20 percent of the population, lived on around 6 percent of the population's total monetary income.

Let us now consider in broad outline the changes in the rural as well as in the urban society.

19-2. Rural Society

As Table 19-1 indicates, in 1999 the rural dwellers amounted to 39.5 million people, that is, to 27 percent of the country's population. The rural birth rates declined during the 1990s, from 15.5 per thousand to 10.0 per thousand in 1997, while the death rates increased from 13.3 per thousand to 16.1 per thousand in 1997. The net growth per thousand fell from 2.2 in 1990 to minus 6.1 per thousand in 1997 – a trend somewhat similar to the urban balances of birth rates and death rates. Eight regions registered small rural population decreases (the Northern, NorthWestern, Central, Volga-Viatka, Central Black Earth, West Siberia, East Siberia, and Far East), while the remaining three registered increases (particularly so in the North Caucasus, as well as in the Lower Volga and the Ural). A number of Russians moved back from abroad and settled in the rural areas, particularly from 1992 to 1995, so that the total rural population remained through the 1990s at roughly 39.5 million. Given the decline in output and employment in the economy as a whole, including agriculture, rural employment decreased from 10.3 million in 1992 to 8.2 million in 1998 – that is, by 2 million – accounting for only 13 percent of the total employment in 1998.

Following the collapse of the USSR, the newly independent Russian Federation set forth its own agrarian program, aiming in principle to bestow private ownership of land and to reorganize the farm enterprises as well as the entire agro-industrial complex. I will examine later on in detail the specific measures involved in this regard, and their policy rationale. For now, note that, by the end of 1997, 27,000 large-scale agricultural enterprises disposed of 50 percent of the agricultural land (149.2 million hectares) and employed 5.7 million workers; on the other hand, 16.3 million household plot owners used only close to 5 percent of the land (10.2 million hectares); finally, 274,000 individual farms were active on over 5.7 percent of the land (11.7 million hectares). The state owned the land used by various large-scale enterprises as well as a land reserve, a land redistribution fund, and a forest fund, while the municipalities controlled about 9 percent of the land (18.5 million hectares). The large-scale agricultural enterprises have been registered as joint companies, agricultural cooperatives, or associations of private farms; some of them have maintained the previous legal status of collective or state farms. Their land and non-land assets belong to the enterprises, which in turn belong to the shareholders, namely to the employees, pensioners, and social workers. The large-scale farms do provide their members with convenient shops, housing, and various social services, as well as household plots, most of whose production is for family use but a growing part of which is being commercialized. Some large-scale farms pay for labor in kind, and in turn the recipients may freely sell these products. The reluctance of individual farm members to strike out on their own, is understandable, given the difficulties that continue to prevail in the countryside.

On the other hand, if one is to believe the Peasants' Party leader Yuri Chernichenko, the chairs of the large-scale farms are in a far more profitable position than they were under the Soviets. They now can dispose of the farms' land, livestock, or crops as they see fit; according to Chernichenko, this explains the fact that much land can be bought and sold on the black market and, while in principle the land belongs to the shareholders, it actually still belongs to the nomenklatura.[1] The farm managers indeed do not necessarily engage in the most appropriate activities for the shareholders but rather those that can attract the highest support from the regional administration. Often such policies have turned out to be costly for the large farms' members, for the taxpayers, and for the consumers. Divergent regional objectives for farm income support and for food security have necessarily led to interregional trade barriers – that is, to restrictions in the circulation of food products on their territories – have fragmented the agricultural food market, and have inhibited specializations based on comparative advantage. Cuts in consumer subsidies and the fall in real incomes have led to important declines in per capita food consumption. In the countryside, these declines were concentrated mostly in potatoes, cereals, meat, and milk products.

---

[1] Chernichenko, Yuri, "Proceeds from Secretly Sold Land Run into the Billions" *Rossiiskiie vesti*, October 10, 1995, transl. in *Current Digest of the Post-Soviet Press*, Vol. XLVII, No. 45, December 6, 1995, pp. 15–16.

Paradoxically, the 27,000 large-scale farms, which control most of the agricultural land, and evidently also the best of the limited technology available in the Russian countryside, produced in 1997 only 40.3 percent of the agricultural output, while the small, backward, but numerous households that worked intensively their minuscule plots accounted for 57.2 percent, and the individual farms for the balance of 2.5 percent. The overall share of agriculture in the economy dropped sharply during the 1990s. Under the impact of both a fall in volume and in agricultural prices, its contribution to the GNP fell from 16.4 percent in 1990 to 6.8 percent in 1997, in an overall declining economy dependent on an increasingly dilapidated base. In 1999 the GNP contracted to 40 percent of its 1991 level.

The agrarian reforms and restructuring have increased the urban-rural inequality. Life in the countryside has become ever more dependent on the household private plot, backward technology, deteriorating infrastructure, decreasing livestock, unfavorable price disparities, unequal terms of trade, limited capital investment, and small monthly wages barely accounting for 41 percent of the average wages in the economy as a whole.

19-3. Urban Society

As we saw in Table 19-1, the total urban population of the Russian Federation finally declined in the decade from 1989 to 1999 after some small variations, from 108.4 million to 106.8 million. Except for the Central Black Earth and the Lower Volga regions, which registered some small urban population increases, all the other regions displayed urban population decreases. During the indicated span of time, the country's main centers, Moscow and Petersburg, also recorded population decreases: Moscow's population shrunk from 8.9 to 8.6 million, that of Petersburg from 5.0 to 4.7 million. Decreases were also registered in seven other towns with populations of over 1 million (Ekaterinensburg, Kazan, Nizhnii Novgorod, Novosibirsk, Perm, Samara, and Cheliabinsk), while unchanged population totals or small increases were recorded in the four other towns with over 1 million inhabitants (Volgograd, Omsk, Rostov, and Ufa).

The processes of privatization and of socioeconomic reorganization during the 1990s, along with the structural changes that they conditioned, led to overall decreases in employment and to an accented differentiation in the society. Total employment declined from 75.3 million to 63.6 million, due *inter alia* to massive decreases in the state's and municipalities' employment (from 62.2 million to 38.3 million) matched only partially by the increases in employment in the private sector. The professional structure also underwent important changes that reduced the employment of unskilled labor. Thus, in 1992, managerial personnel accounted for 9.0 percent of the total employment, specialists of all kinds for 27.5 percent, and workers for 63.5 percent. By 1998, managers accounted for 7.6 percent, specialists for 44.8 percent, and lower skilled workers for the balance of 47.6 percent. All this was accompanied by continuous and massive increases in unemployment. Total unemployment increased from 3.8 million in 1992 to 8.8 million in 1998, and in the urban setting only, from 3.2 million in 1992 to 6.7 million in 1998.

Real disposable income fell through the 1990s; taking 1990 as equal to 100, the percentage reached in 1992 was 52.5, in 1995 57.9, and in 1998 49.8 percent. Real wages also fell through the 1990s from 100 in 1991 to 67.0 in 1992, 46.2 in 1995, and 44.6 in 1998. Similarly the monthly pension allowances decreased from 100 in 1991 to 52.0 in 1992, 53.5 in 1995, and 52.6 in 1998.[2] The fall in the overall economic activity is illustrated by the continuous decline of the GNP through the 1990s. According to World Bank data, the Russian GNP in purchasing power parity reached in 1998 579.8 billion U.S. dollars – that is, 3,950 dollars per capita – ranking the Russian Federation one hundredth in world per capita income. In the same year, the rankings of the industrialized G7 were the following with regard to per capita income: the United States third (with 29,340 dollars); Canada ninth; Japan fourteenth; France seventeenth; Germany twentieth; the United Kingdom twenty-second; and Italy twenty-fourth. In 1999, the GNP grew officially by 1.5 percent. But the government did little to create the appropriate foundations for real growth: Russia remained indeed plagued by the lack of a firm legal framework, of a coherent set of interadministrative connections, and of market relations capable of surmounting the still heavy tendencies toward widespread corruption and capital flight.[3]

The slowdown in economic activity through the 1990s in relation to 1990 weighed heavily on the lower strata of the urban population. The share of consumption in total expenditures rose from 31 percent in 1990 to 49.5 percent in 1995 and to 43.7 percent in 1997. Calories from foodstuffs per urban household fell from 2,511 in 1990 to 2,123 in 1997. Urban housing construction fell from 37,000 apartments built in 1992, to 30,000 per year in 1995, and then to 13,000 per year in 1998. Basic "technological products" – such as telephones and televisions – were available to only a small percentage of the urban population.

At the same time, many former members of the Soviet nomenklatura took over the decisive positions in the state apparatus, in the economy, and in the life of the country in general. Boris Yeltsin himself and his prime ministers and highest regional officials, such as Victor Chernomyrdin, Evgenii Primakov, and Vladimir Putin, came from the party's production or administrative hierarchies or from its old Komsomol. Moscow became the center of the new "bourgeoisie" that grew out of the nomenklatura. As lenders of the banks and

[2] See Goskom, *Rossiiskii statisticheskii ezhegodnik, 1998*, Moscow, 1998, sections "Population" and "Labor"; Goskom, *Rossiia v tsifrakh*, Moscow, 1999, same sections.

[3] *Entering the 21st Century. World Development Report 1999/2000*, Oxford, Oxford University Press for the World Bank, 2000, p. 231; *Transition*, Vol. 10, No. 6, December 1999, p. 3.

of the large enterprises of industry and trade, the official manipulators of the new economic relations, in close relationship with the top levels of the administration, knew how to base economic relations on the old methods of barter and blat (bribes). The new openings of the country to the world market allowed many members of Russia's new business community to place large sums offshore and to undertake few investments in the domestic economy. By the end of the 1990s, capital flight was estimated to have reached close to 3 billion dollars, an appreciable sum for the Russian Federation. The shake-up of the old state and economic setup led to curious readaptations and to important shares for the former state employees. According to various sources, the KGB, for instance, "lost" about half of its personnel in Moscow to the private sector, where they created and managed private coercive structures – namely defense or protection organizations of bankers, managers, politicians, as well as various groups, some of which were connected with the mafia. The mafia is said to have divided the country into regions in which it operates barely challenged by the new administrations. Following an article in the *Izvestia* of September 7, 1994, at the time some 12 percent of the wealthiest Moscow lenders and businesspeople had a previous successful career in the CPSU. Of the rest of the new millionaires, as many as 40 percent had been engaged in marketing fashionable products ranging from advanced electronic goods to high-priced clothing. *Izvestia* listed such well-known figures as Yeltsin, Gorbachev, Yegor Gaidar, Anatoli Chubais, and Nikolai Ryzhkov as among the wealthiest Moscovites. The managerial apex of industry and agriculture, as well as of central and regional state administrations including the parliament and the official organizations, continue to bear the ineffaceable imprint of the old nomenklatura. Indeed, a Russian *Who Is Who* (entitled *The Federal Elite*, compiled by A. A. Muklin and published in 1999) listed about two thousand biographies of the country's leaders of 1989–99, most of whom came from the old top Soviet strata.

19-4. The Command and Control System

As legacies of the Soviet Union, the Federation's leadership hold certain attitudes about how to carry out economic operations. These attitudes explain both the highly personalistic order that eventually succeeded the Soviet Union and the long-lasting institutional contradictions (or more accurately incoherences) of the Federation's government. As a former high Soviet leader Sergei Vasilev pointed out, at the collapse of the USSR, the upper tier of the state became suddenly empty as the party was removed from power, a fact that led the emerging presidential center to assume a set of tasks far higher than it actually could carry out.[4]

---

[4] Vasilev, Sergei, *Ten Years of Russia's Economic Reform: A Collection of Papers*, Bury St. Edmunds, Suffolk, St. Edmundsbury Press, 1999, pp. 49–50.

While the center lost the power to regulate directly the economic processes, it maintained the capacity to issue money and to keep control over the organization of payments and settlement relations. This allowed it to retain control over certain budget revenues, but, in the absence of the appropriate methods of fulfilling the inherited obligations, it could resort only to the solution of compensation through budget deficits and through excessive printing of money. Further, the state's incapacity to retain any effective control over any kind of coercion facilitated the spontaneous commercialization of the state economic structures utilizing the fixed assets that they had controlled. The disintegration led to a situation in which certain regions felt free to pursue their own plans, issue local currencies, and levy taxes, while the center's difficulties in gathering taxes to maintain military and security services led to the emergence of private or local militias, and to the spread of all kinds of crime and corruption.

Until 1993, the Russian Federation continued to be run according to its Soviet constitution; that is, its supreme legislative power was the Congress of People's Deputies, while its governing body was the Supreme Soviet. On Yeltsin's initiative, starting in the summer of 1990, a constitutional commission began work on a new constitution aiming at the eventual buildup of a powerful country presidency. In the meantime, after his election to the presidency of Russia on June 12, 1991, Yeltsin pursued a systematic struggle against the Supreme Soviet, and concentrated through a variety of means executive, legislative, financial, and military powers in the presidency. Eventually he strove to boost the power of the center over the regions, by granting to a majority of them subsidies from the federal budget, while on the other hand strengthening the power of the local governments as counterweights to the regional governors.

The new constitution, adopted by a national referendum on December 12, 1993, divided the state power among the presidency, a bicameral legislature, the executive branch of the government, and a Constitutional Court. However, it defined only ambiguously the center-periphery relations. Various bilateral treaties between the central authorities and the subjects of the Federation, not always consistent with the Constitution, were eventually signed, notably between 1994 and 1996. These treaties granted various degrees of autonomy to certain autonomous republics and *oblasts*, but left many of the practical relations open to further changes. In the system created under the prodding of Yeltsin, the president of the Russian Federation acquired vast powers that made the Federation a presidential republic. The president became indeed the one who appoints the prime minister, heads the Defense Council, and controls the country's foreign policy. Moreover, the heads of the ministries of Defense, Interior, and Foreign Affairs are required to report directly to him. In addition, the president also commands a presidential administration with some two thousand people assuming in practice many of the functions and coordinating powers of the former Communist Party's Central Committee. Yet, on the other hand, to create a counterweight to the power of the political parties in the state Duma, Yeltsin had to rely heavily on the representatives of the republics, *oblasts*, *krais*, and *okrugs*, grouped in the Federation Council, to whom he had to grant extensive economic and political privileges (see Figure 19-2). Yeltsin's presidential system then combined apparently unlimited powers with complete lack of accountability for his actions.[5] In practice, the personification of power in the president allowed him to distribute as he saw fit parcels of this power to unreliable allies in exchange for limited loyalty or conformity to his wishes. Thus grew without any defined limits the autonomy of the component regions of the Russian Federation.

The ascent to power of Yeltsin's successor, Putin, changed Yeltsin's policies and methods of balancing powers in the country by relying on the Federation's Council members and granting them and their constituencies privileges and political liberties. Indeed, soon after his accession to power, Putin sealed various agreements with the Duma's leaders and then corralled the governors of the eighty-nine components of the Federation into seven new administrative districts, each overseen by a regional official directly responsible to him. He then replaced the Federation's Council members and changed the composition of the Federation Council. The groups that predominate now among representatives of governors and regional legislative bodies and businesspeople, are deputies to regional parliaments and former federal-level officials: Putin thus helped not only to limit the power, political influence, and the independence of Russia's eighty-nine regional centers, but also enhanced further the real powers of the presidency.

19-5. Concluding Comments

The Yeltsin era began unexpectedly on March 26, 1989, when the Communist leader Boris Yeltsin, who had been fired in November 1987 from his post of Moscow's party chief, and who had been afterward ousted from the Politburo in February 1988, made an outstanding return to a crucial seat purposely vacated for him by a delegate who had won election to the newly established Soviet of Nationalities Chamber of the Soviet Union's Supreme Soviet. The Yeltsin era – a rightful term, given its crucial historical implications – ended also unexpectedly after a little over ten years, on December 31, 1999, when Yeltsin announced his resignation as president of the Russian Federation and appointed his successor Putin as acting president until the elections of March 26, 2000.

Yeltsin's role in the crushing collapse of the Soviet Union, in the pushing to independence of its republics – first of the Russian Federation – and in the carrying out under his autocratic rule of the beginnings of the transition of the

---

[5] Interview with Lilia Shestova (*Trud*, June 18, 1999), transl. in *Current Digest*, Vol. 51, No. 24 (1999), July 14, 1999, p. 9.

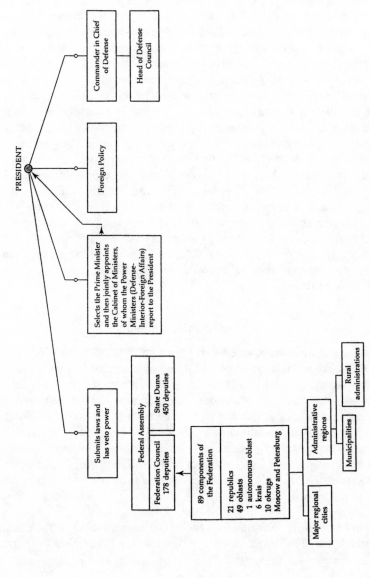

Figure 19-2. The Presidential Republic's State Command System

Federation to the market has called forth all kinds of conflicting evaluations. As late as 1998, his enemy, Gorbachev, dismissed Yeltsin's actions as a failure because he had broken up "the production and market integration that linked Russia and other Soviet republics," had put forward "uncoordinated financial and economic policies," had precipitated the decontrol of prices which thus "led to a sharp decline in real income," had opened Russia to foreign products, and had thus "destroyed the chances of many Russian industries to restructure and marketize themselves."[6] Others, who opposed the preservation of the old, cruel, and inefficient Soviet system pointed out that the Russian Federation's proclamation of sovereignty was in itself "an epoch-making event, one with no analogues in the thousand year history of that state," an event involving "a complete reassessment of all the highest values on which first autocrats and later Bolshevist Russia [were] based."[7]

It is against these two opposing views that numerous conflicts have developed in the Russian Federation and will continue to develop for years to come. I will analyze in the following chapters the problems raised in the debates concerned with the socioeconomic transformation of Russia, and the policies and the measures that Yeltsin proposed or actually carried out for privatization and the drive toward the market. For now, let me sketch in broad outline the framework within which these policies were initiated, debated, rejected, or implemented, namely the main dates of the Yeltsin era. First, recall that Yeltsin returned to active political life in March 1989. The following year, in May 1990, he was elected chair of Russia's Supreme Soviet, a fact which made him virtually the president of the Russian Federation. In February 1991, he resigned from the Communist Party and declared war on the Soviet government. In June of the same year, he was effectively elected the first president of the Russian Federation.

Between August 19 and 21, 1991, Yeltsin crushed the putsch of the Soviet leaders (during Gorbachev's absence) and later issued a decree banning the Communist Party of the Soviet Union. In December of that same year, he helped to extricate Russia from its imperial past by establishing new relations with the newly independent republics. In September 1993 he successfully used the army against a new plot led by Alexander Rutskoi, who, with the help of the Communist parliament, proclaimed himself "the provisional president of Russia." By December 12, 1993, the new constitution, framed under Yeltsin's supervision, gave Yeltsin sweeping powers as the first legal president of the Republic. Subsequently, on July 3, 1996, Yelstin was reelected president. Two years later, by August 17, 1998, Russia faltered under a heavy domestic debt

---

[6] Glad, Betty, "Yeltsin and the New Political [Dis]Order," in *The Russian Transformatin*, Glad, Betty, and Shirver, Eric, eds., New York, St. Martin's Press, 1999, pp. 91–2.

[7] For a detailed discussion of the privatization debates and of the privatization processes of 1992–4, see the important study of Aslund, Anders, *How Russia Became a Market Economy*, Washington, DC, Brookings Institution, 1995, pp. 223–59.

and its economy collapsed. By February 19, 1999, a parliamentary panel finalized impeachment charges against Yeltsin, but eventually he defeated this move. By August 1999, he fired the prime minister (one of numerous such dignitaries dismissed by Yeltsin without much ado) and appointed as acting prime minister the head of the Federal Security Service, Putin. Finally, by December 31, Yeltsin resigned and appointed as his successor, – that is, as acting president – Putin. In his resignation declaration, Yeltsin justified as follows his departure from power before the end of his term: "I have realized that is what I had to do. Russia must enter the next millennium with new positions, with new personalities, with new, smart, strong and energetic people."

It would be erroneous not to recognize the immense challenges Russia has faced and will be facing. Yeltsin's rule animated the sociopolitical scene not only with critical decisions but also with disastrous political combinations and maneuvers in the preservation of his power and in the inevitable drive toward the market. All these decisions and moves are of great interest for anyone who wants to understand the complex processes of transition from a *sui generis* state capitalism toward a *sui generis* market-directed economy. These issues and moves are precisely the subject of the following chapters.

CHAPTER 20

The Transition Issues

20-1. Principles of Action

To better assess the nature and the range of the actual processes of the Soviet transition to the market, it is useful to recall briefly the positions that crystallized there in 1990 with regard to the eventual emergence from the Soviet matrix of a new economy. Recall (as indicated in Section 11-4) the different views that coalesced into three "plans" of transition before the collapse of the USSR: the so-called Ryzhkov plan, the Shatalin (later called Yeltsin's) plan, and the Gorbachev plan. The first set as the transition's objective a regulated market economy, preceded by a preparatory stage of appropriate changes in the legal and the institutional framework. The second plan rejected immediate price liberalization and stressed the need for denationalization followed by the implementation of strict monetary, financial, and credit policies. The third plan, a *sui generis* combination of the other proposals, suggested first monetary and financial measures, then a gradual transition to price liberalization, the broadening of market relations in various directions, and finally the accelerated formation of "self-regulatory mechanisms."

Also at the time, the International Monetary Fund (IMF), the World Bank, and the OECD issued a study entitled *The Economy of the USSR: Summary and Recommendations*, which pointed out two basic orientations in transition policies: a conservative and a radical one. In essence, the conservative approach emphasized the need to proceed slowly to structural reforms, with prices remaining largely under administrative control and macrostabilization achieved gradually. The radical approach asserted that actually the old system could be left to "decay by itself" and that what was needed was to focus simultaneously on the liberalization of most prices, the beginnings of privatization, and macrostabilization. By 1991, the radical approach embodying Western suggestions already in application in Poland (since January 1990) was put forward by Yeltsin's chief reformer, Yegor Gaidar (with help from Jeffrey Sachs of Harvard and Anders Aslund of the Stockholm School of Economics).

In its application, the radical approach was to involve a speedy drive toward rapid market transformation. It was to embody a "shock therapy" that left prices free to find market-clearing levels, freed the private sector from bureaucratic restrictions, set in motion the processes of privatization, and maintained macrostability by restructuring credits and balancing the budgets. As Sachs put it, such a reform was "a seamless web, piecemeal changes cannot work." This policy, adopted by Yeltsin in December 1991, was launched in January 1992. As applied, the "shock therapy" involved immediate price liberalization, unsuccessful attempts to bring down the rapidly rising inflation, conflicting fiscal policies, the continuance of state subsidies mainly to noncompetitive industries, failure to reduce the growing unemployment, absence of coordination with regard to capital markets, and, along with all this, the beginnings of the processes of privatization involving the auctioning of state property with large concessions to the nomenklatura of managers and to the worker collectives.

As these operations began to unfold, the leaders of the Congress of People's Deputies – who were to rise in open revolt against Yeltsin in 1993 – asserted continually that the consequences of price liberalization were the high inflationary increases and the drop in the prevailing standard of living, the fall in production, economic disorganization, miscalculations of the budget deficit, and the collapse of the ruble. According to the chair of the Supreme Soviet, R. I. Khasbulatov, these disastrous consequences were due to Yeltsin's and to his supporters' "miscalculations in the economic strategy, careless attitude towards the most difficult internal problems, even most likely ignorance of these problems."[1] By 1994, Grigory Yavlinsky, a former vice-chair of the RFSSR Council of Ministers and one of the key contributors to the Shatalin plan, affirmed that when the Soviet Union collapsed, the managers of the state-owned enterprises were left in full operational control of vast amounts of state property, and that the launch of the shock therapy gave them complete liberty to act as they saw fit. The trouble is that when the socialist state collapsed, it was not replaced in time "by a developed institutional framework for a market economy." Rather, added Yavlinsky, the managers of the new privately owned enterprises were neither ready nor willing to change their old behavioral patterns to fit into a new economic environment. Their improper manipulations and double bookkeeping continued as in the past. As before, they continued to trade in barter and to set up small enterprises parallel to their "privatized" center, using them as channels to sell most of their own outputs and to shift the proceeds elsewhere, including foreign banks. Buildings, equipment, and plots of land continued to be leased to dubious outside businesses. In short, the process of "mafiasization" of the whole economy got thus in full swing, hampering the development of the national industry, distorting the objectives

---

[1] Khasbulatov, R. I., *The Economic Reform in the Russian Federation (1992–1993)*, Moscow, Poligran, 1993, p. 9.

of privatization, and preventing the expansion of financial stability and of banking for savings, investment, and growth.[2]

Yeltsin's partisans rejected these interpretations and offered very different explanations of the consequences of their "transition strategy," and particularly of their attitude toward the old nomenklatura. Gennady Burbulis, one of Yeltsin's ideologists (who, however, had to resign from the government in December 1992), affirmed that Yeltsin did adopt, deliberately at the beginning, a policy of "compromise with the former elite," aiming at having the former nomenklatura "grow into the new structure, the new system, in a peaceful, evolutionary way." If that compromise had not been made, the progress on the path of reforms would have been much more radical, or a civil war inspired by the nomenklatura would have begun. But, added Burbulis, as the government continued on the path of privatization, detachments of yesterday's nomenklatura were ruined and lost both power and property. The time of compromises with the remnants of the old elite – compromises that in no way fit the reform – was finally over.[3] The government's attempts to control the march toward a free market economy remained, however, in many respects clumsy and ineffective. Several years of inflation, privations, declines in output, and unending economic and social crises followed, providing unparalleled opportunities for "mafiasization," theft, and widespread corruption. In these conditions, the post-Soviet economy moved not toward free markets, but in many respects toward a manipulated noncash economy, in which barter became the key in the transactions among enterprises and an instrument for avoiding tax payments, subduing small businesses, and obstructing the interests and the needs of the consumer. I will return in detail to these issues further in Section 20-4.

20-2. Russia and the West's Economic Patterns

How did the Russian Federation's leaders envisage their rapport with the West? In which way did the emerging Russian market economy diverge from or become similar to such diverse capitalist models as the American, the European, the East Asian, or the Latin American ones? The Yeltsin-Gaidar tendency aimed at forging a market economy broadly coordinating, as in the West, the economy's complexities, overcoming the Soviet heritages and the powers of the old elite, surmounting the vast regional diversities and instabilities, and consolidating economic power and influence notwithstanding the evident weaknesses and limitations of the social groups rejecting state

[2] Yavlinsky, Gregory, *Laissez-Faire versus Policy-Led Transformation, Lessons of the Economic Reforms in Russia*, Moscow, Center for Economic and Political Research, 1996, pp. 11, 13, 58–9.
[3] Burbulis, Gennady, "The Nomenklatura's Death Throes Are Fraught with Upheavals," (*Izvestia*, Oct. 15, 1993), transl. in *Current Digest . . .*, Vol. XLV, No. 44, 1993, pp. 6–7.

privileges and subsidies. Disregarding the assertions of the critics, Gaidar rejected, however (in August 1992), the contentions that he and his colleagues were "Chicago boys" aiming to restructure Russia's economy just on the basis of "standard Western recipes." He pointed out that the authorities needed either to set in motion a market mechanism, even if imperfect, or face a state of emergency encouraging attempts to bring order on the basis of a coup de force. In practice, he added, we could either "enter the community of world's developed countries as equals," or let the country be pulled into a "closed, self-isolated position behind high custom fences." Recall, he added, that the first path led Japan into the ranks of world superpowers, while the second threw one of the richest world countries, Argentina, into the embraces of underdevelopment. Clearly, Gaidar's choice was Japan's path.[4]

A different path was proposed by Gregory Yavlinsky. During and after the launching of the Yeltsin-Gaidar experience, he stressed first that in a huge country like Russia, a conglomerate of vastly heterogenous regions, one cannot simply discard all previous reforms and start from a "blank canvas." Then he added that the state must and should play a very significant role notably in shaping the future industrial structure, along with a system of state and private banks. What had to be taken also into consideration, according to Yavlinsky was that the time and the cost of adjustment based only on market self-regulation would be too huge. In short, Russia first had to create an internal market within the country and open itself only in a limited way to the world market, because Russia could not yet withstand international competition.[5] In sum, Yavlinsky's model was that of an interventionist state similar to Germany's state of the late nineteenth century or Japan's in the nineteenth and twentieth centuries.

In its process of transformation, should Russia rely on Western aid? In which specific ways, and to what extent? In this respect, also, the leaders' opinions were divided. Early in 1992, a member of Yeltsin's consultative council, Nikolai Shmelëv, while broadly agreeing with Gaidar on the path of economic transition – though he designated the actual carrying out of this policy as "harsh and brutal" – asserted that without Western support, Russia could not accomplish either its short-term objectives ("especially the conversion of the ruble from sawdust to currency") or its long-term goal, namely the "gigantic reorganization" of the entire country. "We are the only one in the world" added Shmelëv, that considers importing capital as something suspicious. Actually, "no one needs our resources and our land," and hence, it will take time to persuade serious capital to invest in Russia (*Rossiiskii vesti*, May 8, 1992). Yet, while Russia was then engaged in negotiations for international support for

---

[4] Gaidar, Yegor, "Russia and the Reforms" (*Izvestia*, August 19, 1992), transl. in *Current Digest . . .*, Vol. XLIV, No. 33, 1992, pp. 4–7.

[5] Yavlinsky, Gregory, *Laissex-Faire versus Policy-Led Transformation . . .*, *op. cit.*, pp. 38–40, 43, 52, 57.

rereforms, the political instability in the country, the conflict between the legislative and the executive branches, and the uncertainty about the impact of the reforms injected in the public opinion caution, even apprehension about the reliance on international aid. While Russia did finally rely heavily on such aid, deep apprehensions continued in the society at large. Characteristically, as late as 1998, the economic historian Anatoli Utkin asserted (in *Nezavisimaia gazeta* of September 1, 1998) that "as it could have been foreseen," Russia had embarked from 1992 on a path that resulted in "the losing of her economic bearings," and in Russia's incapacity to resolve such fundamental issues as "a stable state structure, a hierarchy of civil authority, the status of land ownership, the management of the state capitalist sector, and the principles of taxation." Everything had allegedly been eclipsed by the most immediate concerns, namely the federal budget, inflation, and convertibility of the ruble, all under the pressure of the West, instead of keeping the focus on the pursuit of "genuine reform." Allegedly, according to Professor Utkin, just as it did back in 1917, the West shut its eyes to the realities of the Russian problem, promising its support only if Russia was "forfeiting the legacy of industrialization" in favor of "vitalizing chaos." Can we say, concluded Utkin, that we are on the right road when our chasms and ruins arouse hatred of the West in a people raised "in the spirit of love of Western culture"?

Interestingly, in the West also, as pointed out by Jeffrey Sachs, Western aid to Russia found lots of support, but for different reasons than in Russia. Those in favor of international aid pointed out that historically, international financial support had enabled reformist governments to surmount institutional changes and to carry out their reform programs. Those opposed to such support claimed that assistance to Russia could play no useful role since the free market reforms were doomed to failure, or that reforms would involve a long, drawn-out process and that haste to provide aid would amount to a waste of money with meager results.[6]

Obviously, the negative opinions were discarded in the West by the appropriate international organization. The Group of Seven (G7), the IMF, the World Bank, and the European Bank for Reconstruction and Development indeed extended, after complex negotiations and helpful suggestions, crucial aid to Russia on its difficult transition to the market. A Russian balance sheet concerning its external debt, drawn at the end of 1998, showed that at the time that debt amounted to $150 billion (half of which involved debt legacies prior to 1992) – that is, a total equal to 90 percent of the GDP – while the scheduled external debt service was set to reach 90 percent of the federal budget revenue. This level was well beyond a realistic capacity for repayment. According to an official statement of the federal government and of the Central Bank,

[6] Sachs, Jeffrey, "Western Financial Assistance and Russia's Reforms," in *Making Markets Economic Transformations in Eastern Europe and the Post-Soviet States*, Islam, Shafiqul, and Mandelbaum, Michael, eds., New York, Council on Foreign Relations, 1993, pp. 143–5.

the country's debt servicing difficulties were expected "to continue for several years," and in these conditions the government had to become well aware of the need for methodic public disclosures in these matters, to maintain market confidence and to promote public awareness of the economic policy options available.

20-3. The Transition Path

In the passage from the Soviet to the market system, privatization – the transmutation from all-embracing state property to widespread private property – represented the most important institutional change. Before the complete breakdown of the USSR, the Supreme Soviet of the RSFSR adopted in mid-1991 a law on the privatization of state and municipal property, and a law on privatization accounts. These laws, however, were not implemented. But in the meantime, the party-state elite did begin illegally and chaotically its own privatization. Then, on the eve of the collapse of the USSR, in December 1991, the Supreme Soviet of the Russian Federation adopted a law on the fundamental provisions of the program of privatization of state and municipal enterprises in 1992, and in April of that year, a presidential decree specified that the program was to be carried out with privatization vouchers to be distributed to the population. (The program covered all state and municipal property except for state farms, land, and housing.) From October 1992, these vouchers, each with a nominal value of 10,000 rubles, could be purchased by all citizens, regardless of age, at the local offices of the state bank, at the price of 25 rubles per voucher. By January 1993, 144 million Russians had purchased almost all the vouchers available. These could then be sold on the market, invested into privatization investment funds, or used for shares in given companies.

According to the program, the employees of an enterprise were to receive free of charge 25 percent of its capital as nonvoting shares, and purchase an additional 10 percent of the voting shares at a 30 percent discount. This package did not appear sufficient to the Parliament, which adopted a second option allowing the workers and the managers of a firm to be privatized the right to purchase at a discount 51 percent of the voting shares of their firm. Ultimately, a majority of the privatizing enterprises adopted this latter version. The voucher privatization program ran from October 1992 to July 1994. Frequently, retained profits were used as payment, and the real beneficiary tended to be management rather than the workforce.[7]

A new phase of the privatization redistribution took place between 1995 and 1997. It involved the largest Russian companies and brought to the fore for the appropriate transactions a variety of procedures, including loans for share auctions, sales of debtor debts, purchases of promissory notes, and so

[7] Schleifer, Andrei, and Treisman, Daniel, *The Economics and Politics of Transition to an Open Economy, Russia*, Paris, Development Center of the OECD, 1998, pp. 57–69.

Table 20-1 *Russian Federation: Number of Privatized Enterprises, 1993–8*

Privatized enterprises	1993	1994	1995	1996	1997	1998
Total	42,924	21,905	10,152	4,997	2,743	2,129
Municipal	26,340	11,108	6,960	3,354	1,821	1,544
Regional	9,521	5,112	1,317	715	548	321
Federal	7,063	5,685	1,875	928	374	264

Source: Rossia v tsifrakh, op. cit., pp. 161–2.

Table 20-2 *Russian Federation: Privatized Industries by Branches, 1993–8, in Percentages*

Branches	1993	1994	1995	1996	1997	1998
Total	100	100	100	100	100	100
Industry	28.1	26.9	20.6	17.3	13.3	10.8
Agricultural	1.7	3.0	1.9	2.2	1.6	2.3
Construction	9.2	11.0	9.3	10.2	6.8	4.9
Auto transport	3.2	3.8	1.9	2.1	0.8	0.8
Trade	34.6	28.8	32.1	29.1	27.3	22.6
Public catering	6.9	5.4	5.8	4.4	4.7	3.3
Other branches	16.3	21.1	28.4	34.7	45.5	55.3

Source: Rossiia v tsifrakh, op. cit., p. 163.

on. These processes took place at a time of vast expansion in the number of enterprises and organizations, due either to the breakup of certain enterprises or to the creation of new ones. Thus, the Russian Federation counted in 1991 a total of 288,000 enterprises and organizations; by 1992 this total increased to 314,000; by 1994 to 1,245,000; and, by 1999 to 2,901,000, about a third of which were counted officially as "small enterprises."

As can be seen in Table 20-1 the total number of the privatized enterprises decreased each year from 1993 to 1999. However, no complete data have been released concerning the various sizes of the enterprises involved in the process. The figures released indicate only that after the 1992–4 privatization drive, 16.5 percent of the country's enterprises were in the hands of the state, 8.8 percent belonged to the municipalities, 2.7 percent to public organizations, while 62.5 percent constituted private property. According to the official data, by 1999, the state's share had decreased to 5.1 percent, the municipalities' to 6.3 percent, the public organizations' also to 6.3 percent, while the private sector accounted for 74.0 percent and the firms of mixed ownership for 8.3 percent.

As Table 20-2 shows, the largest number of enterprises involved in privatization were, besides the industrial firms, the trade and public catering services.

Information released by the IMF and the OECD indicates that during the first privatization drive, most of the privatized enterprises in trade and consumer service were purchased locally by members of the workers' collectives who enjoyed significant concessional terms. On the other hand, for the large enterprises included in the program, *corporatization* – that is, transformation into joint-stock companies – had been mandatory. As of July 1994, some thirty thousand enterprises were included in the *Register of Enterprises Subject to Transformation into Joint Stock Companies*. The majority of these were either medium-sized or large firms. The privatization of joint-stock companies through voucher action involved a total of 13,500 enterprises. During the second privatization drive, through the initiative of the largest financial groupings and with active government support, the largest Russian companies became the major targets. Foreign participation in privatization and in share transaction had been limited, particularly in "strategic enterprises" in the energy and the financial sectors.

Corporate governance and enterprise restructuring have been handicapped by the dominant role of insiders in the enterprises' structure. In over 65 percent of Russia's eighteen thousand medium-sized and large enterprises, management and employees have majority ownership while the nonstate outsiders control only 20 percent of these companies. Manipulation of voting procedures and obstacles to broad representation have been used as mechanisms for preserving inside control. Only some 25 percent of the medium and large-scale corporations are engaged in serious restructuring. Former Prime Minister Evgenii Primakov suggested in November 1999 that the privatization of certain enterprises should be reconsidered if any of them are idle, their workers are dismissed, or if there are other irregularities or illegalities for which they are accountable. Primakov's suggestions were dismissed by Putin, who affirmed, however, that the privatized state enterprises must certainly go only to responsible "effective private owners." Notwithstanding the vast privatization, the proportion of the assets owned by the federal government is still far in excess of the norms for developed countries. By the end of 1999, 13,700 large enterprises still were wholly owned by the state, which also held shares in an additional 3,800 large enterprises. It seems that the state does not know exactly what it owns. A full register of the federal estate has not be completed, and no mechanism is available to determine the market value of the properties that the state owns.

20-4. Alternatives

In the early Russian Federation, at the end of 1991, there was a widely shared feeling that the country was entering a new stage, one in which Gorbachev's policy of late socialist reformism was finally over and was fully replaced by a new policy focused on the Post-Communist transition to a market economy. The political struggle seemed to have drawn to a close, and the popular

President Yeltsin could supposedly focus his attention on economic reforms. The status quo could be preserved for the state organization, and what mattered immediately was to smooth relations with the former Soviet republics on the basis of both denouncing the 1922 agreement on the formation of the USSR and creating the Commonwealth of Independent States.

Alas, what appeared very soon was not the end but the deepening of the political struggle between the old Soviet power setup and the new president. Yeltsin was unable to seize full control of the institutional framework even after the defeat of the putsch of 1993, and had to rely on the intriguing delegates to the Federation Council of the autonomous republics, *oblasts*, *krais*, and *okrugs* against a hostile Duma. The new leadership lacked useful direct links to many hostile groups that were achieving real controls in various parts of the economy.

Who was actually in control of the economy, the media, and certain key aspects of the power structure? According to one of the great moguls of Yeltsin's Russia, Boris Berezovsky, by 1996, the real economic power was in the hands of seven top bankers and businesspeople who controlled half of the economy and whose economic power enabled them to call many of the shots in the government policies. Berezovsky did not spell out the names of the *seven*, but according to Rose Brady, who interviewed Berezovsky and many other top members of Russia's political and economic establishment, the seven in question were all of a group that had financed Yeltsin's presidential campaign in 1996: Vladimir Potanin, of Un-Exim Bank; Mikhail Khodorowsky, founder of Menatep; Vladimir Vinogradov, founder and chief executive of Inkombank; Vladimir Gusinsky, of Most Group; Mikhail Friedman, president of Alfa Group; Vagit Alekperov, president of Lukoil; and Rem Vyakhirev, chair of Gazprom.[8] According to *Sevodnia*, of August 12, 1999, five of the persons listed by Grady were among the six main controllers of the Russian media (see Figure 20-1). Certainly the number *seven* given by Berezovsky was not necessarily accurate. Potanin noted at the time in more general terms, as reported also by Brady, that "the concentration of the capital in the country of course is very high. If you take maybe 30 or 35 of the biggest companies they really control more than half of the gross national product. But it is 30 to 35, not seven."[9] In short, not all the mechanisms of the market economy were operating fully and in the best possible ways, nor is it certain that the role of the state – still in control of large assets – was well defined. Then, what kind of economy resulted from the processes that unfolded during the Yeltsin era? The theoretical transition toward a market-oriented, Western-style democracy is in principle still in process, but what has already emerged is a formal democratic framework within which the state and many successors of the old

---

[8] Brady, Rose, *Kapitalizm, Russia's Struggle to Free Its Economy*, New Haven, Yale University Press, 1999, pp. 207–8.

[9] *Ibid.*, p. 212.

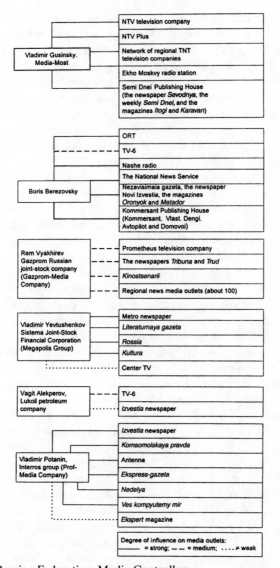

Figure 20-1. Russian Federation: Media Controllers
Source: *Sevodnia*, August 12, 1999 transl. in *Current Digest...*, Vol. 51, No. 33, September 15, 1999, p. 14.

nomenklatura continue to ignore its rules and procedures, because nothing is really powerful enough to stop them. All this involves widespread corruption, crime on a large scale, and multiple illegalities.

Since Putin's arrival to power, certain Russian analysts have asserted that he would finally open the way toward the "dictatorship of the law." By May 2000 his governmental agencies began indeed to lodge all kind of charges – in particular accusations of illicit acquisitions of state properties, their wasteful management, and tax evasion – against some of the country's new "oligarchs" and their companies, involving notably Berezovsky, Gusinsky, Potanin, Alekperov, Vyakhirev, and others. Following these accusations, Berezovsky and Gusinsky were sent packing, while the Duma, which was on good political terms with President Putin, took aim against various big companies in order to reassert state control. Examples include the cases of certain newspapaers (such as *Sevodnia*), television networks (especially NTV and TV6), and the dominant gas company Gazprom and its electricity monopoly. (Gazprom allegedly sold illegally a stake to foreigners when part of the state company was auctioned to the public in 1992.) In short, all this has been leading to the restoration of Gostelradio (the Soviet-era All Union State Television and Radio Company).

Some observers have asserted that beyond all this, what has been taking place is the reassertion of the state and of the new president's close circle to settle scores against some of "oligarchs" of the Yeltsin era, by using against them the appropriate state structures and law enforcement bodies. Other analysts have stated that Putin was giving his close circle the authority to go against Yeltsin's tycoons, "both for potential gain and for the immense riches that the tycoons control, and which the government would like to tap."[10] In any case, one must not forget that Putin, a former fifteen-year member of the KGB, has brought along with him to power some of his former KGB companions. The conflict with Yeltsin's "oligarchs" is not only a conflict among illicitly competing businesspeople, but also a conflict among various parts, or successor parts, of the nomenklatura.

20-5. Concluding Comments

Notwithstanding its important, valid, and necessary changes, the Yeltsin era has also, unfortunately, been disastrous in many respects for Russia's economy and society, and the prospects for improvement under Putin are still uncertain. As can be seen in Table 20-3, the 1990s have been economically devastating: Real GDP has kept decreasing continually, reaching a loss of some 40 percent for the period considered; GDP per capita has also fallen from 26,700 rubles in 1991 to 16,400 in 1998. Inflation reached calamitous levels between 1992 and 1994; it fell significantly by 1997, but the prospects for stabilization decreased again sharply after new economic troubles began in the middle of 1998. The fluctuations in monthly wages and pensions had been catastrophic up to 1995 and then again from mid-1998 on. The population with incomes below the minimum subsistence level amounted to 35.0 million by 1998.

---

[10] See *New York Times*, "Moscow Mogul Case Reflects Power Shift" (June 19, 2000); "Russia Is Charging Tax Evasion by Executives of No. 1 Carmaker" (July 2000); "Russian Puzzle: What Does War on Tycoons Mean?" (July 15, 2000).

Table 20-3 *Russian Federation: Selected Economic Indicators, 1991–9*

Indicators	1991	1992	1993	1994	1995	1996	1997	1998	1999
Real change in GDP percent	–5.0	–14.5	–8.7	–12.7	–4.1	–3.5	0.8	–4.6	–5.2
GDP per capita in 1,000 rubles[a]	26.7	22.8	20.8	18.2	17.4	16.9	17.1	6.4	—
Consumer price inflation	161.0	2,508.8	839.9	215.1	131.3	21.8	11.0	84.4	37.0
Change in monthly wage percent	–3.5	–32.9	4.0	5.6	–16.5	5.4	5.0	–4.4	—
Change in pensions percent	—	–48.0	31.0	3.2	–19.5	8.7	–5.4	–4.8	—
Millions with below subsistence income	—	50.2	46.9	33.3	36.6	32.7	30.7	35.0	—
Unemployment in millions	—	3.6	4.2	5.5	6.4	7.0	7.8	8.5	—

Note:
[a] At 1997 prices.
Sources: European Bank of Reconstruction and Development, *Transition Report Update 1999*, p. 6; Biuro ekonomicheskogo analiza (Bureau of Economic Analysis), *Obzor ekonomicheskoi politiki Rossii za 1998 god* (*Survey of the economic policy of Russia in 1998*), Moscow, Rosspen, 1999, pp. 584, 590, 596; Goskomstat, *Rossiia v tsifrakh, op. cit.*, pp. 102, 111.

The capitalism that emerged under Yeltsin has been, according to a remark of Gaidar, "repulsive, ghastly, thievish and socially unjust." However, as Gaidar noted subsequently (in 2001), the reforms undergone by Russia may be likened to the "transition from dinosaurs to mammals: Russia lost in size but gained speed and maneuverability." Yet what has been created thus far is a highly divided and unstable society, corroded by widespread corruption and misappropriations. In the absence of an appropriate legal framework, of adequate monitoring of the movements of capital, and of the skill patterns nurtured by smoothly operating market conditions, the problems of widespread criminalization cannot be overcome. As Jeni Klugman has pointed out in her book *Poverty in Russia*, there were more poor in that country in the posttransition period than in the pretransition period. The poor comprise the same vulnerable groups, namely the lower working strata, the houses affected by unemployment, and the pensioners. Particularly affected besides the old have been the female heads of households and the children.[11]

As the levels of output have fallen, the duration and amounts of all kinds of social benefits have been reduced, and the eligibility criteria have been

---

[11] *Poverty in Russia, Public Policy and Private Responses*, Klugman, Jeni, ed., Washington, DC, World Bank, 1997, pp. 58–63, 116.

tightened. Unemployment benefits have been brought down sharply. The readjustments of the social protection items have been affected by a host of problems, concerning notably the restructuring of pensions and the scrutiny of all kinds of allocations, including in particular family allowances and health care. The financing and administration of all the systems' programs remain in question. Note that the inherited health care system, though highly inefficient and providing low-quality service, was nonetheless easily accessible, combined curative and preventive functions, and was affordable to the general public. Its reform, like that of pensions and of family allowances, had in view first cost containment. In addition, at the same time, deep changes have taken place through the privatization of the pharmaceutical industry and certain hospitals. Cost containment has entailed essentially a lowering of standards, deterioration of preventive services, and significant increases in copayments, along with stricter rules for access to hospital services. Neither the health care providers (administrators, physicians, nurses, technicians) nor the customers have acquired proper knowledge of the costs of medical services and of the risks associated with providing them inefficiently. Since large changes in the structure of output and employment are bound to continue given necessary shifts in industrial production and in reallocation of resources, the consequences will continue to affect adversely income inequality, poverty, and the programs of benefits and of allowances that address them.

Careful analysts of Russia's evolving patterns, such as Vladimir Popov, have asserted that it was more than probable that Russian capitalism ultimately would not duplicate the European or East Asian patterns but that rather it would eventually resemble a Latin American model, marked with "a highly uneven distribution of wealth and income," and plagued by capital flight, growing foreign debt, and low savings investment and growth.[12] Another analyst, Vladimir Mau of the Moscow Institute for the Economy in Transition, has asserted that if Russia could not break through into an efficient economic system integrated into the world economic linkages, it would pass into the hands of forces intent to build a system of "nationally oriented capitalism" – a kind of economically closed, highly protected entity, involving widespread state interventions.[13]

Initially at least – as was often the case in Russia's historical past – Russia's new leaders assumed that the development of their country would easily and rapidly duplicate the European patterns of advanced capitalist development. However, the heritage of the Soviets' deeply unbalanced sectoral interrelations, the weighty burden of the nomenklatura's habits, methods, and

---

[12] Popov, Vladimir, *A Russian Puzzle*, Helsinki, UNU World Institute for Development Economic Research, 1996, p. 61.

[13] Mau, Vladimir, *The Political History of Economic Reform in Russia 1985–1994*, London, Centre for Research into Communist Economies, 1996, p. 107.

inner conflicts, the diverging patterns of Russia's regional developments, and Russia's conflicting institutional setup excluded the possibility of a break-through into the efficient economic system dreamt by Yeltsin and Gaidar in 1991. Whether the evolving nationally oriented Russian capitalism will ulti-mately represent a *sui generis* combination or just something somewhat close to a Latin American pattern is still an open question, undetermined historically.

CHAPTER 21

The Economic Policies

21-1. Agricultural Policy

The primary objective of the leader of the Russian Federation after the collapse of the USSR was to devise the set of policies that would ensure the transition to the market. The key instrument of this transition was the methodic change of the pattern of ownership in the primary, secondary, and tertiary sectors, that is, the privatization of state property. How did the privatization powers affect the decollectivization of agriculture, the right to sell and purchase land, the prices of agricultural products, and the upstream and the downstream connections of agriculture with other sectors?

First, it should be noted that the privatization of agriculture was carried out in a *sui generis* fashion. Three state committees were involved in this field: The State Land Committee became responsible for all land privatization; the Ministry of Agriculture was in charge of the privatization of all non-land assets; and finally, the State Management of State Property was responsible for preparing legal documents as well as for privatizing the upstream and downstream industries connected with agriculture. During the first stage of this process, from 1991 to 1993, the legislation concentrated on establishing procedures for determining land and non-land entitlements. During the second stage, from 1994 to 1996, the emphasis shifted to ensuring that the holders of entitlements knew their rights and were able to dispose of them properly. For the move toward decollectivization, the government sought to stop the "spontaneous" nomenklatura privatization, curb the interferences and unnecessary administrative controls, and create rapidly a new class of property owner in this sector. The workers and the managers of the collectives were given rights to acquire under preferential terms substantial parts of the assets of the privatized collectives. The government aimed to create an appropriate competitive environment for these changes, increase its budgetary revenues, and encourage a large flow of foreign investments in this field. The process, started in 1992 on the basis of the Law on Privatization of 1991, focused accordingly on the rapid denationalization and transfer of land and non-land assets to the collectives of workers as well as to pensioners and social workers attached to this sector. The legislation also allowed that non-land assets be given to the farms' members who chose to establish their own individual farms.

The 1993 constitution legalized the private ownership of land, and the 1994 Civil Code defined the legal forms of the agricultural enterprises and the procedures for exercising ownership. A number of subsequent documents aimed at providing the legal means for transfering ownership and establishing a land market. By the end of 1993, about 95 percent of large-scale farms registered in the new legal farms – mainly as joint-stock farms – and only a few broke up into separate successor enterprises. A number of dispositions concerning reorganization and restructuring clarified certain key legal issues concerning closed and open sales of farm land and assets. By 1997 a vast majority of large-scale agricultural enterprises reregistered under a new form – they were converted mainly into production cooperatives – but changed little in terms of structure, management, and techniques. The following pattern of land ownership resulted by 1999 out of all these changes. About 27,000 large-scale agricultural enterprises controlled 80.4 percent of the agricultural land (165.8 million hectares); 274,000 family farms managed about 5.6 percent of the agricultural land (namely, 11.7 million hectares); and 16 million family household-plot owners disposed of less than 5 percent of the land (10.2 million hectares), leaving in the hands of the state and municipalities the balance of over 9 percent (18.7 million hectares).

Conflicting discussions continued at various levels of the Russian administration concerning owners' freedom to sell or mortgage their land. While some regions allowed the free sale, purchase, and mortgage of farms, other regions, often under Communist leadership, opposed such sales and obstructed the creation of a countrywide land market. The continuing uncertainty over land ownership rights has also discouraged investments in this sector. Unequal developments occurred in the emergence of private farms; moreover, the decentralization of agricultural policy and of central management has allowed regional governments to tailor farm support measures largely according to their priorities, a fact that has contributed to the uneven development of the private farming sector throughout the country. As late as October 2001, the land code was finally signed into law, allowing private ownership and trade in land – a measure affecting urban land, that is, urban housing and industrial real estate. This, however, is the introductory step for a separate law eventually allowing the purchase and sale of agricultural land.

The state procurement system that established delivery targets and allocated products to the downstream enterprises – for example to the food industries – was officially dismantled at the beginning of the privatization process. But remnants of the old system have persisted in the form of so-called food stocks acquired through downstream enterprises registered as government agencies. These stocks, purchased at administratively set prices for the national reserve and the military, have been run and financed by regional administrators and accordingly have varied throughout the Federation. Some regions have limited the free flow of goods, services, or production factors, and prohibited the export of particular goods, while other regions have introduced region-specific quality standards. In short, lack of competition in handling, processing, and trading agricultural products has continued to dominate the agrofood market. The process of transition has been affected by increasing regional disparities in levels of development and poverty and in income patterns.

The general principles of privatization have affected in this sector not only the position of land ownership but also the ramified connections of reorganized agriculture with upstream enterprises – the enterprises servicing agriculture with spare parts, fuels, and other material supplies – and downstream enterprises, – the enterprises involved in processing agricultural products, 93 percent of which were rapidly fully or partially privatized. These processes have affected also the retail food trade and Centrosoiuz (the dominant operator of retail stores in rural areas) as well as the most important foreign trade organizations in the food area. The general process of transition was carried under the aegis of the state – without pressures from the peasantry. The state defined the range of reform operations, exercised through legislation a direct influence on the operations of farms, and affected through its financial levers productivity and the environment in which the farms operate. Yet, the state failed to encourage numerous farm members to create private farms. Thus far, the state has also failed to use the land more effectively or make more agricultural enterprises fully productive, and has lacked the capacity to create a market environment with effective market channels.[1]

21-2. Industrial Policy

In industry, as in the other sectors of the economy, the primary objectives of Yeltsin's government were to operate a vast transformation of ownership, remove the state's controls, and turn all the managers and workers of the former nationalized enterprises into the main winners. Yet, as pointed out in *A Study of Voucher Privatization Funds in Russia* by a collective of writers,[2] while granting benefits to insiders early did soften their resistance to privatization and ensure a speedy transfer of assets from the state to these insiders,

---

[1] For extensive analyses, see notably OECD, *Agricultural Policies, Markets, and Trade in Transition Economies, Monitoring and Evaluation 1996*, Paris, OECD, 1996; OECD, *Review of Agricultural Policies Russian Federation*, Paris, OECD Centre for Cooperation with Non-Members, 1998; Wegren, Stephen K., *Agriculture and the State in Soviet and Post-Soviet Russia*, Pittsburgh, PA, University of Pittsburgh Press, 1998.

[2] Frydman, Roman, Pistor, Katharina, and Rapaczynski, Andrzey, *A Study of Voucher Privatization Funds in Russia*, Wien Oesterreichiche Nationalbank, December, 1995, p. 87.

the process simultaneously weakened the effectiveness of postprivatization corporate governance mechanisms, delayed restructuring, and nourished little confidence in the government's related operations. The subsequent privatization through auctions in the mid-1990s opened the way to big venture capitalists and at the same time weakened the protection of the shareholders and creditors, brought forth high-profile corporate scandals, and encouraged share declination, manipulation of debt offsets, and diversion of cash flows and assets to related corporations. The privatization of 1993–4 involved relatively small redistributions of controls to outsiders. The second scheme of "share for loans" implemented from 1995 on took place as many of the key resource companies fell into the hands of a small group of financiers, popularly called "oligarchs." This led to very sharp increases in wealth and income in a few hands and to widespread poverty throughout the country, and helped to generate an investment climate marked by corruption and nontransparent business practices including widespread barter, cronyism, and illicit deals. Eventually, as already noted, the state took back into its hands some of the ownerships of the "oligarchs."

In 1992 the Russian Federation had 50,525 industrial enterprises (of which 25,244 were small enterprises created mainly after 1991). Out of the total, 51.7 percent (26,105) belonged to the state and the municipalities, 47.4 percent (23,944) constituted the private sector, and the balance of 0.9 percent (476) were owned by various public organizations. Between 1992 and 1998, the process of privatization affected a total of 27,257 enterprises, most of which were denationalized in 1993–4. Privatization had the greatest effect on the light and the food industries (the agricultural downstream establishments), as well as the metal working industries (some of the upstream agricultural industries). Besides the privatized enterprises, there were in 1998 134,810 small industrial enterprises with one hundred or fewer workers each, in which the state and the municipal capital amounted to 25 percent at the most. The complex, murky interconnections between the management of the grand industrial privatized companies, the state's executive power, and the private shareholders, domestic or foreign, are not easily traceable. Yet, it is possible to illustrate some of the connections involved, notably those among such giants as Russia's main electricity company and the crucial oil and gas industries.

The United Energy System (UES) controls virtually all of Russia's electric power industry. It is one of the largest utilities in the world. In 1998 Yeltsin appointed as its chief executive Anatoli B. Chubais, the well-known chief of the privatization drive of the early 1990s and of other market changes carried out under the patronage of President Yeltsin. Many foreigners who held shares in the company considered him for quite a while a champion of the free market and of shareholders' rights. Soon, however, his name became one of the most hated in the country, both by nationals and by foreigners. As pointed out abroad by correspondents of the *New York Times*, Chubais has been blamed notably by Russia's farmers, the unemployed factory workers, and the elite pensioners for playing the key role in "selling off factories and farms that had become way-stations of a welfare state." He was also blamed by UES shareholders for various murky operations of the company's leadership. Thus, at the beginning of the year 2000, the UES conducted a restructuring program involving mergers and sale of some of its subsidiaries – a process that was supposed to be "transparent," with clear independent appraisals of the deals and of the properties involved. UES carried out the program, however, without conveying any information to the shareholders, who contended that UES ignored how the hasty merger with a key conglomerate (the OKSA aluminum company) and other planned deals "fit into the long-term strategy of the utility." Such deals, which seemed to benefit executives and politicians close to Chubais, appear to be "far from the interests of the company and of a large number of shareholders."[3]

Consider now the complexities involved in the oil and gas deals, and their unexpected – at least for a while – international complications. The oil and gas industries, which play a decisive role both domestically and in Russia's exports, were broken down into a number of privatized units, forming a group of giant firms in control of the country's vast natural and industrial resources. Privatization did not mean, however, full passage into the hands of the private sector. As we will see later in this chapter, the government kept important shares of all these companies in its hands. In the peculiar conditions of Russia's transition to the market, big business could exist only if it had developed close ties with the state, above all directly with the executive power. The latter could indeed turn the life of any company (or bank) into "hell," or by the same token, through political deals, into "heaven." Russia's oil tycoons have indeed founded and run their empires through murky deals with the government, and in particular, with the group around President Yeltsin. As it has become known internationally, the oil and gas industry became legendary for schemes to launder oil money, mislabel products, and manipulate sale prices to move profits into offshore banks and away from shareholders and government authorities.

The major oil companies in operation, by order of assets, magnitude, and revenue, are Lukoil, Iukos, Surgutneftgaz (also called Surgut), Tafneft, and Sibneft. Lukoil (presided by Vagit Alekperov) has been one of the largest vertically integrated companies in Russia. It has comprised seven oil-extracting companies, two refineries, and eleven wholesale and retail companies, and has employed over one hundred thousand people. In 1998, it controlled approximately 16 percent of the country's oil reserves and pumped 21 percent of Russia's oil. In that year, Lukoil's official revenues amounted to $8.4 billion, Iuko's to $2.7 billion, Surgut's also to $2.7 billion, Tafneft's to $1.8 billion, and

[3] Specter, Michael, "A Shrewd Act of Self-Preservation," *New York Times*, June 21, 1996; Banerjee, Neela, "A Big Nyet to Shareholder Input," *New York Times*, February 12, 2000.

Sibneft's to $1.6 billion.[4] The "oil barons" have obtained crucial holdings also in various other industries. Boris Berezovsky (whom I mentioned in relation to his media holdings and to Putin's campaign against him) included in his empire Sibneft, as well as control over the enormous aluminum industry, whose stock owners, once part of Yeltsin's inner circle, tried unsuccessfully to preserve influence in the new political cluster around Putin. The giant Gazprom, the world's largest natural gas company, has been controlling almost all of Russia's gas. It holds 22 percent of the world's reserves and accounts for 33 percent of the world's gas production. It exercises a monopoly on Russia's gas exports, and has enjoyed a particularly great political influence under the premiership of Victor Chernomyrdin (1992–8), a former Gazprom executive. Until 1998 the state held 40 percent of the shares of Gazprom; that year it sold 2.5 percent of this total to a German company (Ruhrgas) and was scheduled to sell another 2.5 percent in 1999. Notwithstanding its large holdings, the state exercised a limited role in Gazprom until May 2001. By that time, in a crucial move, President Putin engineered the replacement of Gazprom's chief executive since 1992, Rem Vyakhirev (who, as I indicated in Figure 21-3, had been also controller of various key media), by Alexei Miller, who had worked for five years as a deputy of Putin.[5]

Gazprom and other giant companies (such as Yukos, the second largest oil producer) that emerged during the privatization drives of the 1990s may face a strangely close and unwanted competition from a newcomer to Russian oil fields. Taking into account the independence of the former Soviet republics bordering the Caspian Sea's large oil fields – Tengiz and Karachaganek in Kazakhstan, and Baku in Azerbaijan – the Clinton administration set as a policy goal, the construction of an oil pipeline fully circumventing Russia and Iran. This $2.4 billion oil line, to be constructed with the participation of B.P. Amoco, was set to begin near Baku, then cross Azerbaijan, Georgia, and Turkey, and end at the Mediterranean port of Ceyhan. In November 1999, Azerbaijan, Georgia, Kazakhstan, and Turkey committed themselves to seeking the full financing of this 1,080-mile pipeline. In the meantime, the United States promoted the construction of a small export pipeline to Georgia's Black Sea port of Supsa, avoiding entirely nearby Russia. Another agreement has proposed the construction of a 1,250-mile companion natural gas pipeline from Turkmenistan's large natural gas reserves to the Turkish city of Erzerum. This proposal was put forward by a partnership including General Electric, the Bechtel Group, and Royal Dutch/Shell. According to the *New York Times*, the United States' aim in the area has been to cut off Russia's oil and gas

---

[4] See Elder, Alexander, *Rubles to Dollars, Making Money on Russia's Exploding Financial Frontier*, New York, New York Institute of Finance, 1998, pp. 172–8; Wines, Michael, "Spiffing Up a Dirty Business, Russia's Oil Barons Say Wildcatter Capitalism Era Is Over," *New York Times*, December 28, 1999.

[5] Elder, Alexander, *Rubles for Dollars . . ., op. cit.*, pp. 178–82.

backyard so that when Russia gets back on its feet, it cannot march back into the Caucasus and Central Asia. Russia, which views the Baku-Caspian project as an implicit threat, aims to enlarge the existing northern oil route to the Black Sea port of Novorossisk – the old oil route from Baku crossing war-torn Chechniia. The United States sees itself as competing with Russia for influence over the Caspian region's energy resources, while Russia sees the pipeline through Turkey not only as an implicit threat in this area, but also as an equivalent to NATO's expansion on Russia's southern flank.[6] These and related considerations seem to direct the policy of Putin on the one hand toward possibly a better understanding with the United States on the question of oil, and on the other hand, back toward reinforcing the currently neglected military industry. Already in 1998 the minister of industry asserted his intention to control the entire field of military-technical cooperation fully and oversee notably the federally owned Russian Arms State Company (*Rosvoruzheniie*), the Manufacture Goods Export Association (*Promexport*), and Russian Technologies (*Rossiiskaia Technologii*).

21-3. Commercial Policy

At the end of 1992, the Russian Federation had a total of 455,000 retail stores and public catering establishments, of which 30,500 were small – that is, they had fewer than thirty workers each – and the state or municipal participation did not exceed 25 percent of their assets. By 1999 the total of retail stores and of public catering enterprises increased to 935,000, of which 386,000 were small establishments with a total workforce of 2 million people. Between 1992 and 1998, during the process of privatization, 43,165 retail stores and 9,922 public catering establishments were transferred to the private sector; the largest transfers took place in 1992–4 as in all other sectors (see Table 21-1). In the majority of cases, employees took over former retail state stores but many unsuccessful stores were eventually sold to other owners. Numerous catering systems became attractive to foreign investors, some of whom established their own foodstore chains. This is the case notably of McDonalds, KFC, and Pizza Hut. In the rural areas, retail trade is still neglected, as it always was.

In foreign trade, Russia's leadership made significant efforts to integrate the country into the world markets, particularly from 1995 on. However, the continuous fall in output, the government's inability to muster the country's

---

[6] See a series of articles in the *New York Times*, viz. LeVine, Steve, "A Cocktail of Oil and Politics," November 20, 1999; Perlez, Jane, "Strategic Issues Aside, Focus on Oil Pipeline Turns to Money," November 21, 1999; Risen, James, "Gore to Meet Kazakh Leader after MIG Case," November 24, 1999; Kaplan, Robert D., "The Great Game Isn't Over," November 24, 1999; and the already quoted article by Wines, Michael, "Spiffing Up a Dirty Business ...," December 28, 1999.

Table 21-1 *Russian Federation: Privatization of Trade and Public Catering, 1992–8*

	1992	1993	1994	1995	1996	1997	1998
Totals	**	23,986	10,189	5,081	2,051	1,074	709
Retail trade	18,598	13,159	5,976	3,060	1,239	689	445
Public catering	4,889	2,850	1,173	590	222	128	70
Wholesale trade	**	661	343	202	213	61	37
Household services	11,960	7,316	2,697	1,229	377	196	157

Sources: (for 1992) *Rossiiskaia Federatsiia v 1992 godu, op. cit.*, p. 74; for the other years, *Rossiia v tsifrakh, op. cit.*, p. 169.

underlying fiscal imbalances, the devaluation of the ruble, the difficulties in restructuring the ruble-denominated government debt, and the establishment of a moratorium in private sector payments on external liabilities have kept Russia's share in the world trade small and decreasing after 1997. Driven by the depreciation of the ruble, inflation, which seemed in process of being tamed in 1997, rose again sharply in 1998 and 1999, severely impacting the country's trade relations. As we will see in detail later on (in Chapter 24), Russia's exports rose between 1992 and 1996 from $53.6 billion to $88.4 billion, stayed at the same level in 1997, and then fell to $73.9 billion in 1998, and to $72 billion in 1999. Imports grew from $43 billion dollars in 1992 to $73.6 billion in 1997, and then fell to $59.5 billion in 1998 and $45.3 billion in 1999. Both exports and imports were dominated by trade with the main capitalist countries, – that is, with the G7, and above all with the United States. Trade with the former Soviet republics continued at far lower levels, amounting to less than 20 percent of Russia's total foreign trade. With both groups – the capitalist countries and the so-called Commonwealth of Independent States (CIS) – Russia's exports consisted essentially of fuels and metals, and the imports mostly of machinery, food, and agricultural products.

Despite the significant progress made in the liberalization of trade, and despite the often repeated assertions that Russia must and wants to expand foreign trade, the country continues to erect all kinds of barriers involving a multiplicity of not always explicit bureaucratic requirements and regulations. Further multiple impediments arise because of the country's federal struc-ture and of the tendency toward regionalization of various policy measures concerning notably taxes and regional controls, as well as protectionism. Cru-cial elements for the expansion of trade for the foreign trades and investors are predictability, consistency, and transparency of trade regulations, as well as consistent adherence to legally established rules. One wonders how long it will take Russia's current system to acquire all the elements necessary to comply with foreign trade policy regulations and rules.

21-4. Financial Policy

We cannot understand the complex shifts in Russia's financial policy if we lose sight of the numerous challenges that prevailed in Russia's economy throughout the 1990s. These multiple challenges concerned notably some now familiar issues: lack of effective management at the enterprise level, an uncertain environment for small business and entrepreneurship, a poorly functioning tax structure, distorted budgetary processes, dubious practices of commercial banking, along with the uncertain operation of financial markets, the spread of barter throughout the economy, and the epidemic expansion of corruption and crime throughout the society at large.

The very high levels of inflation that plagued the country between 1992 and 1994 were fueled by the enormous increase in the volume of credits provided by the Central Bank. These credits were to cover the continuous federal government budget deficits fueled in turn by the support provided to most of the country's enterprises. The stabilization achieved by 1995 brought down the inflation, and progress seemed readily achievable toward the decrease of state interferences in the economy and toward sustainable growth. But, in fact, the government proved incapable of addressing seriously and methodically the causes of the macroeconomic imbalances, and in particular, the distorted budgetary processes. The government did replace the monetary financing of the deficit with noninflationary borrowing at home and abroad, but the ensuing growing interest rates and payments forced it to increase continually the volume of its debt. Starting in 1995, the government financed much of the deficit by issuing short-maturity treasury bills, so-called GKOs, and longer-dated coupon-bearing bonds, OFZs.

As a result of further sharp increases in government spending, the market value of GKOs and OFZs increased steadily, drawing in foreign investors, who by 1997 held in their hands one-third of the issues. In early 1997, the government embarked on a number of changes, including a revised budget for 1997, a more realistic budget for 1998, as well as a new tax code. But the unfortunate advent of the Asian crises in July 1997, which affected all the emerging markets, had a disastrous impact on the Russian Federation, prompting a broad flight of investors and increasing the government's difficulties in attracting buyers for the roughly $1 billion U.S. Treasury bills it needed to roll over each week. In that same month, the IMF agreed to provide an emergency rescue package of $17.1 billion in new loans (bringing its total assistance package to $22 billion) – but, by mid-August, the Russian government had already spent the first advance of the IMF assistance ($4.4 billion) while the Russian commercial banks began to default on their obligations. By August 17, the government gave up its defense of the ruble. The crisis became unmanageable. The payment system became largely frozen, imports declined appreciably, and a major recession started to unfold. As the Russian government and the chairman of the Central Bank indicated at the close of 1999,

Given the inability to advance structural reform and fiscal adjustment, the macro-economic strategy followed since 1996 ..., a heavy reliance on external borrowing, proved unsustainable. We recognize that a durable solution to the serious economic difficulties facing Russia requires a more comprehensive program addressing the underlying fiscal problem and providing for the implementation of wide-ranging market reforms.[7]

To deal with the crisis, the government decided in October 1998 to develop more effective industrial and trade measures concerning notably restructuring failing enterprises, relying on a less liberal foreign exchange regime, and adopting fundamental reforms in social protection. However, Russia's debt situation remained, according to the World Bank, critical, and its credit-worthiness only marginal. Yet, to avoid a further decline, the IMF, in coordination with the European Bank of Reconstruction and Development and the European Union, launched an intensive international effort to support an immediate Russian plan for solving the banking crisis, for restructuring Russia's disastrous finances, and for coping with the most pressing reforms, in particular those of pensions, health, and education. Of course, Russia's needs for transformation are staggering and these problems will take years to come before finding satisfactory solutions. (I will return in detail to some of these issues in Chapter 25.)

21-5. Concluding Comments

Why did the privatization of state enterprises not turn out as well as many people had hoped? What mattered ultimately was *who* had been entrusted with the ownership of these enterprises and whether these new owners encouraged all kinds of inside and outside shady dealings, and whether they ultimately swamped the achieved profits with a combination of official corruption, a distorted tax system, and organized crime. As a number of reliable writers have remarked, the early mass privatization (of 1992–4), which was thought to be "tolerably honest," did encourage inside dealings as well as outright theft, while the subsequent "auctions" privatization – a massive liquidation at bargain prices of Russia's most important companies – benefited a small number of "kleptocrats" who had achieved wealth through both shabby deals and outright state larceny.[8] Some of the kleptocrats lost control of part of their empires already during the summer 1998 economic collapse, but their losses continued to increase under Putin.

[7] Russia Ministry of Finance, Statement of the Government of the Russian Federation and Central Bank of Russia on Economic Policy, www.Minfin.ru/Sdds/sep. htn, January 3, 2000, 9:01 P.M.

[8] Black, Bernard, Kraakman, Reinier, and Tarassova, Anna, "Russian Privatization and Corporate Government: What Went Wrong?" black@stanford.edu. 1999.

In the meantime, the overall critical standard of living has substantially deteriorated. The share of the population living below the poverty line amounted in 1998 and in the first half of 1999 to 35 percent of the total population. Living standards deteriorated soon after 1991 following sharp declines in output and employment, the erosion of real wages and benefits, and increases in unemployment. The reforms of the social security system have been slow and limited. The array of cash and in-kind benefits has remained complicated and poorly administered, and the gap between the de jure and de facto benefits has remained unbridgeable. The problems of pensions and unemployment benefits along with those of the unskilled and public sector workers have proven persistent. The 38 million pensioners (1997 data) have been indeed some of the biggest losers.

In the country as a whole, the population with incomes below the minimum subsistence level decreased officially from 49.7 million in 1992 to 36.6 million in 1995 and to 35 million in 1998. Wide variations exist, however, in the Russian Federation among various republics, *oblasts*, and *krais*. According to 1997 data, the official percentage of the population with incomes below the subsistence level was 20.8 percent of the total population. The regional variations ranged, however, between 16 and 60 percent of the respective populations. In many republics, the variation ranged from roughly 40 percent to over 60 percent; this was the case, for instance, for the republics of Altai, Adygea, Buriatiia, Dagestan, Kabardino-Balkaria, Kalmykiia, Karachai-Cherkassia, Mordovia, Mari El, and worst of all, the republic of Tyva. According to the official data, between 1991 and 1997, the essential nutrition elements decreased for the country's households for proteins from 72 grams to 59; for fats, from 93 to 80; for carbohydrates, from 347 to 344; and for total calories, from 2,527 to 2,337.

Notwithstanding the rise of the country's bureaucratic corruption, crime, and impoverishment, the enactment of an appropriate criminal justice legislation is still uncertain. An effective system of commercial and criminal laws would likely help rid business of corruption and organized crime and would facilitate the transition to broader market-based relations. But this still proves a slow and difficult process. Russian legislators do not yet seem ready to agree on the scope of this kind of substantive legislation. Yeltsin vetoed an early draft of a penal code passed by the Duma, overriding a negative vote of the upper chamber, the Federal Council. But since then, the lack of consensus still delays a proposed law on money laundering. On top of all this, the judiciary is still devoid of the necessary independence to enforce laws without fear of retaliation.

The system that has taken root in Russia has oriented itself toward building interconnected, bureaucratically organized and directed markets, rather than fostering true competition and demonopolization. It has tended to fit logically in the traditional framework of Russian despotism rather than in the desired democratic, Western market-directed paradigm. The anarchic processes that started to unfold in the twilight of the perestroika have continued to grow ever since then and are likely to roll for years to come.

Such developments recall another "time of trouble" that marked Russia's tragic history. In the early seventeenth century, grievous misfortunes affected Russia after the death of Ivan the Terrible. A so-called period of confusion (*smutnoe vremia*) followed the breakup of his despotically centralized state and the explosion of violence, pillage, and brutal impoverishment that this demise generated. The old term *smutnoe vremia* sorely fits again the years following the collapse of the dictatorial Soviet state and empire, the slow and still uncertain coalescence of new, economically healthy, and valid forces, and the drive toward brighter horizons.

CHAPTER 22

The Problems of Agriculture

22-1. Landholding

This chapter focuses first on the respective positions of Russia's three types of agricultural producers – namely, agricultural enterprises, holders of household plots, and family farms – with respect to their land use, sown areas, and livestock holding. The chapter thus centers its attention on the technological basis of each of the indicated category of producers, and on employment and unemployment in this sector. Given the respective positions of each of the indicated categories of producers with respect to the means of production, I present the results in terms of output and yields and compare them to the achievements of the Group of Seven (G7) industrial countries. After the chapter considers the position of agriculture with regard to exports and imports, the concluding section summarizes the overall sectoral results.

Russia's agricultural population increased slightly through the 1990s, from 39.1 million people in 1991 to 39.5 million in 1999, accounting for 27 percent of the population. Total employment in agriculture decreased during these years from 9.9 million to roughly 8.5 million, accounting throughout the period for around 13 to 14 percent of the total employment, because the latter decreased even faster during those years. The land in use by all agricultural producers amounted to 41 percent of the total land of the Federation, while the arable land accounted for as little as 7.3 percent of the total land. When considering land uses and output, one must not lose sight of such familiar issues as technology, investments, subsidies, income, profitability, and so on, but one also must not overlook such specific Russian factors, namely that the average quality of the Russian land is poor, that soils are lost through severe water and soil erosion, and that losses are further amplified by poor technology, poor farming practices, and severe inefficiencies. As for soil loss, it is interesting to note that in 1999 it was officially stated that of the 5.5 million hectares of irrigated land of which Russia disposed in 1991, only 2 million hectares remained in use in 1999.

In the category of producers, the respective shares in the use of total agricultural land, arable land, and pasture varied appreciably during the period under review. The share of land in use of the agricultural enterprises and institutions fell from 613 million hectares in 1991 to 549 million in 1997, while the share of household plots increased from 6.1 million hectares to 10.2 million, and that of family farms from 7.4 million to 11 million. For a more detailed view of the shifts in the type of land used, let us focus on one year, 1997, when general stability seemed (erroneously) to be finally in sight. In that year, the number of agricultural enterprises had increased from 25,900 in 1991 (still consisting then of 12,900 collective farms and of 13,000 state farm) to 27,000 enterprises in 1997, while the number of their workers decreased sharply, from 7.9 million to 5.7 million. As can be seen in Table 22-1, the 27,000 agricultural enterprises held in 1997 over 80 percent of the agricultural area, that is, 165.8 million hectares, on average 6,140 hectares per enterprise. The number of citizens holding plots of land (part of which was used for gardening) decreased from 19.2 million in 1991 to 16.3 million in 1997, working in the latter year on 10.2 million hectares, that is, on 6.2 hectares per plot. Finally, the number of family farms increased from 4,400 in 1991 to 278,000 in 1997, operating on 11.7 million hectares, that is, on 42 hectares per unit. Notwithstanding the basic objectives of the privatization process, clearly there was not by 1997 the significant shift toward family farms, as agricultural reformers, starting in 1910 with Peter Stolypin, had long desired. As we see in Table 22-1, out of the crucially important 124.6 million hectares of arable land, the agricultural enterprises held over 87 percent, while, the holders of the plots of land and family farms disposed jointly of only 10.8 percent.

The vast amounts of land held by the agricultural enterprises allowed them to keep by far the commanding positions in the country's sown areas of grains, industrial crops, and fodder, and also to raise certain types of livestock. Thus, as shown in Table 22-2, close to 90 percent of the total sown area and close to 92 percent of the areas sown with grain were in the hands of the agricultural enterprises, leaving about 10 percent jointly to the plot holders and family farms. The plot holders held the dominant share only in potatoes.

In livestock raising, the divisions among the three types of producers were significantly different. The dominant controllers of pasture land and fodder crops, the agricultural enterprises held in 1997 only 65 percent of the cattle, 55 percent of the cows, 58 percent of the pigs, and less than 40 percent of the sheep and goats. On the other hand, the plot holders, the only ones ready and willing to take care of the livestock with much hard work and with reliance on the old primitive methods, secured decisive positions with all types of livestock; they cared for as much as 33 percent of the cattle, 43 percent of the cows, 40 percent of the pigs, and 53 percent of the sheep and goats. The family farms remained at the margin of all these operations.

While the agricultural enterprises held by far the commanding positions in the control of all types of land, their shares in output and yields declined

Table 22-1 *Russian Federation: Land in Use by Category of Producers, 1997, in Millions of Hectares and in Percentages*

Lands	All producers	Percent	Agricultural enterprises	Percent	Citizens' plots	Percent	Family farms	Percent	State & municipalities	Percent
Land in use	699.9	100	549.0	78.4	11.0	1.6	29.5	4.2	110.4	15.8
Agricultural area	206.2	100	165.8	80.4	10.2	4.9	11.7	5.7	18.5	9.0
Arable land	124.6	100	108.6	87.1	4.6	3.7	8.8	7.1	2.6	2.1
Pasture	77.6	100	54.8	70.6	4.2	5.4	2.8	3.6	15.8	20.4

Source: Based on *Rossiiskii statisticheskii ezhegodnik 1998, op. cit.*, pp. 441–2.

331

Table 22-2 *Russian Federation: Sown Areas by Category of Producers, 1997, in Millions of Hectares and Percentages*

Areas	All producers	Percent	Agricultural enterprises	Percent	Citizens' plots	Percent	Family farms	Percent
Sown area	96.6	100	86.5	89.5	4.6	4.8	5.5	5.7
Grains	53.6	100	49.2	91.8	0.3	0.6	4.1	7.6
Industrial crops	5.4	100	4.7	87.0	0.1	1.9	0.6	11.1
Potatoes	4.3	100	0.6	14.0	3.6	83.7	0.1	2.3
Fodder crops	33.3	100	32.0	96.1	0.6	1.8	0.7	2.1

Source: Rossiiskii statisticheskii ezhegodnik 1998, op. cit., p. 459.

continually and were disappointing throughout the period considered, as we will see later. This crucial discrepancy was due both to their inefficient ways of management and to the continuous shrinking of their technological basis, as I point out in the following section.

22-2. Farming Methods

The growth and structure of agricultural production are highly dependent on the natural framework and on its annual variations, but also, and to a very large extent, on the management's capacity to obtain the appropriate financial means needed to acquire the agricultural machinery and the indispensable fertilizers, as well as on management's ability to secure the qualified specialized personnel and the appropriate labor force for producing the best mix of marketable products. From these points of view, the management of the Russian agricultural enterprises and family farms has proven patently deficient. For instance, according to the official data, for plant growing in 1988, only 62 percent of the agricultural enterprises were stated to be in a "satisfactory" financial condition, while 37 percent were in an unsatisfactory state and 11 percent were roughly at the same level as in previous years. For livestock breeding, the situation was worse: Only 24 percent of the agricultural enterprises were in a "satisfactory" financial condition, while 59 percent were not, and 17 percent were unchanged from the past.[1]

With regard to its technical base, Russian agricultural enterprises, the holders of most of the machines in use in this sector, registered continuous declines through the 1990s. As can be seen in Table 22-3, the amount on hand of tractors and grain combines in the agricultural enterprises declined substantially through the period considered; per 1,000 hectares, the number of tractors decreased from 10.7 to 8.0, while the number of grain combines shrank from 6.5 to 5.1. Sharp decreases were also registered in the purchase of mineral fertilizers – which fell per hectare from 44 kilograms in 1992 to 14 kilograms in 1997 – and of the gasoline and diesel fuel needed for all kinds of machines and for the transport of goods.

Employment in agriculture as a whole amounted in 1996 to 9.5 million. According to the official data, the structure of employment in this sector was at that time the following: The administrative leadership accounted for 8.6 percent of the total; the specialists, for 29.3 percent; employees in various occupations, for 3.2 percent; and finally, the workers, for the balance, 58.9 percent. Appreciable variations were registered among the country's regions in employment and unemployment. The rates of unemployment in the rural areas were stated to be the lowest in the Northwest regions, and the highest in the North-Caucasus, Siberian, and Far East regions. In 1990, the average monthly wage in agriculture as a whole amounted to 95 percent

---

[1] *Rossiiskii statisticheskii ezhegodnik 1998, op. cit.*, p. 503.

Table 22-3 *Russian Federation: Inventory of Agricultural Enterprises, 1991–7*

Inventory item	1991	1992	1993	1994	1995	1996	1997
Tractors[a] (1,000 units)	1,500	1,290	1,243	1,147	1,052	966	856
Grain combines (1,000 units)	349	370	346	317	291	264	231[b]
Mineral fertilizer delivered (1,000 tons)	10,102	5,510	3,721	1,398	1,601	984	972
Gasoline delivered (1,000 tons)	10,633	9,456	6,223	3,670	3,345	2,945	[c]
Diesel fuel delivered (1,000 tons)	19,428	16,522	12,767	7,846	7,105	6,212	[c]

Notes:
[a] Amount on hand.
[b] October 1998.
[c] Data not available.
Sources: *Review of Agricultural Policies in the Russian Federation*, Paris, OECD Center for Economic Cooperation and Development, 1998, p. 54; *Rossiia v tsifrakh, op. cit.*, p. 211.

of the national average, but afterward declined continually reaching by 1997 only 45 percent of the national average. Finally, no fully reliable statement can be made on agricultural profitability, as many farm transactions are done by barter and by unreported ways, and as the Russian notions of "profit" and "loss" are still not fully concordant with Western ones. According to the official data, in 1998, 62 percent of the agricultural enterprises were stated to be in a "satisfactory" financial situation, while only 24 percent of the livestock breeding field were similarly satisfactory. This stresses the poorer results and the more difficult situation in the livestock area, but does not yield a general result. According to the OECD publication *Review of Agricultural Policies in the Russian Federation*, the general result concerning profitability of large-scale agricultural farming (measured as a ratio of net profits to cost of production) fell continually during the period considered; thus, the number of profitable farms, as a percentage of all farms, decreased from 91 percent in 1991 to 21.9 percent and then to 16.9 in 1997 – that is, the loss-making farms increased continually from 5 percent in 1991 to 83.1 percent in 1998. However, as the study itself, notes, "there are numerous methodological problems related to the measurement of 'profitability,'" and this result should be viewed only as indicative rather than as final.[2]

22-3. Output and Yields

Following these changes in the means of production – namely the declines in land use, sown areas, livestock raising, technology, and employment – sharp

[2] OECD, *Review of Agricultural Policies in the Russian Federation, op. cit.*, p. 503.

Table 22-4 *Russian Federation: Volume of Agricultural Production,*
1992–8 by Category of Production, 1990 = 100

Years	Total agricultural output	By the agricultural enterprises	By the population
1992	86.5	75.3	117.5
1993	82.7	68.4	120.7
1994	72.7	57.4	115.0
1995	66.9	48.6	118.9
1996	63.5	43.7	119.4
1997	64.5	44.7	118.7
1998	56.0	36.3	112.8

Source: *Rossiia v tsifrakh, op. cit.*, p. 204.

decreases were registered in almost all the agricultural outputs. On the basis 1990 = 100, by 1997 the output of grains decreased by 24 percent (of which wheat decreased by 11 percent, barley by 24 percent, and rye by 54 percent), and the output of sugar beets by 57 percent, and of sunflower by 18 percent. The output of animal products followed the same pattern of decline. On the basis 1990 = 100, by 1997 total meat output shrank by 52 percent (for beef by 46 percent, for pork by 55 percent, and for poultry by 65 percent), for milk by 39 percent, and for eggs by 33 percent.

The analysis by category of producers shows that the sharp and continuous sectoral output declines were largely attributable to the agricultural enterprises while both the plot holders and the family farms registered increases. As can be seen in Table 22-4, the total agricultural output fell continually through most of the 1990s. On the basis 1990 = 100, it decreased to 56.6 percent, while that of the agricultural enterprises fell even further, namely to 36.3 percent. In contrast, the population's outputs – that is, of both household plots and family farms – increased to around 112–5 percent (all computed at comparable prices).

Analyzed by type of outputs, the results are similar. The agricultural enterprises held the determinant shares only in the outputs of grain and sugar beets (92.2 percent and 95.2 percent in 1998), but in all the other fields, the agricultural enterprises had only small shares (7.8 percent in the output of potatoes, 18.6 percent of vegetables, 41.7 percent of meat, and 50.2 percent or milk).

Little progress was registered in yields. The yield of grains, measured in tsentners per hectare, which had reached between 1986 and 1990 15.9 per year, between 1991 and 1995 amounted to 14.4 per year, in 1996 to 12.9, and in 1997 to 16.5. Similar small variations were registered for the other types of agricultural products. Interesting variations took place between regions. In 1997, the highest yields (20 and above tsentners per hectare) were registered

Table 22-5 *Russian Federation: Sale of Agricultural Produce, 1993 and 1997*

			In percent			
	Total in million tons		Government purchases		Market sales	
Produce	1993	1997	1993	1997	1993	1997
Grains	37.8	37.7	63	25	37	75
Sugar beets	7,143	2,418	98	9	2	91
Potatoes	2,131	1,059	52	29	48	71
Vegetables	2,817	1,762	71	40	29	60
Cattle & fowl	7.0	3.6	79	45	21	55
Milk & milk products	25.3	13.6	97	82	3	18
Eggs[a]	26.2	20.4	92	75	8	25

Note:
[a] millions of pieces.
Source: *Rossiiskii statisticheskii ezhegodnik, op. cit.*, p. 452.

in the Central Black Earth regions (20.0) and in North Caucasus (21.2); the lowest (below 10 tsentners per hectare) were in the Far East (9.2).[3]

The domestic decreases in output and yields were reflected in the fall of sales of most agricultural products. As can be seen in Table 22-5, the sale of basic agricultural products decreased sharply by 1997, and in addition involved a crucial shift from direct government purchases to a significant increase of the market sales of most agricultural products, a situation that paradoxically several political leaders, viewed with dismay. For instance, the liberal Grigory Yavlinsky believes that only the maintenance of firm guarantees of levels of government purchases of agricultural produce makes it possible for agriculture enterprises to secure clear guarantees that they will be supplied with the equipment they need for agricultural production.[4]

The liberalization of price, the discontinuation of high consumer subsidies, along with the fall in incomes have resulted in sharp changes in the pattern of consumer demand. According to the data presented by OECD, in the 1990s the per capita consumption of products with high income elasticities such as meat and dairy products decreased, while the demand for staples such as potatoes and cereal products increased. Between 1990 and 1997, for instance, the per capita consumption in kilogram per person per year fell for meat and meat products from 75 kilograms to 51; for milk and milk products (in fluid milk equivalent) from 386 to 235; for eggs (pieces) from 297 to 200; for sugar from 47 to 32; for vegetables and melons from 89 to 74; and for fruits and

[3] *Rossiiskii statisticheskii ezhegodnik 1998, op. cit.*, pp. 463–4.
[4] Mitrokin, Sergei, "It's Time to Decide on a Strategy," *Nezavisimaia gazeta*, March 14, 2000, transl. in *Current Digest. . .*, Vol. 12, No. 10, April 5, 2000, p. 16.

Table 22-6 *Russian Federation and the G7: Agricultural Production and Grain Yields, 1992 and 1996*

Total production (1990 = 100)	Russia	U.S.	Japan	Germany	France	Italy	U.K.	Canada
1992	86	108	99	93	105	110	102	98
1996	63	114	95	90	104	105	103	110
Tsentners per hectare								
1992	17.2	53.2	57.5	53.1	63.6	46.2	66.9	24.3
1996	16.5	51.4	57.8	62.0	69.3	47.4	70.0	27.5

Source: Rossiiskii statisticheskii ezhegodnik 1998, op. cit., pp. 781–2.

berries from 35 to 28. Small increases were registered only for potatoes and cereal products (including flour, groats, and pulses). In line with the decline in food consumption, the registered output of the food industry also contracted dramatically. Compared to 1990, in 1997 the food industry's output fell for meat products by 78 percent, for whole milk products by 77 percent, for total canned goods by 74 percent, for granulated sugar by 82 percent, for bread and bakery products by 81 percent, and for margarine and vegetable oil by 41 and 53 percent. In both food consumption and food production, what is worrisome in addition to the wide imbalances between regions is the growing income differentiation and the impact of price liberalization on a large part of the urban pensioners and other urban groups. These urban dwellers have to live on very low incomes and have less scope for producing for themselves than do the rural dwellers.[5]

A comparison between the Russian Federation and the countries of the group of industrial countries, the G7, of agricultural output and yields clearly illustrates the very low levels of Russian performance. As can be seen in Table 22-6, on the basis 1990 = 100, the Russian production fell to levels far below those of the G7 countries; in yields per hectare for the key grain cultures, the discrepancy was even more striking and will be hard to bridge in the near future.

22-4. Exports and Imports

Russia has been a net importer of agrofood products since the 1960s. In the 1990s, its agrofood trade has continued to represent a small portion of its exports, and a substantial part of its imports. As can be seen in Table 22-7, the export of agrofood products has varied between $2.5–3 billion per year from

[5] OECD, *Review of Agricultural Policies in the Russian Federation, op. cit.*, pp. 55–7.

Table 22-7 Russian Federation: Exports and Imports, 1994–7, Totals and Shares of Agrofood Products, in Millions of Dollars and Percentages

Years	Total	Of which agrofood	To OECD	Of which agrofood	To NIS	Of which agrofood	Shares of total	OECD	NIS
			Exports in billion dollars[a]					In percent	
1994	66.9	2.8	53.0	2.3	13.9	0.5	4.2	4.3	3.7
1995	79.9	2.7	65.6	2.3	14.3	0.4	3.3	3.5	2.8
1996	86.9	3.2	71.0	2.7	15.9	0.5	3.7	3.8	3.2
1997	86.6	2.4	70.0	1.8	16.6	0.6	2.8	2.6	3.6
			Imports in billion dollars[a]					In percent	
1994	38.7	10.7	28.4	8.6	10.3	2.1	27.7	30.4	20.1
1995	46.7	13.2	33.1	9.7	13.6	3.5	28.2	29.4	25.4
1996	47.4	12.0	32.8	8.1	14.6	3.8	25.2	24.9	26.1
1997	53.5	13.4	39.4	10.2	14.1	3.2	25.1	26.0	22.6

Note:
[a] Excluding nonofficially registered trade.

Source: Rossiiskii statisticheskii ezhegodnik 1998, op. cit., pp. 747–9.

Table 22-8 *Russian Federation: Indicators of Agricultural Decline, 1990–7*

Category Shares	1990	1991	1992	1993	1994	1995	1996	1997
GDP	15.4	13.7	7.2	7.4	6.0	6.9	6.7	6.5
Employment	12.9	13.2	14.0	14.3	15.0	14.7	14.0	13.9
Investments	15.0	17.8	10.8	7.9	5.0	3.5	2.9	2.5
Exports	2.1	2.6	3.9	3.8	4.2	3.3	3.7	2.8
Imports	20.3	27.9	26.0	22.2	27.7	28.2	25.2	25.1

Source: Various sources.

1994 to 1997, while Russia's imports have ranged between $10–3 billion. Russia has been a net importer of such products from both the OECD countries, mainly from the United States and the European Union, the new independent states (NIS), and the Central and East European countries. Since 1994 the share of agrofood imports from both the OECD and NIS has amounted to over 25 percent of Russia's total imports, while the same products' share has amounted to only 2 to 4 percent of Russia's exports.

As shown in Table 22-8, in 1997 Russia's agrofood exports typically consisted mainly of fish and crustaceans, grain, and alcoholic beverages. Russia's main imports were far more varied and substantial; they included, particularly from the OECD countries, meats, butter, fish, oil, sugar, tea, alcoholic beverages, as well as tobacco and cigarettes. From the NIS countries, the main imported goods were meats, grain, sugar, and the apparently indispensable alcoholic beverages.

Russia's food security is increasingly dependent on imports. For instance, Russia's grain harvest reached in 1998 only 45 million tons and in 1999 at the most 60 million tons, compared to 116.6 million in 1990, leaving the country a serious grain deficit. All this has been happening while the financial plight of the countryside has continued to increase. Given this situation, the relatively new Agrarian Party of Russia proposed in July 1999, in order to rescue agriculture, to revive immediately the old kind of machines and tractor stations (that is, the old Soviet system of administering the pooled farm equipment through centralized storage and maintenance) along with a 50 percent reduction in fuel and electricity rates, easy-term loans, and forgiveness of farm tax arrears.[6]

The OECD's study *Review of Agricultural Policies in the Russian Federation*, issued in 1998, advances an essentially opposite view. According to the OECD study, comparative advantage may compel Russia to continue to be a net importer of agrofood products for some time to come, but this should not be a cause of concern. Nor should it encourage attempts to restrict imports and to support agro-exports since such policies would only reduce overall economic

[6] Kucherenko, Vladimir, "Agrarians and Government Reach an Accommodation," *Rossiiskaia gazeta*, July 10, 1999, transl. in *Current Digest. . .*, Vol. 51, No. 28, April 11, 1999, p. 14.

efficiency. This does not mean, however, that every effort should not be made to increase efficiency all along the agrofood chain.[7]

22-5. Concluding Comments

Table 22-8 summarizes the key characteristics of the declining trends in Russian agriculture. These characteristics include GDP, employment, investments, exports, and imports. The decline in the GDP is evidenced from 1991 on; in investments, since 1992; and in exports and imports, by the relative shares in the respective branches, which yielded the following trade deficits in billion dollars from 1994 to 1997: 7.9, 9.5, 8.8, and 11 billion. The shares of employment reflect only slight variations around 14 percent, because the declines in total employment were even sharper than the declines in agriculture.

Concerning this overall decline, certain Russian authors point out that the market transition in agriculture occurred in a sector already depressed by the time of the collapse of the Soviet system. Moreover, the transition was enacted in half measures, particularly with regard to ownership, which the government granted collectively to the workers and managers of the state and collective farms instead of aiming at the destruction of the Soviet framework. The ensuing inflation, with its high rates and short-term credits, also exercised a bad influence on this sector, as did various policies, such as those affecting imports. Furthermore, the Russian agricultural statistics may not reflect fully or correctly the actual volume of production. Under the Soviet system, it was customary to present lower performance data to avoid subsequent higher plan targets. Following the old practice, managers – particularly in the agricultural enterprises – might provide lower output data to avoid the appropriate tax assessments.[8]

In any case, the questions of the land reform and of what to do with agriculture in general are still hotly debated in the Russian Federation. On February 23, 2000, the agricultural ministry presented to an official Agrarian Policy Council a draft program concerning the development of the agro-industrial complex over the period running up to the year 2010. The program, developed in accordance with the instructions of President Putin, proposed reinforcing the chain of command in agriculture, awarding government contracts for the main types of equipment and material fertilizers, and supporting domestic producers via a policy of "reasonable" protectionism. Since the deterioration of the performance in agriculture is also due to the unavailability of loans, the program also proposed opening a number of lending institutions, including an Agricultural Bank and an Agrarian Bank of Reconstruction and Development, which would provide long-term loans to the agro-industrial

---

[7] OECD, *Review of Agricultural Policies in the Russian Federation, op. cit.*, pp. 24–5.

[8] *Ekonomika perekhodnogo perioda* (Economics of the Transition Period), Moscow, Institut ekonomicheskikh problem perekhodnogo perioda, 1998, pp. 815–6.

complex. Private companies, however, have opposed this plan since, as they pointed out, the government contracts fail in practice to reach their goal, as was proven, for instance, by the government's failure to prevent the collapse of related complex industries such as the agrochemical industry.

Another problem under debate is that of market-based purchase and sale of agricultural land and the enactment of a code covering such transactions. Some have proposed the recognition of the "fundamental principle" that farmland is to be excluded from the market trade. Others have insisted that the country's "most valuable land," the black earth areas, be put under the state's care as federal property. Strangely enough, leaders of the liberal party, the Yabloko of Gregory Yavlinsky, have asserted that land must be used for farming and "must not be bought by foreigners." Before land can become marketable, a whole set of measures must be taken, notably a government cadastre, an appraisal system, and mechanisms for selling, mortgaging, and insuring land. In addition, a federal contract system would have to be established, which would include in its contract mechanisms clear-cut guarantees that both the government purchaser and the contractor would meet their commitments. Such a system would make it possible for the agricultural enterprises to be supplied with equipment on a competitive-bidding basis, against a portion of their output furnished to the state food reserves.[9]

The conception and the whole set of measures already enacted concerning the agrofood complex – namely the pattern of privatization of agriculture, as well as the debates still in progress about the role of the state and the question of agricultural land selling and purchasing – reflect the still deep influences of the old Soviet approaches to the matters relating to agricultural property, to the issues concerning its handling by law, to the scope of the market in its functioning, and to the role of the state in agriculture's performance and eventual development. *Nil novi sub sole.*

---

[9] See "Farm Land Policy under Debate," including "General Program for Agricultural Recovery Will Be Developed" (*Nezavisimaia gazeta*, March 1, 2000), "A Referendum Won't Solve Farm Sector Problems" (*Ibid.,*), and "It's Time to Decide on a Strategy" (*Nezavisimaia Gazeta*, March 14, 2000), all transl. in *Current Digest...*, Vol. 52, No. 10, April 5, 2000, pp. 14–16.

CHAPTER 23

The Industrial Changes

23-1. Pattern of Growth

Russian statistics concerning the manufacturing organization and enterprises, the scope of their privatization, and the resulting shares of the state and of the private sector are neither consistent nor easily disentangled. According to the official data, the number of manufacturing organizations and enterprises amounted in 1944 to 212,000 and in 1998 to 339,000. The number of manufacturing enterprises was given as 138,000 and 161,000 during the same period. Subtracting the latter data from the former, we find that the number of manufacturing organizations amounted to 74,000 in 1994 and to as much as 178,000 by 1998. As I already indicated in Chapter 20, the large and medium-sized enterprises included in the privatization program had to change into joint-stock companies, and the state, as we will see immediately, retained various positions within them. Many other groups of manufacturing enterprises followed undoubtedly the same legal transformation. Much of the growth of the manufacturing enterprises was due to the rapid creation of numerous small industrial enterprises. In 1992, for instance, the number of manufacturing enterprises totaled 25,244; by 1998, their total number was 161,000, out of which 134,180 were officially described as small enterprises. In both cases, the number of large enterprises amounts to 25,281 and 27,000 respectively, figures not far from the total of such enterprises in 1990, namely 26,900.[1]

Table 23-1 presents the numbers and composition of the manufacturing enterprises by main branches. As the table shows, the number of the enterprises in all the sectors grew or decreased in the 1990s at various speeds yet changed only in small ways the interrelations among their percentage shares. More significant changes took place in those years between the totals of heavy industry compared to the joint percentages of the various light industries. Total heavy

---

[1] See notably *Rossiiskaia Federatsiia v 1992 godu, op. cit.*, p. 76; *Rossiia v tsifrakh, op. cit.*, pp. 154–6.

Table 23-1 *Russian Federation: Manufacturing Enterprises, by Main Branches,
in Thousands and in Percentages, 1992, 1995, and 1998*

Industry	1992		1995		1998	
Total manufacturing, main branches, %	50,525	100	137,000	100	161,000	100
Electroenergy	943	1.8	1,165	0.8	1,260	0.8
Fuel	725	1.3	952	0.7	1,485	0.9
Ferrous metallurgy	349	0.7	904	0.6	1,401	0.9
Nonferrous metallurgy	327	0.7	1,303	0.9	1,814	1.1
Chemicals[a]	1,479	2.9	4,881	3.5	6,082	3.8
Machine construction	13,505	26.7	47,728	34.8	57,987	36.0
Timber and woodworking	8,187	16.2	16,424	11.9	20,765	12.9
Construction materials	5,053	10.0	7,925	5.7	9,953	6.2
Light industry	10,150	20.0	22,347	16.3	21,136	13.1
Food industry	7,073	13.9	13,902	10.1	22,372	13.9

Note:
[a] Including oil-chemicals.
Sources: *Rossiiskaia Federatsiia v 1992 gody, op. cit.*, p. 68; *Rossia v tsifrakh, op. cit.*, pp. 186–196.

manufacturing – loosely defined herein as including both manufacturers and
mining activities, that is, the first eight entries – registered an increasing share
at around 60 percent plus of the total number of the indicated enterprises.
Meanwhile, the share of light industries – including textiles and the food industry – fell from 33.9 percent in 1992 to 27.0 percent in 1998. As the heading
of the table indicates, the data cover the main manufacturing branches only.
The totals of the percentages presented in the table amount to 94.1 percent for
1992, to 85.7 percent for 1995, and to 89.6 percent for 1998. Put differently, the
balances not accounted for in the table amount to 5.9, 14.3, and 10.4 percent.
A part of these balances may be attributed to the military establishment. According to certain sources, the number of military manufacturing enterprises
amounted in 1992 to 888, with 7.1 million workers, of whom 5.6 million worked
in the defense establishment and 1.5 million in the military research and development (R&D). In 1998, the minister of industry and trade asserted that he
intended to control the entire field of military-technical cooperation, and on
this occasion he indicated that this implied overseeing the following giant federally owned enterprises: *Rosvoruzheniie* (the Russian Arms State Company),
Promexport (Manufactured Goods Export Association), and *Rossiiskoe Technologii* (Russian Technology). All three enterprises are involved in exporting
military hardware.[2]

[2] Dawisha, Karen, and Parrott, Bruce, *Russia and the States of Eurasia, The Politics of Upheaval*,
Cambridge, Cambridge University Press, 1994, p. 171; Korotchenko, Igor, and Masliukov,
Yuri, "Russia Doesn't Have an Investment or an Industrial Policy" (*Nezavisimaia gazeta*,
August 12, 1998), transl. in *Current Digest . . .*, Vol. 50, No. 33, September 1998, p. 10.

Table 23-2 *Russian Federation: Shares in Manufacturing Ownership, Workers, and Output, 1992, 1995, and 1998, in Percentages*

Shares	Ownership			Workers			Output		
	1992	1995	1998	1992	1995	1998	1992	1995	1998
State	45.5	4.9	3.1	81.3	15.9	13.6	84.4	9.7	9.9
Municipal	5.9	2.8	2.0	1.7	1.9	2.0	0.7	1.8	1.5
Public org.	0.9	0.9	0.5	0.7	0.6	0.6	0.2	0.2	0.2
Private	47.4	72.3	88.1	15.4	27.3	37.4	14.0	18.9	27.0
Mixed	0.3	19.1	6.3	0.9	54.3	46.4	0.7	69.9	61.4
TOTAL	100	100	100	100	100	100	100	100	100

Sources: For 1992, *Rossiiskaia Federatsia v 1992 goduv, op. cit.*, p. 68; for the other years, *Rossiiski statisticheskii ezhegodnik 1999* (Russian Statistical Yearbook 1999), Moscow, Goskomstat, 1999, p. 309.

Manufacturing productivity decreased during and after the big inflation years. In 1992, the range of profitability for all industries was quite high, namely from close to 30 percent to as much as 50 or 60 percent (for the production of gas, ferrous and nonferrous metallurgy, chemicals, machinery, and light industries), but then fell by 1995 for the same industries to around 20 percent, and by 1998 to less than 10 to 12 percent – and much lower for all the other industries, except for gas and nonferrous metallurgy, which still registered profits of around 30 percent in relation to costs.

What was the overall impact of privatization on the state's ownership, both in the manufacturing enterprises and in the industrial organizations? As I indicated in Section 20.3, according to the official data, privatization in manufacturing affected between 1992 and 1998 a total of 27,257 enterprises (most of them, 25,809, between 1992 and 1995). Following these measures, the state's ownership, as shown in Table 23-2, decreased to 3.1 percent of the total manufacturing enterprises, that is, to a total of 4,991 enterprises employing 13.6 percent of the industrial workers and accounting for 9.9 percent of this sector's output. As the table shows, the dominant position for ownership shifted from the state to the private sector, but for manufacturing employment and above all for output, the shift toward the mixed companies was pronounced. Various other data point clearly toward the fact that the state's actual shares in the manufacturing enterprises and in the organizations controlling them are much higher than the numbers in Table 23-2 suggest. As of 1998–9, the number of enterprises wholly owned by the ministries or by the federal government in the economy as a whole amounted to 23,089 and to 13,786 respectively. In addition, the state owned stocks in 3,896 enterprises: For 697 of them, blocks of shares were reserved for federal property and were not subject to early sale. Out of the total indicated number in which the state owned some capital, its shares were accounted for as follows: It held 100 percent of the shares in 382 joint-stock companies; blocks of more than 50 percent in 470 companies; blocks of 25 to 50 percent in 1,291 companies; and less than 25 percent of the shares in 1,173 companies. Finally, it also held a "golden share" (a share conferring veto power on certain decisions) in 580 other companies. For the most part, the latter were described as enterprises involved in the production of oil, gas, cola, electric power, pipeline transportation, and arms manufacturing. According to a 1999 declaration of the head of the State Property Ministry, during "the next two to three years," the number of wholly owned state enterprises will be reduced to between one thousand and fifteen hundred. The methodology for cutting down the inventory will involve shutdowns, outright sales, and transformation into joint-stock companies.[3] Clearly, a substantial share of the manufacturing mixed companies and of the industrial organizations is in the hands of the state, and the data on its ownership in manufacturing of 4,991 enterprises confer only an incomplete view of its actual holdings in this sector.

23-2. The Workforce

The Russian statistics furnish three sets of figures concerning the workforce. The first indicates the workforce available, that is, the so-called active population, including the unemployed; the second gives the data of the actually employed personnel, that is, all the employees of an establishment; and the third gives, separately, the number of production workers only. As shown in Table 23-3, the workforce in the economy as a whole decreased in 1998 compared to 1990, to 84.5 percent. The decreases in manufacturing of the workforce, the personnel, and the workers were much sharper, namely down to 61–3 percent. While the number of manufacturing enterprises increased more than three times compared to 1992 (as shown in Table 23-1), their total personnel fell to around 66 percent of the 1992 level – that is, on the average, the number of workers per enterprise decreased appreciably. This was due both to the industrial structural changes of all kinds and to the surge of small enterprises. When considering the decline of personnel in each of the main manufacturing branches, one may note that the decreases affected all of them except electroenergy. Particularly heavy were the decreases in machine construction (a loss of 3,383,000 positions in 1998 compared to 1992), in the woodworking industries (a loss of 753,000), in construction materials

---

[3] Zagorodnaia, E., "Government to Turn over Its Property to the Regions" (*Vremiia*, Dec. 14, 1999), transl. in *Current Digest...*, Vol. 51, No. 50, January 12, 1999, p. 15; Granik, Irina, "Cleaning of State-Owned Property Is Under Way" (*Kommersant*, December 9, 1999), transl. in *Current Digest...*, Vol. 51, No. 49, January 5, 1999; "For Your Information," *Current Digest*, Vol. 50, No. 52, December 1998, p. 15.

Table 23-3 *Russian Federation: Workforce and Employment, 1990–8, in Thousands and in Percentages*

Workforce	1990		1992		1995		1998	
In the economy	75,325	100	72,071	95.7	66,441	88.2	63,642	84.5
In manufacturing	22,809	100	21,324	98.1	17,182	80.6	14,150	62.0
Manufacturing personnel	20,998	100	20,020	104.8	16,006	79.9	13,173	62.7
Production workers	17,001	100	16,344	104.0	13,000	79.5	10,395	61.1

Sources: Rossiiskii statisticheskii ezhegodnik 1999, op. cit., pp. 297, 375; *Rossiia v tsifrakh, op. cit.*, pp. 81, 174.

(a loss of 396,000), in chemicals (of 283,000), and in heavy industry as a whole (5,089,000).

The contractions in the entire economy brought down wages to very low levels throughout the country. On the basis 1990 = 100, the real average monthly wage rate in the economy as a whole decreased in 1991 to 96.5 percent; then, in the high inflation period, it went down to 45.5 percent by 1995; then it began to stabilize in the following years at around 50 percent of the old level. In manufacturing, according to the April 1999 *Transition Report Update* of the European Bank of Reconstruction and Development, the monthly wages decreased between 1993 and 1998 by 28.9 percent. The minimum monthly wage rate in the economy as a whole fell to the minimum subsistence level from 31.3 percent in 1992 to 15.0 percent in 1998. In some key branches of manufacturing, the average monthly wage rate declined continually throughout the 1990s; this was the case in electroenergy, fuel, nonferrous metallurgy, machine construction, and light industry. On the other hand, in 1998, the highest wage rates were still paid in the gas, fuel, nonferrous metallurgy, and coal industries, while the lowest were disbursed in machine construction, which since 1990 had the largest number of small industries, and in light industry. In the economy as a whole, the share of wages in the population's money income – an income supplied from a variety of sources, including the sale of agricultural products and income earned in neighboring countries – amounted to 40.5 percent in 1996 and then to 42.4 percent in 1998.[4] In the structure of manufacturing expenditures, the wage level declined from 13 percent in 1990 to 10.6 percent in 1995, and then increased to 12.8 percent in 1998, while continuing to account for low shares in certain branches (such as 7.2 percent in the oil industry, 8.2 percent in electroenergy, and 9.2 percent in the gas industry).

---

[4] Nikiforov, A., and Lubkov, A., "Osnovnye napravleniia reformirovoniia zarabotnoi platy" (Basic Direction of the Reform of Wages), *Ekonomist*, April 1999, pp. 38–44; also *Ekonomika perekhodnogo perioda, op. cit.*, p. 905; *Obzor ekonomicheskoi politiki v Rossii za 1998 god* (Survey of the Economic Policy of Russia for 1998), Moscow, Rosspen, 1999, p. 596.

23-3. Output Levels

The percentages of Russian changes in gross output, productivity, and real wages in manufacturing between 1993–8 were in summary the following, according to the European Bank of Reconstruction and Development:

	1994	1995	1996	1997	1998	1993–8
Manufacturing gross output	−24	−3.9	−6.8	2.0	−5.2	−34.2
Productivity in manufacturing	−17.7	4.8	0.2	7.9	—	—
Real wages in manufacturing	−17.5	−31.3	9.6	7.6	6.4	−28.9

All the declines over this period conform to the overall declines in the GDP. All the regions of the country experienced massive decreases in their manufacturing output: In 1998 the smallest degrees of output declines varied between 40 and 50 percent in relation to the 1990 level; the biggest declines varied between 50 and close to 70 percent. The smallest declines were registered by the Northern region (59 percent of the 1990 output), the Lower Volga (51 percent), and the Central Black Earth and West Siberia regions (50 percent each). The biggest decreases were suffered by the North Caucasus (which reached 32 percent of the 1990 level) and by the North Western and the Central regions (35 percent each); like Russia as a whole, which in 1998 produced only 46 percent of the 1990 level, the remaining regions also produced about 40 percent of that level. They ranged as follows: Far Eastern (40 percent), Ural (41 percent), Volga-Viatka (44 percent), and East Siberia (48 percent).[5]

The smallest levels of output reached in the main manufacturing branches in the 1990s ranged in 1998 between 24 and 48 percent of the 1990 levels, while the largest ranged between 51 and 88 percent. In the latter group were the ferrous and the nonferrous metallurgies (53 percent each of their 1990 level), the fuel industry (66 percent), and electroenergy (76 percent). In the first group, the lowest level was reached by light industry (only 12 percent of the 1990 levels), construction materials (33 percent), timber and woodworking (36 percent), machine construction (37 percent), chemicals (42 percent), and the food industry (49 percent). The rankings of the shares in the main branches' total output of each year (1992, 1995, and 1998) did not change appreciably: The highest shares were still accounted for by fuel, electroenergy, and the food industry, the lowest by light industry, construction materials, and timber and woodworking.

In the output of manufacturing as a whole, the largest state shares (in machine construction, electroenergy, construction materials, and chemicals) were

---

[5] *Rossiiskii statisticheskii ezhegodnik 1999* (Russian Statistical Yearbook 1999), Moscow, Goskomstat, 1999, pp. 300–1.

Table 23-4 *Russian Federation and the G7: Manufacturing
Output, 1992–7, in Percentages, 1990 = 100*

Country	1992	1993	1994	1995	1996	1997
Russia	75	65	51	50	48	49
U.S.	101	105	111	115	118	124
Japan	96	91	92	95	98	101
Germany	98	91	94	96	96	102
France	97	94	98	99	99	104
Italy	98	96	102	108	105	108
U.K.	96	98	104	106	107	108
Canada	97	102	108	112	114	120

Sources: Rossiiskii statisticheskii ezhegodnik 1998, op. cit., p. 775;
Rossiia v tsifrakh, op. cit., p. 404.

far below the shares of the private sector and even more so of the mixed companies, which dominated by far the other two sectors except in the light industry,
food industry, and construction materials. The enormous shares of the mixed
companies in almost all the branches confirm their dominant position in total
manufacturing output (61.4 percent in 1998). Officially, the dominant positions
in the domestic market were held in 1998 by 258 manufacturing corporations,
most of whom were likely mixed companies.

Comparisons between the levels of industrial production of Russia and of
the G7, from 1992 and 1997 (on the basis 1990 = 100), are shown in Table 23-4.
Clearly, Russia's profound industrial changes after the collapse of the Soviet
Union and of its centrally oriented planned economy, led to the continuous
decline of its manufacturing production. By 1998, close to 50 percent of manufacturing enterprises were working at a loss, compared to 7 percent in 1992.
The Russian decline is sharply evidenced when compared to the performance
of the G7. During the same period, the United States increased its output by
nearly a quarter; by 1997, all the other powers of the group moved from the
level of 1990, from 101 to 120.

Russia did assert its strength in the world at large in some outputs, but
according to the data released by Goskom, these were in other fields than
advanced machinery and equipment. Russia acquired indeed the first world
position in the production of natural gas; the second in the output of heavy
coal, potatoes, and milk; the third in the production of oil; the fourth in the
productions of electroenergy, cast iron, iron ore, steel, wood, cotton fabrics,
grains, and sugar beets; the fifth in the output of mineral fertilizers and saw
timber; and so on.[6] These outputs alone hardly characterize a highly developed
economy.

---

[6] *Rossiiskii statisticheskii ezhegodnik 1998, op. cit.,* p. 780.

23-4. Exports and Imports

The structural changes of manufacturing and its outputs impacted the compositions of exports and imports, which in turn affected the structure of production. The Central State Statistical Office releases two sets of data on foreign trade. The first set includes the registered and nonregistered trade transactions, the second excludes the nonregistered data. Thus the 1998 exports are officially evaluated as amounting, in the first case, to $73.9 billion, and the imports to $59.5 billion. In the second case, exports were stated to have reached in 1998 $72.6 billion, and imports only $44.1 billion. As an OECD survey has pointed out, besides carrying registered imports, shuttle trades bring in to Russia on international flights an enormous quantity of goods in shopping bags at preferential conditions, much of it even duty free. In addition, a large quantity of goods is carried through as unaccompanied luggage (textiles, leather goods, furs, electronics, and even cars in kits). The porousness of Russia's long borders facilitates much of this smuggling. Nonrecorded trade flows have tended to increase particularly in order to circumvent import taxation.[7]

As can be seen in Table 23-5 from the 1998 data, the bulk of exports (34.4 percent) consisted of mineral products, including crude oil, natural gas, and oil products, as well as metals and precious stones (35.8 percent). The largest shares of imports were machinery and equipment (35.6 percent), foodstuffs (24.5 percent), and chemicals (15.4 percent). As I pointed out in Chapter 22, foodstuffs' high import share shows the enormous role they play in ensuring the country's food security. In the structure of imports from the capitalist countries and from NIS as well, the key items are the same: Machinery and equipment account for the largest share (39.4 and 25.1 percent respectively), followed by foodstuffs (26.6 and 18.4 percent) and chemicals (15.7 and 13.8 percent). Interestingly the exports of machinery and equipment to the West and to NIS have amounted to $5.5 billion and $2.4 billion respectively, a total of $7.9 billion, while the imports of machinery and equipment from the West and NIS have accounted for $12.9 billion and $2.8 billion, a total of $15.7 billion, almost double the value of the corresponding exports. Clearly, in this crucial field, Russia does not hold a first rank.

What are the relations between the levels of the main manufacturing exports and imports and the respective levels of Russia's industrial outputs? The highest share of exports in Russia's output was in rolled metals (63.5 percent of production), tractors (46.9 percent), and natural gas (34.5 percent). Also high percentage shares of output exported were recorded for timber, paper, and cellulose, while small percentage output shares were registered for the exports of coal, iron ore, and heavy cars. Imports covered Russia's needs by 35.4 percent for pneumatic tires, 16.7 percent for heavy cars, and 15.6 percent for light cars,

[7] OECD, *Economic Surveys 1997–1998 Russian Federation*, Paris, OECD, 1997, p. 67.

Table 23-5 *Russian Federation: Structure of Exports and Imports with OECD and NIS in 1998, in Totals and in Percentages*

Structure	Exports			Imports		
	OECD	NIS	Total	OECD	NIS	Total
Machinery and equipment	9.3	17.5	10.9	39.4	25.1	35.6
Mineral products (and fuels)	40.2	9.2	34.4	2.8	15.0	5.9
Metals and precious stones	31.7	53.8	35.8	4.6	14.0	7.0
Chemicals	8.2	9.2	8.4	15.7	13.8	15.4
Wood, pulp, and paper	5.5	2.8	5.0	4.5	2.1	3.9
Textiles	1.0	1.7	1.1	2.7	7.3	3.9
Leather and fur products	0.6	0.2	0.5	6.3	0.4	0.2
Food and agriculture products	2.8	4.1	3.0	26.6	18.4	24.5
Other	0.7	1.5	0.9	3.4	3.9	3.6
TOTAL	100	100	100	100	100	100

Source: *Rossia v tsifrakh, op. cit.*, pp. 387–93.

and by as much as 51.9 percent for tractors. (No such interesting interrelations are given for machinery and equipment.) In the 1997 imports, the enterprises with participating foreign capital accounted for a total of $6.4 billion (7.2 percent of the total exports), of which the industrial products accounted for only $2.6 billion (2.9 percent of the total exports).

23-5. Concluding Comments

As can be seen from the data grouped from various sources in the summary Table 23-6, manufactures accounted in the 1990s for 27 to slightly over 30 percent of the GDP, for 22 percent of total employment (toward the end of the 1990s), and for about 35–40 percent of the total investments. In foreign trade, the crucial share of machinery and equipment amounted in exports to 9–11 percent, and in imports to as much as 32–9 percent. Clearly machinery and equipment play a decisive role on dependence on foreign sources. So far Russia has not advanced much in the information revolution in which the United States and the advanced Western countries have engaged ever more decisively since the 1950s. Along with the Internet and its endless Web sites of information and instant communications, this revolution is bringing deep technological changes in many aspects of production, in the pattern of investments, in the formation of companies combining banking with other services, in the relations between companies' inside functions and wide outsourcing, in the connections between suppliers and customers – in short, in the scope, complexity, range, and speed of changes. All these changes outweigh the transformations brought about by the industrial revolution.

Table 23-6 *Russian Federation: Manufacture's Shares in GDP, Employment, Investments, and Foreign Trade, 1992–8, in Percentages*

Shares in	1992	1993	1994	1995	1996	1997	1998
GDP	34.5	32.4	31.5	31.4	27.5	26.8	—
Employment	29.5	29.3	27.1	25.8	24.8	23.0	22.2
Investments	41.3	37.0	32.3	34.4	34.8	36.5	39.9
Exports[a]	9.3	9.0	8.3	9.9	9.8	10.3	10.9
Imports[a]	39.2	35.0	35.2	33.7	32.0	35.3	35.6

Note:
[a] Shares only of machinery and equipment.

Can Russia accomplish these changes over the next few years? It seems both difficult and improbable. What various Russian leaders emphasize now is that their country needs first to create "favorable conditions for business," starting with the elementary protection of property rights and with lower taxes. Russia's "economic challenge," according to Vladimir Mau, the director of the Russian government's Working Center for Economic Reforms, is "a rapid transition to a post-industrial society," a challenge, which he adds, is comparable in scope to the problem of industrialization that Russia faced in the early 1920s. Mau seems to imply that Russia must make the transition to an age of broad and rapid technological changes in which the state cannot set simple targets as during the Soviet industrialization drive (for coal, steel, cement, oil, and so on) and then achieve rapid increases in production. In a period of rapid technological changes, the problem for "postindustrial societies" that want to meet the challenge of "catching up and overtaking" is to create the most favorable conditions possible for vast technological changes within a truly liberal framework – a challenge that Russia will not easily meet.[8]

Russia's progress in information technology changes in data processing and data communications has certainly been slow, modest, and handicapped by many other pressing needs. Academician Mikhail Kirpichnikov noted that in 1999 the most significant event for science and technology was that in that year, for the first time, "the federal budget allocations for science and technology were fully funded." Kirpichnikov then added that in 1999, an advanced telecommunications network was set up for science and institutions of higher education encompassing forty-five regions and having about a million users. Also in 1999, plans were announced to create three industrial innovation complexes on the basis of existing centers, and the government decided to increase its support for defense research. In hard currency, the expenditures involved

[8] Mau, Vladimir, "Renaissance of Liberalism, the Hard-Line Variety," interview with *Izvestia*, April 5, 2000, transl. in *Current Digest...*, Vol. 52, No. 15, May 10, 2000, pp. 1–2.

in the science allocations mentioned by Kirpichnikov amount roughly to $500 million per year.[9]

For post-Soviet Russia, these are some of the basic approaches to the problems of the technological revolution. Will the measures in question be as fruitful as their advocates believe? This, according to Russian historian Sergei Karaganov, is doubtful. Indeed, according to him, Russia's current dynamics will make the federation "lag behind the world of the developed economies for another 15 to 20 years," even if it pursued successful economic policies. And Karaganov adds, "we are already beginning to lag behind even countries falling in the middle range of economic development.... To a significant degree the world information revolution is leaving Russia behind." Meanwhile, most of Russia's industrial sector continues to be stifled by excessive concentration, vertical integration, and geographic segmentation.[10]

Given the strongly entrenched management control of most of Russia's corporations, and given also the old customs of barter deals along with extensive bribe taking, what is continually at the *ordre du jour* are all kinds of high-profile corporate governance scandals. Asset stripping continues to be in evidence and to involve transfer prices, share dilution, manipulation of cash flows and of assets in related companies, along with continuous projects of "restructuring" (an example is the project of the giant Russian Electricity Company run by A. B. Chubais) adversely affecting the shareholders. With the appointment of lenient administrators, the bankruptcy process itself is often used as another channel for asset stripping. Despite a bankruptcy law of March 1998 and of a number of legislative acts of 1999, budgetary constraints for the enterprise sector remain soft or hardly enforceable. (I will return to some of these issues in more detail in Chapter 25.)

---

[9] Kirpichnikov, Mikhail, "We Are Now Creating a Technological Culture," interview in *Nezavisimaia gazeta*, February 8, 2000, transl. in *Current Digest...*, Vol. 52, No. 13, April 2000, pp. 10, 20.

[10] Karagonov, Sergei, "What Is Russia to Do? What Is to Be Done with Russia?" *Moskovzkie novosti*, February 29–March 6, 2000, transl. in *Current Digest...*, Vol. 52, No. 10, April 5, 2000, pp. 1–2; Broadman, Harry G., "Competition and Business Entry in Russia," International Monetary Fund, *Finance and Development*, Vol. 38, No. 2, June 2001, p. 22.

CHAPTER 24

Domestic and Foreign Trade

24-1. The Domestic Trade Network

Post-Soviet Russia has provided the population with consumer goods and services through an expanding network of retail stores, public catering establishments, wholesale trading organizations, and a number of household service institutions involved in information, health, dwellings, culture and science, credit and finance, and so on. What is the pattern of ownership in this sector? How many trading enterprises and workers are engaged in this field? What exactly is the commodity composition of this trade? What is the structure of the households' and of the companies' expenditures in domestic trade? These are the main questions that I consider in this chapter.

As I pointed out previously (in Chapter 21), the privatization drive affected between 1992 and 1998 a total of 43,166 retail stores, 9,922 public catering enterprises, and, from 1993 to 1998, 1,517 wholesale trade establishments. During this period, the ownership shares in retail trade turnover changed as indicated in Table 24-1. The share of the state fell from 41 to 7 percent while that of the private sector increased from 52 to 80 percent and that of mixed enterprises from 7 to 13 percent. However, the state still holds blocks of stocks in the large private companies as well as in the mixed ones.

Over the period 1993 to 1998, the number of retail and public catering stores increased appreciably, but the number of their workers decreased sharply. The totals changed as follows: At the beginning of 1993, 319,000 stores had 2,813,000 workers; by 1998 the corresponding figures were 852,000 stores with 2,785,000 workers. These changes were due in particular to an appreciable expansion of the number of new stores, some of which were very small. Thus in January 1993, the number of new stores amounted to 30,500, with 244,000 workers; by 1998 the number of new small stores expanded to 359,000, with 2,203,000 workers. The number of workers per unit (per one retail and public catering store) fell from ten in 1994 to close to six in 1995, five in 1996, four in 1997, and three in 1998.

Table 24-1 *Russian Federation: Shares in Retail Trade Turnover by Forms of Ownership, 1992–8, in Percentages*

Years	Total	State	Private	Mixed	Retail trade	Public catering
		Forms of ownership			Branches	
1992	100	41	52	7	95	5
1993	100	23	70	7	96	4
1994	100	15	76	9	96	4
1995	100	13	73	14	97	3
1996	100	9	77	14	96	4
1997	100	8	78	14	97	3
1998	100	7	80	13	97	3

Source: Rossiiskii statisticheskii ezhegodnik 1999, op. cit., p. 443.

The volume of retail trade decreased during the 1990s, on the basis 1990 = 100, to 97 percent in 1991, and, after various fluctuations around 90 percent, it declined to 86 percent by 1998. The trade volume of food products decreased more sharply. The volume of foodstuffs traded fell from 99 percent in 1991 to 77 percent in 1998, while the volume of alcohol sold increased to 106 percent in 1991 and then decreased (after 1995), reaching 90 percent by 1998. The trade in nonfood products also shrank from 93 percent in 1991 to 89 percent by 1998. Given the decreases in domestic production, the reliance on food and nonfood products imported increased sharply, as we will see later on. In 1991, 86 percent of retail sales were of products of domestic origin, and only 14 percent of the sales involved imported products. In 1998 the latter share increased to 48 percent. The largest share of imported foods was in meat and meat products, fish, macaroni, flour, fats, and alcoholic beverages; for nonfood products, the largest share of imports was in televisions, radios, and other such technological products. A detailed examination of the changes in sales shows significant decreases, notably of basic foods such as meat and poultry, eggs, sugar, bread flour, and fruits.

The inflationary pressures had unfavorable consequences for both food and nonfood consumption *prices*. Food prices increased percentagewise compared to the preceding year, from 236 in 1991 to 2,626 in 1992, after which they started to decrease, reaching 109 in 1997, but then increased again to 196 by December 1998. For nonfood prices, the changes were similar but on a somewhat higher plateau, namely from 310 in 1991 to 2,673 in 1992, then falling to 108 in 1997 and rising again to 199.5 in 1998. The structure of household expenditures shows a serious increase in the home expenditure on food and a significant decrease in nonfood expenditures.

During the 1990s, an increasing number of retail and public catering stores and establishments operated at a loss. In 1992, 16 percent of them were in this situation; throughout the 1990s, the number of catering trade establishments continued to increase, affecting by 1998 42.6 percent of them. A significant number of wholesale trade firms handling technological products also operated at a loss; this was the case of 10 percent of such firms in 1992, and of 46.3 percent of them in 1998. The commodity exchange establishments decreased appreciably in number during this period, namely from 159 in 1993 to 47 in 1998.

24-2. Trade Interconnections

Let us consider now the interconnections of trade with the towns and the countryside, the country's regions, and the domestic and foreign origin of the supplies. First, note that the overwhelming share of the sales of retail trade and of public catering is being directed toward the towns. From 1992 to 1998, the percentage of these sales has increased continually, namely from 85 percent of the total in 1991 to 93 percent in 1998, while the sales to the countryside have decreased correspondingly, from 15 percent to 7 percent. Moreover, while the urban population decreased from 1991 to 1998 from 109.8 million to 107.1 million, during the same period the rural population increased from 38.7 million to 39.6 million in 1998, which showed clearly that the rural dwellers' income and capacity to purchase decreased appreciably.

As far as the interrelations between trade stores, sales, and regions are concerned, it is interesting to note that by the end of 1998, for instance, the central regions – the region with Moscow at its heart – concentrated over 37 percent of the retail, wholesale, and state purchasing channels, as well as over 37 percent of sales, while it accounted only for 20 percent of the total population. The other main regions with high proportions of trade channels, sales, and population, were: the Lower Volga (with the center of Volgograd) with 11.5 percent of the total population; North Caucasus (including seven republics at the country's southwestern frontier) with 12.1 percent of the population; the Ural region (with its centers of Perm and Oranenburg) with 13.9 percent of the population; and East Siberia (with its Krasnoiarsk and Irkutsk centers) with 10.3 percent of the country's population.

The resources of retail trade consisted of domestic products and imports. The domestic deliveries included factory productions, intermediary wholesale and retail trade products, and citizens' traded goods. Between 1995 and 1998, the shares of domestic and foreign traded resources fluctuated each around 50 percent of the total. (Before 1995, however, the share of the domestic resources declined from 1991 to 1995 from 77 percent down to the 50 percent, while that of imports increased from 23 percent to around 50 percent.) Consider now the structure of domestic traded resources. During the period 1995–8, it counted for one-third (or less) of factory products, for 45 to 50 percent of intermediary wholesale and retail deliveries, and for around 16–20 percent of households' sales. Around 70 percent of all the goods involved were traded through trade organizations, and slightly less than 30 percent were traded through the market.

Table 24-2 *Russian Federation and the G7ᵃ: Foodstuffs per Person per Year,*
in Kilograms

Foodstuffs	Russia 1998	U.S. 1996	Japan 1996	Germany 1996	France 1996	Italy 1994	U.K. 1994
Meat and meat products	44	114	45	86	63	78	73
Milk and milk products	219	304	93	442	317	270	306
Butter	3.1	1.9	0.8	7.3	4.9	2.0	3.5
Eggs (pieces)	217	236	320	226	199	222	189
Fish	9.8	10.2	59.8	15.1	14.7	17.6	11.6
Sugar	33	23.6	15	18.3	34	24.5	37
Potatoes	123	60	102	77	60	43	108
Vegetables	78	117	123	90	63	179	76
Fruits	31	99	60	136	85	169	95
Bread products	118	111	112	78	92	118	87

Note:
ᵃ No data provided for Canada.
Source: Rossiiskii statisticheskii ezhegodnik 1999, op. cit., p. 588.

As we have seen on the basis of many indicators, the 1990s constituted a particularly trying period for the production and sale of foodstuffs as well as of nonfoodstuffs. The relative share of the consumption by households in the GDP first fell from 41.4 percent in 1991 to 33.7 percent in 1992, and then began to rise, reaching 55.9 percent by 1998. However, the Russian GDP decreased continually during that period, amounting by 1998 to less than 50 percent of its 1990 level. Further, a careful examination of the foodstuffs per person (per year, in physical terms, for example, in kilograms) shows the great gap existing between Russia and, for instance, most of the G7. As Table 24-2 shows, according to the official figures released by Goskomstat, in 1998 Russia surpassed all the countries considered in the per person consumption of sugar and potatoes, and also all the other countries except Italy in the consumption of bread products. On the other hand, all the other countries far surpassed Russia in such basic per capita foodstuffs as meat and meat products, milk and milk products, fish, and fruits. Clearly the Russian diet worsened appreciably during these years.

24-3. Concerns in Foreign Trade

The Russian Federation has faced persistent problems with regard to the appropriate framework for its foreign trade. Particular problems include the complicated structure of its tariffs, its trade and investment policies (notably in their connection with banking, financial, and telecommunications services), the still not fully clarified scope and functions of its state trading, and the policies that should govern direct foreign investments. Since 1994 Russia has manifested great interest in membership in the World Trade Organization (WTO) seeking to integrate its markets with the international trading community. Yet, with or without such membership, truly bringing Russia into the rule-based WTO system requires both intensive reviews and vast modifications of Russia's trade regime, economic policies, and laws so that Russia would eventually achieve effective compliance with the WTO rules.

Meanwhile, in June 1994, Russia signed a Partnership and Cooperation Agreement (PCA) with the European Union (EU), set to come into force in 1997. Concurrently, in February 1996, Russia and the EU signed an interim trade agreement – the trade part of the PCA – that accorded to each other most favored nation (MFN) status and freed the goods traded between them of quantitative restrictions (except for the nuclear sectors, steel, and textiles). Despite the PCA, the EU, until April 1998, imposed the contentious and in some cases harmful requirement that Russia (and China) maintain the status of a "non-market economy." After the April 1998 changes, Russia and China were still not designated as market economies but new rules were established, according to which in certain cases their actions would be considered as fulfilling "market conditions." The EU then suggested that it would be important that Russia did join the WTO, holding out the long-term possibility of a "free trade zone" between Russia and the EU. Besides these relations, Russia continued to develop bilateral and multilateral initiatives to enforce its economic and political links with the former Soviet republics, and signed Free Trade Agreements (FTA) with all of the newly independent states (NIS), as well as a number of agreements of regional economic cooperation. However, on the whole, all these efforts have yielded only limited results in modifying Russia's trade system. The NIS countries normally have no tariffs on each other's goods but do apply varying tariff rates and resort to other import measures on goods coming from outside. Furthermore, harmonizing the NIS policies with third countries has proven impossible.

As part of the discussions on the structural reforms that Russia would have to undertake to join effectively the WTO, the World Bank undertook the complex and difficult task of carefully examining the prevailing key issues concerning Russia's foreign trade system, in particular, its tariffs, financial services related to trade, state trading, and policies on the system of foreign investment. The World Bank's study,[1] published in December 1998 and entitled *Russian Trade Policy Reform for WTO Accession*, throws an intensive light on the difficult problems Russia faces in this respect. First, with regard to tariffs – the centerpiece of trade policy in a market economy – the analysts of the World Bank point out that there is little economic justification in providing, as Russia does, differentiated tariff protection to various branches of industry and agriculture, and that the most efficient alternative would be to

---

[1] *Russia Trade Policy Reform by WTO Accession*, edited by Broadman, G. Harry, World Bank Discussion Paper No. 401, Washington, DC, World Bank, December 1998.

adopt a uniform tariff rate. According to the World Bank suggestions, Russia should indeed eliminate all technical barriers to trade and should rely on protection only by tariffs; the federation should reduce the maximum tariff (from the prevailing 13 percent to 10 percent) while eliminating exemptions. Finally Russia should bind its WTO tariff rates closer to applied rates.

With regard to nondiscrimination among trading policies, especially in financial and telecommunication services, the World Bank analysts note that the legal and policy framework devised by the WTO's General Agreement on Trade and Services (GATS) offers a blueprint for the appropriate reforms of the services sectors of the Russian economy. What is needed in this respect is openness of the key sectors to international competition, and transparency and predictability in the regulatory and administrative regime for the service sectors in Russia. The analysts stress notably the need of the publication of the legislation and of the regulation measures affecting trade, the free transfers for current transactions, and subjection to IMF obligations with respect to restrictions on capital transfers. Russia's policies are still evolving in all those regards, and as the World Bank analysts remark, Russia would gain if it would decisively aim at clarifying its property rights regime, commit to market access for most foreign providers in most industries, and commit to a clear timetable for liberalization of the key services industries.

Concerning the problems of state trading, the World Bank analysts point out that Russia has inherited a complex system of centralized exports and imports through specialized trading organizations (the so-called foreign trade organizations, FTO), whose role has been reduced over time, notably through the privatization drive. But elements of state trading continue to persist in three areas: in companies that exercise monopoly (notably in the exports of natural gas demands and of pipelines); in companies that do not have monopoly positions but enjoy various privileges and advantages in trade; and in companies that engage in barter trade with the newly independent states. In sum, to accede to the world markets, Russia must decisively reduce the role of monopolies in trade, create transparent relations between the state and the companies that enjoy privileges in this field, and terminate state trading aspects of the intergovernmental agreements.

Concerning the policy regime governing foreign investment, the World Bank analysts stress that foreign investments bring not only capital, productive facilities, and technology, but also new employment opportunities, all particularly important to today's Russia, where pressures for firms to compete are still low. In the view of the World Bank analysts, the Russian Federation still adheres to the wrong conception that there are only two motivations for foreign investments, namely access to inputs for production and to markets for outputs. Russia is in fact getting relatively small amounts of these two types of investments, and very little of the new and most efficient kind of investments, namely investments in state-of-the-art technology and world-class competitive production.

In short, Russia's effective interconnection of its markets with the world markets posits the need of vast transformations in Russia's prevailing foreign trade framework. These transformations would notably require eliminating the prevailing technical barriers to trade so that protection is based only on reduced tariffs, discarding secret legislative measures affecting various foreign trade transactions and hidden state participation, clarifying the status and privileges of certain firms engaged in foreign trade, eliminating the existing restrictions on foreign direct investments into a limited number of activities, and opening Russia's markets to a far larger degree to the participation of direct foreign investments. Russia's concerns in the field of foreign trade are hence not limited to the usual preoccupation of any country with such questions as the pattern of trade – its direction, volume, and particular structure – or only to the adhesion to WTO's rules, but concomitantly and to a greater extent with the underlying conceptions that have been shaping Russia's trade, many of which are inherited from the Soviet past concerning the objectives, importance, and benefits of foreign trade.

24-4. The Foreign Trade Network

In which ways does Russia's foreign trade structure and its main trade centers reflect Russia's pattern of economic development? Consider first overall characteristics of Russia's exports and imports. As Table 24-3 shows, Russia is now basically an exporter of raw materials – which account roughly for 70 percent of Russia's exports – and secondarily only an exporter of finished products, which amount roughly to a quarter of Russia's exports. Foodstuffs and agroproducts play a small role. On the other hand, on the side of imports, finished products (mostly machinery and equipment) account for 52 to 60 percent of the total, followed by food and agricultural products, which account for about a quarter or more. Raw materials play a small role.

In many respects, this kind of foreign trade reflects the characteristics of a medium developed economy – an exporter mainly of raw materials and heavily dependent on the imports of machinery and equipment for economic construction and/or reconstruction as well as on all kinds of foods and agroproducts. Russia's changes in size, pattern of industrial development, and overall volume and direction of its investments – from a country for many years centered on military production with the support of the entire economy inflexibly guided by the central Soviet planners, to an economy now oriented in various respects toward reconstruction and toward the market, controlled by both a relatively weak state and by an oligarchy with deep roots and interests in the country's raw materials bases – allows us to better perceive the real level and limits of Soviet "industrialization" policy and its impact on the country's overall development. That policy endowed Russia with numerous militarily oriented establishments that began to decay rapidly after the fall of the USSR, as the interest in rapid military expansion decreased, as industry as a whole declined

Table 24-3 *Russian Federation: The Structure of Foreign Trade, 1994–8, in Percentages*

Structure	Exports					Imports				
	1994	1995	1996	1997	1998	1994	1995	1996	1997	1998
1. Raw materials	71.5	68.1	70.8	71.8	69.8	13.2	14.8	16.2	12.9	12.5
Mineral products	45.1	42.0	47.3	47.8	42.3	6.5	6.4	6.4	5.8	5.4
Metals & precious stones	26.4	26.1	23.5	24.0	27.5	6.7	8.4	9.8	7.1	7.1
2. Finished products	23.0	27.3	24.0	24.5	26.3	55.1	52.9	54.8	58.1	59.3
Machinery & equipment	8.3	9.9	9.8	10.3	11.3	35.2	33.7	32.0	35.3	36.2
Chemicals	8.2	9.9	8.5	8.3	8.5	10.0	10.9	14.4	14.4	15.0
Woodwork, cellulose, paper	3.9	5.6	4.2	4.3	4.8	1.5	2.4	3.3	3.6	3.8
Textiles	2.0	1.5	1.1	1.1	1.2	7.9	5.5	4.7	4.5	4.0
Leather & fur products	0.6	0.4	0.4	0.5	0.5	0.5	0.4	0.4	0.3	0.3
3. Food & agricultural products	4.2	3.3	3.7	2.8	3.0	27.7	28.2	25.3	25.1	24.6
4. Other	1.3	1.3	1.5	0.9	0.9	4.0	4.1	3.7	3.9	3.6
TOTAL	100	100	100	100	100	100	100	100	100	100

Source: Rossiiskii statisticheskii ezhegodnik 1999, op. cit., pp. 569–70.

as the investors' interests shifted in other directions, and as the economy tried to reach and achieve new equilibria. With the decline of the military sector, it became increasingly evident how limited externally was the process of the country's industrial change, and how circumscribed was Russia's real economic transformation.

With regard to the volume of foreign trade, it is interesting to note the role played by a limited number of the country's regions. As in the case of domestic trade, the overwhelming role is played by the Central region, with Moscow at its core. That region accounted in 1998 for over 34 percent of exports, and for 47.9 percent of imports, with Moscow alone responsible for 19 and 39 percent of these totals respectively. The Central region was followed in exports, but at an appreciably lower level, by three regions: the Ural, with Ekaterinburg at the core (13 percent); the West Siberian region, centered at Novosibirsk but with the gas and oil rich Tiumen (12.3 percent); and the Northwestern region, with St. Petersburg (10 percent). These four regions hence account jointly for close to 70 percent, leaving small shares for the remaining seven regions in the balance of 30 percent. With regard to imports, the Central region was again followed at far lower levels by three regions: Northwestern (10.6 percent) and the Ural (6.1 percent), and finally Eastern Siberia, with the Irkutsk center (5.7 percent) – again leaving to seven regions a balance of 30 percent. In short, the Central-Moscow core of the country plus three other regions carry out most of the country's foreign trade.

During the late Tsarist regime, the Imperial transport network, consisting mainly of the railway system, was strongly oriented toward servicing foreign trade. The Soviet system deemphasized foreign trade and shifted its attention to developing its links mostly with the East European satellites, and shipping armaments to a limited number of countries, such as Syria. International transport represented then only a small component of direct air, rail, and sea transport. The post-Soviet Russian Federation is again trying to emphasize international foreign trade connections and to develop an appropriate system for this purpose. But it faces enormous difficulties in this regard due to the loss of the best, most modern locations to former fellow republics (namely to the Baltic states, the Ukraine, and Georgia), multiple deficits in handling capacity involving all kinds of transport equipment, plus inadequate means to build and repair maritime vessels, railway locomotives, and freight cars. According to the official data, transport freight by all the means of transportation decreased continually through the 1990s, from a total of 4,849 million tons in 1992 to 2,337 million in 1998. All forms of transportation – railroad, cars and trucks, sea vessels, internal water transport – exhibit significant freight declines.[2]

24-5. Concluding Comments

The bulk of both domestic and foreign trade is carried out through the Central region, dominated by Moscow, and followed at an appreciably lower level by a very limited number of other regions – the Ural, Lower Volga, and West Siberia for domestic trade, and the Ural, West and East Siberia, along with the Northwestern region for foreign trade. This domestic trade depends heavily on imports, is directed mainly toward the country's towns, and is carried out through the trading organizations and, for about 30 percent, directly through markets.

The country's foreign trade is directed primarily toward the Western capitalist countries, and to a much smaller extent toward the former fellow Soviet republics. Indeed, around 80 percent of the Russian Federation exports move toward the West, and around 75 percent of its imports come from there. Russia's participation in world trade remains, however, quite small and much smaller than that of any industrialized country with whom Russia aims to identify itself. As can be seen in Table 24-4 Russia's shares in world exports or imports are far exceeded by each member of the G7. In comparison to a far less populated country such as Canada, Russia's share of world exports

---

[2] See North, Robert N., "Transport in a New Reality," in *Geography in Transition in the Post-Soviet Republics*, Bradshaw, Michael, J., ed., New York, John Wiley & Sons, 1997, pp. 222–7; *Rossiia v tsifrakh, op. cit.*, p. 243.

Table 24-4 *Russian Federation and the G7: Shares in World Exports and Imports, 1990–7, in Percentages*

	Russia	U.S.	Japan	Germany	France	Italy	U.K.	Canada
Exports:								
1990=100	2.1	11.5	8.4	11.9	6.1	5.0	5.4	3.7
1992=100	1.5	12.2	9.3	11.5	6.3	4.9	5.2	3.7
1995=100	1.6	11.8	8.9	10.2	5.8	4.7	4.9	3.9
1997=100	1.6	12.0	7.9	9.6	5.4	4.5	5.3	4.0
Imports:								
1990=100	1.6	12.9	6.6	9.7	6.6	5.1	6.3	3.5
1992=100	2.3	14.5	6.1	10.6	6.3	5.0	5.8	3.4
1995=100	1.2	15.3	6.7	8.8	5.5	4.15	5.3	3.3
1997=100	1.0	16.4	6.2	8.1	4.9	3.8	5.6	3.7

Source: Rossiiskii statisticheskii ezhegodnik 1999, op. cit., p. 610.

amounted to 1.6 percent and that of Canada to 4.0 percent; in world imports, these two countries accounted for 1.0 percent and 3.7 percent respectively.

The limits of Russia's participation in world trade appear even more modest when expressed in the underlying U.S. dollars data. Thus, Russia's exports in 1997 – a good year for Russia compared with the preceding and the following year – amounted to $87 billion compared to $688 billion for the United States, $421 billion for Japan, $512 billion for Germany, $290 billion for France, $238 billion for Italy, $282 billion for the United Kingdom, and $214 billion for Canada. Even more striking differences are to be noted in the magnitude of imports: Russia's imports amounted in 1997 to $53.6 billion U.S., compared to $889 billion for the United States, $339 billion for Japan, $445 billion for Germany, $270 billion for France, $210 billion for Italy, $307 billion for the United Kingdom, and $201 billion for Canada.

Certainly, Russia's efforts to expand its connections with the world market are hindered by the difficult tasks of home reconstruction and by the need for a vast economic reorientation within the framework of a declining economy still shackled in a variety of ways by the unfortunate inheritance of Soviet habits, concepts, and methods. It is hoped, however, that time and the everyday experience will eventually help Russia overcome many aspects of this inheritance, and open its economy more decisively to the beneficial influence of expanding market relations and concepts.

CHAPTER 25

Money and Banking

25-1. The Monetary System

During the 1990s, the Russian Federation experienced powerful inflationary pressures, marked notably by three peak periods. During the first period, between January 1992 and January 1994, Russia reached its highest inflationary levels; during the second, between August 1994 and January 1995, Russia hit a lower plateau; then after a significant decrease of inflationary levels and the achievement of what turned out to be a transitory stabilization in 1997, inflation pushed upward again between August 1998 and March 1999 (see Figure 25-1). All along, Russia was unable to address successfully its underlying fiscal imbalances, which were preventing both a sustained fiscal consolidation and a durable stabilization. The continual fiscal imbalances (to which I will refer in detail further on) left the economy particularly vulnerable to changes in world commodity prices (notably in 1998 due to the fall in oil prices, that is, in Russia's key export item). In addition, these imbalances affected deeply Russia's broadest access to international capital markets. By August 1998, faced with dwindling reserves despite high increases in interest rates, the government launched a series of emergency measures, including a de facto devaluation (namely one new ruble equal to 1,000 old rubles). After the August crisis, the government indicated that its monetary policy would henceforth be conducted in the framework of a flexible exchange rate, a policy guided primarily by the evolution of reserve money.

Throughout the 1990s, the consumer price index increased sharply during certain peak periods; as can be seen in detail in Figure 25-1, the monthly inflation rate varied in 1992 between 40 and 25 percent, in 1993 between 25 and 13 percent, in 1994 between 13, 5, and again 13 percent, falling by the end of 1995 to about 4 percent. After further small variations between August 1996 and July 1998, the consumer price index rose again sharply in mid-August during a major recession, finally falling down again from the beginning of 1999 on.

363

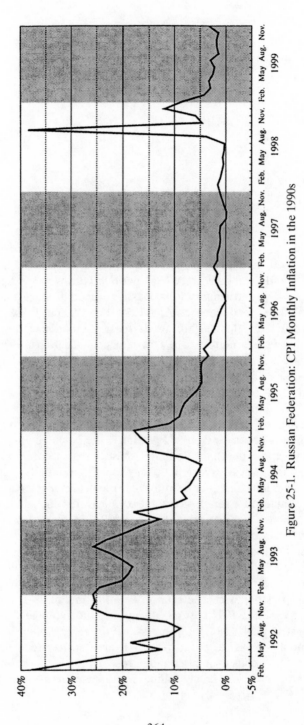

Figure 25-1. Russian Federation: CPI Monthly Inflation in the 1990s

According to the data of Goskomstat, the official money supply increased from 33.2 trillion rubles in 1994 to 295.2 trillion by 1997 (and after the devaluation of the ruble to 1,000 to 1, to 448.3 billion rubles in 1999). However, one must not overlook the fact that in addition to these enormous increases, throughout the 1990s a vast amount of money surrogates were involved in barter, transactions, payments of wages in kind, arrears, offsets, and other forms of quasimonies that have become very common in Russia since the early 1990s. Huge swaths of the economy continue to deal through barter; transactions are manipulated by insiders, avoiding both taxes and the the market. A survey of 350 enterprises made in October and November 1998 found that almost 90 percent of them had exposure to both barter and tax offsets – that is, the payments to the government in goods and services in exchange for the government waiving suppliers' tax obligations. According to certain views, both federal and regional governments have accepted these and other partial retreats from the market, conscious of the fact that a major economic reconstruction could not occur without massive dislocations in employment, output, and investment, and that it was better to accept all kind of "tricks" to keep alive a large part of the secondary economy dominated by unprofitable enterprises.[1]

As for the other forms of money surrogates, *veksel* (promissory note) issues in particular, have performed the function of a variety of debt instruments such as certificates of deposit, commercial paper, simple IOUs, and bonds, issued by banks, enterprises, regional and local authorities, as well as federal authorities. But official statistics are not available for the total of all the outstanding *veksels*. According to certain estimates, the total of the outstanding *veksels* of the subjects of the Federation varied in the late 1990s between 200 to 500 billion rubles, that is, between two-thirds or one and one-half of the volume of ruble M_2. Interestingly, *veksel* issuers can easily refuse to honor *veksels*, invoking formal defects that emerged during their circulation, but on the other hand, counterfeit *veksels* are quite abundant and are deemed to have incurred serious losses for the government in tax revenues.[2]

As a valuable 1998 OECD study, points out *veksels* have certainly provided in various situations needed liquidity and have reduced transaction costs. On the other hand, they have been widely associated with tax evasion, fraud, as well as the manipulation of commercial banks' balance sheets. *Veksels* have been and continue to be in essence a phenomenon related to the complex conditions of a transitional period in a devastated agro-industrial economy with a still slowly growing and insecure private sector and with underdeveloped financial markets. The OECD asserts that, "over time veksels are bound to give way to more conventional forms of financing."[3] This may

---

[1] Shleifer, Andrei, and Treisman, Daniel, *Without a Map, Political Tactics and Economic Reform in Russia*, Cambridge, MA, MIT Press, 2000, pp. 97, 105–6.

[2] *OECD Economic Surveys 1997–1998, Russian Federation, op. cit.*, pp. 178–85.

[3] *Ibid.*, p. 185.

certainly be so. However, what is difficult to determine is how long "over time" will be.

25-2. Development of Banking

As a saying goes, in the market economy, money is the lifeblood, and the banking system is the heart. As we will soon see, in the Russian Federation this heart is often subject to acute arterial fibrillations. Two fundamental laws are the basis of Russian banking: the Law on the Central Bank of the Russian Federation, and the Law on Banks and Banking Activity, along with parts of the Civil Code. These laws date back to before the dissolution of the Soviet Union (1990) but have been revised and redefined with regard to the relationship of the Central Bank and the banking system, notably by the Law on Banks and Banking Activity of February 1996. That law specifies that the country's banking system includes, besides the Central Bank, the credit organizations, as well as their branches and the representatives of foreign banks. According to the specialized literature, however, many gaps continue, to exist in the legislation and the regulation of commercial banking, especially with regard to the lack of deposit insurance, the peculiarities of the bankruptcy process, and the rights of commercial creditors in cases of default. Comprehensive restructuring changes are expected in the Law on the Central Bank and in the Civil Code.

An additional complex problem in the monitoring of appropriate banking regulations has been brought forward by the blossoming of financial-industrial groups – similar in concept to the centralized ministerial arrangements and orientations prevalent in the Soviet system – involving the unification of certain industrial and financial resources and the direction of their investments into diverse branches of production. In essence, the core banks of the Soviet system have been maintained in the Russian Federation, but have been reorganized to fit into a new framework. To start with, the Central Bank now participates in the elaboration of the economic policy of the Federation and in various aspects of its application, has monopoly power in the emission and control of cash circulation, registers the emission of bank notes, exercises control over foreign currency, and has the sole right to issue and revoke banking licenses. In 1990, at the emergence of the Russian Federation, the government owned the Savings Bank (*Sberegatel'nyi bank*, or *Sberbank*) as well as the State Bank of Foreign Trade (*Vneshtorgbank*), and fully controlled a number of commercial banks in foreign countries, notably in Europe, including Eurobank in Paris, Moscow Popular Bank in London, and East-West Handelsbank in Frankfurt am Mein. In that year, Russia transformed Sberbank into a joint-stock commercial bank, and its main shares were handed over to the Central Bank. The same procedure was followed with Vneshtorgbank, the crucial bank managing foreign credits for import-export operations and investments. Also at that time, the former USSR Agroprom Bank was transformed into a joint-stock company and renamed the Russian Agricultural Bank (*Rosselkhozbank*). The latter was substantially reorganized and then returned back to its original name. However, due to low credits and to bad debts, Rosselkhozbank was finally purchased in mid-1996 by the Capital Savings Bank (*Stolichnyi bank sberezhenii*), but allowed to continue its activities under its own name. Also in the early 1990s, the government resuscitated the Foreign Trade Economic Bank of Russia (*Vnesheconombank*), which the Soviet government formed in 1924 to focus on financing foreign trade, but which had collapsed upon the breakup of the USSR. This bank is now charged with the surveillance of operations concerning the country's foreign debt as well as of other foreign trade deals.

When the Soviet Union disintegrated, more than one thousand commercial banks emerged within the financial system of the former planned economy. Some of these banks grew at a rapid pace by taking advantage of the unregulated financial markets. Under the prevailing conditions, such commercial banks provided the government with loans in exchange for the right to manage the state's remaining shares in selected large operations, which if the state failed to repay the loans, would be transferred to the banks. Some such banks also combined with small "pocket banks," set up for the needs of their investors and benefiting from illegal financing of industrial and agricultural enterprises on the basis of subsidies from the Central Bank. Still other small banks serviced foreign currency exchange and short-term trade operations. A number of these banks declined or were eliminated subsequently because of the deep changes in the country's economic conditions. By 1994, the number of commercial banks was 2,457; by 1998 that number decreased to 1,697, and after the August 1998 crisis, to 1,476.

A variety of indicators suggest that Russian commercial banks are much smaller than large Western banks. With regard to their own capital, as of December 1996, the largest Russian banks ranged from $183 million dollars (Mosbusinessbank) to $908 million (Vneshtorgbank), while the largest Western banks ranged between $15.7 billion U.S. (the Union Bank of Switzerland) to $25 billion (Mitsubishi). Besides Sberbank and Vneshtorgbank, which benefit from a highly privileged status, most of the largest commercial banks have been concentrated in Moscow. Among them, the banks with the largest shares of credits in assets have been Oneskimbank and Menatep, which have greatly expanded due to the controversial "shares for loans" privatization scheme of late 1995. As pointed out in 1998 by the *OECD Economic Survey 1997–1998* on the Russian Federation, Oneskimbank has been at the center of a large financial empire that has placed priority on penetrating Russian regions with regard to investments and joint developments. By other criteria, such as the volume of their profits, the largest commercial banks besides Oneskimbank and Menatep have been Inkombank (well known for its extensive web of branches throughout the country), Autobank (associated with automobile producers), Alphabank (important in financial exports and also in the administration of subsidized credits to agriculture), Rossiiskii Kredit (with strong interests in mining), Gazprom (with direct relations with the gas monopoly), and various other banks.

Unlike many commercial banks that have been eliminated by unfavorable economic conditions from the mid-1990s on, the so-called financial-industrial groups (in Russian, *FPG*) that have also emerged from the old government and planning structures have enjoyed rapid development, especially from 1996 on. In that year, there were already thirty-four officially registered FPGs employing over 2 million people. By 1997 their number grew to forty-six FPGs, unifying nine hundred enterprises and organizations, ninety credit institutions, including forty-eight banks and 3 million employees. By 1998 there were eighty-two FPGs integrating banking and industrial capital with emphasis on internal projects and investments of the component units, and on increasing the efficiency of their production and markets. The biggest among the FPGs have been involved in the conversion of certain war-industrial facilities producing all types of metallurgical products, machine construction, telecommunications, chemicals, and so on. The biggest FPGs were in 1998 notably Magnitogorskaia Stal', Uralskie Zavody, Rossiiskii aviatsionnyi Konsortium, and Metalloindustriia.

As pointed out by a study entitled *Banking System of Russia*, issued by the Russian Academy of Science in 1999, the Russian banking system expresses in many ways the conflicting tendencies and characteristics of the period of transition from a centrally directed economy to a market-directed one. The majority of the commercial banks, notes this study, can hardly be called "private," given the fact that their constituency has emerged from the preceding fully owned state structures, and that moreover they are now achieving and adjusting to various modifications of the state's ownership and remaining dependent on the government for credit resources. The basic principles of a functioning banking system in the market framework are self-dependency, real orientations in function of supply and demand, and true market relations between the banks and their customers – conditions that the Russian Federation has not yet come close to achieving.[4]

Clearly the Russian government is conscientious of at least some of these problems and of the need to restructure the banking system thoroughly. As the *Statement of the Government of the Russian Federation and Central Bank on Russia's Economic Policy*, issued on January 3, 1999, indicated, "the current legislative framework for bank restructuring and bank liquidation represents

[4] See notably Zhivalov, V. N., *Finansovaia sistema Rossii* (The Financial System of Russia), Moscow, Ekonomika, 1999; Rossiiskaia Akademiia Nauk (Russian Academy of Science), *Ekonomicheskie i sotsial' nye problemy Rossii, 1999–1: Bankovskaia sistema Rossii, problemy i perspektivy razvitiia* (Economic and Social Problems of Russia: The Banking System of Russia, Problems and Perspectives of Development), Moscow, Inion Ran, 1999.

a major roadblock in our efforts to reconstitute the banking system." What is needed, adds the statement, is to develop a more suitable legal framework. With this objective in view, the government has set forth a Bank Restructuring Law along with amendments to the Law on the Central Bank, the Civil Code, and the Bank Bankruptcy Law, as well as regulations to limit the activities of banks in poor conditions, revoke the licenses of insolvent banks, and redefine the criteria for the licensing of banks. An Agency for Restructuring Credit Organizations (ARKO), established jointly by the Central Bank and by the government, is to have the sole responsibility for restructuring banks that receive funds for recapitalization; it will also provide liquidity support only to solvent banks. The Central Bank will revise the criteria for bank licensing. The revisions will include changes in the calculation of the initial capital, elimination of cross-holdings as a source of capital, consideration of the viability of the bank's business plan, and assessment of the transparency of corporate shareholder groups.

All this indicates first how lax the conditions set by the Central Bank have been traditionally for granting bank licenses up to 1999, and second, how little the new reforms could or would change the real nature of the existing banking system with regard to its state roots, its inherited methods and concepts of management, and its continuing heavy dependence on the state. It is estimated that the state still owns over 30 percent of the total bank assets. Despite transferring its block shares in the key Sberbank and Vneshtorgbank to the Central Bank, the state is the single largest shareholder in many large industrial enterprises that own a majority of banks. While these enterprises have been privatized, the state is still the largest shareholder in many of them. In addition, regional governments are also deeply involved in the operation of many banks located on their territory. Finally the potential disastrous effects of corruption are as significant in banking as they are in other branches of the economy. It will take time to devise and apply adequate measures tailored to the specific problems of the Russian banking system, including *inter alia* public disclosure of the state's direct and indirect ownership in banks, public disclosure of basic information on bank performance, income, credits, and balance sheets, and the training of bank supervisors capable of controlling risk-taking in a salubrious liberal environment.[5]

25-3. Foreign Capital

In the process of globalization of world economic relations, of growing intercountry and interindustry connections, of expanded trade flows, of increased

---

[5] Malyshev, N., "Practical Barriers to Restructuring the Banking System in the Russian Federation," in OECD Proceedings, *A Regional Approach to Industrial Restructuring in the Tsarist Region, Russian Federation*, Paris, OECD, 1998, pp. 253–9.

Table 25-1 *Russian Federation: Foreign Trade and Foreign Investments,
1995–8, in Millions of U.S. Dollars*

	1995	1996	1997	1998
Foreign trade				
Exports	81,096	88,599	88,326	741,457
Imports	60,945	68,828	73,613	58,935
Foreign investments	2,983	6,970	12,295	11,773
Direct investments	2,020	2,440	5,333	3,361
Portfolio investment	39	128	681	191
Credits and other	924	4,402	6,281	8,221

Source: Rossiiskii statisticheskii ezhegodnik 1999, op. cit., pp. 542, 565.

direct foreign investments, Russia accounts for far less than one might expect – for instance, in foreign investments – considering its size, resources, and potential development. On the other hand, Russia's lack of economic and political stability and the absence of an appropriate climate conducive to the attraction of foreign capital have decisively affected both trade flows and direct foreign investments. In 1997, Russia's shares in the world trade accounted for 1.6 percent of the world exports and for 1.0 percent of the imports – very small shares when compared to the lowest and the highest levels attained by the G7 countries, namely with regard to the lowest, 4.0 and 3.7 percent respectively (for Canada) and for the highest, 12.0 and 16.4 percent respectively (reached by the United States). Even compared to Russia's low trade flows, direct foreign investment appears relatively tiny. Thus, in 1997 – when the total foreign investment reached its highest levels in the 1990s – the totals were only of the order of 13.9 percent of the level of exports and 16.7 percent of the level of imports. These relative levels increased in 1998, as the volume of exports and imports fell appreciably.

The analysis of the structure of capital investments shows that the joint ventures of Russia and of foreign capital reached by 1996 only 3 percent of the total investments, and by 1998, 4 percent. In addition, direct foreign investments have risen from 1.2 percent in 1997 to 3.2 percent of the total in 1999 (in that same year, the share of state investments still ran as high as 21.3 percent). As can be seen in Table 25-1, the relative share of direct foreign investments has substantially decreased between 1995 and 1998, while the share of indirect foreign investments, namely in the form of commercial credits, has sharply increased. Percentagewise, the share of direct investments in total foreign investments has fallen from 67.7 percent in 1995, to 35.0 percent in 1996, 43.4 percent in 1997, and 28.5 percent by 1998. Conversely, the share of commercial credits has risen from 31.0 percent in 1995, to 63.2 percent in 1996, 51.1 percent in 1997, and then to 69.9 percent in 1998. Direct foreign investments have tended to concentrate in industry, finance, credit, and commercial operations. Within industry itself, the highest shares of the total have been

Table 25-2 *Russian Federation: Main Investing Foreign Countries, 1995–8, in Percentages*

Country	1995	1996	1997	1998
U.S.	27.9	25.4	24.1	19.0
U.K.	6.1	7.3	19.6	13.5
Switzerland	14.6	19.3	14.3	3.5
Germany	10.3	4.8	13.4	24.2
Netherlands	2.8	14.0	4.4	7.5
Cyprus	1.4	11.8	8.1	7.8
Austria	2.7	2.9	3.1	0.7
France	3.6	0.6	1.7	13.1
Japan	2.5	0.3	1.1	0.5
Sweden	2.1	2.3	0.6	1.2
Total Foreign Investment	100	100	100	100

Source: Rossiiskii statisticheskii ezhegodnk 1999, op. cit., p. 544.

absorbed by the fuel industry, and somewhat paradoxically also by the food industry. In 1998, for instance, 16.0 percent of the total foreign investments went to the fuel industry, and 12.5 percent to the food processing enterprises. The regional pattern of foreign investments shows again, as in other fields, the critical importance of Moscow and the Central region. Moscow's share in foreign investments amounted to 46.9 percent of the totals in 1995, 65.5 percent in 1996, 68.9 percent in 1997, and after the economic collapse of August 1998, 49.8 percent. The Central region's share (including Moscow) amounted to 57.9 percent of the total in 1995, 73.0 percent in 1996, 71.1 percent in 1997, and 59.1 percent in 1998.

The main foreign investors, as indicated in Table 25-2, were continually the United States, the United Kingdom, and Germany. In 1998, the share of the United States amounted to 19.0 percent, or $2.238 billion, that of the United Kingdom to $1.591 billion, and that of Germany to $2.848 billion. Yet all these figures pale beside other statistical data that show that Russia's investments abroad are becoming far larger than that which any other country is now receiving from the developed countries. Thus the investments abroad of the Russian enterprises reached in 1999 $8.038 billion (compared to a total of $9.560 billion that entered Russia from abroad). These figures represent only the legal movement of capital. But, there is also a large amount of illegal capital moving in Russia; according to some sources, the clandestine export of capital is at least as high as the amount exported legally. Finally, as indicated in Table 25-2, the small republic of Cyprus has also become a great investor in Russia; in U.S. dollars, Cyprus invested, according to the official data, $825 million in 1996, $996 million in 1997, $918 million in 1998, and, according to supplementary data, $923 million in 1999. But, as Otto Latsis has pointed out in *Novaia Izvestiia* of March 11, 2000, Cyprus is a major offshore zone, and the capital

Table 25-3 *Russian Federation: External Government Debt, 1994–8, in Billions of U.S. Dollars*

	1994	1995	1996	1997	1998
1. Debt (post-1/1/92)	11.3	17.4	27.7	35.6	55.4
Multilateral creditors	5.4	11.4	15.3	18.7	26.0
IMF	4.2	9.6	12.5	13.2	19.4
World Bank	0.6	1.5	2.6	5.3	6.4
Other official creditors[a]	5.9	6.0	12.4	16.9	29.4
2. Former Soviet debt (pre-1/1/92)	116.2	110.6	108.4	99.0	102.8
Official creditors[b]	69.6	62.6	61.9	56.9	59.5
Commercial creditors	36.0	38.3	37.8	33.9	35.2
All other	10.3	9.7	8.7	8.2	8.1
3. Total sovereign debt	127.5	128.0	136.1	134.6	158.2
In percent of GDP	45.8	36.8	31.6	30.2	48.1

Notes:

[a] Including government to government creditors and official export credits.

[b] Including Paris Club, COMECON, and other creditors.

Source: *Russian Federation: Recent Economic Developments*, IMF Country Report No. 99/100, Washington, DC, 1999, p. 122.

coming from there to Russia is Russia's own capital diverted through Cyprus to evade taxation.[6]

25-4. Credit and Public Debt

The external debt of the Russian government consists of the debts it contracted *after* January 1, 1992, and of the former Soviet debt contracted before the emergence of the Russian Federation, *before* January 1, 1992. Russia's medium- and long-term loans have been granted after January 1, 1992, mainly by the IMF and the World Bank. About 60 percent of the former Soviet debt is owned by official creditors, countries grouped in the "Paris and London Club of Creditors," while the debt to private creditors includes now 16 billion Eurobonds. Except for some arrears, the former Soviet debt and all of the Russian federation's debt is of medium- and long-term maturity. As can be seen in Table 25-3 Russia's total debt amounted in 1998 to $158.2 billion (48 percent of Russia's GDP), including the $102.8 billion debt from the Soviet era and $55.4 billion contracted by Russia after January 1, 1992, including also the liabilities toward other countries of the COMECON. In addition, according to official data, Russia's national debt is almost equal to its foreign debt (around $55 billion).

---

[6] Latgis, Otto, "Poverty Leaves Nowhere to Invest Money" (*Novye Izvestiia*, March 11, 2000), transl. in *Current Digest . . .*, Vol. 52, No. 11, April 12, 2000, p. 17.

Table 25-4 *Russian Federation: Foreign Currency Debt Service, 1994–8, in Billions of U.S. Dollars*

	1994	1995	1996	1997	1998
Debt service due	*18.78*	*19.15*	*17.94*	*11.76*	*13.01*
Principal	13.99	12.65	11.68	5.84	5.76
Interest	4.79	6.50	6.26	5.92	7.25
Debt service paid	3.66	6.40	6.92	5.89	7.77
Principal	2.27	3.32	2.86	1.68	3.49
Interest	1.39	3.08	4.06	4.21	4.28

Source: *Russian Federation: Recent Economic Developments*, IMF, *op. cit.*, p. 123.

Given the continued national financial imbalances and the country's deteriorating economic conditions – its damaged industrial base and decreasing overall production, the traffic of the new "oligarchs," and the fragmented, illiquid, and nontransparent stock market – the Russian government proved incapable of meeting its foreign debt obligations for either the principal repayments or the interest. As shown in Table 25-4, Russia's debt service paid constantly fell below the debt service due. In addition, the Russian "nonsovereign debt" – that is, the external obligations of local governments, banks, and non-bank corporations – amounted in late 1998 to $31.7 billion (9.6 percent of GDP). Put differently, the sovereign and nonsovereign debt amounted jointly to $189.9 billion ($158.2 billion plus $31.7 billion), equal to 57.7 percent of the Russian GDP. The August crises also affected adversely the ability of the "nonsovereign" debtors to meet their obligations. All in all, the creditworthiness of the country for additional credits is marginal.

Yet, Russia itself is also a creditor to a number of less developed countries. By December 1998, Russia's claims on the former socialist and other less developed countries amounted to $114 billion. An agreement finalized in September 1997 between Russia and the Paris Club creditors facilitated the regularization of the Russian claims, with discounts for the poorest countries.

25-5. Concluding Comments

In the Russian Federation, economic policy is, as a rule, contradictory, distorted, and ineffective due to complex underlying factors, particularly the often hidden interrelations among industry, finance, various concealed operations abroad, and, last but not least, the media and their connections to politics. These interconnections have profound roots, which Vladimir Putin wishes to change with the support of his former KGB colleagues and with the help of variously camouflaged alliances in the Duma. However, the roots of the Russian Federation's economy lie deeply implanted in the numerous legacies of Soviet industrialization and social change, and in the Gorbachev-Yeltsin shifts and readjustments involved in the transitions from Soviet to post-Soviet management and ownership. These inheritances, as we have seen, consist of a string of massive, largely obsolete industries that are still employing a large chunk of the workforce (in and around the far-off cities created in the era of industrialization), whose management has had to combine at its summit, particularly since the privatization of the mid-1990s, with some of the new "oligarchs" controlling certain of the country's valuable industrial and financial establishments. Efforts to render more transparent the industry interrelations, and the interindustry and the banking and financial relations, have remained unsuccessful. In some cases, the managers have successfully blocked the efforts to protect the shareholders' rights, to disentangle certain monopolies (for example, the electricity, crude oil, and natural gas monopolies), to implement real bankruptcy laws, and to eliminate all kinds of state subsidies. The politicians have been incapable of drawing sharp distinctions between public and private property or imposing budget constraints on the enterprises. The inability to rein in government spending, weak tax discipline, and a great devolution of revenue to regional governments have, as we shall see, continually nourished budget deficits. The government's position has deteriorated and the push toward borrowing domestically and internationally has increased but has not yielded the desired results.

Without a transparent and flexible banking system on the one hand, and without an open, attractive, expanding capital market on the other hand, Russia may find itself unable to cope properly with a financial crisis like that of August 1998. Furthermore, without changes in the business climate – affected by the prevalence of barter, the arbitrary tax and custom administration, the lack of effective enterprise management, and rampant crime and corruption – a similar crisis may arise again. The Duma is proving incapable of disciplining the government, and the civil society is still far too weak to assert proper checks on the widespread corruption and cronyism.

CHAPTER 26

State Finance

26-1. Size and Structure of the Budget

The General Government Budget of the Russian Federation includes the federal government budget and the subnational budgets – that is, the regional and local budgets – as well as the main social extra budgetary funds comprising the Pension Fund, the Employment Fund, the Social Insurance Fund, and the Federal Medical Insurance Fund. The federal and the subnational budgets are jointly designated as the *consolidated budget*. As can be seen in Table 26-1, between 1994 and 1998, at the core of the system, the federal revenues declined from 11.8 percent of the GDP in 1994, after various rises from 1995 to 1997, to only 10.7 percent by 1998. Outlays, moving on a higher level, contracted from 23.2 percent of the GDP in 1994 to 16.6 percent in 1998. All this left a federal deficit amounting to −5.9 percent of the GDP. I will examine further on in detail the multiple causes of the general decreasing trends. For now, let me note only that the critical reasons of the contractions have been, on the one hand, the continuous fall in profitability throughout the economy and, on the other hand, the manifest incapacity of the government to limit spending.

Consider now the structure of the budgetary system. The capital instrument of budget receipts, taxation, has been continually hampered by the excessive number of taxes and by the granting of numerous exemptions that have encouraged tax evasion. By 1998 a new tax code reduced to sixteen the number of federal taxes and charges (value-added tax, excises on individual type of goods and services, taxes on profit, taxes on revenues from capital, income tax, contributions to state social off-budget funds, state duty, customs duty and charges, taxes on the use of subsoil, taxes on mineral raw materials bases, taxes on revenues from extracting hydrocarbons, taxes on fauna and aquatic biological resources, and forest, water, ecology, and license charges). Further, the tax code relegated to regional taxes and charges the tax on property, immovables, road transport and sales, as well as the tax on gambling business and various regional licenses, and it left local taxes and charges on land, property,

375

Table 26-1 *Russian Federation General Government Operations, 1994–8, in Percentages of GDP*

	1994	1995	1996	1997	1998
Federal government					
Revenues	11.8	12.9	12.5	12.0	10.7
Outlays	23.2	18.6	20.9	19.0	16.6
Balance	–11.4	–5.7	–8.4	–7.0	–5.9
Subnational accounts					
Revenues	18.0	15.0	15.2	16.0	14.6
Outlays	17.5	15.4	15.6	17.5	15.8
Balance	0.5	–0.4	–0.4	–0.9	–1.2
Off-budget funds					
Revenues	9.0	8.0	8.1	9.7	8.4
Outlays	8.6	8.0	8.2	9.6	9.3
Balances	0.4	0.0	–0.1	0.1	–0.9
General government					
Revenues	38.8	35.9	35.8	38.3	33.7
Outlays	49.3	42.0	44.7	46.1	41.7
Balance	–10.5	–6.1	–8.9	–7.8	–8.0

Source: IMF, *Russian Federation: Recent Economic Developments*, IMF Country Report No. 99/100, Washington, DC, September 1999, p. 67.

advertising, inheritance, gifts, and various local charges. The principle of "tax responsibility" was to sit side by side with the criminal, civil, administrative, and other types of responsibility under the law, and the tax code referred to tax violations in a style reminiscent of the criminal code. Yet, while debates continue in the Duma, there are still too many taxes and exemptions, instability in rules and numerous "emergency collections," to combat effectively the adverse impact of the system on incentives and on tax compliance. Moreover, one should not overlook the relation within receipts, between cash and noncash revenues (tax offsets). Between 1994 and 1998, for instance, the tax offsets increased from 3.5 percent of the 1994 federal revenues, to 14.8 percent in 1995, 26.1 percent in 1996, and 18.9 percent in 1997, and decreased finally to 15.7 percent in 1998. The tax offsets arrangements and negotiated tax payments undermine the functioning of the tax system, hide the real extent of liabilities and collections, and overstate the total value added in the economy. While by the end of the 1990s some large enterprises improved tax compliance, only limited advances have been registered toward improving tax administration, strengthening overall tax compliance, and phasing out privileges. Federal tax arrears continue to remain significant, while Russia as a whole accumulates arrears, particularly in its Soviet-era debt.[1]

[1] See *Tax Code of the Russian Federation (Part One)*, transl. by Butler, W. E., London, Simmonds & Hill Publishing, 1999, Introduction, and pp. 12–13, 64.

With regard to outlays, the federal government is evidently unable to rein in excessive spending. Pressures to spend have come both from the Duma, inclined to adopt unrealistic budget dispositions, and from the government itself, where line ministers have resisted attempts by the Ministry of Finance to control their spending engagements. Compared to the government's resources and tax collections, the federal obligations have proven excessive, and so also its borrowings. The government's main expenditures have centered in 1998, for instance, on defense, law enforcement, and social policy (3.0, 1.6, and 1.4 percent of the GDP respectively), transfers to other levels of government (1.4 percent of GDP), and government debt service (4.4 percent of GDP). To finance the obvious needs of the deteriorated defense establishment, the government has issued an increasing volume of short-term government bonds. As for the complex federal-regional relations, the government has asserted its intentions to adopt an "improved formula" for allocating transfers to regions, making these transfers subject to greater conditionality, in particular on the nonaccumulation of arrears on wages, payroll taxes, and utility payments.[2]

With regard to the off-budget social funds, the government's concerns, particularly with the Pension Fund (PF), have been continuously heavy. To ensure the financial stability of the PF, the federal government has affirmed that it will avoid any indexing of general increases in benefits that could not be fully financed by PF revenues, including allocations from the federal budget. To increase the rate of payroll collections, the government decided to restructure tax arrears and provide incentives for early repayment. On the other hand, the government indicated that it was especially concerned by the fact that any "cuts in spending fall heavily on the poorest segments of the population, notably pensioners," and that henceforth proceeds of the sales of humanitarian assistance will be used to clear pensions arrears. Actually, as we will see further on, the PF is suffering a worsening financial situation, one due, among other causes, to a shrinking payroll tax base, a decline in payroll tax compliance, and insufficient transfers from the federal budget to cover the cost of social pensions.

The Russian government's usual approaches to spending, particularly its obvious incapacity to control any outlay since the time of Victor Chernomyrdin, its gerrymandering, and its continuous assertions that it is ready to cut any overspending have led a Russian journalist, Alexei Uliukaev, to draw the following sarcastic description of the real official procedures: "So something has to be done – excess spending has to be cut. How? Very simply – by paying out less money than promised, sitting on requests, making decisions and then shelving them, and not fulfilling commitments unless put under extreme

---

[2] IMF, *Russian Federation: Recent Economic Developments*, IMF Staff Country Report No. 99/100, IMF, Washington, DC, September 1999, pp. 64–5.

pressure. On the other hand, additional spending commitments are constantly being assumed, only to go unfulfilled later on."[3]

Various Russian writers have put forward serious proposals to address Russia's economic transition and its specific problems, including the budgetary ones. For instance, an interesting project, entitled *Strategy of Development of the Russian Federation up to the Year 2010*, has been issued in the year 2000 by a Moscow "Center of Strategic Elaboration." According to this project, what Russia needs first is the establishment of a legal basis of budgetary reform (tax reform, reduction of commitments, and limitations of plenary power) along with an inventory of the budgetary outlays, completion of the budget code, and acceleration of the passage to a Treasury system. Second, Russia must transform the system of social protection, increase the transparency of the budgetary system, ensure effective estimation of outlays, and maximize the utilization of off-budget funds. Third, Russia must move to a new structure of outlays characterized by the lowest share of subsidy economics and the highest share of social duties. Fourth and finally, Russia needs a new distribution of power (after lowering the debt burden on the federal budget) involving the lowering of the tax load.[4]

All this is certainly reasonable, yet incomplete; more is indeed tied into the complex budgetary context. As a World Bank progress report on *Assistance Strategy*, also of the year 2000, points out, Russia has made little progress in addressing the pervasive "nonpayment culture," fiscal and financial indiscipline, institutional weakness, and deterioration and corruption of the social safety net. As the report points out, "with very high debt levels and financial options narrowly constrained, all plausible development scenarios balance on a razor's edge."[5] Indeed, beyond the budgetary questions, deep problems remain to be addressed in every sector and branch of Russia's current socioeconomic framework.

26-2. Analysis of Receipts

Schematically, as can be seen in Table 26-2, the budget receipts rely at the federal level mainly on the value-added tax, profit taxes, and the taxes on trade. Since the early 1990s, Russian revenue collection at the federal level has been affected by a host of factors, including the severe decline of the profitability of enterprises and organizations throughout the economy, the top-level

---

[3] Uliukaev, Alexei, "Chernomyrdin the Monetarist, and Gaidar the Solid Economic Manager," *Sevodnia*, April 29, 1994, transl. in *Current Digest . . .*, Vol. XLVI, No. 17, 1994, p. 16.

[4] Tsentr Strategicheskikh Razrabotok (Center of Strategic Elaboration), *Strategiia Razvitiia Rossiiskoi Federatsii do 2010 goda* (The Strategy of Development of the Russian Federation until the Year 2010), draft, Moscow, 2000, p. 178.

[5] World Bank, Russian Federation. Country Assistance Strategy (CAS) Progress Report, Washington, DC, 2000, p. 7.

Table 26-2 *Russian Federation: Federal Budget Receipts, 1994–8, in Percentages[a]*

Source of budget receipt	1994	1995	1996	1997	1998
VAT	43.6	39.3	43.0	38.0	36.4
Excises	6.2	8.9	19.2	17.2	18.8
Profit taxes	23.7	20.7	13.0	10.7	12.1
Personal income taxes	0.0	1.7	1.9	0.5	0.0
Natural resources taxes	1.4	1.5	1.7	2.2	1.1
Taxes on trade	13.3	15.0	10.3	9.7	14.3
Other	11.8	12.9	10.9	21.7	17.3
TOTAL	100	100	100	100	100

Note:
[a] Underlying data in billions of rubles.
Sources: Based on IMF, *Russian Federation: Recent Economic Developments, op. cit.*, p. 68.

Table 26-3 *Russian Federation: Enterprises and Organizations with Net Operating Losses, Percentage of Total Establishments in the Economy and in the Given Branch*

Enterprise or organization	1992	1995	1996	1997	1998	1999	2000
Industry	7.2	26.4	43.5	46.9	48.8	39.1	38.7
Agriculture	14.7	55.0	76.5	78.1	84.4	52.7	54.1
Construction	7.6	17.7	33.4	36.6	40.6	37.7	36.0
Transport	20.7	31.5	54.0	54.0	53.4	47.9	45.8
Communications	11.0	28.9	35.0	29.4	44.3	28.4	23.2
Trade & public catering	16.0	30.8	45.9	43.4	45.3	32.7	29.5
Wholesale, technoproducts	10.0	22.0	39.1	42.8	47.0	38.7	36.4
Communal economy	33.5	42.6	53.8	50.7	60.1	61.4	64.3
TOTAL	15.3	34.2	50.6	50.1	53.2	40.6	41.6

Source: Rossüskü Statisticheskü ezhegodnik 1999, op. cit., p. 509; *Rossia v tsifrakh, 2001, Goskomstat Rossii*, Moscow, 2001, p. 295.

hesitations to implement comprehensive tax reforms, the inability to organize an effective tax administration and to achieve taxpayer compliance, the excessive scope of various informal fiscal relations, the overlapping institutional responsibilities for tax administration, and, last but not least, the obsolescence of a large number of accounting procedures (underlying, for instance, the critical tax on profits). Let me consider these issues in turn.

The spread of continually declining profitability throughout the economy up to 1998 is readily illustrated in Table 26-3. As shown in the table, the number of enterprises and organizations with operating losses continued to increase dramatically, particularly from 1995 to 1998. The situation changed in 1999 and 2000, but the operating losses remained severe in the economy as a whole. The state proved incapable of liquidating the large insolvent companies, a fact that according to certain sources notably encouraged commodity exporters to masquerade as bankrupt ones. In contrast to the indulgence toward the large enterprises, the fully private small companies and the foreign companies had to operate in a different, often hostile and costly, environment.

Between 1995 and 1998, as we saw in Table 26-1, the federal revenues in relative terms decreased from 12.9 percent of the GDP to 10.7 percent. A close look at the federal receipts shows that they involved cash and noncash revenues, that is, tax offsets revenues amounting respectively to 14.8 percent, 26.1 percent, 18.8 percent, and 15.6 percent of the total. Structural reforms of the fiscal system have so far been only partial. Limited advances have been made toward strengthening tax compliance, and typically, tax arrears have continued to remain significant. Before and after the collapse of August 1998, which was marked by a series of tax defaults by big corporations and banks, the government proved incapable of avoiding massive asset stripping involving transfer price manipulations, share dilution, juggling with debt offsets, and diversion of cash flow and assets to various related companies.

On another plane, to limit the widespread rise of tax offsets and ad hoc negotiated tax payments, the Russian government indicated in 1999 that it would remove from the budget code the articles permitting offsets and that it would also henceforth cease to proclaim tax amnesties. To generate immediate revenues the federal organs introduced at the end of 1998, the government levied temporary export taxes on oil, petrochemicals, timber, ferrous and nonferrous metals, and other products. To enhance the authority of the tax administration, the government authorized the administration to use liens on the delinquent tax payers' bank accounts.

A major obstacle to improving the activities of the Russian State Tax Service (STS), which numbered in 1997 about 180,000 persons, has been – as pointed out by the director of the Fiscal Affairs Department of the IMF, Vito Tanzi – the overlapping of institutional responsibilities for tax administration. Thus, to solve certain high-profile individual tax cases, Russia has been resorting to the establishment of special commissions outside the STS. These commissions are made up of officials of the highest levels of government, including the prime minister. Large taxpayers routinely negotiate their tax payments independent of the statutory liability and of the investigative functions of the STS. Resorting to high-level special commissions contrasts with the procedures of tax administrations in market economies, where tax administration is highly autonomous. The complicated Russian tax procedures defuse accountability in the public sector for collection enforcement and reinforce the view that taxes are not rigid obligations but commitments subject to negotiations. Compounding these problems are the widespread activities of criminal groups; many sources indicate indeed that the extortion of "protection payments" that crime groups often require and acquire from medium-sized and small businesses undermine these business's tax obligations and render the work of tax administrators more difficult and dangerous.[6]

The modernization of Russia's tax administration requires the discarding of well-entrenched practices and the use of considerable financial resources, two giant obstacles hard to overcome. The erosion of federal revenues, especially of cash payments, the excessive reliance on external borrowing, the hesitation or incapacity to enforce payments of statutory tax liabilities, and the government's own inability to pay its own bills on time weigh heavily on the tax administration. In fact, the prevailing system, as Anders Aslund has pointed out, continues in many respects a disastrous combination of certain practices of the old Soviet tax system, including hasty partial reforms, dubious changes motivated by rent-seeking, and inconsistent and often questionable distributions of the tax burden.[7]

26-3. Analysis of Outlays

As I indicated in Section 26-1, the Russian Federation's main outlays concern defense, law enforcement, social policy, intergovernment transfers, and interest payments. As you can see in Table 26-4, in the budgetary outlays of 1998, defense absorbed 12.7 percent of the total spending, followed by law enforcement (10.5 percent), intergovernment transfers (10.1 percent), social policy (8.1 percent), and above all the enormous interest obligations (27.4 percent). In relation to the federal outlays of 1994, the budget shares in the federal outlays of 1998 declined for defense (from 19.7 to 12.7 percent), subsidies to the economic sector (from 12.8 to 3.5 percent), and for intergovernment transfers (from 17.7 to 10.1 percent). On the other hand, they increased notably for law enforcement (from 7.6 percent to 10.5 percent), social policy (from 0.7 to 8.1 percent), and interest payments (from 8.4 to 27.4 percent). By 1998, limits were set on ministerial expenditures, and each ministry had to submit a plan to achieve the set limits. To strengthen the ministry's control over spending units, the Treasury was expected to cover all non-defense ministries' spending. As can be seen in Table 26-4, first of all the share of defense shrank appreciably. The decrease does not reflect the fact that the army needs far less spending; actually, the situation of the military has continued to deteriorate since the early 1990s. Most soldiers and officers receive poor pay and with considerable delays; the number of suicides has increased among the soldiers, while the officers have taken extra jobs to nourish their families. The military equipment has enormously deteriorated, and even the nuclear facilities are not properly

---

[6] Tanzi, Vito, "Creating Effective Tax Administrations: The Experience of Russia and Georgia," paper presented at the Focus Group Meeting at the Collegium Budapest, Institute for International Study, March 27–8, 1998.

[7] Aslund, Anders, "Why Has Russia's Economic Transformation Been So Arduous?" paper for the World Bank Conference on Development Economics, draft, March 14, 1999, p. 14.

Table 26-4 *Russian Federation: Federal Budget Outlays, 1994–8,*
in Percentages[a]

Sector	1994	1995	1996	1997	1998
Government	10.2	1.6	1.2	2.0	2.2
Defense	19.7	16.6	14.3	16.3	12.7
Law enforcement	7.6	6.7	6.4	8.9	10.5
Education	3.9	3.0	2.5	2.9	4.0
Health	1.6	2.1	1.8	3.2	2.7
Social policy	0.7	1.3	2.2	4.6	8.1
Economic	12.8	11.3	7.9	8.7	3.5
Intergovernment	17.7	10.2	11.4	10.2	10.1
Interest payments	8.4	19.0	28.3	24.1	27.4
Other	17.4	28.2	24.0	19.1	18.8
TOTAL	100	100	100	100	100

Note:
[a] Underlying data in billions of rubles.
Source: Based on *Russian Federation: Recent Economic Developments, op. cit.*, p. 68.

maintained, a serious potential danger not only for Russia, but for the globe as a whole.

The social outlays are disbursed via the four extrabudgetary funds (pensions, employment, social insurance, and medical insurance), which are scheduled to extend help to the most exposed segments of the Russian population. In the Soviet and the post-Soviet systems, pensions have been viewed primarily as an earned transfer accumulated by the workers through their years of service. That delayed remuneration for services rendered, however, has become an increasingly difficult burden for the Russian government to bear. Russia's aging population counted as of 1998 30.5 million people (close to 21 percent of the total population) past pension age (sixty for men, fifty-five for women). About this total number of citizens were registered to receive state pensions for old age. However, great difficulties are associated with the distribution of pensions; many of the elderly are concentrated notably in the rural areas, where the service provisions are relatively low in comparison with the urban areas, and in some regions, pensioners represent as many as 80 percent of those in poverty. The worsening financial situation because of, among other factors, the decreasing payroll tax base (as employers have been moving toward nonwage forms of payment) have limited the Pension Fund's ability to borrow from the banking system and have taken the form of pension arrears.

The other important social extrabudgetary funds have benefit systems that are poorly targeted and unable to provide the support they are supposed to give. The Employment Fund (funded by a 1.5 percent payroll tax) is unable to organize an effective social safety net for the unemployed workers. Only about one-quarter of the unemployed actually receive modest benefits, which are highly differentiated across regions. The Social Insurance Fund (funded by a 5.4 percent payroll tax) – which is set to provide allowances for birth, maternity, sickness, as well as for various indigent people – is in fact not targeted to needy groups, and amounts to little more than a nonwage benefit for workers. Finally, the Medical Insurance Fund is affected not only by the fact that some employers, and the subnational governments avoid making their required contributions to the system, but also by the general health crisis, in which the morbidity of working-age people has been increasing significantly. In short, the resources channeled into the health care system do not approach the level needed to provide the health care promised by the Russian constitution to all of Russia's citizens.[8]

26-4. Subnational Accounts

Schematically, as can be seen in Table 26-5, in the subnational accounts the main budgetary receipts include, besides federal transfers, the profit taxes, personal income taxes, value-added tax (VAT), and property taxes. On the side of outlays, the principal spending is on education, health, housing, and, to a lesser extent, social security.

Fiscal trends in the regions have been less favorable than at the federal level. Most regional authorities have been confronted by very tight constraints on borrowing, leading to a decline in the regional budgetary expenditures. As we saw in Table 26-1 in the consolidated subnational accounts, revenues fell from 18.0 percent of the GDP in 1994 to 14.6 percent in 1998, while outlays shrank from 17.5 percent of the GDP to 15.8 percent, yielding a growing deficit.

Continuous contradictions exist between the theoretically highly centralized fiscal federalist system, and the actual large degree of financial authority exercised at the subfederal level through all kinds of informal arrangements. The majority of the regional fiscal organs have a formal federal subordination, but they depend for part of their financing on the regional and local administrations. The informal dual subordination results in many confusing and confronting interbudgetary relations. The new budgetary code has aimed to establish some basic order in the division of spending responsibilities between the federal and the subfederal budgets, but many issues have been left in the dark. In principle, the regional and the local governments possess limited fiscal authority; a large share of their obligations derive from federal laws

---

[8] See the valuable collection of essays in *Russia's Torn Safety Net*, Field, Mark, G., and Twigg, Judith, L., eds., New York, St. Martin's Press, 2000, pp. 25, 46–7, 56–7, 251, 257, 260, 272; see also IMF, *Russian Federation: Recent Economic Development, op. cit.*, pp. 64–6; Vasiliev, Sergei, *Ten Years of Russian Economic Reforms*, St. Edmunds, Suffolk, St. Edmundsbury Press, 1999, p. 108; Russian Ministry of Finance, "Statement of the Government of the Russian Federation and Central Bank of Russia on Economic Policy," draft, January 3, 2000, *op. cit.*, p. 5.

Table 26-5 *Russian Federation: Subnational Accounts, 1994–8, Receipts and Expenditures in Percentages*[a]

	1994	1995	1996	1997	1998
Receipts	100	100	100	100	100
VAT	10.5	12.2	12.2	12.7	13.2
Excises	2.7	2.8	2.5	2.9	0.0
Profit taxes	28.8	32.7	19.6	16.1	15.7
Personal income taxes	15.8	14.3	15.7	17.1	18.1
Natural resources taxes	1.8	4.0	5.1	6.6	4.8
Property taxes	4.3	6.9	11.2	10.9	11.8
Federal transfers	22.8	11.6	18.4	18.3	12.1
Other	13.3	15.5	15.3	15.4	24.3
Outlays	100	100	100	100	100
Education	20.6	20.2	21.6	20.9	19.8
Health	16.3	15.8	15.7	14.8	14.0
Housing & municipal	31.7	25.9	26.7	23.8	22.5
Social security	6.1	7.1	8.0	7.2	6.6
Other	25.3	31.0	28.0	33.3	37.1

Note:
[a] Underlying data in billions of rubles.
Source: Based on *Russian Federation: Recent Economic Developments, op. cit.*, p. 69.

and regulations. But the federal legislation and regulations do not indicate clearly which level of government bears responsibility for certain actions, with all kinds of unexpected results. For instance, certain outlays are carried out at the subnational level, even though formally these outlays are supposed to be a federal responsibility.

With regard to budgetary fulfillment, the subfederal levels of government are in many respects in a difficult situation. As a consequence of this, the regional and local officials operate in various ways around the formal fiscal federalist relations. A crucial means of making ends meet is to underfulfill the spending obligations. In addition, the subnational authorities may resort to all kinds of pressures on the regional and local firms and organizations in their jurisdiction for whom various means for achieving and maintaining good relations with these authorities are a prerequisite for successful business. For instance, as Daniel Treisman noted in an article on "Russia's Taxing Problem," "in many regions a few large enterprises predominate, and governors can look the other way when profits are kept off the books – in return for a 'contribution' to off-budget funds for local development or to the governor's personal retirement fund."[9]

[9] Treisman, Daniel, "Russia's Taxing Problem," *Foreign Policy*, October 1, 1998.

Money surrogates are also a crucial means for manipulating regional and local budgetary accounts involving preexisting debts as well as settlements of current transactions, and also offsets of tax debts against government payments. No less important as tools of independent fiscal policies are the extrabudgetary funds (for pensions, employment, social insurance, and medical insurance). The regions plan the allocation of these funds and may therefore have more liberty in their spending than is true for the explicit budget. Given the entire system of intrabudgetary relations, the subnational authorities pursue, whenever possible, the accumulation of debts and guarantees. Often, the nagging shortages in budgetary receipts push them to borrow even beyond the budgetary requirements, in order to finance, for instance, wages and subsidies. The continuous attempts of the federal government to cut off much of the fiscal decentralization and to subject the receipts and outlays of the subnational authorities to rigid federal regulations obviously have not reached their target. In many respects, fiscal federalist relations remain in disarray.

26-5. Concluding Comments

One of the greatest challenges of post-Soviet Russia has been the restructuring of the economy and the achievement of a sustained revival. It has long since become obvious that what was needed for a sustained revival was a massive infusion of investment, not only by and through government channels, but also through the decisive mobilization of the firms' capacity both to direct their resources and also attract the needed foreign capital. Conscious of this situation, the government decided in 1997 to create a so-called Development Budget, officially part of the state budget, but with a particular status and specific sources of finance, similar to an extrabudgetary fund. The Development Budget was scheduled to be financed partly through borrowing from the World Bank and the European Bank of Reconstruction and Development. A plan was then established to increase as follows the level of investment until the year 2000 (see Table 26-6). Actually, according to the official data, capital investment continued to decline through 1998. This decline had in fact never stopped since the beginning of the 1990s. Total investments evolved indeed as follows, on the basis 1995 = 100 (all at 1997 prices): From 325.8 in 1990, it declined to 276.9 in 1991, 166.1 in 1992, 146.2 in 1993, 111.4 in 1994, 100 in 1995, 81.9 in 1996, 77.8 in 1997, and 72.8 in 1998.[10] In 1997 and 1998, the structure of capital investment clearly indicated the declining role of the state (see Table 26-7).

Several factors create in the Russian economy powerful disincentives to invest. The crucial factors continue to be the tax system and the complex fiscal relations that have emerged among the various levels of government. Further,

---

[10] *Obzor ekonomicheskoi politiki v Rossii za 1998 god* (Survey of the Economic Policy in Russia for 1998), Moscow, Rosspen, 1999, p. 591.

Table 26-6 *Russian Federation: Planned Sources of Investment, 1997–2000,*
in Percentages[a]

	1997	1998	1999	2000
I. Development Budget	4.4	7.8	7.9	8.2
Related foreign credits	2.4	3.2	2.5	2.3
II. Capital investment financed by the federal budget (other than the Development Fund)	9.0	8.6	8.2	7.5
III. Capital investment financed by the regional budgets	9.0	9.3	9.6	9.8
IV. Private funds	77.6	74.3	74.3	74.5
TOTAL	100	100	100	100

Note:
[a] Underlying data in trillions of rubles; prices of 1997.
Source: Based on *OECD Economic Surveys 1997–1998, Russian Federation*, Paris, OECD, 1998, p. 129.

Table 26-7 *Russian Federation: Structure of*
Capital Investments, 1997 and 1998,
in Percentages

	1997	1998
Firms' own means	60.8	53.6
Attracted sources	39.2	46.4
Budgetary means	20.7	19.2
Federal budget	10.2	6.6
Subnational budgets	10.5	12.6
TOTAL	100	100

Source: Rossiiskii statisticheskii ezhegodnik 1999, op. cit.,
p. 533.

the chronic receipts shortcomings have led to the proliferation of taxes and duties and to incessant changes in rates and assessments. Moreover, the continuous dominance of insiders in most of the firms has impeded restructuring and the development of capital markets. The ability of the majority of enterprises to raise outside capital has been severely limited. Only the big firms in fuels, energy, metals, chemicals, and food processing have been able to raise outside capital channeled to them through a handful of Moscow-based financial-industrial groups.[11] Yet, after ten years of stalling with the creditors, Russia has been paying up, from the ample oil revenues, interests and payments for 2001 and 2002.

[11] See the discussion of these issues in OECD, *Economic Surveys 1997–1998, Russian Federation, op. cit.*, pp. 123–9, and OECD, *Economic Surveys 1999–2000, Russian Federation*, Paris, OECD, 2000, pp. 62–3.

CHAPTER 27

Overall View

27-1. Transition and the Agricultural Economy

Consider now the similarities and the differences among the three transitions toward modernization in general, the structural transformations they called forth, the changes they set in motion within the different frameworks in which they arose, and the conceptions advanced during their unfolding by the reformers who proposed the measures. In the pursuit of the same goal, namely "catching up" with the continually developing countries of Western Europe, the three Russian transitions toward modernity called forth many valid proposals and set in motion methods of changes; yet all ultimately yielded only limited results. Poor and underdeveloped Tsarist Russia aimed quite decisively from the 1890s on to surmount its backwardness, notably by supporting the expansion of some of Russia's industries oriented toward export, and forcefully developing Russia's railway network with substantial help from foreign capital. Yet, the succeeding Soviet Russia still inherited a backward, war-ravaged economy that in its turn tried to develop by emphasizing from 1928 on the rapid growth of heavy industry (oriented primarily toward military production), deliberately neglecting the civilian needs, and rejecting the import of foreign capital. After all this, however, Soviet Russia also failed to "catch up" and, as its leaders had pretentiously sought, to "surpass" the West. Finally, the patrimonial state of Boris Yeltsin and then of Vladimir Putin inherited the largely obsolescent Soviet industry within the limits of a former empire shattered in all its structural components. This state also turned out to be incapable of surmounting the country's widespread backwardness and establishing the necessary reliable framework for broadly expanding market relations. In short, notwithstanding the vast, complex, protracted Russian efforts set forth during the three transitions, the target of reaching the Western levels and pace of development has turned out to be still largely unreachable.

Reconsider now, in broad outline, the transition processes in each of the economy's main sectors, starting with agriculture. Recall that since way back

387

to the time of Ivan III (the Great), in the fifteenth century or earlier, arrangements were made for regulating the relationships of the landlord and the peasant through communal setups. The peasant cultivator was organized in a collective unit known as the *commune* (*mir* or *obschina*) set to regulate any needed relations between him and the landlord. The landlord established the communes on each hereditary estate and on each state-granted land, since he was interested in preventing the peasant from moving elsewhere. Thus the peasant became bound in perpetuity to the soil and to the master he served. After the liberation of the serfs in 1861, liberty for the emancipated peasant was only half liberty: He was still bound to the commune and unable to leave his locality and to look for permanent employment elsewhere. Peter Stolypin tried without success after the 1905 revolution to break with the tradition and dissolve the commune in a system of peasant ownership. Between 1906 and 1910, the collective responsibility of the commune for its peasants was in part canceled, but the commune still ruled the life of the majority of the peasants until 1917.

After the 1917 Communist power seizure, during the unstable War Communism and the NEP economic recovery, the peasantry enjoyed limited liberty until 1928, when the Soviet regime engaged itself forcefully in rapid industrialization and the forced collectivization of the peasantry. Only 1.7 percent of the peasantry was organized in collective farms in the early 1920s. Stalin's brutal and overwhelming effort toward complete peasant collectivization began in 1928, and by 1931 the effort involved 52.7 percent of the peasantry, by 1937 93 percent, and by 1940 96.9 percent. After World War II, the peasantry was encased into 36,900 collectives; subsequently the number of collectives declined and landholdings expanded, totaling 27,000 in 1987.

The special organization of the peasantry into collectives managed and controlled by state appointees and by the state's administrations aimed to ensure the carrying out of the state's commands on patterns of cultivation and on levels of output. In essence, the collective farms revived the old type of communes, with the peasantry tied to the state-owned land, devoid of the freedom to quit the collective, and compelled to execute steadfastly the orders of the new landlord, the state. As in the communes, all questions concerning the collectives were handled directly by their managers and the state. As Lenin once put it (in 1899), no particular form of land ownership can be "fundamentally an insurmountable obstacle to capitalism." Indeed, while the regime theoretically aimed to transform the entire peasantry into "proletarians" working in agricultural enterprises, and while it thus established state farms, until the end of the regime the mass of the peasantry actually continued to be confined in the traditional, largely backward framework.

After the collapse of the Soviet Union, efforts to change land tenure fundamentally and to reform large-scale management and organization along with legal ownership clashed with the attempts of the Communist organizations, farm managers, and a large share of the rural population itself that wanted to preserve the old system. By the end of 1997, in the majority of large-scale farms, collective or state reorganizations did not proceed beyond reregistration under a new legal form. Regardless of the variety of such forms, the majority of the farms were converted into production cooperatives in which fixed assets belonged to the collectives under share-based ownership (the shareholders are employees, pensioners, and social workers). Only about 10 percent of large farms underwent more substantial restructuring that broke them up into smaller production units. As a result of this privatization and reorganization process, by November 1997, 62 percent of the agricultural land in Russia was officially considered as privately owned, while the remaining 38 percent was still owned by the municipalities and the state. The majority of the "privately owned" land was in fact under collectively shared ownership, while the rest of the privately owned land was owned by individual farms (5.7 percent of the land) and by household plots (3.0 percent of the total agricultural land). The majority of the large-scale enterprises converted into production cooperatives are *sui generis* versions of the old commune, upon which the peasants depend in the difficult conditions now prevailing in the countryside for employment, social services, state subsidies, and a safety net determined by the capacity of the managers to pull the appropriate strings. In 1997 there were 27,000 collective producers, of which 82 percent were unprofitable collective enterprises, sharing 80 percent of the land in use but accounting for only 49.9 percent of the agricultural production.[1] The government under Putin has been considering the formulation of a complex land program that would ensure agricultural economic recovery and would surmount the conflicting problems of land ownership and government subsidies. But opinions continue to be divided on these issues. Some administrators favor recognizing the real legal equality of all forms of land ownership, the partial sale of certain farmland, and the principle that farmland in general be excluded from free market trade. Others hope that the regime will in all cases accept the principle of free market trade. Others still hope that the adoption of the principle of free market in land will exclude the black earth land, which should instead become federal property. Even the leader of the Yabloko liberal party, Grigori Yavlinski, has proposed that land reform should be carried out gradually, that a set length of time should elapse before a piece of land can be sold, and finally, that no land should be sold to foreigners.

A program for agriculture for the period 1996–2000 aimed to increase Russia's food self-sufficiency and to reduce its dependence on food imports. But in the meantime, Russian agriculture has continued to register sharp declines in output, which fell on the basis 1990 = 100 from 66.9 in 1995 to 63.5 in 1996, 64.7 in 1997, and 56.6 in 1998. During the same period, the production of the agricultural enterprises declined even more sharply. The policy makers

---

[1] OECD, *Review of Agricultural Policies Russian Federation, op. cit.*, pp. 15–17; Amelina, Maria, "The (Not So) Mysterious Resilience of Russia's Agricultural Collectives," *Transition*, Vol. 10, No. 6, December 1999, pp. 19–21.

have been increasingly preoccupied with the rising volume of high-priced processed foods. In the 1990s, agricultural and food trade fluctuated around 25 percent of Russia's imports and accounted for only 3 to 4 percent of Russia's exports. Since the start of the transition, these continuous imbalances have led certain analysts – such as those of the OECD who issued in 1998 the study entitled *Review of Agricultural Policies Russian Federation* – to suggest that "comparative advantage" would dictate that for a time at least Russia should be a net importer of food and agricultural products. These analysts claim that this "should not be cause for concern" nor lead to attempts to restrict imports since such policies would only reduce overall economic efficiency. The writers of the *Review* knew certainly, however, that the Russian government is under constant pressure from producers' interests groups to increase border protection against agricultural and food imports. Of course, such trade restrictions, including tariff barriers, rarely yield the expected results, and rather encourage corruption and rent-seeking behavior.

Let us now turn to the patterns of transition in the secondary sector.

27-2. Transition and the Industrial Economy

During the three transitions, the crucial industrial sector experienced notable transformations to its structure, types of output, phases of growth, levels of technological change, and role in the economy and in the society. On the eve of the first transition, Russia had only 9,500 industrial enterprises with 505,000 workers. Fifty years later, on the eve of the First World War, the Empire counted some 27,000 industrial enterprises with 2.3 to 3 million workers – a level still far below those reached by the Western European countries and by the United States. The biggest development during that transition occurred in the 1890s, during Sergei Witte's tenure as minister of finance (1893–1903). The earlier beginnings of the construction of the Trans-Siberian Railroad (1891) and then its completion, and the construction of the railway interconnections between the centers of European Russia, stimulated the growth of various industries supplying the railroads, fulfilled the pressing needs of expansions of certain exports, and gave impetus to the development of mining, metallurgy, and fuels.

During the second transition, the Communists opened important avenues to differentiation in industry. From the beginning, they viewed the inherited Tsarist industrial base as far too narrow for reaching their key goal of catching up with and of surpassing Western capitalism. From 1928 on, Stalin imposed on the USSR the target of rapid industrialization. Developing and relying upon a far larger industrial labor force than the United States (in 1986, Russia employed 38.2 million persons in industry compared to 18.8 million in the United States) but using backward technology, the USSR achieved industrial output that accounted for only one-fourth of that produced by the United States. Russia's continuous lag in technology hurt its productivity and the quality of its products and kept Soviet commercial goods from gaining an edge in the Western market. The vast Soviet industry remained far behind that of the West. Mikhail Gorbachev hoped in the mid-1980s to revamp the entire Soviet industrial production through the massive introduction of new machines and techniques, but for a variety of reasons, his regime registered little progress. Incentives to promote quality and technological change remained indeed weak and engendered opposition to discarding a large part of the industry's aged equipment, much of which predated World War II. Although most of the Soviet Union's major heavy industrial plants had been located in the Russian Republic (RSFSR), the other Soviet republics had also been centers of diverse industries and mines. By the time of the collapse of the USSR, the Russian Republic accounted for an important part of the products of the machine building and chemical industries, as well as for dominant shares in the output of crude oil, natural gas, and electricity.

From its beginnings, the third transition exhibited sharp declines in the investments in fixed capitals, in the industrial outputs, and in production in all the other sectors – agriculture, construction, trade, transport, communications, and services. The changes in industry were due to the interplay of a number of factors, including first the nature of the Soviet industrial heritage, the structure and quality of the equipment, the industrial methods of management and production, and the impact on all these factors of the political decisions of the new regime. From the moment of its accession to power, the government of the Russian Federation had to reduce sharply the old emphases on heavy industry and military goods and largely leave the rest of industry to find its own ways to the market. The results throughout the 1990s were disastrous. On the basis 1990 = 100, the declines of the industrial outputs of the Russian Federation as a whole ranged from 92 percent in 1991 to 50 percent in 1995, 46 percent in 1998, and then again to 50 percent by 1999. Declines were heavy in all the countries' regions, ranging by 1998, to between 32 to 35 percent of the 1990 level in the North Caucasus, North Western, and the Central regions, to between 40 and 48 percent in the Far Eastern, Ural, Volga-Viatka, and Eastern Siberia regions, and between 50 and 59 percent in the Central Black Earth, Lower Volga, and Northern regions.[2]

During the early years of the transition, the massive privatization of 1992–4 transferred many enterprises to their managers and workers. But the economy as a whole could not find its proper equilibrium in the absence of the legal and institutional framework needed to support the normal development of a market economy. As an IMF study pointed out, the key changes necessary to restructure the economy and improve efficiency had been hampered by the weak role of the enterprises' shareholders and by the big role of the enterprise managers, who focused their efforts on maintaining their control

---

[2] *Rossiiskii statisticheskii ezhegodnik 1999, op. cit.*, pp. 300–1.

and on maximizing their personal gain rather than on restructuring the enterprises and maximizing the shareholders' benefits. The managers continued to hold majority ownership in around 60 percent of the large and medium-sized enterprises; moreover, even where the enterprise managers were not enjoying formal majority ownership, they were able to keep effective control in their hands.[3]

A continuing challenge in restructuring the ailing basis inherited from the Soviet era is to overcome its traditional inefficiency, poor management habits, and wasteful use of labor and material resources. Restructuring on a mass scale is impeded because it would conflict with the interests of influential groups that in fact prosper from the inefficiency of private enterprise. These groups include top managers and owners, regional authorities, bank leaders, and trade unions. A directly related issue is that of bankruptcy legislation, which theoretically aims to increase the role of creditor committees against insolvent enterprises, and to ensure quicker appointment of proper trustees authorized to replace the deficiencies of the failed management with proper observance of time limits for debt liquidation procedures. In the widely corrupt Russian situation, the bankruptcy system (based on the bankruptcy law of March 1998 and then on a decree of January 1999) is setting debt limits as low as $5,000, sufficient to topple a company if it leaves its bills unpaid for three months. This system has become a takeover tool that powerful and unscrupulous competitors, supported by corrupted local authorities, use to take over healthy companies. According to an interesting article by Sabrina Tavernise (published on October 7, 2000, in the *New York Times*), the management of an important active Russian enterprise, the Novokuznetsk Aluminum Plant (which produces yearly 10 percent of Russian aluminum output), was toppled by the local governor of Novokuznetsk in conjunction with the leadership of a competing firm. The law indeed allows healthy companies to fall into bankruptcy just as often as sick ones, because the amount of debt required to start their liquidation is small. The aluminum plant was put into receivership with its debts frozen and its cash flow in the hands of a certain Sergei Chernyshiov, who, as soon as he became receiver, challenged the very debt that had driven the aluminum plant into bankruptcy. A court let him reevaluate the debt to less than 2 percent of what all the creditors had expected to collect. After that, a former competitor consolidated in his hands control over the enterprise and directed its exports through companies affiliated with the Russian Aluminum Company, which controls 70 percent of the country's aluminum. Thus, certain creditors know how to use the bankruptcy law to grab a competing company.

In sum, restructuring on a massive scale has so far proven impossible because its aims and procedures collide inevitably with the interests of interrelated influential groups – enterprises owners, top managers, regional

[3] IMF, *Russian Federation: Recent Economic Developments, op. cit.*, pp. 126–9.

authorities, banks, and trade unions – that in fact prosper from inefficiency and corruption. Moreover, many companies resort to tax manipulations and the avoidance of legal registration, while others fall prey to the pernicious use of certain laws. As has often been noted, many Russian "inside owners" see their position more in terms of power, and are only secondarily interested in structural changes, efficiency, competitiveness, and growth. On the other hand, government-controlled companies or groups of companies as well as unofficially driven financial-industrial groups have become significant factors in reshaping the industrial economy in various ways. The top seventy-five officially registered financial-industrial groups, for instance, produced in 1998 about 10 percent of the Russian GDP and employed five million people, or 35 percent of the industrial workforce. In addition, huge industrial-financial alliances emerged from the institution of unofficial associations, including industrial trading, investment banking, and insurance companies focused on financing their group and on working out appropriate investment projects. Yet, such arrangements have not been able to avoid the fact that the Russian Federation continues to function essentially as a dual economy, particularly with regard to its industry: On the one hand, it is endowed with a dynamic industrial mining and partial export sector – including particularly oil, gas, raw materials, and certain finished products (the latter directed mainly toward the former Soviet republics) – and, on the other hand, it still relies for its domestic needs on a vast, inefficiently restructured industry, competitive only in the home markets.[4]

Let us consider now the various changes in the ensemble tertiary sector.

27-3. Transition and the Tertiary Sector

During Russia's socioeconomic transitions, the transformations in its tertiary sector involved increases and diversifications in its domestic and foreign trade, movements of domestic and foreign capital, development of banking, formation of a pattern of investment, growth of public debt, intricacies of public finance, and, in broader terms, direct impact of various state actions. Notable differences arose between the three transitions with regard to the determinant factors that were called into play in each one of them. In the first transition, domestic and foreign resources were mobilized for the development of railroads and certain exports. In the second, most of the country's resources were concentrated in the hands of the state in order to emphasize heavy industry and the military, while neglecting the rest of the economy's patterns of development. In the third, finally, the country's presidents and their governments deployed numerous attempts to surmount at least some of the deleterious effects of the

[4] Sutela, Peka, "Russia: Rise of a Dual Economy," *Transition*, Vol. 10, No. 5, October 1999, pp. 20–1; Polonsky, Genady, and Aivazian, Zaven, "Restructuring Russian Industry: Can It Really Be Done?" *Post-Communist Economics*, Vol. 12, No. 2, 2000, pp. 229–39.

inherited Soviet deficiencies, by opening various ways to the market and by mending the consequences of certain of their own erroneous "strategies" of change. They failed, however, in their basic targets of restructuring the economy and achieving a sustained revival, proving incapable of decisively mobilizing the country's resources and mastering an appropriate influx of foreign capital.

During the first transition, the Tsarist government did not display any particular interest in domestic trade, focusing its primary attention on the growth of foreign exports (which by 1914 reached eight times their 1860 level) in order to pay for both imports and services (for which it was highly indebted to foreign creditors). Russia's state and private credit institutions grew and diversified from the 1860s until the early 1900s, and the Ministry of Finance played through the State Bank (Gosbank) a non-negligible role in the provision of credits for various industrial developments, But the more decisive role in this regard was discharged by the influx of foreign capital from many sources, accounting by 1916–17 for over 35 percent of the total, for 60 percent in mining, metallurgy, machinery, and metal working, and for over 80 percent in certain municipal and public services. The Russian government's contribution to the interconnecting of the country's developing centers through the expansion of the railroad network provided crucial help in these developments.

During the second transition, the main instrument for the forced mobilization of the country's investable resources was the division of the economy into two spheres: a crucial noncash transactions system involving the production and distribution interrelations, and a cash transaction system enclosing the relations of the state system with the households as well as the interhouseholds transactions. The state's share in the country's retail trade fluctuated around 75 percent of the total, that of non-state sources around 25 percent. As for the foreign trade, the share directed toward the so-called socialist countries amounted in 1950 to 78 percent and by 1989 to 62 percent; conversely, the share toward the capitalist and developing countries increased during that period from 22 to 28 percent. Until 1988 the State Bank serviced all the currency, credit, and payment needs of the economy, active as the fiscal agency of the government and as an all-encompassing center for settling and clearing transactions of all associations and organizations.

After the collapse of the Soviet Union, the new Russian Federation was forced to cope with the needs of reducing inflation, reorganizing money and credit as well as all banking institutions operations and trade, and negotiating Russia's relations with its foreign creditors both before and after the existence of the USSR. In the crucial process of reorganization of banking, the new government decided to rely on the barely transformed core of the Soviet system, and only partially on the emerging small or medium-size commercial banks and on the not always cooperative groups of financial-industrial organizations. For the domestic and foreign trade, appreciable shifts were in process for both structure and goods traded.

During the third transition, the state's share in the domestic trade fell from 67 percent in 1991 to as low as 7 percent by 1998. Correspondingly, the share of the private and mixed forms of ownership increased from 33 percent to 93 percent. In foreign trade, the progress made by the Russian Federation was rather modest: Between 1992 and 1998, total exports increased from $53.6 billion to $74.1 billion, imports from $42.9 billion to $58.9 billion. A crucial share in exports has been accounted for by oil and oil products; Russia has been exporting yearly between 46 to 53 percent of their output, increasingly to the capitalist countries.

The interest of foreign capital in investment in Russia has remained, however, limited given the numerous barriers that it has confronted there. Various changes are now under consideration, concerning in particular the legal framework of such activities, but much remains to be done to attract foreign capital at the levels needed to restructure the country's deteriorated production base. In 1998, the inflow of foreign capital reached only $3.5 billion, but Russia's debts to the IMF and the World Bank's assistance support are already far more significant. On the other hand, paradoxically, Russia's investments abroad exceeded the total that entered Russia in the late 1990s, an excess even larger than the one officially reported, if one takes into account the illegal movements of Russian capital. Without an open, attractive, expanding capital market, Russia might find itself unable to cope properly with its unstable, nagging financial problems.

A further important issue to solve is the restructuring of the taxation system, of its unpredictable and unstable rates, and of its damaging effects on incentives and tax compliance. Equally still insoluble are the questions concerning the structure and volume of government outlays and the appropriate measures for reducing spending. Related to all this are the complex federal-regional relations that oppose the center and the regions. The center views as unacceptable the regions' independence in assessing their own needs with regard to receipts and expenditures. While the regions attempt to limit openly or indirectly, in hidden ways, the center's activities, the latter is trying to assert its activities increasingly both openly and slyly; the establishment by President Putin of the new division of the country into seven centers ruling, supervising, and controlling the regions is a decisive step in this direction.

What has been the impact of all these changes in the distribution of income and the overall wealth level?

27-4. Income and Wealth

As could be expected, during the first transition the structure of Russia's national income changed appreciably, notably between 1883–7 and 1909–13. As I indicated in Part I (in Table 9-5), the key changes during these periods concerned agriculture, industry, and transport. Agriculture remained the overwhelming economic sector, but its share in the national income decreased from 57.0 percent to 50.7 percent, while the shares of industrial factories and transport increased respectively from 9.6 to 14.9 percent, and from 2.2 to 5.8 percent. On the other hand, the share of trade and services decreased from 20.0 to 17.0 percent with the balance accounted for by handicrafts and construction.[5] The Central Bank along with various joint-stock companies focused their attention especially on the development of railroads, metallurgy, and armaments. The legislative pattern along with the general weakness of the financial market and of the middle classes left the door wide open to speculative operations by the banks of Germany, Austria, and particularly France, notably with regard to industrial and commercial stocks and government bonds.

Thanks to Russia's geographical size and to its voluminous agricultural output in 1913, Russia's total output ranked as the world's fourth largest, almost equivalent to that of the United Kingdom. On a per capita basis, however, Russia ranked among Europe's poorest countries. Russia's per capita income was indeed equal to one-third of that of France, one-fourth of that of Germany, one-fifth of that of the United Kingdom, and 15 percent of that of the United States. By 1917 Russia was the most backward major European country. It had failed to participate early in the process of modern capitalist industrial development that began in England in the mid-eighteenth century and then spread to Western Europe and to North America.

On the basis of numerous false assumptions about the "march toward socialism and then to communism," of the creation of a "proletarian basis," and of a planned organization of the economy competing with the West, the Communist regime itself set up in fact a state capitalist system operating as a war economy with the supreme target of rapid industrialization. It should not be forgotten that in the Communist conception – as expressed, for instance, by the Bolshevik leader Nikolai Bukharin in his 1920 book *The Economics of the Transition Period* (favorably commented upon by Lenin) – modern, "mature" capitalism had already proceeded before the twentieth century to the transformation of the national economy into a completely united, combined trust, in which all the separate enterprises had ceased to be enterprises and had become merely "separate workshops, branches of the trust." Thus the entire economy has been transformed into a "completely united enterprise" submitted to the bourgeois state. Bukharin then added, "The existence of a planned organization within capitalist countries, . . . the existence in a certain period of a system of *state capitalism*, is the empirical proof of the 'possibility' of budding communism" – that is, of its establishment on this type of base.[6]

---

[5] See Gregory, Paul R., *Russian National Income 1885–1913, op. cit.*, pp. 73, 199; Gregory, Paul R., *Before Command, An Economic History of Russia, op. cit.*, p. 35.

[6] Burkharin, Nikolai's 1920 work *Ekonomika Perekhodnogo perioda* has been translated by Oliver Field in a book including also other writings of Bukharin, entitled *The Politics and Economics of the Transition Period*, Tarbuck, Kenneth J., ed., London, Routledge and Kegan Paul, pp. 64–76.

According to the careful computations of the CIA, after the destructive World War II, Russia's GDP nearly doubled between 1950 and 1963–4, and again nearly doubled between 1964 and 1980–1. During the entire period 1950–80, the contribution of industry to the national product increased continually from 20.4 percent in 1950 to 36.8 percent in 1980. Concomitantly the share of agriculture fell from 30.6 percent in 1950 to 13.9 percent in 1980.[7] As I have indicated previously, during Gorbachev's perestroika, notwithstanding significant achievements in heavy industry and armaments, Russia continued to remain technologically far behind the United States and the Western European countries in all the other industries and in the economy as a whole.

Russia's GDP decreased dramatically before the beginning of the third transition and then throughout the transition. Thus, on the basis 1989 = 100, the GDP fell from 78.8 percent in 1992 to 55.9 percent by 1998 and to 60.67 percent by 1999. The sharp and continuous decreases of all the sectors through the 1990s – particularly in agriculture – are illustrated in Figure 27-1. Concomitantly, the continuous obsolescence of the entire production apparatus is readily observable from the evolution of the coefficients of renewal and change of the basic capital. In 1970, these coefficients – as percentages of the basic capital at the end of the year – amounted to 11.3 percent in industry, 14.9 percent in agriculture, 16.6 percent in construction, and 7.3 percent in transport. The coefficients decreased continually through the following years, amounting by the end of the Soviet regime, in 1991, to 5.2, 5.9, 9.3, and 3.9 respectively. The decreases continued even more substantially under the regimes of the Russian Federation, amounting by 1998 to only 0.9, 0.5, 1.3, and 1.2 for the respective sectors.[8]

Notwithstanding Russia's vast potential, foreign direct investment continues to remain low. A host of factors continue to hinder all inward investments. These factors include uncertainty about macroeconomic stability and shortcomings in the protection of property rights as well as in the enforcement of contracts. The banking system as a whole has indeed to face many problems after the financial collapse of mid-1998. As an IMF study has pointed out, there are widespread reports of banks shifting assets to various entities, asset stripping, and initiation of unilateral restructuring of balance sheets. Though consisting of a large number of banks, Russian banking still accounts for a relatively small portion of economic activity. While total commercial bank assets accounted for 30 percent of the GDP, in 1998 their deposit base was relatively small; nongovernment deposits accounted indeed only for 12 percent of the GDP. The private sector as a whole was stated to have accounted for 70 percent of the GDP in 1996, but given a continuous lack of financial discipline, the desired large-scale benefits of private ownership have yet to be accomplished.

---

[7] *USSR: Measures of Economic Growth and Development 1950–1980*, Studies, Joint Economic Committee, Congress of the U.S., Washington, DC, 1992, pp. 59–62.

[8] *Rossiskii statisticheskii ezhegodnik 1999, op. cit.*, p. 265.

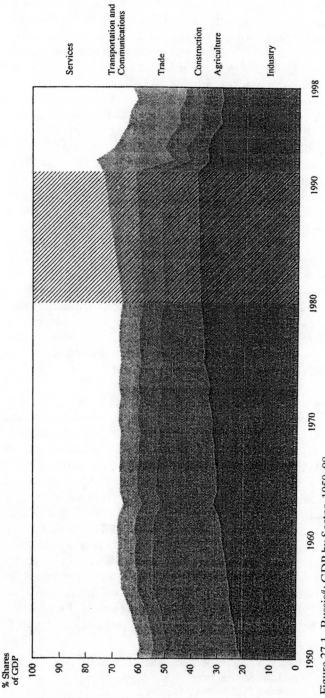

Figure 27-1. Russia[a]: GDP by Sector, 1950–98

Notes:

[a] USSR, 1950–80; Russian Federation, 1991–8.

Services include finance, credit, insurance, real estate operations, science and research, housing, geology, subsoil resources, exploration, meteorology, computer services, state administration and defense, education, culture and art, health care, physical education and social security, utilities, nonproduction activities services to households, and people's associations.

Sources: USSR: Measures of Economic Growth and Development 1950–1980, Studies, Joint Economic Committee, Congress of the United States, Washington, DC, 1982, pp. 59–62; Russian Federation, 1991–8, Goskomstat and IMF estimates.

The main ways of labor market adjustments to declines in real outputs have consisted of wage payments in kind, losses in real wages, and growing wage arrears. The latter have increased each year from 1992 to 1998 in industry from 3.6 million rubles to 79 million, and in agriculture from 1.4 million to 23.7 million (all these data are in constant 1992 prices).

The GDP per capita has also fallen continually from 4,100 rubles in 1991 to 3,500 in 1992, and then, after continuous declines, to 2,400 in 1998 (all these data are in 1990 prices). The share in the total population of those with incomes below the minimum standard increased from 26.2 percent in 1995 to 34.1 percent in 1999. All the social indicators – including rising mortality, increasing income inequality, increasing poverty, and declining real income – show a significant worsening of the situation for a large part of the population throughout the third transition. The regional per capita variations are also discouraging. With the Russian Federation per capita equal to 100 for 1997, the highest levels were reached in West Siberia (145), Moscow (110), and the Far Eastern (110) regions; the lowest levels were accounted for by North Caucasus (46), followed by the Central Black Earth (62) and Volga Viatka (67). The remaining regions had incomes between 80 and 87 percent.

27-5. Concluding Comments

The transitions analyzed in this book have shaped Russia's transformations into a capitalist economy, first through the late transformation of the feudal economy, second through the persistent emphasis of the Soviet state on a certain pattern of industrialization, and third, after the collapse of the USSR, through the hesitant and as yet incomplete economic restructuring within a market framework not always consistently defined.

What kind of capitalism emerged after the first transition? Leon Trotsky sketched as follows the characteristics of the early Russian capitalist development, in his book, *The Russian Revolution of 1905*. He noted that Russian handicraft did not detach itself from agriculture, had not concentrated itself in the towns, and had remained tied to the peasant homestead under the form of house industry. The intermediaries between the home handicraftsmen (the *Kustari*) and the consumers were traveling traders; the commercial capital had not yet created any commercial centers. The early, limited beginnings of industry had been carried out by the state and not by the home industry or by great traders. Peter the Great had indeed built certain manufacturing establishments needed to supply the army and the navy. Eventually, after many changes, foreign capital came in under special privileges. By 1861, the domestic capitalist stratum that grew within the dominant feudal system was far too weak to bring about the needed antifeudal reforms. It was again the state that opened the way toward capitalist development. The state pursued the expansion of the railroads and enacted measures that helped the inflow of foreign capital and the building of big industry. Trotsky then added, on the basis of the data available to him, that Russian industry had developed as follows: Fifteen percent of the industrial establishments had been created before 1861; 23.5 percent had been added between 1861 and 1880; then, over 61 percent had been built between 1881 and 1900, 40 percent of which were accounted for by the expansion between 1890 and 1900. In short, Trotsky pointed out that Russia's pre–World War I capitalist development had been initiated and pursued by the state, eventually with significant help from foreign capital. The capitalist growth was, however, rather limited. Indeed, according to the data furnished by Trotsky, in 1902 Russia counted 19,213 industrial enterprises, compared to 14,650 establishments in 1896 Belgium; Russia surpassed Belgium in the number of workers, namely 1.8 million compared to 542,000, but Russian workers' productivity was very low.[9]

Russia's massive industrial development began only after the Communist takeover and its establishment of a state capitalist system and of a German-type war economy (*Kriegswirtschaft*), installed through brutal means and based on a host of wrong assumptions about the transition from capitalism to "socialism." As Lenin asserted, in the Communist conception an "inexorable war" existed between the advanced Western countries and Russia, a fact that placed before Russia the alternative either to perish or be overtaken and outstripped.[10] This led the Communist Party to concentrate in the hands of the leaders the country's entire production apparatus, to be run as a single unified industrial enterprise operating on the basis of a state plan. This plan aimed to create a powerful military-industrial capacity, increase its overall productivity and technological characteristics, and "outstrip" the West. To raise the productive forces, the Soviet system allocated most of its investable resources to industrial development during successive five-year plans; indeed, more than a third of total investments went to manufacturing, of which as much as 90 percent were provided for producer goods and intermediate products and equipment.

The Soviet leaders assumed that large-scale production was synonymous with scientific-technological progress and that the integration of production processes into higher complexes was the key to efficiency and to higher productivity. As the number of industrial establishments increased, the drive toward concentration of the bulk of large enterprises and toward the creation of associations and production complexes was guided by the center's wish to fit the main producing units into a controllable system that would allow the "simplest" and most effective supervision of all the country's production activities. Eventually, both the center and the managers of such colossal production associations learned through experience that many strategies were possible, and that the extensive scope of the elements involved – the showing of all the moves, the real dimensions of the information set, the payoff structure – could

[9] Trotsky, Leon, *Die Russische Revolution 1905, op. cit.*, pp. 21–8.
[10] Quoted by Stalin, Joseph, in "Industrialization and the Right Deviation" (1928), in *Foundations of Soviet Strategy for Economic Growth*, Spulber, Nicolas, ed., *op. cit.*, pp. 268–9.

not be fully specified. The encasing of the enterprises into a hierarchical setup with multiple objectives defined by volume, type, assortment, quality of goods, and financial indicators finally led to multiple negotiations both between the central manipulators of the system and the managers of the enterprises, and among these managers themselves. The scope of these negotiations shifted from plan indicators to all kinds of unaccountable deviations from the tasks set.

By 1989, the Soviet industrial labor force was twice as large as that of the United States; but while the Soviets relied on masses of low-skilled workers, the United States relied on labor-saving technologies. In terms of output per worker, the Soviets reached about half of the U.S. level. The stock of productive capital was huge in both countries, but the Soviet Union had an increasing amount of obsolete, backward plants and equipment. The Soviet hope of completing retooling the economy on the basis of both domestic production and massive imports of machinery and equipment largely failed. For a long time, the economic transformation made by the Communists – the creation of a centralist government, state ownership of the means of production, banking, transport, and trade, and the replacement of the market in the sphere of production with commands and central allocations – had been proclaimed by them to be "irreversible." In fact, however, all kind of alterations and deviations had to be practiced in the day-to-day operations of the system long before its complete collapse.

The calamitous economic legacies left by the Soviet system's methods of running the economy and society, along with the system's failure to "catch up" with advanced Western capitalism, have left all kinds of obstacles to a rapid, coherent, easy passage to a fully market-directed economy. Yet, besides many negative legacies, the Soviet "state capitalism" has left to the Russian Federation's capitalism an industrial and mining establishment that is still extensive, though obsolete in many respects. This successor capitalism has from its beginnings been a *sui generis* mixture of certain nineteenth century capitalist features, of the peculiar Soviet inheritance, of the conflicting, emerging tendencies in the move toward all-encompassing markets, and of useful outside influences (such as those of the IMF and of the World Bank). In many respects, Russia remains, a strange combination of features, displaying the traits so perceptively drawn by the great Russian poet Alexander Blok early in the twentieth century:

Yea, Russia is a Sphinx. Exulting, grieving,
And sweating blood, she cannot sate
Her eyes that gaze and gaze and gaze
At you [old World] with stone-lipped love for you, and hate.[11]

---

[11] Blok, Alexander, translation of his poem "Skify" (The Scytians), in *An Anthology of Russian Verse 1812–1960*, Yarmolinsky, Avrahm, ed., New York, Doubleday, 1961, p. 121.

Certain nineteenth-century features of the new Russian capitalism – perhaps best exemplified by the emergence of the group of "oligarchs" who surged on the Russian scene after the privatization of 1992–5 – are at least in some respects similar to the emergence of the great capitalists of the end of the nineteenth century in the United States. Putin's forceful raid against certain "tycoons" (such as Vladimir Gusinsky, Boris Berezovsky, and Rem Valkhirev) aims not only at eliminating the new media moguls but also at transferring the control of certain crucially important industries and mines to his own managers (some from the old KGB). Putin's administration is attempting indeed to force the new tycoons to "return to the state" the shares sold by the state itself (for instance, big metal firms such as Norisk Nikel) or allegedly illegally sold stocks to foreigners (for example, stock of Russia's electricity company monopoly).

On the other hand, many former Soviet managers, along with part of their workforce, have taken hold at a critical moment, perhaps abusively, of certain crucial positions in the economy, and have succeeded afterward to obtain all kinds of subsidies, credits, and opportunities for tax evasion. These are not only ghost impacts of the old system, though many leaders of the old system's organization continue to hold key economic positions. Perhaps the best example in this respect is the case of Victor Chernomyrdin, who had been minister of gas production under Mikhail Gorbachev, and then prime minister under Boris Yeltsin. Chernomyrdin became the leader of Gazprom, in which the state still holds a share of close to 40 percent and which the state still uses for various maneuvers against the other "moguls." Unfortunately, the Russian state apparatus is still preventing many spontaneous attempts to develop a freely operating market economy.

The free development of Russian capitalism will still take decades to set in place a fully effective, objective, legal framework. Macroeconomic reform, price liberalization, and mass privatization have clearly proven insufficient to get the private sector and the market fully operational in Russia. On the other hand, it is evident that broad-based institutional reforms involving civil reform, financial reforms, and laws governing the rules of the market require time and the discarding of many persistent Soviet ghosts. Eventually, along with these changes, the restructuring role of the former nomenklatura, along with more free entrepreneurial activity, growing specialization and technological advance, increased exports, and broad interconnections with the foreign capital may eventually expand the domestic market and increase the money income of the widely impoverished and discouraged population of the Russian Federation. In the meantime, the country's government still cannot and indeed has not managed to break away from either the Tsarist or the Soviet legacies and symbols. Indeed, as provided by its constitution, the Russian Federation retains as the state's flag the three-hundred-year-old Tsarist tricolor of white, blue, and red with the Tsarist double-headed eagle as the national seal. On the other hand, Putin and the Federation's Parliament have decided to restore the USSR's national anthem as the new state's hymn (but with changed words) and to bring back the Soviet red banner – without the hammer and sickle – as the official flag of the armed forces. Thus, the leaders of the new Russian Federation connect symbolically the country's third transition with the good or bad legacies of its historical predecessors.

Why did the Russian/Soviet economy (and its successor, the post-Soviet economy) not succeed over the long run in bridging more of the gap with the West? First, Russia's mentality and society have been shaped by the four hundred years of the Tsarist autocratic, centralized, and patriarchal traditions, built on the Mongolian heritage, and by decades of the Communists' powerful and cruel dictatorial system. Under both, the principle of a dominant state apparatus and of a weak and submissive population have created a setup foreign to private property and to citizens' rights. Notwithstanding the attempts, after 1861, to catch up with the West and to change the country's underlying structures, Russia remained by the end of the nineteenth century an agrarian state marked by many feudal characteristics. The further attempts at a broad industrialization during the Communist regime – with its military emphasis – created a further distorted economy lagging behind in many respects the advancing market-directed Western economies. Decades of central planning resulted in massive misallocations of resources and in the creation of a huge industrial setup with both monopolistic power and inefficient production. The post-Soviet transition, aiming as usual to "catch up with the West," faced Russia and its leaders with the challenge of properly manipulating its inherited distortions, a fact as impossible, or improbable, as certain commentators have put it of "starting a new reasonable chess game" with a damaged chess board, chess figures set up in an abnormal way, and chess players not agreeing on the rules by which to play.[12]

Both the Soviet past as well as the post-Soviet state's unbalanced and unsuccessful reforms are to blame for the corrupt tendencies that they are steadily nurturing. As Gregory Yavlinsky, the leader of the Russian liberal party, pointed out, Poland, the Czech Republic, and Hungary have largely overcome their Communist heritage, while Russia has been failing to do so, because in 1989–91 these East European countries endured democratic revolutions that not only changed the power system but also the ruling elites, while Russia has not endured a revolution, but only a reconstruction of the old regime. Russia has indeed endured a kind of "nomenklatura Thermidor" that kept in power people from the Communist Party's Central Committee, its Politburo, and its secret services who have simply changed their guise and started speaking of "reforms, democracy, and the market."[13] Russia's eight premiers of the 1990s were either former Communist functionaries or KGB officers. One of the

[12] *Restructuring, Stabilizing and Modernizing the New Russia*, Welfens, Paul J. J., and Gavrilenkov, Engeny, eds., Berlin, Springer, 2000, p. 7.
[13] Yavlinsky, Gregory, "Lecture on the Future of Russia and its Economy" (*Obshchaia Gazeta*), No. 82/1, 2001.

main problems of the resulting official Russian economy has been its "shadow economy," an unreported economy that, according to the official data, accounts for 40 percent of all transactions. In addition, the economy is plagued by the continuing operation in its center of the military-oriented industry, operating with negative productivity but providing jobs for 25 percent of the industrial labor force. Russia's economy depends now essentially on its natural resources – oil and gas – and will continue to do so for years to come. Russia's march to the free market and to harmonious development stumbles largely because, it has not been able to discard the old system but has simply adapted it for the new tasks for which it is unfit and which it cannot muster.

Index

Abalkin, Leonid I., 269
Achievements of the Soviet Power in Forty Years, 225
Adygea, 290, 327
Aganbegyan, Abel, 205
Agency for Restructuring Credit Organizations (ARKO), 369
Agrarian Bank of Reconstruction, 340
Agrarian Party of Russia, 339
Agrarian Policy Council, 340
Agricultural Bank, 207, 340
agricultural policy, 50–5, 192–7, 317–19
  aims of, 51–2
  decentralization of, 318
  evolution of, 70, 72
agriculture
  changes in, 214
  decline in, 339t
  developments in, 38
  employment in, 333
  failure of, 84
  foreign trade and, 81–3
  Gorbachev, Mikhail, on, 273
  grain yields in, 337t
  inventory of, 334t
  investments in, 78
  landholding and, 139
  liberation of, 50
  output, 79–81, 239, 335, 389
  peasants and, 139
  policy changes regarding, 164
  post–World War II, 218

  privatization of, 341
  production volumes in, 335t
  prominence of, 395–6
  reforms in, 14, 330
  reorganization of, 221
  Russian Federation, in, 293
  sales in, 336t
  serfs and, 13
  sown areas and, 332t
  technology in, 77
  transitions in, 138–41, 271–3, 387–90
  Yavlinsky, Grigory, on, 336
  yields in, 334–7
Agro-Industrial Bank, 252
Agro-Industrial Committee, 216
Agro-Industrial Complex, 216
  structure of, 217t
Agroprom Bank, 366
Aksakov, Ivan, 34
Aksakov, Konstantin, 34
  Alexander II and, 35
Alaniia. *See* North Ossetia
Albakin, L., 234
alcoholic beverages
  taxes on, 62–3, 130
Alekperov, Vagit, 311, 321
Alexander I, 112
Alexander II, 3, 10, 59
  Aksakov, Konstantin, and, 35
  assassination of, 41–2, 83
  hierarchy under, 20
  Zemstva created by, 24

Printed in the United States
103163LV00003B/37-60/A